THE
GREEK ANTHOLOGY
*   *
THE GARLAND OF PHILIP

VOLUME I

THE
GREEK ANTHOLOGY

* *

THE GARLAND OF PHILIP

AND SOME
CONTEMPORARY EPIGRAMS

EDITED BY

A. S. F. GOW

M.A., F.B.A.

FELLOW OF TRINITY COLLEGE AND SOMETIME BRERETON READER
IN CLASSICS IN THE UNIVERSITY OF CAMBRIDGE

AND

D. L. PAGE

LITT.D., F.B.A.

MASTER OF JESUS COLLEGE AND REGIUS PROFESSOR OF GREEK
IN THE UNIVERSITY OF CAMBRIDGE

VOLUME I

INTRODUCTION, TEXT AND TRANSLATION
INDEXES OF SOURCES AND
EPIGRAMMATISTS

CAMBRIDGE
AT THE UNIVERSITY PRESS
1968

Cambridge University Press
Road, London, N.W. 1
Street, New York, N.Y. 10022

Library of Congress Catalogue Card Number: 68–10149
Standard Book Numbers:
521 05875 9 vol. I
521 05876 7 vol. II
521 05874 0 set of two vols.

Printed in Great Britain
at the University Printing House, Cambridge
(Brooke Crutchley, University Printer)

CONTENTS

VOLUME I

Foreword   *page* vii

INTRODUCTION

List of Abbreviations   x

I The *Garland* of Philip and its contributors   xi

  (i)   Evidence for the making of the *Garland* by
       Philip of Thessalonica   xi

  (ii)   Identification of contributors to the *Garland*.
       Alphabetical sequences, disordered blocks,
       and isolated epigrams. Origins of the present
       arrangement in the Palatine Anthology.
       List of identifiable *Garland*-authors   xi

  (iii) Doubtful claimants. The evidence of *A.P.*
       9.1–125. Other evidence. List of doubtful
       claimants included in this book. Authors ex-
       cluded. Comparison with lists compiled by
       predecessors   xxi

  (iv)   Ascriptions   xxix

  (v)   Homonymous authors. List of *Garland*-
       authors, with namesakes. List of authors with
       Roman names   xxx

  (vi)   General observations on the *Garland*-authors xxxii

  (vii) Styles and subjects   xxxiii

  (viii) Dialects   xxxvi

  (ix)   Lengths of epigrams   xxxvii

  (x)   Metres. Variety of metres. Mixed metres.
       Prosody.   xxxvii

  (xi)   The date-limits of the *Garland*   xlv

  (xii) The dedication of the *Garland*   xlix

v

II The text   *page* 1

   (i) The Palatine Anthology   1

   (ii) The Planudean Anthology   li

   (iii) The Relation between the two   li

   (iv) The Reproductions   liii

   (v) Suidas. The *Syllogae minores*. The *apographa*   liv

III The arrangement of epigrams in the present edition   lv

TEXT

Sigla   2

Text and Translation: 3

  I Authors included in the *Garland*   3

  II Doubtful claimants   391

Index of Sources   445

Index of Epigrammatists   451

VOLUME II

List of Abbreviations   2

Commentary   3

Appendix: List of Texts consulted   470

Indexes

  I To Commentary

     A. Greek   475

     B. English   481

  II Of Epigrammatists   490

FOREWORD

The present volume was begun by myself soon after I began to collaborate with Mr Gow in the production of *The Greek Anthology: Hellenistic Epigrams*. When the end of that work was in sight Mr Gow undertook the commentary on Antipater of Thessalonica; and the relation between us has been much the same as in the former volume but with our parts reversed. A. S. F. G. is primarily responsible for Antipater; I am primarily responsible for the rest. Each has made comments on the other's contribution, and there is not much in the book which we should not both endorse. For the translations (including Antipater) the responsibility is mine.

We begin where the former volume ended, and assemble all epigrams assignable to authors included in the second principal source of the Palatine Anthology, the *Garland* compiled by Philip of Thessalonica. The *Garland* comprised a large number of epigrams from the period beginning with Philodemus and ending (probably) about the time of the death of the emperor Gaius. We have appended the epigrams of a number of contemporary authors who are not known to have been included in Philip's *Garland*.

Our collection thus includes almost all the epigrams in the Palatine and Planudean Anthologies more or less certainly datable between *c.* 90 B.C. and A.D. 40. A few of the authors are of high quality, most are mediocre, a few are worthless. Whatever their literary merits, they constitute the only large body of Greek poetry which has survived from this period. The background of some of them is rather the Roman than the Greek world; these were read and occasionally imitated by the celebrated Roman poets of the late Republican and early Imperial ages. If they had been lost and recently recovered from the sands of Egypt they would have attracted widespread interest and prolonged attention; denied the advantages of a startling renaissance, they have been generally neglected or despised. We are not blind to their faults, but we think that even the least talented deserve the passing glance which we bestow upon them here; and a few of them deserve much more.

The translations are intended merely to show what we suppose the meaning to be; and the Commentary is so much the shorter. Elegance of style, which could only be achieved by loose paraphrase, is incompatible with this humble utilitarian purpose and is not to be expected. Experience has taught me to respect the accuracy, and often the ingenuity, of the translations by Paton in the Loeb edition, Mackail in *Select Epigrams from the Greek Anthology* (Longman, Green & Co., London 1911), and Shane Leslie in *The Greek Anthology* (E. Benn, London, 1929). I have checked my versions against theirs; I have of course found many fortuitous coincidences, but it is proper that I should declare openly that I have quite often borrowed a turn of phrase from my predecessors.

D. L. P.

Cambridge
February 1968

INTRODUCTION

ABBREVIATIONS

A.P.	*Anthologia Palatina.*
A.Pl.	*Anthologia Planudea.*
Cichorius *Röm. Stud.*	K. Cichorius *Römische Studien* (Leipzig, 1922).
Gow *GA*	A. S. F. Gow *The Greek Anthology: sources and ascriptions* (Hell. Soc. Suppl. Paper 9, 1958).
HE	A. S. F. Gow and D. L. Page *The Greek Anthology: Hellenistic Epigrams* (Cambridge, 1965).
RE	Pauly–Wissowa *Realencyclopädie* (1894–).
Weisshäupl *Grabged.*	R. Weisshäupl *Grabgedichte d. gr. Anthologie* (Abh. Arch. Sem. d. Univ. Wien 7, 1889).

INTRODUCTION

I. THE 'GARLAND' OF PHILIP AND ITS CONTRIBUTORS

(i) *Evidence for the making of the 'Garland' by Philip of Thessalonica*

A.P. 4.2, an introductory poem headed Φιλίππου στέφανος, states that its author (who is not named in its text) has composed a 'Garland' of epigrams, similar to that of Meleager,[1] by relatively recent authors. Thirteen contributors are named and others are included in the summary term οἱ περισσοί at the end.

The existence of an ancient anthology including all the authors named here could have been inferred from certain alphabetically arranged sequences of epigrams in the Palatine manuscript, and it would have seemed a likely guess that the anthologist was Philip of Thessalonica. Although he is one of the two authors[2] most fully represented in the alphabetical sequences, and plainly one of the latest contributors to the anthology in question, he is not named in the *Proem*,[3] and it would have been a natural inference that he himself was the author of the *Proem*.

(ii) *Identification of contributors to the 'Garland'*

Epigrams by Philip and by all the authors named in the *Proem* are found in certain alphabetically ordered sequences in *A.P.*[4] It

---

[1] See *HE* 1.xiv ff.

[2] The other is Antipater of Thessalonica, whose epigrams in the main alphabetical sequences just outnumber Philip's if those with rival ascriptions are included in the count.

[3] Throughout this book, 'the *Proem*' = *A.P.* 4.2 (= Philip 1).

[4] There are no comparable sequences in the Planudean, but it may be significant that wherever two or more Philippan epigrams stand together in *A.Pl.* 4 the epigram-initials are the same (103–4, 136–7, 165–6, 198–9) or in sequence (175–7 HKK, 214–16 CCω), except at 239–43 (AωωωA) and in two places where two epigrams by the same author stand together (49–50, 333–4).

has long been recognised that these sequences[1] are extracts from Philip's *Garland*, an anthology arranged either as a whole or in sections[2] according to the initial letter of each epigram in the normal alphabetical order.

Twenty-six[3] authors not named in the *Proem* are represented in one or more of eleven main alphabetical sequences. We refer to these hereafter, in addition to those named in the *Proem*, as '*Garland*-authors'.

Many epigrams ascribed to *Garland*-authors occur outside the alphabetical sequences. We have seldom found reason to doubt the ascriptions, and we have included such epigrams in the present collection although we do not suppose that all of them were included in the *Garland*; some of the epigrams by *Garland*-authors outside the alphabetical sequences may have found their way into the *Anthologies* by some route other than the *Garland*.

The only epigrams by a *Garland*-author found solely in sources other than the *Anthologies* are on certain inscriptions bearing the name of Honestus; these we have included for the sake of completeness.

The main alphabetical sequences in *A.P.* occur as follows:

> 5.104–33
> 6.88–108[4] and 227–61
> 7.364–405 and 622–45
> 9.215–312, 403–23,[5] and 541–62[6]
> 10.17–25
> 11.23–46[7] and 318–27[8]

These eleven sequences include 334 epigrams.[9] The other

---

[1] They are not the only alphabetical sequences in P. Fragments of others are found in 11.388–413 and 417–36; 6.134 ff. (Anacreon); and 7.507ᴬ–513 (Simonides). See *HE* 1.xviii n. 3.   [2] See pp. xv ff. below.

[3] Including Philip himself and Antimedon, whose solitary epigram occurs not within but at the end of a sequence.

[4] This sequence may begin with the anonymous epigram 6.87.

[5] Perhaps rather 403–23 + 428–30; see p. xx.

[6] The sequence is interrupted by 547, a single anonymous iambic.

[7] The alphabetical order is in reverse.

[8] The sequence is interrupted by 323, ascribed to Palladas.

[9] Not counting 9.547 and 11.323.

epigrams ascribed to *Garland*-authors, between 200 and 250 in number,[1] are widely scattered. Traces of the original alphabetical sequence may be discernible in 7.174–6 (OOO), 692–4 (ΓΓΗ), 700–3 (IIIΘ); 9.428–30 (CTT)[2] and 706–9 (ΔEEE); but the order in any short sequence may be fortuitous, and is likelier to be so if the letters are widely spaced, as in 6.348–50 (AIT), 9.149–51 (EΠΠ), 10.100–3 (AHMT) and 11.346–8 (MXω).[3]

The alphabetical order is not preserved in the following blocks of more than two[4] successive epigrams ascribed to *Garland*-authors: 5.30–4 (ΠXΠEO), 306–8 (ΔXE); 7.38–40 (ΘOA), 73–5 (ATC), 183–7 (ΠAAHΔ),[5] 233–40 (AAMOOHΦT),[6] 286–9 (ΔKOA), 741–3 (OOE); 9.34–6 (MAO), 58–60 (KTΠ), 81–9 (MMNNNΠMMΛ), 112–14 (TOΠ), 776–8 (ZIΓ), 790–2 (TMN); 11.65–7 (ΛKY).

Most of the small orderly sequences and disordered blocks owe their present positions to the coherence of their subject-matter with their contexts. The same is true of most of the numerous epigrams which stand alone, but it is important to recognise the fact that this is by no means true of all. Some are so wholly isolated that it is impossible to understand why they should have been placed where they are. Opinions will differ about the number of these misplaced epigrams; the following selection serves merely to exemplify the fact:

6.161 stands in the middle of four epigrams from Meleager's *Garland*. 6.333 is a misplaced amatory epigram. 7.554, in the

---

[1] It is impossible to be more precise. We do not know how many homonymous authors are involved, or how many epigrams ascribed simply to 'Antipater' should be assigned to the Thessalonican.

[2] But this may have cohered originally with the main sequence 9.403–23; see p. xx.

[3] In this connexion we ignore alphabetical sequences of only two epigrams: 5.3–4; 9.10–11, 13[B]–14, 92–3, 438–9, 516–17; 12.34–5 ('Antipater' unqualified is not counted; nor is Euenus, a name common to several different poets).

[4] The only places where two (but not more) such epigrams occur in reversed alphabetical order are: 6.198–9; 7.530–1; 9.29–30 (again excluding 'Antipater' unqualified and Euenus).

[5] The first line of 7.183 is missing.

[6] But this block includes an epigram by Alpheus, who is not known to be a *Garland*-author.

middle of a Byzantine block, has no special relation to its context. 9.178, inserted together with 177 and 179 into a sequence from Palladas, has no special relation to its context. 9.342 is an epigram which one would not expect to find in this Book, let alone in this context. 9.570 is a misplaced amatory epigram. 9.575 stands isolated in the most miscellaneous of contexts. In two places, 9.438–9 and 516–17, a couple of epigrams by *Garland*-authors stand together unrelated to each other or to their contexts.

This general survey prompts certain questions about the sources of the Palatine Anthology and the principles governing its arrangement.

The Lemmatist on Meleager's *Proem* says that Constantinus Cephalas (*Protopapas* at the palace at Constantinople in A.D. 917) distributed epigrams from Meleager's *Garland*[1] among separate chapters, referring especially to Books 5, 6, 7 and 9 in the Palatine. That Cephalas created the division into amatory, dedicatory, sepulchral, and epideictic sections is implied by the phrasing here (cυνέχεεν αὐτὰ ἀφορίcαc εἰc κεφάλαια διάφορα, ἤγουν ἐρωτικὰ ἰδίωc καὶ ἀναθεματικὰ καὶ ἐπιτύμβια καὶ ἐπιδεικτικὰ ὡc νῦν ὑποτέτακται ἐν τῶι παρόντι πτυκτίωι) and is confirmed by the heading to Book 7 (ἀρχὴ τῶν ἐπιτυμβίων ἐπιγραμμάτων ὦν ἐcχεδίαcεν ὁ κύριοc Κωνcταντῖνοc ὁ Κεφαλᾶc).

The principles underlying Cephalas' arrangement of epigrams from Meleager's *Garland* can be recognised to some extent in the Palatine manuscript.[2] The arrangement of epigrams from Philip's *Garland* is in some respects less, in others more, complex and enigmatic. It comprises such different elements as long alphabetical sequences, very short alphabetical sequences, small blocks or single epigrams arranged by subject-matter, and apparently motiveless scattering of epigrams in isolation.

[1] The Lemmatist says that this was arranged alphabetically; it was not, but Philip's was. We doubt, however, whether the Lemmatist's statement represents a telescoping of statements about both *Garlands*.

[2] See *HE* I.xvii ff.

It was observed by Weisshäupl[1] that six of the eight main alphabetical sequences in Books 5, 6, 7 and 9 are immediately followed by blocks from Meleager's *Garland*, and that there is a specially close connexion between the components of 6.88–163 (Philip—Meleager—older poets, viz. Anacreon, Callimachus— mixed Meleager and Philip) and 7.364–546 (Philip—Meleager— older poets, viz. Simonides, Callimachus—mixed Meleager and Philip). These coincidences are plainly not fortuitous, but we must make further inquiries before we draw any conclusion from them, in particular any conclusion about the activity of Cephalas. Our problem is part of a much larger whole;[2] we confine ourselves to a few questions and comments.

(1) Was the *Garland* of Philip originally monolithic, i.e. in a single block alphabetically ordered from start to finish, or stratified,[3] i.e. divided into separate categories, each in its own alphabetical order?

We have found no means of answering this question. We observe that epigrams within an alphabetical sequence are not invariably all of the same species:[4] e.g. 5.108 is a sepulchral epigram among the amatory, 6.88 an amatory epigram among the dedications; 6.256 is out of place among the dedications; among the sepulchral epigrams, 7.379 describes the harbour-mole at Puteoli, 7.626 the capture of lions in Africa, 7.641 the workings of a water-clock; among the epideictic epigrams, 9.263 and 554 are satirical; many other examples could be quoted.

How might these aliens have been introduced to their present contexts? The fact that the intruders all preserve the alphabetical order makes it almost certain that they belonged to these contexts in the original *Garland*. If Philip's *Garland* was stratified, the original division into categories may have been imperfect; but we prefer to suppose that the aliens were introduced by the

[1] *Grabged.* 25 f.
[2] See especially Susemihl *Gesch. d. gr. Litt. in der Alex.* 2.568 ff.
[3] So Reitzenstein *RE* 6.105 and apparently also Weisshäupl *Grabged.* 26 n. 1.
[4] See Hecker *Comm. Crit.* 2.168, Weisshäupl 43 ff.

inadvertence of a later compiler, who might carelessly include, e.g., a sepulchral epigram while selecting amatory epigrams from a monolithic *Garland*.

We draw attention here to two other features of the arrangement within the alphabetical sequences. An anthologist who arranges epigrams alphabetically, whether *en bloc* or in categories, might possibly be expected to arrange the authors alphabetically under each epigram-initial; at least he will surely place together all the epigrams by the same author with the same epigram-initial. Neither of these expectations is fulfilled.

(*a*) Authors grouped under the same epigram-initial are not placed in alphabetical order. In 9.215–312, for example, under the epigram-initial A, the order of authors' initials is A-O-MC--A-Δ-Θ-MA-A-B-K-O-Z-B-A-A-O-A-Φ-E-K-BΛ. This random pattern is the rule. No epigram-initial including more than three author-entries has all its authors in alphabetical order.[1] Within the lengthier entries there are two sequences of five authors in alphabetical order;[2] these we suppose to be fortuitous.[3] There is no significant repetition of any particular sequence of authors.[4]

(*b*) Epigrams by the same author under the same epigram-initial are about as often as not separated from each other. In 9.215–312, for example, under the epigram-initial A, the order is Antipater[a], Honestus[a], Scaevola, Aemilianus, Diodorus, Thallus, Argentarius[a], Antiphilus, Bianor[a], Crinagoras[a], Honestus[b], Zonas, Bianor[b], Apollonides, Argentarius[b], Honestus[c],

---

[1] There are twenty-eight examples of more than three entries under the same epigram-initial. Of the nine examples with three (but not more) entries in one of the main sequences, six have the authors in alphabetical order.

[2] Under H and K in 9.215–312.

[3] We regard as fortuitous also the few orderly runs of more than four authors spread over several epigram-initials (six in order, 9.215–312 under Γ to E; five, 7.622–45 under H–K, 9.403–23 under A to Z, 10.17–25 under A to K, 11.23–46 under O to K). The letter A is so common in author-initials (at least 130 in 334 entries) that chance might well have produced more and longer sequences than these.

[4] The order Antipater–Antiphilus occurs ten times in the main sequences. The order Crinagoras–Antipater–Antiphilus–Apollonides occurs twice, by chance we suppose.

Antipater[b], Philip, Erucius, Crinagoras[b,c], Bassus. In 6.88–108, under A, the order is Antiphanes, Maccius, Philip[a], Thallus, Philip[b], Antipater, Philip[c]. In 9.541–62, under K, the order is Crinagoras, Antiphilus[a], Bianor, Antiphilus[b], Antipater[a], Antiphilus[c], Antipater[b]. There are about four dozen places where two epigrams by the same author stand together under the same epigram-initial in the main sequences; there are only five places where more than two epigrams by the same author stand together.[1]

Whereas there is no particular reason why authors grouped under the same epigram-initial should themselves be placed in alphabetical order under that initial, the fact that epigrams by the same author under the same epigram-initial are so often separated calls for an explanation; and this we are unable to provide.

The problem is the same, whether the *Garland* was monolithic or stratified. The man who compiles an anthology from the epigrams of some fifty authors, contemporary or recent, living in various parts of the world, must do his work from published copies of their epigrams.[2] Suppose now that the *Garland* is to be monolithic; how will the anthologist proceed? He might take up, e.g., Adaeus and copy out the first epigram he comes to beginning with the letter A. Will he now put down his text of Adaeus and take up, e.g., Bassus and copy out his first A-epigram; and so on throughout all his authors, occasionally reverting to previously excerpted authors? We cannot imagine why a man should put himself to so much trouble and waste so much time. The simple method was to copy out all the A-epigrams (or all he wanted) from, e.g., Adaeus, and then all the

---

[1] Under Ζ, P and C in 6.88–108, Φιλίππου + τοῦ αὐτοῦ thrice; under E and H in 9.215–312, Φιλίππου + τοῦ αὐτοῦ twice. In 7.286–9 four epigrams ascribed to Antipater stand together ('Α. Θεσσ.–'Α.–τοῦ αὐτοῦ 'Α.–'Α. Μακεδόνος). In 5.102–5, three by Argentarius (interrupted by one from Rufinus). In 11.324–6, three by Automedon.

[2] There is no plausible alternative. It is almost inconceivable that Philip should have known the epigrams of, e.g., Philodemus, Crinagoras, or Zonas except from published copies. See further Gow *GA* 25.

A-epigrams from each of his other authors in turn. The result would be that all the A-epigrams by the same author would stand together; but that is not the result in fact achieved.

It is no help to suppose that the *Garland* was stratified. The simple method was to copy out, e.g., all the *epitaphia* from one author, then all from another author, and so forth. We cannot imagine why a man should adopt the method apparently attested in, e.g., *A.P.* 9.215 ff. under the initial A: he takes single epigrams from each of ten authors, then reverts to one of them (Honestus), then takes up Zonas, then reverts to Bianor, then takes up Apollonides, then reverts to Argentarius and (yet again) Honestus, then takes up Philip, then Erucius, then reverts to Crinagoras (for two epigrams this time), then takes up Bassus. The confusion on his table and in his mind can be imagined; what we cannot imagine is a plausible reason for adopting such a procedure. It may be suggested that Philip thought that his readers would find his anthology less monotonous if he shuffled his authors; we think the motive inadequate and the result neither attained nor likely to be, considering the nature of the material.

We do not think it helpful to transfer the inquiry from Philip to a later compiler. If epigrams by the same author were grouped together in his source, we cannot explain why a compiler should go out of his way to separate them in his selection.

(2) Did Cephalas use a copy of Philip's *Garland*? There is no very obvious reason why this relatively unimportant book should have been among the privileged few that survived the Dark Ages; there is, however, good evidence that it did survive for at least half a millennium,[1] and the combination of order and disorder in the Palatine may suggest that Cephalas inherited a conglomerate anthology in which Philip's authors were represented by the more or less isolated epigrams and that he added the main alphabetical sequences from an independently surviving copy of the *Garland*.

[1] The *Cycle* of Agathias includes imitations of Philippan originals.

This question too seems to us unanswerable; we can only draw attention to some further peculiar features of the main alphabetical sequences.

(*a*) If Cephalas inserted these alphabetical sequences, why did he include more than one within the same chapter? There are two sequences in Book 6, two in Book 7, three in Book 9; why not one in each Book? If we look for an answer in the relation of these *Garland*-sequences to their contexts, we merely find further inconsistencies. Of the eight main alphabetical sequences in these Books, four[1] make a smooth and plainly intentional transition from the end of the *Garland*-sequence into the following block, whereas the other four[2] make an abrupt break in the context at their end.[3]

(*b*) Six of these eight alphabetical sequences are prefixed to blocks from the *Garland* of Meleager. The coherence is presumably planned, and we cannot explain the contrary facts that one sequence (9.403–23) is an exception to the apparent rule and that another (6.227–61) is thrust into the middle of an excerpt from Meleager, breaking into a group of epigrams by one of Meleager's authors and interrupting the coherence of the subject-matter.[4]

(*c*) The epigram-initials most frequently represented in the main alphabetical sequences are A, E, and H;[5] these three account for 123 of the 334 entries. The selection for the third sequence in Book 9 starts with the letter Θ, as if it had suffered a loss at the top. It is worth noticing also that the first sequence in Book 6 has no epigram under four of the seven commonest

---

[1] 6.88–108, 7.364–405, 7.622–45, 9.403–23. All but the last are followed by blocks from Meleager.

[2] 5.104–33, 6.227–61, 9.215–312, 9.541–62. All are followed by blocks from Meleager.

[3] None of these *Garland*-sequences coheres closely in context with what precedes.

[4] It is to be noticed also that 6.348–50 separate two epigrams by Callimachus, and that 7.233–40 interrupt a block from Meleager.

[5] The frequencies are: A 53, H 40, E and K 30, T 21, O 19, Π 15, Λ 14, Δ 13, Γ and C 12, B 9, Θ, M, and Ѡ 8, I, N and Y 7, Φ and Ψ 5, Z, Ξ, P, and X 3.

initials, E, H, O, and Π; there may have been some loss in the middle here.[1]

(d) It is not even certain that the one presumably deliberate act in the arrangement—the prefixing of Philippan to Meleagrian sequences—was the work of Cephalas using a copy of Philip's *Garland*. For, if it were so, we could not explain why an isolated iambic line (9.547) was inserted into one of the alphabetical sequences and an epigram by Palladas (11.323) into another.[2] We notice moreover that the main sequence 9.403–23 appears to be continued, after a brief interruption, in 9.428–30; and we are reluctant to believe that it was Cephalas who first inserted four Byzantine epigrams into one of the Philippan sequences which he was selecting from a copy of the *Garland*. We doubt whether a copy of Philip's *Garland*, surviving into the tenth century, would have included these intruders; nor is it likely that they were first inserted during the brief interval between Cephalas and the date of our Palatine manuscript. If Cephalas himself inserted them, the fact would neither tell us anything about his source for the Philippan sequences nor help us to understand his principles of arrangement. It seems more reasonable to suppose that he found these intruders already embedded in the Philippan sequences; if so, his source for the sequences was probably not an independent copy of the *Garland* but a conglomerate anthology which had been exposed to accretions for a long time. He will then not have been responsible for the incorporation of the Philippan sequences, though he may have been responsible, to some indefinable extent, for the present positions of some of them in the Palatine.

The following are identified as contributors to the *Garland* of

[1] 7.692–4, ΓΓΗ, +700–3, IIIΘ, may originally have belonged to the same sequence.

[2] We cannot simply ignore this example on the ground that Cephalas' activity may not have extended to Book 11. If some other person or persons inserted the Philippan sequences into Books 10 and 11, he (or others) may have been responsible for the preservation of the sequences in Books 5, 6, 7, and 9, and Cephalas may have done nothing more than rearrange what he found preserved for him by others.

Philip on the evidence of the *Proem*[1] and of at least one of the nine main alphabetical sequences in the Palatine:

Adaeus	Boethus	Macedonius
Aemilianus	*Crinagoras	Myrinus
*Antigonus	Diocles	*Parmenion
Antimedon[2]	*Diodorus	Philip
*Antipater	Diotimus	*Philodemus
*Antiphanes	Epigonus	Polemon
*Antiphilus	Erucius	Quintus
Antistius	Etruscus	Sabinus
Apollonides	*Euenus	Scaevola
Argentarius	*Geminus[3]	Secundus
*Automedon	Heraclides	Serapion
Bassus	Honestus	Thallus
*Bianor	Maccius	*Zonas

(iii) *Doubtful claimants*

(a) The evidence of *A.P.* 9.1–125

This section includes and to some extent intermingles epigrams by authors who were,[4] authors who may have been, and authors who were not,[5] contributors to the *Garland*. It will later prove convenient to refer to the following list of ascriptions and epigram-initials.

The names of *Garland*-authors are printed in italics. The initial letters of epigrams which are or might be by *Garland*-

---

[1] An asterisk marks those named in the *Proem*.

[2] Not quite so certain as the others; see Antimedon, Introd.

[3] Assuming that Tullius Geminus is the 'Tullius' of the *Proem*; see vol. 2.330.

[4] The passage includes thirty-eight epigrams ascribed to established *Garland*-authors (not counting 'Antipater' unqualified or Euenus). Seven of these have double ascriptions, and in two of them at least (9.53 and 107) the ascription to a *Garland*-author is, we believe, erroneous.

[5] The passage includes at least twenty-seven epigrams which were certainly not in the *Garland*. Of the twenty-one anonymous epigrams, we judge that almost if not quite all come from sources other than the *Garland*.

authors are placed on the left. Entries with the same arabic
number suspended on the right are similar in subject-matter.

9.1	Δ	Polyaenus of Sardis[1]		37	C	Flaccus[10]
2	K	Tiberius Illustrius[1]		38	E	anon.[10]
3	E	Antipater or Plato[2]		39	A	Musicius
4	H	Cyllenius[2]		40	O	Zosimus[11]
5		Palladas[2]		41		Theon of Alexandria[11]
6		Palladas[2]		42		Julius Leonidas[11]
7	E	Julius Polyaenus[3]		43	A	*Parmenion*[25]
8	E	Julius Polyaenus		44	X	Plato or Flaccus[12]
9	Π	Julius Polyaenus[3]		45	X	Flaccus or Plato or
10	Π	*Antipater of Thessa-*				Antipater[12]
		lonica[4]		46	Π	*Antipater of Macedon* or
11	Π	*Philip* or Isidorus[5]				'Callenius'
12		Leonidas of Alex-		47	T	anon.
		andria[5]		48	Z	anon.
13[A]	A	Plato Junior[5]		49	E	anon.[13]
13[B]	A	*Antiphilus*[5]		50		Mimnermus[12]
14	A	*Antiphilus*[4]		51	A	Plato[13]
15	A	anon.		52		Carpyllides
16		Meleager		53		Nicodemus or *Bassus*
17	O	Germanicus[6]		54		Menecrates[14]
18	E	Germanicus[6]		55		Lucillius or Mene-
19	O	Archias of Mytilene[7]				crates[14]
20	O	anon.[7]		56	E	*Philip*
21	C	anon.[7]		57		Pamphilus[17]
22	N	*Philip*		58	K	Antipater
23	Γ	Antipater		59	T	Antipater
24		Leonidas[8]		60	Π	*Diodorus*
25		Leonidas[8]		61	Γ	anon.
26	T	*Antipater of Thessa-*		62	Ƶ	Euenus of Sicily[17]
		lonica[8]		63		Asclepiades[15]
27	E	Archias or *Parmenion*		64	A	Asclepiades or Archias[15]
28	E	Pompeius or Marcus		65	Γ	anon.
		Junior[17]		66		Antipater of Sidon[15]
29	T	*Antiphilus*[9]		67	C	anon.[16]
30	E	Zelotus or *Bassus*[9]		68	M	anon.[16]
31	E	Zelotus[9]		69	M	*Parmenion*[17]
32	A	anon.[9]		70		Mnasalces[17]
33	O	Cyllenius[9]		71	K	*Antiphilus*
34	M	*Antiphilus*[9]		72	E	Antipater
35	A	*Antiphilus*[9]		73	E	*Antiphilus*
36	O	*Secundus*[9]		74	A	anon.

75	K	Euenus of Ascalon[22]	98	O	Flaccus[21]
76	Δ	Antipater	99		Leonidas[22]
77	Π	*Antipater of Thessa-lonica* or Ariston or Hermodorus	100	Λ	Alpheus
			101	H	Alpheus[23]
			102	H	Antonius[23]
78		Leonidas of Alex-andria[18]	103	H	Mundus[23]
			104	A	Alpheus[23]
79		Leonidas of Alex-andria[18]	105	E	anon.[24]
			106		Leonidas[24]
80		Leonidas of Alex-andria	107	T	Leonidas or *Antipater of Thessalonica*[24]
81	M	*Crinagoras*	108	O	anon.
82	M	*Antipater of Thessa-lonica*[19]	109	O	*Diocles*[11]
			110	O	Alpheus[25]
83	N	*Philip*[19]	111	Θ	Archias of Mytilene
84	N	*Antiphanes*[19]	112	T	*Antipater of Thessa-lonica*
85	N	*Philip*[19]			
86	Π	*Antiphilus*	113	O	*Parmenion*
87	M	*Argentarius*[20]	114	Π	*Parmenion*
88	M	*Philip*[20]	115[A]	A	anon.[26]
89	Λ	*Philip*	115[B]	K	anon.[26]
90	N	Alpheus	116	A	anon.[26]
91	E	Archias Junior	117	Π	Flaccus
92	A	*Antipater of Thessa-lonica*	118		Besantinus
			119		Palladas
93	A	*Antipater of Thessa-lonica*	120		Lucian
			121	C	anon.
94	Π	Isidorus[4]	122	A	anon. or Euenus[20]
95	X	Alpheus	123		Leonidas of Alex-andria
96	A	*Antipater of Thessa-lonica*			
			124	Π	anon.
97	A	Alpheus[21]	125	Θ	anon.

This block includes a number of authors whose claim to a place in the *Garland*, not attested by the *Proem* or by any of the main alphabetical sequences, depends wholly or mainly on such evidence as their connexion with established *Garland*-authors in this passage may supply.

It is immediately apparent that no certain claim is established. Epigrams from a variety of sources are assembled here, and subject-matter, not alphabetical order, is the chief principle governing the arrangement. There seems to be a confused trace of the *Garland's* alphabetical order in 81–9, MMNNNΠMMΛ. No other sequence from known *Garland*-authors preserves the alphabetical order for more than two successive epigrams (10–11, ΠΠ; 13ᴮ–14, AA; 92–3, AA); and in these the order may well be fortuitous. We cannot guess the significance of the fact that this block contains an unusually high proportion of contested ascriptions, both within the Palatine and between the two sources.[1]

The following authors represented in this block are included in the present collection. We hold that there is no proof, and for most of them no evidence at all, that they were included in the *Garland*; the nature of their claims is stated in the Introduction to each: Alpheus, Antonius, Archias, Flaccus, Isidorus, Mundus, Polyaenus of Sardis, Julius Polyaenus, and Pompeius.

(*b*) Other evidence

In five places an anonymous epigram begins or ends a short alphabetical sequence. The claims of these are discussed in the Introduction to the *Adespota*; two of them are included in this book.

There are a few places where an epigram, ascribed to an author not otherwise attested as a contributor to the *Garland*, occurs in a disordered *Garland*-block or stands next to one or two epigrams by *Garland*-authors beginning with the same initial letter:

Alpheus 9.90 (I) is last in the disordered block MMNNN ΠMMΛN. 7.237 (VI) is fifth in the disordered block AAMOOHΦT. 6.187 (V), 9.95 (VII), 97 (VIII) and 110 (IV) stand next to single epigrams by *Garland*-authors.

Glaucus 9.774–5 (I–II) begin a short disordered block AHZΓ surrounded by Byzantine epigrams. Subject-matter is the ruling principle of arrangement.

Pintyus 7.16 (I) follows an epigram by Antipater, perhaps the Thessalonican (LXXIV), beginning with the same letter, O; it is

---

[1] There are double ascriptions for as many as ten of the first fifty-five epigrams in Book 9.

followed by Laurea and Antipater of Thessalonica, beginning
AA. Subject-matter is the ruling principle of arrangement.

Laurea 7.17 (1), following Pinytus, precedes an epigram by
Antipater of Thessalonica beginning with the same letter.
Subject-matter is the ruling principle of arrangement.

The following are included in this collection as examples of
authors who were or may have been contemporary with the
contributors to the *Garland*, and who may have been included
in the *Garland*, though the evidence is insufficient to prove that
they were: Alpheus, Antonius, Archias, Flaccus, Glaucus,
Isidorus, Laurea, Mundus, Pinytus, Polyaenus of Sardis,
Julius Polyaenus, Pompeius.

(c) We have examined but rejected certain other claims. Five
of these deserve special mention:

1. *Thyillus.* 6.170 has no connexion with the *Garland*. 10.5
was put next to an epigram by Argentarius because of its theme;
7.223, next to one by Philodemus, for the same reason.[1]

2. *Dionysius of Andros.*[2] A couplet on a convivial theme is
ascribed to this name at 7.533. 7.526-9 are Meleagrian; 530-1,
Antipater of Thessalonica; 532, Isidorus; 534 is headed 'Aetolian
Automedon';[3] another block from Meleager follows. The
epigram-initials between the Meleagrian blocks are MAEKA.
Thus Dionysius stands between two epigrams whose authors are
not known to be Philippan, in a block in which alphabetical
order is not preserved; and it should be added that two-line
epigrams are relatively uncommon in Philip's *Garland*.[4]

3. *Gaetulicus.* An epigram ascribed to this name occurs in an
alphabetical sequence from a later collection (11.409). The
name recurs in eight other places, and in three of them (5.17,
7.244-5, 7.275), Gaetulicus stands next to isolated epigrams by
Garland-authors; all these have been placed where they are
because of their subject-matter, and there remains no evidence

[1] The epigram-initials are EH, two of the commonest; the pair is preceded by an
anonymous epigram beginning A, but this is surely Byzantine.
[2] See *HE* 2.231. [3] See vol. 2.186. [4] See p. xxxvii.

whatsoever that an author of this name was included in the *Garland*.

4. *Archimedes*. 7.50, the only epigram ascribed to this name, stands between isolated epigrams by *Garland*-authors. The alphabetical order is incoherent, and the collocation of these three epigrams is due to their subject-matter.

5. *Plato Junior*. 9.13 stands next to an isolated epigram on the same theme by Antiphilus. 9.748 is preceded by 'Plato', who may be 'Plato Junior'; if so, 9.747–8 are a pair preceded by an isolated epigram by a *Garland*-author; the epigram-initials are EEH, but the collocation is plainly due to the subject-matter and the sequence must be regarded as fortuitous. 9.751 stands between Archias and 'Asclepiades [= XLIV in *HE*] or Antipater of Thessalonica'. Other epigrams ascribed simply to Plato (not to Plato Junior) stand next to epigrams by *Garland*-authors: 7.670 precedes an epigram headed ἄδηλον, οἱ δὲ Βιάνοροc; 9.44, by Flaccus (PPl) or Plato (C), stands next to Flaccus (C) or Plato or Antipater (Pl); 9.823 stands next to Erucius. There is plainly no evidence here for including Plato Junior in the *Garland*.

We have also excluded the following authors, who have no connexion with the *Garland* except that the epigrams cited stand next to isolated epigrams by *Garland*-authors, none of them having the same epigram-initial as its *Garland*-neighbour: Andronicus 7.181; Capito 5.67 (if 5.68 is by Polemon), Cillactor 5.29 and 45, Cyllenius 9.4 (if 9.3 is by Antipater, and if this is the Thessalonican) and 33, Demiurgus 7.52, Zelotus 9.30–1 (but 9.30 may belong to Bassus), Zosimus 6.183–5 (and 6.15 stands next to Archias).

The following, whose epigrams stand next to epigrams by the doubtful claimants, have even less claim to consideration: Germanicus 9.17–18 (next to Archias of Mytilene, who may be a Meleagrian author; see vol. 2.433), Longus 6.191 (next to Archias) Satyrius 6.11 (following Antipater, unqualified), 10.6 and 11 (both next to Archias), Xenocritus 7.291 (next to Flaccus).

The present collection includes all the epigrams assigned to Philip's *Garland* by Weisshäupl,[1] with the following exceptions:

(*a*) Seven *adespota*: 6.87, 9.15, and 705, discussed in the Preface to the *Adespota* (vol. 2.418); 7.691, four hexameters, and 7.704, two iambics, surely not from the *Garland*; 9.105, which has no connexion with the *Garland*; and 9.741, between Geminus and Philip, on Myron's *Cow*, not in alphabetical order.

(*b*) The following named authors: Archimedes 7.50, Plato Junior 9.13, Plato 9.747, and Plato Junior 9.748. See p. xxvi.

All the authors in the present collection are included in Weisshäupl's Philippan list except four of the doubtful claimants: Glaucus, Pinytus, Polyaenus of Sardis, and Pompeius.

The present collection includes also all epigrams marked 'Fr. Cor. Phil.'[2] in Stadtmüller's edition, with the following exceptions:

(*a*) 6.37, anonymous, between two epigrams by Philip; not in alphabetical order; and Thyillus 7.223 (see p. xxv).

(*b*) 9.370–6 (he omits 374, arbitrarily): between a couple of Byzantine epigrams and a series from Palladas there stands an epigram by Tiberius Illustrius followed by anonymous epigrams, the initials running ΟΔΛΤΤΤ. We see no reason whatever to connect this block with the *Garland*.

Beckby, in the introduction to his edition, includes in his list of Philip's contributors the names of Aceratus, Aeschines, Diophanes, Gaetulicus, 'Satrius', and Thyillus. No epigram by any of these occurs in the main or the shorter alphabetical sequences, and there is no other evidence that any of them was a contributor to the *Garland*. If the criterion of possibility unsupported by evidence were to be applied systematically, we should have to add (among others) Andronicus, Archimedes, Capito, Cillactor, Cyllenius, Dionysius of Andros, Germanicus, Plato Junior, Zelotus, and Zosimus.

---

[1] *Grabged.* 13–20, following but improving upon Passow *Opusc. Acad.* 188 ff. and Weigand *Rh. Mus.* 3.541 ff.

[2] Usually in the left-hand margin of the text, but sometimes omitted there and to be sought (not always to be found) in the page-headings.

No doubt it will be said that we ought to have included all epigrams from the *Anthology* within our date-limits, whether they are connected with Philip's *Garland* or not. Our own opinion is that our second series goes far enough in this direction, if not a little too far. For the rest (and we have given careful consideration to the claims of twenty[1] excluded authors) we are quite at the mercy of subjective impression, a most unreliable guide to the dating of epigrams in the *Anthology*. For some of the excluded authors (notably Aceratus, Archimedes, Capito, Cillactor, Cornelius Longus, Dionysius Andrius, and Ptolemaeus) there is no reason to prefer the period covered by the *Garland* to the period following it; for a few (Dionysius Sophistes, Satyrius, and Zosimus; perhaps also Andronicus and Xenocritus) the preceding period is well within the range of possibility. Merely guessing, we should say that the likeliest to come from the *Garland's* period are Cyllenius, Thyillus, and Zelotus, perhaps also Gallus and Plato Junior; these would contribute a dozen epigrams altogether.

We may be at fault in excluding Germanicus Caesar, the only datable author among those at present under consideration; but the evidence seems to us too doubtful to justify the ascription of any extant epigram to this famous name.[2]

[1] Those named below, with the addition of Gaetulicus (see p. xxv) and Demiurgus (*A.P.* 7.52).

[2] *A.P.* 9.17 and 18 are headed Γερμανικοῦ Καίσαρος by the Corrector, who however added γρ. Ἀδριανοῦ in the margin at 9.17, an addition which we suppose to cover both epigrams. Pl heads 9.17 Γερμανοῦ, 9.18 τοῦ αὐτοῦ.

A.P. 9.387 is headed Ἀδριανοῦ Καίσαρος by the text-hand, and the Corrector adds οἱ δὲ Γερμανικοῦ, Ἡσύχιος δὲ εἰς Τιβέριον τὸν Καίσαρα ἀναφέρει αὐτό; Pl heads it Ἀδριανοῦ Καίσαρος, οἱ δὲ Γερμανικοῦ.

It looks rather as though these epigrams started life under the heading Καίσαρος, to which Γερμανικοῦ, Τιβερίου, or Ἀδριανοῦ was later added according to taste. It is at least clear that the ascription of these epigrams to Germanicus was, and remains, doubtful.

We agree with Stadtmüller and Kroll (*RE* 10.464) in rejecting absolutely Pl's ascription of *A.P.* 7.73–4 to Germanicus.

(iv) *Ascriptions*

There are remarkably few gaps or ambiguities in the transmission of author-names for *Garland*-epigrams in P. In the main alphabetical sequences, of 334 epigrams only three[1] lack an author's name, and doubt is raised about the authorship of only five.[2] Of the epigrams by *Garland*-authors outside the main sequences, only three[3] lack an author's name in P, and doubt is raised about the authorship of ten.

Pl leaves thirty-nine epigrams[4] without an author's name, including eight marked ἄδηλον,[5] and its author-names differ from P's in twenty-seven places.[6] In the main alphabetical sequences there is only one epigram[7] for which Pl supplies a name lacking in P; three epigrams[8] outside the alphabetical sequences are ascribed to *Garland*-authors by Pl but not by P.

Turning now to the epigrams by the doubtful claimants, we find that only one[9] of them lacks an author's name in P, and that doubt is raised there about the authorship of only six. Pl leaves two without an author's name and supplies a name different from P's in five places.[10]

Where the Palatine shows doubt (e.g. ᾿Αντιπάτρου, οἱ δὲ Φιλίππου) we ascribe the epigram to the author first named unless there seems to us to be positive cause for preferring the

[1] 7.626, 9.252, both marked ἀδέσποτον; 9.553.
[2] 6.246, 7.405, 9.264, 406 and 408.
[3] 6.22, 9.13[B] and 742 (Pl's ascription of 9.742 (=Philip LXXIX) to a *Garland*-author is almost certainly erroneous). We do not count here the special case of 6.291 (=Antipater CI), where P has ᾿Αντιπάτρου, whereas C marks it ἀδέσποτον when it occurs the second time, after 9.164.
[4] Reckoning epigrams both in and out of the alphabetical sequences.
[5] See Gow *GA* 20 ff. So far as the *Garland*-epigrams in the present collection are concerned, Pl has ἄδηλον, not ἀδέσποτον, whereas P has ἀδέσποτον, not ἄδηλον except at 7.671 and in the peculiar case of 7.741.3–8 (=Crinagoras 1885–90).
[6] In about one-third of these, the discrepancy may be due to misunderstanding the reference of τοῦ αὐτοῦ.
[7] 9.252 ἀδέσποτον P, Βιάνοροϲ Pl.
[8] As in n. 3 above.
[9] 9.8. We do not count here 9.122, ἀδέσποτον P[a], Εὐήνου P[b].
[10] In two of these the discrepancy may be due to confusion about the reference of τοῦ αὐτοῦ.

alternative. Where the Palatine and Planudean are in conflict, we generally prefer the former.[1]

(v) *Homonymous authors*

An insoluble problem arises when the evidence proves that more than one author is represented by one name or indicates that this may be so.

(1) Epigrams are divided between 'A' and 'A of X'; e.g. 'Thallus' and 'Thallus of Miletus'. In some instances it is likely, in others unlikely, that the ethnic or other epithet was added to distinguish different authors of the same name.

(2) Epigrams are divided between 'A', 'A of X', and 'A of Y', not to mention greater multiples. It is usually impossible to determine how many authors are represented or to make a proper distribution among them of those epigrams which lack the ethnic or other epithet. Antiphanes, Antiphanes of Macedon, and Antiphanes of Megalopolis may be one author (for one of the ethnics may be erroneous) or two authors or even three authors. If there are two, a Macedonian and a Megalopolitan, we cannot judge which is the author of any epigram headed simply 'Antiphanes'.

The following lists summarise such opinions as we have found it possible to form; reasons are given in the Introductions to the authors:

(*a*) Established *Garland*-authors, with namesakes. Square brackets signify that the combination of name and epithet is found only with epigrams detached from the alphabetical sequences. Sinuous brackets ({) couple pairs who may represent a single author. Asterisks mark names which may, in each case, represent two authors.

All recorded ethnics and other epithets[2] are included in these lists.

---

[1] The merits of Pl's ascriptions are always to be carefully considered; we accept them as a rule readily enough where P has no name, as in 6.22, 9.8, 9.13[B], 9.252. But unless there is a positive reason for the alternative, it is prudent to prefer the source which makes far the fewer demonstrable mistakes.

[2] On the question whether these go back to Philip himself, see Gow *GA* 18 ff.

Adaeus of Macedon
[Addaeus of Mytilene]
Aemilianus of Nicaea
Antigonus of Carystus
Antimedon of Cyzicus
Antipater of Thessalonica[1]
{ Antiphanes of Macedon
{ Antiphanes of Megalopolis
Antistius
Apollonides
[Apollonius of Smyrna]
Argentarius
Automedon
Bassus
[Bassus of Smyrna]
*Bianor *grammaticus* of Bithynia
Boethus
Crinagoras of Mytilene
*Diocles of Carystus
Diodorus of Sardis
*Diodorus *grammaticus* [of Tarsus]
Diotimus of Miletus
Epigonus of Thessalonica
{ Erucius of Thessaly
{ [Erucius of Cyzicus]

Etruscus of Messene
Euenus *grammaticus*
[Euenus of Ascalon]
[Euenus of Athens]
[Euenus of Sicily]
Geminus
Heraclides of Sinope
{ Honestus of Byzantium
{ [Honestus of Corinth]
Maccius
{ Macedonius
{ Macedonius of Thessalonica
Myrinus
Parmenion of Macedon
Philip of Thessalonica
Philodemus
Polemon the King
Quintus
*Sabinus [*grammaticus*]
Scaevola
Secundus of Tarentum
Serapion of Alexandria
Thallus of Miletus
Zonas of Sardis

(*b*) Doubtful claimants, with namesakes.

Alpheus of Mytilene
Antonius of Argos
Archias of Byzantium
Archias *grammaticus*
Archias Junior
Archias of Macedon
Archias of Mytilene[2]
Flaccus

Glaucus of Athens
Isidorus of Aegae
Laurea
Mundus
Pinytus
Polyaenus of Sardis
Polyaenus, Julius
Pompeius

This is perhaps the most convenient place to add the only point of nomenclature omitted in the foregoing lists,—the full names of the Italians and Romanised Greeks:

[1] The ethnics Θετταλοῦ (once) and Μακεδόνος (five times) also are applied to the name Antipater; we suppose that these refer to the Thessalonican.

[2] In addition to these, Archias of Antioch has a claim to inclusion; see vol. 2.435.

praenomen	nomen	cognomen
—	Tullius	Laurea
—	Lollius	Bassus
—	Mucius	Scaevola
—	Munatius	Mundus
—	Statilius[1]	Flaccus
—	Tullius	Geminus
—	Tullius	Sabinus
Quintus	Maccius	—
—	Antistius	—
—	Antonius	—
—	Erucius	—
—	Pompeius	—[2]
Marcus	—	Argentarius
—	—	Aemilianus
—	—	Etruscus
—	—	Honestus
—	—	Secundus
Quintus	—	—

We use the *cognomen* if it is known; if not, the *nomen*; only Quintus must be called by his *praenomen*.

(vi) *General observations on the 'Garland'-authors*

The majority of these authors are mere names to us. Much is known of Philodemus, something of Mucius Scaevola and Polemon. We hear a little from other sources about Crinagoras, Diodorus of Sardis, and Zonas; conjecture supplies some information about Antistius, Apollonides, Argentarius, Diocles, Diodorus of Tarsus, and Geminus. Among the doubtful claimants there is no familiar figure except Laurea, unless Archias of Antioch is to be recognised; and conjecture supplies Pompeius with an identity.

The ethnic adjectives indicate that Philip chose freely among his own compatriots: Adaeus, Antiphanes, and Parmenion are Macedonians; Antipater, Epigonus, and Macedonius come from Thessalonica. Professors of rhetoric and similar studies are well

---

[1] Spelt as if 'Statyllius' in our sources.
[2] Conjecture supplies the *cognomen* 'Macer'.

represented: Bianor, Diodorus of Sardis, Euenus, and Zonas; perhaps also Aemilianus, Apollonides, Argentarius, Diocles, Diodorus of Tarsus, Polyaenus of Sardis, and Sabinus. Several of Philip's authors sought or enjoyed patronage in high society, including the imperial household, notably Philip himself, Antipater, Antiphilus, Apollonides, Bassus, Diodorus of Sardis, Honestus, and Thallus; Crinagoras and Philodemus are far above the common herd, acceptable associates of the great. But high society itself is sparsely represented: only by Scaevola, Crinagoras, and Polemon,[1] unless Antistius, Geminus, and Pompeius are correctly identified.

(vii) *Styles and subjects*

Philip's *Garland* includes two remarkably interesting authors, Crinagoras and Philodemus; and a third who is much better than the rest, Argentarius. The first of these is in a class by himself. The epigrams of Crinagoras reflect high affairs of state and other aspects of contemporary life, mostly at Rome and mostly in the loftiest ranks of society; and the impress of the poet's personality is clearly marked. His language is vigorous, often plain and sometimes unpolished; his metre is rough. He is the only one of these authors, except to some extent Antipater and Philodemus, whose epigrams are as a rule inspired by the passing scene and coloured by strong emotions. Personal reaction to realities is not very often discernible elsewhere in the present collection, though a humbler species of the same genus is found in certain epigrams by authors of lower social standing who seek the favour of the imperial household; hereabout is the only new ground broken for the cultivation of the epigram in this period.

Philodemus and Argentarius are the principal exceptions to the general rule that the amatory epigram, especially the paederastic, is quite out of fashion; the contrast with contemporary Roman poetry is in this respect extreme and surprising.

---

[1] There is no evidence that the celebrated Germanicus was included (see p. xxviii n. 2). If he had been, one might have expected him to be named in the *Proem*; but King Polemon was omitted from the *Proem*.

These two authors and Automedon are the principal exceptions to another general rule, that the satirical epigram is out of fashion.

The present collection includes a few other competent and pleasing authors, notably Adaeus, Antiphanes, Antistius, Diodorus of Sardis, and Erucius. These compose as a rule in a relatively straightforward style on conventional themes; but a much stronger impression is left on the reader's mind by those epigrammatists who reflect the baneful influence of the Tarentine Leonidas. The mannerisms of this school have indeed left their mark on only a minority of the *Garland*-authors, but it is a minority which includes some of those most fully represented, notably Philip, Antiphilus, and Bianor. The characteristics of the style are too familiar to need more than a summary description here. It can be broadly defined as the exercise of ingenuity in word-coining and phrase-making, extravagantly picturesque, applied to the description of commonplace objects or the narration of uncommon events. Such elaboration of vocabulary and phrasing, often over-strained and occasionally ludicrous, is applied also to descriptions of dedications or of works of art. The themes are as a rule conventional or novel variations on the conventional, and the epigram is designed simply to exhibit the composer's skill in the Leonidean style. That style is much less often employed in the only other type of epigram common in this period, the epitaph (whether inscriptional or fictitious); the epitaphs are as a rule appreciably less exotic in word and phrase.

The most accomplished of the Leonideans—superior to Leonidas himself—are Maccius and Zonas; far the worst is Philip himself. Antiphilus is a fair representative of the school. One of the epigrams of Myrinus (II) is a successful application of the Leonidean style to a satirical theme.

There are some highly competent composers among the doubtful claimants. Pompeius writes well, and we should like more of Julius Polyaenus. Isidorus was a pleasing epigrammatist; so were Antonius, Laurea, and Mundus, if they are fairly represented. Alpheus is mediocre, and no more can be said for Flaccus and Glaucus. The Leonidean style is seldom found in this group of authors except in the miscellany which passes under the name of Archias.

The long life and popularity of these authors may seem to be much beyond their deserts, but the explanation is not, we believe, very far to seek. The epigram in this period, as before, deals for the most part with topics of common interest, an interest by no means confined to the sophisticated circles for which they were primarily intended. The love-poems and dedications and epitaphs, however artificial in conception and execution, were felt by many people, especially people in the middle and humbler walks of life, to be closely related to their own experience; even the tall stories are often not far from the actual experience of men and women in the villages on the coasts and hills, and probably not at all far from their talk about unusual events. What we should have wished to say on this theme has already been said by F. L. Lucas in *Greek Poetry* (Everyman's Library (1966) pp. 240 ff.) :[1]

History is largely preoccupied with crises and cataclysms; but the daily life of ordinary men and women remains harder to recall. Towering masterpieces like Homer's epics, or the Parthenon, or the pediments of Olympia are, of their nature, exceptional and rare; far more light may be thrown on the common folk of Hellas by the delicacy of some painted vase, the grace of a Tanagra statuette, the quiet sorrow of a grave-relief from the Cerameicus, or by small and unpretending poems such as these...These can tell us of a people's simple yet enduring joys and sorrows, hopes and fears. A girl mourns for the pet rabbit, or cricket, she has loved and lost; or is mourned herself by the playmates her gay stories will never gladden again. A young bride offers the dolls and drums of her childish years to the Maiden-Goddess who has watched over her maidenhood; or is lit to her own untimely tomb by the same torches as made gay her marriage-feast. Lovers warn their coy mistresses how fast a rose must fall; or curse their fickleness; or chide their own despair. Of Love's goddess a wife begs only that her husband be always one with her in heart; a courtesan prays to the same Aphrodite, whom, according to

[1] See also Mackail *Select Epigrams from the Greek Anthology* (1911) 32–90.

her lights, she also has always truly served; or puts aside the too truthful mirror in which it has grown terrible to look. A young hunter lies, his hunting ended, among the wild creatures that now leap heedlessly across his grave. The tired traveller plunges his parched face in the cool of the wayside spring, or sprawls, relaxed at last, under its plane-trees' shade. A shepherd listens to Pan piping among his nymphs in the windless silence of the hills; or prays still to hear, even in his grave, the flocks quietly nibbling at the turf above him. A ploughman turns out his faithful ox to grass for its few remaining years; or recalls his own lifelong warfare with the briars and brambles that now triumphantly invade his final resting-place. The sailor lies happily lazy beside the bubble of his cooking-pot; or finds a friendless grave in some grey, surf-pounded shingle, or amid the waste seas of the Levant. The old man, life's journey done, passes to his rest with quiet resignation, or a smile of irony.

It matters little or nothing if the style is second-rate and second-hand, and the subject inspired in the author by nothing more than a desire to impress the sophisticated city-folk. Many of these epigrams reflect, as Lucas says, 'the joys and sorrows, hopes and fears' of simple people; there were, and still are, many homes in the remote villages of Greece and Crete where they ring truer than they ever did in the minds of their composers.

(viii) *Dialects*

The majority of the epigrams in the present collection are written in a literary Ionic dialect long established by tradition for elegiac verse of this kind. Some are written in a similarly traditional Doric, which seldom differs in anything more than the use of ᾱ for η.[1] There are numerous epigrams in which these dialects are mixed, and in editing these we adopt the practice described in *HE* 1.xlv ff.:[2]

(1) Where the sources agree on a mixture of Ionic and Doric, we make no change unless there is only one aberrant form.

(2) Where the sources offer a choice between Ionic and Doric, we choose the form which best matches the rest of the epigram. If the dialect of the rest is mixed, we generally prefer

[1] The Doric is somewhat severer in Erucius II and Zonas III.
[2] We refer to this for a fuller discussion.

the Doric; there is a tendency in our sources, as elsewhere, rather to change from ᾱ to η than *vice versa*. P has many more examples of ᾱ where Pl has η than *vice versa*.

(ix) *Lengths of epigrams*

There is a single exception to the general rule that no elegiac epigram composed by a *Garland*-author exceeds eight lines: 9.26, ascribed to Antipater of Thessalonica (XIX), has ten lines.[1] In *HE*, as many as seventy-one epigrams exceed eight lines.[2]

The favourite length is six lines[3] (327 epigrams); four-line epigrams (112) and eight-line (98) are much less common; two-line (39) are relatively rare. The pattern is much the same in the doubtful claimants: half their epigrams have six lines, and none exceeds eight lines except three in the miscellany under the name 'Archias'.[4]

The epigrams in non-elegiac metres show a preference for an even number of lines; the exceptions are Crinagoras XL (7), Philip XIV (7) and LXII (5).[5]

(x) *Metres*

(1) Variety of metres

The following are composed in metres other than the elegiac:
(*a*) Hendecasyllables: Alpheus IV, Antipater LXII.
(*b*) Dactylic pentameters: Philip LXII.

---

[1] There is no evidence that this epigram was included in the *Garland*. *A.Pl.* 131 and 133, ascribed simply to 'Antipater' (LXXXVI and LXXXVII), have each ten lines; we think it quite possible that he is the Sidonian.

[2] Ten lines, 48; twelve lines, 14; fourteen lines, 3; sixteen lines, 3; Theocritus XX has 18, Meleager CXXII has 20, Antipater of Sidon LXIV has 24.

[3] Here too is a change of fashion. In *HE*, the favourite length is four lines (343; especially among some of the older poets); then six lines (216) and eight lines (112); two-line epigrams are relatively rare (78).

[4] Archias IX, XVI, XIX.

[5] Seven lines also in Philip LII, but we believe that a line is missing. Among the doubtful claimants, Flaccus II has five lines; and 'Lacon or Philip' LXXVI has eleven.

In *HE*, four of the five epigrams by Leonidas in iambic trimeters have an uneven number of lines; so have Aeschrion I (scazons) and Phalaecus II (ia. trim. catal.).

(*c*) Iambic trimeters: Antipater cvii, cx, Apollonides xviii, Crinagoras xl, l, Flaccus ii, Heraclides i, Isidorus ii, iii, Philip xii–xiv, xvi, xx, xxvi, xxxiv, xlviii, lii, lxiv–lxvi and (probably not by Philip) lxxvi, lxxix.[1]

(*d*) Scazons: Apollonides ix.

(2) Mixed metres

Epigrams in a mixture of different metres were popular only in the third century B.C.;[2] there is no example in the present collection, unless one is to be recognised in Crinagoras vii.

(3) Prosody

The following general rules and preferences are characteristic of the versification of most of the *Garland*-authors and their contemporaries. No account is taken here of non-elegiac metres:

A. Short vowels before mute + liquid or nasal consonants

(*a*) Within a word or word-group[3] a short vowel is normally lengthened by following mute + liquid or nasal consonants.

Exceptions (about 150) include twenty proper-names otherwise intractable and eighteen examples of a vowel left short at the point of junction in compounds otherwise intractable.[4] Certain words are proner than others to exceptional treatment, notably ἀλλότριος, βότρυς, δάκρυον, Κύπρις; and in a dozen places the syllabic augment is left short.

In word-groups such vowels are very seldom left short: Adaeus 19 τὸ πρίν, 51 ὁ πρεσβυς, Crinagoras 2053 τὶ πλεον,

---

[1] In *HE*: Scazons, Aeschrion i, Theocritus xiii; Hendecasyllables, Phalaecus iii, Theocritus xvi; Iambic trimeters, Leonidas ii, xxiii, lxviii, lxxix, xc, Phaedimus ii, anon. lviii B. Other unmixed metres in *HE*: ia. trim. catal., Phalaecus ii; ia. dim. catal., Callimachus xvii; ia. tetr. catal. + ia. trim. catal., Asclepiades xxxiii; ia. trim. + cr. ba., Theodoridas xv; tro. pent. catal., Callimachus lxviii; Greater Asclepiad, Callimachus lxix; Pherecr., Callimachus lxx; Archilochian, Theodoridas vi.

[2] In *HE*: ia. trim. + dact. tetr. catal., Phaedimus iii; ia. trim. + hendecas., Theocritus xv; tro. tetr. catal. + reiz., Theocritus xvii; Archiloch. + ia. trim. + ia. trim. catal., Theocritus xiv; 2 ia. dim. catal. + Archiloch., Callimachus xvii; Archiloch. + hendecas., Callimachus xlviii; hendecas. + Archiloch., Theocritus xi; ia. dim. catal. + hendecas., Callimachus xx.

[3] Especially article + noun or adj.; preposition + noun or adj.; τί πλέον, *sim.*

[4] E.g. μουσὸπροσωπος.

Philip 2897 ὅ πρεσβυς; Archias 3588 τὅ κρηγυον, Glaucus 3869 ὅ γλυπτας.

(*b*) The number of places where a final vowel stands before initial consonants of these types is small enough[1] to suggest that the collocation was avoided. Where it occurs, two features are noticeable:

(i) The vowel is normally left short. There are only about fifty exceptions; fourteen of these involve lengthening of γε, δέ, με, τε, three involve lengthening before βλ, γλ, γν, and seven may be explained as extensions of the word-group principle.[2] The remaining exceptions[3] are Antipater 216, 254, 297, 523, 552, 619, 711, Apollonides 1237, 1296, [Antiphilus] 1097, 1098, Argentarius 1430, Bianor 1666, Crinagoras 1828, 1937, 2011, Erucius 2239, 2253, Philodemus 3214, 3311, Zonas 3449; Antonius 3587, Archias 3795.

(ii) The collocation is avoided especially in the first half of either line; there are only about 30 exceptions, a third of them in Antipater.

Some epigrammatists are strict in their observance of these rules. Few exceptions will be found in Argentarius, Diodorus, Erucius, Maccius and Philodemus; Crinagoras, Parmenion and Philip are much laxer.

B. *Correptio epica*[4]

(*a*) Correption at the end of the dactyl is confined as a rule to the first dactyl in the hexameter and pentameter and to the bucolic diaeresis in the former and the corresponding place in the latter line. There are very few exceptions: Antipater 715, Antiphilus 921, Apollonides 1161, Crinagoras 1831, Diodorus 2106; Flaccus 3855 (all at the end of the fifth dactyl).[5]

---

[1] About 140 examples.

[2] I.e. adj. or adverb + noun or verb, as in μεγᾱ κλαιουσα, δολιχᾱ πρυμνησια, ενᾱ τροπον, τοδὲ προκαλυμμα, βαρῡ βρυχημα, δονακᾱ τριτανυστον.

[3] Excluding Antipater 257, where ἔθανεν βρέφος could be written.

[4] In the following we take no account of καί, μοι, τοι, που, *sim.*

[5] In *HE* there are only eighteen certain examples of correption at the end of the fifth dactyl (not counting the monosyllables, as in the previous note; there are about two dozen examples of these in correption).

(b) Correption between the short syllables of the dactyl (e.g. αcταῖ εcαν) is avoided. There are less than eighty exceptions, a quarter of them in Crinagoras. Such correption is particularly uncommon

(i) at the feminine caesura in the hexameter (about twenty exceptions, of which six are in Crinagoras);[1]

(ii) in the fifth dactyl in the hexameter (only Antipater 711, Crinagoras 1827, 1877, 1893; and καί treated thus in Laurea 3927).[2]

(c) The syllables most commonly so treated are -μαι, -εαι, -cαι, -ται of verbs and -οι, -αι of nouns, adjectives, and participles. Correption of -η, -ηι, -ᾱ, -ει, -οῖ, -ου, -ω and -ωι is relatively rare except in Crinagoras.

Some authors are strict in their observances of these rules, notably Apollonides, Argentarius, Diodorus, Geminus, Maccius, and Philodemus.

It is a remarkable feature of Philip's versification that he avoids *correptio epica* in all circumstances.[3]

C. Hiatus

Hiatus is avoided.[4] Exceptions are very rare except in Antipater and Crinagoras: Adaeus 3, Antipater 87, 149, 153, 171, 177, 212, 381, 463, 495, 601, 713, Antiphilus 1073, Bianor 1651, 1673, Crinagoras 1799, 1842, 1845, 1851, 1867 (*bis*), 1875, 1879, 1891 (*bis*), 1927, 1939, 1946, 1951, 1954, 1965, 1967, 1969, 1981, 1991, 2036, 2046, 2054, 2057, Erucius 2248, 2262, 2270, Macedonius 2544, Philodemus 3314 (*dub.*), Philip 2821, 2923 (*fort. bis*), Zonas 3475; Archias 3742, 3748, Glaucus 3873 (*dub.*), Laurea 3917.

---

[1] Correption in this place is very rare in *HE*: only twenty-five examples, not counting καί (twenty-three), ἤ, ναί, Ζεῦ, where the true caesura is the masculine.

[2] Correption in this place is very rare in *HE*: seven certain examples, not counting correption of monosyllables (thirteen examples).

[3] Correption occurs in Philip only six times: 2852, 2995, 3009, 3035, 3082–3.

[4] Excluding hiatus in correption; and before the pronoun οἱ, of which there are a dozen examples (and only one where the digamma is not effective in οἱ: Geminus 2386; in *HE*, Hegesippus 6.166.3 = 1907, Phalaecus *ap.* Athen. 10.440 D = 2938 n.).

There are about as many examples in Crinagoras as in all the other *Garland*-authors together. A writer who begins a line καὶ αὐτὴ ἤχλυcεν is plainly indifferent to the normal rules. Most remarkable is his tolerance of those monosyllables which are commonly subject to correption (καί, coί, *sim.*) as true long syllables capable of standing in hiatus.

It is a general rule in these authors that hiatus is not obviated by digamma except before the pronoun οἱ. There may be an exception in Crinagoras 1891 μὴ εἴπῃιc and possibly another in 2054 ἐπὶ ἐλπίcι; but Crinagoras is so tolerant of hiatus that he may have written thus without any thought of digamma. The phenomenon is introduced by a likely conjecture in Diodorus 2138.

Hiatus at the diaeresis of the pentameter is contrary to rule. We believe that there is no true exception in the *Garland*-authors[1] (see Antiphilus (?) 1094, Crinagoras 1854, anon. 3509; Alpheus 3561, Archias 3619).

D. We draw attention here to a fact discussed by Maas, *Gk Metre* (1962) §22: it is a general rule that the syllable which ends the first half of the pentameter should be, or contain, a long vowel or diphthong. Lengthening by position is avoided, and lengthening by means of paragogic *nu* is particularly rare (Adaeus 40, Antipater 162, Antiphilus 806, 956, Crinagoras 1840, 1900; in *HE*, seventeen examples, none in Meleager's lengthy contribution).

There are only about seventy exceptions[2] to this rule in 1,895 lines in the present collection; there is not a single exception in Philip's lengthy contribution, a fact which surely rules out the operation of mere chance.[3]

---

[1] In *HE*, the only exception is anon. 3765. *HE* has four apparent examples of a short syllable counting as a long in this place (Antipater 289, 389, Phaedimus 2906, anon. 3869); Glaucus 3874, the only apparent example in the present collection, is surely corrupt.

[2] Forty-three of these in Antipater, Antiphanes, Antiphilus, and Crinagoras.

[3] There had long been a tendency in this direction, and it becomes more habitual as time goes on. Leonidas and Meleager have 68 exceptions in 712 lines (i.e. about as many as the present collection has in 1,895 lines). Theocritus has 11 exceptions

E. Elision

(*a*) Elision of -αι is avoided.[1] The only exceptions are Adaeus 4, Antipater 190, 424, Antiphanes 764, Apollonides 1283, Argentarius 1314, Crinagoras 1882, Euenus 2323, Maccius 2476, 2477, 2482, Philip 3119, Secundus 3384, Zonas 3493.

(*b*) Elision is avoided

(1) in the hexameter,

(i) at the masculine caesura;[2] the only exceptions are Adaeus 11, Antipater 241, Automedon 1577, Bassus 1639, Crinagoras 1831, 1875, Parmenion 2586, Philip 2927 (δ᾽);

(ii) at the feminine caesura; elision at this place is confined to disyllables,[3] so that there is always a preceding masculine caesura, and the disyllables are of types (prospective pronouns and prepositions; ὅτε and τότε once each) which allow the masculine caesura to predominate. The only exception is Antipater 169, where enclitic ποτέ is elided in this place;

(iii) at the bucolic diaeresis;[4] the only exceptions are Antiphanes 731, Crinagoras 1941, and a few examples of elision of δέ.

in 48 lines (in the epigrams; in *Id.* 8.33 ff., 6 in 14). Asclepiades, 12 in 107. Callimachus, 18 in 137 (in the epigrams; in *Lav. Pall.*, 9 in 71). Hermesianax *Coll. Alex. fr.* 6, 6 in 47.

It is to be noticed also that when the main caesura in the hexameter is masc. as a rule the syllable preceding the caesura is or contains a long vowel or diphthong. Lengthening by position occurs in Philip's *Garland*-authors about 78 times in 753 chances; in Philip himself, only thrice in 116 chances. That the facts are not fortuitous is clearly indicated by the contrast with *HE*, which has about 132 exceptions in 745 chances; in Meleager alone, 29 in 120.

It is noteworthy that in both hexameter and pentameter an appreciable number of the exceptions involve lengthening by means of the final consonant + *two* initial consonants, as in e.g. πλεξω λευκοῖον | πλ-.

[1] It is not quite so rare in *HE*: Meleager has nine examples, Leonidas six or seven, Asclepiades four, Posidippus two, Dioscorides, Hedylus, Nicias, Nossis, Pancrates and Theocritus one each, anon. three examples.

[2] This too is not quite so rare in *HE*: twenty-six examples, including four of elision of δέ or τε.

[3] In *HE* there is a single exception (Meleager 4558 τοὔνομ᾽ | ἐμοί) to the rule that only disyllables may be elided in this place. The disyllables are mostly pronouns or prepositions; other non-enclitic words are seldom elided here (ἵνα, θαμά, ἔτι, ὅτε, τίνα, φέρε once each); of verb-forms, only ἔχε and θέτο once each; of enclitics, ποτέ four times, τινά once.

[4] In *HE*, δέ is elided in this place nine times (five of them in Meleager), τε and με once each. Otherwise the elision is very rare: Antipater 318, Ariston 794, Asclepiades 980 (*dub.*), Damagetus 1381, Dioscorides 1575, Leonidas 2269, Perses 2883, Theocritus 3383, Meleager 4168, 4714.

(iv) in the fifth dactyl, especially

(*a*) between its short syllables;[1] only Antipater 499, Antiphilus 909, Apollonides 1257, 1283, Argentarius 1303, Diodorus 2154, Euenus 2306, Honestus 2414, Philip 3013, Philodemus 3172, Secundus 3384, 3390; Flaccus 3811, 3815, Isidorus 3885;

(*b*) after its second short syllable;[2] only Antipater 455, ἵνα in Parmenion 2578 and Philip 2817, and a few examples of δέ elided here.

(2) In the pentameter,

(i) between its halves;[3] only Adaeus 20, Antiphanes 750, Antiphilus 868, Bianor 1666, Crinagoras 1968 (*s.v.l.*), Parmenion 2607, 2609, Quintus 3361; Archias 3619 (*coni.*);

(ii) in its second half, where elision becomes the rarer the farther the line advances: after –, many examples; after – ∪, 26; after – ∪ ∪, 13; after – ∪ ∪ –, 10; after – ∪ ∪ – ∪,[4] 3 (Apollonides 1222, Argentarius 1440, Philodemus 3181).

An unparalleled elision is attested in Erucius 2261, ἄρτ(ι).

F. Masculine caesura in the hexameter is commonly followed by bucolic caesura, preferably with pause in the latter place. There are only two or three exceptions in Bianor, Geminus, Honestus, and Maccius together, not many in Antipater, Antiphilus, Apollonides, and Argentarius; Crinagoras, Parmenion, Philip, and Philodemus are much laxer.

G. A break between the short syllables of the fourth dactyl in the hexameter is avoided unless the first of the two shorts is a

---

[1] Here we take no account of elided γε, δέ, με, σε, τε, ἔτι, ὅτε, ποτε, τότε, and prepositions. In *HE* (with the same exclusions) there are twenty-eight exceptions.

[2] In *HE*, elision here is severely restricted: prepositions twenty-six times, δέ fourteen (never τε), ποτέ five, τινά three, ἄρα, γε, ἐμέ (never με), ὅτε, τόδε once each. There are three striking abnormalities: Hedylus 1887 ἔθιγ’, Mnasalces 2613 χερμάδι’, Phanias 2994 εἰνόδι’.

[3] In *HE*, thirty-five examples, twenty-four of them in Asclepiades, Callimachus, Leonidas, Posidippus, and Meleager. We do not count, for either *Garland*, elision of δέ, με, σε, τε in this place; the first and last of these are quite often elided.

[4] In *HE*, elision at this place occurs in Alcaeus 149, Asclepiades 893, Theocritus 3403.

prospective monosyllable (e.g. Crinagoras 1875 τί πρόωρον ἐφιείς). The only exceptions are Philip 2929, 3120, [Philip] 3158, Philodemus 3314.[1]

H. If the second foot of the hexameter is spondaic, no word except a prospective monosyllable may end with the foot. The only exceptions are Antipater 477, 575, Maccius 2490, Zonas 3444; Archias 3770.

I. If the fourth foot of the hexameter is spondaic, no word except a prospective monosyllable may end with the foot. There is no exception in the *Garland*-authors,[2] but see Archias 3730 n.

J. A break after the first syllable of the fifth dactyl in the hexameter is avoided, unless that place is occupied by a prospective monosyllable (τὴν ἁλὶ πιστήν) or followed by a post-positive word (Φιλοπρήγμων δὲ καλεῖται). Exceptions are absent from Bianor and Honestus, rare in Antiphilus, Apollonides, and Argentarius, quite common in Crinagoras, Philip, and Philodemus.

K. Words of the form ∪ –, not being part of a coherent word-group (τὸν ἐμόν, τί πλέον, *sim.*) should not stand before the main caesura in either line. Breaches of the rule are notably common in Antipater and Philip.

L. The spondee in the fifth foot of the hexameter is not common. Of the forty-one examples, Antipater (8), Crinagoras (7), Bianor (5) and Zonas (4) account for the majority. The last word of such lines always consists of either four or six syllables,[3] except Crinagoras 1835 διαπρύσιον σάλπιγγος.[4]

M. The addition of paragogic *nu* to 'make position' is uncommon, especially (i) *in thesi* (Antipater 706; Alpheus 3565),

---

[1] In *HE*, only Meleager 4132; Theaetetus 3366 involves a coherent word-group.
[2] In *HE*, Aratus 762, Leonidas 2213, Nicarchus 2749.
[3] I.e. either | ∪∪ – – – – or | – – – –.
[4] Automedon 1563 merely repeats an example from Homer. In Antipater 351, ἐσβέσθη δέ may count as a word-group, parallel to *HE* Leonidas 2379, 2433. The spondaic fifth foot is much rarer in *HE*, except in Leonidas (fifteen examples; three consecutive in 2375–9, 2429–33); the other authors have only eleven examples, of which five involve proper-names. Meleager has only two, both proper-names.

and (ii) at the end of the first half of the pentameter (see D above). It is unlikely to be fortuitous that this device occurs only once in forty-eight out of forty-nine epigrams assigned to Antiphilus, only twice each in Argentarius and Philodemus, and only thrice in Philip's lengthy contribution.

N. A few other anomalies are assembled here:

(*a*) A short final vowel is not lengthened by initial λ (exceptions: Adaeus 30, Erucius 2226)[1] or by initial ρ (exceptions: Argentarius 1371, 1390, Erucius 2229).[2] (*b*) The placing of monosyllabic forms of the definite article before the division of the pentameter, a common practice in Meleager's authors,[3] is hardly permitted by Philip's (exceptions: Antipater 364, Philodemus 3337, Zonas 3483). (*c*) Other rare anomalies are the placing of a monosyllabic enclitic before the masculine caesura in either line (Antipater 86, 198, 278, 590, Crinagoras 1797, 1901, Geminus 2388) or after it (Philip 3099, Philodemus 3191); diaeresis with pause after initial – ‿‿ – ‿ ‿ in the hexameter (Crinagoras 2030); the word-division εὔχετο γραῦν before the masculine caesura in Parmenion 2618; Crinagoras 1842, ἐν | παντί bestriding the division in the pentameter; Crinagoras 2033–4 and 2039–40, ending a sentence with the first word of the hexameter.[4]

(xi) *The date-limits of Philip's 'Garland'*

(1) The upper limit

All evidence, both external and internal, is consistent with the received opinion that Philip's *Garland* began where Meleager's ended, probably in the first decade of the first century B.C. Philodemus, who was just too late for Meleager's *Garland*,[5] was included in Philip's. There is no evidence that any author earlier than Philodemus and Zonas was included by Philip.

---

[1] In *HE*, only Leonidas 2496 for certain, but see also Leonidas 2021, Antagoras 166 n.

[2] In *HE*, Antipater 208, 452, Anyte 713, Asclepiades 1003, Callimachus 1105, Hedylus 1844, Pancrates 2847, Rhianus 3227, 3230, Theocritus 3392.

[3] See *HE* 2.131, 366, 619.   [4] In *HE*, cf. Nicias 2780–1.

[5] See *HE* 1.xv f.

(2) The lower limit

External evidence establishes or suggests dates extending from the first decade of the first century B.C. down to, but not necessarily beyond, the end of the principate of Gaius (A.D. 37–41).[1]

Zonas was a well-known person at the time of the Mithridatic wars; Philodemus was in his twenties between 90 and 80 B.C. Tullius Laurea and Mucius Scaevola were more or less contemporary with Cicero. Crinagoras served on embassies to Rome from Mytilene in 48/7, 45 and 26/5 B.C. Argentarius, if he was the pupil of Cestius Pius, lived in the Augustan period.[2] Diodorus of Sardis was a friend of Strabo (c. 64 B.C. to c. A.D. 21). Antipater of Thessalonica was familiar with L. Calpurnius Piso Frugi (consul 15 B.C.). Antistius, if he is C. Antistius Vetus, suffered banishment in A.D. 21. Apollonides, if he is the rhetorician from Nicaea, was contemporary with Tiberius. Pompeius, if he is Pompeius Macer Junior, committed suicide in A.D. 33. Polyaenus of Sardis is said to have lived under Gaius, by whom Polemon was appointed king of Pontus in A.D. 37. Geminus, if he is C. Terentius Tullius Geminus, was *consul suffectus* in A.D. 46 and a young man between A.D. 25 and 35.

Internal evidence is provided by the following:[3]

(a) From the beginning up to and including the principate of Tiberius.

Philodemus: XVII, the poet is thirty-seven years of age; XXIII, addressed to Piso, presumably Julius Caesar's father-in-law.

Crinagoras: see the Introduction to him. Most of the epigrams were composed before the beginning of the Christian era, one or two come from the second decade A.D.

Erucius: VI is Augustan at latest.

Diodorus of Sardis: XVIII describes a portrait of Arsinoê, who died in 41 B.C.; I, on Tiberius, probably 24 B.C.; VIII, probably on Drusus the brother of Tiberius, about the same time.

[1] For what follows, see the Introductions to each author.
[2] So also Diocles and Automedon, if they are correctly identified.
[3] See the Introductions to each author, and Prefaces and notes on the epigrams cited.

Antipater: see the Introduction to him; I, on Piso's victory over the Bessi, 11 B.C.; XLI may refer to the same campaign; XLVI and XLVII, to Gaius Caesar, not far from 1 B.C.; XLVIII, to Cotys, who was killed in A.D. 19.

Apollonides: XXI, probably on D. Laelius Balbus, consul in 6 B.C.; XXVI, probably to L. Calpurnius Piso Frugi, not earlier than 10 B.C.; XXIII, on Tiberius, not before A.D. 4; XXV, probably on C. Vibius Postumus, A.D. 13–15 or a little later.

Thallus: II, probably on Gaius Caesar, who died in A.D. 4; or on Germanicus, who died in A.D. 19.

Honestus: XXI, almost certainly on Livia, who died in A.D. 29.

Adespota: I, probably late Augustan.

Bianor: XVI, on the destruction of Sardis, A.D. 17.

Bassus: V, on the death of Germanicus in A.D. 19.

Philip: IV, later than A.D. 14, upper limit uncertain; II, likelier to be in the time of Tiberius than of Gaius.

(*b*) From the principate of Gaius (A.D. 37–41).[1]

Philip: III, probably A.D. 37; LX and LXI, probably in the time of Gaius; VI, probably A.D. 39.

(*c*) From a period later than the principate of Gaius.

Antiphilus VI uses the expression Καῖσαρ Νέρων in an epigram on the restoration of liberties to Rhodes. If the emperor is, as we believe, Nero, and the occasion an event of the year A.D. 53, this will be the only epigram in the present collection certainly later than the principate of Gaius. It is therefore the more important to draw attention to the fact[2] that this epigram stands in isolation, at a distance from all alphabetical sequences or other blocks of epigrams by *Garland*-authors. It may have been taken into the *Anthology* from some other source; it must not be used as evidence that Philip's *Garland* was first published later than the principate of Gaius.

[1] Philip LVII and Antiphilus III are not to be counted here. These epigrams were probably composed earlier than the building of the bridge of boats at Puteoli by Gaius; how much earlier, there is no means of determining.

[2] It is a fact which escaped the notice of Müller (see Antiphilus VI Pref.), Peek (*RE* 19.2340), and Beckby (3.777).

The evidence is plainly consistent with the conclusion that the *Garland* was first published before the end of the principate of Gaius; and there are one or two additional arguments which have been alleged to reinforce this belief.

First, in view of the conduct and character of Gaius during the last two years of his principate, it is not likely that a courtier-poet would include epigrams complimentary to him in an anthology first published after his death. If the occasions of Philip III and VI are correctly identified, this argument seems to us to have appreciable, perhaps decisive, weight. The death of Gaius was the cause of almost universal rejoicing; the syco-phantic versifier would not be likely thereafter to include in an anthology an epigram (Philip III) describing his own and the world's distress at the illness of that emperor a few years earlier.

Secondly, the exclusion of Gaetulicus from the *Garland* may be significant. *A.P.* preserves ten epigrams under this name, none connected with a *Garland*-sequence. If the author is Cn. Cornelius Lentulus Gaetulicus, consul in A.D. 26, thereafter *legatus* in Upper Germany, the exclusion of so eminent a person[1] may seem to require a particular explanation, and this could be found in the fact that he was executed for conspiracy against Gaius in A.D. 39;[2] there would have been no motive to exclude him if the *Garland* had been first published after the death of Gaius. Thus the date-limits for publication of the *Garland* would be narrowed to the period between October A.D. 39 and January A.D. 41. It is very far from certain, however, that the epigrammatist is the same person as the consul; the *cognomen* 'Gaetulicus' is not uncommon in this period, and there is no other apparent connexion between the two except the fact that both composed verses.[3]

---

[1] He was a well-known poet, and a friend of the sisters of the emperor Gaius.
[2] The point is made by Cichorius *Röm. Stud.* 356 ff.
[3] A positive case against the identification is stated by Skutsch *RE* 4.1386, approved by von Radinger *RE* 7.465 and Peek *RE* 17.2340. We attach no import-ance to the argument that the epigrams are not the sort of thing that the consul's Latin verses (see Skutsch *l.c.* 1385 f.) lead us to expect.

In general, the evidence suggests, but cannot be said to prove beyond all question, that the *Garland* was first published during the principate of Gaius; the year A.D. 40 is the likeliest.

(xii) *The dedication of the 'Garland'*

In the fifth line of his *Proem* (2632) Philip addresses the friend or patron to whom the *Garland* is being offered, ἐcθλὲ Κάμιλλε. Among the known bearers of the *cognomen* 'Camillus' in this period there is one who has a strong claim to recognition here, namely L. Arruntius Camillus Scribonianus, consul in A.D. 32 together with the father of the future emperor Nero, Cn. Domitius Ahenobarbus. Philip was a poet of the court, and it is likely that he dedicated his *Garland* to a patron of influence in high society.

This identification,[1] if it could be proved, would have an important consequence. It would then be certain that the *Garland* was published not later than A.D. 41; for this is the Camillus who revolted against the emperor Claudius in A.D. 42,[2] and it is obvious that Philip would not have dedicated the *Garland* to him after the outbreak of the revolt.

The identification, though likely, falls short of certainty, for there is a possible alternative in M. Furius Camillus, *frater arualis* in A.D. 38.[3]

---

[1] Proposed by Hillscher *Jahrb.* Suppl. 18.421; Cichorius agreed.

[2] His army (he was *legatus* in Dalmatia) refused to follow him; he killed himself, or was killed by a soldier. See Tac. *Ann.* 6.1, 12.52; *Hist.* 1.89, 2.75; Suet. *Claud.* 13, 35; *Otho* 1 f.; Plin. *Ep.* 3.16.7; Dio Cass. 55.23.4, 58.17.1, and especially 60.15 f.; *RE* 2.1264.

[3] Perhaps a brother or half-brother of Camillus Scribonianus (*RE* 2.1264, 7.350). But we think it very unlikely that Philip would have sought a patron in any member of this family after the revolt, at least during the principate of Claudius.

II. THE TEXT[1]

The principal sources for almost all epigrams in the present collection are the *Anthologia Palatina*[2] and the *Anthologia Planudea*.[3] There are many quotations in Suidas, very few in other authors. A few of the epigrams recur in the *Syllogae Minores*. There are no papyrus-texts. Inscriptions have added nothing except a few epigrams by Honestus.

(i) *The Palatine Anthology*

This is a manuscript written in several hands, all assigned to the tenth century. Its text is divided into fifteen Books,[4] of which 1–3, 8 and 14 do not concern us. The various hands are distinguished as follows:

> 4–9.384.8, by the scribe A
> 9.384.9–9.563, by the scribe J
> 9.564–11.66.3, by the scribe B
> 11.66.4–11.118.1, by the scribe B 2
> 11.118.1–13.31, by the scribe B

The scribe J made corrections and added ascriptions and *lemmata* in the part written by A. A corrector, designated 'C', or called 'the Corrector', took the text in hand after J had finished with it, made innumerable corrections in the parts written by A and J, and added many author-names, ethnics, and *lemmata*. It is certain that C used an exemplar[5] different from A's and that J's exemplar was different from both; it is likely that B's exemplar was different from all these.

---

[1] Discussed more fully in *HE* i.xxxii ff.
[2] Heidelberg, *cod. gr.* 23 + Paris, Bibl. Nationale *cod. gr. suppl.* 384.
[3] Venice, *cod. Marc.* 481.
[4] This is the modern practice. In *A.P.*, the modern 'Book 11' is divided after 11.64 by a second heading introducing the satirical epigrams. See Gow *GA* 54.
[5] It is not to be supposed that all C's contributions are taken from his exemplar. Some appear to be conjectural; at least it seems very unlikely that his source contained such blunders as φιλεράστρι' ἄκοιτις at 5.4.5, ἡμέρα at 5.107.6, ὑδασιτεγγῆ at 6.90.5, φοίβαις at 6.158.2, τελείηι at 7.278.8, ἐπεὶ δή at 7.377.5. See also Waltz i.xlv nn. 1, 2.

The text-hand, whether A or J or B or B 2, we designate throughout as 'P'. The labours of J and C do not extend beyond 9.563; we distinguish with these letters their contributions up to that point.

Where one of the text-hands corrects himself, we do not report the fact unless the original lection seems better than the correction or seems worth reporting for some other particular reason.

If the same epigram appears twice in *A.P.*, we cite the earlier appearance as 'P^a', the second as 'P^b'.

In these and other respects we follow the practices more fully described in *HE* i.xxxii ff.

(ii) *The Planudean Anthology*

Folios 2–76 of this manuscript (Planudes' autograph), herein designated 'Pl A', contain a selection, in seven chapters, from the anthology of Cephalas. Folios 81^v–100, herein designated 'Pl B', contain supplements to the first four of the seven chapters of Pl A. Planudes expressly says that Pl A and Pl B depend on different exemplars. Though Pl coincides with the text of P as corrected by C in innumerable places, it is certain that P was not Planudes' only source for either Pl A or Pl B.[1] We therefore recognize at least five different exemplars, those of A, J, C, Pl A and Pl B, and probably a sixth, that of B.

(iii) *The relation between P and Pl*

(1) It is obvious that Pl contains many editorial conjectures and supplements. It must suffice to cite a few places where Pl, faced with a serious corruption, indulges in rewriting:

5.132.6 (3233) θύεμε P, κλῶμαι Pl; 7.51.3 (13) ὑπαὶ μακε τῆιδ' P, ὑπαὶ μακέτϊ∗δ' C, ὑπέκβαλε Pl; 7.382.5 (2805) κενοῦσα C, κρατοῦσα Pl; 7.401.3 (2008) τ' ἐπεκρείκοντα P, τ' ἐποκριόεντα J, τε πλεῖα δόλοιο Pl; 9.275.3 (2548), at the verse-

---

[1] This conclusion is now firmly established by F. Lenzinger *Zur griechischen Anthologie* (diss. Bern, Zürich 1965). Our work was already in the press when Dr Lenzinger's book reached us.

end, ἐναίθρι P, ἀν' αἰθέρα Pl. A large collection of such examples could be assembled from our *apparatus*; add the apparent supplements[1] to fill gaps in 5.25.5 (3178), 7.305.3 (49), 7.631.1 (1159), 9.265.3 (1233), 9.267.1 (2833), 9.438.5 (2991), and the attempt to restore order out of chaos in 7.362.4–5 (3150–1).

(2) On the other hand there are many places where Pl's differences from P cannot reasonably be explained as editorial interventions. The following list, which could be much extended,[2] argues decisively in favour of Pl's independence; opinions may differ about particular examples, but the cumulative force is irresistible:

5.102.3 (1321) ἀλλ' ἐπὶ λεπτά P, ἐς δὲ ποθεινά Pl; 5.118.1 (1351) ἡδύπνευστε P, ἡδύπνοιε Pl; 5.124.6 (3223) μεγαλῆς P, πολλῆς Pl; 6.102.4 (2744) κάρυον...ἐκφανές P, κάρυα... ἐκφανέ' Pl; 6.22.4 (3443) χλωρῆς P, λεπτῆς Pl; 6.106.6 (2653) εὐαγρεῖ τῶιδε πέταccον ὄρος P, εὐαγρεῖν τῶιδ' ἐπίνευσον ὄρει Pl; 6.240.6 (2653) κάπρον P, ταῦρον Pl; 6.252.1 (791) ἀπὸ προτέρης P, ἀφ' ὁπλοτέρης Pl; 7.147.8 (3687) cὺ cῆι P, τεῆι Pl; 7.278.3 (3652) ὑπὸ δειράcιν P, ποτὶ χοιράcιν Pl; 9.13ᴮ.3 (961) αἴρων P, ἄρας Pl; 9.85.5 (2897) ἤγαγε δ' εἰς λιμένας με P, ἤγαγεν εἰς λιμένας δέ Pl; 9.117.6 (3832) φθιμένης P, φθίμενος Pl; 9.252.4 (1694) δραξάμενος P, πλεξάμενος Pl; 9.260.3 (3388) οὐ μὰ Κύπριν· τί δὲ Κύπρις ἐμοὶ ἔτι πλὴν ὅcον ὅρκος P, οὐ μὰ Κύπριν οὐδὲ Κύπρις ἔτι ἐμοὶ ὅcον ὅρκος Pl; 9.438.6 (2992) πρὸς κύτος P, πρὸς τάχος Pl; 9.561.2 (3002) βορραίου P, ἢ βορέου Pl; 9.708.1 (3015) τόλμηι PPlA, λύccηι PlB; 9.756.1 (63) οἶδε βρυάζειν P, ἄδε βρυάζει Pl; 9.824.2 (2219) ὀρειώτα P, ὀρειβάτεω Pl; 11.49.3 (2326) δὲ τριcὶν Νύμφαιcι τέταρτος P, τριcὶ Νύμφαιc τέτρατος αὐτός Pl; 11.72.1 (1637) Κοτυτταρίς P, Κυτώταρις Pl; 11.318.6 (3339) μαλακῶc P, μαλακός τ' Pl; 12.172.1 (2330) λυτρῶν (for λυγρῶν, the obvious correction) P, λοιπόν Pl.

---

[1] 'Apparent', because a few of them may be true tradition; see the notes *ad locc.*
[2] E.g. 7.278.3 (3652), 9.224.4 (1900), 9.244.3 (1211), 9.281.2 (1252), 11.67.2 (2575).

In the following places, where P is or may be corrupt, Pl has what is evidently in most instances the true reading; we think it very improbable that most are conjectural:

5.16.1 (1301) περιλάμπει P, πυριλαμπεῖc Pl (where conjecture would have given περιλαμπεῖc); 5.89.3 (1315) ἰοῖc P, οἴcτρωι Pl; 5.114.4 (2477) ἤλλακται P, ἠλλάχθαι Pl, and two lines below οὐ καλῶc P, οὐκ ἄλλωc Pl; 5.307.3 (863) κατέcθετε P, καταίθετε Pl; 7.36.5 (2266) ἀγανόc P, ἀένναοc Pl; 7.278.1 (3650) θηρcὶν P, Θῆριc Pl; 7.623.4 (56) παιδοτοκεῖν P, παιδο-κομεῖν Pl; 9.94.6 (3908) ζωόν P, ζωῆc Pl; 9.101.1 (3560) ὀνόματι P, ἐν ὄμμαcι Pl; 9.242.1 (901) νηcαίοιο P, Νεccαίοιο Pl; 9.250.1 (2422) κατηριφίην P, κατ' ἠριφίην C, κατηρείφθην Pl; 9.404.5 (1047) γλαυκοῦ P, γαυλοῦ Pl; 9.406.1 (67) κρήνη ἐμέ P, κρηνίc με Pl (where conjecture would have given κρήνη με).

Moreover, Pl is not wholly dependent on P for its author-names: 6.22, nameless in P, is ascribed to Zonas in Pl; only four other epigrams are ascribed to Zonas in Pl, and the name here cannot be a mere guess. 9.13 and 13[B], combined in P, are properly separated in Pl, and 13[B] is there very plausibly ascribed to Antiphilus. 9.252, ἀδέcποτον in P, is ascribed to Bianor in Pl; this cannot be a mere guess. 9.742, nameless in P, is ascribed to Philip in Pl with the ethnic Μακεδόνοc, which is not elsewhere applied to this author; we believe the ascription to be erroneous, but it is not likely to be a mere guess.

(iv) Reproductions of MSS

Reproductions of P[1] and Pl[2] have been fully collated throughout for the present edition. The exceptionally detailed reports in Stadtmüller's *apparatus* are almost invariably reliable so far as he goes (to *A.P.* 9.563), with one important reservation: his

---

[1] *Anthologia Palatina: codex Palatinus et codex Parisinus phototypice editi: praefatus est Carolus Preisendanz* (Leiden 1911).

[2] There is no published facsimile; we have used a reduced photostat made for A.S.F.G.

judgment of what was originally written in erasures is sometimes speculative and occasionally incompatible with the plain evidence of the photographs.[1] From *A.P.* 9.564 onwards we have occasionally improved upon the collations of P made for Jacobs and Dübner; we have corrected some errors and supplied some omissions in previous reports of the readings in Pl.[2]

(v) *Suidas*[3]

Numerous quotations from epigrams in the present collection are preserved in the lexicon nowadays commonly called 'The Suda'. The quotations are as a rule introduced by the phrase ἐν ἐπιγράμμασιν, never with an author's name. We believe that the lexicon's excerpts come from a source different from those represented in P and Pl, but its variants are seldom anything but trivialities or errors, and we report only those which contribute something to the understanding of the tradition or the constitution of the text.

Syllogae minores

We record the presence in the following *Syllogae* of epigrams included in this book, together with their ascriptions.[4] We disregard their readings, especially the variants which are trivialities or errors, unless there is some point of special interest in them.

Syll.E = *Sylloge Euphemiana*, 82 epigrams preserved in three manuscripts of the sixteenth century: *Paris.* 2720 (collated by Schneidewin *Progymn. in Anth. Gr.* Göttingen 1855), *Paris.* 1773 and *Flor.* 57.29 (collated by Stadtmüller).

Syll. Σπ = a collection of 58 epigrams written on blank pages at the beginning and end of P and in sundry spaces in between; closely akin to *Syll.E.*

Syll.S = a collection of 118 epigrams preserved in *Paris. Suppl.* 352 (13th cent.), published by Cramer *An. Par.* 4.365.

[1] See *HE* I.xxxvii n. 2.
[2] A collation of Pl by Preisendanz was at Beckby's disposal; his *apparatus* is a notable improvement on the past, but is not altogether free from error and omission.
[3] The following notes are abbreviations of *HE* I.xli–xlv.
[4] If any; there are none in *Syll.S*, four in *Syll.E.*

App.B.-V. = *Appendix Barberino-Vaticana*, 54 amatory epigrams preserved in two manuscripts of the sixteenth century, *Barber. gr.* 1.123 and *Vat. gr.* 240, published by L. Sternbach *Anth. Plan. Appendix Barberino-Vaticana* (Leipzig 1890).

Apographa

The *apographa* are manuscripts containing epigrams selected by various scholars from P, for the most part because they were not to be found in Pl. They are useful only as sources for early corrections and conjectures. We have not collated them, and have reason to doubt whether (in many instances) such early corrections and conjectures have been ascribed to their proper authors, especially when the help of Stadtmüller is no longer available.[1]

Ap.G. = *Guietianum*, 700 epigrams with corrections probably by F. Guyet (1575–1655).

Ap.R. = *Ruhnkenianum*, given by D. Ruhnken (*ob.* 1798) to J. Pierson, from whom it passed to H. de Bosch.

Ap.L. = *Lipsiense*, 650 epigrams transcribed by J. Gruter (1560–1627); this is the source from which J. J. Reiske published a number of epigrams with corrections.

Ap.B. = *apographon codicis Buheriani*, a copy by J. G. Schneider of an apograph made by J. Bouhier (1673–1746). There are other copies of this apograph in Paris, one of them containing notes by Salmasius and Guyet as well as Bouhier's own contributions.

III. THE ARRANGEMENT OF EPIGRAMS IN THE PRESENT EDITION

We have presented the identifiable *Garland*-authors and the doubtful claimants separately; the authors in each of these two sequences are arranged in alphabetical order.

It is impossible to confine the former sequence to epigrams which were included in the *Garland*. Some epigrams preserved

---

[1] See *HE* i.xliv f.

in detachment from the alphabetical sequences may have entered the *Anthology* from sources other than the *Garland*; and, where homonymous authors are involved, it is impossible to determine how their epigrams should be distributed.[1]

The variety of the problems is so great that it has proved impossible to formulate a consistent principle of arrangement. Our practice may be summarily stated as follows:

Polyaenus of Sardis, and *Julius Polyaenus*: there is no reason to doubt that these are different authors; we present them separately.

Adaeus of Macedon, and *Addaeus of Mytilene*: the single epigram ascribed to the latter has no connexion with the *Garland*; we place it at the end of those ascribed to Adaeus of Macedon or Adaeus alone. If two authors are represented, it is possible that one or more of those ascribed to Adaeus without ethnic belong to the Mytilenaean.

The same applies to *Bassus*, and *Bassus of Smyrna*, and to *Honestus of Corinth*, and *Honestus of Byzantium*: in each pair, a single epigram unconnected with the *Garland*-sequences is ascribed to the second name and ethnic; these we place at the end of the other epigrams ascribed to Bassus and Honestus.

Consistency would require the same treatment of *Erucius of Thessaly* and *Erucius of Cyzicus*: but in this instance we incline to believe that one of the ethnics is erroneous, and we therefore make no distinction, but place the epigrams bearing the ethnics in the positions most appropriate to their subject-matter.

Bianor of Bithynia, and *Bianor Grammaticus*: epigrams ascribed to both occur in alphabetical sequences; we believe that only one author is represented and therefore adhere to the principle adopted for Erucius.

Macedonius, and *Macedonius of Thessalonica*: epigrams ascribed to both occur in alphabetical sequences; we suspect that two authors are represented, and place the Thessalonican's epigram before the others.

---

[1] See pp. xxx f. above; it follows that not only non-*Garland*-epigrams but also non-*Garland*-authors are included.

Tullius Sabinus, and *Sabinus Grammaticus*: the former's epigram is, the latter's is not, in an alphabetical sequence; we place the former's first.

Antiphanes, Antiphanes of Macedon, and *Antiphanes of Megalopolis*: epigrams under all three headings occur in alphabetical sequences; we have acted on the very doubtful assumption that only one author is represented, and we have arranged the epigrams according to their subject-matter.

Diocles, Diocles of Carystus, and *Julius Diocles*: we place first the epigram ascribed to the Carystian, the only one in an alphabetical sequence; next, those ascribed to Julius; finally the epigram ascribed simply to Diocles.

Euenus: the name appears sometimes alone, elsewhere qualified by four different adjectives; we place the epigrams with the fuller headings first, beginning with Euenus Grammaticus, whose epigram is the only one in an alphabetical sequence.

Archias: we believe that several different authors are represented, none of them included in the *Garland*; we have arranged the epigrams in groups as described in the Introduction to Archias.

Diodorus, Diodorus of Sardis, Diodorus Grammaticus, and *Diodorus of Tarsus*: the Sardian and Grammaticus are represented in alphabetical sequences; the Tarsian is not, but he may be the same person as Grammaticus. We place the Sardian first, followed by all but one (xv) of the 'Diodorus'-epigrams from the alphabetical sequences; then comes Grammaticus; then the Tarsian, followed by five 'Diodorus'-epigrams which may belong to him; finally a couple of 'Diodorus'-epigrams which we do not know how to distribute.

Epigrams whose authorship is contested are not placed at the end of an author's contribution unless we are inclined positively to reject their ascription to that author. To this practice we have made an exception in Antipater; sixteen epigrams with double ascriptions are placed at the end of his contribution.

In arranging the epigrams of each author we have generally

followed P's order of subjects,[1] refraining from rearrangement
of all but the most obviously misplaced epigrams. Argentarius
needed more disturbance than most in order to bring together
the amatory, the sympotic, the satirical, and certain other
personal epigrams. In Antiphilus and Philip, contrary to our
general principle, we have picked out certain epigrams of
personal or historical interest and placed them at the beginning.
In Crinagoras also we have brought together the epigrams of
special autobiographical or other historical interest.[2] Antipater
called for special treatment, described in the Introduction to him.

In order to facilitate cross-reference and indexing[3] it has
seemed to us necessary to number the lines consecutively
throughout the book. It follows that in all epigrams succeeding
the first in the book each line has two numbers—an internal
number in the epigram to which it belongs and a higher in the
continuous enumeration. We use the internal numbers in our
apparatus criticus and in the commentary on the epigram concerned; the higher elsewhere. The higher alone is sufficient to
enable the reader to find the line, but since he will sometimes
wish to know without more ado to what author he is being
referred, we add the name unless it is that of the author on whom
he is already engaged. And since many of the authors here
included bear relatively unfamiliar names, we have thought it
best not to use abbreviations even when the references are to
poets well-known outside the *Anthology*. To take an illustration:
A.P. 6.5 is here Philip viii, and is so cited when we wish to refer,
not to a particular line, but to the epigram as a whole, except
that, if the reference is from another part of the commentary on
Philip, we do not give the author's name. This epigram occupies
vv. 2680-7 in the continuous enumeration of lines, and except in

---

[1] We have not, as in *HE*, united the amatory epigrams distributed in P between
Books 5 and 12.

[2] These have an inner classification: love-affairs; gifts; dedications; epitaphs;
the Caesars and other great persons; travels; a few miscellaneous personal epigrams;
a couple of satirical epigrams; and a quite miscellaneous remainder.

[3] This paragraph is repeated, with the appropriate modifications and additions,
from *HE* i.xlix f.

its own *apparatus* and commentary (where it is 1) we refer to its first line as Philip 2680 if the commentary is on another author, but simply as 2680 if it is on another epigram by Philip.

In referring to authors included in *Hellenistic Epigrams* we give the name in full followed by book, number, and (where appropriate) line of the epigram in *A.P.* or *A.Pl.* and also its place in the continuous enumeration of lines, omitting '*A.P.*' but including '*A.Pl.*'; e.g. 'Dioscorides 7.708.4 = 1620', 'Leonidas *A.Pl.* 236.3 = 2484'. It follows that, e.g., 'anon. 6.48.1 = 3812' would refer to an anonymous epigram in *HE*, whereas 'anon. 3500' refers to the present book; but to eliminate all doubt we have consistently printed 'anon. (*HE*)' where the reference is to the earlier work.

In our *apparatus criticus* we disregard the evidence of the manuscripts concerning accents, aspiration, word-division, and the presence or absence of *iota* subscript or adscript and of paragogic *nu*, except in certain corrupt or doubtful passages where it seemed advisable to reproduce the reading exactly as it stands in our sources. We correct without note minor errors in *lemmata* and we expand the names of authors where abbreviated in the ascriptions.[1]

We refer to epigrams in Book 5 by their old numbers, which are higher by one than in Stadtmüller's edition.

---

[1] In reporting *lemmata*, we place the author's name first whether (as is most common) it stands first in the source or not; e.g. *A.P.* 7.39 εἰc Αἰcχύλον ᾽Αντιπάτρου Θεcc. is reported by us as ᾽Αντιπάτρου Θεcc. εἰc Αἰcχύλον. This is a departure from the practice in *HE*.

TEXT
AND
TRANSLATION

SIGLA

P Codex *Anthologiae Palatinae* (Palat. 23 + Paris.Suppl.Gr. 384)

Pᵃ Pᵇ epigr. eorum quae in P bis exarantur prima et altera transcriptio
J cod. P partium librarius, alibi lemmatista
C cod. P libr. i–ix corrector

Pl Codex *Anthologiae Planudeae* (Ven.Marc. 481)

PlA ff. 2–76 capita vii Anthologiae complectentia
PlB ff. 81 v.–100 supplementa ad cap. i–iv complectentia

Syllogae Minores (vide p. liv)

Syll.E   Sylloge Euphemiana
Syll.Σπ   Sylloge Σπ
Syll.S   Sylloge S
App.B.-V. Appendix Barberino-Vaticana

Apographa Codicis P (vide p. lv)

Ap.B.   Apographon cod. Buheriani
Ap.G.   Apographon Guietianum
Ap.L.   Apographon Lipsiense
Ap.R.   Apographon Ruhnkenianum

Suid. Suidae Lexicon

Salm. Salmasius

s.a.n. sine auctoris nota

I

AUTHORS INCLUDED IN THE 'GARLAND'

ΑΔΑΙΟΥ

I

αὔλακι καὶ γήραι τετρυμένον ἐργατίνην βοῦν   (1)
Ἄλκων οὐ φονίην ἤγαγε πρὸς κοπίδα
αἰδεσθεὶς ἔργων· ὁ δέ που βαθέηι ἐνὶ ποίηι
μυκηθμοῖς ἀρότρου τέρπετ' ἐλευθερίηι.

II

τὰν ὄιν, ὦ Δάματερ ἐπόγμιε, τάν τ' ἀκέρωτον   5
μόσχον καὶ τροχιὰν ἐν κανέωι φθοΐδα
σοὶ ταύτας ἐφ' ἅλωος, ἐφ' ἇι πολὺν ἔβρασεν ἄντλον
Κρήθων καὶ λιπαρὰν εἶδε γεωμορίαν,
5 ἱρεύει, πολύσωρε· σὺ δὲ Κρήθωνος ἄρουραν
πᾶν ἔτος εὔκριθον καὶ πολύπυρον ἄγοις.   10

III

οὔ σε κυνῶν γένος εἷλ', Εὐριπίδη, οὐδὲ γυναικός
οἶστρος τὸν σκοτίης Κύπριδος ἀλλότριον,
ἀλλ' Ἀίδης καὶ γῆρας, ὑπαὶ Μακέτηι δ' Ἀρεθούσηι
κεῖσαι ἑταιρείηι τίμιος Ἀρχέλεω.
5 σοὶ δ' οὐ τοῦτον ἐγὼ τίθεμαι τάφον, ἀλλὰ τὰ Βάκχου   15
βήματα καὶ σκηνὰς ἐμβάδι †πειθομένας†.

I *A.P.* 6.228 Ἀδαίου Μακεδόνος Pl A Ἀδδαίου Μακεδόνος Suid. s.vv. τετρυμ-
μένον (1–3 ἔργων), κοπίς (2 οὐ–3 ἔργων)
1 ἐργατίνην Pl: -τίην PSuid.   2 Ἄλκων PSuid.: ἕλκων CPl   4 ἀρότρου
P: ἀρότου Pl

II *A.P.* 6.258 Ἀδαίου Suid s.vv. ὄγμος (1–2 μόσχον), ὄιν (eadem), φθοΐς (2 καὶ–
3 ἅλωος; pergit ὦ Δάματερ φέρω), ἀντλία (3–4), γεωμόριον (3 ἐφ' ἇι–4)   caret Pl
5 ἱρεύει Ap.G.: ἱερ- P

ADAEUS

I

Alcon turns his ox out to pasture in old age

His labouring ox, worn out by furrow and age, Alcon led not
to the slaughter-knife, in reverence for work done. Somewhere
in the deep pasture loud-lowing it rejoices in freedom from the
plough.

II

A farmer's offerings to Demeter

Demeter, guardian of the ploughland, Crethon consecrates to
you, Lady of many corn-heaps, this ewe and hornless heifer
and wheel-shaped cake in its basket, upon this threshing-floor
where he has winnowed a great pile of sheaves and seen a
splendid harvest. Do you make Crethon's field every year rich
in barley and plentiful in wheat.

III

The death and fame of Euripides

It was not dogs that killed you, Euripides, nor passion for
women (for you were no friend to love in darkness), but
Hades and old age; and you lie beneath Macedonian Arethusa,
honoured for the companionship of Archelaus. Yet not this I
reckon your tomb, but Dionysus' stages and scenes ⟨trodden⟩
by the buskin.

III *A.P.* 7.51 'Αδδαίου εἰς τὸν αὐτόν   Pl в s.a.n.   Suid. s.v. ὑπαίμακε
(1 οὔ–Εὐρ., pergit 3 ἀλλ'–ὑπαίμακεν)
2 τὸν Pl: τὸ P   **3** ὑπαὶ Μακέτηι δ': ὑπαὶ μακε τηῖδ' P,   ὑπαὶ μακέτἰ⁕δ' C,
ὑπέκβαλε· τῆι δ' Pl,   ὑπαίμακεν (cett. om.) Suid.   **4** κεῖσαι Pl: κεῖται P
6 βήματα Jacobs: ἤματα P, ἤματα Pl | ἐμβάδι Hermann: ἔμβαλε PPl | πειθο-
μένας CPl: ἐρειδομένας (vel φειδομένας) P

IV

Ἠμαθίην ὃς πρῶτος ἐς ἄρεα βῆσα Φίλιππος
Αἰγαίην κεῖμαι βῶλον ἐφεσσάμενος,
ῥέξας οἷ᾽ οὔπω βασιλεὺς τὸ πρίν. εἰ δέ τις αὐχεῖ
    μεῖζον ἐμεῦ, καὶ τοῦθ᾽ αἵματος ἡμετέρου.   20

V

τύμβον Ἀλεξάνδροιο Μακηδόνος ἤν τις ἀείδηι,   (21)
ἠπείρους κείνου σῆμα λέγ᾽ ἀμφοτέρας.

VI

ἢν παρίηις ἥρωα, Φιλοπρήγμων δὲ καλεῖται
πρόσθε Ποτειδαίης κείμενος ἐν τριόδωι,
εἰπεῖν οἷον ἐπ᾽ ἔργον ἄγεις πόδας· εὐθὺς ἐκεῖνος   25
εὑρήσει σὺν σοὶ πρήξιος εὐκολίην.

VII

ταύρωι φρικαλέον νάπος ἐκβαίνοντι Δοβήρου
Πευκέστης ἵππωι καρτερὸς ἠντίασεν.
ἀλλ᾽ ὁ μὲν ὡρμήθη πρηὼν ἅτε, τοῦ δ᾽ ἀπαλοῖο
    Παιονίδα λόγχην ἧκε διὰ κροτάφου,   30
5 συλήσας κεφαλῆς δὲ διπλοῦν κέρας, αἰὲν ἐκείνωι
    ζωροποτῶν ἐχθροῦ †κόμπον μὴ θανάτου†.

IV *A.P.* 7.238 Ἀδαίου   εἰς Φίλιππον [J] τὸν [P] βασιλέα [J] τὸν πατέρα
Ἀλεξάνδρου   Pl B s.a.n.
3 εἰ δέ Pl: οὐδέ P

V *A.P.* 7.240 Ἀδαίου   εἰς τὸν αὐτόν [J] Ἀλέξανδρον   Pl B Παρμενίωνος

VI *A.P.* 7.694 [C] Ἀδδαίου   [J] εἰς Φιλοπράγμονα τινὰ δυσνόητον   caret Pl
3 ἐκεῖνος Salm.: -νο P

IV

On Philip II of Macedon

I who first moved Emathia to war, I, Philip, lie clothed in
Aegae's earth, having done such deeds as no king yet before me.
If there is one whose claim is greater than mine, that too is of my
parentage.

V

On the tomb of Alexander the Great

Whoever sings of the tomb of Macedonian Alexander, say that
both continents are his monument.

VI

On Philopregmon

If you pass by the Hero—his name is Philopregmon, and his
grave is at the road-fork in front of Potidaea—tell him to what
work you are walking, and straightway he will discover, together with you, ease of accomplishment.

VII

Peucestes makes a wine-vessel from a bull's horns

A bull, as it emerged from Doberus' dangerous glen, Peucestes
met steadfast on horse-back. Huge as a cliff it came rushing, but
through its soft temple he drove his Paeonian spear. Both horns
from the head he stripped, and ever, as he drinks his neat wine
therein, ⟨boasts of his enemy's death⟩.

VII *A.P.* 9.300 Ἀδαίου   [C] εἰς Πευκέστην ταῦρον τὸν καλούμενον ʒόμβρον
λογχεύσαντα, τίς δὲ ὁ Πευκέστης οὐκ οἶδα   caret Pl
3 πρηὼν Ruhnken: -ειῶν C, -είων P   **4** κροτάφου Salm.: -φων P

VIII

τῆι βαιῆι Καλαθίνηι ὑπὸ σκυλάκων μογεούσηι
Λητωὶς κούφην εὐτοκίην ἔπορεν·
μούναις οὔ τι γυναιξὶν ἐπήκοος, ἀλλὰ καὶ αὐτάς   35
συνθήρους σώιζειν Ἄρτεμις οἶδε κύνας.

IX

Ἰνδὴν βήρυλλόν με Τρύφων ἀνέπεισε Γαλήνην
εἶναι καὶ μαλακαῖς χερσὶν ἀνῆκε κόμας.
ἠνίδε καὶ χείλη νοτερὴν λειοῦντα θάλασσαν
καὶ μαστούς, τοῖσιν θέλγω ἀνηνεμίην.   40
5 ἢν δέ μοι ἡ φθονερὴ νεύσηι λίθος, ὡς ἐν ἑτοίμωι
ὥρμημαι, γνώσηι καὶ τάχα νηχομένην.

X

ἤν τινα καλὸν ἴδηις, εὐθὺς τὸ πρᾶγμα κροτείσθω·
βάζ' ἃ φρονεῖς, ὄρχεων δράσσεο χερσὶν ὅλαις.
ἢν δ' εἴπηις, τίω σε καὶ ἔσσομαι οἷά τ' ἀδελφός,   45
αἰδώς σου κλείσει τὴν ἐπὶ τοὔργον ὁδόν.

ΑΔΔΑΙΟΥ ΜΥΤΙΛΗΝΑΙΟΥ

XI

ὁ γριπεὺς Διότιμος, ὁ κύμασιν ὁλκάδα πιστήν
κἢν χθονὶ τὴν αὐτὴν οἶκον ἔχων πενίης,

VIII *A.P.* 9.303 Ἀδαίου   [C] εἰς κύνα ἐγκυμονοῦσαν σκύλακας   Pl b Ἀδαίου
IX *A.P.* 9.544 Ἀδδαίου   εἰς λίθον βήρυλλον   caret Pl
3 λειοῦντα Jacobs: πλείοντα P   **5** νεύσηι Brunck: -σει P

VIII

On the birth of puppies to Calathina

To little Calathina, in labour with puppies, Leto's daughter brought light ease of bearing. Not only to women she listens; Artemis knows how to protect also her fellow-hunters the hounds.

IX

The goddess of calm seas engraved on a beryl

Me, a beryl from India, Tryphon persuaded to be goddess of calm waters, as with delicate fingers he set my tresses flowing. Look too at my lips, how they bring smoothness to the rainy sea, and my breasts, whereby I charm the winds away. As I am ready and eager, so shall you see me presently swimming, if the grudging stone will give me leave.

X

The ardent lover

If you see a beauty, strike while the iron is hot. Say what is in your mind, seize him in handfuls. For if what you say is this, 'I respect you, I will be as a brother to you', then shame will bar the road to action.

ADDAEUS OF MYTILENE

XI

On a fisherman whose boat served as funeral-pyre

Diotimus the fisherman, whose boat was his trust amid the waves, and the same on land the abode of his poverty, fell into

X *A.P.* 10.20 'Αδαίου   caret Pl
2 ὄρχεων Jacobs: ὄρκῶν P
XI *A.P.* 7.305 [C] 'Αδδαίου Μιτυληναίου   [J] εἰς γριπέα Διότιμον ἐπιτύμβιον θαυμαστόν   Pl A 'Αδδαίου Μιτυληναίου

νήγρετον ὑπνώσας ⟨'Αίδην⟩ τὸν ἀμείλιχον ἴκτο
αὐτερέτης ἰδίηι νηὶ κομιζόμενος.   50
5 ἦν γὰρ ἔχε ζωῆς παραμύθιον, ἔσχεν ὁ πρέσβυς
καὶ φθίμενος πύματον πυρκαϊῆς ὄφελος.

ΑΙΜΙΛΙΑΝΟΥ

I

ἕλκε, τάλαν, παρὰ μητρὸς ὃν οὐκέτι μαστὸν ἀμέλξεις,
ἕλκυσον ὑστάτιον νᾶμα καταφθιμένης·
ἤδη γὰρ ξιφέεσσι λιπόπνοος. ἀλλὰ τὰ μητρός   55
φίλτρα καὶ εἰν 'Αίδηι παιδοκομεῖν ἔμαθεν.

II

ἀβάλε χειμερίου με κατέκλυσε κύματα πόντου
δειλαίην νεκύων φόρτον ἀμειψαμένην.
αἰδέομαι σωθεῖσα· τί μοι πλέον ὅρμον ἱκέσθαι
δευομένηι φωτῶν πείσματα δησομένων;   60
5 Κωκυτοῦ με λέγοιτε βαρὺ σκάφος. ὤλεσα φῶτας,
ὤλεσα, ναυηγοὶ δ' εἰσὶν ἔσω λιμένος.

III

τέχνας εἵνεκα σεῖο καὶ ἁ λίθος οἶδε βρυάζειν,
Πραξίτελες· λῦσον, καὶ πάλι κωμάσομαι.

---

3 'Αίδην hic inseruit Hecker: ὑπν. τὸν ἀμείλικτον ἱκέτοτο ut vid. P,   ὑπν. τὸν ἀμείλιχον ἴκτο, tum γρ. 'Αίδαν supra rasuram C, ὑπν. τὸν ἀμείλιχον ἴκτο πρὸς ᾽Αίδην Pl

I A.P. 7.623 [C] Αἰμιλιανοῦ   [J] εἰς παῖδα τῆς μητρὸς τεθνηκυίας θηλάζοντα Pl A Αἰμιλιανοῦ
1 μαστὸν P: μαζ- Pl | ἀμέλξεις Pl: ἀν- P   2 ὑστάτιον Pl: ὑστάστ- P
3 λιπόπνοος Pl: -πνυος ut vid. P   4 καὶ εἰν Pl: κ' ἦν εἰς, voc. εἰς punctis deleto, P | παιδοκομεῖν Pl: -τοκεῖν P

sleep unwaking and went to Hades the implacable, conveyed by his own ship, himself his own crew. The boat which he had for comfort of his life, the old man had also in death for the final service of a funeral-pyre.

AEMILIANUS

I

On a portrayal of a woman slain with a child at the breast

Suck from your mother, poor child, the breast that you shall never milk again, suck the last stream from the slaughtered; already by the sword she lies breath-bereft, yet a mother's love knows how to nurse her child even in death.

II

On a ship coming to harbour with its crew dead

Would that the waves of the stormy sea had drowned me, wretch that I am, who have changed my cargo for corpses. I am shamed by my safety. What good is it to me, to reach moorings deprived of men to make fast my cables? Let my name be Grievous Barque of the Wailing River. I have destroyed my men, destroyed them; they are as ship-wrecked men, although inside the harbour.

III

On a sculpture by Praxiteles

If it depended only on your art, Praxiteles, the marble itself would know how to frisk and frolic. Set me free, and I shall

II *A.P.* 9.218 [C] Αἰμιλιανοῦ Νικαέως   εἰς ναῦν ἀπολέσασαν τοὺς πλωτῆρας
Pl A Αἰμιλιανοῦ Νικαέως
4 δησομένων Stephanus: λυσομ- PPl

III *A.P.* 9.756 εἰς Αἰμιλιανοῦ [εἰς Ceιληνοὺς Αἰμιλιανοῦ coni. Jacobs]   Pl A
Αἰμιλιανοῦ
1 οἶδε βρυάζειν P: ἄδε βρυάζει Pl   2 πάλι Pl: -λιν P | κωμάσομαι P: -cεται Pl

νῦν δ' ἡμῖν οὐ γῆρας ἔτ' ἀδρανές, ἀλλ' ὁ πεδητὰς   65
Ceιληνοῖc κώμων βάcκανός ἐcτι λίθοc.

ΑΝΤΙΓΟΝΟΥ

I

ἀργυρέη κρηνίc με τὸν οὐκέτι μακρὰ βοῶντα
βάτραχον οἰνηραῖc ἔcχεν ὑπὸ cταγόcιν·
κεῖμαι δ' ἐν Νύμφαιc, κείναιc φίλοc, οὐδὲ Λυαίωι
ἐχθρός, ὑπ' ἀμφοτέρων λουόμενοc cταγόcιν.   70
5 ὀψέ ποτ' εἰc Διόνυcον ἐκώμαcα. φεῦ τίνεc ὕδωρ
πίνουcιν μανίην cώφρονα μαινόμενοι.

ΑΝΤΙΜΕΔΟΝΤΟC

I

ἄνθρωποι δείληc ὅτε πίνομεν· ἢν δὲ γένηται   (73)
ὄρθροc, ἐπ' ἀλλήλουc θῆρεc ἐγειρόμεθα.

ΑΝΤΙΠΑΤΡΟΥ ΘΕCCΑΛΟΝΙΚΕωC
A. ΑΝΤΙΠΑΤΡΟΥ ΘΕCCΑΛΟΝΙΚΕωC

I

coί με, Θρηϊκίηc cκυληφόρε, Θεccαλονίκη   75
μήτηρ ἡ πάcηc πέμψε Μακηδονίηc,
ἀείδω δ' ὑπὸ coὶ δεδμημένον Ἄρεα Βεccῶν
ὅcc' ἐδάην πολέμου πάντ' ἀναλεξάμενοc.
5 ἀλλά μοι ὡc θεὸc ἔccο κατήκοοc, εὐχομένου δέ
κλῦθι. τίc ἐc Μούcαc οὔατοc ἀcχολίη;   80

3 πεδητάc Brunck: πεδιταc P, πεδητὴc Pl   4 Ceιληνοῖc κώμων Pl: Ciλ-
(marg. scr. ει) κομῶν P | ἐcτι Pl: ἔcται P
I A.P. 9.406 [C] Ἀντιγόνου Καρυcτίου (in rasura; Ἀντιπάτρου ut vid. P, cum
ethnico potius Ciδωνίου quam Θεccαλονικέωc)   εἰc βάτραχον ἀποπνιγέντα ἐν
οἴνωι Pl A Ἐπιγόνου Θεccαλονικέωc

be revelling again. But now, for us Silens, what fetters our
revelling is no longer impotent old age but jealous marble.

ANTIGONUS

I

On the figure of a frog in a silver wine-vessel

Me, a frog no longer loud-croaking, the silver fountain gripped
fast beneath its showers of wine. Among the Nymphs I lie,
beloved of them, yet no less dear to Bacchus, washed by the
showers of both. At long last I came to Dionysus' revelling; I
pity those whose drinking is water, mad with the madness of
sobriety.

ANTIMEDON

I

Men are kindly in their cups, beastly when they wake up

When we drink in the evening we are human beings, but when
dawn comes we are wild beasts that start up against one another.

ANTIPATER OF THESSALONICA

I

On Piso's defeat of the Bessi

Thessalonica, the mother of all Macedonia, has sent me to you,
the bearer of the spoils of Thrace. I put together all I learnt of
the war, and my song is of the Bessian fighting-men subdued
beneath you. Listen to me, as a god may, and hear my prayer;
how can the ear lack leisure for the Muses?

1 κρηνίς με Pl: κρήνη ἐμὲ P   **2** ἔςχεν PPl: γρ. χεῦεν marg. P   **2** cταγό-
ciν P: -ci Pl   **3** bis scr. P, secundo loco recte, primo κ. δὲ Νύμφαις φίλος
κεῖνος οὐδὲ κ.τ.λ.   **5** ἐκώμαca Pl: ἐκόμ- P

I *A.P.* 11.46 ᾽Αντιμέδοντος Κυζικηνοῦ   Pl a ᾽Αντιμέδοντος Κυζικηνοῦ

I *A.P.* 9.428 [J] ᾽Αντιπάτρου Θεσσαλονικέως   εἰς τὴν κατάπτωcιν τῶν Βεccῶν
Pl a ᾽Αντιπάτρου

II

ἀρκεῖ τέττιγας μεθύσαι δρόσος, ἀλλὰ πιόντες
ἀείδειν κύκνων εἰσὶ γεγωνότεροι.
ὡς καὶ ἀοιδὸς ἀνὴρ ξενίων χάριν ἀνταποδοῦναι
ὕμνους εὐέρκταις οἶδε παθὼν ὀλίγα.
5 τοὔνεκά σοι πρώτως μὲν ἀμείβομεν, ἢν δ' ἐθέλωσιν   85
Μοῖραι πολλάκι μοι κείσεαι ἐν σελίσιν.

III

ὦ Ἑλικὼν Βοιωτέ, σὺ μέν ποτε πολλάκις ὕδωρ
εὐεπὲς ἐκ πηγέων ἔβλυσας Ἡσιόδωι,
νῦν δ' ἡμῖν ἔτι κοῦρος ὁμώνυμος Αὔσονα Βάκχον
οἰνοχοεῖ κρήνης ἐξ ἀμεριμνοτέρης.   90
5 βουλοίμην δ' ἂν ἔγωγε πιεῖν παρὰ τοῦδε κύπελλον
ἓν μόνον ἢ παρὰ σεῦ χίλια Πηγασίδος.

IV

Ὀρφεὺς θῆρας ἔπειθε, σὺ δ' Ὀρφέα· Φοῖβος ἐνίκα
τὸν Φρύγα, σοὶ δ' εἴκει μελπομένωι, Γλάφυρε,
οὔνομα καὶ τέχνης καὶ σώματος. οὔ κεν Ἀθήνη   95
ἔρριψεν λωτοὺς τοῖα μελιζομένη
5 οἷα σύ, ποικιλοτερπές. ἀφυπνώσαι κεν ἀκούων
αὐτὸς Πασιθέης Ὕπνος ἐν ἀγκαλίσιν.

II *A.P.* 9.92 [C] Ἀντιπάτρου Θεσσαλονικέως   [J] ἐπὶ φιλοξενίαι τινὸς σοφοῦ ὃς
τῶι ξενίσαντι ταῦτα προσεῖπε τὰ μέλιτος γλυκερώτερα ἔπη. προοίμιον ὁ τέττιξ
Pl A Ἀντιπάτρου Θεσσαλονικέως
5 ἐθέλωσιν P: -λουσι Pl   6 μοι P: μου Pl | κείσεαι Ascensius: -σεται PPl
III *A.P.* 11.24 τοῦ αὐτοῦ [sc. Ἀντιπάτρου]   Pl A τοῦ αὐτοῦ [sc. Ἀντιπάτρου
Θετταλοῦ]

II

The poet thanks his patron

Dew is enough to make cicadas tipsy, but when they have drunk they sing louder than swans. Even so the poet, in thanks for acts of friendship, knows how to give songs to his benefactors in return, though it be little that he has received. Therefore I make this first response to you, and if the fates are willing your name shall often lie on my pages.

III

On a cupbearer named Helicon

Boeotian Helicon, there was a time when you often spouted from your springs the water of sweet speech for Hesiod; and still today a boy like-named pours us Italian wine from a fountain more care-free. Rather would I drink one single cup from his hand than a thousand of the Pegasaean from yours.

IV

To Glaphyrus, a piper

Orpheus made beasts obedient, but you make Orpheus so. Phoebus defeated the Phrygian, but yields to your minstrelsy, Glaphyrus,—the name is for your art and your person alike. Athena would not have thrown the pipes away if she had made such music as you, master of variety's delights. Sleep himself, in Pasithea's arms, would wake up when he heard you.

3 ἔτι Gow: ἔθ' ὁ PPl | Βάκχον Pl: -χου P

IV *A.P.* 9.517 [J] Ἀντιπάτρου Θεσσαλονικέως   Pl в Ἀντιπάτρου
2 coì Pl: cù P | εἴκει Lascaris: ἤ (in rasura) κει P, ἤκει Pl | μελπομένωι Pl: -να P | Γλάφυρε P: -ρα Pl   5 ποικιλοτερπές. ἀφυπνώσαι Eldick: -τερπε cάφ' ὑπνώσαι Pl, -τερπε cάφ' ὑπνώcca P

V

τρὶς δέκα με πνεύσειν καὶ δὶς τρία μάντιες ἄστρων
φασίν, ἐμοὶ δ' ἀρκεῖ καὶ δεκὰς ἡ τριτάτη.   100
τοῦτο γὰρ ἀνθρώποις βιοτῆς ὅρος, οἱ δ' ἐπὶ τούτοις
Νέστορι. καὶ Νέστωρ δ' ἤλυθεν εἰς Ἀίδην.

VI

πάντα καλῶς τό γε μὴν χρυσῆν ὅτι τὴν Ἀφροδίτην
ἔξοχα καὶ πάντων εἶπεν ὁ Μαιονίδης.
ἢν μὲν γὰρ τὸ χάραγμα φέρῃς, φίλος, οὔτε θυρωρός   105
ἐν ποσὶν οὔτε κύων ἐν προθύροις δέδεται,
5 ἢν δ' ἑτέρως ἔλθῃς, καὶ ὁ Κέρβερος. ὦ πλεονέκται
†οἱ πλούτου πενίην ὡς ἀδικεῖτε μόνοι.†

VII

ὄρθρος ἔβη, Χρύσιλλα, πάλαι δ' ἠῶιος ἀλέκτωρ
κηρύσσων φθονερὴν Ἠριγένειαν ἄγει.   110
ὀρνίθων ἔρροις φθονερώτατος ὅς με διώκεις
οἴκοθεν εἰς πολλοὺς ἠιθέων ὀάρους.
5 γηράσκεις, Τιθωνέ, τί γὰρ σὴν εὐνέτιν Ἠῶ
οὕτως ὀρθριδίην ἤλασας ἐκ λεχέων;

VIII

τὴν ξηρὴν ἐπὶ νῶτα Λυκαινίδα, τὴν Ἀφροδίτης   115
λώβην, τὴν ἐλάφου παντὸς ἀπυγοτέρην,

V A.P. 9.112 [C] Ἀντιπάτρου Θεσσαλονικέως   [J] εἴς τινα μαντευσάμενον περὶ τῆς ἑαυτοῦ ζωῆς ἕως πόσων ἐκταθήσεται χρόνων   Pl A Ἀντιπάτρου Θεσσαλονικέως
1 τρὶς Pl: τρεῖς P   3 τούτοις Pl: -τους P

VI A.P. 5.30 Ἀντιπάτρου Θεσσαλονικέως   [J] ὅτι πόρναι τὸν χρυσὸν μᾶλλον ἢ τοὺς ἐραστὰς ἀσπάζονται   Pl A Ἀντιπάτρου Θεσσαλονικέως

V

A long life not desired

The astrologers say that I shall live thrice ten and twice six years, but the third decade is enough for me. That is the landmark of man's life; those that follow are for Nestor,—and even Nestor went to Hades.

VI

Love is mercenary

Homer said all things well, but best of all that Aphrodite is golden. For if you bring the cash, my friend, there is neither porter in your path nor dog chained at the door. But if you come otherwise, Cerberus himself is there. O greedy for gain...

VII

Untimely cock-crow

The dawn-twilight has passed, Chrysilla, and the early-morning cock has long been proclaiming and bringing on the envious break of day. A curse upon you, most envious of fowls, for driving me from home to my pupils' endless discourses. Tithonus, you are growing senile; or why have you driven your bedfellow Aurora thus early from your couch?

VIII

An unloveable woman

That woman with the dried-up posterior, Lycaenis, Aphrodite's plague, smaller-haunched than any deer, with whom (as

---

1 ὅτι Brunck: ἔτι PPl   **2** Μαιονίδης Pl: Μαιωνίδας P   **3** φέρηις Pl: -ρεις P   **6** πλούτου P^{pc}Pl: -τοι P^{ac}

VII *A.P.* 5.3. Ἀντιπάτρου Θεσσαλονικέως   [J] εἰς Χρύσιλλαν τὴν ἑταίραν   Pl A τοῦ αὐτοῦ [sc. Ἀντιπάτρου Θεσσαλονικέως]   **3** φθονερώτατος P: -τατε Pl

VIII *A.P.* 11.327 Ἀντιπάτρου Θεσσαλονικέως   caret Pl

αἰπόλος ἦι μεθύων οὐκ ἄν ποτε, φασί, συνώικει—
γοῖ, γοῖ, τοιαῦται Cιδονίων ἄλοχοι.

IX

ἡ τὰ πέδιλα φέρουσα Μενεκρατίς, ἡ δὲ τὸ φᾶρος
Φημονόη, Πρηξὼ δ᾽ ἢ τὸ κύπελλον ἔχει.   120
τῆς Παφίης δ᾽ ὁ νεὼς καὶ τὸ βρέτας, ἄνθεμα δ᾽ αὐτῶν
ξυνόν, Cτρυμονίου δ᾽ ἔργον Ἀριστομένους.
5 αἱ τρεῖς ἀσταὶ ἔσαν καὶ ἑταιρίδες, ἀλλὰ τυχοῦσαι
Κύπριδος εὐκταίης νῦν ἑνός εἰσι μία.

X

Βιθυνὶς Κυθέρη με τεῆς ἀνεθήκατο, Κύπρι,   125
μορφᾶς εἴδωλον λύγδινον εὐξαμένα.
ἀλλὰ σὺ τῆι μικκῆι μεγάλην χάριν ἀντιμερίζου
ὡς ἔθος, ἀρκεῖται δ᾽ ἀνδρὸς ὁμοφροσύναι.

XI

οὗτος ὁ Λειάνδροιο διάπλοος, οὗτος ὁ πόντου
πορθμὸς ὁ μὴ μούνωι τῶι φιλέοντι βαρύς.   130
ταῦθ᾽ Ἡροῦς τὰ πάροιθεν ἐπαύλια, τοῦτο τὸ πύργου
λείψανον, ὁ προδότης ὧδ᾽ ἐπέκειτο λύχνος.
5 κοινὸς δ᾽ ἀμφοτέρους ὅδ᾽ ἔχει τάφος εἰσέτι καὶ νῦν
κείνωι τῶι φθονερῶι μεμφομένους ἀνέμωι.

IX *A.P.* 6.208 [=Pª] Ἀντιπάτρου   ἀνάθημα τῆι Ἀφροδίτηι παρὰ γυναικῶν,
et post 9.365 [=Pᵇ] Ἀντιπάτρου Θεσσαλονικέως   εἰς τρεῖς πάλαι πόρνας
λαβούσας δὲ ἄνδρας καὶ σωφρονισθείσας   [C marg.] ἐπὶ τρισὶ γυναιξίν   Pl A
Ἀντιπάτρου
1 ἡ δὲ PªPl: ἅ δὲ Pᵇ   2 ἡ PªPl: ἅ Pᵇ   3 δ᾽ ὁ CᵇPl: ὁ Pªᵇ
4 Ἀριστομένους Pᵇ: Ἀριστομάχου PªPl   5 αἱ τρεῖς Pᵇ: πᾶσαι δ᾽ PªPl
6 εὐκταίης Pᵇ: εὐκρίτου Pª, εὐκρήτου Pl

the saying is) a drunken goatherd would not consort,—filthy beast, such are the wives of the Sidonians.

IX

Dedication by three women

She who carries the shoes is Menecratis; she who bears the robe is Phemonoê; the one holding the cup is Prexo; the temple and the statue are the Paphian's; their offering is in common, and is the work of Aristomenes from the Strymon's country. The three were citizens and courtesans; they got the love they prayed for, and now each belongs to one man.

X

Dedication of a statue to Aphrodite

Bithynian Cythera dedicated me, the marble image of your form, Cyprian goddess, according to her vow. Do you make a large gift in return for a small one, as your custom is; a husband's loving heart is all she asks.

XI

Where Hero and Leander died

This is Leander's crossing, these the sea's straits, grievous not only to the man who loved. This is where Hero dwelt of old, this is the relic of her tower, on this the traitor-lamp was placed. And this tomb holds both in common, reproaching to this day that envious gale.

X *A.P.* 6.209 〚παρὰ〛 τοῦ αὐτοῦ [sc. ᾿Αντιπάτρου Θεσσαλονικέως]   ἀνάθημα τῆι αὐτῆι [sc. ᾿Αφροδίτηι]   caret Pl

XI *A.P.* 7.666 ᾿Αντιπάτρου [C] Θεσσαλονικέως   εἰc τὸν Λεάνδρου διάπλουν καὶ τῆc ῾Ηροῦc   [J ad v. 4] εἰc Λέανδρον καὶ τὴν ῾Ηρῶ τὴν Cεcτιάδα   Pl A ᾿Αντιπάτρου   εἰc ῾Ηρῶ καὶ Λέανδρον

1 Λειάνδροιο Pl: Λεάν- P   **5** κοινὸc Pl: -νοὺc P

XII

ἀνέρα μὴ πέτρηι τεκμαίρεο· λιτὸς ὁ τύμβος   135
ὀφθῆναι μεγάλου δ' ὀcτέα φωτὸς ἔχει.
εἰδήcειc Ἀλκμᾶνα λύρης ἐλατῆρα Λακαίνης,
ἔξοχον ὃν Μουcέων ἐννέ' ἀριθμὸς ἔχει.
5 κεῖται δ' ἠπείροιc διδύμαιc ἔριc εἴθ' ὅ γε Λυδός
εἴτε Λάκων. πολλαὶ μητέρες ὑμνοπόλων.   140

XIII

ὁ τραγικὸν φώνημα καὶ ὀφρυόεccαν ἀοιδήν   (141)
πυργώcαc cτιβαρῆι πρῶτος ἐν εὐεπίηι
Αἰcχύλοc Εὐφορίωνος Ἐλευcινίης ἑκὰς αἴης
κεῖται κυδαίνων cώματι Τρινακρίην.

XIV

δύcμορε Νικάνωρ πολιῶι μεμαραμμένε πόντωι,   145
κεῖcαι δὴ ξείνηι γυμνὸς ἐπ' ἠϊόνι
ἢ cύ γε πρὸς πέτρηιcι, τὰ δ' ὄλβια κεῖνα μέλαθρα
φροῦδα †πάcης ἐλπὶc ὄλωλε Τύρου,
5 οὐδέ τί cε κτεάνων ἐρρύcατο. φεῦ ἐλεεινέ,
ὤλεο μοχθήcαc ἰχθύcι καὶ πελάγει.   150

XV

μηδ' ὅτ' ἐπ' ἀγκύρης ὀλοῆι πίcτευε θαλάccηι,
ναυτίλε, μηδ' εἴ τοι πείcματα χέρcος ἔχοι,

XII *A.P.* 7.18 Ἀντιπάτρου Θεccαλονικέωc   εἰc Ἀλκμᾶνα   Pl A Ἀντιπάτρου
Θεccαλονικέωc   εἰc Ἀλκμᾶνα   Suid. s.vv. λιτός (1 λιτὸc–2), λύρα (3), ἐλατήρ,
εἰδήcειc (3 s.), Λυδιάζων (5 s.), ὑμνοπόλος (π. μ. ὑ.)
4 Μουcέων P: -cῶν PlSuid.   **5** διδύμαιc Pl: -μοιc PSuid.   **6** μητέρες
PSuid.: πατρίδες Pl

XIII *A.P.* 7.39 Ἀντιπάτρου Θεccαλονικέωc εἰc Αἰcχύλον   Pl A Ἀντιπάτρου
εἰc Αἰcχύλον   Suid. s.v. πυργοφόρος (1–3 Αἰcχύλοc)
1 φώνημα CPl: φρόν- PSuid.   **4** Τρινακρίην C^{γρ}: Ταιναρίην PPl

XII

On the tomb of Alcman

Judge not the man by the stone; the tomb is not much to see, but it holds a great man's bones. You shall recognize Alcman, striker of the Laconian lyre, whom the nine Muses, one and all, hold pre-eminent. Here he lies, cause of dispute to both continents, whether he was a Lydian or Laconian. Singers have many mothers.

XIII

On the tomb of Aeschylus

He who first with robust and noble speech raised aloft the utterance of Tragedy and its high-browed songs, Aeschylus the son of Euphorion lies far from Eleusis' land, making Sicily glorious by his remains.

XIV

On Nicanor, lost at sea

Ill-starred Nicanor, wasted by the gray sea, naked you lie on a foreign shore or by the rocks; that wealthy home is lost to you ⟨   ⟩; the hopes of all Tyre are perished, and no part of your possessions saved you. Ah pitiable, your life is over, and your labours served only fishes and the sea.

XV

On a man drowned in harbour

Trust not the fatal sea, mariner, not even when at anchor, not even if the beach holds your stern-cables. Ion fell into the har-

XIV *A.P.* 7.286 Ἀντιπάτρου [C] Θεσσαλονικέως   [J] ἕτερον εἰς ναυηγὸν Νικάνορα Τύριον πλουσιώτατον   Pl в Ἀντιπάτρου
1 Νικάνωρ P: -ᾶνορ Pl | μεμαραμμένε P: μεμορημένε Pl   **4** φροῦδα⁛πάσης P: φροῦδά τε καὶ πάσης Pl

XV *A.P.* 9.82 [C] Ἀντιπάτρου Θεσσαλονικέως   [J] εἰς ναυηγὸν ἐν τῶι λιμένι ναυηγήσαντα διὰ μέθην. παραινεῖ οὖν ὁ γράψας μὴ πιστεύειν θαλάσσηι   Pl A Ἀντιπάτρου
1 ἀγκύρης Jacobs: -ρηι PPl | πίστευε Pl: -τεύετε P   **2** ἔχοι P: ἔχει Pl

καὶ γὰρ Ἴων ὅρμωι ἐνικάππεcεν, ἐc δὲ κόλυμβον
ναύτου τὰc ταχινὰc οἶνοc ἔδηcε χέραc.
5 φεῦγε χοροιτυπίην ἐπινήιον. ἐχθρὸc Ἰάκχωι   155
πόντοc. Τυρcηνοὶ τοῦτον ἔθεντο νόμον.

XVI

Αὐcονίη με Λίβυccαν ἔχει κόνιc ἄγχι δὲ Ῥώμηc
κεῖμαι παρθενικὴ τῆιδε παρὰ ψαμάθωι,
ἡ δέ με θρεψαμένη Πομπηίη ἀντὶ θυγατρόc
κλαυcαμένη τύμβωι θῆκεν ἐλευθερίωι   160
5 πῦρ ἕτερον cπεύδουcα· τὸ δ’ ἔφθαcεν οὐδὲ κατ’ εὐχήν
ἡμετέρην ἦψεν λαμπάδα Φερcεφόνη.

XVII

κύματα καὶ τρηχύc με κλύδων ἐπὶ χέρcον ἔcυρεν
δελφῖνα ξυνῆc κοινὸν ὅραμα τύχηc,
ἀλλ’ ἐπὶ μὲν γαίηc ἐλέωι τόποc, οἱ γὰρ ἰδόντεc   165
εὐθύ με πρὸc τύμβουc ἔcτεφον εὐcεβέεc.
5 νῦν δὲ τεκοῦcα θάλαccα διώλεcε· τίc παρὰ πόντου
πίcτιc ὃc οὐδ’ ἰδίηc φείcατο cυντροφίηc;

XVIII

πούλυποc εἰναλίηι ποτ’ ἐπὶ προβλῆτι τανυcθείc
ἠελίωι ψύχειν πολλὸν ἀνῆκε πόδα.   170
οὔπω δ’ ἦν πέτρηι ἴκελοc χρόα, τοὔνεκα καί μιν
αἰετὸc ἐκ νεφέων ὀξὺc ἔμαρψεν ἰδών,

XVI A.P. 7.185 [C] Ἀντιπάτρου Θεccαλονικέωc   [J] εἰc κόρην Λίβυccαν ἐν
Ῥώμηι τελευτήcαcαν   Pl A Ἀντιπάτρου Θεccαλονικέωc
1 Ῥώμηc PPl: -μαc C   4 κλαυcαμένη Pl: -να P   6 ἡμετέρην Pl:
ἀμετέραν P | Φερcεφόνη CPl: Περ- P
XVII A.P. 7.216 [C] Ἀντιπάτρου Θεccαλονικέωc   [J] εἰc τὸν αὐτὸν [sc. δελφῖνα]
ὁμοίωc ἐκβραcθέντα   Pl B s.a.n.   Suid. s.v. τόποc (3–6 πίcτιc)

bour, and the sailor's hands, so swift to dive, were fettered by wine. Avoid dances on deck; the sea is the wine-god's enemy. This law was passed by the Tyrrhenians.

XVI

For a slave-girl's tomb

The dust of Italy lies over me, a Libyan maid; not far from Rome I lie beside these sands. And she who reared me like a daughter, Pompeia, mourned me and did not bury me in a slave's tomb. Quite different was the flame she was eager for; but this one came first, and contrary to our prayer it was Persephone who lit the torch.

XVII

A stranded dolphin

The waves and the rough surf dragged me, a dolphin, to the beach, a spectacle for all men of their common fate. Yet on land there is a place for pity; those who saw me at once adorned me for the grave with pious hands. As for the sea that bore me, it has destroyed me now. What trust is in the ocean, that had no mercy even for its own brood?

XVIII

An octopus and an eagle

An octopus, stretched one day on a rock-spit in the sea, spread its many feet for the sun to dry. Its colour had not yet become like the rocks, and so an eagle, sharp of sight from the clouds,

1 ἔςυρεν P: -ραν CPl   **2** ξυνῆς Opsopoeus: ξείνοις PPl   **4** εὐθύ PPlᵖᶜSuid.: εὐθύς Plᵃᶜ | τύμβους PSuid.: -βον Pl   **5** πόντου Gow: -τωι PPlSuid.

XVIII *A.P.* 9.10 Ἀντιπάτρου Θεσσαλονικέως   [J] εἰς πολύπουν καὶ ἀετὸν διὰ τὸ τὸν ἀετὸν δραξάμενον αὐτὸν ὑπὸ τῶν ἐκείνου πλεκτανῶν ἀγρευθῆναι   Pl A Ἀντιπάτρου Θεσσαλονικέως

5 πλοχμοῖς δ᾽ εἱλιχθεὶς πέσεν εἰς ἅλα δύςμοροс. ἦ ῥα
  ἄμφω καὶ θήρης ἤμβροτε καὶ βιότου.

XIX

τάσδε θεογλώссους Ἑλικὼν ἔθρεψε γυναῖκας   175
  ὕμνοις καὶ Μακεδὼν Πιερίας σκόπελος,
Πρήξιλλαν, Μοιρώ, Ἀνύτης στόμα, θῆλυν Ὅμηρον
  Λεσβιάδων Σαπφὼ κόσμον ἐυπλοκάμων,
5 Ἤρινναν, Τελέσιλλαν ἀγακλέα, καὶ σέ, Κόριννα,
  θοῦριν Ἀθηναίης ἀσπίδα μελψαμέναν,   180
Νοссίδα θηλύγλωссον, ἰδὲ γλυκυαχέα Μύρτιν
  πάσας ἀενάων ἐργατίδας σελίδων.
ἐννέα μὲν Μούσας μέγας Οὐρανὸς ἐννέα δ᾽ αὐτά
10 Γαῖα τέκεν, θνατοῖς ἄφθιτον εὐφροσύναν.

XX

φεύγεθ᾽ ὅσοι λόκκας ἢ λοφνίδας ἢ καμασῆνας   185
  ἄιδετε, ποιητῶν φῦλον ἀκανθολόγων,
οἵ τ᾽ ἐπέων κόσμον λελυγισμένον ἀσκήσαντες
  κρήνης ἐξ ἱερῆς πίνετε λιτὸν ὕδωρ.
5 σήμερον Ἀρχιλόχοιο καὶ ἄρσενος ἦμαρ Ὁμήρου
  σπένδομεν· ὁ κρητὴρ οὐ δέχεθ᾽ ὑδροπότας.   190

XXI

Ἀντιγένης ὁ Γελῶιος ἔπος ποτὲ τοῦτο θυγατρί
  εἶπεν ὅτ᾽ ἦν ἤδη νεύμενος εἰς Ἀίδην·

---

5 δ᾽ Pl: om. P | δύσμορος Pl: -ροι P

XIX A.P. 9.26 [C] Ἀντιπάτρου Θεссαλονικέως   [J] εἰς τὰς ἐννέα λυρικὰς
ποιητρίας ἤγουν Πρήξιλλαν Μοιρώ Ἀνύτην Σαπφὼ Ἤρινναν Τελέσιλλαν
Κόρινναν Νοссίδα Μύρτιν Pl a Ἀντιπάτρου Θεссαλονικέως
2 σκόπελος CPl: -λον P   3 Μοιρώ P: Μυρώ Pl   6 Ἀθηναίης P:
Ἀθαν- Pl   9 αὐτά Stadtmüller: αὐτάς PPl   10 τέκεν P: τέκε Pl

seized it. Entangled in the coils the ill-fated eagle fell into the sea, losing both its prey and its life.

XIX

Nine poetesses

These are the women of heavenly voice whom Helicon and Pieria's Macedonian rock nourished on songs,—Praxilla; Moero; the lips of Anytê; the female Homer, Sappho, the glory of the fair-tressed ladies of Lesbos; Erinna; illustrious Telesilla; and you, Corinna, who sang of Athena's warlike shield; Nossis, the tender-voiced; and sweet-singing Myrtis; all craftswomen of immortal pages. The great heavens created nine Muses, and Earth herself nine others for mortals' undying delight.

XX

The old poets better than the new

Away with you, all who sing of 'loccae' and 'lophnides' and 'camasenes', tribe of thorn-gathering poets, and you who drink frugal water from the holy spring, practising contortions as your verses' ornament. Today we pour wine for the birthday of Archilochus and manly Homer; our bowl is not at home to water-drinkers.

XXI

A dying man's advice to his daughter

One day when Antigenes of Gela was already on his way to death, he spoke to his daughter thus: 'Pretty maiden, my little

XX A.P. 11.20 Ἀντιπάτρου Θεσσαλονικέως   Pl A Ἀντιπάτρου Θετταλοῦ
1 καμασῆνας edd. vett.: καμ cῆνας P, καμιcήνας Pl   3 λελυγιcμένον P: λελιγυc- Pl   6 κρητὴρ Pl: κρατ- P
XXI A.P. 9.96 [C] Ἀντιπάτρου   [J] εἰc Ἀντιγένην τὸν γελωτοποιὸν παραίνεcιc ἐπὶ τῆι ἰδίαι θυγατρὶ βιωφελής   Pl A Ἀντιπάτρου Θεσσαλονικέωc
2 νεύμενος Pl: -ματος P | Ἀίδην Pl: -δαν P

'παρθένε καλλιπάρηιε κόρη δ' ἐμή, ἴσχε συνεργόν
  ἠλακάτην, ἀρκεῖν κτῆμα πένητι βίωι,
5 ἢν δ' ἴκηι εἰς ὑμέναιον 'Αχαιίδος ἤθεα μητρός   195
  χρηστὰ φύλασσε, πόσει προῖκα βεβαιοτάτην.'

XXII

μούναν σὺν τέκνοις, νεκυοστόλε, δέξο με, πορθμεῦ,
  τὰν λάλον· ἀρκεῖ σοι φόρτος ὁ Τανταλίδης.
πληρώσει γαστὴρ μία σὸν σκάφος· εἴσιδε κούρους
  καὶ κούρας, Φοίβου σκῦλα καὶ 'Αρτέμιδος.   200

XXIII

αὐτά τοι τρέσσαντι παρὰ χρέος ὤπασεν ἅιδαν
  βαψαμένα κοίλων ἐντὸς ἄρη λαγόνων
μάτηρ ἅ σ' ἔτεκεν, Δαμάτριε, φᾶ δέ, σίδαρον
  παιδὸς ἑοῦ φύρδαν μεστὸν ἔχουσα φόνου,
5 ἀφριόεν κοναβηδὸν ἐπιπρίουσα γένειον,   205
  δερκομένα λοξαῖς οἷα Λάκαινα κόραις,
'λεῖπε τὸν Εὐρώταν· ἴθι Τάρταρον. ἀνίκα δειλάν
  οἶσθα φυγὰν τελέθεις οὔτ' ἐμὸς οὔτε Λάκων.'

XXIV

Κρῆσσα κύων ἐλάφοιο κατ' ἴχνιον ἔδραμε Γοργώ
  ἔγκυος ἀμφοτέρην "Αρτεμιν εὐξαμένη   210

---

4 ἀρκεῖν Pl: ἀρ κεῦ P

XXII A.P. 7.530 'Αντιπάτρου Θεσσαλονικέως   [J] εἰς Νιόβην καὶ τοὺς αὐτῆς
παῖδας   Pl A 'Αντιπάτρου   εἰς αὐτό
2 Τανταλίδης P: -δος Pl   4 σκύλα Pl: σκῦλλα P

XXIII A.P. 7.531 [C] 'Αντιπάτρου Θεσσαλονικέως   [J] εἰς Δαμάτριον τὸν
Λάκωνα ὃν ἡ μήτηρ ὡς φυγοπόλεμον ἀπέσφαξεν   Suid. s.vv. "Αρης (2), φᾶ δέ

girl, keep your distaff as your work-mate, a possession that suffices for the life of poverty. And should you come to marriage, hold fast to your mother Achaeis' virtuous ways, securest of dowries for a husband.'

XXII

On Niobe's children

Take me with my children, and none beside, ferryman of the dead; I am the one who would not hold her tongue. The load from the house of Tantalus is big enough for you; a single mother's womb shall fill your boat. Behold my sons and daughters, the spoils of Apollo and Artemis.

XXIII

A Spartan mother kills her cowardly son

The mother who bore you, Damatrius, herself gave you death, sinking the sword within your hollow flanks after you had fled in defiance of duty. And thus she spoke, holding the steel covered and dripping with her own son's blood, with foaming lips and gnashing teeth, looking with eyes askance, the image of a Spartan matron: 'Begone from the Eurotas; on your way to Tartarus; since cowardly flight is among your skills, you are neither son of mine nor Spartan.'

XXIV

A bitch has puppies while killing a deer

Gorgo, a Cretan bitch, being pregnant, ran in the track of a hind, with a prayer to both Dianas. In the act of killing she

σίδαρον, φύρδην (3 φᾶ–4), ἀφριόεν, κόναβος (5), λοξὴ φάλαγξ (6), Εὐρώταν (7s.) caret Pl
2 βαψαμένα P: -νη Suid. | κοίλων Suid.: -λαν P   7 δειλάν P: -λήν Suid.
8 φυγὰν P: -γὴν Suid. | τελέθεις C: -θει P, -θειν Suid.

XXIV *A.P.* 9.268 [C] Ἀντιπάτρου Θεσσαλονικέως   εἰς κύνα θηρευτικὴν ἐν αὐτῆι τῆι ἄγραι τεκοῦσαν ἐννέα σκύλακας   Clem. Al. 4 p. 592 (1)   caret Pl
1 ἴχνιον Clem.: ἴχνος P | Γοργώ Jacobs: -γῆ P, -γῶς Clem.

τίκτε δ' ἀποκτείνουσα, θοὴ δ' ἐπένευσεν Ἐλευθώ
ἄμφω, εὐαγρίης δῶρα καὶ εὐτοκίης·
5 καὶ νῦν ἐννέα παισὶ διδοῖ γάλα. φεύγετε, †Κρῆσσαι
κεμμάδες, ἐκ τοκάδων τέκνα διδασκόμεναι.†

B. ΑΝΤΙΠΑΤΡΟΥ ΜΑΚΕΔΟΝΟΣ

XXV

αἰεὶ θηλυτέρηισιν ὕδωρ κακὸν Ἑλλήσποντος·   215
ξεῖνε Κλευνίκης πεύθεο Δυρραχίδος.
πλῶε γὰρ ἐς Cηστὸν μετὰ νυμφίον, ἐν δὲ μελαίνηι
φορτίδι τὴν Ἕλλης μοῖραν ἀπεπλάσατο.
5 Ἡροῖ δειλαίη, cὺ μὲν ἀνέρα Δήιμαχος δέ
νύμφην ἐν παύροις ὠλέσατε σταδίοις.
                                                             220

XXVI

Ἀνθέα τὸν ναυηγὸν ἐπὶ στόμα Πηνειοῖο   (221)
νυκτὸς ὑπὲρ βαιῆς νηξάμενον cανίδος
μούνιος ἐκ θάμνοιο θορὼν λύκος ἄσκοπον ἄνδρα
ἔκτανεν. ὢ γαίης κύματα πιστότερα.

XXVII

ξεῖνοι, παρθένος εἰμὶ τὸ δένδρεον. εἴπατε δάφνης   225
φείcαcθαι δμώων χερcὶν ἑτοιμοτόμοις,
ἀντὶ δ' ἐμεῦ κομάρου τις ὁδοιπόρος ἢ τερεβίνθου
δρεπτέcθω χθαμαλὴν ἐς χύσιν, οὐ γὰρ ἑκάc.
5 ἀλλ' ἀπ' ἐμεῦ ποταμὸς μὲν ὅσον τρία, τοῦ δ' ἀπὸ πηγῶν
ὕλη πανθηλὴς δοιὰ πέλεθρ' ἀπέχει.   230

XXV *A.P.* 9.215 Ἀντιπάτρου Μακεδόνος   εἰς Κλεονίκην   Pl A Ἀντιπάτρου
Μακεδόνος
1 αἰεὶ Pl: ἀεὶ P   2 Κλευνίκης Jacobs: Κλεονίκ- P, Κλεοννίκ- Pl   5 Ἡροῖ
Pᵃᶜ: Ἡρὼ Pl, ἠνοῖ Pᵖᶜ
XXVI *A.P.* 7.289 [C] Ἀντιπάτρου Μακεδόνος   [J] εἰς Ἀνθέα τὸν ναυηγὸν ἐκ

gave birth; swiftly Eleutho granted both gifts, of good hunting and easy travail. And now she has nine babies to suckle. Fly, Cretan prickets, learning....

XXV

On a bride drowned in the Hellespont

Stranger, the Hellespont was ever an evil sea for women. Ask Cleonicê of Dyrrachium. She was sailing to Sestos to meet her bridegroom, and in her black ship she copied the fate of Hellê. Unhappy Hero, who lost your man, Deïmachus his bride, within a few furlongs.

XXVI

A man saved from drowning is killed by a wolf

The shipwrecked man, Antheus, swam to the mouth of the Peneüs at night on a small plank, but a lone wolf sprang from a thicket and killed him off his guard. O waves trustworthier than land!

XXVII

The sacrosanct bay-tree

Strangers, a maiden am I, this tree here; bid the slaves' hands, all ready for cutting, to spare the bay. Let the wayfarer pluck for strewing on the ground from arbutus or terebinth instead of me; they are not far off. The river is about a hundred yards from me, and seventy distant from its springs is a luxuriant forest.

τῆς θαλάccηc cωθέντα ὑπὸ θηρὸc δὲ χερcαίου ἀναιρεθέντα   Pl A τοῦ αὐτοῦ [sc. 'Αντιπάτρου]

3 θάμνοιο CPl: θαλάμοιο P | λύκοc CPl: om. P   4 πιcτότερα C: πικρότ- PPl

XXVII A.P. 9.282 [C] 'Αντιπάτρου Μακεδόνοc   εἰc δάφνην τὸ φυτὸν ὑπό τινων κοπτόμενον   caret Pl

2 φείcαcθαι Reiske: -θε P   5 ἀπ' Salmasius: ὑπ' P

XXVIII

νῆσοι ἐρημαῖαι, τρύφεα χθονός, ἃς κελαδεινός
ζωστὴρ Αἰγαίου κύματος ἐντὸς ἔχει,
Cίφνον ἐμιμήcαcθε καὶ αὐχμηρὴν Φολέγανδρον,
τλήμονες, ἀρχαίην δ᾽ ὠλέcατ᾽ ἀγλαΐην.
5 ἦ ῥ᾽ ὑμᾶc ἐδίδαξεν ἑὸν τρόπον ἤ ποτε λευκή   235
Δῆλοc ἐρημαίου δαίμονοc ἀρξαμένη.

XXIX

Μηδείηc τύποc οὗτοc. ἴδ᾽ ὡc τὸ μὲν εἰc χόλον αἴρει   (237)
ὄμμα τὸ δ᾽ εἰc παίδων ἔκλαcε cυμπαθίην.

C. ΑΝΤΙΠΑΤΡΟΥ [CΙΔΩΝΙΟΥ]

XXX

—Αὐcονίωι Πείcωνι cυναcπιcτὴc Διόνυcοc
ἵδρυμαι μεγάρων φρουρὸc ἐπ᾽ εὐτυχίηι.   240
—ἄξιον, ὦ Διόνυc᾽, ἐcέβηc δόμον. ἔπρεπεν ἄμφω
καὶ μέγαρον Βάκχωι καὶ Βρόμιοc μεγάρωι.

XXXI

Ἀντίπατροc Πείcωνι γενέθλιον ὤπαcε βίβλον
μικρὴν ἐν δὲ μιῆι νυκτὶ πονηcάμενοc.
ἵλαοc ἀλλὰ δέχοιτο καὶ αἰνήcειεν ἀοιδόν   245
Ζεὺc μέγαc ὡc ὀλίγωι πειθόμενοc λιβάνωι.

XXVIII A.P. 9.421 Ἀντιπάτρου [C] Μακεδόνοc   [P] εἰc τὰc Κυκλάδαc νήcουc
[C] ὅτι ἔκπαλαι ἦcαν ἔρημοι διὰ τὴν τῶν πολέμων cυνέχειαν   caret Pl
5 ἑὸν Heringa: ἕνα P | ποτε apogr.: τότε P

XXIX A.Pl. (A) 143 Ἀντιπάτρου Μακεδόνοc   εἰc τὸ αὐτό [sc. ἄγαλμα
Μηδείαc]   caret P

XXVIII

Deserted islands

Deserted islands, fragments of land which the Aegean wave's loud-sounding cincture holds within, you have copied Siphnos and parched Pholegandros; poor wretches, you have lost your ancient splendour. Surely you have been taught her own ways by Delos, once so bright, the first to meet a doom of desolation.

XXIX

On a picture of Medea

This is a picture of Medea. See how one eye is raised in anger, the other softened to compassion for her children.

XXX

On a statue of Dionysus

—I, Dionysus, comrade-in-arms of Italian Piso, am placed here for good luck, to guard his house.

—Worthy, Dionysus, is the home you have entered. Both are as they should be, the house for Bacchus and Bromios for the house.

XXXI

A birthday-present for Piso

Antipater has given Piso a book on his birthday, a little one, the labour of a single night. May he receive it graciously and praise the poet, like great Zeus won over by a little frankincense.

XXX *A.Pl.* (A) 184 ᾽Αντιπάτρου Cιδωνίου   εἰc ἕτερον ἄγαλμα τοῦ αὐτοῦ [sc. Διονύcου]   caret P
4 Βάκχωι Pl: Βρομίωι Gow

XXXI *A.P.* 9.93 [J] ᾽Αντιπάτρου Cιδωνίου [C supra] Θεccαλονικέωc [J] πρὸc Πείcωνα γενεθλιακὴ βίβλοc δῶρον ἐκπονηθὲν ἐν μιᾶι νυκτί   Pl A ᾽Αντιπάτρου
4 πειθόμενοc PPl: cπειcόμ- C

XXXII

Ἁρπαλίων ὁ πρέσβυς, ὁ πᾶς ῥυτίς, οὑπιλινευτής,
τόνδε παρ' Ἡρακλεῖ θῆκέ με τὸν σιβύνην,
ἐκ πολλοῦ πλειῶνος †ἐπεὶ βάρος οὐκέτι χεῖρες
ἔσθενον† ἐς κεφαλὴν δ' ἤλυθε λευκοτέρην.   250

XXXIII

εἰδότα κἠπ' Ἄτλαντα τεμεῖν πόρον, εἰδότα Κρήτης
κύματα καὶ Πόντου ναυτιλίην Μέλανος,
Καλλιγένευς Διόδωρον Ὀλύνθιον ἴσθι θανόντα
ἐν λιμένι πρώιρης νύκτερον ἐκχυμένου
5 δαιτὸς ἐκεῖ τὸ περισσὸν ὅτ' ἤμεεν. ἆ πόσον ὕδωρ   255
ὤλεσε τὸν τόσσωι κεκριμένον πελάγει.

XXXIV

δμώιον Ἱπποκράτευς ἔθανε βρέφος ἐς πλατὺ πόντου
χεῖλος γειτοσύνης ἑρπύσαν ἐκ καλύβης
πλεῖον ἐπεὶ μαζῶν ἔπιεν ποτόν. ἔρρε, θάλασσα,
ἢ βρέφος ὡς μήτηρ ψεύσαο δεξαμένη.   260

XXXV

αὔην με πλατάνιστον ἐφερπύζουσα καλύπτει
ἄμπελος ὀθνείηι δ' ἀμφιτέθηλα κόμηι

XXXII *A.P.* 6.93 Ἀντιπάτρου [C] Σιδωνίου   [P] ἀνάθημα τῶι Ἡρακλεῖ παρὰ
Ἁρπαλίωνος   Suid. s.vv. σιγύνη (2 τόνδε–3), πλειών (3 ἐκ π. π.)   caret Pl
1 οὑπιλινευτής C: οὐλινευτής P   2 σιβύνην P: σιγύνην Suid.   4 ἐς P: εἰς C
XXXIII *A.P.* 7.625 [J] Ἀντιπάτρου Σιδωνίου   εἰς Διόδωρον τὸν Καλλιγένους
ναυαγὸν τὸν Ὀλύνθιον   caret Pl
5 ἐκεῖ Jacobs: ἐπεὶ P

XXXII

Dedication of a hunting-spear

Harpalion, the old man, the mass of wrinkles, the trapper, set me, this hunting-spear, by the side of Heracles. By reason of his many years his hands had no more strength for the weight; he had come to the season of gray hairs.

XXXIII

On a man drowned in harbour

This is to tell you that Diodorus of Olynthus, son of Calligenes, —he who was skilled to cleave a crossing even as far as Atlas, skilled too in the Cretan waves and the sailing of the Black-water sea,—died of a fall at night from the prow in harbour while vomiting there the excess of his dinner. So little water killed a man tested in oceans so great.

XXXIV

On a drowned child

The slave-child of Hippocrates crawled to the broad sea-rim from the cottage near-by and died, for it drank more than from its mother's breast. A curse upon you, sea, for receiving the child as a mother and then cheating it.

XXXV

A vine is trained on a dead plane-tree

A creeping vine hides me, the dried-up plane-tree. Another's

XXXIV *A.P.* 9.407 [J] ’Αντιπάτρου Cιδωνίου   εἰc βρέφοc ἀποπνιγὲν ἐν θαλάccηι   Pl a ’Αντιπάτρου

XXXV *A.P.* 9.231 [C] ’Αντιπάτρου Cιδωνίου   εἰc πλάτανον ξηρὰν βαcτά-
ζουcαν ἄμπελον   Pl a ’Αντιπάτρου

ἡ πρὶν ἐμοῖς θαλέθουσιν ἐνιθρέψας' ὁροδάμνοις
βότρυας, ἢ ταύτης οὐκ ἀπετηλοτέρη·
5 —τοίην μέντοι ἔπειτα τιθηνείςθω τις ἑταίρην   265
ἥτις ἀμείψαςθαι καὶ νέκυν οἶδε μόνη.

C. ΑΝΤΙΠΑΤΡΟΥ

XXXVI

ὕδατος ἀκρήτου κεκορημένωι ἄγχι παραστάς
χθιζὸν ἐμοὶ λεχέων Βάκχος ἔλεξε τάδε·
'εὕδεις ἄξιον ὕπνον ἀπεχθομένων 'Αφροδίτηι.
εἰπέ μοι, ὦ νήφων, πεύθεαι 'Ιππολύτου;   270
5 τάρβει μή τι πάθηις ἐναλίγκιον.' ὡς ὁ μὲν εἰπών
ᾤχετ', ἐμοὶ δ' ἀπὸ τῆς οὐκέτι τερπνὸν ὕδωρ.

XXXVII

οὔ μοι Πληϊάδων φοβερὴ δύσις οὐδὲ θαλάσσης
ὥριον στυφελῶι κῦμα περὶ σκοπέλωι,
οὐδ' ὅταν ἀστράπτηι μέγας οὐρανὸς ὡς κακὸν ἄνδρα
ταρβῶ καὶ μύθων μνήμονας ὑδροπότας.   275

XXXVIII

ὠκύμορόν με λέγουσι δαήμονες ἀνέρες ἄστρων.
εἰμὶ μὲν ἀλλ' οὔ μοι τοῦτο, Σέλευκε, μέλει.
εἰς 'Αίδην μία πᾶσι καταίβασις, εἰ δὲ ταχίων
ἡμετέρη Μίνω θᾶσσον ἐποψόμεθα.   280
5 πίνωμεν, καὶ δὴ γὰρ ἐτήτυμον εἰς ὁδὸν ἵππος
οἶνος ἐπεὶ πεζοῖς ἀτραπὸς εἰς 'Αίδην.

---

3 ὁροδάμνοις Pl: -νους P   4 ἀπετηλοτέρη Pl: ἀποτ- P   6 μόνη PPl:
-νην Gow

XXXVI A.P. 9.305 'Αντιπάτρου   [C] εἰς ἑαυτὸν διὰ τὸ ὑδροποτεῖν κακῶς
διατεθέντα καὶ πάλιν τὸν οἶνον ἀσπάσαςθαι   Pl A 'Αντιπάτρου
1 ἀκρήτου Pl: ἄκρίτ- P   2 λεχέων P: κοτέων Pl   3 ἀπεχθομένων Pl:
-νην P | 'Αφροδίτηι Pl: -την P   4 πεύθεαι Pl: πεύθεσθαι P

foliage flourishes about me, who once nursed clusters with my own growing branches, and was not less leafy than the vine. —Such a mistress hereafter let men cherish, one who alone knows how to recompense them after their death.

XXXVI

On the folly of temperance

I had drunk my fill of undiluted water, when Bacchus stood beside my bed, yesterday, and spoke thus: 'You sleep the sleep of those whom Aphrodite hates; tell me, my sober friend, have you heard of Hippolytus? You should be afraid of suffering a fate like his.' Thus he spoke, and went away; and since then water is no longer any pleasure to me.

XXXVII

A worse danger than storm and lightning

The setting of the Pleiads is no such terror to me, nor the sea-wave roaring around a rugged cliff, nor when the great skies flash lightning, as is my fear of the wicked man and of the water-drinkers who remember all I say.

XXXVIII

The short and merry life is best

The experts in astrology tell of an early death for me; though it be so, I care nothing for that, Seleucus. All men have the same way down to Hades; if mine is quicker than others', I shall be face to face with Minos the sooner. Let us drink, for surely it is a true saying that wine is like a horse for the highway, while your foot-traveller must go to Hades by a lane.

XXXVII *A.P.* 11.31 ’Αντιπάτρου   Pl A ’Αντιπάτρου
2 ὡρῦον Salmasius: ὡρυμον P, ὀρνύμενον Pl

XXXVIII *A.P* 11.23 ’Αντιπάτρου   Pl B s.a.n.
3 μία πᾶσι P: πάντεσσι Pl | ταχίων Bothe: -χειον P, -χιον Pl   4 Μίνω Pl:
Μηνω P   5 πίνωμεν Pl: -νομεν P | δὴ γὰρ P: γὰρ δὴ Pl

XXXIX

Τριτογενὲς σώτειρα, Διὸς φυγοδέμνιε κούρα
Παλλάς, ἀπειροτόκου δεσπότι παρθενίης,
βωμόν τοι κεραοῦχον ἐδείματο τόνδε Σέλευκος   285
†Φοιβείαν ἰαχὰν φθεγγομένου στόματος†.

XL

Φοῖβε Κεφαλλήνων λιμενοσκόπε θῖνα Πανόρμου
ναίων τρηχείης ἀντιπέρην Ἰθάκης,
δός με δι' εὐπλώτοιο πρὸς Ἀσίδα κύματος ἐλθεῖν
Πείσωνος δολιχῆι νηὶ συνεσπόμενον,   290
5 καὶ τὸν ἐμὸν βασιλῆα τὸν ἄλκιμον εὖ μὲν ἐκείνωι
ἵλαον εὖ δ' ὕμνοις ἄρτισον ἡμετέροις.

XLI

καυσίη ἡ τὸ πάροιθε Μακηδόσιν εὔκολον ὅπλον
καὶ σκέπας ἐν νιφετῶι καὶ κόρυς ἐν πτολέμωι
ἱδρῶ διψήσασα πιεῖν τεόν, ἄλκιμε Πείσων,   295
Ἠμαθὶς Αὐσονίους ἦλθον ἐπὶ κροτάφους.
5 ἀλλὰ φίλος δέξαι με· τάχα κρόκες αἵ ποτε Πέρσας
τρεψάμεναι καὶ σοὶ Θρῆικας ὑπαξόμεθα.

XLII

καὶ Μακεδὼν ὁ σίδηρος ἐν ἄορι καὶ τὰ πρὸς ἀλκήν
τῆς ἀπ' Ἀλεξάνδρου χειρὸς ἐπιστάμενος,   300
Πείσων, σὴν ποθέων ἱκόμην χέρα, τοῦτο δὲ φωνῶ·
'χαίρων δεξιτερὴν εὖρον ὀφειλομένην.'

XXXIX A.P. 6.10 Ἀντιπάτρου   εἰς βωμὸν ἀνατεθέντα τῆι Ἀθηνᾶι παρὰ
Σελεύκου   Suid. s.v. φυγοδέμνιος (1 σώτ.)   caret Pl
1 Διὸς P: om. Suid.   3 τόνδε C: τοῖσδε P
XL A.P. 10.25 Ἀντιπάτρου   caret Pl

XXXIX

An altar made of horns for Athena

For you, Triton-born saviour Pallas, daughter of Zeus, who
run from the marriage-bed, queen of childless maidenhood,
Seleucus built this altar with horns upon it. . . .

XL

Prayer for a safe sea-passage

Phoebus, the Cephallenians' harbour-watchman, dweller on
Panormus' beach, opposite craggy Ithaca, grant me to go with
fair sailing through the waves to the Asian land in the wake of
Piso's long vessel. And dispose my valiant sovereign to gracious
favour towards him, gracious also to my songs.

XLI

A hat for Piso

A broad-brimmed hat, from olden times the Macedonian's comfortable gear, shelter in snow-storm and helmet in war, thirsting
to drink your sweat, valiant Piso, I come, an Emathian to
Italian brows. Take me in friendship; it may be that my felt-
nap, which once routed the Persians, will beneath you subdue
the Thracians too.

XLII

A sword for Piso

Macedonian is the sword's iron, and from Alexander's hand it
has learnt what makes for valour. And now, Piso, I have reached
your hand that I yearn for, and these words I speak: 'To my
delight I have found the destined hand.'

XLI *A.P.* 6.335 'Αντιπάτρου   *Et.M.* 487.39 ('Αντίπατρος Θεσσαλονικεύς)
Suid. s.vv. καυcία, cκεπανόν (1 s.)   caret Pl
1 ἡ τὸ P: ἤτοι *Et.M.*, τὸ (om. ἡ) Suid. s.v. cκεπ.   4 'Ημαθὶc Ap.B.: -θιὰ P,
-θίαc C
XLII *A.P.* 9.552 'Αντιπάτρου   caret Pl

XLIII

ἡ κόρυς ἀμφοτέρην ἔλαχον χάριν, εἰμὶ δ' ὁρᾶσθαι
καὶ τερπνὴ φιλίοις καὶ φόβος ἀντιπάλοις,
ἐκ δὲ Πυλαιμένεος Πείσων μ' ἔχει. ἔπρεπεν ἄλλαις   305
οὔτε κόρυς χαίταις οὔτε κόμαι κόρυθι.

XLIV

Θειογένης Πείσωνι τὰ τεχνήεντα κύπελλα
πέμπει, χωροῦμεν δ' οὐρανὸν ἀμφότερα.
δοιὰ γὰρ ἐκ σφαίρης τετμήμεθα, καὶ τὸ μὲν ἡμῶν
τοὺς νοτίους τὸ δ' ἔχει τείρεα τὰν Βορέηι.   310
5 ἀλλὰ σὺ μηκέτ' Ἄρητον ἐπίβλεπε, δοιὰ δ' ἐν ἀμφοῖν
μέτρα πιὼν ἄθρει πάντα τὰ Φαινόμενα.

XLV

λαμπάδα κηροχίτωνα, Κρόνου τυφήρεα λύχνον,
σχοίνωι καὶ λεπτῆι σφιγγομένην παπύρωι,
Ἀντίπατρος Πείσωνι φέρει γέρας· ἢν δέ μ' ἀνάψας   315
εὔξηται λάμψω φέγγος ἀκουσίθεον.

XLVI

τέσσαρες αἰωροῦσι τανυπτερύγων ἐπὶ νώτων
Νῖκαι ἰσηρίθμους υἱέας ἀθανάτων,

XLIII *A.P.* 6.241 [=Pᵃ] Ἀντιπάτρου, et post 9.754 [=Pᵇ] Ἀντιπάτρου εἰς κράνον   Pl A fol. 55ᵛ [=Plᵃ] Ἀντιπάτρου εἰς κράνος, et fol. 68ʳ [=Plᵇ] Ἀντιπάτρου
3 ἔπρεπεν PᵃPlᵇ: ἔπρεπε δ' PᵇPlᵃ   **4** χαίταις CᵃPᵇPlᵃˑ ᵇ: -ται Pᵃ | κόμαι PᵃPlᵇ: -μη PᵇPlᵃ

XLIV *A.P.* 9.541 Ἀντιπάτρου εἰς ποτήριον   Pl A Ἀντιπάτρου
4 τὰν Brunck: τὰ P, τοὺν Pl   **5** Ἄρητον P: ἐς ἄρκτον Pl | δοιὰ δ' ἐν Pl: δισσὰ γὰρ P

XLIII

A helmet for Piso

I am a helmet endowed with a double gift,—a sight both for my friends' rejoicing and for my foes' affright. Piso has received me from Pylaemenes. No other's hair was so well fitted for the helmet, nor helmet for the hair.

XLIV

Bowls for Piso

Theiogenes sends Piso these well-made bowls; between us we contain the heavens, for we are both cut from a sphere, and the one of us has the southern stars, the other the constellations in the north. You need no longer look up your Aratus; drink double measure from the pair, and behold all the Phaenomena.

XLV

A candle for Piso

Antipater sends Piso a present of a wax-robed light, rush-lamp of Cronos, bound with cord and thin papyrus. If he kindles me and prays, I will blaze with the light of the god's attention.

XLVI

On four figures of Victory, each upholding a divinity

Four Victories lift on their wide-winged backs as many children

XLV *A.P.* 6.249 ᾿Αντιπάτρου   Pl A ᾿Αντιπάτρου   Suid. s.vv. πάπυρος, τυφήρεα (1 s.), ἀκουσίθεον (3 ἦν–4).
2 cφιγγομένην PSuid.: -νον Pl   3 ἀνάψαc CPlSuid.: -αιc P   4 εὔξηται PPl: εὔχη- Suid.

XLVI *A.P.* 9.59 [C] ᾿Αντιπάτρου   [J] εἰc οἶκόν τινα ἐν ῾Ρώμηι ἔχοντα γραφὴν ἐν ἧι ἦcαν Νῖκαι ἐγγεγραμμέναι τέccαρεc καὶ τέccαρεc δαίμονεc, ᾿Αθηνᾶ ᾿Αφροδίτη ῾Ηρακλῆc ῎Αρηc· καὶ διὰ μὲν τοῦ ῾Ηρακλέουc τὸ τῆc ῾Ρώμηc ἀνίκητον αἰνίττεται, διὰ δὲ τῆc [cetera deleta]   Pl A τοῦ αὐτοῦ [sc. ᾿Αντιπάτρου]
1 αἰωροῦcι τανυπτερύγων Pl: -cιν τὰν πτερύγων P   2 Νῖκαι Pl: νίκα καὶ Pᵃᶜ, νίκα Pᵖᶜ

ἇ μὲν ᾿Αθαναίαν πολεμαδόκον, ἇ δ᾽ ᾿Αφροδίταν,
ἇ δὲ τὸν ᾿Αλκείδαν, ἇ δ᾽ ἀφόβητον ῎Αρη 320
5 σεῖο κατ᾽ εὐόροφον γραπτὸν τέγος, ἐc δὲ νέονται
οὐρανόν. ὦ ῾Ρώμαc Γαῖε πάτραc ἔρυμα,
θείη ἀνίκατον μὲν ὁ βουφάγοc ἁ δέ cε Κύπρις
εὔγαμον, εὔμητιν Παλλάc, ἄτρεστον ῎Αρηc.

XLVII

cτέλλευ ἐπ᾽ Εὐφρήτην, Ζηνὸc τέκοc, εἰc cὲ γὰρ ἤδη 325
ἠῶιοι Πάρθων αὐτομολοῦcι πόδεc.
cτέλλευ, ἄναξ, δήειc δὲ φόβωι κεχαλαcμένα τόξα,
Καῖcαρ, πατρώιων δ᾽ ἄρξαι ἀπ᾽ ἐντολέων,
5 ῾Ρώμην δ᾽ ᾿Ωκεανῶι περιτέρμονα πάντοθεν αὐτόc
πρῶτοc ἀνερχομένωι cφράγιcαι ἠελίωι. 330

XLVIII

Ζηνὶ καὶ ᾿Απόλλωνι καὶ ῎Αρεϊ τέκνον ἀνάκτων
εἴκελον, εὐκταίη μητέροc εὐτοκίη,
πάντα τοι ἐκ Μοιρέων βαcιλήια, πάντα τέλεια
ἦλθεν, ἐποιήθηc δ᾽ ἔργον ἀοιδοπόλων.
5 Ζεὺc cκῆπτρον βαcίλειον, ῎Αρηc δόρυ, καλλοcύνην δέ 335
Φοῖβοc ἔχει, παρὰ coὶ δ᾽ ἀθρόα πάντα, Κότυ.

XLIX

᾿Αντιπάτρου ῥητῆροc ἐγὼ τάφοc, ἡλίκα δ᾽ ἔπνει
ἔργα Πανελλήνων πεύθεο μαρτυρίηc.

3 ᾿Αθαναίαν Pl: ᾿Αθην- P   4 τὸν Pl: τὰν P | ἀφόβητον Pl: ἀμφίβοντον P
5 εὐόροφον PPl: -φου C   6 Γαῖε Lascaris: γαῖαν P, γαῖα Pl   7 μὲν ὁ Pl:
ὁ μὲν ὁ P | cε Brunck: γε Pl, om. P
XLVII A.P. 9.297 ᾿Αντιπάτρου   [C] εἰc τὸν Καίcαρα μέλλοντα ἀπαίρειν ἐπὶ
τοὺc Πάρθουc ἤδη ὑποcπόνδουc γενομένουc   caret Pl
1 ἐπ᾽ Salm.: ἀπ᾽ P   3 δήειc Brunck: δηίειc P   4 ἐντολέων
Emperius: ἀντ- P   6 ἠελίωι Salmasius: ἠελένωι P

of the Immortals. One holds Athena the warrior, one Aphrodite, one Alcides, one fearless Ares, painted on your fine ceiling; and they are on their way to heaven. Gaius, bulwark of your country Rome, may the ox-devourer make you invincible, the Cyprian happy in marriage, Pallas wise in counsel, Ares unflinching.

XLVII

The Parthians subdued

Be on your way to the Euphrates, son of Zeus; to you already the Parthians in the East are deserting apace. Be on your way, my prince; you shall find their bows unstrung through terror, Caesar. Rule in accord with your father's precepts, and be yourself the first to certify to the rising sun that Rome is bounded by the ocean on all sides.

XLVIII

Praise of Cotys

Son of kings, the image of Zeus and Apollo and Ares, blest child for whom your mother prayed, all kingly gifts and all perfections have come to you by Fate's decree, and you are made the theme of poesy. Zeus has his royal sceptre, Ares his spear, and Phoebus his beauty; but in you, Cotys, all are united.

XLIX

Epitaph for an orator

I am the tomb of Antipater the orator. You may ask all Greeks everywhere to bear witness, how great were the works of his

XLVIII *A.Pl.* (B) 75 'Αντιπάτρου   caret P
2 εὐκταίη...εὐτοκίη Graefe: -ηι...-ηι Pl

XLIX *A.P.* 7.369 [C] 'Αντιπάτρου   [J] εἰς 'Αντίπατρον ῥήτορα   θαυμαστὸν [C] ἢ μᾶλλον ἱερέα   Pl B s.a.n.
1 ῥητῆρος CPl: -τορος P

κεῖται δ' ἀμφήριστος, 'Αθηνόθεν εἴτ' ἀπὸ Νείλου
ἦν γένος, ἠπείρων δ' ἄξιος ἀμφοτέρων.　　　　340
5 ἄστεα καὶ δ' ἄλλως ἑνὸς αἵματος, ὡς λόγος Ἕλλην,
κλήρωι δ' ἡ μὲν ἀεὶ Παλλάδος, ἡ δὲ Διός.

L

Στρυμόνι καὶ μεγάλωι πεποτισμένον Ἑλλησπόντωι
ἠρίον 'Ηδωνῆς Φυλλίδος 'Αμφίπολι,
λοιπά τοι Αἰθοπίης Βραυρωνίδος ἴχνια νηοῦ　　　　345
μίμνει καὶ ποταμοῦ τἀμφιμάχητον ὕδωρ,
5 τὴν δέ ποτ' Αἰγείδαις μεγάλην ἔριν ὡς ἁλιανθές
τρῦχος ἐπ' ἀμφοτέραις δερκόμεθ' ἠϊόσιν.

LI

μὴ κλαίων τὸν Ἔρωτα δόκει, Τηλέμβροτε, πείσειν
μηδ' ὀλίγωι παύσειν ὕδατι πῦρ †ἀπνεές.　　　　350
χρυσὸς Ἔρωτος ἀεὶ παιώνιος, ἐσβέσθη δέ
οὐδὲ τότ' ἐν πολλῶι τικτόμενος πελάγει.

LII

βουκόλος ἔπλεο, Φοῖβε, Ποσειδάων δὲ καβάλλης,
κύκνος Ζεύς, Ἄμμων δ' ὠμφιβόητος ὄφις,
χοἳ μὲν ἐπ' ἠϊθέας σὺ δὲ †παιδικός†, ὄφρα λάθοιτε·　　　　355
ἐστὲ γὰρ οὐ πειθοῦς εὐνέται ἀλλὰ βίης.
5 Εὐαγόρας δ' ὢν χαλκὸς ἄτερ δόλου αὐτὸς ἐναργής
πάντας καὶ πάσας οὐ μεταβαλλόμενος.

5 Ἕλλην P: ἐστίν Pl

L A.P. 7.705 [C] 'Αντιπάτρου　　3τ τὸ ἐπίγραμμα ὅτι δυσνόητόν ἐστι καὶ ἐσφαλ-
μένον　　caret Pl
1 πεποτισμένον Dübner (-νη iam Hecker): πεπολησμ- P　　2 'Αμφίπολι
Bentley: -λει P　　3 Αἰθοπίης Bentley: -θιόπης P | νηοῦ Bentley: νηῶι P
5–6 tamquam peculiare epigramma distinxit P, marg. v. 5 3τ et ἄδηλον ἐν τίνι
scr. J　　5 Αἰγείδαις Wesseling: -δεσιν P | ἁλιανθές Boivin: -θείς P

42

inspiration. He lies here, and men dispute whether his stock was from Athens or the Nile; but both continents might be proud of him. You must know too that their cities are of a single ancestry, so Greek legend tells; the one belongs ever to Pallas by allotment, the other to Zeus.

L

On the ruins of Amphipolis

Amphipolis, tomb of Edonian Phyllis, washed by the Strymon and the great Hellespont, nothing remains of you but the ruined temple of the maid of Aethopion and Brauron and the battlefield of your river's waters. Her who was once the high strife of the sons of Aegeus, now we see like a torn rag of sea-purple on both banks.

LI

Love yields to nothing but money

Think not that you will win Love over by weeping, Telembrotus, or put an end to ⟨   ⟩ fire with a drop of water. The remedy for Love was ever gold; his fire was not even then extinguished when he was born in the deep seas.

LII

On Euagoras, a greater lover than the gods

You were an ox-herd, Phoebus, Poseidon was a nag, Zeus was a swan, Ammon was the celebrated snake. They were after girls, you were for a boy, all of you hoping to go undetected; you were mates not by persuasion but by brute force. But Euagoras, being made of brass, without deception and with no change of shape does it to every boy and every girl too.

LI A.P. 9.420 Ἀντιπάτρου   εἰς ἐρῶντα   [C] πρὸς Κλεόμβροτον   Pl A Ἀντιπάτρου
2 ἀπνεές P: om. Pl (add. man. rec.)

LII A.P. 9.241 [C] Ἀντιπάτρου   εἰς Ἀπόλλωνα καὶ Ποσειδῶνα καὶ τὸν Δία καὶ Ἄμμωνα. ἁρμόττει δὲ μᾶλλον εἰς τὸν Εὐαγόραν. τωθαστικόν   Pl A Ἀντιπάτρου   2 ὠμφιβόητος C: ἀμφι- PPl   5 ἐναργής P: ἁλίσκει Pl

LIII

δραχμῆς Εὐρώπην τὴν Ἀτθίδα μήτε φοβηθείς
μηδένα μήτ' ἄλλως ἀντιλέγουσαν ἔχε,   360
καὶ στρωμνὴν παρέχουσαν ἀμεμφέα χὠπότε χειμών
ἄνθρακας. ἦ ῥα μάτην, Ζεῦ φίλε, βοῦς ἐγένου.

LIV

γηραλέον νεφέλας τρῦχος τόδε καὶ τριέλικτον
ἰχνοπέδαν καὶ τὰς νευροτενεῖς παγίδας
κλωβούς τ' ἀμφιρρῶγας ἀνασπαστούς τε δεράγχας   365
καὶ πυρὶ θηγαλέους ὀξυπαγεῖς στάλικας
5 καὶ τὰν εὔκολλον δρυὸς ἰκμάδα τόν τε πετηνῶν
ἀγρευτὰν ἰξῶι μυδαλέον δόνακα
καὶ τρυφίου τρίκλωστον ἐπισπαστῆρα βόλοιο
ἄρκυν τε κλαγερῶν λαιμοπέδαν γεράνων   370
σοί, Πὰν ὦ σκοπιῆτα, γέρας θέτο παῖς Νεολάιδα
10 Κραῦγις ὁ θηρευτὰς Ἀρκὰς ἀπ' Ὀρχομενοῦ.

LV

ἥρωος Πριάμου βαιὸς τάφος οὐχ ὅτι τοίου   (373)
ἄξιος ἀλλ' ἐχθρῶν χερσὶν ἐχωννύμεθα.

LIII A.P. 5.109 Ἀντιπάτρου   εἰς πόρνην τινὰ καλουμένην Εὐρώπην   caret Pl
1 Ἀτθίδα C: Ἀστθίδα P | φοβηθείς Valckenaer: -θῆις P   3 ἀμεμφέα C:
ἀφεμφ- P
LIV A.P. 6.109 Ἀντιπάτρου   ἀνάθημα τῶι Πανὶ παρὰ Κραύβιδος   Pl A Ἀντιπάτρου   Suid. s.v. γλάγος (8).
2 ἰχνοπέδαν P: ἰσχνο- Pl   3 τε δεράγχας P: δέ τε ῥαγχας Pl   5 εὔκολ-

LIII

A complaisant girl

You can have Europa, the woman from Attica, for a drachma, without fear of anyone or refusal from her for any other cause. She provides a bed beyond cavil and a fire in the winter. There was no need, Zeus, to turn yourself into a bull.

LIV

Dedication to Pan by a hunter

This old rag of hunting-net, and the triply-twisted foot-snare, and these traps with stretched sinews, and broken cages, and neck-nooses to be drawn tight, and fire-sharpened pointed stakes, and the sticky moisture of the oak, and the cane dripping with mistletoe, catcher of birds, and the triple-spun drawer-to of the tattered spring-net, and the neck-trapping snare for clamorous cranes,—Craugis the huntsman, son of Neolaidas, an Arcadian from Orchomenos, dedicated these in your honour, Pan of the heights.

LV

On the tomb of Priam

Small is the tomb of the hero Priam; not because it is what such a man deserves but because we were heaped by the hands of enemies.

λον CPl: εὖ κῶλον P | τόν Pl: τῶν P | πετηνῶν P^pc: πετειν- P^acPl   8 κλα-
γερῶν C: γλαγ- PPlSuid.   10 Κραῦγις Brunck: Κραῦβις P, Κράμβις Pl |
θηρευτὰς P: -τὴς Pl

LV *A.P.* 7.136 [C] 'Αντιπάτρου   [P] εἰς Πρίαμον   Pl A 'Αντιπάτρου   εἰς
Πρίαμον

LVI

οἵδ' Ἀΐδαν στέρξαντες ἐνόπλιον οὐχ ἅπερ ἄλλοι   375
στάλαν ἀλλ' Ἀρετὰν ἀντ' ἀρετᾶς ἔλαχον.

LVII

ῥιγηλὴ ναύταις Ἐρίφων δύσις ἀλλὰ Πύρωνι
πουλὺ γαληναίη χείματος ἐχθροτέρη,
νῆα γὰρ ἀπλοίηι πεπεδημένου ἔφθασεν αὔτως
ληϊστέων ταχινὴ δίκροτος ἐσσυμένη,   380
5 χεῖμα δέ μιν προφυγόντα γαληναίωι ὑπ' ὀλέθρωι
ἔκτανον. ἆ λυγρῆς, δειλέ, καχορμισίης.

LVIII

καὶ νέκυν ἀπρήϋντος ἀνιήσει με θάλασσα
Λῦσιν ἐρημαίηι κρυπτὸν ὑπὸ σπιλάδι
στρηνὲς ἀεὶ φωνεῦσα παρ' οὔατι καὶ παρὰ κωφόν   385
σῆμα. τί μ', ὤνθρωποι, τῆιδε παρωικίσατε
5 ἢ πνοιῆς χήρωσε, τὸν οὐκ ἐπὶ φορτίδι νηί
ἔμπορον ἀλλ' ὀλίγης ναυτίλον εἰρεσίης
θηκαμένη ναυηγόν; ὁ δ' ἐκ πόντοιο ματεύων
ζωὴν ἐκ πόντου καὶ μόρον εἱλκυσάμην.   390

LVI A.P. 7.252 [C] Ἀντιπάτρου   [J] εἰς τοὺς αὐτούς [sc. τοὺς μετὰ Λεωνίδου πεσόντας]   Pl B s.a.n
1 ἐνόπλιον Casaubon: ἐνύπνιον PPl | ἅπερ Pl: ἅτερ P | ἄλλοι Aldus: ἄλλος PPl
2 ἔλαχον P: ἔλαβον Pl
LVII A.P. 7.640 [C] τοῦ αὐτοῦ [sc. Ἀντιπάτρου]   [J] εἰς Πύρωνά τινα οὐκ ἐν τῆι θαλάσσηι ναυαγήσαντα ἀλλ' ὑπὸ ληιστῶν ἤγουν πειρατῶν πεφονευμένον caret Pl

LVI

On a warrior's grave

These men, having welcomed death in arms, got no grave-stone as others do, but Valour in return for their valiance.

LVII

On a man becalmed at sea and killed by pirates

The setting of the Kids is the sailor's terror, but to Pyron the calm was much more an enemy than the storm. For his boat, as he lay a prisoner of becalming, was overtaken by a swift pirates' ship, fast driven with double oar-bank. He escaped the storm, but they killed him with a death in the doldrums. Alas, poor wretch, for your grievous ill-harbourage.

LVIII

On a man drowned and buried on the beach

The implacable sea shall vex even the corpse of me, Lysis, hidden beneath a lonely rock; it sounds ever harshly by my ear and alongside my unhearing sepulchre. Why, fellow-men, did you make me neighbour to her who bereaved me of breath and shipwrecked me, not as merchant on a trade-ship but as sailor of a little rowing-boat? While I sought my living from the sea, I caught my death too from the sea.

2 πουλὺ Dorville: πουλῆς P   3 ἀπλοίηι Salm.: ἀλιπλόη P | πεπεδημένου Dorville: -νην P | ἔφθασεν αὕτως Ellis: -σε ναύταις P   4 ἐσσυμένη apogr.: ἐσσομ- P   6 ἔκτανον Jacobs: -νεν P

LVIII *A.P.* 7.287 [C] Ἀντιπάτρου   [J] εἰς Λῦσιν ναυηγόν   Pl в Ἀντιπάτρου
3 στρηνὲς CPl: στην- P   5 ἐπὶ Schneider: ἔτι PPl

LIX

πᾶσα θάλασσα θάλασσα. τί Κυκλάδας ἢ στενὸν Ἕλλης
κῦμα καὶ ᾿Οξείας ἠλεὰ μεμφόμεθα;
ἄλλως τοὔνομ᾿ ἔχουσιν· ἐπεὶ τί με τὸν προφυγόντα
κεῖνα Σκαρφαιεὺς ἀμφεκάλυψε λιμήν;
5 νόστιμον εὐπλοίην ἀρῶιτό τις· ὡς τά γε πόντου   395
πόντος ὁ τυμβευθεὶς οἶδεν ᾿Αρισταγόρης.

LX

οὐδετέρης ὅλος εἰμὶ θανὼν νέκυς ἀλλὰ θάλασσα
καὶ χθὼν τὴν ἀπ᾿ ἐμεῦ μοῖραν ἔχουσιν ἴσην,
σάρκα γὰρ ἐν πόντωι φάγον ἰχθύες ὀστέα δ᾿ αὖτε
βέβρασται ψυχρῆι τῆιδε παρ᾿ ἠϊόνι.   400

LXI

Πύρρος ὁ μουνερέτης ὀλίγηι νεῖ λεπτὰ ματεύων
φυκία καὶ τριχίνης μαινίδας ἐκ καθέτης
ἠϊόνων ἀποτῆλε τυπεὶς κατέδουπε κεραυνῶι
νηῦς δὲ πρὸς αἰγιαλοὺς ἔδραμεν αὐτομάτη
5 ἀγγελίην θείωι καὶ λιγνύι μηνύουσα,   405
καὶ φράσεν ᾿Αργώιην κοὐκ ἐπόθησε τρόπιν.

LIX A.P. 7.639 [C] ᾿Αντιπάτρου   [J] εἰς ᾿Αρισταγόραν τινὰ ἐν τῶι Σκαρφαιεῖ
λιμένι ναυαγήσαντα   Pl a ᾿Αντιπάτρου
1 Κυκλάδας Pl: -δος P

LX A.P. 7.288 [C] τοῦ αὐτοῦ ᾿Αντιπάτρου   [J] ὁμοίως εἰς ναυηγὸν ἀνώνυμον
Pl a ᾿Αντιπάτρου
3 γὰρ Pl: μὲν γὰρ P

LIX

On a man drowned in harbour

All seas are simply seas; why do we idly blame the Cyclades or the narrow waters of Hellê or the Needles? The repute they have is vain. For why, when I had escaped them, did the harbour of Scarphea close over me? Let who will pray for fair weather homeward; that the sea's ways are the sea is known to Aristagores buried here.

LX

A drowned man's skeleton is washed ashore

In death my corpse is not wholly of either element; the portions of me that sea and land possess are equal. Fishes ate my flesh in the sea, but my bones have been washed up on this chill beach.

LXI

On a fisherman killed by lightning at sea

Pyrrhus, sole oarsman in his little boat, looking for wrasse-fry and sprats with a sunk line of hair, far from the shore was struck by lightning and fell dead. And his boat ran of its own motion to the beaches, making plain its message by sulphur and smoke; it told its tale, and needed no Argo's keel.

LXI *A.P.* 7.637 [C] Ἀντιπάτρου   [J] εἰς Πύρρον τὸν ἁλιέα κεραυνόβλητον γενόμενον   Pl в Ἀντιπάτρου
1 μουνερέτης Pl: μουνορ- P | νεῖ Scaliger: νηὶ PPl   2 καθέτης P: -του Pl
6 κοὐκ P: δ' οὐκ Pl

LXII

Κυλλήνην ὄρος Ἀρκάδων ἀκούεις·
αὕτη cῆμ' ἐπίκειτ' Ἀπολλοδώρωι.
Πίcηθέν μιν ἰόντα νυκτὸς ὥρηι
ἔκτεινεν Διόθεν πεcὼν κεραυνός,   410
5   τηλοῦ δ' Αἰγανέηc τε καὶ Βεροίηc
νικηθεὶc Διὸc ὁ δρομεὺc καθεύδει.

LXIII

Αὔcονος Ἡγερίου με λέγειν νέκυν ὧι μετιόντι
νύμφην ὀφθαλμοὺc ἀμβλὺ κατέcχε νέφος,
ὄμμαcι δὲ πνοιὴν cυναπέcβεcε μοῦνον ἰδόντος   415
κούρην. φεῦ κείνης, Ἥλιε, θευμορίηc.
5   ἔρροι δὴ κεῖνο φθονερὸν cέλαc, εἴθ' Ὑμέναιος
ἧψέ μιν οὐκ ἐθέλων εἴτ' Ἀίδης ἐθέλων.

LXIV

χειμερίου καίουcαν ἐφ' ἑcτίηι ἄνθρακα Γοργώ
τὴν γρηὺν βροντῆc ἐξεπάταξε φόβος,   420
πνεύμονα δὲ ψυχθεῖcα κατήμυcεν. ἦν ἄρα μέccη
γήρωc καὶ θανάτου λειπομένη πρόφαcιc.

LXII *A.P.* 7.390 [C] Ἀντιπάτρου   [J] εἰc Ἀπολλόδωρόν τινα ὑπὸ κεραυνοῦ
τελευτήcαντα· ἦν δ' ἄρα cταδιοδρόμος   Pl в Ἀντιπάτρου
3 ὥρηι Pl: ὥρηc P   6 Διὸc P: om. Pl
LXIII *A.P.* 7.367 [C] Ἀντιπάτρου   [J] εἰc νυμφίον τινὰ ἐπὶ τῆc παcτάδοc
τελευτήcαντα   caret Pl
1 Αὔcονοc apogr.: -cooc C, -cιc (?) P | λέγειν Reiske: -γει P   3 ὄμμαcι C:

LXII

*An athlete, homeward bound from Olympia,
is killed by lightning*

You have heard of Cyllenê, the Arcadians' mountain; that it is
which lies as a tombstone on Apollodorus. He was travelling at
night-time from Pisa when lightning fell from Zeus and killed
him. Far from Aeganea and Beroea the runner sleeps, defeated
by Zeus.

LXIII

Death of a bridegroom

Call me the corpse of Egerius, an Italian, whose eyes, as he
went to meet his bride, a dim cloud covered, extinguishing his
breath together with his sight, when he had no more than seen
the maiden. Alas, Sun, what a doom was that. A curse upon
that envious flame, whether unwilling Hymen kindled it, or
Hades willing.

LXIV

An old woman dies of fright in a thunderstorm

As Gorgo was kindling coals on her hearth in winter, fright at
a thunderclap struck the old woman out of her wits. Chilled to
the lungs, she closed her eyes for ever; thus midway between
old age and the grave still another cause of death was left.

-ατι P | ἰδόντος apogr.: -τες P   **4** κούρην Salm.: -ρον P   **5** κεῖνο
C: -νον P

LXIV *A.P.* 9.309 [C] ᾽Αντιπάτρου   εἰς γραῦν πῦρ ἀνακαίουςαν καὶ ὑπὸ ψόφου
βροντῆς θανοῦςαν   Pl A ᾽Αντιπάτρου
1 ἄνθρακα Pl: -κι P   **3** μέςςη Pl: -ηι P

LXV

οὐκ οἶδ᾽ εἰ Διόνυσον ὀνόσσομαι ἢ Διὸς ὄμβρον
μέμψομ᾽, ὀλισθηροὶ δ᾽ εἰς πόδας ἀμφότεροι,
ἀγρόθε γὰρ κατιόντα Πολύξενον ἔκ ποτε δαιτός   425
τύμβος ἔχει γλίσχρων ἐξεριπόντα λόφων.
5 κεῖται δ᾽ Αἰολίδος Cμύρνης ἑκάς. ἀλλά τις ὄρφνης
δειμαίνοι μεθύων ἀτραπὸν ὑετίην.

LXVI

χειμερίου νιφετοῖο περὶ θριγκοῖσι τακέντος
δῶμα πεσὸν τὴν γραῦν ἔκτανε Λυσιδίκην,   430
σῆμα δέ οἱ κωμῆται ὁμώλακες οὐκ ἀπ᾽ ὀρυκτῆς
γαίης ἀλλ᾽ αὐτὸν πύργον ἔθεντο τάφον.

LXVII

εἴκοσιν Ἑρμοκράτεια καὶ ἐννέα τέκνα τεκοῦσα
οὔθ᾽ ἑνὸς οὔτε μιῆς αὐγασάμην θάνατον,
οὐ γὰρ ἀπωίστευσεν ἐμοὺς υἱῆας Ἀπόλλων   435
οὐ βαρυπενθήτους Ἄρτεμις εἷλε κόρας,
5 ἔμπαλι δ᾽ ἃ μὲν ἔλυσεν ἐμὰν ὠδῖνα μολοῦσα,
Φοῖβος δ᾽ εἰς ἥβαν ἄρσενας ἀγάγετο
ἀβλαβέας νούσοισιν. ἴδ᾽ ὡς νίκημι δικαίως
παισί τε καὶ γλώσσηι σώφρονι Τανταλίδα.   440

LXVIII

εἶχεν Ἀριστείδης ὁ βοκέρριος οὐκ ἀπὸ πολλῶν
πολλὰ μιῆς δ᾽ ὅιος καὶ βοὸς εὐπορίην,

LXV *A.P.* 7.398 [C] Ἀντιπάτρου   [J] εἴς τινα μεθυσθέντα Πολύξενον καὶ
ἐξολισθήσαντα τελευτῆσαι, et ad v. 3 εἰς Πολύξενον Cμυρναῖον οἰνωθέντα καὶ
ἐξολισθήσαντα καὶ τελευτῆς δι᾽ αὐτὸ τοῦτο τυχόντα   Pl A Ἀντιπάτρου
1 εἰ P: ἢ Pl | Διόνυcον Pl: -νυccον P | ὀνόσσομαι CPl: ὀνομάσc- P

LXVI *A.P.* 7.402 [C] Ἀντιπάτρου   [J] εἰς γραῦν τινα Λυσιδίκην ἣν ἡ οἰκία
καταπεσοῦσα ἀπέκτεινε   caret Pl

LXV

A drunken man falls to his death

I know not whether to blame the wine-god or the rain from Zeus; both are slippery for the feet. The tomb holds Polyxenus, who fell from treacherous slopes one day while returning from the country after dinner; and far from Aeolian Smyrna he lies. If a man is drunk, let him fear the rain-soaked path in darkness.

LXVI

The house falls and kills an old woman

When the winter snow melted round the copings, her house fell down and killed old Lysidicê. Villagers who were her neighbours made as her sepulchre not a tomb of dug earth but the house itself.

LXVII

A fortunate mother

I, Hermocrateia, bore nine and twenty children and saw not the death of one, either boy or girl. Neither Apollo shot my sons down, nor Artemis bereaved me of my daughters to my sorrow. Rather the one came and eased my travail, while Phoebus brought my boys to young manhood unharmed by sickness. See how justly I surpass the daughter of Tantalus in my children and in my modesty of speech.

LXVIII

Suicide of a poor man

Aristides the ⟨   ⟩ had not much or from many sources,

LXVII *A.P.* 7.743 Ἀντιπάτρου   [J] εἰс Ἑρμοκράτειάν τινα γυναῖκα τεκοῦсαν κθ τέκνα καὶ μηδενὸс ἑωρακυῖαν θάνατον. сημεῖον θαυμαстόν   caret Pl
3 υἱῆαс C: υἱῆναс P   **4** εἷλε Salm.: ἧλε P   **5** ἐμὰν Stadtmüller: ἐμῶν P   **8** τε Salm.: om. P | Τανταλίδα apogr.: -δη P, -δαс J

LXVIII *A.P.* 9.149 [C] Ἀντιπάτρου   εἰс Ἀριстείδην πένητα οὗ βίοс ὅλοс ἦν ἐπὶ δάμαλιν καὶ πρόβατον ἅπερ ἐν ἡμέραι μιᾶι ἀπώλεсεν   Pl A Ἀντιπάτρου

53

ἀλλὰ γὰρ οὐδ᾽ ὁ πένης ἔφυγε φθόνον, ἤματι δ᾽ αὐτῶι
θῆρες ὄιν τὴν βοῦν δ᾽ ὤλεσε δυστοκίη.
5 μισήσας δ᾽ ἀβληχὲς ἐπαύλιον ἅμματι πήρης   445
ἐκ ταύτης βιοτὴν ἀχράδος ἐκρέμασεν.

LXVIIIA

πλοῦτος ᾽Αριστείδηι δάμαλις μία καὶ τριχόμαλλος
ἦν ὄις· ἐκ τούτων λιμὸν ἔλαυνε θύρης.
ἤμβροτε δ᾽ ἀμφοτέρων· ἀμνὴν λύκος, ἔκτανεν ὠδίς
τὴν δάμαλιν, πενίης δ᾽ ὤλετο βουκόλιον.   450
5 πηροδέτωι δ᾽ ὅγ᾽ ἱμάντι κατ᾽ αὐχένος ἅμμα λυγώσας
οἰκτρὸς ἀμυκήτωι κάτθανε πὰρ καλύβηι.

LXIX

τὸ βρέφος ῾Ερμώνακτα διεχρήσασθε, μέλισσαι,
φεῦ κύνες, ἑρπηστὴν κηρία μαιόμενον,
πολλάκι δ᾽ ἐξ ὑμέων ἐψισμένον ὠλέσατ᾽, αἰαῖ,   455
κέντροις. εἰ δ᾽ ὀφίων φωλεὰ μεμφόμεθα
5 πείθεο Λυσιδίκηι καὶ ᾽Αμύντορι μηδὲ μελίσσας
αἰνεῖν· κἀκείναις πικρὸν ἔνεστι βέλος.

LXX

θηρευτὴν Λάμπωνα Μίδου κύνα δίψα κατέκτα
καίπερ ὑπὲρ ψυχῆς πολλὰ πονησάμενον,   460

LXVIIIA *A.P.* 9.150 [J] τοῦ αὐτοῦ [sc. ᾽Αντιπάτρου]   [C ut vid.] εἰc τὸν
αὐτὸν ᾽Αριστείδην τὸν ἐλεεινότατον   Pl A τοῦ αὐτοῦ [sc. ᾽Αντιπάτρου]   εἰc τὸν
αὐτόν
2 ἔλαυνε Pᵖᶜ: ἤλ- PᵃᶜPl   3 ἤμβροτε CPl: quid fuerit in P incertum
LXIX *A.P.* 9.302 ᾽Αντιπάτρου   [C] εἰc παιδίον ἕρπον ὅπερ διεχρήcαντο
μέλιccαι Pl A ᾽Αντιπάτρου

but provision enough from a single sheep and cow. Yet not even the pauper escaped Envy: on the same day, wild beasts killed his sheep and a hard birth killed his cow. In disgust with a farm where no sheep bleated, with the strap from his wallet he hung his life from this wild pear-tree.

LXVIIIA

On the same

For Aristides, one heifer and a fleecy sheep were all his wealth. Through them, he drove starvation from the door. Then he lost both: a wolf killed the sheep, pangs of birth the cow; his poverty's consolation perished. He tied a knot against his neck with the strap of his wallet, and died in his misery beside the cabin where no cattle lowed.

LXIX

On a child stung to death by bees

You have killed the infant Hermonax, savage pack of bees, as he was crawling in search of your combs. One whom you had so often fed, alas, you have slain with your stings. If we caution against the lairs of snakes, be taught by Lysidicê and Amyntor not to praise bees either; in them too there lies a bitter weapon.

LXX

Death of a hunting-dog

Lampon, the hunting-hound of Midas, died of thirst, hard though he worked for his life; for he dug the damp earth

2 ἑρπηστὴν Pl: -πυστὴν P   3 ἐψισμένον P: ἐcτιγμ- Pl | αἰαῖ Pl: αἰεὶ P
4 εἰ δ' Jacobs: οἶδ' Pl, δ' οἶδ' P   6 βέλος Jacobs: μέλι PPl
LXX A.P. 9.417 ᾽Αντιπάτρου   εἰς τὸν κύνα Μίδου [C] διψήcαντα καὶ διὰ τοῦτο
ἀπαλλάξαντα   Pl A ᾽Αντιπάτρου

ποccὶ γὰρ ὤρυccεν νοτερὸν πέδον, ἀλλὰ τὸ νωθέc
πίδακοc ἐκ τυφλῆc οὐκ ἐτάχυνεν ὕδωρ.
5 πῖπτε δ' ἀπαυδήcαc, ἡ δ' ἔβλυcεν. ἦ ἄρα, Νύμφαι,
Λάμπωνι κταμένων μῆνιν ἔθεcθ' ἐλάφων;

LXXI

γειαρότηc ᾿Άρχιπποc ὅτ' ἐκ νούcοιο βαρείηc   465
ἄρτι λιποψυχέων ἔρρεεν εἰc ᾿Άίδην
εἶπε τάδ' υἱήεccιν· 'ἰώ, φίλα τέκνα, μάκελλαν
καὶ τὸν ἀροτρίτην cτέρξατέ μοι βίοτον.
5 μὴ cφαλερῆc αἰνεῖτε πόνον cτονόεντα θαλάccηc
καὶ βαρὺν ἀτηρῆc ναυτιλίηc κάματον.   470
ὅccον μητρυιῆc γλυκερωτέρη ἔπλετο μήτηρ
τόccον ἁλὸc πολιῆc γαῖα ποθεινοτέρη.'

LXXII

οἱ μέν cευ Κολοφῶνα τιθηνήτειραν, ᾿Όμηρε,
οἱ δὲ καλὰν Cμύρναν, οἱ δ' ἐνέπουcι Χίον,
οἱ δ' ᾿Ίον, οἱ δ' ἐβόαcαν εὔκλαρον Cαλαμῖνα,   475
οἱ δέ νυ τῶν Λαπιθέων ματέρα Θεccαλίαν,
5 ἄλλοι δ' ἄλλην γαῖαν ἀνίαχον· εἰ δέ με Φοίβου
χρὴ λέξαι πινυτὰc ἀμφαδὰ μαντοcύναc
πάτρα cοι τελέθει μέγαc οὐρανὸc ἐκ δὲ τεκούcηc
οὐ θνατᾶc ματρὸc δ' ἔπλεο Καλλιόπαc.   480

5 πῖπτε Pl: -τεν P | ἡ Jacobs: αἱ PPl | ἔβλυcεν Brunck: -cαν PPl | ἦ ἄρα Reiske:
παρὰ PPl   6 κταμένων Stephanus: -νωι PPl

LXXI A.P. 9.23 [C] ᾿Αντιπάτρου   [J] εἰc γεηπόνον μέλλοντα θνήιcκειν καὶ τοῖc
υἱοῖc παραινοῦντα ἔχεcθαι τῶν ἐπὶ γῆc ἔργων, φεύγειν δὲ τὴν ναυτιλίαν καὶ τὰ
θαλάccηc ἔργα Pl A ᾿Αντιπάτρου
2 ᾿Άίδην Pl: -δαν P   3 ἰώ P: ὦ Pl   4 ἀροτρίτην P: -τρητὴν Pl
6 ἀτηρῆc Pl: ἄτειρ- P

with his paws, but the sluggish water would not hurry from the hidden spring. He gave up and fell; and then the spring welled up. Did the Nymphs charge to Lampon's account their anger for the deer he had killed?

LXXI

A dying farmer's advice to his sons

Thus to his sons spoke the ploughman Archippus, when in a swoon through grievous sickness he was just slipping away towards death: 'Dear children, be well content with the mattock and the life that is of the plough. Approve not the grievous labour of the treacherous ocean or the heavy toil of perilous seafaring. As a mother is more delightful than a step-mother, by so much is the earth more desirable than the gray sea.'

LXXII

On Homer's birthplace

Homer, some say that your nurse was Colophon, others lovely Smyrna, some Chios, some Ios, others declare happy Salamis, some Thessaly the mother of the Lapiths. These have proclaimed one land, those another. But if I must declare openly the knowing utterances of Phoebus, the great heavens are your fatherland; no mortal gave you birth, but Calliopê was your mother.

LXXII *A.Pl.* (A) 296 'Αντιπάτρου   εἰς τὸν αὐτὸν [sc. Ὅμηρον]   Ps.-Plut. *Vit. Hom.* 87 (Allen)   caret P

3 ἐύκλαρον PlPlut.: -κληρον Pl^sscr   **4** τῶν Λαπιθέων Pl: τᾶν Λαπιθᾶν Plut. | Θεσσαλίαν Plut.: -ίην Pl   **5** ἄλλην γαῖαν Pl: ἄλλο μέλαθρον Plut. | Φοίβου Plut.: -βος Pl   **6** πινυτὰς Pl: -τὰν Plut. | ἀμφαδὰ Plut.: ἄνδιχα Pl | μαντοσύνας Pl: -ναν Plut.   **7** coι Pl: τοι Plut. | τεκούσης Pl: γυναικός Plut.

LXXIII

οὔνομά μευ Σαπφώ, τόσσον δ᾽ ὑπερέσχον ἀοιδῶν   (481)
θηλειᾶν ἀνδρῶν ὅσσον ὁ Μαιονίδας.

LXXIV

Στασίχορον ζαπληθὲς ἀμέτρητον στόμα Μούσας
ἐκτέρισεν Κατάνας αἰθαλόεν δάπεδον
οὗ, κατὰ Πυθαγόρεω φυσικὰν φάτιν, ἁ πρὶν Ὁμήρου   485
ψυχὰ ἐνὶ στέρνοις δεύτερον ᾠκίσατο.

LXXV

νεβρείων ὁπόσον σάλπιγξ ὑπερίαχεν αὐλῶν
τόσσον ὑπὲρ πάσας ἔκραγε σεῖο χέλυς,
οὐδὲ μάτην ἁπαλοῖς ξουθὸς περὶ χείλεσιν ἑσμός
ἔπλασε κηρόδετον, Πίνδαρε, σεῖο μέλι.   490
5 μάρτυς ὁ Μαινάλιος κερόεις θεὸς ὕμνον ἀείσας
τὸν σέο καὶ νομίων λησάμενος δονάκων.

LXXVI

ἦ χθαμαλὴν ὑπέδυς ὁ τόσος κόνιν; εἰς σέ τις ἀθρῶν,
Σώκρατες, Ἑλλήνων μέμψεται ἀκρισίην.

LXXIII *A.P.* 7.15 ᾽Αντιπάτρου   εἰς τὴν αὐτήν   Pl A fol. 1ᵛ [=Plᵃ] s.a.n., et fol. 95ᵛ [=Plᵇ] s.a.n.   εἰς Σαπφώ, et fol. 123ᵛ [=Plᶜ] s.a.n.   cod. Bodl. Lat. class. d 5 (Ellis *J.Phil.* 24.162) s.a.n. ἐπίγραμμα εἰς Πέργαμον ᾽Ασίας περὶ Σαπφοῦς   *CIG* 3555 s.a.n.
1 ὑπερέσχον PPlᵇ cod. Bodl. *CIG*: -έσχων Plᵃ, -εσέχων Plᶜ | ἀοιδῶν Plᵃᵇᶜ cod. Bodl. *CIG*: -δᾶν P   2 θηλειᾶν P (accent. θήλ-): -ῶν Plᵇ cod. Bodl. *CIG*, θηλύων Plᵃᶜ | ordinem ἀνδρῶν θήλειαν P, corr. C | Μαιονίδας PPlᵃ cod. Bodl.: -δης Plᵇᶜ *CIG*

LXXIV *A.P.* 7.75 ᾽Αντιπάτρου   εἰς Στησίχορον   Pl B ᾽Αντιπάτρου   εἰς Στησίχορον   Suid. s.v ζαπληθές (1 s.)

LXXIII

Sappho

My name is Sappho. I surpassed female poets as greatly as Homer surpassed the male.

LXXIV

The tomb of Stesichorus

Stesichorus, the Muse's rich and infinite voice, is buried in the scorched land of Catana. In his breast, so runs Pythagoras' pronouncement on man's nature, the former soul of Homer made a second home.

LXXV

Praise of Pindar

As a trumpet sounds above the fawn-bone pipes, so loud above all others rang your lyre; it was not for nothing, Pindar, that the tuneful swarm moulded its wax-bound honey about your tender lips. Witness the horned god of Maenalus, who forgot his own pastoral reeds and sang your song.

LXXVI

On the death of Socrates

Can it be that so great a man as you went under the lowly dust? He who looks at you, Socrates, shall blame the ill-judgment of

1 Cτασίχορον P: Cτηc- CPlSuid. | Μούcαc Stadtmüller: -cηc PPlSuid.
2 Κατάναc PlSuid.: κτάναc P   3 Πυθαγόρεω CPl: -ρου P | φυcικὰν CPl: -κὴν P   4 ἐνὶ C: ἐν PPl | ὠικίcατο Pl: -κήcατο P

LXXV *A.Pl.* (A) 305 ᾿Αντιπάτρου   εἰc εἰκόνα Πινδάρου   Eust. 1498.36 caret P
3 ἁπαλοῖc Brunck: -λὸc PlEust. | ξουθὸc περὶ χείλεciν ἐcμόc Pl: περὶ χείλεciν ἐcμὸc ἐκεῖνοc Eust.

LXXVI *A.P.* 7.629 [C] ᾿Αντιπάτρου   [J] εἰc Cωκράτην τὸν Cωφρονίcκου τὸν ᾿Αθηναῖον   Pl A ᾿Αντιπάτρου   εἰc Cωκράτην
1 εἰc Pl: εἰ P

νηλέες, οἳ τὸν ἄριστον ἀπώλεσαν οὐδὲ ἐν αἰδοῖ   495
δόντες· τοιοῦτοι πολλάκι Κεκροπίδαι.

LXXVII

Διογένευς τόδε σῆμα, σοφοῦ κυνὸς ὅς ποτε θυμῶι
ἄρσενι γυμνήτην ἐξεπόνει βίοτον,
ὧι μία τις πήρα, μία διπλοῖς, εἷς ἅμ' ἐφοίτα
σκίπων, αὐτάρκους ὅπλα σαοφροσύνας.   500
5 ἀλλὰ τάφου τοῦδ' ἐκτὸς ἴτ', ἄφρονες, ὡς ὁ Σινωπεύς
ἐχθαίρει φαῦλον πάντα καὶ εἰν 'Αίδηι.

LXXVIII

αὐτὸν βακχευτὴν ἐνέδυ θεὸν ἡνίκα Βάκχας
ἐκ Θηβῶν 'Ιταλὴν ἤγαγε πρὸς θυμέλην
ἀνθρώποις Πυλάδης τερπνὸν δέος οἷα χορεύων   505
δαίμονος ἀκρήτου πᾶσαν ἔπλησε πόλιν.
5 Θῆβαι γιγνώσκουσι τὸν ἐκ πυρός, οὐράνιος δέ
οὗτος ὁ παμφώνοις χερσὶ λοχευόμενος.

LXXIX

ὁ σταδιεὺς 'Αρίης ὁ Μενεκλέος οὐ κατελέγχει
Περσέα, σὸν κτίστην, Ταρσέ, Κίλισσα πόλι.   510
τοῖοι γὰρ παιδὸς πτηνοὶ πόδες, οὐδ' ἂν ἐκείνωι
οὐδ' αὐτὸς Περσεὺς νῶτον ἔδειξε θέων.
5 ἢ γὰρ ἐφ' ὑσπλήγων ἢ τέρματος εἶδέ τις ἄκρου
ἠίθεον, μέσσωι δ' οὔποτ' ἐνὶ σταδίωι.

3 νηλέες PPl: -λεεῖς, sscr. -λεῖς, C | οὐδὲ ἐν αἰδοῖ Brunck: οὐδὲ ἐν "Αιδου P, οὐδὲν
ἐν "Αιδου Pl   4 τοιοῦτοι Pl: οἱ τοσσοῦτοι P
LXXVII A.P. 7.65 'Αντιπάτρου εἰς τὸν αὐτόν [sc. Διογένην]   Pl a 'Αντιπάτρου εἰς τὸν αὐτόν   Suid. s.v. γυμνῆται (1 ὅς–2)

the Greeks; merciless, they slew the best of men, conceding nothing to the sense of shame. How often have the Athenians acted thus!

LXXVII

Epitaph for Diogenes the Cynic

This is the tomb of Diogenes, the wise Cynic, who once with manly spirit practised an ascetic life; who had one wallet, one cloak, one staff to accompany his steps, the armour of self-sufficient moderation. Immoderate fools, keep clear of this tomb; even in Hades the Sinopean hates all men that are base.

LXXVIII

On Pylades the pantomimus

When he brought the Bacchants from Thebes to the Italian stage, Pylades put on the form of the Bacchanal god himself, to all men's delight and terror, for by his dancing he filled the whole city with that deity's intemperate fury. Thebes knows the one born of fire; the heavenly god is this one here, brought to birth by these all-expressive hands.

LXXIX

Praise of a young sprinter

Tarsus, Cilician city, the sprinter Aries, son of Menecles, does no disgrace to your founder Perseus. Such are the boy's winged feet,—not even Perseus himself would have shown him his back in the race. The youth might be seen at the start or at the finish, but never in the middle of the course.

3 πήρα μία CPl: cπείρα (?) P | διπλοῖc Pl: -πλιος P, -πλοος C **4** cκίπων PPl: cκῆπ- C | caοφροcύναc P: -νηc Pl

LXXVIII A.Pl. (A) 290 Ἀντιπάτρου εἰc cτήλην Πυλάδου ὀρχηcτοῦ caret P

LXXIX A.P. 9.557 Ἀντιπάτρου Pl A Ἀντιπάτρου εἰc Ἀρίαν **2** cὸν Pl: τὸν P **5** ὑcπλήγων P: -ήγγων Pl

LXXX

διccῶν ἐκ βροχίδων ἁ μὲν μία πίονα κίχλαν   515
ἁ μία δ' ἱππείαι κόccυφον εἷλε πάγαι.
ἀλλ' ἁ μὲν κίχλαc θαλερὸν δέμαc ἐc φάοc Ἠοῦc
οὐκέτ' ἀπὸ πλεκτᾶc ἧκε δεραιοπέδαc,
5 ἁ δ' αὖθιc μεθέηκε τὸν ἱερόν. ἦν ἄρ' ἀοιδῶν
φειδὼ κἤν κωφαῖc, ξεῖνε, λινοcταcίαιc.   520

LXXXI

δένδρεον ἱερόν εἰμι· παρερχόμενόc με φυλάccευ
πημαίνειν. ἀλγῶ, ξεῖνε, κολουομένη.
μέμνεο, παρθένιόc μοι ἔπι φλόοc, οὐχ ἅπερ ὠμαῖc
ἀχράcιν. αἰγείρων τίc γένοc οὐκ ἐδάη;
5 εἰ δὲ περιδρύψειc με παρατραπίην περ ἐοῦcαν   525
δακρύcειc. μέλομαι καὶ ξύλον Ἡελίωι.

LXXXII

ἴcχετε χεῖρα μυλαῖον, ἀλετρίδεc, εὕδετε μακρά
κἤν ὄρθρον προλέγηι γῆρυc ἀλεκτρυόνων,
Δηὼ γὰρ Νύμφαιcι χερῶν ἐπετείλατο μόχθουc,
αἱ δὲ κατ' ἀκροτάτην ἀλλόμεναι τροχιήν   530
5 ἄξονα δινεύουcιν, ὁ δ' ἀκτίνεccιν ἑλικταῖc
cτρωφᾶι Νιcυρίων κοῖλα βάρη μυλάκων.
γευόμεθ' ἀρχαίου βιότου πάλιν εἰ δίχα μόχθου
δαίνυcθαι Δηοῦc ἔργα διδαcκόμεθα.

LXXX *A.P.* 9.76 [C] Ἀντιπάτρου   [J] εἰc κόccυφον καὶ κίχλην ὑπὸ πάγηc
ἀγρευθέντων [sic] καὶ τοῦ κοccύφου διά τινα τύχην ἢ καὶ τὸ μουcικὸν ἀποδρά-
cαντοc   Pl β Ἀντιπάτρου
3 ἀλλ' ἁ P: ἀλλὰ τὸ Pl | κίχλαc Pl: -ληc P   4 δεραιοπέδαc Pl: δερειο- P
LXXXI *A.P.* 9.706 Ἀντιπάτρου   caret Pl
4 αἰγείρων Schneider: αιηρων P   5 περιδρύψειc Chardon: -ψηιc P

LXXX

The sacrosanct song-bird

Of two nooses, the one caught a fat thrush, the other a black-bird, in its horse-hair trap. Now the one did not thereafter release the plump body of the thrush to the light of day from the twisted neck-bonds, while the other set its holy bird free again. Thus even among insensate snares, friend, there is mercy for the songster.

LXXXI

The sacrosanct poplar

A holy tree am I; when you pass by, beware of harming me. He who damages me, friend, gives me pain. Remember, the bark upon me is virginal, not as on the crude wild-pear. Who does not know the pedigree of poplars? If you strip my bark, though of a mere wayside tree, you shall weep for it. I am only wood, but the Sun-god is my guardian.

LXXXII

On a water-mill

Hold back the hand that works the millstone, women grinders; sleep long, though the cock's crow proclaim the morning twi-light. For Demeter has enjoined upon the Nymphs the labours of your hands; and they, leaping upon the wheel's topmost part, whirl the axle, which revolves with its twisting rays the hollow weights of the millstones from Nisyros. We taste again the joys of our fore-fathers' life, if we learn to feast without labour on Demeter's works.

LXXXII *A.P.* 9.418 τοῦ αὐτοῦ [sc. ᾿Αντιπάτρου]   εἰς μύλην [C] ὅτι τὸ παλαιὸν γυναῖκες ἠλέτρευον πρὶν ἢ τὴν ἐξ ὕδατος τέχνην φανῆναι, ὡς δηλοῖ τὸ ἐπίγραμμα caret Pl
2 προλέγηι Salm.: -γει P   **3** χερῶν Boivin: χορ- P   **4** τροχιήν J: προ- P   **5** δινεύουσιν Ap.B.: δινεῦσιν P   **6** Νισυρίων Hecker: πισύρων P

LXXXIII

βούπαις ὠπόλλων· τόδε χάλκεον ἔργον Ὀνατᾶ   535
ἀγλαΐης Λητοῖ καὶ Διὶ μαρτυρίη,
οὔθ᾽ ὅτι τῆςδε μάτην Ζεῦς ἤρατο χὤτι κατ᾽ αἶνον
ὄμματα καὶ κεφαλὴν ἀγλαὸς ὁ Κρονίδης.
5 οὐδ᾽ Ἥρηι νεμεσητὸν ἐχεύατο χαλκὸν Ὀνατᾶς
ὃν μετ᾽ Ἐλειθυίης τοῖον ἀπεπλάσατο.   540

LXXXIV

[ἁ δάμαλις δοκέω μυκήσεται·] ἦν δὲ βραδύνηι   (541)
χαλκὸς ὁ μὴ νοέων αἴτιος, οὐχὶ Μύρων.

LXXXV

Νικίεω πόνος οὗτος. ἀειζώουσα Νέκυια
ἤσκημαι πάσης ἠρίον ἡλικίης,
δώματα δ᾽ Ἀϊδωνῆος ἐρευνήσαντος Ὁμήρου   545
γέγραμμαι κείνου πρῶτον ἀπ᾽ ἀρχετύπου.

LXXXVI

Τανταλὶς †ἅδε ποχ᾽ ἅδε δὶς ἑπτὰ τέκνα† τεκοῦσα
γαστρὶ μιῆι Φοίβωι θῦμα καὶ Ἀρτέμιδι,
κούρα γὰρ προύπεμψε κόραις φόνον, ἄρσεσι δ᾽ ἄρσην,
διςςαὶ γὰρ διςςὰς ἔκτανον ἑβδομάδας.   550

LXXXIII *A.P.* 9.238 [C] Ἀντιπάτρου   εἰς Ἀπόλλωνα καὶ Λητὼ τὴν αὐτοῦ
μητέρα   Pl A Ἀντιπάτρου   εἰς Ἀπόλλωνα
1 ὠπόλλων Lascaris: ὤ πολλόν P, ἀπόλλων Pl | Ὀνατᾶ PPl: ἐνατᾶ C
2 ἀγλαΐης Pl: αἰγλ- P | μαρτυρίη P: -ίην Pl   6 Ἐλειθυίης Salm.:
Ἐλειθ- Pl, Εἴληθ- P

LXXXIII

On a bronze statue of Apollo

A fine big boy is Apollo. This bronze by Onatas bears witness to Zeus and Leto of their beauty,—that Zeus was not idle in loving her, and that the son of Cronos is 'glorious in eyes and head', as we are told. Not even Hera can be angry with Onatas' pouring of this bronze, which with the aid of the goddess of birth he has moulded to such grace.

LXXXIV

On Myron's Cow

⟨The herdsman calls the cow to him⟩: if it delays, the fault is of the senseless bronze, not Myron's.

LXXXV

On a portrayal of the Underworld

This is the work of Nicias. The artist has made me an ever-living Home of the Dead, every generation's sepulchre. It was Homer who first explored the house of Aidoneus, and from him as my first model I am copied.

LXXXVI

On a portrayal of Niobe and her children

This is the daughter of Tantalus, who in bygone days bore in her single womb twice seven children, victims for Phoebus and Artemis. The maiden sent forth death upon the maidens, the male upon the males, the two killing two groups of seven.

LXXXIV *A.P.* 9.728 Ἀντιπάτρου   Pl A Ἀντιπάτρου   εἰς τὴν αὐτήν
1 initium ex *A.P.* 9.724 perperam transscriptum damnavit Gow
LXXXV *A.P.* 9.792 Ἀντιπάτρου   caret Pl
1 Νικίεω Brunck: Νίκεω P | ἀειζώουσα Jacobs: ἀεὶ ζώει ὅς P | Νέκυια Jacobs: νεκυα P
LXXXVI *A.Pl.*(A) 131 Ἀντιπάτρου   εἰς τὸ αὐτὸ [sc. ἄγαλμα Νιόβης]   caret P

5 ἁ δὲ τόσας ἀγέλας μάτηρ πάρος, ἁ πάρος εὔπαις,
    οὐδ᾽ ἐφ᾽ ἑνὶ τλάμων λείπετο γηροκόμωι,
    μάτηρ δ᾽ οὐχ ὑπὸ παισίν, ὅπερ θέμις, ἀλλ᾽ ὑπὸ ματρός
    παῖδες ἐς ἀλγεινοὺς πάντες ἄγοντο τάφους.
    Τάνταλε, καὶ δὲ σὲ γλῶσσα διώλεσε καὶ σέο κούραν,   555
10 χἁ μὲν ἐπετρώθη σοὶ δ᾽ ἔπι δεῖμα λίθος.

LXXXVII

τίπτε, γύναι, πρὸς Ὄλυμπον ἀναιδέα χεῖρ᾽ ἀνένεικας
    ἔνθεον ἐξ ἀθέου κρατὸς ἀφεῖσα κόμαν;
Λατοῦς παπταίνουσα πολὺν χόλον, ὦ πολύτεκνε,
    νῦν στένε τὰν πικρὰν καὶ φιλάβουλον ἔριν.   560
5 ἁ μὲν γὰρ παίδων σπαίρει πέλας, ἁ δὲ λιπόπνους
    κέκλιται, ἅι δὲ βαρὺς πότμος ἐπικρέμαται,
καὶ μόχθων οὔπω τόδε σοι τέλος ἀλλὰ καὶ ἄρσην
    ἔστρωται τέκνων ἑσμὸς ἀποφθιμένων.
ὦ βαρὺ δακρύσασα γενέθλιον, ἄπνοος αὐτά   565
10 πέτρος ἔσηι, Νιόβα, κἀδεῖ τειρομένα.

LXXXVIII

καὶ Κύπρις Σπάρτας· οὐκ ἄστεσι δ᾽ οἷά τ᾽ ἐν ἄλλοις
    ἵδρυται μαλακὰς ἑσσαμένα στολίδας,
ἀλλὰ κατὰ κρατὸς μὲν ἔχει κόρυν ἀντὶ καλύπτρας
    ἀντὶ δὲ χρυσείων ἀκρεμόνων κάμακα.   570
5 οὐ γὰρ χρὴ τευχέων εἶναι δίχα τὰν παράκοιτιν
    Θραικὸς Ἐνυαλίου καὶ Λακεδαιμονίαν.

LXXXVII *A.Pl.* (A) 133 Ἀντιπάτρου   εἰς τὸ αὐτὸ [sc. ἄγαλμα Νιόβης]
caret P
1 χεῖρ᾽ ἀνένεικας Huschke: χεῖρα νένευκας Pl   10 κἀδεῖ Jacobs: κἄιδι Pl

66

And she who had once been the mother of so great a flock, once so blest in children, was left in misery without a single one to comfort her old age. The children were all carried by their mother,—not, as was meet, the mother by her children,—to the mournful grave. Tantalus, your tongue was fatal to you and your daughter alike; she was turned to stone, and over you a stone was set for you to dread.

LXXXVII

On the same

Why, woman, lift up your shameless hand to Olympus, letting godlike tresses fall from a godless head? Looking at Leto's great wrath, O mother of many, bewail at once your bitter and foolhardy strife. Of your daughters, this one is gasping beside you, that one lies breath-bereft, over this one a heavy doom impends. Nor is that yet your troubles' end; the swarm of your male children too lies low in death. Deep-lamenting the day you were born, your own body shall become a lifeless rock, Niobe, worn out by sorrowful cares.

LXXXVIII

On the Spartan Aphrodite in armour

The Cyprian belongs to Sparta too, but is not set up as in other cities draped in soft folds. She has a helmet instead of a veil over her head, and a spear instead of golden branches. The Spartan, the bed-fellow of Thracian Enyalius, must not be without armour.

LXXXVIII *A.Pl.* (A) 176 Ἀντιπάτρου   εἰς τὴν ἐν Cπάρται [sc. Ἀφροδίτην]
caret P
1 ἄcτεcι δ' Jacobs: -εcιν Pl

LXXXIX

τίς δὴ σὰς παλάμας πρὸς κίονα δῆσεν ἀφύκτοις
ἅμμασι; τίς πυρὶ πῦρ καὶ δόλον εἶλε δόλωι;
νήπιε, μὴ δὴ δάκρυ κατὰ γλυκεροῖο προσώπου   575
βάλλε, σὺ γὰρ τέρπηι δάκρυσιν ἠϊθέων.

XC

τρίζυγες αἱ Μοῦσαι τᾶιδ' ἔσταμεν. ἁ μία λωτούς,
ἁ δὲ φέρει παλάμαις βάρβιτον, ἁ δὲ χέλυν.
ἁ μὲν Ἀριστοκλῆος ἔχει χέλυν, ἁ δ' Ἀγελάδα
βάρβιτον, ἁ Κανάχου δ' ὑμνοπόλους δόνακας.   580
5 ἀλλ' ἁ μὲν κράντειρα τόνου πέλει, ἁ δὲ μελωιδός
χρώματος, ἁ δὲ σοφᾶς εὑρέτις ἁρμονίας.

XCI

καὶ κραναᾶς Βαβυλῶνος ἐπίδρομον ἅρμασι τεῖχος
καὶ τὸν ἐπ' Ἀλφειῶι Ζᾶνα κατηυγασάμαν
κάπων τ' αἰώρημα καὶ Ἡελίοιο κολοσσόν   585
καὶ μέγαν αἰπεινᾶν πυραμίδων κάματον
5 μνᾶμά τε Μαυσωλοῖο πελώριον, ἀλλ' ὅτ' ἐσεῖδον
Ἀρτέμιδος νεφέων ἄχρι θέοντα δόμον
κεῖνα μὲν ἠμαύρωτο †δὲ κ' ἦν ἴδε† νόσφιν Ὀλύμπου
Ἅλιος οὐδέν πω τοῖον ἐπηυγάσατο.   590

LXXXIX *A.Pl.* (A) 197 Ἀντιπάτρου   εἰς τὸ αὐτὸ [sc. ἄγαλμα Ἔρωτος δεδε-
μένου]   Syll.S   caret P
1 δὴ σὰς Meineke: δήσας Syll.S, διςςὰς Pl

XC *A.Pl.* (A) 220 Ἀντιπάτρου   εἰς εἰκόνας Μουςῶν   caret P
4 Κανάχου Gow: -χὰ Pl

LXXXIX

On a figure of Eros bound

Whoever bound your hands to the pillar with inescapable knots? Who has taken fire prisoner by fire, and stealth by stealth? Silly child, let not ever a tear fall on your sweet face; when young men weep you are happy enough.

XC

Three Muses

A trio are we, the Muses standing here. One bears in hand the pipes, one the barbitos and one the lyre. Aristocles' Muse holds the lyre, Ageladas' the barbitos, and Canachus' the musical reeds. The one is ruler of diatonic, one makes melody of chromatic, and one is inventor of the subtle enharmonic mode.

XCI

On the temple of Artemis at Ephesus

I have seen the Walls of rock-like Babylon that chariots can run upon, and the Zeus on the Alpheus, and the Hanging Gardens, and the great statue of the Sun, and the huge labour of the steep Pyramids, and the mighty Tomb of Mausolus; but when I looked at the house of Artemis soaring to the clouds, those others were dimmed, ⟨　⟩ apart from Olympus, the sun never yet looked upon its like.

XCI *A.P.* 9.58 [C] Ἀντιπάτρου　[J] εἰc τὸν ἐν Ἐφέcωι ναὸν τῆc Ἀρτέμιδοc ὅτι πάντων τῶν θεαμάτων ὑπερεῖχεν. νῦν δὲ πάντων ἐcτὶν ἐρημότεροc καὶ κακοδαιμονέcτεροc τῆι τοῦ Χριcτοῦ χάριτι καὶ Ἰωάννου τοῦ θεολόγου　Pl A Ἀντιπάτρου
2 Ζᾶνα P: Ζῆνα Pl | κατηυγαcάμαν Page: -μην PPl　　　3 κάπων PPl: πόντου C
7 δὲ P: τε Pl　　　8 ἐπηυγάcατο Brunck: ἐπαυγ- PPl

XCII

τίς ποκ' ἀπ' Οὐλύμποιο μετάγαγε παρθενεῶνα
τὸν πάρος οὐρανίοις ἐμβεβαῶτα δόμοις
ἐc πόλιν 'Ανδρόκλοιο θοῶν βαcίλειαν 'Ιώνων,
τὰν δορὶ καὶ Μούcαιc αἰπυτάταν "Εφεcον;
5 ἦ ῥα cὺ φιλαμένα, Τιτυοκτόνε, μέζον 'Ολύμπου   595
τὰν τροφὸν ἐν ταύται τὸν cὸν ἔθευ θάλαμον;

XCIII

λιτόc τοι δόμος οὗτος ἐπεὶ παρὰ κύματι πηγῶι
ἵδρυμαι νοτερῆc δεcπότιc ἠϊόνος,
ἀλλὰ φίλος, πόντωι γὰρ ἐπὶ πλατὺ δειμαίνοντι
χαίρω καὶ ναύταιc εἰc ἐμὲ cωιζομένοιc.   600
5 ἱλάcκευ τὴν Κύπριν, ἐγὼ δέ coι ἢ ἐν ἔρωτι
οὔριος ἢ χαροπῶι πνεύcομαι ἐν πελάγει.

XCIV

κλεινὴν οὐκ ἀπόφημι, cὲ γὰρ προπάροιθεν ἔθηκαν
κλήιζεcθαι πτηνοί, Τῆνε, Βορηϊάδαι,
ἀλλὰ καὶ 'Ορτυγίην εἶχεν κλέος, οὔνομα δ' αὐτῆc   605
ἤρχετο 'Ριπαίων ἄχριc 'Υπερβορέων.
5 νῦν δὲ cὺ μὲν ζώειc ἡ δ' οὐκέτι. τίc κεν ἐώλπει
ὄψεcθαι Τήνου Δῆλον ἐρημοτέρην;

XCII *A.P.* 9.790 'Αντιπάτρου   Pl в s.a.n.
6 ἐν ταύται P: ἐνταυθοῖ Pl
XCIII *A.P.* 9.143 [J] 'Αντιπάτρου   εἰc Πρίηπον ἢ καὶ Πᾶνα ἑcτῶταc ἐπ'
αἰγιαλῶι, μᾶλλον δ' εἰc 'Αφροδίτηc ἄγαλμα   Pl A 'Αντιπάτρου

XCII

On the same

Whoever was it that brought from Olympus the maiden-room,
the one that stood formerly in Heaven's house, to the city of
Androclus, Ephesus, queen of the fleet-footed Ionians, topmost in war and in the arts? Was it you, slayer of Tityus, loving
your nurse more dearly than Olympus, and so placing your
own chamber in this city?

XCIII

On a temple of Aphrodite beside the sea

Simple is this dwelling (for I am enshrined beside the white
waves, as queen of the sea-wet beach), but dear to me, for I
rejoice in the ocean whose wide expanses fear me and in the
sailors who reach me in safety. Conciliate the Cyprian, and I
will breathe favourable winds for you whether in love or on
the sparkling waves.

XCIV

On the islands Tenos and Delos

Your fame I deny not; the winged sons of Boreas made you
celebrated, Tenos, in bygone days. But Ortygia was famous
too, and its name travelled as far as the Hyperboreans of Rhipae.
And now you are alive, she lives no longer; who would have
thought to see Delos more deserted than Tenos?

I τοι P: μοι Pl

XCIV *A.P.* 9.550 Ἀντιπάτρου   Pl A Ἀντιπάτρου
I κλεινὴν Salm.: κείνην PPl   2 Τῆνε J^margPl: Δῆλε P | Βορηϊάδαι P: -δα Pl
3 εἶχεν Page: -χε PPl   5 ζώεις P^pcPl: ζώης P^ac

XCV

εὔκολος Ἑρμείας, ὦ ποιμένες, ἐν δὲ γάλακτι
χαίρων καὶ δρυΐνωι σπενδομένοις μέλιτι·   610
ἀλλ' οὐχ Ἡρακλέης, ἕνα δὲ κτίλον ἢ παχὺν ἄρνα
αἰτεῖ καὶ πάντως ἓν θύος ἐκλέγεται.
5 —ἀλλὰ λύκους εἴργει.—τί δὲ τὸ πλέον εἰ τὸ φυλαχθέν
ὄλλυται εἴτε λύκοις εἴθ' ὑπὸ τοῦ φύλακος;

XCVI

ἤδη τοι φθινόπωρον, Ἐπίκλεες, ἐκ δὲ Βοώτου   615
ζώνης Ἀρκτούρου λαμπρὸν ὄρωρε σέλας.
ἤδη καὶ σταφυλαὶ δρεπάνης ἐπιμιμνήσκονται
καί τις χειμερινὴν ἀμφερέφει καλύβην.
5 σοὶ δ' οὔτε χλαίνης θερμὴ κροκὺς οὔτε χιτῶνος
ἔνδον, ἀποσκλήσηι δ' ἀστέρα μεμφόμενος.   620

XCVII

αἰάζει πήρη τε καὶ Ἡράκλειον ἀρίστου
βριθὺ Σινωπίτου Διογένευς ῥόπαλον
καὶ τὸ χύδην ῥυπόεντι πίνωι πεπαλαγμένον ἔσθος
διπλάδιον κρυερῶν ἀντίπαλον νιφάδων
5 ὅττι τεοῖς ὤμοισι μιαίνεται· ἦ γὰρ ὁ μέν που   625
οὐράνιος σὺ δ' ἔφυς οὖν σποδιῆισι κύων.
ἀλλὰ μέθες μέθες ὅπλα τὰ μὴ σέθεν· ἄλλο λεόντων
ἄλλο γενειητῶν ἔργον ὄρωρε τράγων.

XCV A.P. 9.72 [C] Ἀντιπάτρου   [J] ὅτι ἡ πρὸς Ἑρμῆν θυσία εὔκολος, ἡ δὲ
πρὸς Ἡρακλέα δύσκολος, βουφάγος γὰρ καὶ γαστρίμαργος   Pl A Ἀντιπάτρου
2 σπενδομένοις Hecker: -νος PPl   5 δὲ τὸ Pl: δὲ P   6 λύκοις Pl: -κος P
XCVI A.P. 11.37 Ἀντιπάτρου   caret Pl
5 κροκὺς Huschke: κροκύαι P

XCV

Hermes preferred to Heracles as protector of the flock

Easy-going is Hermes, shepherds, pleased at libations of milk
and honey from the oak. Not so Heracles; he demands a whole
ram or a fat sheep, or anyway exacts a whole victim.—But he
keeps the wolves away.—But what good is that if what is protected is killed, whether by wolves or by the protector?

XCVI

Autumn

It is already autumn, Epicles, and the flame of Arcturus rises
bright from the girdle of Boötes. Already the grape-clusters
turn their thoughts to the pruning-hook, and men are roofing
their winter huts. But you have at home no warm and woolly
cloak or tunic; you will be shrivelled up, while you put the
blame on the star.

XCVII

Diogenes the Cynic's properties abused

The wallet laments; the heavy Herculean club of Sinopean
Diogenes, best of men, and the double cloak, all stained with
filth and dirt, that contends against the chilly snowflakes, lament
that they are polluted by your shoulders. You are the dog that
lies in the dust, the other is the one of Heaven. Put off the gear
that is not yours, put it off I say; the lion's business is one thing,
the bearded goat's another.

XCVII *A.P.* 11.158 Ἀντιπάτρου   Pl a Ἀντιπάτρου
1 ἀρίστου Gow: -του PPl   2 Cινωπίτου Pl: -πείου P | Διογένευc Pl:
-νουc P   3 ῥυπόεντι P: -πόωντι Pl

XCVIII

οὐ προσέχω. καίτοι πιστοί τινες. ἀλλὰ μεταξύ,
πρὸς Διός, εἴ με φιλεῖς, Πάμφιλε, μή με φίλει.   630

XCIX

ἑστηκὸς τὸ Κίμωνος ἰδὼν πέος εἶφ' ὁ Πρίηπος·   (631)
'οἴμοι, ὑπὸ θνητοῦ λείπομαι ἀθάνατος.'

D. ΑΜΦΙCΒΗΤΗΤΑ

C

ὥριον ἀνθήσαντας ὑπὸ κροτάφοισιν ἰούλους
κειράμενος γενύων ἄρcενας ἀγγελίας
Φοίβωι θῆκε Λύκων πρῶτον γέρας, εὔξατο δ' οὕτως   635
καὶ πολιὴν λευκῶν κεῖραι ἀπὸ κροτάφων.
5 τοίην ἀλλ' ἐπίνευε, τίθει δέ μιν ὡς πρό γε τοῖον
ὡς αὖτις πολιῶι γήραϊ νιφόμενον.

CI

Βακχυλὶς ἡ Βάκχου κυλίκων cποδὸς ἔκ ποτε νούcω
κεκλιμένα Δηοῖ τοῖον ἔλεξε λόγον·   640

XCVIII *A.P.* 11.219 Ἀντιπάτρου   Pl A Ἀντιπάτρου
XCIX *A.P.* 11.224 Ἀντιπάτρου   Pl A Ἀντιπάτρου
C *A.P.* 6.198 Ἀντιπάτρου Θεσσαλονικέως   ἀνάθημα τῶι Ἀπόλλωνι παρὰ
Λύκωνος   Pl A ἄδηλον   Suid. s.vv. ἴουλος (1–3 γέρας), τοῖιν (4–5 ἐπίνευε)
1 ὥριον CPl: αὔρ- P, ὅρ- Suid. v.l.   2 ἄρcενας PPl: -νος Suid.   5–6 om.
Pl   5 τοῖον P: τοῖιν Suid.   6 νιφόμενον C: νηφ- P

XCVIII

The vice of Pamphilus

I pay no heed,—though not all men are liars; meantime, for
heaven's sake, Pamphilus, if you love me, don't kiss me.

XCIX

The jealousy of Priapus

Said Priapus, seeing Cimon's yard erect, 'Woe is me, immortal
as I am, a mortal is my better'.

C

Lycon shaves his first beard

Having shaved the down that flowered in its season under his
temples, Lycon dedicated to Phoebus his cheeks' messengers of
manhood, a first offering, and prayed that he might so shave
gray hairs from his whitened temples. Grant him these, and
even as you made him earlier, so make him hereafter, with the
snows of white old age upon him.

CI

How a wine-loving woman evaded fulfilment of a vow

Bacchylis, that soaker of Bacchus' cups, being one day prostrate with sickness, addressed Demeter thus: 'If I escape the

CI *A.P.* 6.291 [=Pᵃ] 'Αντιπάτρου, et post 9.164 [=Pᵇ] [C] ἀδέσποτον   [J]
εἰς γραῦν μέθυσον εὐξαμένην ἐν ἀρρωστίαι ἐπὶ ἑκατὸν ἡλίοις μὴ γεύσασθαι οἴνου
ἀλλ' ὑδροποτήσειν, ἐγερθεῖσα δὲ ἐπὶ κοσκίνωι εἶδεν ἡλίου ἀκτῖνας τῶν ἑκατὸν
πλείονας καὶ πάλιν ἤρξατο πίνειν   Pl A ἄδηλον   Suid. s.vv. σποδός (1–2 κεκλ.),
ἀβρόμιος (3 ss.–ἄοινος), μῆχος (6–8)
1 Βακχυλὶς PᵃSuid.: ἡ γραῦς PᵇPl | ἐκ PᵃSuid.: ἐν PᵇPl   2 κεκλιμένα Pᵃ:
-νη PᵇPlSuid. | Δηοῖ Pᵃ: Διὶ PᵇPl | ἔλεξε λόγον Pᵃ: -ξεν ἔπος PᵇPl

'ἢν ὀλοοῦ διὰ καῦμα φύγω πυρὸς εἰς ἑκατόν coι
ἠελίους δροcερᾶν πίομαι ἐκ λιβάδων
5 ἀβρόμιος καὶ ἄοινος.' ἐπεὶ δ' ὑπάλυξεν ἀνίην
αὐτῆμαρ τοῖον μῆχος ἐπεφράcατο,
τρητὸν γὰρ θεμένα χερὶ κόcκινον εὖ διὰ πυκνῶν   645
cχοίνων ἠελίους πλείονας ηὐγάcατο.

CII

'εὐχέcθω τις ἔπειτα γυνὴ τόκον' εἶπε Πολυξώ
γαcτέρ' ὑπὸ τριccῶν ῥηγνυμένη τεκέων,
μαίης δ' ἐν παλάμηιcι χύθη νέκυς· οἱ δ' ἐπὶ γαῖαν
ὤλιcθον κοίλων ἄρcενες ἐκ λαγόνων   650
5 μητέρος ἐκ νεκρῆς ζωὸς γόνος. εἷς ἄρα δαίμων
τῆς μὲν ἄπο ζωὴν εἴλετο τοῖς δ' ἔπορεν.

CIII

βίβλοι Ἀριcτοφάνευς θεῖος πόνος αἷcιν Ἀχαρνεύς
κιccὸς ἐπὶ χλοερὴν πουλὺς ἔcειcε κόμην·
ἠνίδ' ὅcον Διόνυcον ἔχει cελὶς οἷα δὲ μῦθοι   655
ἠχεῦcιν φοβερῶν πληθόμενοι χαρίτων.
5 ὦ καὶ θυμὸν ἄριcτε καὶ Ἑλλάδος ἤθεcιν ἶcε
κωμικέ, καὶ cτύξας ἄξια καὶ γελάcας.

CIV

πηρὸς ἄπαις ἢ φέγγος ἰδεῖν ἢ παῖδα τεκέcθαι
εὐξαμένη δοιῆς ἔμμορεν εὐτυχίης,   660

3 καῦμα Pl: κῦμα P^{ab}Suid.   4 δροcερᾶν...λιβάδων P^{a}: -ρᾶc...-δος P^{b}Pl
5 ἀνίην P^{a}: ἀνάγκην P^{b}Pl   7 τρητὸν P^{a}PlSuid.: λεπτοῦ P^{b} | θεμένα P^{a}:
-νη P^{b}PlSuid. | χερὶ P^{a}PlSuid.: χειρὶ P^{b} | πυκνῶν PlSuid.: ποικνῶν P^{a}, πυκνὴν P^{b}
CII A.P. 7.168 Ἀντιπάτρου Θεσσαλονικέως   εἰς Πολυξώ δυστοκήcαcαν ἐπὶ τριcὶ
βρέφεcιν Pl β ἄδηλον
4 ἄρcενες PPl: ἄρρεν- C   6 ζωὴν CPl: ζωῆς P

cursèd fever's heat, I promise you, beerless and wineless, to drink nothing but dew-like water-drops till I have seen a hundred suns.' But on the very day when she was quit of her pains she planned the following trick: she took a fretted sieve in her hand, and through its close-set rush-work she could perfectly well see more suns than that.

CII

Death of a woman in child-birth

'After this, let women pray for children', cried Polyxo, her belly torn by triplets. She sank dead in the midwife's hands, and her boys slipped from her hollow flanks to the ground, a living birth from a mother's corpse. One and the same god took life from her and gave life to them.

CIII

On the plays of Aristophanes

These are the books of Aristophanes, a work divinely inspired; the Acharnian ivy waved its green foliage over them in masses. See how deep in Dionysus are his pages, how clear-voiced his plays, so full of dangerous charms. Incomparable spirit, comedian well-suited to the character of Greece, both hater and mocker of what deserved it.

CIV

A blind and barren woman sees and gives birth

A blind and barren woman prayed either to see the daylight or to bear a child, and was granted the double blessing. Not long

CIII *A.P.* 9.186 [C] Ἀντιπάτρου Θεσσαλονικέως εἰς Ἀριστοφάνην τὸν κωμικόν Pl A ἄδηλον

3 Διόνυcον CPl: -coc P   5 ἴcε Platnauer: ἴcα PPl   6 cτύξαc P: cτίξ- Pl | ἄξια Pl: ἄξιε P

CIV *A.P.* 9.46 [C] Ἀντιπάτρου Μακεδόνος εἰς γυναῖκα τυφλὴν [J] ἔγκυον οὖσαν καὶ τεκοῦσαν ἀναβλέψαι παρ' ἐλπίδα   Pl A Καλλινίου

τίκτε γὰρ †εὐθὺϲ† ἄελπτα μετ' οὐ πολὺ καὶ τριπόθητον
αὐτῆμαρ γλυκερὸν φέγγοc ἐϲεῖδε φάουϲ.
5 Ἄρτεμιϲ ἀμφοτέροιϲιν ἐπήκοοϲ ἥ τε λοχείηϲ
μαῖα καὶ ἀργεννῶν φωϲφόροϲ ἡ ϲελάων.

CV

τίϲ ϲοῦ, Μεντορίδη, προφανῶϲ οὕτωϲ μετέθηκεν   665
τὴν πυγὴν οὖπερ τὸ ϲτόμ' ἔκειτο πρὸ τοῦ;
βδεῖϲ γὰρ κοὐκ ἀναπνεῖϲ, φθέγγηι δ' ἐκ τῶν καταγείων.
θαῦμά μ' ἔχει τὰ κάτω πῶϲ ϲου ἄνω γέγονεν.

CVI

εἰνοδίην καρύην με παρερχομένοιϲ ἐφύτευϲαν
παιϲὶ λιθοβλήτου παίγνιον εὐϲτοχίηϲ,   670
πάνταϲ δ' ἀκρεμόναϲ τε καὶ εὐθαλέαϲ ὀροδάμνουϲ
κέκλαϲμαι πυκιναῖϲ χερμάϲι βαλλομένη.
5 δένδρεϲιν εὐκάρποιϲ οὐδὲν πλέον· ἦ γὰρ ἔγωγε
δυϲδαίμων ἐϲ ἐμὴν ὕβριν ἐκαρποφόρουν.

CVII

Γλύκων, τὸ Περγαμηνὸν Ἀϲίδι κλέοϲ,   675
ὁ παμμάχων κεραυνόϲ, ὁ πλατὺϲ πόδαϲ,
ὁ καινὸϲ Ἄτλαϲ αἵ τ' ἀνίκατοι χέρεϲ
ἔρρονti, τὸν δὲ πρόϲθεν οὔτ' ἐν Ἰταλοῖϲ
5   οὔθ' Ἑλλάδι †τὸ πρῶτον† οὔτ' ἐν Ἀϲίδι
ὁ πάντα νικῶν Ἀίδαϲ ἀνέτραπεν.   680

4 φάουϲ Pl: φάοϲ P   5 ἐπήκοοϲ Brunck: ὑπ- PPl
CV A.P. 11.415 Ἀντιπάτρου ἢ Νικάρχου   Pl в s.a.n.
1 οὕτωϲ P: -τω Pl   3 καταγείων Pl: κατογ- P
CVI A.P. 9.3 Ἀντιπάτρου, οἱ δὲ Πλάτωνοϲ   [J] εἰϲ καρύην πεφυτευμένην ἐν

after, against all hope, she gave birth, and on the same day saw
the sweet longed-for radiance of light. Both prayers were heard
by Artemis, midwife in child-bed and light-bringer of white-
gleaming rays.

CV

On the foul breath of Mentorides

Who can it be, Mentorides, who has so obviously transferred
your breech to the place where your mouth used to be? You do
not breathe, you break wind; your voice comes from the base-
ment. I cannot understand how your lower became your upper
parts.

CVI

The tormented nut-tree

Men planted me, a wayside nut-tree, for children passing by,
the sport of their well-aimed stone-throwing. All my branches
and my growing twigs are battered and broken by showers of
pebbles. It is no use for a tree to be fruitful; I at least have been
a fruit-bearer only to my own misery and insult.

CVII

Death of a great athlete

Glycon, Pergamum's glorious gift to Asia, the pancratiasts'
thunderbolt, broad of foot, the modern Atlas, is gone from
us, and with him those unconquerable hands. All-conquering
Hades has overthrown a man never ⟨thrown⟩ before in
Italy or in Hellas or in Asia.

ὁδῶι   Pl A ’Αντιπάτρου, οἱ δὲ Πλάτωνος   schol. rec. Theocr. 7.138 (3–4
κέκλ.)
5 ἦ Pl: εἰ P

CVII *A.P.* 7.692 [C] ’Αντιπάτρου, οἱ δὲ [P] Φιλίππου Θεσσαλονικέως   [J] εἰς
Γλύκωνα Περγαμηνὸν ἀθλητήν   caret Pl
5 τὸ πρῶτον P: πτωτόν ποτ’ Emperius   **6** ’Αίδας Page: -δης P

CVIII

ἵμερον αὐλήσαντι πολυτρήτων διὰ λωτῶν
εἶπε λιγυφθόγγωι Φοῖβος ἐπὶ Γλαφύρωι·
'Μαρσύη, ἐψεύσω τεὸν εὕρεμα, τοὺς γὰρ Ἀθήνης
αὐλοὺς ἐκ Φρυγίης οὗτος ἐληίσατο.
5 εἰ δὲ σὺ τοιούτοις τότ' ἐνέπνεες οὐκ ἂν Ὕαγνις   685
τὴν ἐπὶ Μαιάνδρωι κλαῦσε δύσαυλον ἔριν.'

CIX

κλασθείσης ποτὲ νηὸς ἐν ὕδατι δῆριν ἔθεντο
διςςοὶ ὑπὲρ μούνης μαρνάμενοι σανίδος.
τύψε μὲν Ἀνταγόρης Πεισίστρατον. οὐ νεμεσητόν,
ἦν γὰρ ὑπὲρ ψυχῆς· ἀλλ' ἐμέλησε Δίκηι.   690
5 νῆχε δ' ὁ μὲν τὸν δ' εἷλε κύων †ἄλός. παναλάστωρ
χήρων† οὐδ' ὑγρῶι παύεται ἐν πελάγει.

CX

ταύρου βαθὺν τένοντα καὶ σιδαρέους
Ἄτλαντος ὤμους καὶ κόμαν Ἡρακλέους
σεμνάν θ' ὑπήναν καὶ λέοντος ὄμματα   695
Μιλησίου γίγαντος οὐδ' Ὀλύμπιος
5 Ζεὺς ἀτρόμητος εἶδεν, ἄνδρας ἡνίκα
πυγμὰν ἐνίκα Νικοφῶν Ὀλύμπια.

CVIII A.P. 9.266 [C] Ἀντιπάτρου   εἰς Μαρσύαν τὸν αὐλητὴν διὰ τὸ γλαφυρὸν
καὶ ἐμμελὲς αὐλεῖν   Pl A Φιλίππου
5 Ὕαγνις Pl: -νης P
CIX A.P. 9.269 [C] τοῦ αὐτοῦ [sc. Ἀντιπάτρου Θεσσαλονικέως]   εἰς ναυηγούς
τινας μαχομένους ἕνεκεν σανίδος ὧν τὸν μὲν κύων θαλάσσιος καταβέβρωκεν ὁ δὲ
διεσώθη   Pl B Φιλίππου
5 νῆχε δ' P: νήχεθ' Pl | ἄλός P: ἄλιος Pl

CVIII

On an eminent piper

Thus Phoebus pronounced upon the clear notes of Glaphyrus, when through his many-holed pipes he fluted the spirit of love: 'Marsyas, you lied about your find; the man who stole Athena's pipes from Phrygia is this one here. If you had breathed into such pipes as these, Hyagnis would not have mourned that fatal piping-match beside the Meander.'

CIX

Reversal of fate at sea

There was once a shipwreck, and two men came to blows in the water, fighting for a solitary plank. Antagores struck Peisistratus,—a pardonable act, for his life was at stake; but Justice was not unconcerned. The one swam off, a shark seized the other. The ⟨avenger⟩ knows no rest, not even in the waters of the sea.

CX

On a successful boxer

Not even Olympian Zeus saw without a shudder the thick bull-neck, the iron shoulders of Atlas, the hair and reverend beard of Heracles, the lion's eyes, of our Milesian giant, at the time when Nicophon beat the men at boxing in the Olympic Games.

CX *A.P.* 6.256 Ἀντιπάτρου   Pl A Ζωνᾶ   Pl в Ἀντιπάτρου   Syll.Σπ Ἀντιπάτρου   Suid. s.vv. ἀτρόμητος (1–5 εἶδε), τένοντας (1 τ. β. τέν.), Ἄτλας, cιδηρέαν (1 cιδ.–2 ὤμους)
1 βαθὺν τένοντα PPl: βαθυτένοντα Suid. s.v. τένοντας | cιδαρέους PPl^AB: cιδηρ- Suid. (ter)   2 κόμαν PPl^AB: -μην Suid.   3 ὑπήναν PPl^AB: -νην Suid.
6 πυγμὰν PPl^A: -μὴν Pl^B

CXI

πριομένα κάλλει Γανυμήδεος εἶπέ ποθ' Ἥρα
θυμοβόρον ζάλου κέντρον ἔχουσα νόωι·   700
'ἄρσεν πῦρ ἔτεκεν Τροία Διί, τοιγὰρ ἐγὼ πῦρ
πέμψω ἐπὶ Τροίαι πῆμα φέροντα Πάριν,
5 ἥξει δ' Ἰλιάδαις οὐκ αἰετὸς ἀλλ' ἐπὶ θοίναν
γῦπες ὅταν Δαναοὶ σῦλα φέρωσι πόνων'.

CXII

χρύσεος ἦν γενεὴ καὶ χάλκεος ἀργυρέη τε   705
πρόσθεν, παντοίη δ' ἡ Κυθέρεια τὰ νῦν,
καὶ χρυσοῦν τίει καὶ χάλκεον ἄνδρ' ἐφίλησεν
καὶ τοὺς ἀργυρέους οὔποτ' ἀποστρέφεται.
5 Νέστωρ ἡ Παφίη· δοκέω δ' ὅτι καὶ Δανάηι Ζεύς
οὐ χρυσός, χρυσοῦς δ' ἦλθε φέρων ἑκατόν.   710

CXIII

εἴθε με παντοίοισιν ἔτι πλάζεσθαι ἀήταις
ἢ Λητοῖ στῆναι μαῖαν ἀλωομένηι·
οὐκ ἂν χητοσύνης τόσον ἔστενον. οἳ ἐμὲ δειλήν,
ὅσσαις Ἑλλήνων νηυσὶ παραπλέομαι
5 Δῆλος ἐρημαίη, τὸ πάλαι σέβας. ὀψέ πηι Ἥρη   715
Λητοῦς ἀλλ' οἰκτρὴν τήνδ' ἐπέθηκε δίκην.

CXI *A.P.* 9.77 [C] Ἀντιπάτρου Θεσσαλονικέως   [J] εἰς Ἥραν καὶ εἰς Γανυμήδην
τὸν ἁρπασθέντα ὑπὸ Διός. ζηλοτυπία θαυμάσιος καὶ βλέπε μοι τὸν σεμνὸν Δία
τὸν τῶν θεῶν ὕπατον παιδικοῦ κάλλους ἡττώμενον   Pl A Ἀρίστωνος ἢ
Ἑρμοδώρου
1 Ἥρα P: -ρη Pl   2 θυμοβόρον P: -ρου Pl   3 ἔτεκεν P: -κε Pl
4 Τροία(ι) P: -αν Pl   5 αἰετὸς Pl: ἀετ- P | θοίναν P: -ναις Pl   6 σῦλα
Gow: σκῦλα PPl

CXII *A.P.* 5.31 τοῦ αὐτοῦ [sc. Ἀντιπάτρου Θεσσαλονικέως]   [J] ὅτι πάσας τὰς

CXI

Ganymede and Paris

Vexed by the beauty of Ganymede, with a soul-consuming sting of jealousy in her mind, thus Hera spoke one day: 'Troy bore for Zeus a flame in a male's guise; therefore shall I send a flame against Troy,—Paris, to bring her woe. There shall come to the sons of Ilus no eagle but vultures to the feast, when Danaans carry off the booty of their toils.'

CXII

Love is mercenary

In bygone days there was a golden age and a bronze and a silver; Cytherea today combines all in one. She honours the man of gold, she loves the man of bronze, she never turns her back on the man of silver. The Paphian is just like Nestor. I even think that Zeus, when he came to Danaê, was not himself gold, but the bearer of a hundred gold coins.

CXIII

Delos deserted

I wish I were still astray at the will of every wind, not stopped to serve as a midwife to wandering Leto; I should not have had all this desolation to bemoan. Alack, how many Greek ships sail past me in my misery, Delos the desert, once a holy place. Late but grievous is this penalty that Hera has laid on me because of Leto.

ὕλας ἡ ἡδονὴ ἀσπάζεται καὶ χωρὶς χρυσοῦ ἑταίρα οὐχ ἁλίσκεται   App.B.-V.
10 Κιλλάκτορος   caret Pl
3–4 καὶ ter P: ἢ ter App.   6 χρυσοῦς CApp.: -coῦ P

CXIII A.P. 9.408 'Ἀπολλωνίδου, οἱ δὲ 'Ἀντιπάτρου   εἰς Δῆλον τὴν νῆcον [C sequ. pag.] 'Ἀντιπάτρου   εἰς Δῆλον τὴν νῆcον   Pl A 'Ἀπολλωνίδου, οἱ δὲ 'Ἀντιπάτρου
2 ἀλωομένηι Pl: -νην P   3 χητοcύνης Gow: -νην PPl   4 νηυcὶ Pl: ναυcὶ P   5 πηι Pl: ποι P

CXIV

Τὴν Μικρήν με λέγουσι καὶ οὐκ ἴσα ποντοπορεύσαις
ναυσὶ διιθύνειν ἄτρομον εὐπλοΐην,
οὐκ ἀπόφημι δ' ἐγώ. βραχὺ μὲν σκάφος, ἀλλὰ θαλάσσηι
πᾶν ἴσον. οὐ μέτρων ἡ κρίσις ἀλλὰ τύχης.   720
5 ἔστω πηδαλίοις ἑτέρηι πλέον, ἄλλο γὰρ ἄλληι
θάρσος, ἐγὼ δ' εἴην δαίμοσι σωιζομένη.

CXV

οὐχὶ Θεμιστοκλέους Μάγνης τάφος ἀλλὰ κέχωσμαι   (723)
Ἑλλήνων φθονερῆς σῆμα κακοκρισίης.

ΑΝΤΙΦΑΝΟΥΣ

I

αὐτή σοι Κυθέρεια τὸν ἱμερόεντ' ἀπὸ μαστῶν,   725
Ἰνώ, λυσαμένη κεστὸν ἔδωκεν ἔχειν,
ὡς ἂν θελξινόοισιν ἀεὶ φίλτροισι δαμάζηις
ἀνέρας· ἐχρήσω δ' εἰς ἐμὲ πᾶσι μόνον.

II

νηὸς ἁλιστρέπτου πλαγκτὸν κύτος εἶδεν ἐπ' ἀκτῆς
μηλοβότης βλοσυροῖς κύμασι συρόμενον,   730

CXIV *A.P.* 9.107 τοῦ αὐτοῦ [sc. Λεωνίδου Ταραντίνου]   [C] ὁμοίως [J] εἰς
μικρὰν ναῦν ἐρίζουσαν ἐπ' εὐπλοίηι ταῖς μεγάλαις ναυσίν   Pl A 'Αντιπάτρου
Θεσσαλονικέως
1 ποντοπορεύσαις Pl: -σαι P

CXV *A.P.* 7.236 [C] 'Αντιπάτρου Θεσσαλονικέως   [J] εἰς τὸν αὐτὸν [sc.
Θεμιστοκλέα] ἐν Μαγνησίαι   Pl B τῆς αὐτῆς [sc. 'Ανύτης]
2 κακοκρισίης C: κακοτροπίης Pl, κεκροπ- P (ex epigr. praeced.)

CXIV

On a small boat

They call me The Little One, and say that I cannot steer a fair
and fearless passage like sea-going ships. And I do not deny it.
I am indeed a little boat, but to the sea all is equal; what decides
is not size but fortune. Let another be better off in rudder-oars
(some put their trust in this, and some in that); for my part, I
pray my safety rest with the powers above.

CXV

On the tomb of Themistocles

This mound is not the Magnesian burial-place of Themistocles,
but a monument to the envious ill-judgment of the Greeks.

ANTIPHANES

I

The charms of Ino

Ino, the Cytherean herself loosed from her breasts the magic
cincture of desire and gave it you to keep, that by its heart-
enchanting charms you might subdue men evermore; yet
against me you have used them, every one.

II

A wrecked boat drowns a shepherd

A shepherd on the shore saw the wandering hull of a sea-
tossed vessel being dragged by the rough waves. He cast his

I *A.P.* 6.88 Ἀντιφάνους Μακεδόνος   ἀνάθημα τῆι Ἀφροδίτηι παρὰ Ἰνοῦς
['Ηνοῦς C, 'Αννοῦς ut vid. A] Pl A Ἀντιφάνους Suid. s.vv. ἱμερόεντα (1–2, om.
Ἰνὼ λυc.), θελξινόοιcιν (3–4)
2 Ἰνὼ Pl: ἠνὼ P | λυcαμένη C: λουc- PC^γ^ρPl

II *A.P.* 9.84 [C] Ἀντιφάνους   [J] εἴc τινα νομέα θεαcάμενον θραῦcμα νηὸc ἐν
θαλάccηι καὶ βουληθέντα ἐξελκύcαι· ὑπεcπάcθη εἰc τὸν βυθὸν καὶ ἀπώλετο
Pl A Ἀντιφάνους
1 πλαγκτὸν Pl: πλακτὸν P | ἐπ' P: ἀπ' Pl   2 βλοcυροῖc Pl: -ρῆc P

χεῖρα δ' ἐπέρριψεν· τὸ δ' ἐπεσπάσατ' ἐς βυθὸν ἅλμης
τὸν cώιζονθ'· οὕτως πᾶcιν ἀπηχθάνετο.
5 ναυηγὸν δ' ὁ νομεὺς ἔсχεν μόρον. ὢ δι' ἐκείνην
καὶ δρυμοὶ χῆροι πορθμίδα καὶ λιμένες.

III

δυсμοίρων θαλάμων ἐπὶ παстάсιν οὐχ Ὑμέναιος   735
ἀλλ' Ἀίδης ἔстη πικρογάμου Πετάλης·
δείματι γὰρ μούνην πρωτόзυγα Κύπριν ἀν' ὄρφνην
φεύγουсαν, ξυνὸν παρθενικαῖсι φόβον,
5 φρουροδόμοι νηλεῖς κύνες ἔκτανον· ἢν δὲ γυναῖκα
ἐλπὶς ἰδεῖν ἄφνως ἔσχομεν οὐδὲ νέκυν.   740

IV

ἥμιсύ μευ зώειν ἐδόκουν ἔτι, κεῖνο δ' ἔφυсεν
ἓν μόνον αἰπυτάτου μῆλον ἐπ' ἀκρεμόνος·
ἡ δὲ κύων δένδρων καρποφθόρος, ἡ πτιλόνωτος
κάμπη καὶ τὸ μόνον βάσκανος ἐξέφαγεν.
5 ὁ φθόνος εἰς πολὺν ὄγκον ἀπέβλεπεν· ὃς δὲ τὰ μικρά   745
πορθεῖ, καὶ τούτου χείρονα δεῖ με λέγειν.

V

ἡ πάρος εὐύδροιсι λιβαзομένη προχοαῖсι
πτωχὴ νῦν Νυμφῶν μέχρι καὶ εἰς стаγόνα·
λυθρώδεις γὰρ ἐμοῖσιν ἐνίψατο νάμαсι χεῖρας
ἀνδροφόνος κηλῖδ' ὕδαсιν ἐγκεράσας·   750
5 ἐξ οὗ μοι κοῦραι φύγον ἥλιον 'εἰς ἕνα Βάκχον'
εἰποῦσαι 'Νύμφαι μισγόμεθ', οὐκ ἐς Ἄρη'.

III *A.P.* 9.245 [C] Ἀντιφάνους εἰς νύμφην κόρην φυγοῦσαν ἐκ τοῦ θαλάμου καὶ ὑπὸ
κυνῶν διασπασθεῖσαν Pl A Ἀντιφάνους
1 παστάсιν Pl: παράстασιν P   3 μούνην P: Μοβοϊν Pl   4 παρθενικαῖсι
P: -κῆιсι Pl   6 ἄφνως Jacobs: ἄφνω P, αἴφνης Pl

IV *A.P.* 9.256 [C] Ἀντιφάνους   εἰς μῆλον τὸ δένδρον οὗ τὸν καρπὸν αἱ κάμπαι
κατέφαγον   caret Pl

86

hand upon it, but it dragged its saviour forth to the depth of the brine, so strong was its spite against all men. The pasturer got the doom of the ship-wrecked. Alas, by that boat's fault both woods and harbours are bereaved.

III
A bride is killed by dogs on her wedding-night

At the doors of the ill-fated chamber of Petalê, bride of sorrow, there stood not Hymen but Hades. As in terror she fled alone through the darkness from Love's first coupling (all maidens share the dread), she was killed by savage house-guardian dogs. To see her a wife was our hope; suddenly we could not even see her corpse.

IV
A caterpillar eats a tree's only apple

I seemed to be still half alive, and that half produced one single apple on the steepest branch. But now that brute, the tree's harvest-killer, that downy-backed caterpillar has spitefully eaten up even that solitary one. Envy turns her eyes to the great of substance; him who makes havoc of the little, I must call names even worse than Envy.

V
On waters polluted by blood-stained hands

I, who once streamed with abundant water's outflow, am now the Nymphs' beggar even for a drop. For a murderer washed his gory hands in my flood, mingling the stain with my waters. Since then the Maidens have fled the sunlight, crying 'We Nymphs mix with Bacchus only, not with Ares'.

3 καρποφθόρος Salm.: -οφόρος P   5 ὄγκον Jacobs: ὄχλον P   6 τούτου Reiske: τούτους P | χείρονα δεῖ με λέγειν Graefe: γηρὰν αει μ᾽ ελεγεν P

V *A.P.* 9.258 [C] Ἀντιφάνους Μεγαλοπολίτου εἰς τὴν αὐτὴν πηγήν Pl A Ἀντιφάνους εἰς τὴν αὐτήν
1 προχοαῖσι P: -οῆισι Pl   4 ἀνδροφόνος Pl: -φώνον P | ἐγκεράσας P: -κεράων Pl

VI

εἴ τινα μὴ τέρπει λωτοῦ †χέλυς† ἢ γλυκὺς ἦχος
ψαλμῶν ἢ τριγέρων νεκτάρεος Βρόμιος
ἢ πεῦκαι κοῦροι στέφανοι μύρα, λιτὰ δὲ δειπνῶν   755
λαθροπόδας τρώκταις χερσὶ τίθησι τόκους,
5 οὗτος ἐμοὶ τέθνηκε, περικνήστην δὲ παρέρπω
νεκρὸν ἐς ἀλλοτρίους φειδόμενον φάρυγας.

VII

ἀνθρώποις ὀλίγος μὲν ὁ πᾶς χρόνος, ὅν ποτε δειλοί
ζῶμεν, κἢν πολιὸν γῆρας ἅπασι μένηι,   760
τῆς δ᾽ ἀκμῆς καὶ μᾶλλον· ὅτ᾽ οὖν χρόνος ὥριος ἡμῖν,
πάντα χύδην ἔστω, ψαλμὸς ἔρως προπόσεις.
5 χειμὼν τοὐντεῦθεν γήρως βαρύς, οὐδὲ δέκα μνῶν
στύσεις· τοιαύτη σ᾽ ἐκδέχετ᾽ ὀρχιπέδη.

VIII

ψηφίζεις, κακόδαιμον, ὁ δὲ χρόνος ὡς τόκον οὕτω   765
καὶ πολιὸν τίκτει γῆρας ἐπερχόμενος,
κοὔτε πιὼν οὔτ᾽ ἄνθος ἐπὶ κροτάφοις ἀναδήσας,
οὐ μύρον, οὐ γλαφυρὸν γνούς ποτ᾽ ἐρωμένιον,
5 τεθνήξηι πλουτοῦσαν ἀφεὶς μεγάλην διαθήκην,
ἐκ πολλῶν ὀβολὸν μοῦνον ἐνεγκάμενος.   770

VI A.P. 9.409 [C] Ἀντιφάνους   εἰς τὸ ἀνέτως ζῆν καὶ μετὰ μουσικῶν καὶ πίνειν
ἐστεφανωμένον   caret Pl
3 πεῦκαι Ruhnken: -κας P   4 τρώκταις Brunck: τρόκτας P   5 περικνήστην Page: περι μνηστιν P   6 φάρυγας Salm.: -γα P
VII A.P. 10.100 Ἀντιφάνους Pl b s.a.n.

88

VI

On a miser

He who has no pleasure in ⟨   ⟩ of flute or sweet sound of strings plucked or thrice-agèd nectar of the Wine-god or torches, boys, garlands, or unguents, but while supping frugally lays up with greedy fingers the stealthy-footed profits of usury,—to me that man is as good as dead; I pass by the cheese-parer's corpse, that miser for the benefit of strangers' throats.

VII

'Gather ye rose-buds while ye may'

Brief for mankind is the whole of time, all that we live, poor creatures, even if gray old age await us one and all; and briefer yet the time of ripeness. Therefore, while time is fresh upon us, let all be overflowing,—song, love, carousals. Thenceforward is the heavy winter of old age; you shall not make love, not even for a thousand drachmas, such is the impotence that awaits you.

VIII

On a miser

You count your cash, poor fool, but Time as it overtakes you breeds the white hairs of age as fast as your interest. Neither having drunk nor bound flowers on your temples, nor ever known unguent or smooth darling boy, you shall be dead, leaving behind a huge testament full of riches, out of so many pence taking with you but the one.

2 μένηι Pl: -νει P   **5** βαρύς Jacobs: βαρύ P, βάρος Pl   **6** cτύcειc P: cτῆc- Pl | c' Pl: om. P

VIII *A.P.* 11.168 ʼΑντιφάνους   Pl A ʼΑντιφάνους
2 ἐπερχόμενος P: -νον Pl   **4** ποτ' ἐρωμένιον P: τι μελιcμάτιον Pl   **6** ὀβολὸν P: -λῶν Pl

IX

γραμματικῶν περίεργα γένη, ῥιζώρυχα μούcηc
ἀλλοτρίηc, ἀτυχεῖc cῆτεc ἀκανθοβάται,
τῶν μεγάλων κηλῖδεc, ἐπ' Ἠρίννηι δὲ κομῶντεc,
πικροὶ καὶ ξηροὶ Καλλιμάχου πρόκυνεc,
5 ποιητῶν λῶβαι, παιcὶ cκότοc ἀρχομένοιcιν,   775
ἔρροιτ', εὐφώνων λαθροδάκναι κόριεc.

X

ὦ θηρῶν βροτὲ μᾶλλον ἀνήμερε, πάντα cε μιcεῖ,
πατρολέτωρ, πάντηι δ' ἐκδέχεταί cε μόροc.
ἢν ἐπὶ γῆc φεύγηιc, ἀγχοῦ λύκοc· ἢν δὲ πρὸc ὕψοc
δενδροβατῆιc, ἀcπὶc δεῖμ' ὑπὲρ ἀκρεμόνων.   780
5 πειράζειc καὶ Νεῖλον, ὁ δ' ἐν δίναιc κροκόδειλον
ἔτρεφεν, εἰc ἀcεβεῖc θῆρα δικαιότατον.

ΑΝΤΙΦΙΛΟΥ

I

λιτὸc ἐγὼ τὰ τύχηc, ὦ δεcπότι, φημὶ δὲ πολλῶν
ὄλβον ὑπερκύπτειν τὸν cὸν ἀπὸ κραδίηc.
ἀλλὰ δέχευ μιαροῖο †βαθυρραίνοιο† τάπητοc   785
ἐνδυτὸν εὐανθεῖ πορφύρηι εἰδόμενον
5 εἴριά τε ῥοδόεντα καὶ ἐc κυανότριχα χαίτην
νάρδον ὑπὸ γλαυκῆc κλειομένην ὑάλου,
ὄφρα χιτὼν μὲν χρῶτα περιcκέπηι, ἔργα δ' ἐλέγχηι
χεῖραc, ὁ δ' εὐώδηc ἀτμὸc ἔχηι πλοκάμουc.   790

IX *A.P.* 11.322 'Αντιφάνουc   Pl A 'Αντιφάνουc
1 ῥιζώρυχα Pl: -ώνυχα P   5 ποιητῶν λῶβαι παιcὶ Pl: ποιητῶν ⟨spat. vac. c.
8 litt.⟩ βαι ποcὶ P

X *A.P.* 11.348 'Αντιφάνουc   Pl B s.a.n.
2 πατρολέτωρ P: παντολ- Pl

90

IX

On pedants of Callimachus' school

Meddlesome tribe of critics, uprooters of others' poetry, miserable book-worms, at home in thorny passages, defilers of the great, so proud of your Erinna, bitter and harsh barkers at Callimachus' command, plague of poets, black night to the child-beginner, away with you, bugs and back-biters of men eloquent.

X

The parricide's doom

Parricide, a human more savage than wild beasts, all things abhor you, and death awaits you everywhere. If you fly by land, the wolf is close upon you; if you climb to the tree-top, the asp is your terror on the boughs. You try the Nile too: it nurses in its pools the crocodile, most just of animals towards the impious.

ANTIPHILUS

I

Gifts to a lady

Slender is my fortune, Sovereign Lady, but I hold that the man who is yours, heart and soul, can raise his head above the wealth of most. Accept this garment that is like the flowered purple of a soft 〈　〉 carpet, and rose-red wool, and nard enclosed in green glass for your dark-tressed hair. So may the tunic shelter your body, and wool-work prove the skill of your hands, and the scented vapour pervade your tresses.

I *A.P.* 6.250 Ἀντιφίλου Suid. s.vv. λιτός (1–2), μνιαρόν (3–4), εἴρια (5 εἴρ.–ῥοδόεντα δέχευ), νάρδος (5 καὶ–6), ἐλέγχομεν (7–8 ἔργα δὲ χεῖρας ἐλέγχει)   caret Pl
1 τὰ τύχης Reiske: τ' ἀτυχὴς PSuid.   4 πορφύρηι CSuid.: -ρίηι P
8 εὐώδης...ἔχηι Ap.G.: εὐειδὴς...ἔχει P

II

μῆλον ἐγὼ στρούθειον ἀπὸ προτέρης ἔτι ποίης
ὥριον ἐν νεαρῶι χρωτὶ φυλασσόμενον,
ἄσπιλον ἀρρυτίδωτον ἰσόχνοον ἀρτιγόνοισιν,
ἀκμὴν εὐπετάλοις συμφυὲς ἀκρεμόσιν,
5 ὥρης χειμερίης σπάνιον γέρας. εἰς δέ c᾽, ἄνασσα,   795
τοίην χὼ νιφόεις κρυμὸς ὀπωροφορεῖ.

III

—εἰπέ, Δικαιάρχεια, τί σοι τόσον εἰς ἅλα χῶμα
βέβληται μέссου γευόμενον πελάγους;
Κυκλώπων τάδε χεῖρες ἐνιδρύσαντο θαλάσσηι
τείχεα· μέχρι πόσου, Γαῖα, βιαζόμεθα;   800
5 —κόσμου νηΐτην δέχομαι στόλον· εἴσιδε Ῥώμην
ἐγγύθεν, εἰ ταύτης μέτρον ἔχω λιμένα.

IV

ἤδη που πάτρης πελάσας σχεδὸν ‘αὔριον’ εἶπον
‘ἡ μακρὴ κατ᾽ ἐμοῦ δυσπνοΐη κοπάσει’.
οὔπω χεῖλος ἔμυσε, καὶ ἦν ἴσος Ἄιδι πόντος,   805
καί με κατέτρυχεν κεῖνο τὸ κοῦφον ἔπος.
5 πάντα λόγον πεφύλαξο τὸν αὔριον· οὐδὲ τὰ μικρά
λήθει τὴν γλώσσης ἀντίπαλον Νέμεσιν.

II *A.P.* 6.252 ’Αντιφίλου   Pl в ’Αντιφίλου   Suid. s.vv. μῆλον (1–4), ποίη (1),
ἄσπιλος (1–στρούθ.), ἀκμή (3s.), ἀκρεμόνες (4), σπάνις (5–γέρας), κρυμός (5 εἰс–6),
νιφετός (eadem)
1 στρούθειον Pl: -θίον PSuid. | ἀπὸ προτέρης PSuid.: ἀφ᾽ ὁπλοτέρης Pl
2 νεαρῶι CPlSuid.: νιαρῶι P   5 δέ c᾽ PSuid.: cè δ᾽ Pl | ἄνασσα PSuid.Pl^ac:
-αν Pl^pc

III *A.P.* 7.379 [C] ’Αντιφίλου Βυζαντίου   [J] εἰς τὴν ἐν Δικαιαρχίαι θάλασσαν καὶ
εἰς τὰ ἐκεῖσε νεώρια καὶ τοὺς λιμένας   caret Pl

II

A quince, preserved in winter, given to a lady

A quince am I, still preserved from last season, fresh, in a young skin, unspotted, unwrinkled, downy like the newly-born, still of one growth with my leafy stems, a rare gift from winter's season; but for you, my Queen, even the snows and frosts bear harvests like this.

III

On the harbour-mole at Puteoli

—Tell me, Dicaearchia, why have you cast so great a mole into the waters, touching mid-ocean? Cyclopean were the hands that planted these walls in the sea. How far, Earth, must we suffer your violence?

—I am harbour to the world's fleet of ships. Look at Rome near-by, and judge if I have not a haven the measure of hers.

IV

On a storm at sea

I was already nearing my fatherland when 'Tomorrow', I cried, 'this long hard wind against me will die down'. My lips were not yet closed, when the sea was like Hades, and those light words destroyed me. Beware of every speech with 'tomorrow' in it; not even small things are overlooked by Nemesis, who challenges all we say.

---

1 Δικαιάρχεια apogr.: -χία P   4 βιαζόμεθα C: -όμενα P   6 εἰ ταύτης Reiske: ἐπ' αὐτῆς P

IV *A.P.* 7.630 [C] 'Αντιφίλου Βυζαντίου   [J] ὅτι οὐ δεῖ λέγειν ἀνθρώπωι, τὸ αὔριον ποιήσω τὸ καὶ τό · ἄδηλον γὰρ τοῦτο καὶ ἄγνωστον· ὡς ὁ παθὼν μαρτύρεται Pl A 'Αντιφίλου
2 δυσπνοίη Hecker: δυcπλοίην P, -πλοίη Pl   4 κατέτρυχεν Pl: -χε P | ἔπος CPl: ἔτος (?) P

V

Εὐβοϊκοῦ κόλποιο παλινδίνητε θάλασσα,
πλαγκτὸν ὕδωρ ἰδίοις ῥεύμασιν ἀντίπαλον,   810
ἡελίωι κἢν νυκτὶ τεταγμένον ἐς τρίς, ἄπιστε,
ναυσὶν ὅσον πέμπεις χεῦμα δανειζόμενον·
5 θαῦμα βίου, θαμβῶ σε τὸ μυρίον, οὐδὲ ματεύω
σὴν στάσιν· ἀρρήτωι ταῦτα μέμηλε φύσει.

VI

ὡς πάρος Ἀελίου, νῦν Καίσαρος ἁ Ῥόδος εἰμί   815
νᾶσος, ἴσον δ᾿ αὐχῶ φέγγος ἀπ᾿ ἀμφοτέρων·
ἤδη σβεννυμέναν με νέα κατεφώτισεν ἀκτίς,
Ἅλιε, καὶ παρὰ σὸν φέγγος ἔλαμψε Νέρων.
5 πῶς εἴπω τίνι μᾶλλον ὀφείλομαι; ὃς μὲν ἔδειξεν
ἐξ ἁλός, ὃς δ᾿ ἤδη ῥύσατο δυομέναν.   820

VII

λαβροπόδη χείμαρρε, τί δὴ τόσον ὧδε κορύσσηι
πεζὸν ἀποκλείων ἴχνος ὁδοιπορίης;
ἢ μεθύεις ὄμβροισι καὶ οὐ Νύμφαισι διαυγὲς
νᾶμα φέρεις, θολεραῖς δ᾿ ἠράνισαι νεφέλαις.
5 ὄψομαι ἡελίωι σε κεκαυμένον, ὅστις ἐλέγχειν   825
καὶ γόνιμον ποταμῶν καὶ νόθον οἶδεν ὕδωρ.

V A.P. 9.73 [C] Ἀντιφίλου Βυζαντίου   [J] εἰς τὸ σύστρεμμα τῆς θαλάσσης
τοῦ Εὐβοϊκοῦ κόλπου τὸ καθ᾿ ἑκάστην ἡμέραν ἐν τῶι Εὐρίπωι γινόμενον   Pl A
Ἀντιφίλου Βυζαντίου
3 ἄπιστε Page: -τον PPl   5 ματεύω Pl: μαντ- P   6 φύσει CPl: de P non
liquet

VI A.P. 9.178 [C] Ἀντιφίλου Βυζαντίου   εἰς Ῥόδον τὴν νῆσον ὅτε Νέρων ἐν
αὐτῆι παρεγένετο διὰ τὸν κολοσσόν Pl A τοῦ αὐτοῦ [sc. Ἀντιφίλου]

V

On the turbulence in the Euboean straits

Back-whirling sea of the Euboean gulf, roaming waters, oppo-
nents to your own streams, how great a flood thrice marshalled
by day and by night you send, inconstant, on short loan to ships.
Wonder of the world, I marvel at you unendingly, yet seek
not the cause of your turbulence; that is the business of mys-
terious Nature.

VI

On Nero, the saviour of Rhodes

I, Rhodes, once the Sun's island, am now Caesar's, and I boast
of equal light from both. Just as my fire was dying, a new
radiance illumined me: O Sun, surpassing your light, Nero
shone forth. How shall I say to whom I owe the more? The
one revealed me from the sea, the other rescued me just as I
was sinking.

VII

A torrent cuts off the poet's path

Violent-rushing torrent, why lift your head so mighty high,
shutting off the journey's footpath? Surely you are drunk with
rains; the flow you bring is not translucent with the Nymphs'
waters, rather the muddy clouds are your contributors. I shall
live to see you parched by the sun, which knows how to test
the true-born river-water and the bastard.

1 ἀελίου PPl^{pc}: ἠελ- Pl^{ac} | ἁ P: ἡ Pl   2 νᾶσος PPl^{pc}: νῆς- Pl^{ac}
3 cβεννυμέναν PPl^{pc}: -νην Pl^{ac} | με νέα Pl^{pc} : γενεὰν P, γενεὴν Pl^{ac} 4 ἅλιε
PPl^{pc}: ἠλ- Pl^{ac} 6 ὃc Pl: ὁ P | δυομέναν P: -νην Pl

VII *A.P.* 9.277 [C] Ἀντιφίλου   εἰc χείμαρρουν ῥαγδαίως καταφερόμενον·
τωθαστικόν Pl A Ἀντιφίλου
1 λαβροπόδη Pl: λαπρο- C, λαμπρο- P   3 ὄμβροιcι P: ὄμβροιο Pl^{pc},
ὄμβριον Pl^{ac} | διαυγέc PPl^{pc}: -γεῖc Pl^{ac} 4 ἡράνιcαι Huet: -ιc' ἐν PPl

VIII

ἡ τερεβινθώδης ὀλιγάμπελος, οἷά τε βαιή
νησίς, ἀλλ᾽ ὁμαλὴ πᾶσα καὶ ἀστύφελος·
αἱ δ᾽ ἀγχοῦ μεγάλαι τε καὶ εὐρέες, ἀλλ᾽ ἐπὶ πουλύ
τρηχεῖαι, μεγέθει †τοῦτο† περισσότεραι.   830
5 καρποῖς, οὐ σταδίοισιν, ἐρίζομεν· οὐδὲ γὰρ αὖλαξ
Αἰγύπτου Λιβύης ψάμμου ἐπιστρέφεται.

IX

κἢν πρύμνηι λαχέτω μέ ποτε στιβὰς αἵ θ᾽ ὑπὲρ αὐτήν
ἠχεῦσαι ψακάδων τύμματι διφθερίδες
καὶ πῦρ ἐκ μυλάκων βεβιημένον ἤ τ᾽ ἐπὶ τούτων   835
χύτρη καὶ κενεὸς πομφολύγων θόρυβος·
5 †καί κε ῥύπτοντα ἴδοιμι† διήκονον, ἡ δὲ τράπεζα
ἔστω μοι στρωτὴ νηὸς ὕπερθε σανίς·
δὸς λαβὲ καὶ ψιθύρισμα τὸ ναυτικόν. εἶχε τύχη τις
πρώιην τοιαύτη τὸν φιλόκοινον ἐμέ.   840

X

Καλχηδὼν δύστηνον ἐρωδιὸν ἐχθρὰ κολάζει.
τεῦ χάριν ὁ προδότης ὄρνις ἀεὶ λέγεται,
Φοῖβος ἐρεῖ· τεναγῖτιν ὅτ᾽ εἰς ἅλα κῶλον ἐλαφρόν
στήσας ψαμμίτην δόρπον †ἐθημολόγει†,
5 δυσμενέες τότ᾽ ἔβησαν ἐπὶ πτόλιν ἀντιπέρηθεν   845
ὀψὲ διδασκόμενοι πεζοβατεῖν πέλαγος.

VIII *A.P.* 9.413 [J] Ἀντιφίλου [C] Βυζαντίου   [J] εἰς νῆσον Τερέβινθον [C] ἐν ἧι
τιμᾶται ὁ ἅγιος μάρτυς Ἀλέξανδρος [idem ad v. 4] εἰς τὴν Τερέβινθον [P sup.
v. 4] ἡ Τερέβινθος νησίδιόν ἐστι σύνεγγυς Πριγκήπου   [J ad v. 4] θαυμαστόν,
accedunt χρήσιμον ter, ὡραῖον semel Pl A Ἀντιφίλου
2 νησίς Pl: -σοις P   3 πουλύ Pl: πολύ P

IX *A.P.* 9.546 Ἀντιφίλου   caret Pl
5 καί κε ῥύπτοντα εἴδοιμι διήκονον ἤδη τράπεζαν P marg. inf., καί κρύπτοντα ᵋ

VIII

On the island Terebinthus

The Terebinthian is of few vines, being a small islet, but all level and smooth. Those near-by are large and broad but mostly rough, ⟨ ⟩ superior in size. We compete not in furlongs but in crops, just as the cornlands of Egypt care nothing for the sands of Libya.

IX

The pleasures of the simple life at sea

Let me have a couch on the poop some day, and the awnings resounding above it with the thud of spray, and fire breaking out from millstones, and the pot upon them, and the hollow tumult of bubbles. Let me have a sight of the ⟨ ⟩ steward and let my table be a plank laid over the ship. Let me hear the words 'Give and take'(?), and the whispering sounds at sea. Only the other day this sort of fortune befell my democratic self.

X

Why Chalcedon calls the heron a traitor

Chalcedon punishes the wretched heron as an enemy. Why the bird is always called 'Traitor', Phoebus will tell you.—While it was gathering its sandy supper, standing its light limbs in shallow waters, the enemy came against the city from the coast opposite, learning at the last moment how to cross the sea on

---

ἰδίδοιμι διήκονον ἤδη τράπεζα (mox in τράπεζαν corr.) P text., ubi ιδιδοι in rasura; latet fortasse διηκο ἴδοιμι διήκονον ηδη τραπεζαν P marg. dext.   ἡ δὲ τράπεζα Reiske   **6** cτρωτὴ Boissonade: πρώτη P   **7** εἶχε Reiske: ει και P
X A.P. 9.551 'Αντιφίλου   caret Pl
1 Καλχηδὼν Meineke: κολχαδὼν Pᵖᶜ, καλχαδὼν Pᵃᶜ   **3** τεναγῖτιν Ruhnken: τ' ἐν ἀγει τον P   **4** ψαμμίτην Ruhnken: -είτην P

βάλλετε δὴ κακὸν ὄρνιν, ἐπεὶ βαρὺν ἤρατο μισθόν
ἐκ δηίων κόχλους καὶ βρύον ὁ προδότης.

XI

ἀρχένεως λιμενῖτα, σὺ μέν, μάκαρ, ἤπιον αὔρην
πέμπε κατὰ σταθερῆς †οἰχομένην ὀθόνην†   850
ἄχρις ἐπὶ Τρίτωνα· σὺ δ' ἠιόνος ἄκρα λελογχὼς
τὴν ἐπὶ Πυθείου ῥύεο ναυστολίην.
5 κεῖθεν δ', εἰ Φοίβωι μεμελήμεθα πάντες ἀοιδοί,
πλεύσομαι εὐαεῖ θαρσαλέος Ζεφύρωι.

XII

εἶπον ἐγὼ καὶ πρόσθεν, ὅτ' ἦν ἔτι φίλτρα Τερείνης   855
νήπια, 'συμφλέξει πάντας ἀεξομένη',
οἱ δ' ἐγέλων τὸν μάντιν· ἴδ' ὁ χρόνος, ὅν ποτ' ἐφώνουν,
οὗτος, ἐγὼ δὲ πάλαι τραύματος ἠισθανόμην.
5 καὶ τί πάθω; λεύσσειν μὲν ὅλαι φλόγες, ἢν δ' ἀπονεύσω,
φροντίδες, ἢν δ' αἰτῶ, παρθένος· οἰχόμεθα.   860

XIII

χεῦμα μὲν Εὐρώταο Λακωνικόν, ἁ δ' ἀκάλυπτος   (861)
Λήδα, χὠ κύκνωι κρυπτόμενος Κρονίδας·
οἱ δ' ἐμὲ τὸν δυσέρωτα καταίθετε. καὶ τί γένωμαι;
ὄρνεον· εἰ γὰρ Ζεὺς κύκνος, ἐγὼ κόρυδος.

8 βρύον Sylburg: βρίον Pᵖᶜ (sed βρύον ut vid. voluit), βρύων ut vid. Pᵃᶜ
XI A.P. 10.17 'Αντιφίλου   caret Pl
1 ἀρχένεως Hecker: ἀρχέλεως P   5 ἀοιδοί Jacobs: -δήν P   6 θαρσαλέος
Hecker: -έως P

foot. Stone the wicked bird, for the shellfish and oyster-green the traitor got were its grievous wages from our foes.

XI

Prayer for a calm sea-passage

Blest god of the harbour, ship-ruler, send a gentle breeze ⟨   ⟩ as far as Triton's realm; and you, who own the shore's extremity, make safe the voyage to the Pythian shrine. From there, if we singers all are dear to Phoebus, I shall sail heartened by a fair-blowing west-wind.

XII

Tereina's dangerous charms

I said it in early days too, when Tereina's charms were still in childhood, 'When she grows up she will burn every man to cinders'. And they laughed at me, the great prophet. Now look, the time I spoke of is here, and I have long felt the wound. What is to become of me? To look at her is to be in flames, nothing else; if I turn towards her, it's a heartache; if I ask the favour,—she's a virgin. There is no hope for me.

XIII

*The lover inflamed by a picture of
Leda and the swan*

The stream is Spartan, of the Eurotas; the woman disrobed is Leda; the one disguised as a swan is Zeus. You set my unhappy lover's heart aflame. What shall I turn into? Surely a bird; for if Zeus is a swan, I can be a lark.

XII *A.P.* 5.111 Ἀντιφίλου   [J] εἰς κόρην τινὰ Τερείνην ὀνομαζομένην κάλλος ἀμήχανον ἔχουσαν   Pl A Ἀντιφίλου
5 λεύccειν Pl: λεύceιν P

XIII *A.P.* 5.307 Ἀντιφίλου   Pl A Ἀντιφίλου
2 Κρονίδαc CPl: -δηc P   **3** καταίθετε Pl: κατέcθετε P

XIV

ἡ κομψή, μεῖνόν με· τί σοι καλὸν οὔνομα; ποῦ σε 865
ἔστιν ἰδεῖν; ὃ θέλεις δώσομεν. οὐδὲ λαλεῖς;
ποῦ γίνηι; πέμψω μετά c᾽ αὖ τινα. μή τις ἔχει σε;
ὦ σοβαρή, ὑγίαιν᾽· οὐδ᾽ ὑγίαινε λέγεις;
5 καὶ πάλι καὶ πάλι σοι προσελεύσομαι. οἶδα μαλάσσειν
καὶ σοῦ σκληροτέρας. νῦν δ᾽ ὑγίαινε, γύναι. 870

XV

βουστρόφον ἀκροσίδαρον ἀπειλητῆρα μύωπα
καὶ πήραν μέτρου σιτοδόκον σπορίμου
γαμψόν τε δρέπανον, σταχυητόμον ὅπλον ἀρούρης,
καὶ παλινουροφόρον χεῖρα θέρευς θρίνακα
5 καὶ τρητοὺς ποδεῶνας ὁ γατόμος ἄνθετο Δηοῖ 875
Πάρμις, ἀνιηρῶν παυσάμενος καμάτων.

XVI

Εἰνοδίη, σοὶ τόνδε φίλης ἀνεθήκατο κόρσης
πῖλον ὁδοιπορίης σύμβολον Ἀντίφιλος·
ἦcθα γὰρ εὐχωλῆιcι κατήκοος, ἦcθα κελεύθοις
ἵλαος· οὐ πολλὴ δ᾽ ἡ χάρις, ἀλλ᾽ ὁσίη. 880
5 μηδέ τις ἡμετέρου μάρψηι χερὶ μάργος ὁδίτης
ἀνθέματος· cυλᾶν ἀcφαλὲς οὐδ᾽ ὀλίγα.

XIV A.P. 5.308 τοῦ αὐτοῦ [sc. Ἀντιφίλου] [C] ἢ μᾶλλον Φιλοδήμου Pl A τοῦ
αὐτοῦ [sc. Φιλοδήμου]
3 c᾽ αὖ Page: cού PPl 5 μαλάσσειν CPl: -ccον P
XV A.P. 6.95 Ἀντιφίλου ἀνάθημα τῆι Δηοῖ παρὰ Πάρμιδος γεωπόνου Suid.
s.vv. μύωψ (1), πήρα (2), γαμψόν (3), θρίναξ (4), ποδεῶνας (5-6) caret Pl

XIV

A street-scene

Wait for me, my charmer. What is your pretty name? Where can one see you? I will pay whatever you like. Won't you even speak to me? Where do you live? I will send someone to fetch you later on. Have you a lover? Miss Airs and Graces, good-bye to you. Won't you even say good-bye? I shall accost you again and yet again; I know how to soften even harder girls than you. So good-bye for now, my lady.

XV

A ploughman's dedication to Demeter

His ox-turning iron-tipped menacing goad; his wallet, holder of the seed-corn's measure; his curved sickle, the field's corn-cutting implement; his pitchfork, the harvest's hand that brings the counter-wind; his riddled funnels,—these Parmis the plough-man has dedicated to Demeter, retired from the pains of labouring.

XVI

The poet dedicates his hat to the Goddess of the Road

To you, Lady of the Road, Antiphilus has dedicated this hat from his own head, a token of his journey; for you listened to his vows, you were propitious to his paths. Slight but pious is my thank-offering. Let not any covetous traveller snatch my dedication; even the smallest sacrilege is at one's peril.

2 μέτρου apogr.: -ον PSuid.   **4** παλινουροφόρον Toup: παλιουρ- PSuid. | θέρευς PSuid.: -ους C

XVI *A.P.* 6.199 Ἀντιφίλου Βυζαντίου ἀνάθημα Ἀντιφίλου Suid. s.vv. πιλήϲεϲι (1–2 πῖλ.), ἦϲθα (2–4 Ῑλ.), ὁϲίη (4 οὐ–ὁϲ.)   caret Pl
1 φίλης Suid.: -λη C, -ληι P   **3** ἦϲθα κελ. Jacobs: ἔνθα κελ. PSuid.

XVII

σῆμα δυωδεκάμοιρον ἀφεγγέος ἠελίοιο
τρισσάκις ἀγλώccωι φθεγγόμενον ctόματι,
εὖτ' ἂν θλιβομένοιο ποτὶ cτενὸν ὕδατος ἀήρ   885
αὐλὸν ἀποcτείληι πνεῦμα διωλύγιον,
5 θῆκεν Ἀθήναιος δήμωι χάριν, ὡς ἂν ἐναργής
εἴη κἠν φθονεραῖc ἠέλιος νεφέλαιc.

XVIII

Βόρχοc ὁ βουποίμην ὅτ' ἐπὶ γλυκὺ κηρίον εἶρπεν
αἰγίλιπα cχοίνωι πέτρον ἐπερχόμενος,   890
εἵπετό οἱ cκυλάκων τις ὁ καὶ βοcίν, ὃc φάγε λεπτήν
cχοῖνον ἀνελκομένωι χραινομένην μέλιτι.
5 κάππεcε δ' εἰc Ἀίδαο, τὸ δ' ἀτρυγὲc ἀνδράcιν ἄλλοιc
κεῖνο μέλι ψυχῆc ὤνιον εἰρύcατο.

XIX

νεκροδόκον κλιντῆρα Φίλων ὁ πρέcβυc ἀείρων   895
†ἔνδον† ὄφρα λάβοι μιcθὸν ἐφημέριον
cφάλματοc ἐξ ὀλίγοιο πεcὼν θάνεν· ἦν γὰρ ἕτοιμοc
εἰc Ἀίδην, ἐκάλει δ' ἡ πολιὴ πρόφαcιc.
5 τὸν δ' ἄλλοιc ἐφόρει νεκυοcτόλον, αὐτὸc ἐπ' αὐτῶι
ἀcκάντην ὁ γέρων ἀχθοφορῶν ἔλαθεν.   900

XVII A.P. 7.641 [C] Ἀντιφίλου [J] ʒτ τὴν τοῦ γράμματος ἔννοιαν, ὅτι
δύcληπτοc   Pl B s.a.n. εἰc ὡρολόγιον
2 φθεγγόμενον Pl: -οc P

XVIII A.P. 7.622 [C] Ἀντιφίλου Βυζαντίου   [J] εἰc Βόρχον τινὰ βουκόλον
κρημνιcθέντα διὰ μέλι Pl B Ἀντιφίλου

XVII

On a water-clock

The twelve-sectioned marker of the rayless sun, thrice giving voice though with tongueless mouth, when the water is compressed towards the narrow pipe and the air sends forth a far-reaching blast,—this for the people's pleasure Athenaeus set up, so that the sun might be clear even amid envious clouds.

XVIII

On the death of Borchus while gathering honey

When Borchus the oxherd went after the sweet honeycomb, attacking the steep cliff with a rope, one of the dogs that followed his cattle followed him and bit through the slender rope, smeared with the honey as it was pulled up. He fell to his death. That honey, unharvested by other men, he had carried off at the cost of his life.

XIX

On the death of an undertaker

Old Philo, lifting a bier for the dead ⟨   ⟩ to get his daily wage, from a slight stumble fell and died. He was ripe for Hades, and his gray hairs were excuse enough to summon him. That bier which he was carrying to lay out the bodies of other men, the old fellow carried unawares for his own person.

1 εἷρπεν CPl: ἦρ- P   3 φάγε CPl: φάετε ut vid. P   5 ἀτρυγὲс CPl: -υτες ut vid. P

XIX A.P. 7.634 [C] 'Αντιφίλου Βυζαντίου   [J] εἰс γέροντα νεκροφόρον βαστά-ζοντα τὸν κράβατον καὶ ἐξολισθέντα τεθνηκότα   Pl A 'Αντιφίλου
2 ἔνδον P: -δοθεν Pl   3 ἕτοιμος CPl: -μως vel -μας P   4 πρόφασις P: -ιν Pl   5 τὸν P: ὃν Pl | ἐπ' αὐτῷ P: ἐφ' αὐτῶι Pl

XX

Γλαῦκος ὁ Νεσσαίοιο διαπλώουσιν ὁδηγός
πορθμοῦ καὶ Θασίων ἔντροφος αἰγιαλῶν,
πόντου ἀροτρευτὴρ ἐπιδέξιος, οὐδ' ὅτ' ἔκνωσσεν
πλαζομένηι στρωφῶν πηδάλιον παλάμηι,
5 μυριέτης, ἁλίοιο βίου ῥάκος, οὐδ' ὅτ' ἔμελλεν   905
θνήισκειν ἐκτὸς ἔβη γηραλέης σανίδος·
τοὶ δὲ κέλυφος ἔκαυσαν ἐπ' ἀνέρι, τόφρ' ὁ γεραιός
πλώσηι ἐπ' οἰκείης εἰς Ἀίδην ἀκάτου.

XXI

δοῦρας Ἀλεξάνδροιο, λέγει δέ σε γράμματ' ἐκεῖνον
ἐκ πολέμου θέσθαι σύμβολον Ἀρτέμιδι   910
ὅπλον ἀνικήτοιο βραχίονος. ἆ καλὸν ἔγχος,
ὧι πόντος καὶ χθὼν εἶκε κραδαινομένωι.
5 ἴλαθι, δοῦρας ἀταρβές· ἀεὶ δέ σε πᾶς τις ἀθρήσας
ταρβήσει μεγάλης μνησάμενος παλάμης.

XXII

τίς με, Διωνύσωι πεπλασμένον ἀμφιφορῆα,   915
τίς με, τὸν Ἀδριακοῦ νέκταρος οἰνοδόκον,
Δηοῦς ἐπλήρωσε; τίς ὁ φθόνος εἰς ἐμὲ Βάκχου
ἢ σπάνις οἰκείου τεύχεος ἀσταχύων;
5 ἀμφοτέρους ἤισχυνε· σεσύληται μὲν ὁ Βάκχος,
Δημήτηρ δὲ Μέθην σύντροφον οὐ δέχεται.   920

XX *A.P.* 9.242 [C] Ἀντιφίλου Βυζαντίου   εἰς Γλαῦκόν τινα πένητα ἐν ἀκατίωι
πλέοντα καὶ τὰ τοῦ βίου ποριζόμενον καὶ ἐν αὐτῶι τῶι ἀκατίωι θνήξαντα [C ad
vv. 2 seqq.] ὅτι τὸν ἐλεεινὸν γέροντα μετὰ τῆς ἰδίας νηὸς κατέκαυσαν   Pl A τοῦ
αὐτοῦ [sc. Ἀντιφίλου]
1 Νεσσαίοιο Pl: νησαί- P   2 πορθμοῦ P: ποθμ- Pl | ἔντροφος Pl et man. rec.
in P: -τροος P   3 ἀροτρευτὴρ PPl^pc: -τῆς Pl^ac | οὐδ' P: ἠδ' Pl | ἔκνωσσεν P:
-σσε Pl   5 ἁλίοιο Pl: ἀιλιοιο P | ὅτ' Pl: ἀρ P | ἔμελλεν P: -λλε Pl   7 ἔκαυσαν
Jacobs: ἔκλυσαν P, ἔκλυσσαν Pl | τόφρ' ὁ Reiske: τόφρα PPl

XX

On the death of Glaucus, a ferryman

Glaucus, the guide of the strait of Nessus for those who sail across it, native of Thasos' shores, skilled ploughman of the sea, who even while he slept turned the rudder with unerring hand, infinitely old, mere rags and tatters of a seaman's life, even on the point of death did not leave his long-lived deck. They burnt the shell over him, that the old man might sail to Hades in his own boat.

XXI

On a spear of Alexander

The spear of Alexander; your inscription says that he dedicated you to Artemis after battle, a weapon symbolic of his unconquerable arm. Ah noble spear, before your brandishing the ocean and the earth gave way. Be merciful, spear that knew not terror; all men for all time shall tremble when they look upon you, remembering that mighty hand.

XXII

On an amphora filled with grain

Who has filled me, a jar moulded for Dionysus,—me, a wine-jar for Adria's nectar,—with the goddess of grains? What is this grudging me of Bacchus, or shortage of proper vessels for corn? He has disgraced both divinities: Bacchus has been plundered, and Demeter is not at home to Drink.

XXI *A.P.* 6.97 Ἀντιφίλου [C] Βυζαντίου   [P] ἀνάθημα τῆι Ἀρτέμιδι παρὰ Ἀλεξάνδρου βασιλέως   Pl A Ἀντιφίλου
I δοῦρας PPl: -ρατ' C | ἐκεῖνον Lascaris: -νου PPl   4 εἶκε Pl: ἧκε P
XXII *A.P.* 6.257 Ἀντιφίλου   Suid. s.vv. ἀμφιφορῆα (1–6), cυλῶ (5)   caret Pl
4 τεύχεος CSuid.: -χους P

XXIII

Θεσσαλὲ Πρωτεσίλαε, σὲ μὲν πολὺς ἄισεται αἰών
Τροίαι ὀφειλομένου πτώματος ἀρξάμενον·
σᾶμα δέ τοι πτελέηςι συνηρεφὲς ἀμφικομεῦσι
Νύμφαι ἀπεχθομένης Ἰλίου ἀντιπέρας·
5 δένδρεα δυσμήνιτα, καὶ ἤν ποτε τεῖχος ἴδωσι   925
Τρώιον αὐαλέην φυλλοχοεῦντι κόμην.
ὅσσος ἐν ἡρώεσσι τότ᾽ ἦν χόλος, οὗ μέρος ἀκμήν
ἐχθρὸν ἐν ἀψύχοις σώιζεται ἀκρεμόσιν.

XXIV

οὕτω πᾶς ἀπόλωλε, γεωπόνε, βῶλος ἀρότροις;
ἤδη καὶ τύμβους νωτοβατοῦσι βόες,   930
ἡ δ᾽ ὕνις ἐν νεκύεσσι; τί τοι πλέον, ἢ πόσος οὗτος
πυρός, ὃν ἐκ τέφρης κοὐ χθονὸς ἀρπάσετε;
5 οὐκ αἰεὶ ζήσεσθε· καὶ ὑμέας ἄλλος ἀρώσει
τοίης ἀρξαμένους πᾶσι κακοσπορίης.

XXV

οὐχ ὅτι με φθίμενον κῆδος λίπεν ἐνθάδε κεῖμαι   935
γυμνὸς ὑπὲρ γαίης πυροφόροιο νέκυς·
ταρχύθην γὰρ ἐγὼ τὸ πρίν ποτε, νῦν δ᾽ ἀροτῆρος
χερσὶ σιδηρείη μ᾽ ἐξεκύλισεν ὕνις.
5 ἦ ῥα κακῶν θάνατόν τις ἔφη λύσιν, ὁππότ᾽ ἐμεῖο,
ξεῖνε, πέλει παθέων ὕστατον οὐδὲ τάφος;   940

XXIII *A.P.* 7.141 Ἀντιφίλου [J] Βυζαντίου   [P] εἰς Πρωτεσίλαον [J] εἰς
Πρωτεσίλαον τὸν ἐν Τροίαι πρῶτον πάντων Ἑλλήνων τελευτήσαντα   Pl A
Ἀντιφίλου εἰς Πρωτεσίλαον   Suid. s.vv. δυσμίσητα (5–6), ἀκμήν (7–8)
3 σᾶμα P: σῶμα Pl   4 Νύμφαι CPl: -αν P | ἀπεχθομένης CPl: ἀπεχομ- P
5 δυσμήνιτα Brodaeus: -μίνητα P, -μίμητα (ex -μίμημα corr.) Pl, -μίσητα Suid. |
ἴδωσι CPl: ἔδωσι P   6 αὐαλέην P: -έαν CPlSuid. | φυλλοχοεῦντι CPl: -χεεῦντι
P, -χοεῦσι Suid.

XXIII

On the elms round the tomb of Protesilaus

Thessalian Protesilaus, long ages shall sing of you, the first to fall a victim owed to Troy. Nymphs put foliage about your tomb, shaded by elms, opposite hated Ilium. Wrathful are those trees, and if ever they see the walls of Troy they shed their withered leaves. How great was then those heroes' anger, if a part of their hostility still survives in lifeless boughs.

XXIV

On a farmer ploughing a burial-ground

Farmer, is every earth-clod thus lost to the plough? Must your oxen now tread even the backs of sepulchres, and the plough-share go even among the dead? How does it profit you? How much wheat is this that you snatch from ashes instead of earth? You will not live for ever; some other shall plough you up as well, for setting men the example of such evil sowing.

XXV

On a corpse disinterred by the plough

It is not because funeral-rites failed me when I died that I lie here a naked corpse above the corn-bearing ground. Once, long ago, I was buried, but now the iron share at the ploughman's hand has tumbled me out. Did someone say that death was deliverance from evils? For me, stranger, not even the tomb is the end of suffering.

XXIV *A.P.* 7.175 [C] 'Αντιφίλου [J] εἰс τάφον ἐξορυχθέντα ὑπὸ ἀρότου [ἀρότρου Boissonade] Pl в s.a.n.
1 οὕτω Pl: οὔπω P | γεωπόνε CPl: -νος P 3 ἠ δ' ὕνιc P: ὕννιc δ' Pl | τοι P: τὸ Pl 4 ἀρπάсετε Pl: -сεται P, -σεαι C 5 ἀρώσει P: ἀρόссει Pl
XXV *A.P.* 7.176 [C] τοῦ αὐτοῦ [sc. 'Αντιφίλου] εἰс τὸ αὐτό [J] ἕτερον ὁμοίωс εἰс τάφον [haec erasa; pergit C] ὑπ' ἀροτῆρος ἐξορυγέντα caret Pl
4 сιδηρείη C: -ην P | ἐξεκύλισεν Jacobs: -ισσεν P

XXVI

δώματά μοι ceιcθέντα κατήριπεν, ἀλλ᾽ ἐμὸc ἀπτώc
ἦν θάλαμοc τοίχων ὀρθὰ τιναξαμένων·
οἷc ὑποφωλεύουcαν ὑπήλυθον αἱ κακόμοιροι
ὠδῖνεc, ceιcμῶι δ᾽ ἄλλον ἔμιξα φόβον.
5 μαῖα δέ μοι λοχίων αὐτὴ Φύcιc, ἀμφότεροι δέ   945
κοινὸν ὑπὲρ γαίηc εἴδομεν ἠέλιον.

XXVII

τηλοτάτω χεύαcθαι ἔδει τάφον Οἰδιπόδαο
παιcὶν ἀπ᾽ ἀλλήλων, οἷc πέραc οὐδ᾽ Ἀίδαc,
ἀλλὰ καὶ εἰc Ἀχέροντοc ἕνα πλόον ἠρνήcαντο,
χὠ cτυγερὸc ζώει κἢν φθιμένοιcιν Ἄρηc.   950
5 ἠνίδε πυρκαϊῆc ἄνιcον φλόγα· δαιομένα γάρ
ἐξ ἑνὸc εἰc διccὰν δῆριν ἀποcτρέφεται.

XXVIII

ναῦν Ἱεροκλείδηc ἔcχεν cύγγηρον ὁμόπλουν,
τὴν αὐτὴν ζωῆc καὶ θανάτου cύνοδον,
πιcτὴν ἰχθυβολεῦντι cυνέμπορον· οὔ τιc ἐκείνηc   955
πώποτ᾽ ἐπέπλωcεν κῦμα δικαιοτέρη.
5 γήραοc ἄχριc ἔβοcκε πονευμένη, εἶτα θανόντα
ἐκτέριcεν, cυνέπλω δ᾽ ἄχρι καὶ Ἀίδεω.

XXVI *A.P.* 7.375 [C] Ἀντιφίλου Βυζαντίου   [J] εἴc τινα γυναῖκα ἔγκυον ἐν
ceιcμῶι τετοκυῖαν τιναccομένου τοῦ δώματοc   caret Pl
3 οἷc Salm.: αἷc P | ὑποφωλεύουcαν Reiske: -cαι P
XXVII *A.P.* 7.399 [C] Ἀντιφίλου   [J] ἕτερον εἰc Ἐτεοκλέα καὶ Πολυνείκην τοὺc
Οἰδίποδοc υἱούc   caret Pl

XXVI

A woman gives birth during an earthquake

My house was shaken and collapsed; only my bed-chamber stayed erect, the walls shaken but upright. As I cowered beneath them, my ill-starred birth-pains came upon me, and I joined to the earthquake a second cause of fear. But Nature herself was midwife to my travail, and we both saw together the sunlight above the earth.

XXVII

On the deathless feud between the sons of Oedipus

Far from each other should tombs have been heaped for the sons of Oedipus. For them, not even death was the end, but they refused a common passage to Acheron. Hatred and strife live in them even among the dead. Look at their pyre's uneven flame: it divides, and turns from one mass into a quarrelsome pair.

XXVIII

On a fisherman whose boat served as funeral-pyre

The boat that Hieroclides had was a shipmate growing old together with him, one and the same companion in life and in death, a loyal fellow-traveller in his fishing. None truer than that boat ever sailed over the waves. Her labours fed him till old age, and when he died she buried him and shared his sailing even to Hades.

3 ’Αχέροντος C: -τα P

XXVIII *A.P.* 7. 635 [C] τοῦ αὐτοῦ [sc. ’Αντιφίλου] ὁμοίως [J] εἰς ‘Ιεροκλείδην ἁλιέα θανόντα ὃν κατέκαυσαν σὺν τῆι ἰδίαι νηί Pl B Μαικίου
3 ἐκείνης Pl: -νος P   6 ἄχρι καὶ ’Αίδεω Jacobs: ἄχρις ’Αίδεω P, ἄχρι καὶ εἰς ’Αίδην Pl

XXIX

ἄμφω μὲν πηροὶ καὶ ἀλήμονες, ἀλλ' ὁ μὲν ὄψεις,
ὃς δὲ βάσεις, ἄλλου δ' ἄλλος ὑπηρεσίη ·   960
τυφλὸς γὰρ χωλοῖο κατωμάδιον βάρος αἴρων
ἀτραπὸν ὀθνείοις ὄμμασιν ἀκροβάτει.
5 ἡ μία δ' ἀμφοτέροις ἤρκει φύσις · ἐν γὰρ ἑκάστωι
τοὐλλιπὲς ἀλλήλοις εἰς ὅλον ἠράνισαν.

XXX

αἰγιαλοῦ τενάγεσσιν ὑποπλώοντα λαθραίηι   965
εἰρεσίηι Φαίδων εἴσιδε πουλυπόδην.
μάρψας δ' ὠκὺς ἔριψεν ἐπὶ χθόνα, πρὶν περὶ χεῖρας
πλέξασθαι βρύγδην ὀκτατόνους ἕλικας ·
5 δισκευθεὶς δ' ἐπὶ θάμνον ἐς οἰκία δειλὰ λαγωοῦ
εἰληδὸν ταχινοῦ πτωκὸς ἔδησε πόδας,   970
εἷλε δ' ἁλούς · σὺ δ' ἄελπτον ἔχεις γέρας ἀμφοτέρωθεν
ἄγρης χερσαίης, πρέσβυ, καὶ εἰναλίης.

XXXI

τόλμα, νεῶν ἀρχηγέ, σὺ γὰρ δρόμον ηὕραο πόντου
καὶ ψυχὰς ἀνδρῶν κέρδεσιν ἠρέθισας,
οἷον ἐτεκτήνω δόλιον ξύλον, οἷον ἔνεικας   975
ἀνθρώποις θανάτωι κέρδος ἐλεγχόμενον.
5 ἦν ὄντως μερόπων χρύσεον γένος, εἴ γ' ἀπὸ χέρσου
τηλόθεν ὡς Ἀίδης πόντος ἀπεβλέπετο.

XXIX *A.P.* 9.13ᴮ s.a.n. [J] εἰς τὸ αὐτὸ περί τε τοῦ τυφλοῦ καὶ τοῦ χωλοῦ ὅτι
ἀλλήλοις τὸ ἐλλειπὲς ἐδάνειζον Pl ᴀ Ἀντιφίλου εἰς τὸ αὐτό
2 ὃς Pl: ὁ P   3 αἴρων P: ἄρας Pl   4 ἀκροβάτει Pl: ἀκριβ- P

XXX *A.P.* 9.14 Ἀντιφίλου Βυζαντίου [J] εἰς πολύπουν ἀγρευθέντα παρὰ
ἁλιέως καὶ ριφέντα ἐπὶ θάμνον ἐν ἧι λαγὼς κοιμώμενος παρὰ τοῦ πολύπου
ἠγρεύθη Pl ᴀ Ἀντιφίλου Βυζαντίου

XXIX

The blind man and the lame help each other

Both were maimed and vagabonds, but the one had lost his eyes, the other his legs, and each was the other's help. The blind man, lifting the lame man's weight on his shoulders, edged his way forward with eyes not his own. Their combined faculties were enough for both; what was lacking in each, they contributed to one another to form a whole.

XXX

A fisherman's double catch

Phaedon saw an octopus floating with furtive oarsmanship below the shallows of the shore. Swiftly he seized it and flung it to land before it could tightly twine the eight strands of its spirals about his hands. Whirled into a bush, on to a hare's timorous home, it bound in its coils the swift cowering creature's feet. So the captive was captor; the old man has an unexpected gift from both elements,—one catch from the land, one from the sea.

XXXI

On the dangers of seafaring

Spirit of adventure, inventor of ships,—for it was you who discovered ocean's highway and excited man's soul with profits,—what treacherous timber you framed, what profit to man you brought, yet subject to death's arrest. Truly it was men's Golden Age, when the sea was viewed from the shore, a long way off, like Hades.

---

2 πουλυπόδην Pl: πολυπ- P   3 ὠκύς P: ὀξύς Pl

XXXI *A.P.* 9.29 [C] 'Αντιφίλου Βυζαντίου   [J] εἰς τόλμαν τὴν ἀρχηγὸν τῶν νεῶν καὶ ὅτι τόλμης ἕνεκα καὶ κέρδους θαλάσσηι ἐγχειροῦσιν ἄνθρωποι   [J ad v. 2] ὅτι κέρδος καὶ τόλμη ναυτικὴν κατεσκεύασαν, καὶ τοῦτο μακάριον ἦν εἰ ἀπὸ τῆς χέρσου μόνον ἔ3ων οἱ ἄνθρωποι   Pl A 'Αντιφίλου Βυζαντίου
3 ἕνεικας P: ἐνῆκ- Pl   5 εἴ γ' Pl: εἰ P

XXXII

μυρία με τρίψασαν ἀμετρήτοιο θαλάσσης
κύματα καὶ χέρσωι βαιὸν ἐρεισαμένην   980
ὤλεσεν οὐχὶ θάλασσα, νεῶν φόβος, ἀλλ' ἐπὶ γαίης
Ἥφαιστος· τίς ἐρεῖ πόντον ἀπιστότερον;
5 ἔνθεν ἔφυν ἀπόλωλα, παρ' ἠϊόνεσσι δὲ κεῖμαι
χέρσωι τὴν πελάγευς ἐλπίδα μεμφομένη.

XXXIII

κλῶνες ἀπηόριοι ταναῆς δρυός, εὔσκιον ὕψος   985
ἀνδράσιν ἄκρητον καῦμα φυλασσομένοις,
εὐπέταλοι, κεράμων στεγανώτεροι, οἰκία φαττῶν,
οἰκία τεττίγων, ἔνδιοι ἀκρεμόνες
5 κἠμὲ τὸν ὑμετέραισιν ὑποκλινθέντα κόμαισιν
ῥύσασθ' ἀκτίνων ἠελίου φυγάδα.   990

XXXIV

παμφάγος ἑρπηστὴς κατὰ δώματα λιχνοβόρος μῦς
ὄστρεον ἀθρήσας χείλεσι πεπταμένον
πώγωνος διεροῖο νόθην ὠδάξατο σάρκα,
αὐτίκα δ' ὀστρακόεις ἐπλατάγησε δόμος·
5 ἁρμόσθη δ' ὀδύναισιν, ὁ δ' ἐν κλείθροισιν ἀφύκτοις   995
ληφθεὶς αὐτοφόνον τύμβον ἐπεσπάσατο.

XXXII *A.P.* 9.34 [C] Ἀντιφίλου Βυζαντίου   [J] εἰς ἑτέραν ναῦν ἣν οὐχὶ θάλασσα κατέφθειρεν ἀλλὰ πῦρ ἀπό τινος τύχης   Pl A Ἀντιφίλου Βυζαντίου
XXXIII *A.P.* 9.71 [C] Ἀντιφίλου Βυζαντίου   [J] εἰς δρῦν διὰ τὸ εὔσκιον τοῦ δένδρου καὶ τὴν ἀνάπαυσιν τῶν ὑπεισερχομένων   Pl A Ἀντιφίλου Βυζαντίου
2 φυλασσομένοις Pl: -νους P   3 φαττῶν Reiske: φωτῶν PPl   5 τὸν Pl: τὴν P | ὑμετέραισιν Brunck: -ροισιν P, -ρηισιν Pl | κόμαισιν P: -μηισι Pl
6 φυγάδα CPl: -δων P

XXXII

On a ship destroyed by fire on shore

I who made a beaten track across the infinite sea's innumerable
waves and rested but a moment on the shore, perished not by
the sea, the vessel's dread, but by fire on the land. Who shall
say that the ocean is the more treacherous? Whence I was born,
thence came my death; on the beaches I lie, reproaching the dry
land for what I expected from the sea.

XXXIII

Shelter from the mid-day sun

Overhanging boughs of the tall oak, shady height so welcome to men sheltering from the intemperate heat, full of
foliage, closer roofing than tiles, home of wood-pigeons, home
of cicadas, branches in the noon-tide, protect me too as I lie
beneath your tresses, a fugitive from the sun's rays.

XXXIV

On a mouse trapped by an oyster

A gluttonous gormandising mouse, creeping through the house,
seeing an oyster with lips wide open, bit the false flesh of its
wet beard. At once the house of shell clapped shut; in pain it
closed tight, and the mouse, caught in a prison with no escape,
brought on itself a suicide's tomb.

XXXIV *A.P.* 9.86 [C] 'Αντιφίλου [J] εἰc μῦν ἐνδακόντα ὄcτρεον καὶ ⟨τελευ-
τήcαντα suppl. Stadtmüller⟩ τοῦ ὀcτρέου cυμπτύξαντοc καὶ ἀποπνίξαντοc αὐτόν
Pl a 'Αντιφίλου
1 δώματα Pl: δῶμα P   3 διεροῖο νόθην Pl: διερίοιο νωθὴν P   6 τύμβον
PPl: πότμον Pl^{γρ}

XXXV

δέρκεο τὸν Τροίας δεκέτη λόχον, εἴσιδε πῶλον
εὐόπλου Δαναῶν ἔγκυον ἡσυχίης·
τεκταίνει μὲν Ἐπειός, Ἀθηναίη δὲ κελεύει
ἔργον, ὑπαὶ νώτου δ' Ἑλλὰς ὅλα δύεται.   1000
5 ἦ ῥα μάταν ἀπόλοντο τόσος στρατός, εἰ πρὸς Ἄρηα
ἦν δόλος Ἀτρείδαις ἐσθλότερος πολέμου.

XXXVI

—αἱ βίβλοι, τίνος ἐστέ; τί κεύθετε;—θυγατέρες μέν
Μαιονίδου, μύθων δ' ἵστορες Ἰλιακῶν·
ἁ μία μὲν μηνιθμὸν Ἀχιλλέος ἔργα τε χειρός   1005
Ἑκτορέας δεκέτους τ' ἄθλα λέγει πολέμου,
5 ἁ δ' ἑτέρα μόχθον τὸν Ὀδυσσέος, ἀμφί τε λέκτροις
χηρείοις ἀγαθᾶς δάκρυα Πηνελόπας.
—ἵλατε σὺν Μούσαισι, μεθ' ὑμετέρας γὰρ ἀοιδάς
εἶπεν ἔχειν αἰὼν ἕνδεκα Πιερίδας.   1010

XXXVII

ἀνέρα θήρ, χερσαῖον ὁ πόντιος, ἄπνοον ἔμπνους
ἀράμενος λοφιῆς ὑγρὸν ὕπερθε νέκυν
εἰς ψαμάθους ἐκόμισσα. τί δὲ πλέον; ἐξ ἁλὸς ἐς γῆν
νηξάμενος φόρτου μισθὸν ἔχω θάνατον.
5 δαίμονα δ' ἀλλήλων ἠμείψαμεν· ἁ μὲν ἐκείνου   1015
χθὼν ἐμέ, τὸν δ' ἀπὸ γῆς ἔκτανε τοὐμὸν ὕδωρ.

XXXV A.P. 9.156 [C] Ἀντιφίλου Βυζαντίου   εἰς τὸν δούριον ἵππον ὃν Ἐπειὸς
κατεσκεύασεν Pl A Ἀντιφίλου   εἰς τὸ αὐτό
4 ὑπαὶ Reiske: ὑπὲρ PPl | ὅλα P: ὅλη Pl   5 μάταν P: -την Pl
XXXVI A.P. 9.192 [C] Ἀντιφίλου Βυζαντίου   εἰς τὰς Ὁμήρου βίβλους ἤγουν
εἰς τὴν Ἰλιάδα καὶ Ὀδύσσειαν· θαυμαστὸν ὅλον τὸ ἐπίγραμμα Pl A Ἀντιφίλου
εἰς Ἰλιάδα καὶ Ὀδύσσειαν

XXXV

On a picture of the Trojan Horse

Behold Troy's tenth-year ambush, look at the horse, pregnant with the Greeks' armed silence. The maker is Epeius; she who enjoins the work, Athena; and all Hellas goes in beneath its back. Truly in vain that great army perished, if deceit was better than battle for the Atridae in their war.

XXXVI

The Iliad and Odyssey

—Whose books are you? What have you inside?

—Daughters of Homer, learnèd in tales of Troy. One of us tells of Achilles' wrath and the deeds of Hector's hand and the trials of the ten years' war; the other, the labours of Odysseus and good Penelope's tears over her widowed bed.

—Be gracious, in the Muses' company; since your songs, the centuries have claimed to possess eleven sisters of Pieria.

XXXVII

A dolphin brings a drowned man to land and dies there

Beast lifting man, the sea-dweller the land-liver, the breathing the breath-bereft, I carried the sodden corpse on my back to the sands. And what good came of it? Having swum from sea to land I have death as the wages of my porterage. We exchanged destinies with each other: his land killed me, my waters killed him who came from the land.

---

1 τίνος Pl: -νες P   3 χειρός Pl: -ρῶν P   4 Ἑκτορέας Pl: -ρέαις P
| τ' Pl: om. P

XXXVII *A.P.* 9.222 [C] Ἀντιφίλου Βυζαντίου   εἰς δελφῖνα βαστάσαντα ἄνδρα ναυηγὸν καὶ διασώσαντα αὐτὸν ἕως τῆς χέρσου   Pl A Ἀντιφίλου
1 ἄπνοον ἔμπνους CPl: ἄπνοος ἔμπνουν P   3 εἰς ψαμ. P: ἐς ψαμ. Pl |
ἐκόμισσα Pl: -μισα P | τί Schaefer: τὸ PPl | ἐς γῆν P: εἰς γῆν Pl

XXXVIII

—πορφυρέαν τοι τάνδε, Λεωνίδα, ὤπασε χλαῖναν
Ξέρξης ταρβήσας ἔργα τεᾶς ἀρετᾶς.
—οὐ δέχομαι. προδόταις αὕτα χάρις. ἀσπὶς ἔχοι με
καὶ νέκυν. ὁ πλοῦτος δ᾽ οὐκ ἐμὸν ἐντάφιον.   1020
5 —ἀλλ᾽ ἔθανες· τί τοσόνδε καὶ ἐν νεκύεσσιν ἀπεχθής
Πέρσαις;—οὐ θνάισκει ζᾶλος ἐλευθερίας.

XXXIX

σκίπων με πρὸς νηὸν ἀνήγαγεν ὄντα βέβηλον
οὐ μοῦνον τελετῆς ἀλλὰ καὶ ἡελίου·
μύστην δ᾽ ἀμφοτέρων με θεαὶ θέσαν, οἶδα δ᾽ ἐκείνηι   1025
νυκτὶ καὶ ὀφθαλμῶν νύκτα καθηράμενος.
5 ἀσκίπων δ᾽ εἰς ἄστυ κατέστιχον ὄργια Δηοῦς
κηρύσσων γλώσσης ὄμμασι τρανότερον.

XL

ὑλοτόμοι, παύσασθε νεῶν χάριν· οὐκέτι πεύκη
κύματος ἀλλ᾽ ἤδη ῥινὸς ἐπιτροχάει·   1030
γομφὸς δ᾽ οὐκέτι χαλκὸς ἐν ὁλκάσιν οὐδὲ σίδηρος,
ἀλλὰ λίνωι τοίχων ἁρμονίη δέδεται·
5 τὰς δ᾽ αὐτὰς ποτὲ πόντος ἔχει νέας, ἄλλοτε γαῖα
πτυκτὸν ἁμαξίτην φόρτον ἀειρομένας.
Ἀργὼ μὲν προτέροισιν ἀοίδιμος, ἀλλὰ Σαβίνωι   1035
καινοτέρην πῆξαι Παλλὰς ἔνευσε τρόπιν.

XXXVIII A.P. 9.294 [C] Ἀντιφίλου Βυζαντίου εἰς τὸν αὐτὸν Λεωνίδην παρὰ
Ξέρξου πορφυρῆι χλανίδι σκεπαζόμενον καὶ μὴ δεχόμενον Pl A Ἀντιφίλου
1 Λεωνίδα Lascaris: -δη PPl   3 ἔχοι P: -ει Pl   6 ἐλευθερίας Pl: -ίης P
XXXIX A.P. 9.298 Ἀντιφίλου εἴς τινα τυφλόν, ὃς ἀνελθὼν εἰς τὸ ἐν Ἐλευσῖνι
ἱερὸν τῆς τελετῆς γινομένης ἀνέβλεψεν, ὁμοῦ δὲ μετεῖχε τῶν μυστηρίων [ad haec
C] οὕτως καὶ σὺ βλέψαις, υἱὲ τῶν ἐξανασκάφων, ὡς ὁ ἐν Ἐλευσῖνι τυφλός [pergit

ANTIPHILUS

XXXVIII

Xerxes and the corpse of Leonidas

—Xerxes has given you this purple cloak, Leonidas, in awe of your valorous deeds.

—I decline. That is the reward of traitors. Let my shield be my covering even in death. Wealth is no winding-sheet for me.

—You were killed; why so full of enmity to Persia even among the dead?

—The love of liberty is never killed.

XXXIX

A blind man sees

My staff brought me up to the temple, uninitiated not only in the ritual but in the sun's light too. The goddesses made me initiate in both, and I know that on that night I was purged also of the night upon my eyes. Staffless I went down to the city, proclaiming the mysteries of Demeter more clearly with my eyes than with my tongue.

XL

On boats made of hide

You may stop work, wood-cutters, for all ships care; it is now hide, no longer pine, that runs over the waves. Bolts are no longer of bronze or iron in ships; the sides' framework is stitched with flax. The same vehicles are carried by the sea as ships today, by land tomorrow, uplifted as a waggon's folded load. Argo was sung by men of old; now Pallas has granted Sabinus the fashioning of a newer kind of keel.

idem paulo infra] Ἀντιφίλου εἰς τυφλὸν ψεῦϲμα παράδοξον Pl A Ἀντιφίλου εἰς τυφλὸν ἀνελθόντα εἰς τὸ ἐν Ἐλευϲῖνι ἱερόν Drac. metr. 84.16 (1)
2 μοῦνον Pl: μόν- P   6 ὄμμαϲι τρανότερον P: ὄμματι τρανοτέρω Pl

XL A.P. 9.306 Ἀντιφίλου [C] εἰς μονόξυλα ἐκ δέρματοϲ κατεϲκευαϲμένα ὑπό τινοϲ Ϲαβίνου ϲτρατηγοῦ Pl A Ἀντιφίλου
1 ὑλοτόμοι Pl: -μου P   6 πτυκτὸν Jacobs: πυκ- PPl | ἁμαξίτην Pl: -ξείτην P | ἀειρομέναϲ CPl: ἀειραμ- P   8 καινοτέρην CPl: καινυτ- P

117

XLI

ψῆγμ᾽ ἄπυρον χρυσοῖο σιδηρείων ὑπ᾽ ὀδόντων
ῥινηθέν, Λιβυκῆς κουφότερον ψαμάθου,
μῦς ὀλίγος βαρὺ δεῖπνον ἐδαίσατο, πᾶσα δὲ νηδύς
συρομένη βραδύπουν θῆκε τὸν ὠκύτατον·   1040
5 ληφθεὶς δ᾽ ἐκ μεσάτης ἀνετέμνετο κλέμματα γαστρός.
ἧς ἄρα κἢν ἀλόγοις, χρυσέ, κακοῦ πρόφασις.

XLII

ἇ καλὸν αὐτοπόνητον ἐν αἰθέρι ῥεῦμα μελισσῶν,
κἄπλαστοι χειρῶν αὐτοπαγεῖς θαλάμαι,
προίκιος ἀνθρώπων βιότωι χάρις, οὐχὶ μακέλλας,   1045
οὐ βοός, οὐ γαμψῶν δευομένα δρεπάνων,
5 γαυλοῦ δὲ σμικροῖο, τόθι γλυκὺ νᾶμα μέλισσα
πηγάζει σκήνευς δαψιλὲς ἐξ ὀλίγου·
χαίροιτ᾽ εὐαγέες καὶ ἐν αἰθέρι ποιμαίνεσθε,
αἰθερίου πτηναὶ νέκταρος ἐργάτιδες.   1050

XLIII

ἤμην καὶ προπάροιθε συνέμπορος ἀνέρι κέρδους
ἡνίκα δημοτέρην Κύπριν ἐναυτολόγει·
κεῖθεν καὶ συνέπηξεν ἐμὴν τρόπιν, ὄφρα με λεύσσηι
Κύπρις τὴν ἀπὸ γῆς εἰν ἁλὶ ῥεμβομένην.
5 ἔστιν ἑταίρειος μὲν ἐμοὶ στόλος, εἰσὶ δὲ λευκά   1055
κάρπασα καὶ λεπτὸν φῦκος ὑπὲρ σανίδων·
ναυτίλοι, ἀλλ᾽ ἄγε πάντες ἐμῆς ἐπιβαίνετε πρύμνης
θαρραλέως· πολλοὺς οἶδα φέρειν ἐρέτας.

XLI A.P. 9.310 [C] 'Αντιφίλου Βυζαντίου   εἰς μῦν φαγόντα ῥίνημα χρυσοῦ καὶ
ὑπὸ βάρους κρατηθέντα καὶ ἀνατμηθέντα   Pl A τοῦ αὐτοῦ [sc. 'Αντιφίλου]
4 θῆκε Pl: ἔθ- P   5 δ᾽ Pl: om. P
XLII A.P. 9.404 'Αντιφίλου   εἰς σμῆνος μελισσῶν   Pl A 'Αντιφίλου
2 κἄπλαστοι Jacobs: αἱ πλασταὶ PPl   3 ἀνθρώπων Pl: -πωι P | μακέλλας
Pl: -αις P   5 γαυλοῦ Pl: γλαυκοῦ P   6 δαψιλὲς PᵞʳPl: δαψηλ- P
7 χαίροιτ᾽ P: -οισθ᾽ Pl | ποιμαίνεσθε P: -οισθε Pl

XLI

On the death of a mouse in a goldsmith's workshop

From unfired gold-dust, scraped by the file's iron teeth, lighter than Libyan sand, a little mouse ate a heavy dinner, and its whole belly dragged and made that swift runner slow of foot. So it was caught and had its thievings cut from mid-stomach. Thus even to brutes, Gold, you are the cause of evil.

XLII

In praise of bees

Beautiful honey-stream, self-made in the sky, and chambers un-fashioned by human hand, self-moulded, free gift to man's life, needing no spade or ox or crooked sickle but only a little pail, where the bee gushes a sweet stream in plenty from its tiny frame; hail, undefiled, go pasture on the flowers, wingèd makers of nectar in the sky.

XLIII

On a ship built from the profits of a brothel

In former days too I was my master's partner in his profitable trade, when the passengers he collected were public Cyprians; hence the keel he built me, that Aphrodite might see me, the land-born, sea-tossed. I have a light-lady's rig and dress of white canvas and dainty dye of sea-weed on my planks. Come, sailors all, take heart and mount my stern; I can take a host of oarsmen.

XLIII *A.P.* 9.415 Ἀντιφίλου [C] Βυζαντίου   [J] εἰς ναῦν [C] ἑταιρικὴν ἐν ᾗ πόρναι διεπέρων τὴν θάλασσαν τὴν κακὴν ἐμπορίαν μετερχόμεναι caret Pl
3 cυνέπηξεν C: -πιξ- J | λεύccηι Ap.B.: -ccει P   **5** ἑταίρειος μὲν Salm.: ἑταίριος
οι
ut vid. P^ac, ἑταίρειος P^pc, denuo post versus finem ἑταιρείοιος ἐμοὶ cτόλος scr. |
λευκά Jacobs: λεπτά P

XLIV

—κρηναῖαι λιβάδες, τί πεφεύγατε; ποῦ τόσον ὕδωρ;
τίς φλὸξ ἀενάους ἔσβεσεν ἠελίου;   1060
—δάκρυσιν Ἀγρικόλαο τετρύμεθα, πᾶν δ' ὅσον ἡμῖν
ἦν ποτὸν ἡ κείνου διψὰς ἔχει σποδιή.

XLV

ἡ πήρη καὶ χλαῖνα καὶ ὕδατι πιληθεῖσα
μᾶζα καὶ ἡ πρὸ ποδῶν ῥάβδος ἐρειδομένη
καὶ δέπας ἐκ κεράμοιο, σοφῶι κυνὶ μέτρα βίοιο   1065
ἄρκια· κἢν τούτοις ἦν τι περισσότερον.
5 κοίλαις γὰρ πόμα χερσὶν ἰδὼν ἀρύοντα βοώτην
εἶπε 'τί καὶ σὲ μάτην, ὄστρακον, ἠχθοφόρουν; '

XLVI

γηράσκει καὶ χαλκὸς ὑπὸ χρόνου, ἀλλὰ σὸν οὔτι
κῦδος ὁ πᾶς αἰών, Διόγενες, καθελεῖ,   1070
μοῦνος ἐπεὶ βιοτᾶς αὐτάρκεα δόξαν ἔδειξας
θνατοῖς καὶ ζωᾶς οἶμον ἐλαφροτάταν.

XLVII

ἡ γραῦς Εὐβούλη, ὅτε οἱ καταθύμιον ἦν τι,
Φοίβου τὸν πρὸ ποδῶν μάντιν ἄειρε λίθον.

XLIV *A.P.* 9.549 Ἀντιφίλου   Pl a Ἀντιφίλου   Pl b Ἀντιφίλου
2 ἠελίου PPl^Aac^Pl^B: ἀελ- Pl^Apc   3 Ἀγρικόλαο Reiske: -λαε PPl^A, -λα Pl^B |
τετρύμεθα Reiske: τετρύμμεθα P, τετύμμεθα Pl^A, τετρίμμεθα Pl^B
XLV *A.Pl.* (A) 333 Ἀντιφίλου Βυζαντίου   εἰς Διογένην   caret P
XLVI *A.Pl.* (A) 334 τοῦ αὐτοῦ [sc. Ἀντιφίλου]   εἰς τὸ αὐτό   Diog.L. 6.78
Suid. s.v. Φιλίσκος Αἰγινήτης   caret P

LI

On the vanity of concealing age with cosmetics

Though you smooth the ragged skin of your channelled cheeks and put coal-black on your lidless eyes and dye your white hair dark and hang round your temples curly fire-crisped ringlets, all that is useless; ridiculous too, whatever else you may do....

ANTISTIUS

I

A priest of the Great Mother puts a lion to flight

These garments and locks of hair the Gallus dedicated to the Mountain-Mother of the gods; and this adventure is the reason why.—A terrible lion met him walking solitary in the woods; a struggle for life was imminent, but the goddess put it in the Gallus' mind to beat his timbrel, and he turned the savage beast to flight in terror of the monstrous sound. That is why his locks of hair hang from the rustling branches.

II

On the death of three athletes

Fatal to you at sea, Menestratus, the outflow of Aoüs, and to you, Menander, the Carpathian's storm-wind, and to you, Dionysius, the Sicilian crossing. Alas, how great a grief to Hellas; for you were the best of all her athletes.

II *A.P.* 7.366 [C] ᾽Αντιϲτίου [J] εἰϲ Μενέϲτρατον καὶ Μένανδρον καὶ Διονύϲιον τοὺϲ ἀθλητάϲ caret Pl
2 πόροϲ Ϲικελόϲ C: πάροϲ Ϲικελικόϲ P   3 πόϲον Salm.: τόϲον P   4 κρέϲ- coναϲ P: κρείϲϲ- C | ἀθλοφόρων P: -φόρουϲ C

III

Εὐμένεος Κλεόδημος ἔτι βραχύς, ἀλλὰ χορεύει
σὺν παισὶν βαιῶι μικρὸς ἔτ᾽ ἐν θιάσωι·
ἠνίδε καὶ στικτοῖο δορὴν ἐζώσατο νεβροῦ   1115
καὶ σείει ξανθῆς κισσὸν ὑπὲρ κεφαλῆς.
5 ὦνα σύ μιν Καδμεῖε τίθει μέγαν, ὡς ἂν ὁ μύστης
ὁ βραχὺς ἡβητὰς αὖθις ἄγοι θιάσους.

IV

ἀγροφύλαξ ἕστηκα πολυκτεάνοις ἐν ἀρούραις
Φρίκωνος καλύβην καὶ φυτὰ ῥυόμενος,   1120
τοῦτο λέγων πρὸς ἕκαστον· ἐπὴν γελάσηις ἐσιδών με
τοῦ σκεύους, χώρει τὴν κατὰ σαυτὸν ὁδόν·
5 ἢν δὲ παρεκβήηις ἐς ἃ μὴ θέμις, οὔτι σ᾽ ὀνήσει
ἡ λάχνη· τρυπᾶν πάντας ἐπιστάμεθα.

ΑΠΟΛΛΩΝΙΔΟΥ

I

τρῖγλαν ἀπ᾽ ἀνθρακιῆς καὶ φυκίδα σοί, λιμενῖτι   1125
Ἄρτεμι, δωρεῦμαι Μῆνις ὁ δικτυβόλος
καὶ ζωρὸν κεράσας ἰσοχειλέα καὶ τρύφος ἄρτου
αὖον ἐπιθραύσας, τὴν πενιχροῦ θυσίην·
5 ἀνθ᾽ ἧς μοι πλησθέντα δίδου θηράμασιν αἰέν
δίκτυα· σοὶ δέδοται πάντα, μάκαιρα, λίνα.   1130

III A.P. 11.40 Ἀντιστίου caret Pl
3 ἐζώσατο Dorville: ἐξώ- P   5 Καδμεῖε Dorville: Κάδμε P   6 ἄγοι
Dorville: ἄγει P
IV A.Pl. (A) 243 Ἀντιστίου   εἰς τὸν αὐτόν   caret P
3 πρὸς Brunck: παρ᾽ Pl   5 παρεκβήηις Hermann: -βαίης Pl

III

On a child dancing

Eumenes' son Cleodemus is still a little one, but small as he is
he dances with the boys in a band of tiny worshippers. See,
he has dressed himself in a dappled fawn's skin and shakes ivy
over his golden head. Cadmean King, make him big, so that
your little devotee may hereafter lead bands of young men.

IV

Priapus threatens the trespasser

Farm-guardian I stand in wealthy fields, protecting the hut and
plants of Phricon, and this I say to one and all: 'When you have
had your laugh at the sight of my equipment, go your own
road; but if you trespass to forbidden ground, shaggy hair will
be no help to you. We are capable of drilling anyone.'

APOLLONIDES

I

A fisherman's offerings to Artemis

I, Menis the net-caster, give a red mullet from the embers
and a wrasse to you, Artemis of the Harbour, and wine that I
have mixed brim-level, and a dry piece of bread that I have
broken, the poor man's sacrifice. In return for this give me
meshes ever filled with prey; given to you, Goddess, are all
our nets.

I A.P. 6.105 Ἀπολλωνί⟨δ⟩ου ἀνάθημα τῆι Ἀρτέμιδι παρὰ Μήνιδος ἁλιέως
Pl A Ἀπολλωνίδου Suid. s.vv. τριγλίς (1–2), φυκίδα (1–2), ἀνθρακιά (1–2 δωρ.),
ζωρότερον (3 καὶ 3.–ἴσοχ.), αὖον (3 καὶ τρ.–4)
1 λιμενῖτι Jacobs: -νῖτιν Pl, -νῆτιν PSuid.   2 Μῆνις PPl: Θῆρις Suid. bis
4 πενιχροῦ Page: -χρὴν PPlSuid.   6 πάντα μάκαιρα CPl: παμμάκαιρα P

II

Εὔφρων οὐ πεδίου πολυαύλακός εἰμ' ὁ γεραιός
οὐδὲ πολυγλεύκου γειομόρος βότρυος,
ἀλλ' ἀρότρωι βραχύβωλον ἐπικνίζοντι χαράσσω
χέρσον καὶ βαιοῦ πίδακα ῥωγὸς ἔχω.
5 εἴη δ' ἐξ ὀλίγων ὀλίγη χάρις· εἰ δὲ διδοίης   1135
πλείονα, καὶ πολλῶν, δαῖμον, ἀπαρξόμεθα.

III

ӡμήνεος ἔκ με ταμὼν γλυκερὸν θέρος †ἀμφινομέων†
γηραιὸς Κλείτων σπεῖσε μελισσοπόνος
ἀμβροσίων ἔαρος κηρῶν μέλι πολλὸν ἀμέλξας,
δῶρον ἀποιμάντου τηλοπέτευς ἀγέλης.   1140
5 θείης ἑςμοτόκον χορὸν ἄπλετον, εὖ δὲ μελιχροῦ
νέκταρος ἐμπλήςαις κηροπαγεῖς θαλάμας.

IV

ἠλλάχθη θανάτοιο τεὸς μόρος, ἀντὶ δὲ ςεῖο,
δέςποτα, δοῦλος ἐγὼ στυγνὸν ἔπληςα τάφον·
ἡνίκα ςευ δακρυτὰ κατὰ χθονὸς ἠρία τεῦχον,   1145
ὡς ἂν ἀποφθιμένου κεῖθι δέμας κτερίςω,
5 ἀμφὶς ἔμ' ὤλιςθεν γυρὴ κόνις. οὐ βαρὺς ἡμῖν
ἔςτ' Ἀίδης· ӡήςω τὸν ςὸν ὑπ' ἠέλιον.

II *A.P.* 6.238 Ἀπολλωνίδου   Suid. s.vv. πολυαύλακος (1 οὐ–γερ.), πολυγλεύκου
(2), κνίӡων (3), ἀπάρχεσθαι (5–6)   caret Pl
3 χαράσσω P: -ων Suid.   4 πίδακα Ap.G.: πήδ- P | ῥωγὸς P: ῥαγ- C
5 εἴη Hecker: εἰμὶ P, εἰ μὴ Suid.

III *A.P.* 6.239 τοῦ αὐτοῦ [sc. Ἀπολλωνίδου]   Suid. s.vv. cμήνη (1–2), τηλοπέτευς (3–4), θεcμοτόκον (5 θείης–ἄπλ.), θαλάμη (5 ἔκ δὲ μελ.–6)   caret Pl
1 ӡμήνεος requirit litterarum primarum ordo: cμή- PSuid. | ἀμφινομέων Pac

II

Dedication by a poor farmer

I, Euphron, in old age, am farmer of no many-furrowed field
or juicy grape-clusters. Small is the plot of land I scratch with
scraping ploughshare, and scant the grape whose fount is mine.
From small possessions let there be a small return of favour; if
you give more, then likewise many, Goddess, the first-fruits
we shall offer.

III

A bee-keeper's offerings

Old Cliton the bee-keeper cut me, harvest of sweetness, from
the hive ⟨   ⟩ and made libation, pressing abundant honey
from the ambrosial combs of Spring, a gift from his unshep-
herded far-flying flock. So make his swarm-bearing choir
innumerable, and full with sweet nectar fill the wax-built cells.

IV

Death of a slave while digging his master's grave

Transferred was your doom of death, and in your stead,
Master, I your slave filled the hateful tomb. When I was
building your grievous sepulchre underground, that I might
bury your body there after death, the domed earth slid about
me. No burden is Hades to me, for I shall live on in the light
of your sun.

-μαίων PᵖᶜC: ἀντινομένων et ἀντινομαίων Suid.   5 ἐϲμοτόκον Salm.: θεϲμο-
PSuid. | εὖ P: ἐκ Suid.

IV *A.P.* 7.180 [C] ᾿Απολλωνίδου   [J] εἰϲ ἕτερον δοῦλον ἀντὶ τοῦ δεϲπότου
τελευτήϲαντα   Pl в ᾿Απολλωνίδου   εἰϲ δοῦλον   Suid. s.v. ἠρία (3–4)
1 θανάτοιο Pl: -του P   3 ϲευ Pl: ϲου P, ϲοι C | δακρυτὰ PPl: δυϲδάκρυτα
(om. ϲευ vel ϲου) Suid. | τεύχων Suid.   5 ἀμφὶϲ Paton: ἀμφὶ δ᾿ PPl | ὤλιϲθεν
γυρὴ P: -θε ξυνὴ Pl

V

ἔφθανεν Ἡλιόδωρος, ἐφέσπετο δ' οὐδ' ὅσον ὥρηι
ὕστερον ἀνδρὶ φίλωι Διογένεια δάμαρ·   1150
ἄμφω δ' ὡς ἅμ' ἔναιον ὑπὸ πλακὶ τυμβεύονται
ξυνὸν ἀγαλλόμενοι καὶ τάφον ὡς θάλαμον.

VI

καὶ τίς ὃς οὐκ ἔτλη κακὸν ἔσχατον υἱέα κλαύσας;
ἀλλ' ὁ Ποσειδίππου πάντας ἔθαψε δόμος,
τέσσαρας, οὓς Ἀίδαο συνήριθμον ἥρπασεν ἦμαρ   1155
τὴν πολλὴν παίδων ἐλπίδα κειραμένου.
5 πατρὸς δ' ὄμματα λυγρὰ κατομβρηθέντα γόοισιν
ὤλετο· κοινή που νὺξ μία πάντας ἔχει.

VII

ἦν ἄρα Μιλήτου Φοιβήιον ὅρμον ἵκησθε,
λέξατε Διογένει πένθιμον ἀγγελίην,   1160
παῖς ὅτι οἱ ναυηγὸς ὑπὸ χθονὶ κεύθεται Ἄνδρου
Δίφιλος Αἰγαίου κῦμα πιὼν πελάγευς.

VIII

Σύρου καὶ Δήλοιο κλύδων μέσος υἷα Μενοίτην
σὺν φόρτωι Σαμίου κρύψε Διαφάνεος
εἰς ὅσιον σπεύδοντα πλόου τάχος. ἀλλὰ θάλασσα 1165
ἐχθρὴ καὶ νούσωι πατρὸς ἐπειγομένοις.

V *A.P.* 7.378 [C] Ἀπολλωνίδου   [J] εἰς Ἡλιόδωρον καὶ Διογένειαν τὴν αὐτοῦ
γαμετήν   Pl A et B, utroque loco Ἀπολλωνίδου
1 ἔφθανεν PPl^B: κάτθανεν Pl^A   3 ἅμ' ἔναιον Tyrwhitt: ὑμέναιον PPl^{AB} | ὑπὸ
Jacobs: ἐπὶ PPl^{AB} | τυμβεύονται PPl^B: -το Pl^A   4 θάλαμον CPl^{AB}: θάνατον P
VI *A.P.* 7.389 [C] Ἀπολλωνίδου   [J] εἰς τοὺς τέσσαρας υἱοὺς Ποσιδίππου ἐν
μιᾶι ἡμέραι τελευτήσαντας   Pl B Ἀπολλωνίδου
2 Ποσειδίππου CPl: Ποσιδ- P | δόμος CPl: δέμας (?) P   4 κειραμένου PPl:
-νον C   5 πατρὸς CPl: -ρὶς (?) P

V

Husband and wife die and are buried together

Heliodorus went first, his wife Diogeneia followed her dear husband not an hour later. Both, as they dwelt together, are buried beneath the stone, happy to share the tomb also, even as the bed-chamber.

VI

On a man who lost four sons and became blind

Who that has wept for a son has not endured the worst of evils? The house of Posidippus buried all he had, four of them, seized by an equal number of days of death that cut short his great hopes in his children. Their father's mournful eyes, flooded with lamentations, lost their light; one might say, a single common darkness holds them all.

VII

On Diphilus, drowned and buried far from home

If you come to Apollo's harbour of Miletus, tell Diogenes this mournful message: that his son Diphilus, shipwrecked, is hidden beneath the earth of Andros, having drunk the waves of the Aegean sea.

VIII

On Menoites, lost at sea

The waves midway between Syros and Delos buried Menoites, son of Samian Diaphanes, together with his freight. Pious was the haste of the voyage he was running, but the sea is no friend even to those who hurry for a father's sickness.

VII *A.P.* 7.631 [C] Ἀπολλωνίδου   [J] εἰς Δίφιλον υἱὸν Διογένους ναυαγὸν τὸν Μιλήσιον   Pl a Ἀπολλωνίδου
1 ὅρμον Pl: om. P   4 πελάγευς P: -γους Pl

VIII *A.P.* 7.642 [C] Ἀπολλωνίδου   [J] εἰς Μενοίτην τὸν Cάμιον ναυηγὸν υἱὸν Διοφάνους   caret Pl
1 Cύρου Reiske: εββρου P | υἶα C: οἶα P

IX

Γλῆνιν παρηιονῖτις ἀμπέχω χερμάς
πικρῆι κατασπασθέντα κύματος δίνηι
ὅτ᾽ ἰχθυάзετ᾽ ἐξ ἄκρης ἀπορρῶγος.
χῶσαν δέ μ᾽ ὅσσος λαὸς ἦν συνεργήτης,   1170
5   Πόσειδον, οὕς σὺ σῶιзε καὶ γαληναίην
    αἰὲν διδοίης ὁρμιηβόλοις θῖνα.

X

καὶ πότε δινήεις ἄφοβος πόρος, εἰπὲ θάλασσα,
εἰ καὶ ἐν ἀλκυόνων ἤμασι κλαυσόμεθα,
ἀλκυόνων, αἶς πόντος ἀεὶ στηρίξατο κῦμα   1175
νήνεμον, ὡς κρῖναι χέρσον ἀπιστοτέρην;
5 ἀλλὰ καὶ ἡνίκα μαῖα καὶ ὠδίνεσσιν ἀπήμων
   αὐχεῖς, σὺν φόρτωι δῦσας ᾽Αριστομένην.

XI

'πρὸς παίδων' εἶπεν 'γουνάзομαι, ἤν με θανοῦσαν
στείληις, μὴ σπεῖσαι δεύτερα φίλτρα γάμου.'   1180
εἶπεν, ὁ δ᾽ εἰς ἑτέρην ἐσπούδασεν· ἀλλὰ Φίλιννα
Διογένην λήθης τίσατο καὶ φθιμένη.
5 νυκτὶ γὰρ ἐν πρώτηι θάλαμον σχάσε μῆνις ἄφυκτος,
   ὡς μὴ λέκτρον ἰδεῖν δεύτερον ἠέλιον.

IX A.P. 7.693 [C] ᾽Απολλωνίδου   [J] ἰαμβικόν· εἰς ναυαγόν τινα Γλῆνιν εἰς
                                                               ω
παρηον [sic] τεθαμμένον   caret Pl
2 πικρῆι Ap.B.: -ῆ P   4 ὅσσος C: -οι P   6 ὁρμιηβόλοις C: ὁρμιὴν βόλοις P
X A.P. 9.271 [C] ᾽Απολλωνίδου   εἰς τὴν ἐν Βοσπόρωι θάλασσαν ὅτι ἐν αὐταῖς
ταῖς καλουμέναις ᾽Αλκυονίδες [sic] ἡμέραις ᾽Αριστομένην κατεπόντωσεν   Pl A
᾽Απολλωνίδου

IX

On Glenis, drowned while fishing

A heap of stones by the beach, I cover Glenis, who was dragged down by a wave's cruel eddy while fishing from a steep rock-top. They made a mound of me, all the folk who worked with him. So keep them safe, Poseidon, and ever grant the line-casters a stormless shore.

X

On Aristomenes, drowned during the halcyon days

And when is the passage of your whirling waters not to be feared, tell me, Sea, if we must have mourning even on the days of the halcyons,—the halcyons, for whom the ocean has always fixed its wave in windless calm, so that they judge the dry land the more treacherous? At the time when you boast yourself a midwife painless to their labour, you have sunk Aristomenes together with his freight.

XI

Philinna's revenge

'In our children's name I implore you', she said, 'if you lay me out in death, not to solemnise the charms of marriage a second time.' So she spoke, but he hastened to another wife. Yet even in death Philinna took vengeance on Diogenes for not remembering her: on the first night her inescapable wrath split the bridal-room asunder, so that no second sun should behold his bed.

---

1 δινήεις ἄφοβος PPl: sup. -ηεις ἄφοβος scr. θεῖσα Βόσπορος C   2 ἐν Pl: om. P
5 μαῖα Muncker: γαῖα PPl

XI *A.P.* 9.422 [J] Ἀπολλωνίδου   [C] παρὰ γυναικὸς Φιλίννης πρὸς τὸν ἄνδρα Διογένην   Pl A Ἀπολλωνίδου
2 σπεῖσαι P: -σαις Pl   3 ἑτέρην Pl: ἑταίρην P   4 Διογένην P: -νη Pl

XII

ἰχθυοθηρητῆρα Μενέστρατον ὤλεσεν ἄγρη   1185
  δούνακος ἐξαμίτης ἐκ τριχὸς ἑλκομένη
εἶδαρ ὅτ᾽ ἀγκίστρου φονίου πλάνον ἀμφιχανοῦσα
ὀξείην ἐρυθρὴ φυκὶς ἔβρυξε πάγην·
5 ἀγνυμένη δ᾽ ὑπ᾽ ὀδόντι κατέκτανεν ἅλματι λάβρωι
  ἐντὸς ὀλισθηρῶν δυσαμένη φαρύγων.   1190

XIII

οὐκέτι, Τιμόκλεια, τεῶν φάος ὤλεσας ὄσσων   (1191)
  κούρους διοτόκωι νηδύι γειναμένη,
ὄμμασι δ᾽ ἐν πλεόνεσσιν ἀθρεῖς πυριθαλπὲς ὄχημα
ἠελίου, προτέρης οὖσα τελειοτέρη.

XIV

ἀγγελίης ἤκουσεν ἀνωίστου Μελίτεια,   1195
  υἱέα σὺν φόρτωι κύμασι κρυπτόμενον·
ἠϊόσιν δ᾽ ἐπικέλσαν ἁλίκλυστον δέμας ἄλλου
δύσμορος οἰκείης σύμβολον εἶδε τύχης,
5 υἱέα δ᾽ ὡς ἔστειλε. Δίων δ᾽ ἐπὶ νηὸς ἀθραύστου
  ἤλυθεν εὐκταίης σῶος ἀπ᾽ ἐμπορίης.   1200
μητέρες ὡς ἀνίσου μοίρης λάχον· ἡ μὲν ἄελπτον
  ζωὸν ἔχει, κείνη δ᾽ ὄψεται οὐδὲ νέκυν.

XII *A.P.* 7.702 [C] Ἀπολλωνίδου   [J] εἰς Μενέστρατον ἁλιέα ἀποπνιγέντα ὑπὸ φυκίδος   Pl β Ἀπολλωνίδου
1 ἰχθυοθηρητῆρα CPl: -τειρα P   2 ἐξαμίτης J. G. Schneider: ἐξαμῆς PPl
3 φονίου Meineke: -ιον PPl   4 ἐρυθρὴ Pl: -ὴν P | ἔβρυξε Meineke: ἔφριξε PPl   5 ἀγνυμένη Pl: ἀγρυμ- P | ὑπ᾽ ὀδόντι P: ὑποδύντα Pl
XIII *A.P.* 7.742 Ἀπολλωνίδου   [J] εἰς Τιμόκλειαν διδυμοτόκον   caret Pl

XII

On a fisherman killed by swallowing his catch

His rod's prey, drawn up by the six strands of hair, killed Mene-stratus the fisherman when the red wrasse, gaping round the murderous hook's wandering bait, swallowed the piercing snare. While he was cracking it in his teeth, it took a violent leap, dived inside his slippery throat, and killed him.

XIII

A blind woman bears twins

No longer, Timocleia, have you lost the light of your eyes, being mother of sons from twin-bearing womb, but with eyes more numerous you look upon the sun's blazing chariot, being more perfect than your former self.

XIV

A mother buries a body mistaken for her son,
who returns safely

Meliteia heard the unlooked-for tidings that her son was sunk beneath the waves together with his freight. Poor woman, she saw a token of her own misfortune in the sea-beaten body of another man driven ashore, and gave it funeral-rites as if it had been her son. But Dion returned safely, on a vessel undamaged, from trading to his heart's desire. So unequal was the mothers' share in destiny: the one holds her son living beyond hope, the other shall not even see the corpse of hers.

1 τεῶν Salm.: τεὸν P   **2** δοιοτόκωι Salm.: δυοτ- P   **3** ἀθρεῖς Salm.: -ροῖς P | πυριθαλπὲς Salm.: περιθ- P

XIV *A.P.* 9.228 [C] ᾽Απολλωνίδου   εἰς Μελίτειάν τινα γυναῖκα τὸν ἴδιον υἱὸν ἀκούσασαν ναυαγῆσαι καὶ ξένου τινὸς ὡς τὸ ἐκείνου σῶμα θάψασαν · εἶτα ἐπανῆλθε καὶ ὁ υἱὸς αὐτῆς   Pl a ᾽Απολλωνίδου
1 Μελίτεια P: Μελίτινα Pl   **6** εὐκταίης Jacobs: ἐκ γαίης PPl

XV

γήθησαν περὶ παιδὸς Ἀριστίπποιο τοκῆες
καὶ κλαῦσαν· μοίρης δ' ἦμαρ ἐν ἀμφοτέρης.
εὖτε γὰρ αἰθόμενον δόμον ἔκφυγεν, ἰθὺ κεραυνοῦ   1205
Ζεὺς κατά οἱ κεφαλῆς ἄσπετον ἧκε σέλας.
5 τοῦτο δ' ἔπος τότ' ἔλεξαν ὅσοι νέκυν ὠδύροντο·
'ὦ πυρὶ δαιμονίωι τλῆμον ὀφειλόμενε'.

XVI

δειματόεις ἐλάφων κεραὸς λόχος, εὖτε κρυώδεις
πλῆσαν ὀρῶν κορυφὰς χιόνεαι νιφάδες,   1210
δείλαιαι ποταμοῖσιν ἐφώρμισαν ἐλπίδι φροῦδοι
χλιῆναι νοτεροῖς ἄσθμασιν ὠκὺ γόνυ,
5 τὰς δὲ περιφράξας ἐχθρὸς ῥόος ἁθρόον ἄφνω
χειμερίηι στυγεροῦ δῆσε πάγοιο πέδηι,
πληθὺς δ' ἀγροτέρων ἀλίνου θοινήσατο θήρης,   1215
ἢ φύγεν ἁρπεδόνην πολλάκι καὶ στάλικα.

XVII

ἡ Καθαρή, Νύμφαι γὰρ ἐπώνυμον ἔξοχον ἄλλων
κρήνηι πασάων δῶκαν ἐμοὶ λιβάδων,
λῃϊστὴς ὅτε μοι παρακλίντορας ἔκτανεν ἄνδρας
καὶ φονίην ἱεροῖς ὕδασι λοῦσε χέρα,   1220
5 κεῖνον ἀναστρέψασα γλυκὺν ῥόον οὐκέθ' ὁδίταις
βλύζω· τίς γὰρ ἐρεῖ τὴν Καθαρὴν ἔτ' ἐμέ;

XV A.P. 9.243 [C] Ἀπολλωνίδου   εἰς Ἀρίστιππον ἐκ πυρὸς σωθέντα καὶ ὑπὸ
κεραυνοῦ ἐν αὐτῆι τῆι ἡμέραι ἀπαλλάξαντα   Pl a Ἀπολλωνίδου
XVI A.P. 9.244 [C] τοῦ αὐτοῦ [sc. Ἀπολλωνίδου]   εἰς ἐλάφους ἐν ποταμῶι
κρυσταλλωθέντι πεδηθείσας καὶ ὑπὸ κυνηγετῶν ἐν αὐτῶι ἀγρευθείσας   Pl a
Ἀπολλωνίδου

XV

The death of Aristippus

His parents both rejoiced and wept for their son Aristippus; the
day of both destinies was one and the same. For when he had
escaped from the burning house, straightway Zeus sent down
upon his head a thunderbolt's indescribable flame. These words
then spoke as many as bewailed him dead: 'Unhappy, fore-
doomed to fire from heaven!'

XVI

On a herd of deer caught in a frozen river

A frightened troop of horned deer, when snow-clouds had filled
the frosty hill-tops, found haven in the river, poor creatures,
setting off in hope to warm their swift limbs in its moist ex-
halations. The unfriendly stream imprisoned them suddenly all
together, and bound them in the wintry fetters of hateful ice.
So a crowd of rustics feasted on a catch without nets, that had
often escaped their cords and stakes.

XVII

On a fountain polluted by blood

I, the Undefiled (for the Nymphs gave my spring that name
above all other fountains), when a brigand had murdered men
who reclined beside me, and washed his bloody hand in my
holy waters,—I turned back that sweet stream, and gush no
more for wayfarers. For who will still call me the Undefiled?

3 ἐφώρμισαν (ex ἐφώρμης- corr.) Pl: ἐφόρμ- P | ἐλπίδι φροῦδοι P: ἐλπίϲι
χρηϲταῖϲ Pl   4 ἄϲθμαϲιν Pl: ἄθμ- P | ὠκὺ γόνυ Pl: ὠκυγόνου P   6 χει-
μερίηι Pl: -ίηϲ P   8 ϲτάλικα P: -καϲ Pl

XVII *A.P.* 9.257 [C] Ἀπολλωνίδου   εἰϲ πηγὴν ὀνομαζομένην Καθαρήν   Pl A
Ἀπολλωνίδου
1 ἡ P: ἦν Pl   3 παρακλίντοραϲ Pl: -ροϲ P   6 ἔτ' ἐμέ Bothe: ἔτι με PPl

XVIII

θάμνου ποτ᾽ ἄκρους ἀμφὶ κλῶνας ἥμενος
τέττιξ, πτερῶι φλέγοντος ἡλίου μέσον
νηδὺν ῥαπίζων, δαίδαλ᾽ αὐτουργῶν μέλη,   1225
ἡδὺς κατωργάνιζε τῆς ἐρημίας.
5   Κρίτων δ᾽, ὁ πάσης ἰξοεργὸς Πιαλεύς
θήρης, ἀσάρκου νῶτα δουνακεύσατο.
τίσιν δ᾽ ἔτισεν· εἰς γὰρ ἠθάδας πάγας
σφαλεὶς ἀλᾶται παντὸς ἱμείρων πτεροῦ.   1230

XIX

ἰοτυπὴς Διὸς ὄρνις ἐτίσατο Κρῆτα φαρέτρης
οὐρανόθεν τόξωι τόξον ἀμυνόμενος·
κεῖνον δ᾽ εὐθὺς ἄκοντι παλινδρομέοντι κατέκτα
ἠερόθεν, πίπτων δ᾽ ἔκτανεν ὡς ἔθανεν.
5   μηκέτ᾽ ἐφ᾽ ὑμετέροις ἀψευδέσι Κρῆτες ὀιστοῖς   1235
αὐχεῖθ᾽· ὑμνείσθω καὶ Διὸς εὐστοχίη.

XX

Αἴλιος Αὐσονίης στρατιῆς πρόμος, ὁ χρυσέοισι
στέμμασι σωρεύσας αὐχένας ὁπλοφόρους,
νοῦσον ὅτ᾽ εἰς ὑπάτην ὠλίσθανε τέρμα τ᾽ ἄφυκτον
εἶδεν ἀριστείην †ἐμφανὲς† εἰς ἰδίην,   1240
5   πῆξε δ᾽ ὑπὸ σπλάγχνοισιν ἑὸν ξίφος, εἶπέ τε θνῄσκων·
'αὐτὸς ἑκὼν ἐδάμην, μὴ νόσος εὖχος ἔχηι'.

XVIII *A.P.* 9.264 [C] Ἀπολλωνίδου, οἱ δὲ Φιλίππου   εἰς τέττιγα ἰξευθέντα παρὰ Κρίτωνος ἰξευτοῦ   caret Pl
1 κλῶνας Salm.: πρῶνας P   3 ῥαπίζων Reiske: ῥανίζ- P | δαίδαλ᾽ Reiske: δαίδαλον P | αὐτουργῶν μέλη Page: -γῶ μέλει P   5 δ᾽ C: om. P

XIX *A.P.* 9.265 [C] τοῦ αὐτοῦ [sc. Ἀπολλωνίδου, οἱ δὲ Φιλίππου]   εἰς ἀετὸν τοξευθέντα ὑπὸ Κρητὸς καὶ τὸν τοξεύσαντα ἐν τῶι πίπτειν ἀποκτείναντα Pl A   τοῦ αὐτοῦ [sc. Ἀπολλωνίδου]

XVIII

The penalty for killing a cicada

The cicada would sit on the bough-tips of a thicket, beating
on its belly with its wing while the sun blazed in mid-course,
inspired creator of varied song, making sweet music through
the loneliness; but Criton of Piala, limer of all kinds of prey,
caught by his reed the fleshless creature's back. He paid the
penalty: baffled, he goes roving to his customary snares, longing
in vain for any kind of feathered prey.

XIX

The archer killed by his victim

Arrow-struck, the bird of Zeus took vengeance on the Cretan
for his quiver, requiting archery with archery from the sky.
Straightway from the air it slew him with returning shaft, and,
falling, killed him even as it had been killed. Cretans, no longer
boast of your unerring arrows; let the true aim of Zeus also be
sung.

XX

Aelius prefers suicide to death by disease

Aelius, leader of the Ausonian army, he whose armoured
shoulders were laden with golden torques, when he slipped
down to his last illness and saw the end inescapable, ⟨   ⟩
drove his own sword into his heart and, dying, spoke: 'I am
vanquished of my own free will, that disease may not have the
glory.'

1 ἰοτυπὴς Pl: -πεὶς P   3 κεῖνον Pl: ξένον P | παλινδρομέοντι κατέκτα Pl:
παλιν, ceteris spatio vacuo relicto omissis, P   4 ἠερόθεν Pl: ἠερίον P
6 αὐχεῖθ' Pl: -εῖςθ' P

XX A.P. 7.233 [C] Ἀπολλωνίδου   [J] εἰς Αἴλιον Ῥωμαῖον στρατιώτην [C]
ἑαυτὸν ἀναιρήσαντα   Pl A Ἀπολλωνίδου   Suid. s.v. ὑπάτη (3–5 ξίφ.)
2 cωρεύcαc CPl: τω- P   3 νοῦcον CPlSuid.: νεῦc- P   5 θνήcκων Pl:
θνά- P   6 ἔχηι P: -οι Pl

XXI

Λαίλιος, Αὐσονίων ὕπατον κλέος, εἶπεν ἀθρήσας
Εὐρώταν· 'Cπάρτης χαῖρε φέριστον ὕδωρ'.
Μουσάων δ' ἐπὶ χεῖρα βαλὼν πολυίστορι βίβλωι   1245
εἶδεν ὑπὲρ κορυφῆς cύμβολον εὐμαθίης·
5 κίτται, μιμηλὸν βιότου πτερόν, ἐν cκιεροῖσιν
ἄγκεσι παμφώνων μέλπον ἀπὸ cτομάτων.
ὡρμήθη δ' ὑπὸ ταῖcι. τί δ' οὐ ʒηλωτὸς ὁ μόχθος,
εἰ καὶ πτηνὰ ποθεῖ ⟨   ⟩;   1250

XXII

ξυνὸν ὁπηνίκα θαῦμα κατείδομεν 'Acìc ἅπαcα,   (1251)
πῶλον ἐπ' ἀνδρομέαν cάρκα φριμαccόμενον,
Θρηϊκίης φάτνης πολιὸς λόγος εἰς ἐμὸν ὄμμα
ἤλυθε· δίʒημαι δεύτερον 'Ηρακλέα.

XXIII

ὁ πρὶν ἐγὼ 'Ροδίοισιν ἀνέμβατος ἱερὸς ὄρνις,   1255
ὁ πρὶν Κερκαφίδαις αἰετὸς ἱστορίη,
ὑψιπετῆ τότε ταρcὸν ἀνὰ πλατὺν ἠέρ' ἀερθείς
ἤλυθον, 'Ηελίου νῆcον ὅτ' εἶχε Νέρων,
5 κείνου δ' αὐλίcθην ἐνὶ δώμαcι χειρὶ cυνήθης
κράντοροc, οὐ φεύγων Ζῆνα τὸν ἐccόμενον.   1260

XXI A.P. 9.280 [C] 'Απολλωνίδου   εἰς Λαίλιον ὕπατον 'Ρωμαῖον   ʒτ τὴν ἔννοιαν
τῆς γραφῆς idem ad v. 5 ʒτ τὴν τοῦ γράμματος ἔννοιαν   Pl A 'Απολλωνίδου
1 Λαίλιος PPl: Λάλλιος C | ὕπατον PPl: -των C   2 Εὐρώταν CPl: -τα P
3 πολυίcτορι CPl: -ίcτορ** P   5 κίτται Salm.: κιττè P, κίτταc Pl   7 ὑπὸ
Page: ἐπὶ PPl   8 post ποθεῖ deficit P, γάρυος ὑμετέρης scr. Pl

XXI

Laelius and the jays

Laelius, consular glory of the Ausonians, looked upon the Eurotas and cried, 'Hail, waters of Sparta unsurpassable'. So having set his hand to the Muses' book of all wisdom, he saw overhead a token of quick learning,—jays, the feathered mimics of our life, sang in the shady glens from throats of every tone. By them he was encouraged; for how should the labour not be enviable, if even birds desire ⟨to repeat man's poetry⟩?

XXII

On a man-eating horse

When we, the whole of Asia, witnessed the portent in common, —a colt loud-neighing for human flesh,—the ancient tale of the Thracian stable came before my eyes; I look for a second Heracles.

XXIII

On the first appearance of an eagle at Rhodes

The holy bird, in former days no visitant of Rhodians,—the eagle, in former days a mere fable to the sons of Cercaphus,— just then I arrived, borne aloft on high-flying wings through the broad sky, when Nero held the island of the Sun. And in his house I lodged, tame to the ruler's hand, not shrinking from the future Zeus.

XXII *A.P.* 9.281 [C] τοῦ αὐτοῦ [sc. ᾿Απολλωνίδου] εἰς πῶλον σάρκας ἀνθρω-
πείας σιτιζόμενον Pl a ᾿Απολλωνίδου
1 ξυνὸν P: ξεῖνον Pl   **2** ἐπ' Pl: ὑπ' P | φριμασσόμενον C: φρισσόμ- P,
φρυασσόμ- Pl   **3** πολιὸς PPl: παλεὸς C

XXIII *A.P.* 9.287 ᾿Απολλωνίδου [C] εἰς ἀετὸν ἐν ῾Ρόδωι παραγινόμενον ὅτε καὶ
Νέρων ἤκμαζεν Pl a ᾿Απολλωνίδου
3 ἀερθείς CPl: -θης P

XXIV

Cκύλλος, ὅτε Ξέρξου δολιχὸς ϲτόλος Ἑλλάδα πᾶϲαν
ἤλαυνεν, βυθίην εὕρετο ναυμαχίην
Νηρῆος λαθρίοιϲιν ὑποπλεύϲαϲ τενάγεϲϲι
καὶ τὸν ἀπ' ἀγκύρης ὅρμον ἔκειρε νεῶν·
5 αὔτανδρος δ' ἐπὶ γῆν ὠλίϲθανε Περϲὶς ἄναυδος   1265
ὀλλυμένη, πρώτη πεῖρα Θεμιϲτοκλέουϲ.

XXV

μητρὶ περιϲτεφέος ϲηκοῦ, Κυθέρεια, θαλάϲϲηι
κρηπῖδας βυθίας οἴδματι πηξαμένη,
χαῖρ', ἔτι δ' ἀμφί ϲε πόντος ἐπὶ Ζεφύροιο πνοῆιϲιν
ἁβρὸν ὑπὲρ νώτου κυανέου γελάϲαι·   1270
5 εἵνεκα δ' εὐϲεβίης νηοῦ θ' ὃν ἐγείρατο ϲεῖο
Πόϲτουμος αὐχήϲει μέζον †αφλουϲι† Πάφου.

XXVI

ἡδὺ παρειάων πρῶτον θέρος ἤματι τούτωι
κείρεο καὶ γενύων ἠϊθέους ἕλικας,
Γάιε, ϲὸν δὲ πατὴρ χερὶ δέξεται εὐκτὸν ἴουλον
Λεύκιος αὐξομένου πουλὺν ἐς ἠέλιον.   1275
5 δωρεῦνται χρυϲέοιϲιν, ἐγὼ δ' ἱλαροῖς ἐλέγοιϲιν·
οὐ γὰρ δὴ πλούτου Μοῦϲα χερειοτέρη.

XXIV A.P. 9.296 [C] Ἀπολλωνίδου εἰς Cκύλλιν τὸν τὰς ἀγκύρας τῶν
Περϲικῶν νεῶν νυκτὸς ἀποκείραντα Pl a Ἀπολλωνίδου
3 Νηρῆος Pl: Νιρ- P | ὑποπλεύϲας P: -πλώϲας Pl
XXV A.P. 9.791 Ἀπολλωνίδου caret Pl
1 περιϲτεφέος Hecker: -ϲτρεφεα P | ϲηκοῦ Hermann: -κὸν P   3 χαῖρ', ἔτι Page:

APOLLONIDES

XXIV

On Scyllus, an under-water swimmer

Scyllus, when the long fleet of Xerxes was harassing all Hellas, invented sea-fighting from the depths, swimming under Nereus' secret shallows, and cut the ships' moorings from anchor. So Persia, with all her men, slipped landward in silence perishing,— Themistocles' first enterprise.

XXV

On a temple of Aphrodite in the sea

Cytherea, who have fixed in the flood the deep-water foundations of your sanctuary encircled by your mother the sea, all hail to you; and still may the ocean around you softly smile on its dark-blue surface at the breeze of Zephyr. Because of his piety and the temple Postumus built for you, you shall be prouder than ⟨   ⟩ of Paphos.

XXVI

Gaius shaves his first beard

On this day, Gaius, cut the sweet first harvest of your cheeks and the youthful curls from your chin. Your father Lucius shall take in his hand the down he prayed for, as you grow up to see many a sun. They make you gifts of gold, of merry verses I; the Muse is not inferior to riches.

χαίρει P   4 ἁβρὸν Jacobs: ἀφρὸν P | κυανέου Jacobs: -εον P | γελάσαι Page: -σας P   5 ἐγείρατο Hecker: ἐγείν- P
XXVI A.P. 10.19 Ἀπολλωνίδου   Pl A Ἀπολλωνίδου
1 παρειάων Jacobs: παρειδων P, παρηΐδων Pl   4 Λεύκιος ed. vet.: -κιον PPl

143

XXVII

ὑπνώεις, ὦ 'ταῖρε, τὸ δὲ σκύφος αὐτὸ βοᾶι σε
'ἔγρεο, μὴ τέρπου μοιριδίηι μελέτηι'.   1280
μὴ φείσηι, Διόδωρε, λάβρος δ' εἰς Βάκχον ὀλισθὼν
ἄχρις ἐπὶ σφαλεροῦ ζωροπότει γόνατος.
5 ἔσσεθ' ὅτ' οὐ πιόμεσθα πολὺς πολύς· ἀλλ' ἄγ' ἐπείγου·
ἡ συνετὴ κροτάφων ἅπτεται ἡμετέρων.

XXVIII

θαύμασε τὸν Κινύρην ὁ πάλαι χρόνος ἢ Φρύγας ἄμφω,   1285
σὸν δέ, Λέων, ἡμεῖς κάλλος ἀεισόμεθα,
Κερκαφίδη περίβωτε. μακαρτάτη ἔστ' ἄρα νήσων
καὶ Ῥόδος, ἢ τοίωι λάμπεται ἠελίωι.

XXIX

εἰ τοιόσδε Λέων λάχεν ἀντίος Ἡρακλῆϊ,
οὐκ ἦν Ἀλκείδεω τοῦτο τὸ δωδέκατον.   1290

XXX

ἄνθετ' Ἀναξαγόρης με τὸν οὐκ ἐπὶ ποσσὶ Πρίηπον   (1291)
ἐν χθονὶ δ' ἀμφοτέρωι γούνατι κεκλιμένον,
τεῦξε δὲ Φυρόμαχος· Χαρίτων δέ μοι ἄγχι καλιήν
ἀθρήσας δίζευ μηκέτι πῶς ἔπεσον.

XXVII *A.P.* 11.25 Ἀπολλωνίδου   Pl A Ἀπολλωνίδου
1 ὑπνώεις Pl: -νώιης P | ὦ ἑταῖρε PPl   5 πολὺς πολύς P: πολὺς χρόνος Pl
6 συνετὴ P: πολιὴ Pl
XXVIII *A.Pl.* (B) 49 Ἀπολλωνίδου   caret P
2 Λέων Pl^pc: Λέον Pl^ac

XXVII

Drink deep while you may

You sleep my, friend, while the cup itself cries out to you,
'Wake up, take no pleasure in practising for death'. Spare not,
Diodorus, slip greedily into the wine, drink it neat even to
the knee's giving-way. Time shall be when we drink not,
long enough. Come, stir yourself; our temples are already
touched by the hand of sober sense.

XXVIII

To a handsome boy

Olden times marvelled at Cinyras and the pair of Phrygians;
we, Leon, shall sing of your beauty, renowned scion of Cercaphus. Most blessed among islands is Rhodes, lit by such a sun.

XXIX

To the same

If such a Lion as you had taken his stand as opponent of Heracles,
there would have been no Twelve Labours of Alcides (?).

XXX

On a kneeling statue of Priapus

Anaxagoras dedicated me, the Priapus not on his feet but
resting on the ground with both knees. Phyromachus made me.
Seeing a precinct of the Graces close by me, seek no longer why
I fell.

XXIX *A.Pl.* (B) 50   cum 49 coniunctum   caret P
XXX *A.Pl.* (A) 239 ᾿Απολλωνίδου   εἰς ἕτερον   caret P
3 ἄγχι καλιήν Jacobs: ἀγχόθι καλὴν Pl

ΑΠΟΛΛΩΝΙΟΥ CΜΥΡΝΑΙΟΥ

XXXI

ἀγροτέρων θεός εἰμι. τί μοι χρυσέοις δεπάεσσι   1295
σπένδετε; ποῦ δ᾽ Ἰταλοῦ χεῖτε μέθυ Βρομίου,
καὶ γυροὺς ταύρων πέτρηι προσδεῖτε τένοντας;
φείσασθ᾽· οὐ τούτοις θύμασι τερπόμεθα.
5 Πὰν ὁ παρωρείτης αὐτόξυλος ἀρνεοθοίνης
εἰμὶ καὶ ἐγχθονίου γλευκοπότης κύλικος.   1300

ΑΡΓΕΝΤΑΡΙΟΥ

I

Μήνη χρυσόκερως, δέρκηι τάδε, καὶ πυριλαμπεῖς
ἀστέρες οὓς κόλποις Ὠκεανὸς δέχεται,
ὥς με μόνον προλιποῦσα μυρόπνοος ὤιχετ᾽ Ἀρίστη,
ἑκταίην δ᾽ εὑρεῖν τὴν μάγον οὐ δύναμαι;
5 ἀλλ᾽ ἔμπης αὐτὴν ζητήσομεν· ἤν, ἐπιπέμψω   1305
Κύπριδος ἰχνευτὰς ἀργυρέους σκύλακας.

II

ποιεῖς πάντα, Μέλισσα, φιλανθέος ἔργα μελίσσης·
οἶδα καὶ ἐς κραδίην τοῦτο, γύναι, τίθεμαι·
καὶ μέλι μὲν στάζεις ὑπὸ χείλεσιν ἡδὺ φιλεῦσα,
ἢν δ᾽ αἰτῆις, κέντρωι τύμμα φέρεις ἄδικον.   1310

XXXI *A.Pl.* (A) 235 Ἀπολλωνίου Cμυρναίου   εἰς ἕτερον ἄγαλμα Πανός   caret P
4 τούτοις Ascensius: τοιούτοις Pl

I *A.P.*5.16 [PJ] Μάρκου Ἀργενταρίου   εἰς Ἀρίστην τὴν ἑταίρην   Pl A Μάρκου
Ἀργενταρίου

APOLLONIUS OF SMYRNA

XXXI

Pan prefers simple offerings

The countrymen's god am I. Why make libation to me from golden cups? Wherefore pour wine of the Italian Bacchus, and bind to the stone the curved necks of bulls? Forbear; these are not the offerings that delight me. I, Pan, a mere wood-block on the hillside, am mutton-feaster and must-drinker from the cup of clay.

ARGENTARIUS

I

Aristê deserts her lover

Do you see this, Moon golden-horned, stars fiery-bright whom Ocean to his bosom takes? How sweet-scented Aristê has left me alone and gone, and this the sixth day I cannot find the witch? Still, we shall search her out; see, I shall send the Cyprian's silver sleuth-hounds on her track.

II

Melissa resembles her namesake, the bee

All your flower-loving namesake does, you do, Melissa; I know this, my lady, and lay it to heart. Sweetly kissing, you drip honey from your lips; but when you ask your fee, with your sting you strike me most unfairly.

I δέρκηι Pl: -κει P | πυριλαμπεῖc Pl: περιλάμπει P   2 ἀcτέρεc Pl: -ραc P
3 με Pl: γε P | μυρόπνοος P: μυρίπ- Pl   6 cκύλακαc Pl: κάλυκαc P
II *A.P.* 5.32 Μάρκου ᾽Αργενταρίου   [J] εἰc Μέλιccαν τὴν ἑταίραν   caret Pl

III

Ἀντιγόνη, Σικελή πάρος ἦcθά μοι· ὡc δ' ἐγενήθηc   (1311)
Αἰτωλή, κἀγὼ Μῆδοc, ἰδού, γέγονα.

IV

οὐκ ἔcθ' οὗτοc ἔρωc, εἴ τιc καλὸν εἶδοc ἔχουcαν
βούλετ' ἔχειν φρονίμοιc ὄμμαcι πειθόμενοc,
ἀλλ' ὅcτιc κακόμορφον ἰδὼν πεφορημένοc οἴcτρωι   1315
cτέργει μαινομένηc ἐκ φρενὸc αἰθόμενοc,
5 οὗτοc ἔρωc, πῦρ τοῦτο· τὰ γὰρ καλὰ πάνταc ὁμοίωc
τέρπει τοὺc κρίνειν εἶδοc ἐπιcταμένουc.

V

—τὴν ἰcχνὴν Διόκλειαν, ἀcαρκοτέρην Ἀφροδίτην,
ὄψεαι, ἀλλὰ καλοῖc ἤθεcι τερπομένην.   1320
—οὐ πολύ μοι τὸ μεταξὺ γενήcεται, ἀλλ' ἐπὶ λεπτά
cτέρνα πεcὼν ψυχῆc κείcομαι ἐγγυτάτω.

VI

αἶρε τὰ δίκτυα ταῦτα, κακόcχολε, μηδ' ἐπίτηδεc
ἰcχίον ἐρχομένη cύcτρεφε, Λυcιδίκη·
εὖ cε περιcφίγγει λεπτὸc cτολιδώμαcι πέπλοc,   1325
πάντα δέ cου βλέπεται γυμνὰ καὶ οὐ βλέπεται.
5 εἰ τόδε cοι χαρίεν καταφαίνεται, αὐτὸc ὁμοίωc
ὀρθὸν ἔχων βυccῶι τοῦτο περιcκεπάcω.

III *A.P.* 5.63 Μάρκου [J] Ἀργενταρίου caret Pl
IV *A.P.* 5.89 Μάρκου Ἀργενταρίου [J] ἐρωτομανέc PlA τοῦ αὐτοῦ [sc.
Ῥουφίνου]
3 οἴcτρωι Pl: ἰοῖc P
V *A.P.* 5.102 [J] Μάρκου [P] Ἀργενταρίου [J] εἰc Διόκλειαν τὴν ἰcχνοτάτην
PlA τοῦ αὐτοῦ [sc. Μάρκου Ἀργενταρίου]

III

The nationality of Antigone

For me in time past, Antigone, you were the girl from Sicily; since you became a Cheque, I have become a No-wagian.

IV

True love is of the plain girl

This is not love, to desire to possess a beauty, merely obedient to judicious eyes; rather he who sees an ill-favoured girl and is gadfly-driven, all aflame, adoring her from a heart distracted,— that is love, that is the true fire; beauty pleases all alike that have the skill to judge a pretty face.

V

How Diocleia's slimness may be an advantage

—You shall see Diocleia, the slender one, a slimmer Aphrodite, but merry in her pretty ways.

—Then there will not be much between us; I shall throw myself on her little bosom and lie as close as may be to her soul.

VI

The seductive charms of Lysidicê

Take off those nets, procrastinator, stop twisting your hips so purposefully as you walk, Lysidicê. How close your thin gown binds you in its folds,—all of you is seen, yet unseen, naked. So you think this is a delightful game? I too have something to be covered straight in gauze.

I 'Αφροδίτην P: -ης Pl   3 ἀλλ' ἐπὶ λεπτά P: ἐς δὲ ποθεινά Pl   4 ψυχῆς Pl: -χεῖς P

VI *A.P.* 5.104 [J] Μάρκου [P] 'Αργενταρίου   [J] εἰς Λυσιδίκην   caret Pl
3 εὖ Paton: οὐ P | περισφίγγει C: -γγω P | λεπτὸς στολιδώμασι Reiske: λεπτοστολ-
P   4 δέ σου C: σοῦ δὲ P

VII

ἄλλος ὁ Μηνοφίλας λέγεται παρὰ μαχλάσι κόσμος,
    ἄλλος, ἐπεὶ πάσης γεύεται ἀκρασίης.   1330
ἀλλ᾽ ἴτε Χαλδαῖοι κείνης πέλας· ἦ γὰρ ὁ ταύτης
    οὐρανὸς ἐντὸς ἔχει καὶ Κύνα καὶ Διδύμους.

VIII

ἔγχει Λυσιδίκης κυάθους δέκα, τῆς δὲ ποθεινῆς
    Εὐφράντης ἕνα μοι, λάτρι, δίδου κύαθον.
φήσεις Λυσιδίκην με φιλεῖν πλέον; οὐ μὰ τὸν ἡδύν   1335
    Βάκχον, ὃν ἐν ταύτηι λαβροποτῶ κύλικι,
5 ἀλλά μοι Εὐφράντη μία πρὸς δέκα· καὶ γὰρ ἀπείρους
    ἀστέρας ἓν μήνης φέγγος ὑπερτίθεται.

IX

ἠράσθης πλουτῶν, Σωσίκρατες, ἀλλὰ πένης ὢν
    οὐκέτ᾽ ἐρᾶις· λιμὸς φάρμακον οἷον ἔχει.   1340
ἡ δὲ πάρος σε καλεῦσα μύρον καὶ τερπνὸν Ἄδωνιν
    Μηνοφίλα νῦν σου τοὔνομα πυνθάνεται,
5 'τίς πόθεν εἰς ἀνδρῶν; πόθι τοι πτόλις; ' ἦ μόλις ἔγνως
    τοῦτ᾽ ἔπος, ὡς οὐδεὶς οὐδὲν ἔχοντι φίλος.

VII *A.P.* 5.105 τοῦ αὐτοῦ [sc. Μάρκου 'Αργενταρίου] [J] εἰς Μηνοφίλαν Pl A
ἄδηλον
1 Μηνοφίλας CPl: Μινο- P   2 πάσης CPl: πάσσης P | ἀκρασίης CPl: -ίας P
3 ἴτε P: ὅτε Pl
VIII *A.P.* 5.110 [J] Μάρκου [P] 'Αργενταρίου [J] εἰς δύο πόρνας, τὴν μὲν
Λυσιδίκην τὴν δὲ Εὐφράντην καλουμένην Pl A τοῦ αὐτοῦ [sc. Μάρκου 'Αργενταρίου]

VII

On the vices of Menophila

Quite different is the world-order of Menophila, so runs the
tale among her sinful sisters, quite different. She leaves no in-
continence unsampled. Go visit her, Chaldaeans: her heaven
keeps both *Canis* and *Gemini* hidden.

VIII

Euphrantê is worth ten of Lysidicê

Pour in ten ladles for Lysidicê, but, waiter, for my darling
Euphrantê give me only one. Will you say I love Lysidicê the
better? Not so, by sweet Bacchus whom I swallow in this cup;
for me, Euphrantê is one to be compared with ten, just as the
moon's one brightness surpasses infinite stars.

IX

The man without money is no longer loved

When you were rich you were a lover, Sosicrates; being poor
you love no longer. Such physic is in hunger. And Menophila,
who used to call you her sweetness, her darling Adonis, now
asks what your name may be,—'What man art thou, and
whence? Where is thy city?' You have had hard learning of
this lesson, that nobody is friend to him who nothing owns.

---

1 Λυϲιδίκηϲ CPl^{pc}: -κη P, -κην Pl^{ac} | κυάθουϲ CPl: κυαίθ- P   4 ταύτηι CPl:
τούτη P   5 Εὐφράντη μία CPl: εὐφραντηρία P

IX *A.P.* 5.113 [J] Μάρκου [P] ᾿Αργενταρίου   [J] εἰϲ Cωϲικράτην πλούϲιον ὄντα
καὶ διὰ τὸ ἀκατάϲχετον τῶν ἐρώτων πένητα γενόμενον   Pl Α τοῦ αὐτοῦ [sc.
Φιλοδήμου]
2 φάρμακον CPl: φάρκαμον P   3 καλεῦϲα P: -οῦϲα Pl   4 ϲου P: ϲοὶ Pl
5 εἰϲ Pl: ἧϲ P | πτόλιϲ CPl: πόλ- P

X

θῆλυς ἔρως κάλλιστος ἐνὶ θνητοῖcι τέτυκται   1345
ὅccοιc ἐc φιλίην cεμνὸc ἔνεcτι νόοc.
εἰ δὲ καὶ ἀρcενικὸν cτέργειc πόθον, οἶδα διδάξαι
φάρμακον ὧι παύcειc τὴν δυcέρωτα νόcον·
5 cτρέψαc Μηνοφίλαν εὐίcχιον ἐν φρεcὶν ἔλπου
αὐτὸν ἔχειν κόλποιc ἄρcενα Μηνόφιλον.   1350

XI

Ἰcιὰc ἡδύπνευcτε, καὶ εἰ δεκάκιc μύρον ὄcδειc,   (1351)
ἔγρεο καὶ δέξαι χερcὶ φίλαιc cτέφανον,
ὃν νῦν μὲν θάλλοντα, μαραινόμενον δὲ πρὸc ἠῶ
ὄψεαι, ὑμετέρηc cύμβολον ἡλικίηc.

XII

παρθένον Ἀλκίππην ἐφίλουν μέγα, καί ποτε πείcαc   1355
αὐτὴν λαθριδίωc εἶχον ἐπὶ κλιcίηι·
ἀμφοτέρων δὲ cτέρνον ἐπάλλετο, μή τιc ἐπέλθηι,
μή τιc ἴδηι τὰ πόθων κρυπτὰ περιccοτέρων.
5 μητέρα δ᾿ οὐκ ἔλαθεν †κείνηc λάλον†, ἀλλ᾿ ἐcιδοῦcα
ἐξαπίνηc ''Ερμῆc κοινόc' ἔφη 'θύγατερ'.   1360

X *A.P.* 5.116 [J] Μάρκου [P] Ἀργενταρίου   [J] ἐρωτικόν, ὅτι ὁ θῆλυc ἔρωc
εὐάρμοcτον τῆι φύcει, ὁ δ᾿ ἄρρην ἀνάρμοcτον καὶ ἀcεβέc   caret Pl
XI *A.P.* 5.118 [J] Μάρκου [P] Ἀργενταρίου   [J] πρόc τινα ἐρωμένην ἧιτινι καὶ
cτέφανον ἐκ ῥόδων ἀπέcτειλεν   Pl A Ἀργενταρίου

X

A remedy for homosexual love

Woman's love is best for mortals, all who have a serious mind for loving. If you cherish desire for males too, I can teach you a remedy to stop that sick-love malady: turn Menophila's fine hips about, and in your mind imagine that you have nothing but a male Menophilus in your embrace.

XI

Beauty, like flowers, will fade

Sweet-breathing Isias, though you smell of perfume ten times over, rouse yourself and take this garland in your dear hands; just now it is blooming, but towards dawn you will see it fading, a symbol of your youth.

XII

The poet and Alcippê interrupted by her mother

I was much in love with a maiden, Alcippê, and one day I prevailed on her and held her secretly on her bed. Both hearts were beating, lest anyone come near, lest anyone see the secrets of our surpassing passion. But her mother noticed ⟨   ⟩ and looked in suddenly and said, 'Half-shares in treasure-trove, my dear'.

1 ἡδύπνευϲτε P: ἡδύπνοιε Pl | ὅϲδειϲ C: εὔδειϲ Pl et ut vid. P   4 ὑμετέρηϲ P: ἡμ- Pl

XII *A.P.* 5.127 [C] Μάρκου [P] ᾿Αργενταρίου   [C] ἐπὶ παρθένωι ᾿Αλκίππηι Pl A τοῦ αὐτοῦ [sc. Μάρκου ᾿Αργενταρίου]
4 περιϲϲοτέρων Meineke: -ρον PPl   5 ἔλαθεν P: -ον Pl

XIII

στέρνα περὶ στέρνοις, μαστῶι δ᾽ ἐπὶ μαστὸν ἐρείσας   (1361)
  χείλεά τε γλυκεροῖς χείλεσι συμπιέσας
᾽Αντιγόνης καὶ χρῶτα λαβὼν πρὸς χρῶτα, τὰ λοιπά
  σιγῶ, μάρτυς ἐφ᾽ οἷς λύχνος ἐπεγράφετο.

XIV

ἤδη, φίλτατε λύχνε, τρὶς ἔπταρες· ἦ τάχα τερπνήν   1365
  εἰς θαλάμους ἥξειν ᾽Αντιγόνην προλέγεις;
εἰ γάρ, ἄναξ, εἴη τόδ᾽ ἐτήτυμον· οἷος ᾽Απόλλων
  θνητοῖς μάντις ἔσηι καὶ σὺ παρὰ τρίποδι.

XV

Ἡσιόδου ποτὲ βύβλον ἐμαῖς ὑπὸ χερσὶν ἑλίσσων
  Πύρρην ἐξαπίνης εἶδον ἐπερχομένην·   1370
βύβλον δὲ ῥίψας ἐπὶ γῆν χερὶ τοῦτ᾽ ἐβόησα,
  ᾽῎Εργα τί μοι παρέχεις, ὦ γέρον Ἡσίοδε; ᾽

XVI

ὄρνι, τί μοι φίλον ὕπνον ἀφήρπασας, ἡδὺ δὲ Πύρρης
  εἴδωλον κοίτης ὤιχετ᾽ ἀποπτάμενον;
ἦ τάδε θρέπτρα τίνεις ὅτι θῆκά σε, δύσμορε, πάσης   1375
  ὠιοτόκου κραίνειν ἐν μεγάροις ἀγέλης;
5 ναὶ βωμὸν καὶ σκῆπτρα Σαράπιδος, οὐκέτι νυκτός
  φθέγξεαι, ἀλλ᾽ ἕξεις βωμὸν ὃν ὠμόσαμεν.

XIII *A.P.* 5.128 τοῦ αὐτοῦ [sc. ᾽Αργενταρίου]   [C] εἰς ἑταίραν ᾽Αντιγόνην
App. B.-V. 17 caret Pl
1 μαστὸν δ᾽ ἐπὶ μαστῶι ἐρείσσας App.

XIV *A.P.* 6.333 [C] Μάρκου [P] ᾽Αργενταρίου Pl A ἄδηλον
2 εἰς P: ἐς Pl

XIII

The poet's passion for Antigone

Breast to breast with Antigone, bosom on bosom pressing, lips on sweet lips fastening, flesh to flesh clasping,—the rest is silence; the lamp is registered witness of it all.

XIV

To a prophetic lamp

Thrice already you have sneezed, my lamp, my good friend; perhaps you foretell that my darling Antigone will come to my bed-chamber? Lord and master, would this might be truly so; you too shall be all men's prophet at the tripod, a second Apollo.

XV

The lover interrupted while reading Hesiod's 'Works and Days'

One day unrolling Hesiod's works in my hands, suddenly I saw Pyrrha coming my way. I flung the book on the ground and shouted 'Why give me the Works, you old fool Hesiod?'

XVI

Untimely cock-crow

Chanticleer, why have you snatched my treasured sleep away? The sweet image of Pyrrha is flown from my bed and gone. Is this your return for my nursing, you villain, for making you sovereign in my palace over all the egg-laying flock? By the altar and sceptre of Sarapis, you shall no longer crow by night; the altar we swore by shall be for you.

XV *A.P.* 9.161 [C] Μάρκου Ἀργενταρίου   εἰς Ἡσίοδον τὸν ποιητήν   Pl B s.a.n.
1 et 3 βύβλον P: βίβ- Pl   **1** ἑλίσσων CPl: -ω P

XVI *A.P.* 9.286 [C] Μάρκου Ἀργενταρίου   εἰς ἀλέκτορα τὸν ὄρνιν τινὰ ἀφυπνί-
σαντα ἡδέως κοιμώμενον   Pl B Ἀργενταρίου
4 ὠιοτόκου...ἀγέλης Pl: -κον...-λην P   **5** ναὶ P: μὴ Pl, μὰ Pl[sscr]

XVII

σάνδαλα καὶ μίτρην περικαλλέα τόν τε μυρόπνουν
βόστρυχον ὡραίων οὖλον ἀπὸ πλοκάμων   1380
καὶ ζώνην καὶ λεπτὸν ὑπένδυμα τοῦτο χιτῶνος
καὶ τὰ περὶ στέρνοις ἀγλαὰ μαστόδετα,
5 ἔμβρυον εὐώδινος ἐπεὶ φύγε νηδύος ὄγκον,
Εὐφράντη νηῶι θῆκεν ὑπ' Ἀρτέμιδος.

XVIII

κέντρα διωξικέλευθα φιλορρώθωνά τε κημόν   1385
τόν τε περὶ στέρνοις κόσμον ὀδοντοφόρον,
†καὶ cυίνην† ῥάβδον ἐπὶ προθύροιcι, Πόcειδον,
ἄνθετό cοι νίκης Χάρμοc ἀπ' Ἰcθμιάδος,
5 καὶ ψήκτρην ἵππων ἐρυcίτριχα τήν τ' ἐπὶ νώτων
μάστιγα ῥοίζου μητέρα θαρcαλέην.   1390
ἀλλὰ cύ, κυανοχαῖτα, δέχευ τάδε, τὸν δὲ Λυκίνου
υἷα καὶ εἰc μεγάλην cτέψον Ὀλυμπιάδα.

XIX

δύcμοροc ἐκρύφθην πόντωι νέκυc, ὃν παρὰ κῦμα
ἔκλαυcεν μήτηρ μυρία Λυcιδίκη
ψεύcτην αὐγάζουcα κενὸν τάφον· ἀλλά με δαίμων   1395
ἄπνουν αἰθυίαιc θῆκεν ὁμορρόθιον
5 Πνυταγόρην, ἔcχον δὲ κατ' Αἰγαίην ἅλα πότμον
πρυμνούχουc cτέλλων ἐκ Βορέαο κάλουc.
ἀλλ' οὐδ' ὡc ναύτην ἔλιπον δρόμον, ἀλλ' ἀπὸ νηόc
ἄλλην πὰρ φθιμένοιc εἰcανέβην ἄκατον.   1400

XVII A.P. 6.201 [C] Μάρκου [P] Ἀργενταρίου   ἀνάθημα τῆι Ἀρτέμιδι παρὰ
Εὐφράντης   caret Pl
1 μυρόπνουν C: -οπτην P   5 ἔμβρυον Hermann: ἄμβροτον P | φύγε C: -γεν P
6 Εὐφράντη Meineke: -τηι P
XVIII A.P. 6.246 Φιλοδήμου, οἱ δὲ Ἀργενταρίου   Pl A Φιλοδήμου   Suid. s.vv.
κημόc (1), διωξικέλευθα (1 διωξ. κέντρα), στέρνοιc (2), ψήκτρα (5-6)

XVII

Dedication after child-birth

Sandals and chaplet passing fair, and scent-breathing curly tress
from her lovely hair, and girdle, and this fine-spun tunic's under-
garment, and shining breast-bands that encircled her bosom,—
these Euphrantê dedicated in the temple of Artemis when she
had been delivered of the burden in her womb with easy pangs.

XVIII

Dedication after victory in a horse-race

Course-pursuing spurs, nose-fondling muzzle, tooth-laden
breast-adornment, wand of willow,—these in your porch,
Poseidon, Charmus has dedicated from victory in the Isthmian
Games, with horses' hair-currying comb, and whip for the
back, bold mother of whistling blows. Do you, the Dark-tressed,
accept these gifts and crown Lycinus' son for the great Olym-
piad also.

XIX

For the cenotaph of Pnytagores, lost at sea

The sea hid my ill-fated corpse, bewept with a myriad tears
beside the wave by Lysidicê my mother, when she looked on
the false-spoken empty tomb. Me, Pnytagores, my destiny set
tossing in the seagulls' company, breath-bereft. I found my
fate in the Aegean sea, making ready the stern-cables because of
the north-wind. Yet not even so could I leave the sailor's
path; from my own ship I embarked on another vessel among
the dead.

7 Λυκίνου Pl: -κείν- P

XIX A.P. 7.374 [C] Μάρκου ᾿Αργενταρίου   [J] εἰς ναυαγὸν Λυσιδίκης υἱὸν Πνυταγόραν   Pl A ᾿Αργενταρίου
1 ἐκρύφθην Reiske: -η PPl   4 ἄπνουν P: -οον Pl | ὁμορρόθιον PPl^{γρ}: ὁμωρόφιον Pl   5 Αἰγαίην Pl: ᾿Αργαί- P | πότμον CPl: πόντον P   6 πρυμνούχους Pl: -νύχ- P | κάλους P: -λως Pl   8 εἰσανέβην Hecker: εἰσεν- PPl

XX

οὗτος ὁ Καλλαίσχρου κενεὸς τάφος, ὃν βαθὺ χεῦμα
ἔσφηλεν Λιβυκῶν ἐκδρομέοντα πόρων,
cυρμὸς ὅτ' Ὠρίωνος ἀνεστρώφηcε θαλάccηc
βένθος ὑπὸ cτυγερῆc οἴδματα πανδυcίηc.
5 καὶ τὸν μὲν δαίcαντο κυκώμενον εἰν ἁλὶ θῆρεc,   1405
κωφὸν δὲ cτήλη γράμμα λέλογχε τόδε.

XXI

ἀκρίδι καὶ τέττιγι Μυρὼ τόδε θήκατο cῆμα
λιτὴν ἀμφοτέροιc χερcὶ βαλοῦcα κόνιν,
ἵμερα δακρύcαcα πυρῆc ἔπι· τὸν γὰρ ἀοιδόν
Ἅιδηc, τὴν δ' ἑτέρην ἥρπαcε Περcεφόνη.   1410

XXII

μηκέτι νῦν μινύριζε παρὰ δρυί, μηκέτι φώνει
κλωνὸc ἐπ' ἀκροτάτου, κόccυφε, κεκλιμένοc·
ἐχθρόν coι τόδε δένδρον· ἐπείγεο δ' ἄμπελοc ἔνθα
ἀντέλλει γλαυκῶν cύcκιοc ἐκ πετάλων.
5 κείνηc ταρcὸν ἔρειcον ἐπὶ κλάδον ἀμφί τ' ἐκείνηι   1415
μέλπε λιγὺν προχέων ἐκ cτόματοc κέλαδον.
δρῦc γὰρ ἐπ' ὀρνίθεccι φέρει τὸν ἀνάρcιον ἰξόν,
ἁ δὲ βότρυν· cτέργει δ' ὑμνοπόλουc Βρόμιοc.

XX A.P. 7.395 [C] Μάρκου Ἀργενταρίου   [J] εἰς Κάλλαιcχρον ναυαγήcαντα ἐν
τῶι Λιβυκῶι πελάγει δύνοντοc Ὠρίωνοc Pl в Ἀργενταρίου
2 ἐκδρομέοντα Page: ἐνδρ- P, εὐδρ- Pl   3 ὅτ' Pl: δ' ὅτ' P   4 πανδυcίηc
CPl: πανcυδίηc P   6 δὲ cτήλη Pl: δ' ἐν cτήληι P

XXI A.P. 7.364 [=Pᵃ] [C] Μάρκου Ἀργενταρίου   [P] εἰς τέττιγα καὶ ἀκρίδα
[Ἀργενταρίου add. P, del. C]]   denuo scr. C in marg. sup. p. 235 post VII 190 [=Pᵇ]
Μάρκου Ἀργενταρίου   caret Pl

XX

For the cenotaph of Callaeschrus, lost at sea

This is the empty tomb of Callaeschrus, whom the deep flood brought low as he ran out of the Libyan straits, when Orion's pull turned the ocean's depths upside down, as they swelled at the time of its hateful setting. The beasts devoured him tossing in the brine, and this dull writing is all his grave gets.

XXI

Epitaph for a grasshopper and a cicada

Myro made this grave for her grasshopper and her cicada, casting a little dust on both with her own hands; and she wept with yearning over the pyre. The songster was seized by Hades, the other by Persephonê.

XXII

The blackbird must avoid the oak-tree

No longer now warble by the oak-tree, blackbird, no longer perch on the topmost bough and call; that tree is no friend to you. Go where the vine rises shady from gray-green leaves; that is the plant for you to press your foot upon, round that you must sing, pouring shrill music from your throat. The oak bears against birds its hateful mistletoe; the other bears the grape-cluster, and singers are dear to the wine-god.

3 ἵμερα Reiske: ἤμερα Pᵃᵇ   4 Περσεφόνη Pᵃ: -φώνη Pᵇ

XXII *A.P.* 9.87 [C] Μάρκου ᾿Αργενταρίου   [J] εἰс κόссυφον παραίνεсιс μὴ καθέζεсθαι αὐτὸν παρὰ δρῦν διὰ τὸ ἰξοφόρον εἶναι τὸ δένδρον καὶ ἁλίсκεсθαι τὸν κόссυφον ὑπὸ τοῦ ἰξοῦ, μᾶλλον μὲν οὖν ἐν ἀμπέλωι καθέζεсθαι   Pl Α ᾿Αργενταρίου
1 νῦν CPl: om. P   3 δένδρον P: -δρεον Pl   6 сτόματος CPl: -των P
8 ἃ P: ἠ Pl

XXIII

Κύπριδι κεῖco, λάγυνε μεθυcφαλέc, αὐτίκα δῶρον,
    κεῖco, καcιγνήτη νεκταρέηc κύλικοc,   1420
Βακχιὰc ὑγρόφθογγε cυνέcτιε δαιτὸc ἐίcηc,
    cτειναύχην ψήφου cυμβολικῆc θύγατερ,
5 θνητοῖc αὐτοδίδακτε διήκονε, μύcτι φιλούντων
    ἡδίcτη, δείπνων ὅπλον ἑτοιμότατον·
εἴηc ἐκ Μάρκου γέραc ἀγλαόν, ὅc cε, φίλοινε,   1425
    ἤινεcεν ἀρχαίην cύμπλανον ἀνθέμενοc.

XXIV

ἀρχαίη cύνδειπνε, καπηλικὰ μέτρα φιλεῦcα,
    εὔλαλε πρηύγελωc εὔcτομε μακροφάρυξ,
αἰὲν ἐμῆc πενίηc βραχυcύμβολε μύcτι λάγυνε,
    ἦλθεc ὅμωc ὑπ' ἐμὴν χεῖρά ποτε χρόνιοc.   1430
5 αἴθ' ὄφελεc καὶ ἄμικτοc ἀνύμφευτόc τε παρείηc,
    ἄφθοροc ὡc κούρη πρὸc πόcιν ἐρχομένη.

XXV

ἐθραύcθηc ἡδεῖα παρ' οἰνοπόταιcι λάγυνε
    νηδύοc ἐκ πάcηc χευαμένη Βρόμιον·
τηλόθε γὰρ λίθοc εἷc cε βαρύcτονοc οἷα κεραυνόc   1435
    οὐ Διὸc ἐκ χειρῶν ἀλλὰ Δίωνοc ἔβη·
5 ἦν δὲ γέλωc ἐπὶ cοὶ καὶ cκώμματα πυκνὰ τυπείcηc
    καὶ πολὺc ἐξ ἑτάρων γινόμενοc θόρυβοc.
οὐ θρηνῶ cε, λάγυνε, τὸν εὐαcτῆρα τεκοῦcαν
    Βάκχον, ἐπεὶ Cεμέλη καὶ cὺ πεπόνθατ' ἴcα.   1440

XXIII A.P. 6.248 Ἀργενταρίου   Suid. s.v. λάγυνοc (1–6)   caret Pl
3 Βακχιὰc P: -χειὰc CSuid.   6 δείπνων C: -νον P
XXIV A.P. 9.229 [C] Μάρκου Ἀργενταρίου   εἰc λάγυνον οἰνηρήν   Pl B
Ἀργενταρίου
2 μακροφάρυξ P: -ρυγξ Pl   5 ἄμικτοc Pl: ἄμυκτ- P | παρείηc P: παρεῖναι
Pl   6 ἄφθοροc Pl: -θονοc P

XXIII

Dedication of a flagon to Aphrodite

Lie here this moment, a gift for the Cyprian, flagon reeling-drunk; lie here, sister of the nectar wine-cup, liquid-voiced Bacchic boon-companion of the common feast, strait-necked child of the bottle-party's pledge, man's self-taught servant, the lover's sweetest confidant, the banquet's readiest instrument. Be the bright gift from Marcus, who has sung your praises, wine-lover, and dedicated you, his ancient fellow-wanderer.

XXIV

To an old flagon

Ancient comrade of the feast, lover of the shopman's measures, sweet-talking, soft-laughing, large-lipped, long-throated, ever sharing my poverty's secrets at small expense to yourself, late, flagon, but at last you have come under my hand. If only I had you pure and unmated, like a maid coming undefiled to her husband.

XXV

A flagon broken

You were smashed, sweet flagon, among the topers, and poured wine from all your belly. A deep-moaning stone came upon you from afar, like a thunderbolt, from hand of Dion, not hand divine. They laughed at you; mockeries came thick and fast when you were struck, and great uproar from our friends. I do not mourn you, flagon, since you gave birth to cheer-chanting Bacchus; your fate and Semelê's were the same.

XXV *A.P.* 9.246 [C] Μάρκου ᾿Αργενταρίου   εἰс οἰνηρὴν λάγυνον κλαcθεῖcαν ὑπὸ βολῆс λίθου   Pl A ᾿Αργενταρίου

1 ἡδεῖα Scaliger: ἡλεῖα PPl | οἰνοπόταιcι P: -τηcι Pl   3 τηλόθε Pl^pc: -θι PPl^ac
5 πυκνὰ P: πολλὰ Pl   6 γινόμενοc P: γιγν- Pl

XXVI

κωμάζω χρύσειον ἐc ἑcπερίων χορὸν ἄcτρων
λεύccων, †οὐδ' ἄλλων λὰξ ἐβάρυνα ὄροc†.
cτέψαc δ' ἀνθόβολον κρατὸc τρίχα τὴν κελαδεινήν
πηκτίδα μουcοπόλοιc χερcὶν ἐπηρέθιcα.
5 καὶ τάδε δρῶν εὔκοcμον ἔχω βίον· οὐδὲ γὰρ αὐτόc   1445
κόcμοc ἄνευθε λύρηc ἔπλετο καὶ cτεφάνου.

XXVII

cφάλλομαι ἀκρήτωι μεμεθυcμένοc. ἀλλὰ τίc ἄρα
cώcει μ' ἐκ Βρομίου γυῖα cαλευόμενον;
ὡc ἄδικον θεὸν εὗρον, ὀθούνεκεν αὐτὸc ἐγώ cε,
Βάκχε, φέρων ὑπὸ coῦ τἄμπαλι παρφέρομαι.   1450

XXVIII

λῦcον ἀπ' εὐόρμων δολιχὰ πρυμνήcια νηῶν,
εὔτροχα δ' ἐκπετάcαc λαίφεα ποντοπόρει,
ἔμπορε, χειμῶνεc γὰρ ἀπέδραμον, ἄρτι δὲ κῦμα
γλαυκὸν θηλύνει πρηΰγελωc Ζέφυροc,
5 ἤδη καὶ φιλότεκνοc ὑπὸ τραυλοῖcι χελιδών   1455
χείλεcι καρφίτην πηλοδομεῖ θάλαμον,
ἄνθεα δ' ἀντέλλουcι κατὰ χθόνα. τῶι cὺ Πριήπωι
πειθόμενοc πάcηc ἅπτεο ναυτιλίηc.

XXVI *A.P.* 9.270 [C] Μάρκου Ἀργενταρίου   ἐπί τινι ἐν νυκτὶ μετὰ κιθάραc
κωμάζοντι   Pl α Ἀργενταρίου
1 ἄcτρων Pl: -ον P   2 λεύccων Pl: λεύcων P | ὄροc P: χορούc Pl   3 cτέψαc
Pl: cτρ- P | ἀνθοβόλον PPl

XXVI

The dancer in harmony with the universe

Looking at the golden dance of the evening stars I revel 〈　　〉.
I crown the hair of my head with flowers; with musical fingers
I wake to passion the tuneful lyre. And so doing I lead a well-
ordered life; the world-order itself is not without its Lyre and
Crown.

XXVII

The wine-god's injustice

Drunk with neat wine I stumble; will there be anyone to rescue
me, my limbs swaying at the wine-god's will? How unjust
have I found this divinity: I myself carry you, Bacchus, and in
return you carry me astray.

XXVIII

Spring and the sailing-season

Loose, trader, the long hawsers from the well-moored ships,
spread out the smooth-running sails and cross the sea. The
storms have fled, and now the west-wind tender-smiling
softens the gray-green wave. Now too the swallow, fond
parent, with lisping lips builds its nest of stalks and clay, and
flowers spring up throughout the land. So give heed to Priapus
and take to all manner of seafaring.

XXVII *A.P.* 11.26 Ἀργενταρίου Pl A Ἀργενταρίου
3 ὅθ' οὕνεκεν Pl: ὅτ' εἵνεκεν P | σε Pl: γε P　**4** τἄμπαλι P: τοὔμ- Pl
XXVIII *A.P.* 10.4 Μάρκου Ἀργενταρίου Pl A Μάρκου Ἀργενταρίου
6 πηλοδομεῖ Pl: -δαμεῖ P

XXIX

Γῶβρυ, Διώνυσός σε καὶ ἡ φιλεράστρια Κύπρις
τέρποι καὶ γλυκεραὶ γράμμασι Πιερίδες·   1460
ὧν μὲν γὰρ σοφίην ἀποδρέπτεο, τῆς δ᾽ ἐς ἔρωτας
ἔρχεο, τοῦ δὲ φίλας λαβροπότει κύλικας.

XXX

πέντε θανὼν κείσηι κατέχων πόδας, οὐδὲ τὰ τερπνά
ζωῆς οὐδ᾽ αὐγὰς ὄψεαι ἠελίου·
ὥστε λαβὼν Βάκχου ζωρὸν δέπας ἕλκε γεγηθώς,   1465
Κίγκιε, καλλίστην ἀγκὰς ἔχων ἄλοχον.
5 εἰ δέ σοι ἀθάνατος σοφίης νόος, ἴσθι Κλεάνθης
καὶ Ζήνων Ἀίδην τὸν βαθὺν ὡς ἔμολον.

XXXI

ἡ Βρόμιον στέρξασα πολὺ πλέον ἢ τροφὸς Ἰνώ,
ἡ λάλος ἀμπελίνη γρηὺς Ἀριστομάχη,   1470
ἡνίκα τὴν ἱερὴν ὑπέδυ χθόνα πᾶν τ᾽ ἐμαράνθη
πνεῦμα πάρος κυλίκων πλεῖστον ἐπαυρομένηι,
5 εἶπε †τάδε· Μίνωι πάλαι† φέρε κάλπιν ἐλαφρήν,
οἴσω κυάνεον τοὺξ Ἀχέροντος ὕδωρ·
καὐτὴ παρθένιον γὰρ ἀπώλεσα.᾽ τοῦτο δ᾽ ἔλεξε   1475
ψευδές, ἵν᾽ αὐγάζηι κἢν φθιμένοισι πίθον.

XXIX *A.P.* 10.18 ᾽Αργενταρίου caret Pl
1 φιλεράστρια Huschke: φιλελάστ- P
XXX *A.P.* 11.28 ᾽Αργενταρίου Pl в s.a.n.
3 ζωρὸν Pl: -ρὸс P 4 ἄλοχον P: ἄκοιτιν Pl

XXIX
Wine, woman, and song

Gobrys, may Dionysus and the amorous Cyprian and the sweet
Muses with their books be your delight; pluck their wisdom,
enter into her passions, swallow his friendly cups.

XXX
Enjoy life while it lasts

Five feet of land shall be your holding when you lie dead; you
shall not see the delights of life or the sun's rays. So take a neat
cup of wine and drain it rejoicing, Cincius, with your beautiful
wife in your embrace. If you think the mind of Philosophy
immortal (?), remember that Cleanthes and Zeno went to the
depths of Hades.

XXXI
A woman drunkard in Hades

That chatterbox, wine-hag Aristomachê, she who loved Bromios much more than his nurse Ino did, when she went down
below the holy earth, and all the breath faded from her who
formerly enjoyed so many a cup, thus spoke ⟨to Minos:⟩
'Bring me a light pitcher; I will fetch the dark water from
Acheron, for I too murdered a bridegroom.' That was a lie she
told, hoping to see a wine-jar even among the dead.

XXXI *A.P.* 7.384 [C] Μάρκου 'Αργενταρίου   [J] εἰς 'Αριστομάχην τινὰ γραῦν
τὴν μέθυσον   Pl A 'Αργενταρίου
1 Βρόμιον CPl: -μον P   3 τ' P: δ' Pl   7 παρθένιον Reiske: -ίην PPl
8 κῆν C: καὶ P, κἂν Pl

XXXII

Ψύλλος ὁ τὰς ποθινὰς ἐπιμισθίδας αἰὲν ἑταίρας
  πέμπων ἐς τὰ νέων ἡδέα συμπόσια,
οὗτος ὁ θηρεύων ἁπαλόφρονας, ἐνθάδε κεῖται
  αἰσχρὸν ἀπ᾽ ἀνθρώπων μισθὸν ἐνεγκάμενος.   1480
5 ἀλλὰ λίθους ἐπὶ τύμβον, ὁδοιπόρε, μήτε σὺ βάλλε
  μήτ᾽ ἄλλον πείσῃς· σῆμα λέλογχε νέκυς.
φεῖσαι δ᾽ οὐχ ὅτι κέρδος ἐπήινεσεν ἀλλ᾽ ὅτι κοινὰς
  θρέψας μοιχεύειν οὐκ ἐδίδαξε νέους.

XXXIII

λάθριος, Ἡράκλεια, καλῶν ὑπὸ χείλεσιν ἕλκεις   1485
  κεῖνο· πάλαι κατὰ σοῦ τοῦτ᾽ ἐβόησε πόλις.
πῶς ἔτλης αἶσχος ῥέξαι κακόν; ἤ σε βιαίως
  εἵλκυσέ τις θαλερῶν δραξάμενος πλοκάμων;
5 ἤ σοι τοὔνομα τερπνὸν ἀφ᾽ Ἡρακλῆος ἐχούσῃ,
  μάχλε, φιλεῖν ἥβην κέκριται ἠιθέων;   1490

XXXIV

Ἀντιγόνην ἔστεργε Φιλόστρατος· ἦν δὲ παλαισταῖς   (1491)
  ὁ τλήμων Ἴρου πέντε πενιχρότερος.
εὗρε δ᾽ ὑπὸ κρυμοῦ γλυκὺ φάρμακον· ἀντία γὰρ σχών
  γούνατ᾽ ἐκοιμήθη, ξεῖνε, μετ᾽ Ἀντιγόνης.

XXXII *A.P.* 7.403 [C] Μάρκου Ἀργενταρίου   [J] εἰς Ψύλλον τινὰ προαγωγὸν
ὃν ἡ κοινὴ συνήθεια καλεῖ μαυλιστήν   Pl A Ἀργενταρίου
1 ποθινὰς P: -θενὰς Pl   5 μήτε CPl: μή τι P

XXXII

Epitaph for Psyllus, a procurer of women

Psyllus, who was for ever sending desirable hire-girls to young men's merry banquets, that hunter of tender souls, here he lies, having earned shameful wages from his fellow men. Yet, traveller, neither cast yourself a stone upon his tomb, nor persuade another thereto; he is dead and buried. Spare him, not because profit was all he approved, but because being keeper of public women he taught young men not to to be adulterers.

XXXIII

A reason for the vice of Heracleia

In secret, Heracleia, you do our pretty boys that service with your lips. The town has long since cried this charge against you. How could you dare to do a crime so base? Did someone grasp your luxuriant hair and drag you to it by force? Or were you fated, wanton girl, having your pretty name from Heracles, to kiss his wife's namesake in young men?

XXXIV

A substitute for Antigone

Philostratus loved Antigone; a sad fellow he, poorer than Irus by five palms' breadth. But the frosty weather taught him a delightful cure: he tucked up his knees in bed, my friend, and so slept with antic o'knee.

XXXIII *A.P.* 9.554 [J] ᾿Αργενταρίου   caret Pl
1 καλῶν Jacobs: -λῶς P
XXXIV *A.P.* 11.320 ᾿Αργενταρίου   Pl A ᾿Αργενταρίου

XXXV

αὐγάζω τὸν ἄφυκτον ἐπὶ cφραγῖδος Ἔρωτα   1495
χερcὶ λεοντείαν ἀνιοχεῦντα βίαν,
ὡς τᾶι μὲν μάςτιγα κατ' αὐχένος, ᾶι δὲ χαλινούς
εὐθύνει, πολλὰ δ' ἀμφιτέθηλε χάρις.
5 φρίccω τὸν βροτολοιγόν, ὁ γὰρ καὶ θῆρα δαμάζων
ἄγριον οὐδ' ὀλίγον φείcεται ἀμερίων.   1500

XXXVI

βουκόλον ἢν ἐcίδηις τὸν ἐμόν, ξένε, τοῦτ' ἔπος αὐτῶι   (1501)
εἶπον, ὅθ' ὁ πλάςτας ὧδέ μ' ἔδηcε Μύρων.

XXXVII

ὥριμος, οἶδα καὶ αὐτός, ὁδοιπόρε· μηκέτ' ἐπαίνει
ἰcχάδα μηδ' ἐcόρα τὸν πέλας ἀκρεμόνα.
καὶ λίην ὁ Πρίηπος ἐφίcταμαι ὀξὺ δεδορκὼς   1505
καὶ φυλακὴν cύκων ἢν ἐπέοικεν ἔχων.
5 ἢν δὲ μόνον cὺ θίγηις τῆς ἰcχάδος, ἰcχάδα δώcεις·
ὡς ἰcότης πάντων ἐcτὶ δικαιοτάτη.

ΑΥΤΟΜΕΔΟΝΤΟΣ

I

τὴν ἀπὸ τῆς Ἀcίης ὀρχηcτρίδα, τὴν κακοτέχνοις
cχήμαcιν ἐξ ἁπαλῶν κινυμένην ὀνύχων,   1510

XXXV *A.P.* 9.221 [C] Μάρκου Ἀργενταρίου   ἐπὶ cφραγῖδι ἐχούcῃ Ἔρωτα
ἡνιοχοῦντα λέοντας Pl a Ἀργενταρίου
3 ὡς P: ὃc Pl | ἆι Pl: ἆ P (?)   **6** ὀλίγον Pl: -γων P
XXXVI *A.P.* 9.732 Μάρκου Ἀργενταρίου Pl a Μάρκου Ἀργενταρίου εἰς
τὸ αὐτό

XXXV

On a seal-stone portraying Eros

I see upon the seal Love the inescapable, charioteering the strength of a lion with his own hands; in the one, the whip against the neck, with the other he guides the reins, and grace abundant blooms about him. I shudder at the man-destroyer: he who subdues even the savage beast will not have the least mercy for mortals.

XXXVI

On Myron's Cow

Stranger, if you see my cowherd, give him this message: I was tied up here by that sculptor Myron.

XXXVII

Priapus protects the fig-tree

It is ripe, I know it as well as you, my traveller-friend; stop praising the fig, keep your eyes off the branch beside you. I, Priapus, am guardian, sharp-sighted enough, keeping due watch over my figs. Just touch a fig, and a fig shall be your forfeit; an eye for an eye is of all things most perfect justice.

AUTOMEDON

I

On a dancing-girl

I praise the dancing-girl from Asia, her who quivers from her tender finger-tips in lascivious postures, not because she com-

2 πλάстας P: -ης Pl

XXXVII A.Pl. (A) 241 ’Αργενταρίου εἰς τὸ αὐτό caret P

I A.P. 5.129 Αὐτομέδοντος [C] εἰς πόρνην ὀρχηστρίδα caret Pl
2 κινυμένην ὀνύχων C: ὀν. κιν. P

αἰνέω οὐχ ὅτι πάντα παθαίνεται οὐδ' ὅτι βάλλει
   τὰς ἁπαλὰς ἁπαλῶς ὧδε καὶ ὧδε χέρας,
5 ἀλλ' ὅτι καὶ τριβακὸν περὶ πάσσαλον ὀρχήσασθαι
   οἶδε καὶ οὐ φεύγει γηραλέας ῥυτίδας·
γλωττίζει, κνίζει, περιλαμβάνει· ἢν δ' ἐπιρίψηι   1515
   τὸ σκέλος, ἐξ Ἅιδου τὴν κορύνην ἀνάγει.

II

πέμπε, κάλει· πάντ' ἐστὶν ἑτοιμά σοι· ἢν δέ τις ἔλθηι,
   τί πρήξεις; σαυτῶι δὸς λόγον, Αὐτόμεδον.
αὕτη γὰρ †λαχάνου σισαρωτέρη†, ἡ πρὶν ἀκαμπής
   ζῶσα, νεκρὰ μηρῶν πᾶσα δέδυκεν ἔσω.   1520
5 πόλλ' ἐπί σοι γελάσουσιν, ἀνάρμενος ἂν παραβάλληι
   πλώειν, τὴν κώπην μηκέτ' ἔχων ἐρέτης.

III

Νικήτης ὀλίγος μὲν ἐπὶ προτόνοισιν ἀήτης
   οἶά τε πρηείης ἄρχεται ἐκ μελέτης,
ἀλλ' ὅταν ἐμπνεύσηι, κατὰ δ' ἱστία πάντα φέρηται,   1525
   λαίφεα πακτώσας μέσσα θέει πελάγη
5 ναῦς ἅτε μυριόφορτος, ἕως ἐπὶ τέρματα μύθων
   ἔλθηι ἀκυμάντους †ἔμπροσθεν† εἰς λιμένας.

IV

εὐδαίμων πρῶτον μὲν ὁ μηδενὶ μηδὲν ὀφείλων,
   εἶτα δ' ὁ μὴ γήμας, τὸ τρίτον ὅστις ἄπαις.   1530
ἢν δὲ μανεὶς γήμηι τις, ἔχει χάριν ἢν κατορύξηι
   εὐθὺς τὴν γαμετὴν προῖκα λαβὼν μεγάλην.

II *A.P.* 11.29 Αὐτομέδοντος caret Pl
3 ἡ Schneider: om. P   6 ἐρέτης Boissonade: -του P
III *A.P.* 10.23 Αὐτομέδοντος Pl A Αὐτομέδοντος

mands every gesture of passion, nor because she flings so tenderly her tender hands this way and that, but because she knows how to dance around the worn-out peg, and does not shun the wrinkles of age. She tongues and tickles and hugs, and when she throws her leg across she resurrects the club from Hades.

II

The impotent lover

Send for her, summon her; you have everything ready. But if anyone should come, what will you do? Consider how things stand with you, Automedon. This ⟨   ⟩ that used to be alive and unbendable, is now dead and all sunk between your thighs. People will laugh aloud at you, if you venture to sail unequipped, a rower who has lost his oar.

III

On the eloquence of Nicetes

Nicetes begins with gentle practising, like a little breeze on the forestays; but when it blows hard and all the sails are let down, he makes the canvas fast and runs over the middle of the sea like a huge merchantman till he reaches the end of his discourse ⟨   ⟩ to waveless harbours.

IV

On the blessings of the bachelor

Happy is he, first, who owes no man anything; next, he who has not married; third, he who is childless. If a man is so mad as to marry, he can be thankful if he buries his wife at once,

4 πελάγη Pl: -γει P   6 ἔμπροσθεν P: ἔμπορος Pl
IV A.P. 11.50 Αὐτομέδοντος   Pl A Αὐτομέδοντος   Syll.S

5 ταῦτ' εἰδὼς coφὸc ἴcθι, μάτην δ' Ἐπίκουρον ἔαcον
  ποῦ τὸ κενὸν 3ητεῖν καὶ τίνεc αἱ μονάδεc.

V

ἀνθρακίων δέκα μέτρα φέρων, ἔco καὶ cὺ πολίτηc·   1535
  ἢν δὲ καὶ ὗν ἀγάγηιc, αὐτὸc ὁ Τριπτόλεμοc.
δεῖ δὲ καὶ Ἡρακλείδηι ὑφηγητῆρι δοθῆναι
  ἢ καυλοὺc κράμβηc ἢ φακὸν ἢ κοχλίαc.
5 ταῦτ' ἔχε καὶ λέγε cαυτὸν Ἐρεχθέα, Κέκροπα, Κόδρον,
  ὅν κ' ἐθέληιc· οὐδεὶc οὐδὲν ἐπιcτρέφεται.   1540

VI

—δέξαι, Φοῖβε, τὸ δεῖπνον ὅ coι φέρω.—ἢν τιc ἐάcηι,
  δέξομαι.—εἶτα φοβῆι καὶ cύ τι, Λητοΐδη;
—οὐδένα τῶν ἄλλων πλὴν Ἄρριον· οὗτοc ἔχει γὰρ
  ἅρπαγοc ἰκτίνου χεῖρα κραταιοτέρην,
5 ἀκνίcου βωμοῖο νεωκόροc· ἢν τελέcηι δέ   1545
  τὴν πομπήν, ἄραc ὤιχεθ' ἅπαντα πάλιν.
ἐν Διὸc ἀμβροcίηι πολλὴ χάριc· εἷc γὰρ ἂν ὑμέων
  ἤμην, εἰ λιμοῦ καὶ θεὸc ἡιcθάνετο.

VII

ἐχθὲc δειπνήcαc τράγεον πόδα καὶ δεκαταῖον
  κανναβίνηc κράμβηc μήλινον ἀcπάραγον   1550
εἰπεῖν τὸν καλέcαντα φυλάccομαι· ἔcτι γὰρ ὀξύc,
  καὶ φόβοc οὐχ ὁ τυχὼν μή με πάλιν καλέcηι.

V A.P. 11.319 Αὐτομέδοντοc Pl B s.a.n.   εἰc...
2 ὁ Pl: om. P   3 ὑφηγητῆρι Pl: -τορι P   4 ἢ (init. vers.) Pl: om. P
(suppl. man. rec.) | καυλοὺc κράμβηc P: -λὸν κράμπηc Pl

having got a large dowry. In this knowledge let your wisdom lie; leave Epicurus vainly to inquire where the void is and what the atoms are.

V

How to become an Athenian citizen

Bring ten measures of charcoal, and you shall be a citizen. If you can bring a pig as well, you shall be Triptolemos himself. To your agent Heraclides you must give cabbage-stalks, lentils, or snails. Possess yourself of these, and you may call yourself Erechtheus, Cecrops, Codrus, whomever you will; nobody cares at all.

VI

On Arrius, a greedy temple-warden

—Phoebus, accept the dinner I bring you.
—If someone will let me, I will accept it.
—What, is even the son of Leto afraid of something?
—Of no man else but Arrius. He has a grasp more powerful than the robber-kite, this temple-minister of a savourless altar. When he has celebrated the procession, he picks everything up and goes home. There is much to be thankful for in the ambrosia which Zeus supplies; otherwise I should be one of you, if a god too could feel hunger.

VII

A miserly dinner-host

Having dined yesterday on goat's foot and a ten-days-old yellow stalk of hemp-like cabbage, I am careful not to say who my host was; he is quick-tempered, and there's an uncommon risk that he might invite me again.

VI *A.P.* 11.324 Αὐτομέδοντος Pl A Αὐτομέδοντος εἰς ἅρπαγον
2 τι P: om. Pl   **5** ἀκνίcου P: -νίccου Pl
VII *A.P.* 11.325 τοῦ αὐτοῦ [sc. Αὐτομέδοντος] Pl A Αὐτομέδοντος

VIII

μέχρι τίνος, Πολύκαρπε, κενῆς παράσιτε τραπέζης,
  λήσηι κερματίοις χρώμενος ἀλλοτρίοις;
οὐ γὰρ ἔτ᾽ εἰν ἀγορῆι σε βλέπω πολύν, ἀλλ᾽ ὑποκάμπτεις   1555
  ἤδη καὶ ζητεῖς ποῖ σε φέρωσι πόδες.
5 πᾶσιν ἐπαγγέλληι 'κόμισαι τὸ σόν· αὔριον ἔρχου
  καὶ λαβέ'· κοὐδ᾽ ὁμόσας οὐκέτι πίστιν ἔχεις.
Κυζικόθεν σε φέρων ἄνεμος Σαμόθραιξι πέλαζε·
  τοῦτό σε τοῦ λοιποῦ τέρμα μένει βιότου.   1560

IX

ἡμίονοι σύγγηροι ἐμὴν κομέουσιν ἀπήνην
  ταῖσιν Ὁμηρείοις πάντα Λιταῖς ἴκελαι,
χωλαί τε ῥυσαί τε παραβλῶπές τ᾽ ὀφθαλμώ,
  Ἡφαίστου πομπή, σκύτινα δαιμόνια,
5 οὔποτε γευσάμεναι μὰ τὸν Ἥλιον οὐδ᾽ ἐν ὀνείρωι   1565
  οὐ θέρεος κριθήν, οὐκ ἔαρος βοτάνην·
τοὔνεκ᾽ ἐμεῦ μὲν ἔκητι βίον ζώοιτε κορώνης
  ⟨   κε⟩νεὴν ἠέρα βοσκόμεναι.

X

πώγων καὶ λάσιαι μηρῶν τρίχες, ὡς ταχὺ πάντα
  ὁ χρόνος ἀλλάσσει· Κόννιχε, τοῦτ᾽ ἐγένου;   1570
οὐκ ἔλεγον 'μὴ πάντα βαρὺς θέλε μηδὲ βάναυσος
  εἶναι· καὶ κάλλους εἰσί τινες Νεμέσεις';
5 ἦλθες ἔσω μάνδρης, ὑπερήφανε. νῦν ὅτι βούλει
  οἴδαμεν· ἀλλ᾽ ἐξῆν καὶ τότ᾽ ἔχειν σε φρένας.

VIII A.P. 11.346 Αὐτομέδοντος Pl B s.a.n.   εἰς δόλιον
2 λήσηι PPl^{ac}: -σεις Pl^{pc} | χρώμενος P: ψευδόμεν᾽ Pl   4 ποῖ Bothe: ποῦ PPl
5 αὔριον P: ἀργύριον Pl   7 πέλαζε P: -λασσεν Pl
IX A.P. 11.361 Αὐτομέδοντος   caret Pl

VIII

A defaulting banker

How long, Polycarpus, parasite of an empty banker's-table, shall you go undetected, spending the pence of other men? I no longer see you much in the market-place; you turn aside at once and look for somewhere to run away. To all comers you cry 'Fetch what is yours; come and get it tomorrow', but you are no longer to be trusted even on oath. 'The wind has carried you from Cyzicus and brought you within reach of the Samothracians'; this is the end that awaits you for the rest of your life.

IX

Old and skinny mules

The mules that wait upon my carriage are grown old together, the living image of Homer's 'Prayers',—'lame and wrinkled and with eyes asquint', fit escort for Hephaestus, ghosts of skin and bone, having never even in a dream—by the Sun I swear it —tasted barley in summer or grass in spring: for all I care you may live the life-span of a crow ⟨   ⟩ feeding on empty air.

X

The passing of youth's charm

Beard and shaggy thigh-hairs, how quickly Time changes all things. Is this, Connichus, what you have come to? Did I not tell you, 'Seek not to be so harsh and rude in all ways; even beauty has its Nemesis'? Proud fellow, you have come within the fold. That you want it now, we know; you might have had as much sense even in those days.

---

1 κομέουcιν Brunck: κοιμ- P   **3** ὀφθαλμῴ Brunck: -μῶν P   **8** κενεὴν ἠέρα Dorville: νεην ἱερὰ P, spat. vac. c. xx litt. ante νεην relicto
X *A.P.* 11.326 τοῦ αὐτοῦ [sc. Αὐτομέδοντοc]   caret Pl
2 ἀλλάccει Brunck: ἀλά- P   **5** ὅτι Brunck: ὅτε P

XI

πρὸς τὸν παιδοτρίβην Δημήτριον ἐχθὲς ἐδείπνουν   1575
πάντων ἀνθρώπων τὸν μακαριστότατον·
εἷς αὐτοῦ κατέκειθ' ὑποκόλπιος, εἷς ὑπὲρ ὦμον,
εἷς ἔφερεν τὸ φαγεῖν, εἷς δὲ πιεῖν ἐδίδου,
5 ἡ τετρὰς ἡ περίβλεπτος. ἐγὼ παίζων δὲ πρὸς αὐτόν
φημί, 'σὺ καὶ νύκτωρ, φίλτατε, παιδοτριβεῖς;'   1580

XII

ἄνθρωπε, ζωῆς περιφείδεο, μηδὲ παρ' ὥρην
ναυτίλος ἴσθι· καὶ ὡς οὐ πολὺς ἀνδρὶ βίος.
δείλαιε Κλεόνικε, σὺ δ' εἰς λιπαρὴν Θάσον ἐλθεῖν
ἠπείγευ Κοίλης ἔμπορος ἐκ Συρίης,
5 ἔμπορος ὦ Κλεόνικε· δύσιν δ' ὑπὸ Πλειάδος αὐτήν   1585
ποντοπορῶν αὐτῆι Πλειάδι συγκατέδυς.

BACCOY

I

οὐ μέλλω ῥεύσειν χρυσός ποτε· βοῦς δὲ γένοιτο
ἄλλος χὠ μελίθρους κύκνος ἐπηιόνιος·
Ζηνὶ φυλασσέσθω τάδε παίγνια· τῆι δὲ Κορίννηι
τοὺς ὀβολοὺς δώσω τοὺς δύο κοὐ πέτομαι.   1590

II

Φωκίδι πὰρ πέτρηι δέρκευ τάφον· εἰμὶ δ' ἐκείνων
τῶν ποτε Μηδοφόνων μνᾶμα τριηκοσίων,

XI *A.P.* 12.34 Αὐτομέδοντος caret Pl
1 παιδοτρίβην edd. vett.: -βη P
XII *A.P.* 7.534 [C] Αἰτωλοῦ Αὐτομέδοντος   [J] εἰς Κλεόνικον ἐν Θάσωι ναυαγήσαντα   Pl B Θεοκρίτου
3-6 om. Pl   5 Πλειάδος Graefe: Πληάδων P   6 ποντοπορῶν αὐτῆι
Pierson: ποντοπόρωι ναύτηι P

XI

A fortunate gymnastics-master

Yesterday I dined with the boys' trainer, Demetrius, of all men
the most fortunate. One lay in his lap, one leant on his shoulder,
one brought him food, one gave him drink, that admirable
quartette. So I said to him in fun, 'And at night, my good
friend, do you exercise them too?'

XII

Epitaph for Cleonicus

Mortal, be careful of your life, go not seafaring out of season;
even so a man's life is not long. Unhappy Cleonicus, you were
in such haste to reach bright Thasos, trading from Hollow
Syria,—trading, Cleonicus, and sailing at the very setting of the
Pleiads; so together with the Pleiads you sank.

BASSUS

I

A love simpler than those of Zeus

I am never going to flow as a shower of gold; let others turn
into bulls or swans melodious on the shore. Such tricks shall be
reserved for Zeus; I shall give Corinna her twopence, and make
no use of wings.

II

On the Spartan dead at Thermopylae

Behold the tomb beside the Phocian rock: I am the memorial
of those three hundred Mede-slayers of old, who fell far from

I *A.P.* 5.125 Βάccου [C] εἰc Κόριννάν ἑταίραν Pl A Βάccου
1 μέλλω CPl: -ει P   2 μελίθρουc Pl: μελόθ- P | ἐπτιόνιοc P: ἐπ' ἠϊόνοc Pl
II *A.P.* 7.243 [PC] Λολλίου Βάccου [P] εἰc [J] τοὺc αὐτοὺc τριακοcίουc Λακε-
δαιμονίουc τοὺc μετὰ Λεωνίδου Pl B Βάccου Suid. s.v. ταγόc (5–6)
2 μνᾶμα P: μνῆ- Pl

οἳ Σπάρτας ἀπὸ γᾶς τηλοῦ πέσον ἀμβλύναντες
Ἄρεα καὶ Μῆδον καὶ Λακεδαιμόνιον.
5 ἦν δ' ἐσορῆις ἐπ' ἐμεῖο †βοόστρυχον† εἰκόνα θηρός,   1595
ἔννεπε τοῦ ταγοῦ μνᾶμα Λεωνίδεω.

III

γαῖα Ταραντίνων, ἔχε μείλιχος ἀνέρος ἐσθλοῦ
τόνδε νέκυν. ψεῦσται δαίμονες ἀμερίων·
ἢ γὰρ ἰὼν Θήβηθεν Ἀτύμνιος οὐκέτι πρόσσω
ἤνυσεν, ἀλλὰ τεὴν βῶλον ὑπωικίσατο·   1600
5 ὀρφανικῶι δ' ἐπὶ παιδὶ λιπὼν βίον εὖνιν ἔθηκεν
†ὀφθαλμόν†· κείνωι μὴ βαρὺς ἔσσο τάφος.

IV

ἥδ' ἐγὼ ἡ τοσάκις Νιόβη λίθος ὁσσάκι μήτηρ,
δύσμορος, †ἦ μαστῶν ἔπηξα† γάλα.
Ἀίδεω πολὺς ὄλβος ἐμῆς ὠδῖνος ἀριθμός   1605
ἦν τέκον. ὢ μεγάλης λείψανα πυρκαϊῆς.

V

κλειδοῦχοι νεκύων, πάσας Ἀίδαο κελεύθους
φράγνυτε, καὶ στομίοις κλεῖθρα δέχοισθε πύλαι·
αὐτὸς ἐγὼν Ἀίδας ἐνέπω· Γερμανικὸς ἄστρων,
οὐκ ἐμός. οὐ χωρεῖ νῆα τόσην Ἀχέρων.   1610

4 Μῆδον P: -δων Pl | Λακεδαιμόνιον Boissonade: -ίαν P, -ίων Pl   5 ἐπ' CPl
Suid.: ὑπ' P | βοόστρυχον PSuid.ᴬ: βόστρυχον PlSuid.ʳᵉˡˡ· | θηρός Bro-
daeus: θήρης PPlSuid.   6 μνᾶμα PPl: μνῆ- Suid.

III A.P. 7.372 [C] Λολλίου Βάccου   [J] εἰς Ἀτύμνιον ὁμοίως ἐπὶ ξένης τελευτήcαντα Pl β Λολλίου
6 ὀφθαλμὸν P: -μῶν Pl

the land of Sparta, having blunted the warrior-might of both
Medes and Lacedaemonians. As for the 〈 〉 wild-beast's
image that you see upon me, proclaim it to be the memorial of
their commander Leonidas.

III

Epitaph for Atymnius

Earth of the Tarentines, hold in kindly embrace this corpse of a
noble man. The guardian-spirits of mortals are deceivers:
coming from Thebes, Atymnius reached no farther, but made
his home under your soil. He died and left his child an orphan;
he made 〈 〉 bereaved. Be not a heavy tomb for him.

IV

On Niobe

Here am I, Niobe, as many times stone as I was a mother; ill-
fated, in whose breast the milk froze hard. Great wealth for
Hades is the number of my offspring that I brought to birth. O
relics of a vast funeral-pyre!

V

On the death of Germanicus

Door-keepers of the dead, block all the roads to Hades; gates,
receive bolts in your sockets. It is I myself, Hades, who speak.
Germanicus belongs to the stars; he is not mine. Acheron has
no room for a vessel large enough.

IV *A.P.* 7.386 [C] Βάccου Λολλίου   [J] εἰc Νιόβην τὴν ἐν Cιπύλωι ἀπολιθωθεῖcαν
ἧcτινοc ἐν μιᾶι ἡμέραι ἑπτὰ υἱοὶ καὶ τοcαῦται θυγατέρεc ἐτελεύτηcαν   caret Pl
1 ἥδ᾽ Ap.B.: ἅδ᾽ P   3 ἀριθμόc P: -μούc C   4 ἦν Ellis: ἤ P
V *A.P.* 7.391 [C] Βάccου Λολλίου   [J] εἰc Γερμανικὸν τὸν Καίcαροc ἀδελφιδοῦν
τὸν πατέρα Νέρωνοc   caret Pl

VI

ἄρρηκτοι Μοιρῶν πυμάτην ἐσφράγισαν ὅρκοι
  τῶι Φρυγὶ πὰρ βωμῶι τὴν Πριάμου θυσίην·
ἀλλὰ σοί, Αἰνεία, στόλος ἱερὸς Ἰταλὸν ἤδη
  ὅρμον ἔχεν, πάτρης φροίμιον οὐρανίης.
5 ἐς καλὸν ὤλετο πύργος ὁ Τρώιος· ἦ γὰρ ἐν ὅπλοις   1615
  ἠγέρθη κόσμου παντὸς ἄνασσα πόλις.

VII

Ληθαίης ἀκάτοιο τριηκοσίους ὅτε ναύτας
  δεύτερον ἔσχ' Ἄιδης πάντας ἀρηϊφάτους,
'Cπάρτας ὁ στόλος' εἶπεν· 'ἴδ' ὡς πάλι πρόσθια πάντα
  τραύματα, καὶ στέρνοις δῆρις ἔνεστι μόνοις.   1620
5 νῦν γε μόθου κορέσασθε καὶ εἰς ἐμὸν ἀμπαύσασθε
  ὕπνον, ἀνικάτου δῆμος Ἐνυαλίου.'

VIII

οὐλόμεναι νήεσσι Καφηρίδες, αἵ ποτε νόστον
  ὠλέσαθ' Ἑλλήνων καὶ στόλον Ἰλιόθεν,
πυρσὸς ὅτε ψεύστας χθονίης δνοφερώτερα νυκτός   1625
  ἦψε σέλα, τυφλὴ δ' ἔδραμε πᾶσα τρόπις
5 χοιράδας ἐς πέτρας· Δαναοῖς πάλιν Ἴλιος ἄλλη
  ἔπλετο καὶ δεκέτους ἐχθροτέρη πολέμου.
καὶ τὴν μὲν τότ' ἔπερσαν, ἀνίκητος δὲ Καφηρεύς,
  Ναύπλιε, σοὶ γὰρ πᾶν Ἑλλὰς ἔκλαυσε δάκρυ.   1630

VI *A.P.* 9.236 [C] Βάccου Λολλίου   εἰς Αἰνείαν τὸν Τρῶα ὅτι ἐξ αὐτοῦ ἠγέρθη
ἡ μεγάλη πόλις Ῥωμαίων   Pl A Βάccου Λολλίου   εἰς τὸ αὐτό
1 ἐσφράγιcαν P: -φρήγ- Pl   2 πὰρ βωμῶι CPl: om. P   3 coὶ Pl: cὺ P
VII *A.P.* 9.279 [C] Βάccου   εἰς τοὺς τριακοσίους ἄνδρας τοὺς Cπαρτιάτας   Pl B
Βάccου

VI

On the Trojan origin of Rome

Unbreakable oaths of Destiny set their seal on the last sacrifice, that of Priam, beside the Phrygian altar. But your holy fleet, Aeneas, was already finding anchorage in Italy, a prelude to your home in heaven. It is well that the towers of Troy perished, for a city that is queen of the whole world arose in arms.

VII

On the Spartan dead at Thermopylae

When for the second time Hades received from the Lethaean boat three hundred men aboard, all slain in war, 'Sparta's is this host', he cried; 'see how again every wound is frontal, and the mark of battle is nowhere but on the breast. Now cease your hunger for strife; come and rest in the sleep I give, People of War invincible.'

VIII

On the dangerous rocks of Caphereus

Fatal to ships are you, the crags of Caphereus that once destroyed the home-coming of the Greeks and their fleet from Ilium, when the deceitful beacon kindled flames gloomier than the underworld's night, and every keel ran blind upon the rocky reefs; that was another Ilium for the Greeks, even more hateful than the ten years' war. Ilium indeed they sacked in those days, but Caphereus was unconquerable; it was for you, Nauplius, that Hellas wept all her tears.

4 καὶ P: κἤν Pl   6 ἀνικάτου P: -κήτ- Pl

VIII *A.P.* 9.289 [C] Βάccου   εἰc τὰc Καφηρίδαc πέτραc ἐν αἷc ἧψε τὰ πυρὰ Ναύπλιοc καὶ τοὺc Ἕλληναc μετὰ τῶν νεῶν ἔθραυcεν   Pl A Βάccου
1 νόcτον Ascensius: -του PPl   3 ψεύcταc P: -τηc Pl   4 cέλα Pl: -αc P
5 ἐc P: εἰc Pl   7 ἀνίκατοc P: -κητ- Pl

IX

μήτε με χείματι πόντος ἄγοι θρασύς, οὐδὲ γαλήνης
ἀργῆς ἠσπασάμην τὴν πολυνηνεμίην.
αἱ μεσότητες ἄρισται· ὅπηι δέ γε πρήξιες ἀνδρῶν,
καὶ πάλι μέτρον ἐγὼ τἄρκιον ἠσπασάμην.
5 τοῦτ' ἀγάπα, φίλε Λάμπι, κακὰς δ' ἔχθαιρε θυέλλας·   1635
εἰσί τινες πρηεῖς καὶ βιότου ζέφυροι.

X

ἡ πολιὴ κροτάφοισι Κυτώταρις, ἡ πολύμυθος
γραῖα, δι' ἣν Νέστωρ οὐκέτι πρεσβύτατος,
ἡ φάος ἀθρήσασ' ἐλάφου πλέον, ἡ χερὶ λαιῆι
γῆρας ἀριθμεῖσθαι δεύτερον ἀρξαμένη,   1640
5 ζώει καὶ λεύσσουσα καὶ ἀρτίπος οἷά τε νύμφη
ὥστε με διστάζειν μή τι πέπονθ' Ἀίδης.

XI

ἐκλάσθην ἐπὶ γῆς ἀνέμωι πίτυς· ἐς τί με πόντωι   (1643)
στέλλετε ναυηγὸν κλῶνα πρὸ ναυτιλίης;

IX A.P. 10.102 Βάccου Pl A s.a.n. Pl B Βάccου
1 ἄγοι PlᴬB: ἄγει P | γαλήνης PPlᴮ: -νην Plᴬ   2 ἀργῆς Plᴮ: -γας P, -γὴν
Plᴬ | πολυνηνεμίην Plᴬ: πάλι νην. P, παλινην. Plᴮ   3 πρήξιες Plᴬᴮ: πράξ-
P   4 πάλι Plᴮ: πάλαι P, μάλα Plᴬ   5 ἀγάπα PPlᴬPlᴮˢˢᶜʳ: -πη Plᴮ

IX

On moderation

Let not the fierce ocean carry me in stormy weather; nor yet
do I embrace the doldrums of idle calm. Middle courses are
best. Where the doings of men are concerned, there again I
embrace moderation as the all-sufficient. Be well-pleased with
this, my dear Lampis, and detest the mischief of the storm-winds.
In life too there are such things as gentle Zephyrs.

X

On a very old woman

That gray-head Cytotaris, that old woman of many words,
through whom Nestor has lost his record for longevity, she
who has seen the sunlight longer than a stag, and has begun to
count her old age a second time on her left hand,—she is living
with eyes wide open and frisky as a bride, so that I am in some
doubt whether Death has not died.

XI

On a fallen tree, better not used for ship's timber

A pine-tree am I that was broken by the wind ashore; why
send me to sea, a stem shipwrecked before sailing?

X *A.P.* 11.72 Βάccου Cμυρναίου εἰc γραῖαν   Pl A Νικάρχου
1 Κυτώταριc P: Κοτυτταρίc Pl   **5** καὶ λεύccουcα Pl: καὶ (αι sscr.) λέccουcα
ut vid. P
XI *A.P.* 9.30 [C] Ζηλώτου, οἱ δὲ Βάccου [J] εἰc πεύκην ὑπὸ ἀνέμου κλαcθεῖcαν
καὶ μέλλουcαν ναῦν γίνεcθαι   Pl A Ζηλώτου

ΒΙΑΝΟΡΟC

I

ἁ Μακέτις σε κέκευθε τάφου κόνις, ἀλλὰ πυρωθείς   1645
Ζανὶ κεραυνείωι γαῖαν ἀπηχθίσαο·
τρὶς γὰρ ἐπαστράψας, Εὐριπίδη, ἐκ Διὸς αἰθήρ
ἥγνισε †τὰν θνατὰν σήματοс† ἱστορίαν.

II

Θειονόης ἔκλαιον ἐμῆς μόρον, ἀλλ' ἐπὶ παιδός
ἐλπίσι κουφοτέρας ἔστενον εἰς ὀδύνας·   1650
νῦν δ' ἐμὲ καὶ παιδὸς φθονερὴ ἀπενόσφισε Μοῖρα·
φεῦ βρέφος, ἐψεύσθην καὶ σὲ τὸ λειπόμενον.
5 Περσεφόνη, τόδε πατρὸς ἐπὶ θρήνοισιν ἄκουσον·
θὲс βρέφος ἐс κόλπους μητρὸς ἀποιχομένης.

III

ἰχθύσι καὶ ποταμῶι Κλειτώνυμον ἐχθρὸς ὅμιλος   1655
ὧσεν ὅτ' εἰс ἄκρην ἦλθε τυραννοφόνος·
ἀλλὰ Δίκα μιν ἔθαψεν, ἀποσπασθεῖσα γὰρ ὄχθη
πᾶν δέμας ἐс κορυφὴν ἐκ ποδὸς ἐκτέρισεν.
5 κεῖται δ' οὐχ ὑδάτεσσι διάβροχος, αἰδομένα δέ
γᾶ κεύθει τὸν ἑᾶς ὅρμον ἐλευθερίας.   1660

I *A.P.* 7.49 Βιάνοροс Βιθυνοῦ [Βυθηνοῦ cod.]   εἰς τὸν αὐτόν   Pl b s.a.n.   εἰς
τὸν αὐτόν
2 κεραυνείωι Stephanus: -ναίωι PPl | γαῖαν C: παιαν P, πᾶσαν Pl | ἀπηχθίσαο
Page: ἀπηχθίασας P, ἀπημφίασας Pl   3 ἐπαστράψας P: ἀπ- Pl
4 θνατὰν...ἱστορίαν P: θνητὰν...ἱστορίην Pl
II *A.P.* 7.387 [C] Βιάνοροс   [J] εἰς Θεονόην τινὰ σὺν τῶι ἰδίωι παιδὶ ἅμα
τελευτήσασαν καὶ ταφεῖσαν   Pl a Βιάνοροс

BIANOR

I

On the tomb of Euripides, struck by lightning

The tomb's Macedonian dust concealed you, yet fire-struck by Zeus the Thunderer you put off the burden of earth. For thrice the sky lightened by the will of Zeus, Euripides, and ⟨consecrated your sepulchre to everlasting fame⟩.

II

On the death of Theionoê and her child

I was weeping for the death of my Theionoê; yet, because of my hopes for her child, lighter were the griefs with which I moaned in harmony. But now envious Fate has bereaved me of the infant as well,—alas, child, I am cheated even of you, all that was left. Persephone, listen to this, at a father's lamentation: lay the child on the bosom of its departed mother.

III

A miraculous burial

A hostile mob thrust Cleitonymus to the fishes and the river when he came as tyrant-killer to the acropolis. Yet Justice gave him burial; for the bank, torn away, honoured with funeral-rites his whole body from head to feet. Undrenched by the waters he lies; the earth in reverence covers the haven of her liberty.

I Θειονόης Pl: -όεις P | μόρον Cᵞᴾ: γάμον PPl   3 φθονερὴ Pl: -ὴν P | ἀπενόσφισε P: τις ἐνόσφ. Pl | μοῖρα Pl: -αν P   5 Περσεφόνη P: Φερ- Pl | ἄκουσον Pl: -σεν P

III *A.P.* 7.388 [C] τοῦ αὐτοῦ Βιάνορος   [J] εἴς τινα Κλειτώνυμον τύραννον. οὐκ οἶδα δ' ὅστις ἐστὶν οὗτος ὁ Κλειτώνυμος   Pl A Βιάνορος   Pl B Βιήνορος
2 τυραννοφόνος CPlᴬᴮ: -φόρος P   3 Δίκα PPlᴮ: -κη Plᴬ | μιν CPlᴬᴮ: μὲν (?) P
5 αἰδομένα PPlᴮ: -νη Plᴬ   6 γᾶ PPlᴮ: γῆ Plᴬ | ἑᾶς PPlᴮ: ἑῆς Plᴬ | ἐλευθερίας edd. vett.: -ίης PPlᴬᴮ

IV

ὕστατον ἐθρήνησε τὸν ὠκύμορον Κλεαρίστη
παῖδα καὶ ἀμφὶ τάφωι πικρὸν ἔπαυσε βίον·
κωκύσασα γὰρ ὅσσον ἐχάνδανε μητρὸς ἀνίη
οὐκέτ᾿ ἐπιστρέψαι πνεύματος ἔσχε τόνους.
5 θηλύτεραι τί τοσοῦτον ἐμετρήσασθε τάλαιναι   1665
θρῆνον, ἵνα κλαύσητ᾿ ἄχρι καὶ Ἀίδεω;

V

πάντα Χάρων ἄπληστε, τί τὸν νέον ἥρπασας αὕτως   (1667)
Ἄτταλον; οὐ σὸς ἔην κἂν θάνε γηραλέος;

VI

Οἰδίποδος παίδων Θήβη τάφος, ἀλλ᾿ ὁ πανώλης
τύμβος ἔτι ζώντων αἰσθάνεται πολέμων.   1670
κείνους οὐδ᾿ Ἀίδης ἐδαμάσσατο· κἠν Ἀχέροντι
μάρνανται· κείνων χὠ τάφος ἀντίπαλος·
5 καὶ πυρὶ πῦρ ἤλεγξαν ἐναντίον. ὢ ἐλεεινοί
παῖδες ἀκοιμήτων ἁψάμενοι δοράτων.

VII

ἀγγελίην πὰρ Ζηνὸς ἐπεὶ φέρεν ἠεροδίνης   1675
αἰετός, οἰωνῶν μοῦνος ἐνουράνιος,

IV *A.P.* 7.644 [C] Βιάνορος γραμματικοῦ   [J] εἴς τινα γυναῖκα Κλεαρίστην τὸν
ἴδιον υἱὸν ὀδυρομένην καὶ διωλύγιον ἀνακράξασαν ⟨ὥστε⟩ τὴν ψυχὴν ἀπορρῆξαι
Pl A Βιάνορος
V *A.P.* 7.671 [C] ἄδηλον, οἱ δὲ Βιάνορος   [J] εἰς Ἄτταλον νεώτερον   Pl A s.a.n.
1 αὕτως C: αὕτως Pl, οὕτως P   2 κἂν P: κεὶ Pl | θάνε CPl: θάνεν P |
γηραλέος CPl: ρηρ- (?) P
VI *A.P.* 7.396 [C] Βιάνορος Βιθυνοῦ [Βυθηνοῦ cod.]   [J] εἰς Ἐτεοκλέα καὶ

IV

The strange death of Clearista

Clearista mourned her last for a child too early dead, and beside
the tomb she ended her bitter life; wailing with all the fullness
of a mother's grief, she could no longer relax her straining
breath. Wretched women, why do you give yourselves such
full measure of lamentation that you weep your way even to
the grave?

V

Epitaph for Attalus

Ever insatiable Charon, why have you stolen Attalus, a mere
child? Was he not yours even if he had died old?

VI

On the undying feud between the sons of Oedipus

Thebes is the grave of the sons of Oedipus; yet the all-destroying
tomb feels their warfare living still. Not even Hades has subdued them; even in Acheron they are fighting, even their tomb
is divided against itself. They have proved that even fire may
be adversary to fire. O pitiable sons, unresting are the spears you
seized.

VII

The archer killed by his victim

As the high-circling eagle, alone of birds a heaven-dweller,
was bearing a message from Zeus, it passed too slowly by the

Πολυνείκην τοὺς Οἰδίποδος παῖδας   Pl A Βιάνορος   εἰς Ἐτεοκλέα καὶ Πολυνείκην   Pl B s.a.n.
2 πολέμων P: δοράτων Pl^A, πολέμων hic, δοράτων v. 6 Pl^B, litteris αβ adfixis
vocabula invicem mutanda notans   3 οὐδ' Pl^B: οὔτ' PPl^A | κὴν PPl^A: κεῖν'
Pl^B   4 ἀντίπαλος CPl^AB: -πυλος P
VII *A.P.*9.223 [C] Βιάνορος εἰς ἀετὸν τοξευθέντα ὑπὸ Κρητὸς καὶ τὸν τοξεύσαντα
διὰ τοῦ αὐτοῦ βέλους κτείναντα   Pl A Βιάνορος

οὐκ ἔφθη τὸν Κρῆτα, θοὴν δ' ἐπετείνατο νευρήν,
πτηνὸν δ' ὁ πτερόεις ἰὸς ἐληίσατο.
5 Ζηνὸς δ' οὔτι δίκην ἔλαθεν φόνος, ἔμπεσε δ' ὄρνις
ἀνδρί, τὰ δ' εὐστοχίης ἀνταπέτισε βέλη·   1680
αὐχένι δ' ἰὸν ἔπηξεν, ὃν ἥπατι κοίμισεν αὐτός,
ἓν δὲ βέλος δισσῶν αἷμ' ἔπιεν θανάτων.

VIII

ἀκταίην παρὰ θῖνα διαυγέος ἔνδοθεν ἅλμας
ἰχθύα πουλυπόδην ἔδρακεν ἰχθυβόλος,
νηχομένωι δ' ἐπόρουσε καὶ ἐξ ἁλὸς ἧκ' ἐπὶ χέρσον   1685
ἁρπάγδην ἄγρης δεσμὸν ὑποφθάμενος.
5 αὐτὰρ ὁ δισκηθεὶς κατακαίριος ἔμπεσε δειλῶι
πτωκί, παχεῖ σχοίνωι κεῖτο γὰρ ὑπναλέος·
τὸν δὲ χυθεὶς περὶ πάντα πεδήσατο· φωτὶ δ' ὑπ' ἄγρης
ἐμβυθίης ἄγρη χερσόθεν ἠντίασε.   1690

IX

ἐς βαθὺν ἥλατο Νεῖλον ἀπ' ὀφρύος ὀξὺς ὁδίτης
ἡνίκα λαιμάργων εἶδε λύκων ἀγέλην·
ἀλλά μιν ἀγρεύσαντο δι' ὕδατος, ἔβρυχε δ' ἄλλος
ἄλλον ἐπουραίωι δήγματι δραξάμενος·
5 μακρὰ γεφυρώθη δὲ λύκοις βυθός, ἔφθανε δ' ἄνδρα   1695
νηχομένων θηρῶν αὐτοδίδακτος ἄρης.

3 ἐπετείνατο P: ἐνετ- Pl   5 φόνος Graefe: μόνος P, νόμος Pl

VIII A.P. 9.227 [C] Βιάνορος εἰς ἁλιέα ἀγρεύσαντα ὀκτάπουν καὶ διὰ τοῦ
ὀκτάποδος λαγωόν   caret Pl
2 ἰχθύα C: -ύων (?) P   6 παχεῖ σχοίνωι Boissonade: παχυσχοίνω P
7 ἄγρης Jacobs: -ην P   8 ἐμβυθίης Jacobs: -ην P

Cretan, who stretched his rapid string against it, and the feathered arrow made the flyer its prize. The justice of Zeus failed not to mark the killing: the bird fell upon the man and paid him out for his shafts of true aim. The eagle pierced his neck with the arrow which he had given a resting-place in its liver; so a single shaft drank the blood of a double death.

VIII

A fisherman's double catch

Beside the sea-beach, within the translucent brine, a fisherman espied the many-footed fish. As it swam he rushed upon it, snatched it and threw it from sea to shore, too quick for his prey's enchaining. So hurled by happy chance it fell on a timorous hare that lay sleeping in the thick rushes. It spread itself all about it and bound it fast; so for the man through his catch from the deep there came a catch from the shore.

IX

How the wolves pursued their victim in the Nile

Swift from the bank the traveller leapt into the deep Nile when he saw the pack of ravenous wolves; but they chased him through the water, and one fastened its teeth on another, gripping with a bite on its tail. So the deeps were bridged by the wolves in a long line, and the self-taught tactics of the swimming beasts overtook the man.

IX *A.P.* 9.252 [C] ἀδέσποτον [J] εἰς ὁδίτην τινὰ ὑπὸ λύκων διωκόμενον καὶ εἰς ποταμὸν ἑαυτὸν ῥίψαντα, ὃν οἱ λύκοι καὶ εἰς αὐτὸ τὸ ὕδωρ ἐδίωκον Pl A Βιάνορος 1 ἐc P: εἰc Pl 2 εἶδε λύκων Pl: λύκων εἶδεν P 3 ἀγρεύσαντο Pl: ἀγεύ- P 4 δραξάμενος P: πλεξάμ- Pl

X

ἤριπεν ἐξ ἄκρης δόμος ἀθρόος, ἀλλ' ἐπὶ παιδί
νηπιάχωι Ζεφύρου πολλὸν ἐλαφρότερος.
φείσατο κουροσύνης καὶ ἐρείπιον· ὢ μεγάλαυχοι
μητέρες, ὠδίνων καὶ λίθος αἰσθάνεται.   1700

XI

καρφαλέος δίψει Φοίβου λάτρις εὖτε γυναικός
εἶδεν ὑπὲρ τύμβου κρωσσίον ὀμβροδόκον,
κλάγξεν ὑπὲρ χείλους, ἀλλ' οὐ γένυς ἥπτετο βυσσοῦ·
Φοῖβε, σὺ δ' εἰς τέχνην ὄρνιν ἐκαιρομάνεις·
5 χερμάδι δ' ὑψηλῶν σφαλερὸν ποτόν, ἅρπαγι χείλει   1705
ἔφθανε μαιμάσσων λαοτίνακτον ὕδωρ.

XII

καύματος ἐν θάμνοισι λαλίστατος ἡνίκα τέττιξ
φθέγξατο διγλώσσωι μελπόμενος στόματι,
δουνακόεντα Κρίτων συνθεὶς δόλον εἷλεν ἀοιδόν
ἤερος, οὐκ ἰδίην ἰξοβολῶν μελέτην.   1710
5 ἄξια δ' οὐχ ὁσίης θήρης πάθεν, οὐ γὰρ ἔτ' ἄλλων
πήξατ' ἐπ' ὀρνίθων εὔστοχον ὡς πρὶν ἄγρην.

X *A.P.* 9.259 [C] Βιάνορος   εἰς δόμον καταπεσόντα ἐν ὧι ἦν βρέφος καὶ διεσώθη
Pl A Βιάνορος   Pl B Βιάνορος
2 ἐλαφρότερος CPl^{AB}: -τατος P   3 ἐρείπιον Pl^{AB}: ἐρίπ- P

XI *A.P.* 9.272 [C] Βιάνορος   εἰς Ἀπόλλωνος ἱερὸν ὄρνεον ἐν τύμβωι γεγλυμμέ-
νον ἄγγος θεασάμενον καὶ ζητοῦντα ἐν αὐτῶι ὕδωρ   caret Pl

X

An infant survives the collapse of a house

The house collapsed in a heap from top to bottom, but over
the infant child far lighter than a Zephyr. Even the ruins were
merciful to childhood. O mothers of proud boast, even the
stones have feeling for your birth-pains.

XI

How the crow reached the water in a pitcher

When Phoebus' servant, parched with thirst, saw a rain-holding
pitcher on top of a woman's tomb, it croaked above the edge,
but its beak could not reach the deeps. So you, Phoebus, inspired your bird to timely artifice: heightening with a pebble
the elusive draught, eagerly with greedy lips it overtook the
stone-stirred water.

XII

The penalty for killing a cicada

When the chatterbox cicada cried out, singing with two-
tongued mouth among the bushes in the heat, Criton fitted
together his deceitful reeds and stole the songster from the air,
a limer bent on business not his own. He was properly punished
for that impious chase: no longer could he fasten his snare on
his other prey, the birds, with true aim as before.

2 ὀμβροδόκον Salm.: -κην P   5 χερμάδι δ' ὑψηλῶν Page: χερμάδα δὲ
ψαλμῶν P | σφαλερὸν Harberton: σφαῖρον P   6 λαοτίνακτον Salm.: -τίτακτον
P
XII *A.P.* 9.273 [C] τοῦ αὐτοῦ [sc. Βιάνοροϲ]   εἰϲ τέττιγα ὃν ἰξοεργόϲ τιϲ Κρίτων
ὥϲπερ ϲτρουθίον ἐθήραϲεν   caret Pl
4 ἰξοβολῶν Salm.: ἐξο- P

XIII

λάρνακα πατρώιων ἔτι λείψανα κοιμίζουσαν
νεκρῶν χειμάρρωι παῖς ἴδε cυρομένην·
καί μιν ἄχος τόλμης ἐπλήcατο, χεῦμα δ' ἀναιδές   1715
εἰcέθορεν· πικρὴν δ' ἦλθ' ἐπὶ cυμμαχίην.
5 ὀcτέα μὲν γὰρ ἔcωcεν ἀφ' ὕδατος, ἀντὶ δὲ τούτων
αὐτὸς ὑπὸ βλοcυροῦ χεύματος ἐφθάνετο.

XIV

πῶλον τὸν πεδίων ἀλλ' οὐχ ἁλὸς ἱππευτῆρα
νηὶ διαπλώειν πόντον ἀναινόμενον   1720
μὴ θάμβει χρεμέθοντα καὶ ἐν ποcὶ λὰξ πατέοντα
τοίχους καὶ θυμῶι δεcμὰ βιαζόμενον·
5 ἄχθεται εἰ φόρτου μέρος ἔρχεται, οὐ γὰρ ἐπ' ἄλλοις
κεῖcθαι τὸν πάντων ἔπρεπεν ὠκύτατον.

XV

φῶρες ὅτ' εἰνάλιοι Τυρcηνίδος ἀγχόθι δίνης   1725
φορμικτὰν ἀκάτου θῆκαν ὑπὲκ βύθιον,
αὐτίκα μιν κιθάρηι λιγυαχέι δέξατο δελφίν
cύνθρονον, ἐκ δὲ βυθοῦ νήχεθ' ἑλιccόμενος
5 μέχρις ἐπ' Ἰcθμὸν ἔκελσε Κορίνθιον· ἦ ρα θάλαccα
ἰχθῦc ἀνθρώπων εἶχε δικαιοτέρους.   1730

XIII A.P. 9.278 [C] Βιάνορος   εἰc λάρνακα λείψανα φέρουcαν ἀνδρὸς ἦν χει-
μάρρους κατέcυρεν   Pl A Βιάνορος
1 πατρώιων CPl: -ωον P, -ωαν C^sscr | κοιμίζουcαν Pl: κομίζουcαν C, κομί-
ζουcα P

XIII

*On a boy drowned while rescuing
his parents' coffin*

A boy saw a casket, still giving repose to the relics of his parents'
bodies, swept away by a torrent. Grief filled him with courage,
and he leapt into the ruthless stream. But the help he came to
offer cost him sore: the bones he rescued from the water, but in
their stead he himself was overtaken by the savage flood.

XIV

A horse on board ship

If the horse—rider of plains, not ocean—refuses to sail the sea
by ship, wonder not at his whinnying and kicking the side-walls
with his hooves and angrily forcing the bonds. He bears it ill,
if he must go as a mere portion of the freight; it was not right
that the swiftest of all creatures should stand at rest on other
conveyances.

XV

Arion and the dolphin

When the sea-brigands near the Tyrrhenian eddies put the harper
overboard into the deeps, straightway a dolphin took him and
seated him together with his clear-sounding cithara, and swam
dancing from the deeps till it came ashore at the isthmus of
Corinth. Truly the sea had fishes more righteous than men.

XIV *A.P.* 9.295 [C] Βιάνοροс   ἐπὶ ἵππωι ὠκυτάτωι μὴ βουλομένωι εἰcελθεῖν ἐν
νηί   Pl A Βιάνοροc
XV *A.P.* 9.308 [C] Βιάνοροc   εἰc 'Αρίωνα τὸν Μηθυμναῖον καὶ τὸν δελφῖνα
Pl A Βιάνοροc
2 ὑπὲκ βύθιον Jacobs: ὑπερβύθιον PPl   3 λιγυαχέι P: -ηχέι Pl
4 cύνθρονον P: -θροον Pl   5 ἦ ῥα Pl^pc: ἄρα PPl^ac

XVI

Cάρδιεc αἱ τὸ πάλαι Γύγου πόλιc αἵ τ' Ἀλυάττου,
Cάρδιεc, αἱ βασιλεῖ Περcὶc ἐν Ἀσιάδι,
αἳ Κροίcωι τὸ παλαιὸν ἐπλινθώσασθε μέλαθρον
ὄλβον Πακτωλοῦ ῥεύματι δεξάμεναι,
5 νῦν δὴ ὅλαι δύστηνοι ἐc ἓν κακὸν ἁρπασθεῖσαι   1735
ἐc βυθὸν ἐξ ἀχανοῦc χάσματος ἠρίπετε.
Βοῦρα καὶ Ἷc' Ἑλίκη κεκλωσμέναι· αἱ δ' ἐνὶ χέρcωι
Cάρδιεc ἐμβυθίαιc εἰc ἓν ἔκεισθε τέλοc.

XVII

κοῦρον ἀποπλανίην ἐπιμάζιον Ἑρμώνακτα,
φεῦ, βρέφος ὡς ἀδίκως εἵλετε, βουγενέεc·   1740
ἠγνοίηcεν ὁ δειλὸc ἐc ὑμέαc οἷα μελίccαc
ἐλθών· αἱ δ' ἔχεων ἦτε χερειότεραι.
5 ἀντὶ δέ οἱ θοίνηc ἐνεμάξατε φοίνια κέντρα,
ὦ πικραί, γλυκερῆc ἀντίπαλοι χάριτος.

XVIII

μὴ πόδα γυμνὸν ἔρεσσε δι' ὑλάεσσαν ἀταρπόν   1745
Αἰγύπτου· χαροπῶν φεῦγε διὲξ ὀφίων,
ἀγρεῦ δουνακοδῖφα, τὸν ἐκ χέρσου δὲ φύλαξαι
ἰόν, ὁ τοξεύειν ὄρνιν ἐπειγόμενος.

XIX

ἠνίδε καὶ χέρσου τὸ γεωτόμον ὅπλον ἐρέccει
καὶ τὸν ὑπουθατίαν μόσχον ἄγει δάμαλιc,   1750

XVI *A.P.* 9.423 Βιάνοροc   εἰc Cάρδειc τὴν πόλιν [C] διὰ τὴν προτέραν εὐδαιμο-
νίαν πρὸc τὴν νῦν ἐρήμωσιν Pl A Βιάνοροc
2 αἱ P: & Pl | Ἀσιάδι Pl: Ἀσίδι P   3 αἵ P: & Pl | κροίcω P^{sscr}Pl: κρυcω P
5 δὴ Hermann: δὲ PPl | δύστηνοι P: -ναι Pl | ἐc Lascaris: εἰc PPl   6 ἀχανοῦc
Pl: ἀφανοῦc P   7 Ἷc' Ἑλίκη Reiske: εἰc Ἑλίκην PPl | κεκλωσμέναι edd. vett.:
-μένα PPl   8 ἐμβυθίαιc Reiske: ἐν βυθίαιc PPl

BIANOR

XVI

On the destruction of Sardis by earthquake

Sardis, of old the city of Gyges, the city of Alyattes, Sardis, for
the Great King an Anatolian Persia, builder in bygone days of
a palace for Croesus, taking wealth from the stream of Pactolus:
now, ill-fated, wholly to a single doom you are swept away,
tumbling to the depths through the earth's vast yawning. Bura
and Helicê had a fate like yours; you, Sardis, on the mainland,
are laid low in the same ending as those cities deep-drowned.

XVII

A child stung to death by bees

Children of the ox, how wrong of you to slay Hermonax, a
nursling boy astray. Poor wretch, he knew you not when he
came to you as if to honey-bees; but you were worse than vipers.
Instead of feasting him, you pressed your murderous stings
into him, bitter creatures, contraries of your sweet gift.

XVIII

Egyptian snakes

Speed not your foot unshod along the forest paths of Egypt;
fly from the grim serpents, reed-hunting fowler. Beware of
the poison from the land, as you hasten to shoot the fowls of
the air.

XIX

A cow suckles while ploughing

See how the heifer both speeds the land's earth-cleaving tool
and leads her suckling calf. The driver-herdsman she dreads,

XVII *A.P.* 9.548 Βιάνορος   Pl A Βιάνορος
3 δειλὸς P: δείλαιος Pl   **5** ἐνεμάξατε Pl: ἐναιμ- P
XVIII *A.P.* 10.22 Βιάνορος   caret Pl
3 δουνακοδῖφα Huschke: -δηφα P
XIX *A.P.* 10.101 Βιάνορος   caret Pl
2 μόσχον Huschke: -χει P

βούταν μὲν τρομέουσα διάκτορα, τὸν δὲ μένουσα
νήπιον, ἀμφοτέρων εὔστοχα φειδομένα.
5 ἴσχε᾽, ἀροτροδίαυλε πεδώρυχε, μηδὲ διώξηις
τὰν διπλοῖς ἔργοις διπλὰ βαρυνομέναν.

XX

τὸ σκάφος οὐ βυθὸς εἷλε· πόθεν βυθός; οὐ γὰρ ἔπλωσεν·   1755
οὐδὲ νότος, πρὸ νότου δ᾽ ὤλετο καὶ πελάγευς.
ἤδη γάρ μιν ἅπασαν ἐπὶ ζυγὰ γομφωθεῖσαν
ἤλειφον πεύκης τῆι λιπαρῆι νοτίδι,
5 πίσσα δ᾽ ὑπερβρασθεῖσα πυρὸς φλογὶ τὴν ἁλὶ πιστήν
τευχομένην γαίηι δεῖξεν ἀπιστοτέρην.   1760

XXI

οὗτος ὁ μηδέν, ὁ λιτός, ὁ καὶ λάτρις, οὗτος ἐρᾶται·   (1761)
ἔστι τινὸς ψυχῆς κύριος ἀλλοτρίης.

XXII

ἔστησεν Περίανδρος ᾽Αρίονος εἰκόνα ταύτην
καὶ τὸν ἀπολλυμένωι σύνδρομα νηξάμενον
εἰνάλιον δελφῖνα. λέγει δ᾽ ἐπ᾽ ᾽Αρίονι μῦθος·   1765
῾κτεινόμεθ᾽ ἀνθρώποις, ἰχθύσι σωιζόμεθα.᾽

4 φειδομένα Page: -η P   5 ἴσχε᾽ Jacobs: ἴσχες P
XX A.P. 11.248 Βιάνορος   Pl A Βιάνορος
XXI A.P. 11.364 Βιάνορος   Pl B s.a.n.

yet lingers for her little one, careful of both, shrewd-guessing. Hold back, earth-delver, as you plough to and fro, press not hard upon her who bears the double burden of double tasks.

XX

On a ship burnt before launching

It was not the deeps that destroyed the ship. How could it be the deeps? She never sailed. Nor the south-wind: she perished too soon for south-wind and sea. She was already all bolted up to her benches, and they were anointing her with the pine's oily juice, when the pitch boiled over in the fire's flame and proved her, though fashioned to be faithful at sea, too faithless on land.

XXI

A lowly man in love

This nobody, this paltry man, this lackey,—even he is loved; he is master of some other's soul.

XXII

On a statue of Arion and the dolphin

Periander set up this image of Arion and of the dolphin that swam in the sea, running alongside as he was perishing. The words on Arion say 'By men we are murdered, by fishes saved'.

I λιτὸς Pl: λειτ- P | ἐρᾶται Scaliger: ὁρᾶτε P, ὁρᾶται Pl
XXII *A.Pl.* (A) 276 Βιάνοροϲ   εἰϲ εἰκόνα Ἀρίονοϲ τοῦ κιθαρωιδοῦ   caret P
3 ἐπ' Ἀρίονι edd. vett.: ὁ παρ' ἠόνι Pl

ΒΟΗΘΟΥ

I

εἰ τοῖος Διόνυσος ἐς ἱερὸν ἦλθεν Ὄλυμπον
κωμάζων Λήναις σύν ποτε καὶ Σατύροις,
οἷον ὁ τεχνήεις Πυλάδης ὀρχήσατο κεῖνον
ὀρθὰ κατὰ τραγικῶν τέθμια μουσοπόλων,
5 παυσαμένη ζήλου Διὸς ἂν φάτο σύγγαμος Ἥρη
'ἐψεύσω, Σεμέλη, Βάκχον· ἐγὼ δ' ἔτεκον.'

1770

ΚΡΙΝΑΓΟΡΟΥ

I

κἢν ῥίψῃις ἐπὶ λαιὰ καὶ ἢν ἐπὶ δεξιὰ ῥίψῃις,
Κριναγόρη, κενεοῦ σαυτὸν ὕπερθε λέχους,
εἰ μή σοι χαρίεσσα παρακλίνοιτο Γέμελλα,
γνώσῃι κοιμηθεὶς οὐχ ὕπνον ἀλλὰ κόπον.

1775

II

τὸν σκοπὸν Εὐβοίης ἁλικύμονος ᾖσεν Ἀριστώ
Ναύπλιον, ἐκ μολπῆς δ' ὁ θρασὺς ἐφλεγόμην.
ὁ ψεύστης δ' ὑπὸ νύκτα Καφηρείης ἀπὸ πέτρης
πυρσὸς ἐμὴν μετέβη δυσμόρου ἐς κραδίην.

1780

I *A.P.* 9.248 [C] Βοηθοῦ τοῦ ἐλεγειογράφου   εἰς Πυλάδην τὸν ὀρχηστὴν ὑποκρι-
νόμενον τὸν Διόνυσον   Pl A Βοηθοῦ
3 ὀρχήσατο P: ὠρ- Pl
I *A.P.* 5.119 Κριναγόρου   [J] εἰς τὴν αὐτοῦ ἐρωμένην Γέμελλαν   Pl A Κριναγόρου

BOËTHUS

I

Praise of a pantomimist

If Dionysus had come in this form to holy Olympus revelling
with Bacchants and Satyrs of old, as Pylades the artist danced
him by the true canons of those who serve the Muses in Tragedy,
then would Hera, the consort of Zeus, have ceased from
jealousy and said 'You lied, Semelê, about Bacchus; it was I
who bore him'.

CRINAGORAS

I

A restless night

Though you throw yourself to the left, though to the right,
Crinagoras, upon your empty bed, unless lovely Gemella re-
clines beside you, when you lie abed you will know not sleep
but suffering.

II

A singing-girl enchants her lover

Aristo sang of Nauplius, watchman of sea-girt Euboea; and I,
the rash lover, was inflamed by her song. That faithless flame
by night from the rock of Caphereus passed into my unhappy
heart.

I λαιἀ CPl: λαιᾶι P   3 Γέμελλα P: -μιλλα Pl

II *A.P.* 9.429 Κριναγόρου   εἰς τὸν ἐν Ναυπλίαι σκοπόν   caret Pl
I 'Αριστώ Salm.: -τωι P   3 ὑπὸ Salm.: ὑπὲρ P | Καφηρείης Brunck: Ταφ-
P   4 δυσμόρου P^(ac) ut vid.: -ρος P^(pc)

III

ἀργύρεόν σοι τόνδε γενέθλιον ἐς τεὸν ἦμαρ,
  Πρόκλε, νεόσμηκτον δουρατίην κάλαμον,
εὖ μὲν ἐυσχίστοισι διάγλυπτον κεράεσσιν,
  εὖ δὲ ταχυνομένην εὔροον εἰς σελίδα,
5 πέμπει Κριναγόρης, ὀλίγην δόσιν ἀλλ᾽ ἀπὸ θυμοῦ   1785
  πλείονος, ἀρτιδαεῖ σύμπονον εὐμαθίηι.

IV

αἰετοῦ ἀγκυλοχείλου ἀκρόπτερον ὀξὺ σιδήρωι
  γλυφθὲν καὶ βαπτῆι πορφύρεον κυάνωι,
ἤν τι λάθηι μίμνον μεταδόρπιον ἐγγὺς ὀδόντων,
  κινῆcαι πρηεῖ κέντρωι ἐπιστάμενον,   1790
5 βαιὸν ἀπ᾽ οὐκ ὀλίγης πέμπει φρενός, οἶα δὲ δαιτός
  δῶρον ὁ πᾶς ἐπὶ σοί, Λεύκιε, Κριναγόρης.

V

χάλκεον ἀργυρέωι με πανείκελον Ἰνδικὸν ἔργον,
  ὄλπην, ἡδίστου ξείνιον εἰς ἑτάρου,
ἦμαρ ἐπεὶ τόδε σεῖο γενέθλιον, υἱὲ Cίμωνος,   1795
  πέμπει γηθομένηι σὺν φρενὶ Κριναγόρης.

VI

εἴαρος ἄνθει μὲν τὸ πρὶν ῥόδα, νῦν δ᾽ ἐνὶ μέσσωι
  χείματι πορφυρέας ἐσχάσαμεν κάλυκας

III A.P. 6.227 Κριναγόρου Μυτιληναίου   Suid. s.v. ἀρτιδαεῖ (1 + πέμπω ἀρτιδ. κ.τ.λ.)   caret Pl
5 πέμπει P: -πω Suid.   6 ἀρτιδαεῖ Suid.: -δαῆ P | σύμπονον apogr.: -πνοον PSuid. | εὐμαθίηι P: ἐργασίηι Suid.
IV A.P. 6.229 Κριναγόρου   caret Pl

III

A birthday-present for Proclus

This spear-like silver pen, fresh-polished, neatly cut with well-divided tips, smooth-flowing on the hurried page, Crinagoras sends you for your birthday, Proclus, a little gift but from a larger heart, to work with you in your lately-learnt scholarship.

IV

Gift of a tooth-pick to Lucius

This pointed wing-tip of a crook-beaked eagle, carved with the knife and purple with dyed lacquer, skilled in shifting with gentle sting whatever remains hidden about the teeth after dinner,—this, Lucius, your devoted friend Crinagoras sends you, a small token of a large affection, a sort of souvenir from our feast.

V

A birthday-present for the son of Simon

A work of bronze from India, very like a silver one, an oil-flask, a gift to a dear friend's house, since this is your birthday, son of Simon, Crinagoras sends with heart rejoicing.

VI

Roses in winter for a lady

Roses once bloomed in spring; now in mid-winter we have opened our crimson cups, glad and smiling on this your birth-

---

1 ἀγκυλοχείλου Salm.: -λος P   5 φρενός C: -νας P | δαιτός Salm.: δαπὸς P
6 ὁ πᾶς Hecker: ὄπασσ' P

V *A.P.* 6.261 Κριναγόρου   Suid. s.v. ὄλπη (1–3 γεν.)   caret Pl
1 'Ινδικὸν CSuid.: εἰδικὸν P   2 ὄλπην P: -πιν Suid.

VI *A.P.* 6.345 τοῦ αὐτοῦ [sc. Κριναγόρου]   caret Pl

cῆι ἐπιμειδήσαντα γενεθλίηι ἄςμενα τῆιδε
   ἠοῖ νυμφιδίων ἀccοτάτηι λεχέων.   1800
5 καλλίcτηc cτεφθῆναι ἐπὶ κροτάφοιcι γυναικόc
   λώιον ἢ μίμνειν ἠρινὸν ἠέλιον.

VII

βύβλων ἡ γλυκερὴ λυρικῶν ἐν τεύχεϊ τῶιδε
   πεντὰc ἀμιμήτων ἔργα φέρει χαρίτων
   †Ἀνακρείοντοc, ἃc ὁ Τήιοc ἡδὺc πρέcβυc   1805
   ἔγραψεν ἢ παρ' οἶνον ἢ cὺν Ἱμέροιc†.
5 δῶρον δ' εἰc ἱερὴν Ἀντωνίηι ἤκομεν ἠῶ
   κάλλευc καὶ πραπίδων ἔξοχ' ἐνεγκαμένηι.

VIII

λαμπάδα, τὴν κούροιc ἱερὴν ἔριν, ὠκὺc ἐνέγκαc
   οἷα Προμηθείηc μνῆμα πυρικλοπίηc   1810
νίκηc κλεινὸν ἄεθλον ἔτ' ἐκ χερὸc ἔμπυρον Ἑρμῆι
   θῆκεν ὁμωνυμίηι παῖc πατρὸc Ἀντιφάνηc.

IX

ἠοῖ ἐπ' εὐκταίηι τάδε ῥέζομεν ἱρὰ τελείωι
   Ζηνὶ καὶ ὠδίνων μειλίχωι Ἀρτέμιδι·
τοῖcι γὰρ οὑμὸc ὅμαιμοc ἔτ' ἄχνοοc εὔξατο θήcειν   1815
   τὸ πρῶτον γενύων ἠϊθέοιcιν ἔαρ.
5 δαίμονεc ἀλλὰ δέχοιcθε, καὶ αὐτίκα τῶνδ' ἀπ' ἰούλων
   Εὐκλείδην πολιῆc ἄχριc ἄγοιτε τριχόc.

---

3 γενεθλίηι Reiske: -ληι P   5 καλλίcτηc Reiske: -τη P
VII *A.P.* 9.239 [C] Κριναγόρου   εἰc βίβλον λυρικὴν Ἀνακρέοντοc   caret Pl
4 ἢ cὺν Ἱμέροιc C (idem ἰαμβικόν addit): caret P   **5** Ἀντωνίηι Dorville:
-ίη P   **6** ἐνεγκαμένηι Dorville: -νην P

day, so near to your bridal-bed. Better to be wreathed on the temples of the loveliest of women than to wait for the sun of spring.

VII

Anacreon's poems a gift to Antonia

The delightful quintet of lyric books inside this case brings works of inimitable charm,—Anacreon's, which that pleasant old man from Teos wrote in his cups or with the Passions' help. We come to her holy day, a gift for Antonia, winner of beauty's and wisdom's highest prize.

VIII

Dedication after victory in the torch-race

Antiphanes, son of a like-named father, having swiftly borne the torch, object of the boys' ritual race, memorial of Prometheus' fire-theft, dedicated to Hermes the glorious prize of victory still alight in his hands.

IX

Euclides cuts his first beard

On the longed-for morning we make these sacrifices to Zeus the fulfiller and Artemis the soother of birth-pangs; for to them my brother, yet beardless, vowed to dedicate the young man's earliest bloom of spring on his cheeks. Accept it, Divinities, and presently bring Euclides from this first growth to the season of gray hair.

VIII *A.P.* 6.100 Κριναγόρου   ἀνάθημα Ἑρμῆι παρὰ ᾽Αντιφάνους   caret Pl
1 λαμπάδα C: -δι P | ἐνέγκας Ap.B.: ἐναγκάς P   **2** πυρικλοπίης P: πυροκ- C
3 ἔτ᾽ apogr.: om. P | χερὸς Dorville: χειρ- P
IX *A.P.* 6.242 Κριναγόρου   caret Pl
3 θήσειν C: -σεις P   **6** τριχός C: τρι⁑χός P

X

ἑσπερίου Μάρκελλος ἀνερχόμενος πολέμοιο
σκυλοφόρος κραναῆς τέλσα παρ' Ἰταλίης   1820
ξανθὴν πρῶτον ἔκειρε γενειάδα. βούλετο πατρίς
οὕτως καὶ πέμψαι παῖδα καὶ ἄνδρα λαβεῖν.

XI

Καλλιμάχου τὸ τορευτὸν ἔπος τόδε· δὴ γὰρ ἐπ' αὐτῶι
ὠνὴρ τοὺς Μουσέων πάντας ἔσεισε κάλως·
ἀείδει δ' Ἑκάλης τε φιλοξείνοιο καλιήν   1825
καὶ Θησεῖ Μαραθὼν οὓς ἐπέθηκε πόνους.
5 τοῦ σοι καὶ νεαρὸν χειρῶν σθένος εἴη ἀρέσθαι,
Μάρκελλε, κλεινοῦ τ' αἶνον ἴσον βιότου.

XII

Ἥρη Ἐληθυιῶν μήτηρ, Ἥρη δὲ τελείη,
καὶ Ζεῦ γινομένοις ξυνὸς ἅπασι πατήρ,   1830
ὠδῖνας νεύσαιτ' Ἀντωνίηι ἵλαοι ἐλθεῖν
πρηείας μαλακαῖς χερσὶ σὺν Ἠπιόνης,
5 ὄφρα κε γηθήσειε πόσις μήτηρ θ' ἑκυρή τε·
ἦ νηδὺς οἴκων αἷμα φέρει μεγάλων.

XIII

Τυρσηνῆς κελάδημα διαπρύσιον σάλπιγγος   1835
πολλάκι Πισαίων στρηνὲς ὑπὲρ πεδίων

X A.P. 6.161 [=Pᵃ] ἀνάθημα παρὰ Μαρκέλλου ⟦Κριναγόρου: hoc del. C, pergit idem in rasura⟧ ὑπάτου Κριναγόρου, denuoque post 6.344 [=Pᵇ] Κριναγόρου Pl A Κριναγόρου Suid. s.v. σκῦλα (1–2)
2 τέλσα Pᵇ: τέρμα PᵃPlSuid.

XI A.P. 9.545 Κριναγόρου Pl B Κριναγόρου Schol. Ar. Equ. 753 s.a.n. (1–2)
2 κάλως edd. vett.: -λους PPl   4 οὓς P: τοὺς Pl   5 νεαρὸν Pᵖᶜ: -ρῶν PᵃᶜPl

X

Marcellus cuts his first beard

Marcellus, returning trophy-laden from the western war to the bounds of craggy Italy, then first cut his flaxen beard. This was his fatherland's desire, to send him out a boy and take him back a man.

XI

Callimachus' 'Hecalê' a gift to Marcellus

This chiselled poem is by Callimachus; the man shook the Muses' sail-reefs all loose above it. He sings of the hut of hospitable Hecalê, and what labours Marathon set for Theseus. May it be granted you to attain his hands' youthful strength, Marcellus, and equal fame for a life of glory.

XII

For Antonia, soon to be a mother

Hera, mother of the goddesses of child-birth, Hera of marriage-rites, and Zeus, common father to all that are born, be gracious and grant that travail come to Antonia gently with the soft hands of Epionê, so that father and mother and wife's mother may rejoice. Truly her womb bears the blood of princely houses.

XIII

For Demosthenes, an Olympic victor

Former times could often tell of the Etruscan trumpet's piercing clangour sounding shrill over Pisa's plains for twofold victory;

XII *A.P.* 6.244 Κριναγόρου   caret Pl
1 Ἐληθυιῶν Ap.B.: Εἰληθυῶν P, Εἰλειθυῶν C | τελείη C: τελέσει (?) P   **2** πατήρ Reiske: -τερ P   **4** πρηείας C: πρησεί- P | Ἠπιόνης C: -νίης P   **5** ἑκυρή Geist: -ρά P   **6** ἣ Sitzler: ἡ P | οἴκων C: -κος (?) P
XIII *A.P.* 6.350 Κριναγόρου   caret Pl
2 πεδίων C: -δίον P

φθεγξαμένης ὁ πρὶν μὲν ἔχει χρόνος ἐν δυσὶ νίκαις·
εἰ δὲ σὺ καὶ τρισσοὺς ἤγαγες εἰς στεφάνους
5 ἀστοὺς Μιλήτου, Δημόσθενες, οὔ ποτε κώδων
χάλκεος ἤχησεν πλειοτέρωι στόματι.   1840

XIV

δειλαίη, τί σε πρῶτον ἔπος, τί δὲ δεύτατον εἴπω;
δειλαίη· τοῦτ᾽ ἐν παντὶ κακοῦ ἔτυμον.
οἴχεαι, ὦ χαρίεσσα γύναι, καὶ ἐς εἴδεος ὥρην
ἄκρα καὶ εἰς ψυχῆς ἦθος ἐνεγκαμένη.
5 Πρώτη σοι ὄνομ᾽ ἔσκεν ἐτήτυμον· ἦν γὰρ ἅπαντα   1845
δεύτερ᾽ ἀμιμήτων τῶν ἐπὶ σοὶ χαρίτων.

XV

Γῆ μευ καὶ μήτηρ κικλήσκετο, γῆ με καλύπτει
καὶ νέκυν· οὐ κείνης ἥδε χερειοτέρη.
ἔσσομαι ἐν ταύτηι δηρὸν χρόνον, ἐκ δέ με μητρός
ἥρπασεν ἠελίου καῦμα τὸ θερμότατον.   1850
5 κεῖμαι δ᾽ ἐν ξείνηι ὑπὸ χερμάδι μακρὰ γοηθείς
Ἴναχος εὐπειθὴς Κριναγόρου θεράπων.

XVI

δείλαιοι, τί κεναῖσιν ἀλώμεθα θαρσήσαντες
ἐλπίσιν ἀτηροῦ ληθόμενοι θανάτου;
ἦν ὅδε καὶ μύθοισι καὶ ἤθεσι πάντα Σέλευκος   1855
ἄρτιος, ἀλλ᾽ ἥβης βαιὸν ἐπαυρόμενος
5 ὑστατίοις ἐν Ἴβηρσι τόσον δίχα τηλόθι Λέσβου
κεῖται ἀμετρήτων ξεῖνος ἐπ᾽ αἰγιαλῶν.

4 εἰς apogr.: εἰ P   5 ἀστοὺς Stadtmüller: -τὸς P   6 ἤχησεν C: ἤχειον (?) P
XIV A.P. 5.108 Κριναγόρου   [J] εἰς κόρην καλουμένην Πρώτην   caret Pl
2 κακοῦ Page: -κῶι P   3 γύναι C: νύμφη P
XV A.P. 7.371 [C] Κριναγόρου   [J] εἰς Ἴναχον τὸν Κριναγόρου θεράποντα ἐπὶ
ξένης τελευτήσαντα Pl B s.a.n.

but when you, Demosthenes, brought Miletus' citizens to a threefold crowning, never was brazen bell that rang with louder voice.

XIV

On the death of Protê

Unfortunate, what shall I say to you first, what last? Unfortunate: that is the true word in our depth of sorrow. You are gone, gracious lady, excelling in beauty's bloom and soul's character. There was truth in the name they gave you, meaning 'First'; for all things were second to your inimitable graces.

XV

Epitaph for a faithful servant

'Earth' was she named who bore me, and earth it is that covers my corpse. No worse is this earth than that: in this I shall rest a long time; from my mother I was taken by the sun's hottest blaze. In a foreign land I lie beneath a stone, loud-lamented, Inachus, obedient servant of Crinagoras.

XVI

Epitaph for Seleucus

Poor fools, why do we wander thus heartened by empty hopes, forgetful of ruinous death? Here was Seleucus, perfect in all his words and ways; yet, enjoying youth's prime but a brief season, among the outermost Iberians he lies, sundered so far from Lesbos, a stranger on untrodden shores.

5 δ' ἐν PPl^ac: δὲ Pl^pc

XVI *A.P.* 7.376 [C] Κριναγόρου   [J] εἰς Cέλευκον νέον τελευτήσαντα   Pl B Κριναγόρου
2 ἀτηροῦ PPl: -ῶι C | ληθόμενοι Salm.: αἰθ- P, αἰcθ- Pl | θανάτου P: θανάτωι C, βιότου Pl

XVII

ἠρνήσαντο καὶ ἄλλαι ἑὸν πάρος οὔνομα νῆσοι
ἀκλεέc, ἐc δ' ἀνδρῶν ἦλθον ὁμωνυμίην·   1860
κληθείητε καὶ ὔμμεc Ἐρωτίδεc. οὐ νέμεσίc τοι,
Ὀξεῖαι, ταύτην κλῆσιν ἀμειψαμέναιc.
5 παιδὶ γάρ, ὃν τύμβωι Διῆc ὑπεθήκατο βώλου,
οὔνομα καὶ μορφὴν αὐτὸc ἔδωκεν Ἔρωc.
ὦ χθὼν cηματόεccα καὶ ἡ παρὰ θινὶ θάλαccα,   1865
παιδὶ cὺ μὲν κούφη κεῖcο, cὺ δ' ἡcυχίη.

XVIII

καὶ αὐτὴ ἤχλυcεν ἀκρέcπεροc ἀντέλλουcα
Μήνη, πένθοc ἑὸν νυκτὶ καλυψαμένη,
οὔνεκα τὴν χαρίεccαν ὁμώνυμον εἶδε Cελήνην
ἄπνουν εἰc ζοφερὸν δυομένην Ἀίδην·   1870
5 κείνηι γὰρ καὶ κάλλοc ἑοῦ κοινώcατο φωτόc
καὶ θάνατον κείνηc μῖξεν ἑῶι κνέφεϊ.

XIX

Ὑμνίδα τὴν Εὐάνδρου, ἐράcμιον αἰὲν ἄθυρμα
οἰκογενέc, κούρην αἱμύλον εἰναέτιν,
ἥρπαcαc, ὦ ἄλλιcτ' Ἀίδη, τί πρόωρον ἐφιείc   1875
μοῖραν τῆι πάντωc cεῖό ποτ' ἐccομένηι;

XVII A.P. 7.628 [C] Κριναγόρου   [J] εἰc παιδίον εὐμορφότατον ἐν νήcωι
τελευτῆcαν καὶ ταφέν, ἐξ οὗ αἱ νῆcοι Ἐρωτίδεc   Pl A Κριναγόρου
3 ὔμμεc Stephanus: ἄμμεc PPl   4 Ὀξεῖαι Geist: ὄξει P, ἕξει C, ὄξει an ἕξει
incertum Pl, sequitur spat. vac. litt. ii vel iii   5 ὑπεθήκατο Grotius: -κατε
PPl   7 χθὼν Lascaris: χθὸν PPl

208

XVII

On the death of a boy named 'Love'

Other islands too in time past have renounced their own in-
glorious names and have come to call themselves the same as
men. So be you called 'Love's islands'; none shall be jealous,
Needles, if you take that name in exchange. For Love himself
gave his name and beauty to the boy whom Diës laid beneath
a mound of earth. Grave-yard land, and sea beside the shore,
lie the one lightly, the other calm, upon this child.

XVIII

On the death of a lady named after
the moon, 'Selenê'

The Moon herself darkened when she rose at nightfall and
veiled her mourning in the blackness, on seeing her lovely
namesake, Selenê, breath-bereft, descending to the gloom of
Hades. With her she had shared the beauty of her light, and
with her death she mingled her own darkness.

XIX

Epitaph for a slave-girl

You have stolen Euander's Hymnis, ever his darling and delight,
born in the house, nine years old, a maiden of winning ways;
implacable Hades, why send so early doom to one who must
anyway be yours hereafter?

XVIII *A.P.* 7.633 [C] Κριναγόρου   [J] εἰς Cελήνην τινὰ [C] γυναῖκα [J]
ὁμώνυμον cελήνηc δι' ὑπερβολὴν κάλλουc ⟦τεθνηκυῖαν erasum⟧   caret Pl
5 κείνηι Ap.G.: -νη P
XIX *A.P.* 7.643 [C] Κριναγόρου   [J] εἰς παιδίcκην Ὑμνίδα [sequitur voc.
corrupt.: παίcτριαν Stadtmüller] τὴν Εὐάνδρου   Pl в Κριναγόρου
2 εἰναέτιν Salm.: οἰνα- P, ἐννα- Pl   3 αλλιcτ' P^ac: ἄλιcτ' P^pc, ἄλληcτ' Pl
4 τῆι...ἐccομένηι Dorville: τὴν...-ην PPl | cεῖό ποτ' Pl: cοὶ ποθ' P

XX

ὦ δύστην᾽ ὄλβοιο Φιλόστρατε, ποῦ σοι ἐκεῖνα
σκῆπτρα καὶ αἱ βασιλέων ἄφθονοι εὐτυχίαι
αἷσιν ἐπηιώρηςας ἀεὶ βίον ἢ ἐπὶ Νείλωι
⟨ἢ παρ᾽ Ἰου⟩δαίοις ὢν περίοπτος ὅροις;
5 ὀθνεῖοι καμάτους τοὺς coὺς διεμοιρήσαντο,
cὸς δὲ νέκυς ψαφαρῆι κείcετ᾽ ἐν Ὀστρακίνηι.

1880

XXI

Ὀθρυάδην, Cπάρτης τὸ μέγα κλέος, ἢ Κυνέγειρον
ναυμάχον ἢ πάντων ἔργα κάλει πολέμων·
Ἄρριος αἰχμητὴς Ἰταλὸς παρὰ χεύμαςι Νείλου
κλινθεὶς ἐκ πολλῶν ἡμιθανὴς βελέων,
5 αἰετὸν ἁρπαςθέντα φίλου στρατοῦ ὡς ἴδ᾽ ὑπ᾽ ἐχθροῖς,
αὖτις ἀρηϊφάτων ἄνθορεν ἐκ νεκύων,
κτείνας δ᾽ ὅς cφ᾽ ἐκόμιζεν ἑοῖς ἀνεςώςατο ταγοῖς,
μοῦνος ἀήττητον δεξάμενος θάνατον.

1885

1890

XXII

μὴ εἴπηις θάνατον βιότου ὅρον· εἰcὶ καμοῦcιν
ὡς ζωοῖς ἀρχαὶ cυμφορέων ἕτεραι.
ἄθρει Νικιέω Κώιου μόρον· ἤδη ἔκειτο
εἰν Ἀίδηι, νεκρὸς δ᾽ ἦλθεν ὑπ᾽ ἠέλιον.
5 ἀcτοὶ γὰρ τύμβοιο μετοχλίσσαντες ὀχῆας
εἴρυσαν ἐς ποινὰς τλήμονα διcθανέα.

1895

XX *A.P.* 7.645 [C] Κριναγόρου [J] εἰς Φιλόστρατόν τινα πλούcιον καὶ εὐτυχῆ ἐπὶ ξένης τελευτήcαντα Pl в Κριναγόρου
4 ἢ παρ᾽ Ἰουδαίοις Cichorius: δαίοις, spat. vac. relicto, PPl, κεῖcαι Ἰου- suppl. man. rec. in P | ὅροις Pl: ὅρρις P
XXI *A.P.* 7.741 in duo epp. discerptum: 1–2 [C] Κριναγόρου [J] εἰς Ὀθρυάδην τὸν Cπαρτιάτην 3–8 [C] ἄδηλον [J] εἰς Ῥωμαῖον cτρατιώτην ἀριστεύσαντα [sequitur voc. dub. lect.] Pl в Κριναγόρου
2 κάλει πολέμων P: καλιπτολέμων Pl 3–4 denuo marg. inf. scripti [=P²]
3 Ἄρριος Scaliger: Ἄρεος PP²Pl | Νείλου PP²: Ῥήνου Pl et C^γρ 6 αὖτις Pl: -θις P 7 ὅς Lascaris: ὅ PPl

XX

On a friend fallen from high estate

Ill-starred in your prosperity, Philostratus, where are those sceptres and abundant princely blessings on which you ever made your life depend, a man of eminence whether on the Nile or within the boundaries of Judaea? Strangers have shared out the fruits of your labour, and your corpse shall lie in sandy Ostracina.

XXI

A Roman saves the legionary Eagle

Call Othryadas to witness, Sparta's great glory, or Cynegeirus the sea-fighter, or the great deeds of any war: Arrius, an Italian warrior, lay by the Nile's streams half-dead from many missiles; but when he saw the eagle snatched from his dear legion in the enemy's power, he leapt up once more from the bodies of the battle-slain, killed the man who was carrying it off, and returned it safe to his commanders. He alone got death without defeat.

XXII

The disinterment of Nicias, tyrant of Cos

Say not that death is the limit of life. For the dead, as for the living, new sufferings may begin. Look at the fate of Nicias of Cos: already he lay in Hades, yet his corpse came back to the daylight. His townsmen forced apart the fastenings of his tomb and dragged the wretch forth to pay his penalty in a second death.

XXII *A.P.* 9.81 [C] Κριναγόρου [J] ὅτι καὶ νεκροὶ πολλάκις πάσχουσιν ἀναίσθητα μέν, ἀλλ᾽ ὅμως πάσχουσιν. καὶ βλέπε τὸν Μαυρικίου τάφον καὶ τὸν Ἀμαντίου, ὧν ὁ μὲν ἐξεβλήθη καὶ κατεσκάφη, ὁ δ᾽ ἐξερρίφη καὶ κατεσπάρη, ὁ μὲν ἐπὶ Λέοντος, ὁ δ᾽ ἐπὶ Ῥωμανοῦ, καὶ ταῦτα βασιλέων. τί δ᾽ ἂν εἴποις περὶ τῶν λοιπῶν ἀνθρώπων; Pl A Κριναγόρου

1 βιότου P: -τῆς Pl | καμοῦσιν Pl: -cι P   2 ἕτεραι P: -ρων Pl   5 ἀστοὶ PPl^pc: αὐτοὶ Pl^ac | μετοχλίccαντεc Pl: -λήcαντεc P   6 ἐc P: εἰc Pl | διcθανέα Stephanus: δυcθ- PPl

XXIII

αἶγά με τὴν εὔθηλον, ὅσων ἐκένωσεν ἀμολγεύς
οὔθατα πασάων πουλυγαλακτοτάτην,
γευσάμενος μελιηδὲς ἐπεί τ' ἐφράσσατο πῖαρ
Καῖσαρ κἢν νηυσὶν σύμπλοον εἰργάσατο.   1900
5 ἥξω δ' αὐτίκα που καὶ ἐς ἀστέρας· ὧι γὰρ ἐπέσχον
μαζὸν ἐμόν, μείων οὐδ' ὅσον Αἰγιόχου.

XXIV

ψιττακὸς ὁ βροτόγηρυς ἀφεὶς λυγοτευχέα κύρτον
ἤλυθεν ἐς δρυμοὺς ἀνθοφυεῖ πτέρυγι,
αἰεὶ δ' ἐκμελετῶν ἀσπάσμασι Καίσαρα κλεινόν   1905
οὐδ' ἂν' ὄρη λήθην ἤγαγεν οὐνόματος·
5 ἔδραμε δ' ὠκυδίδακτος ἅπας οἰωνὸς ἐρίζων
τίς φθῆναι δύναται δαίμονι 'χαῖρ'' ἐνέπειν.
Ὀρφεὺς θῆρας ἔπεισεν ἐν οὔρεσιν, ἐς σὲ δέ, Καῖσαρ,
νῦν ἀκέλευστος ἅπας ὄρνις ἀνακρέκεται.   1910

XXV

ἄγχουροι μεγάλαι κόσμου χθόνες, ἃς διὰ Νεῖλος
πιμπλάμενος μελάνων τέμνει ἀπ' Αἰθιόπων,
ἀμφότεραι βασιλῆας ἐκοινώσασθε γάμοισιν,
ἓν γένος Αἰγύπτου καὶ Λιβύης θέμεναι.
5 ἐκ πατέρων εἴη παισὶν πάλι τοῖσιν ἀνάκτων   1915
ἔμπεδον ἠπείροις σκῆπτρον ἐπ' ἀμφοτέραις.

XXIII A.P. 9.224 [C] Κριναγόρου   ἐπὶ τῆι αἰγὶ ἧς ὁ Καῖσαρ τὸ γάλα ἤσθιεν
καὶ πλέων σύμπλουν ταύτην ἐκόμιζεν   Pl A Κριναγόρου
3 ἐφράσσατο Pl: -άσατο P   4 εἰργάσατο P: ἠγάγετο Pl
XXIV A.P. 9.562 [C] Κριναγόρου   εἰς τὸν Καίσαρος ψιττακόν   Pl A Φιλίππου
1 λυγοτευχέα P: λογοτ- Pl   2 ἐς P: εἰς Pl   6 δαίμονι PPl: Καίσαρι

XXIII

On a royal milch-goat

I am the milch-goat, milkiest of all whose udders the dairy-pail ever drained; and Caesar, when he had tasted and marked my richness, sweet as honey, made me his fellow-voyager even on board. Soon I shall reach even to the stars; for the man to whom I gave my breast is not the least inferior to the Aegis-bearer.

XXIV

A parrot teaches other birds to say 'Hail, Caesar'

Man's mimic, the parrot, left its wicker-work cage and went to the woods on flowery wings, and ever practising for its greetings the glorious name of Caesar, forgot it not even among the hills. So all the birds, quickly taught, came running in rivalry, who should be first to say 'Greetings' to the god. Orpheus made beasts obey him on the hills; to you, Caesar, now every bird tunes up unbidden.

XXV

On the wedding of Juba II and Cleopatra-Selenê

Great neighbour-regions of the world, which the Nile, swollen from dusky Ethiopia, severs, you have made common kings for both by marriage, making a single race of Egyptians and Libyans. May the kings' children hold from their fathers in their turn firm dominion over both mainlands.

P^{marg}   **7** ἐc cὲ δέ Jacobs: ἄιcαι δὲ P, ἐc δὲ cὲ Pl   **8** ἀκέλευcτοc Lascaris: -λευτ- PPl

XV *A.P.* 9.235 [C] τοῦ αὐτοῦ [sc. Κριναγόρου]   εἰc τὴν γῆν Αἰγύπτου καὶ Λιβύηc ὅτι τὸ τῶν βαcιλέων κῆδοc ἀμφοτέραc cυνῆψεν, τῶν Πτολεμαίων δηλονότι caret Pl

XXVI

οὔρεα Πυρηναῖα καὶ αἱ βαθυαγχέες Ἄλπεις,
αἳ Ῥήνου προχοὰς ἐγγὺς ἀποβλέπετε,
μάρτυρες ἀκτίνων, Γερμανικὸς ἃς ἀνέτειλεν
ἀστράπτων Κελτοῖς πουλὺν Ἐνυάλιον.   1920
5 οἱ δ᾽ ἄρα δουπήθησαν ἀολλέες, εἶπε δ᾽ Ἐνυώ
Ἄρεϊ 'τοιαύταις χερσὶν ὀφειλόμεθα'.

XXVII

οὐδ᾽ ἢν Ὠκεανὸς πᾶσαν πλήμυραν ἐγείρηι,
οὐδ᾽ ἢν Γερμανίη Ῥῆνον ἅπαντα πίηι,
Ῥώμης δ᾽ οὐδ᾽ ὅσσον βλάψει σθένος, ἄχρι κε μίμνηι   1925
δεξιὰ σημαίνειν Καίσαρι θαρσαλέη.
5 οὕτως καὶ ἱεραὶ Ζηνὸς δρύες ἔμπεδα ῥίζαις
ἑστᾶσιν, φύλλων δ᾽ αὖα χέους᾽ ἄνεμοι.

XXVIII

ἀντολίαι δύσιες κόσμου μέτρα· καὶ τὰ Νέρωνος
ἔργα δι᾽ ἀμφοτέρων ἵκετο γῆς περάτων.   1930
ἥλιος Ἀρμενίην ἀνιὼν ὑπὸ χερσὶ δαμεῖσαν
κείνου, Γερμανίην δ᾽ εἶδε κατερχόμενος.
5 διccὸν ἀειδέσθω πολέμου κράτος· οἶδεν Ἀράξης
καὶ Ῥῆνος δούλοις ἔθνεσι πινόμενοι.

XXVI *A.P.* 9.283 [C] Κριναγόρου   εἰς Γερμανικὸν τὸν πατέρα Νέρωνος ὅτε τοὺς Κελτοὺς κατεπολέμησεν   Pl A Βάccου   εἰς Γερμανικόν
1 Πυρηναῖα Pl: Πυρρήν- P

XXVII *A.P.* 9.291 Κριναγόρου   [C] εἰς Ῥώμην τὴν πόλιν διὰ τὸ ἀήττητον αὐτὴν τότε εἶναι, νυνὶ δὲ πάσης δρυὸς ἐστιν ἐλεεινοτέρα   Pl A Κριναγόρου   εἰς Ῥώμην

XXVI

On Germanicus, conqueror of the Celts

Pyrenean mountains and deep-valleyed Alps that face the Rhine's flood near-by, you bear witness to the rays that Germanicus made to dawn with lightnings of mighty battle against the Celts. They in their masses crashed to earth, and Enyo said to Ares 'To such hands as these our services are due'.

XXVII

Rome is invincible while she trusts Caesar

Not even though Ocean rouse all her flood, not even though Germany drink all the Rhine, not the least will it injure the strength of Rome, so long as she remains confident in Caesar, that he rules aright. Even so the holy oaks of Zeus stand rooted firm while the withered leaves are scattered by the winds.

XXVIII

On Nero, victorious from the Rhine
to the Araxes

Sunrise and sunset mark the world's limits, and the deeds of Nero have passed through both boundaries of the earth. The sun at its rising has seen Armenia subdued under his hand, and Germany at its going down. Let us sing his twofold victory in war; it is known to the Araxes and the Rhine, now drunk by peoples enslaved.

1 πλήμυραν P: πλήμμ- CPl   2 Γερμανίη P: -νη Pl | ἅπαντα CPl: πάντα P
3 δ' P: om. Pl   5 οὕτως P: -τω Pl
XXVIII A.Pl. (A) 61 Κριναγόρου   εἰς Νέρωνος [sc. εἰκόνα]   caret P
3 'Αρμενίην edd. vett.: ἁρμον- Pl

XXIX

κἢν μυχὸν Ὀρκυναῖον ἢ ἐς πύματον Cολόεντα   1935
ἔλθηι καὶ Λιβυκῶν κράσπεδον Ἑσπερίδων
Καῖσαρ ὁ πουλυσέβαστος, ἅμα κλέος εἷσιν ἐκείνωι
πάντηι· Πυρήνης ὕδατα μαρτύρια.
5 οἷσι γὰρ οὐδὲ πέριξ δρυτόμοι ἀπεφαιδρύναντο,
λουτρὰ καὶ ἠπείρων ἔccεται ἀμφοτέρων.   1940

XXX

ἔρδοι τὴν ἔμαθέν τις, ὅπου καὶ ὑπ' Ἄλπιας ἄκρας
ληϊcταὶ λαcίαις ἀμφίκομοι κεφαλαῖc
φωρῆς ἀπτόμενοι φύλακας κύνας ὧδ' ἀλέονται·
χρίονται νεφροῖς πῖαρ ἔπεστιν ὅcον
5 ψευδόμενοι ῥινῶν ὀξὺν cτίβον. ὢ κακὸν εὑρεῖν   1945
ῥηίτεραι Λιγύων μήτιες ἢ ἀγαθόν.

XXXI

νῆcον, τὴν εἰ κἀμὲ περιγράψαντες ἔχουσιν
μετρῆcαι βαιήν, ἑπτὰ μόνον cταδίους,
ἔμπης καὶ τίκτουσαν ἐπ' αὔλακα πῖαρ ἀρότρου
ὄψει καὶ παντὸς κάρπιμον ἀκροδρύου   1950
5 καὶ πολλοῖς εὔαγρον ὑπ' ἰχθύcι καὶ ὑπὸ Μαίρηι
εὐάνεμον λιμένων τ' ἤπιον ἀτρεμίηι,
ἀγχόθι Κορκύρης Φαιηκίδος· ἀλλὰ γελᾶcθαι
†τῶι ἐπεωρίcθην† τοῦτ' ἐθέμην ὄνομα.

XXIX A.P. 9.419 Κριναγόρου   εἰς τὸν cεβαστὸν Καίcαρα [C] τὸν Αὔγουcτον
θαυμαστόν   caret Pl
2 ἔλθηι Dorville: -ηιc P
XXX A.P. 9.516 Κριναγόρου   ἀδιανόητον παντελῶc   Pl A Κριναγόρου [om.
1–4]

XXIX

Pyrenaean waters attest the fame of Augustus

Though Caesar the Most August should journey to the depths
of Hercynia's forest or outermost Soloeis and the fringe of the
Libyan Hesperides, glory shall go with him everywhere. The
waters of the Pyrenees are witness: in them not even the neighbouring wood-cutters washed, yet now they shall be baths for
both continents.

XXX

How Alpine bandits put dogs off their track

'Every man to his trade': the shaggy shock-headed bandits on
the Alpine peaks, when they take a robbery in hand, escape
the watch-dogs in this way: they grease themselves with the
fat that covers kidneys, and so deceive the muzzle's keen track-
ing. Ligurian cleverness is readier at finding the villainous than
the virtuous way.

XXXI

On a little island with a ludicrous name

An island,—the tiny one, if men can mark about and measure
such as me, not more than seven stades,—you shall nevertheless
see me bringing forth to the furrow the plough's fat harvest,
with a crop too of every tree-fruit, and good hunting-ground
with many fishes, with cool winds under the dog-star, and
gentle in my harbour's stillness, close to Phaeacian Corcyra.
But this name I took ⟨   ⟩ to be mocked at.

4 ἔπεστιν Heyne, ὅσον Scaliger: ἀπεστινόσου P   5 κακὸν Pl: καλ- P
6 ῥηίτεραι Pl: -ροι P | ἀγαθόν P^margPl: -θῶν P
XXXI *A.P.* 9.555 Κριναγόρου caret Pl
I κἀμὲ Page: καί με P   2 cταδίουc P^ac: -οιc P^pc

XXXII

πλοῦς μοι ἐπ' Ἰταλίην ἐντύνεται· ἐς γὰρ ἑταίρους   1955
στέλλομαι, ὧν ἤδη δηρὸν ἄπειμι χρόνον.
διφέω δ' ἡγητῆρα περίπλοον, ὅς μ' ἐπὶ νήσους
Κυκλάδας ἀρχαίην τ' ἄξει ἐπὶ Σχερίην.
5 σύν τί μοι ἀλλά, Μένιππε, λάβευ φίλος, ἵστορα κύκλον
γράψας, ὦ πάσης ἴδρι γεωγραφίης.   1960

XXXIII

ῥιγηλὴ πασῶν ἔνοσι χθονός, εἴτε σε πόντου   (1961)
εἴτ' ἀνέμων αἴρει ῥεῦμα τινασσόμενον,
οἰκία μοι ῥύευ νεοτευχέα. δεῖμα γὰρ οὔπω
ἄλλο τόσον γαίης οἶδ' ἐλελιζομένης.

XXXIV

φρὴν ἱερὴ μεγάλου Ἐνοσίχθονος, ἔσσο καὶ ἄλλοις   1965
ἠπίη, Αἰγαίην οἳ διέπουσιν ἅλα·
κἠμοὶ γὰρ Θρήικι διωκομένῳ ὑπ' ἀήτῃ
ὤρεξας πρηεῖ' ἀσπασίῳ λιμένας.

XXXV

εἰ καί σοι ἑδραῖος ἀεὶ βίος, οὐδὲ θάλασσαν
ἔπλως, χερσαίας τ' οὐκ ἐπάτησας ὁδούς,
ἔμπης Κεκροπίης ἐπιβήμεναι, ὄφρ' ἂν ἐκείνας   1970
Δήμητρος μεγάλων νύκτας ἴδῃς ἱερῶν.
5 τῶν ἄπο κἠν ζωοῖσιν ἀκηδέα, κεῦτ' ἂν ἵκηαι
ἐς πλεόνων, ἕξεις θυμὸν ἐλαφρότερον.

XXXII *A.P.* 9.559 Κριναγόρου   [C] διὰ τὸν πλοῦν τὸν ἐπ' Ἰταλίας   caret Pl
3 διφέω Ap.B.: δηφ- P
XXXIII *A.P.* 9.560 τοῦ αὐτοῦ [sc. Κριναγόρου]   caret Pl
1 ἔνοσι χθονός Jacobs: ἐνοσίχθονος P   2 αἴρει Chardon: ἔρρει P | τινασσό-
μενον Pᵖᶜ: -νων Pᵃᶜ   4 οἶδ' Chardon: εἶδ' P

XXXII

Preparation for a journey to Italy

I am getting ready to sail to Italy. I am going to join my friends, from whom I have been away so long a time, and I am looking for a circumnavigator-guide to the island Cyclades and ancient Scheria. Now, Menippus, give me a little help, my friend, writing me a scholarly Tour, my expert in all geography.

XXXIII

An earthquake

Most dreaded of all shocks, earthquake, whether it be ocean's or wind's shuddering storm that uplifts you, spare my new-built house; so great a terror as earthquake I have never known.

XXXIV

Safe landing after a storm at sea

Holy spirit of the great earth-shaker, be gentle to others also who cross the Aegean sea; to me, pursued by the wind from Thrace, you were gracious and offered harbours to my delight.

XXXV

A stay-at-home advised to see the Eleusinian mysteries

Though your life is always sedentary, and you have neither sailed the sea nor trodden roads ashore, still, set foot in Attica to see those nights of Demeter's great mysteries. Thence you shall get a heart that is care-free among the living and less heavy when you go to join the majority.

XXXIV *A.P.* 10.24 Κριναγόρου   caret Pl
1 μεγάλου Meineke: -λη P

XXXV *A.P.* 11.42 Κριναγόρου   Pl a Κριναγόρου
3 ἂν P: ἐν Pl | ἐκείναc Brunck: -ναιc PPl   **4** Δήμητρος Pl: -ριος P | μεγάλων Brunck: -λαc PPl   **5** κῆν P: κἂν Pl

XXXVI

γείτονες οὐ τρισσαὶ μοῦνον Τύχαι ἔπρεπον εἶναι,   1975
  Κρίσπε, βαθυπλούτου σῆς ἕνεκεν κραδίης,
ἀλλὰ καὶ αἱ πάντων πᾶσαι· τί γὰρ ἀνδρὶ τοσῶιδε
  ἀρκέσει εἰς ἑτάρων μυρίον εὐσο⟨ίην⟩;
5 νῦν δέ σε καὶ τούτων κρέσσων ἐπὶ μεῖζον ἀέξοι
  Καῖσαρ· τίς κείνου χωρὶς ἄρηρε τύχη;   1980

XXXVII

οἵους ἀνθ᾽ οἵων οἰκήτορας, ὦ ἐλεεινή,
  εὕραο· φεῦ μεγάλης Ἑλλάδος ἀμμορίη.
αὐτίκα καὶ †γαίηι† χθαμαλωτέρη εἴθε, Κόρινθε,
  κεῖσθαι καὶ Λιβυκῆς ψάμμου ἐρημοτέρη,
5 ἢ τοίοις διὰ πᾶσα παλιμπρήτοισι δοθεῖσα   1985
  θλίβειν ἀρχαίων ὀστέα Βακχιαδῶν.

XXXVIII

τῆς ὄιος γενεὴ μὲν Ἀγαρρική, ἔνθα τ᾽ Ἀράξεω
  ὕδωρ πιλοφόροις πίνεται Ἀρμενίοις,
χαῖται δ᾽ οὐ †μήλοις ἅτε που μαλακοῖς ἐπὶ μαλλοῖ†,
  ψεδναὶ δ᾽, ἀγροτέρων τρηχύτεραι χιμάρων·   1990
5 νηδὺς δὲ τριτοκεῖ ἀνὰ πᾶν ἔτος, ἐκ δὲ γάλακτος
  θήλη ἀεὶ μαστοῦ πλήθεται οὐθατίου·
βληχὴ δ᾽ ἀσσοτάτω τερένης μυκήματι μόσχου·
  ἄλλα γὰρ ἀλλοῖαι πάντα φέρουσι γέαι.

XXXVI A.Pl. (A) 40 Κριναγόρου   εἰς εἰκόνα Κρίσπου   caret P
4 εὐσοίην suppl. Page: post εὐσο deficit Pl
XXXVII A.P. 9.284 [C] Κριναγόρου   εἰς τὴν κατάπτωσιν τῆς Κορίνθου   caret
Pl
3 γαίη ut vid. P: γᾶς ἤ C   **5** δοθεῖσα Salm.: δεθεῖσα P

XXXVI

Compliments to Crispus

You deserve not only the three Fortunes as your neighbours, Crispus, for the sake of your heart's deep riches, but all the good fortunes of all men too. Nothing can be too much for so great a man, whose aim is the infinite prosperity of his friends. Now may Caesar, who is mightier even than these, raise you to higher things. What man's fortune stands firm without him?

XXXVII

The degradation of Corinth

O pitiable, what dwellers you have found for yourself, and in what others' place! Woe for the misery of great Hellas! O Corinth, I would have you lie more prostrate than ⟨   ⟩, more deserted than the sands of Libya, rather than be surrendered whole to such shop-soiled slaves, and vex the bones of the ancient Bacchiads.

XXXVIII

An Armenian sheep

The sheep is of the breed of Agarra, where the water of the Araxes is drunk by felt-capped Armenians. The fleece is not ⟨soft wool like that on our sheep⟩, but sparse-haired, rougher than wild goats'. But it bears thrice every year, and its udder's teat is always full of milk. Its bleat is very near the lowing of a tender calf. Thus diverse countries bear all things different.

XXXVIII A.P. 9.430 Κριναγόρου   εἰς πρόβατον τριτόκον   [C] καὶ νῦν εἰςι τοι-
αῦτα πρόβατα οὐκ ἐν ᾿Αρμενίαι μόνον ἀλλὰ καὶ ἐν Cκυθίαι   [J ad fin.] θαυμαστόν
caret Pl
1 ἔνθα τ᾿ Schneider: ἐντὸς P | ᾿Αράξεω apogr.: -ξεο P   3 χαῖται Salm.:
χεῖται P

XXXIX

θάρcει καὶ τέτταρcι διαπλαcθέντα προcώποιc   1995
μῦθον καὶ τούτων γράψαι ἔτι πλέοcιν·
οὔτε cὲ γὰρ λείψουcι, Φιλωνίδη, οὔτε Βάθυλλον
τὸν μὲν ἀοιδάων, τὸν δὲ χορῶν χάριτεc.

XL

εἰ καὶ τὸ cῆμα λυγδίνηc ἀπὸ πλακόc
καὶ ξεcτὸν ὀρθῆι λαοτέκτονοc cτάθμηι,   2000
οὐκ ἀνδρὸc ἐcθλοῦ. μὴ λίθωι τεκμαίρεο,
ὦ λῶιcτε, τὸν θανόντα· κωφὸν ἢ λίθοc,
5   τῆι καὶ ζοφώδηc ἀμφιέννυται νέκυc.
κεῖται δὲ τῆιδε τὠλιγηπελὲc ῥάκοc
Εὐνικίδαο, cήπεται δ᾽ ὑπὸ cποδῶι.   2005

XLI

τήνδ᾽ ὑπὸ δύcβωλον θλίβει χθόνα φωτὸc ἀλιτροῦ
ὀcτέα μιcητῆc τύμβοc ὑπὲρ κεφαλῆc
cτέρνα τ᾽ ἐποκριόεντα καὶ οὐκ εὔοδμον ὀδόντων
πρίονα καὶ κώλων †δούλιον οἰοπέδην†,
5   ἄτριχα καὶ κόρcην, Εὐνικίδου ἡμιπύρωτα   2010
λείψαν᾽ ἔτι χλωρῆc ἔμπλεα τηκεδόνοc.
χθὼν ὦ δυcνύμφευτε, κακοcκήνευc ἐπὶ τέφρηc
ἀνδρὸc μὴ κούφη κέκλιcο μηδ᾽ ὀλίγη.

XXXIX *A.P.* 9.542 Κριναγόρου   caret Pl
2 μῦθον Reiske: -θῶν P | γράψαι ἔτι Reiske: γραψα ἐνι P   **3** Φιλωνίδη
Porson: -δι P   **4** χορῶν Porson: -ρὸν P
XL *A.P.* 7.380 [C] Κριναγόρου   [J] εἰc Εὐνικίδαν τινὰ οὗτινοc ἡ λάρναξ ἀπὸ
λυγδίνηc πλακὸc ἐχρημάτιζεν   [C] ἰαμβικόν   caret Pl
4 ὦ C: ὁ P   **6** τὠλιγηπελὲc Salm.: -γωπ- P   **7** cήπεται C: -πετε P

CRINAGORAS

XXXIX

Encouragement to a writer of pantomimes

Never fear, write a story shaped for four parts or for even more; grace shall not fail you, Philonides, or Bathyllus, the one in singing, the other in the dance.

XL

On a bad man buried in a fine tomb

Though the tomb be of white marble-slab and polished by the stonemason's straight rule, it is not a good man's. Judge not the dead, my good friend, by the grave-stone. The stone is senseless; even the blackest corpse has such a covering. Here lie the feeble rags and tatters of Eunicidas, rotting under the dust.

XLI

On the same

In this foul-clodded earth, the tomb above his odious head crushes a scoundrel's bones and ridgy chest and the evil-smelling saw-line of his teeth and his limbs' ⟨   ⟩ and his hairless head, the half-burnt relics of Eunicidas, still full of green corruption. Earth with your evil bed-mate, lie neither light nor little on the ashes of this foul-bodied fellow.

XLI *A.P.* 7.401 [C] Κριναγόρου   [J] ἕτερον ἀνώνυμον εἰς Εὐνίδικον οὖτινος τὰ ὀστᾶ ἀτημέλητα   Pl в Κριναγόρου
3 στέρνα CJ^sscrPl: -νον P | τ' ἐποκριόεντα J^sscr: τ' ἐπεκρείκοντα P (ï sup. ρεί scr. C), τε πλεῖα δόλοιο Pl | ὀδόντων CPl: -τα P   5 Εὐνικίδου Brunck: Εὐνιδίκου CPl et J in lemmate, Εὐνίδικον P   8 κέκλισο μηδ' CPl: κεκλίσομαι δ' P

XLII

βότρυες οἰνοπέπαντοι ἐυςχίστοιό τε ῥοιῆς
θρύμματα καὶ ξανθοὶ μυελοὶ ἐκ στροβίων   2015
καὶ δειναὶ δάκνεςθαι ἀμυγδάλαι ἥ τε μελιςςῶν
ἀμβροςίη πυκναί τ᾽ ἰτρίνεαι ποπάδες
5 καὶ πότιμοι γέλγιθες ἰδ᾽ †ὑελακυκάδες† ὄγχναι
δαψιλῆ οἰνοπόταις γαςτρὸς ἐπειςόδια·
Πανὶ φιλοςκίπωνι καὶ εὐςτόρθυγγι Πριάπωι   2020
ἀντίθεται λιτὴν δαῖτα Φιλοξενίδης.

XLIII

ςπήλυγγες Νυμφῶν εὐπίδακες αἱ τόςον ὕδωρ
εἴβουςαι ςκολιοῦ τοῦδε κατὰ πρεόνος,
Πανός τ᾽ ἠχήεςςα πιτυςτέπτοιο καλιή,
τὴν ὑπὸ Βαςςαίης ποςςὶ λέλογχε πέτρης,   2025
5 ἱερά τ᾽ ἀγρευταῖςι γερανδρύου ἀρκεύθοιο
πρέμνα, λιθηλογέες θ᾽ Ἑρμέω ἱδρύςιες,
αὐταί θ᾽ ἱλήκοιτε καὶ εὐθήροιο δέχοιςθε
Ϲωςάνδρου ταχινῆς ςκῦλ᾽ ἐλαφοςςοΐης.

XLIV

ποιμὴν ὦ μάκαρ, εἴθε κατ᾽ οὔρεος ἐπροβάτευον   2030
κἠγὼ ποιηρὸν τοῦτ᾽ ἀνὰ λευκόλοφον
κριοῖς ἀγητῆρςι †ποτὲ βληχημένα† βάζων
ἢ πικρῆι βάψαι νήοχα πηδάλια
5 ἅλμηι· τοιγὰρ ἔδυν ὑποβένθιος, ἀμφὶ δὲ ταύτην
θῖνά με ῥοιβδήςας Εὖρος ἐφωρμίςατο.   2035

XLII *A.P.* 6.232 Κριναγόρου   [C] ἀνάθημα Φιλοξενίδου τῶι Πανί   Suid. s.vv. οἰνοπέπαντοι (1–2 θρύμμ.), στρόβιλος (2 καὶ–στροβ.), ἀμυγδαλῆ (3 καὶ–ἀμυγδ.), ποπάδες (3 ἥ–4), γέλγιθες (5–6), ἐπειςόδια (γέλγιθες καὶ ὄγχναι καὶ ῥοιαὶ καὶ ςταφυλαί+6)   caret Pl
1 ἐυςχίστοιό C: ἐυιςχ- P   **2** στροβίων Page: -βίλων PSuid.   **3** δειναὶ Toup: δειλαὶ PSuid.   **5** γέλγιθες PSuid.: -γηθες C | ὑελακυκάδες P: ἠδέ τε Suid.   **7** φιλοςκίπωνι C: -ςκήπ- P

XLII

Dedication to Pan and Priapus

Wine-ripe grape-clusters, and fragments of split pomegranate, and yellow marrow from cone-kernels, and almonds hard to bite, and bees' ambrosia, and piles of honey-cakes, and tasty garlic-heads, and ⟨   ⟩ pears, plentiful diversions for the wine-drinker's belly,—Philoxenides dedicates a modest festival to Pan, lover of the shepherd's staff, and to Priapus with his goodly spike.

XLIII

Dedication by a hunter

Caves of the Nymphs, many-fountained, slow-pouring all your waters down this winding headland; echoing cabin of pine-crowned Pan, his home under the foot of Bassae's crags; stumps of aged juniper, sacred to hunters; stone-heaped seats of Hermes,—be gracious, and accept from this lucky huntsman, Sosander, the spoils of his swift stag-chasing.

XLIV

The drowned sailor envies the pastoral life

Happy shepherd, would that I too were tending a flock down the hillside on this grassy white crest, talking to my leader-rams ⟨   ⟩ instead of plunging the ship's rudders in the bitter brine. So I went down under the deep waters, and the whirling east-wind brought me to rest on this beach.

XLIII *A.P.* 6.253 Κριναγόρου   Suid. s.vv. εἴβεσθαι (1–2), σπήλυγγες (1–2 εἴβ.), πρῶνες (1 αἰ–2), πρεών (eadem), πίτυς (3), καλιά (3)   caret Pl
2 πρεόνος P: φρέατος Suid. (εἴβ.)   6 λιθηλογέες Ap.B.: λιθολ- P   7 δέ-χοισθε P: -εσθε C
XLIV *A.P.* 7.636 [C] Κριναγόρου   [J] εἴς τινα ναυαγήσαντα καὶ μακαρίζοντα τοὺς ὀριπλάνους ποιμένας   caret Pl
4 πικρῆι Salm.: πι μικρῆι P   6 ἐφωρμίσατο Jacobs: ἐφημ- P

XLV

παίδων ἀλλαχθέντι μόρωι ἔπι τοῦτ᾽ ἐλεεινή
μήτηρ ἀμφοτέρους εἶπε περισχομένη·
'καὶ νέκυν οὐ σέο, τέκνον, ἐπ᾽ ἤματι τῶιδε γοήσειν
ἤλπισα, καὶ ζωοῖς οὐ σὲ μετεσσόμενον
5 ὄψεσθαι. νῦν δ᾽ οἱ μὲν ἐς ὑμέας ἠμείφθησαν   2040
δαίμονες, ἄψευστον δ᾽ ἵκετο πένθος ἐμοί'.

XLVI

λῶπος ἀποκλύζουσα παρὰ κροκάλαισι θαλάσσης
χερνῆτις διεροῦ τυτθὸν ὕπερθε πάγου
χέρσον ἐπεκβαίνοντι κατασπασθεῖσα κλύδωνι
δειλαίη πικροῦ κῦμ᾽ ἔπιεν θανάτου,   2045
5 πνεῦμα δ᾽ ὁμοῦ πενίηι ἀπελύσατο· τίς κ᾽ ἐνὶ νηί
θαρσῆσαι πεζοῖς τὴν ἀφύλακτον ἅλα;

XLVII

βρέγμα πάλαι λαχναῖον ἐρημαῖόν τε κέλυφος
ὄμματος ἀγλώσσου θ᾽ ἁρμονίη στόματος,
ψυχῆς ἀσθενὲς ἕρκος, ἀτυμβεύτου θανάτοιο   2050
λείψανον, εἰνόδιον δάκρυ παρερχομένων,
5 κεῖσο †πέλας κατὰ† πρέμνοιο παρ᾽ ἀτραπόν, ὄφρα ⟨   ⟩
ἀθρήσας τί πλέον φειδομένωι βιότου.

XLV *A.P.* 7.638 [C] Κριναγόρου   [J] εἰς γυναῖκα δύο τέκνα ἔχουσαν ὧν τὸ μὲν
ἠσθένει τὸ δ᾽ ἕτερον ὑγιὲς ἦν· τοῦ μὲν οὖν ἀσθενοῦντος ἐγερθέντος ὁ ὑγιὴς τέθνηκεν
caret Pl
XLVI *A.P.* 9.276 [C] Κριναγόρου   εἰς γραῦν πενιχρὰν ἐν τῶι ἀποπλύνειν τὰ
ἑαυτῆς ῥάκη ἀποπνιγεῖσαν   Pl a Κριναγόρου

XLV

Reversal of fate for two brothers

Thus spoke a pitiable mother over her sons' reversal of destiny, embracing both of them: 'Neither *your* corpse, my child, I thought to mourn this day, nor to see *you* among the living. Now destinies are shifted round for you, but there is no deception in the sorrow that has come to me.'

XLVI

On a woman drowned while washing clothes

Washing a robe by the sea-shingle, a little above a dripping rock, a hire-woman was dragged down by a surge that mounted the shore; poor wretch, she drank the wave of bitter death and renounced her breath together with her poverty. Who will dare the sea on ship-board, when the landsman is not safe from it?

XLVII

The moral of the wayside skull

Skull's once hairy crown, eye's deserted shell, frame of a tongue-less mouth, soul's feeble fence, relic of death without burial, wayside weeping for passers-by, lie there under the tree-stump beside the path, that looking on you ⟨a man may learn⟩ what profit there is in being careful of life.

1 κροκάλαισι P: -ληισι Pl

XLVII *A.P.* 9.439 [C] Κριναγόρου   εἰc κρανίον ἀνθρώπου κείμενον ἀτημέλητον   Pl A 'Αντιφίλου
2 ἁρμονίη Pl: -ην P   5 παρ' ἀτραπὸν P: παρὰ πρόπον Pl   6 ἀθρήcαc P: -cαιc Pl

XLVIII

ἄχρι τεῦ, ἆ δείλαιε, κεναῖc ἐπὶ ἐλπίcι, θυμέ,
πωτηθεὶc ψυχρῶν ἀccοτάτω νεφέων   2055
ἄλλοιc ἄλλ᾽ ἐπ᾽ ὄνειρα διαγράψειc ἀφένοιο;
κτητὸν γὰρ θνητοῖc οὐδὲ ἓν αὐτόματον.
5 Μουcέων ἀλλ᾽ ἐπὶ δῶρα μετέρχεο, ταῦτα δ᾽ ἀμυδρὰ
εἴδωλα ψυχῆc ἠλεμάτοιcι μέθεc.

XLIX

δράμαcιν ἐν πολλοῖcι διέπρεπεc ὅccα Μένανδροc   2060
ἔγραφεν ἢ Μουcέων cὺν μιῆι ἢ Χαρίτων.

L

καὶ κλαῖε καὶ cτέναζε †cυcφίγγων† χεροῖν
τένονταc, ὦ 'πίβουλε· τοῖά τοι πρέπει.
οὐκ ἔcθ᾽ ὁ λύcων· μὴ 'λεείν᾽ ὑπόβλεπε·
αὐτὸc γὰρ ἄλλων ἐκ μὲν ὀμμάτων δάκρυ   2065
5 ἔθλιψαc, ἐν δὲ πικρὰ καρδίαι βέλη
πήξαc ἀφύκτων ἰὸν ἔcταξαc πόθων,
Ἔρωc, τὰ θνητῶν δ᾽ ἐcτί cοι γέλωc ἄχη.
πέπονθαc οἷ᾽ ἔρεξαc· ἐcθλὸν ἡ δίκη.

LI

αὐτόc cοι Φοίβοιο πάιc λαθικηδέα τέχνηc   2070
ἰδμοcύνην, πανάκηι χεῖρα λιπηνάμενοc,
Πρηξαγόρη, cτέρνοιc ἐνεμάξατο. τοιγὰρ ἀνῖαι
ὄρνυνται δολιχῶν ὁππόcαι ἐκ πυρετῶν

XLVIII *A.P.* 9.234 [C] Κριναγόρου   περὶ φιλοcοφίαc καὶ ὅτι μόνη ἀρετὴ
τίμιον κτῆμα   Pl A Κριναγόρου
1 ἆ PPl^pc: ὦ Pl^ac | ἐπὶ Pl: ἐπ᾽ P   6 μέθεc Pl^pc: -θαιc P et ut vid. Pl^ac

XLVIII

A foolish ambition

How long, poor fool, fluttering on hopes as high as the chilly clouds, my soul, will you sketch dream upon dream of riches? Nothing comes to man's possession of its own accord. Pursue rather the Muses' gifts, and leave these dim phantoms of the mind to fools.

XLIX

Praise of an actor

You excelled in the many dramas that Menander wrote with one of the Muses' or the Graces' help.

L

On a statue of Eros in bonds

Weep and groan, schemer, the sinews of your arms bound fast; such are your deserts. There is no one to untie you. Let us have no more piteous glances up. You, Eros, were the one to squeeze tears from others' eyes; you fixed your bitter arrows in the heart, and instilled the poison of passions inescapable. The agonies of mortals are your mirth. What is done to you is what you did; justice is an excellent thing.

LI

On a portrait of the physician Praxagoras

Phoebus' son himself, anointing his hand with All-heal, rubbed pain-stilling science of your art into your breast, Praxagoras. Therefore however many anguishes arise from long fevers,

XLIX *A.P.* 9.513 Κριναγόρου caret Pl
L *A.Pl.* (A) 199 Κριναγόρου εἰς τὸ αὐτό [sc. ἄγαλμα Ἔρωτος] caret P
LI *A.Pl.* (A) 273 Κριναγόρου εἰς εἰκόνα Πραξαγόρου ἰατροῦ caret P

5 καὶ ὁπόσαι τμηθέντος ἐπὶ χροός, ἄρκια θεῖναι
φάρμακα πρηείης οἶσθα παρ' Ἠπιόνης.   2075
θνητοῖσιν δ' εἰ τοῖοι ἐπήρκεον ἰητῆρες,
οὐκ ἂν ἐπορθμεύθη νεκροβαρὴς ἄκατος.

ΔΙΟΚΛΕΟΥϹ

I

μή με κόνι κρύψητε (τί γάρ;) πάλι, μηδ' ἐπὶ ταύτης
ἠιόνος οὐκ ὀνοτὴν γαῖαν ἐμοὶ τίθετε.
μαίνεται εἴς με θάλασσα καὶ ἐν χέρσοισί με δειλόν   2080
εὑρίσκει ῥαχίαις, οἶδέ με κἢν Ἀίδηι.
5 χέρσωι ἐπεκβαίνειν εἰ ἐμεῦ χάριν ὕδατι θυμός,
ἀρκεῦμαι σταθερῆι μιμνέμεν ὣς ἄταφος.

II

δίκτυα σοὶ τάδε, Πάν, ἀνεθήκαμεν οἶκος ἀδελφῶν
οἱ τρεῖς ἐξ ὀρέων, ἠέρος, ἐκ πελάγευς·   2085
δικτυβόλει μὲν τῶιδε παρ' ἠιόνων κροκάλαισιν,
δικτυβόλει τούτωι δ' ἄγκεσι θηροτόκοις,
5 τὸν τρίτον ἐν πτηνοῖσιν ἐπίβλεπε· τῆς γὰρ ἁπάντων,
δαῖμον, ἔχεις ἡμέων δῶρα λινοστασίης.

5 ὁπόσαι Wolters: ὁπόσα ex ὁππόσα corr. Pl

1 *A.P.* 7.393 [C] Διοκλέους Καρυστίου   [J] εἰς τὸν αὐτὸν ναυηγὸν Τλησιμένην
οὕτινος τὰ λείψανα ἐπὶ τῶν αἰγιαλῶν καλινδεῖται ταφῆς οὐ δεόμενα   caret Pl
1 πάλι C: -λαι P | ταύτης Salm.: -τας P   2 ἠιόνος Salm.: -νας P | τίθετε
Salm.: τίσετε P   3 μαίνεται Brunck: μαίνετε δ' P | εἴς με Salm.: εἰς ἐμὲ C,
ἐμὲ P   4 κἢν P ut vid.: κεῖν C   5 χέρσωι ἐπεκβαίνειν εἰ Jacobs: χ. δ'
ἐπεκβαίνει P   6 ἀρκεῦμαι Meineke (-κοῦμαι iam Jacobs): πάρκειμαι P

230

however many when the flesh is cut, you have been taught by gentle Epionê to apply remedies sufficient. If mortals had enough such physicians, the boat would never have crossed the ferry with its load of corpses.

DIOCLES

I

On a drowned man washed out of his grave

Hide me not (what use is it?) with dust again, nor place upon me the blameless earth of this beach. The sea is enraged against me; it finds me, poor wretch, on the land's rocky shores, it knows me even in death. If for my sake it is the waters' will to trespass on land, I am content to stay thus unburied on the ground.

II

Dedications by three brothers

A family of brothers, the three of us, from hills, air, and sea we have dedicated these nets, Pan, to you. Cast nets for this one by the shore-shingle, cast nets for that one in the glen-cradles of wild beasts, look kindly upon the third one among his birds. For the gifts you have, Divine Being, come from the netting of each of us.

II *A.P.* 6.186 Ἰουλίου Διοκλέους   εἰς τὸ αὐτό   Pl A Ἰουλιανοῦ Διοκλέους   εἰς τὸ αὐτό   Suid. s.v. ἄγχη (4)
2 πελάγευς Pl: -γους P   3 versum spat. vac. relicto om. P, inseruit C; spat. vac. relicto om. Pl | μὲν τῶιδε Page: τούτωι δὲ C   4 δικτυβόλει PPl: θηροβόλει Suid.

III

οὐκ οἶδ' εἴτε σάκος λέξαιμί σε, τὴν ἐπὶ πολλούς   2090
ἀντιπάλους πιστὴν σύμμαχον ὡπλισάμην,
εἴτε βέβαιον ἐμοὶ πόντου σκάφος, ἥ μ' ἀπὸ νηός
ὀλλυμένης κόμισας νηκτὸν ἐπ' ἠϊόνος.
5 Ἄρεος ἐν πολέμοις ἔφυγον χόλον ἔν τε θαλάσσηι
Νηρῆος· σὺ δ' ἄρ' ἧς ὅπλον ἐν ἀμφοτέροις.   2095

IV

χαῖρέ ποτ' οὐκ εἰπόντα προσεῖπέ τις· 'ἀλλ' ὁ περισσός   (2096)
κάλλεϊ νῦν Δάμων οὐδὲ τὸ χαῖρε λέγει.
ἥξει τις τούτου χρόνος ἔκδικος, εἶτα δασυνθείς
ἄρξει χαῖρε λέγειν οὐκ ἀποκρινομένοις.'

ΔΙΟΔΩΡΟΥ

I

αἰγιβότου Σκύροιο λιπὼν πέδον Ἴλιον ἔπλω   2100
οἷος Ἀχιλλείδης πρόσθε μενεπτόλεμος,
τοῖος ἐν Αἰνεάδηισι Νέρων ἀγὸς ἄστυ Ῥέμοιο
νεῖται ἐπ' ὠκυρόην Θύμβριν ἀμειψάμενος,
5 κοῦρος ἔτ' ἀρτιγένειον ἔχων χνόον· ἀλλ' ὁ μὲν ἔγχει
θῦεν, ὁ δ' ἀμφοτέροις, καὶ δορὶ καὶ σοφίηι.   2105

III *A.P.* 9.109 [C] Ἰουλίου Διοκλέους   [J] εἰς ἀσπίδα στρατιώτου ἐν ἧι καὶ ἐν πολέμοις ἐσώθη καὶ ναυαγήσας ἔπλευσε μετ' αὐτῆς ὡς ἐπὶ σχεδίης νηξάμενος Pl a Ἰουλίου Διοκλέους
2 ὡπλισάμην Pl: ὁπ- P   3 βέβαιον Meineke: δὲ βαιὸν PPl   4 ὀλλυμένης CPl: -νους P | ἠϊόνος Page: -νας PPl   5 ἔν τε P: ἐν δὲ Pl

III

On a man saved from drowning by his shield

I know not whether to call you 'shield', my faithful ally with
whom I armed myself against so many foes, or 'my steadfast
sea-boat', since you carried me swimming to shore from a
doomed vessel. In wars I escaped the wrath of Ares, at sea of
Nereus; and you were my defence in both.

IV

On Damon's haughtiness

One day a man spoke to a boy who would not say 'good
morning': 'So our great beauty Damon will not even say
"good morning" now. A time shall come to punish him for
this; then, grown all bushy, he will begin to say "good morning" to those who will not reply.'

DIODORUS

I

Nero returns to Rome

As of old Achilles' son, steadfast in war, left the land of goat-
pasturing Scyros and sailed to Ilium, so Nero, leader among the
sons of Aeneas, changes his ground to the city of Remus, returning to the swift-flowing Tiber, still a boy with the down
fresh upon his chin. The other was vigorous with the spear,
this one both in war and in wisdom.

IV *A.P.* 12.35 Διοκλέους   caret Pl
4 ἄρξει apogr.: ἄρχηι P

I *A.P.* 9.219 [C] Διοδώρου Cαρδιανοῦ   εἰc Νέρωνα τὸν βαcιλέα [idem add. et
del.] ⟦ὅτε ἀπέπλει ἀπὸ Cκύρου πρὸc τὴν Ἴλιον⟧   Pl A Διοδώρου Cαρδιανοῦ
τοῦ Διοπείθους
I ἔπλω Lascaris: -ων PPl   **2** μενεπτόλεμος P: Νεοπτ- Pl

233

II

μὴ σύ γε, μηδ' εἴ τοι πολὺ φέρτερος εἴδεται ὅccων
ἀμφοτέρων, κλεινοῦ κοῦρε Μεγιcτοκλέουc,
κἢν cτίλβηι Χαρίτεccι λελουμένοc, ἀμφιδονοίηc
τὸν καλόν· οὐ γὰρ ὁ παῖc ἤπιοc οὐδ' ἄκακοc,
5 ἀλλὰ μέλων πολλοῖcι καὶ οὐκ ἀδίδακτοc ἐρώτων·   2110
τὴν φλόγα ῥιπίζειν δείδιθι, δαιμόνιε.

III

'ἥ τε Cάμου μεδέουcα καὶ ἣ λάχεc Ἴμβραcον, Ἥρη,
δέξο γενεθλιδίουc, πότνα, θυηπολίαc,
μόcχων ἱερὰ ταῦτα, τά cοι πολὺ φίλτατα πάντων
ἴcμεν, ὅcοι μακάρων θεcμὸν ἐπιcτάμεθα.'   2115
5 εὔχετ' ἐπιcπένδων τάδε Μάξιμοc· ἡ δ' ἐπένευcεν
ἔμπεδα, Μοιράων δ' οὐκ ἐμέγηρε λίνα.

IV

Καρπαθίην ὅτε νυκτὸc ἅλα cτρέψαντοc ἀήτου
λαίλαπι βορραίηι κλαcθὲν ἐceῖδε κέραc,
εὔξατο κῆρα φυγών, Βοιώτιε, cοί με, Κάβειρε   2120
δέcποτα, χειμερίηc ἄνθεμα ναυτιλίηc
5 ἀρτήcειν ἁγίοιc τόδε λώπιον ἐν προπυλαίοιc
Διογένηc· ἀλέκοιc δ' ἀνέρι καὶ πενίην.

II *A.P.* 5.122 Διοδώρου   [C] εἰc ἔρωτα παραίνεcιc   caret Pl
3 ἀμφιδονοίηc Boissonade: -δοναίηc P
III *A.P.* 6.243 Διοδώρου   Pl A Διοδώρου
1 τε Cάμου CPl: τε ἅμου ut vid. P   2 γενεθλιδίουc CPl: -ίδια ut vid. P |
θυηπολίαc CPl: -ίηc P   4 ἴcμεν Pl: εἴη P   6 ἐμέγηρε CPl: ἐπέγειρε ut vid. P

II

On a much-courted youth

Forbear—even if he seems to you more precious than both
eyes, son of famed Megistocles, and though he gleams from the
Graces' bathing,—forbear to go dancing round that beauty;
the boy is neither gentle nor without malice, but much-courted,
no illiterate in the book of Love. Beware, my friend, of fanning
the flame.

III

Sacrifice by Maximus to Hera

'Hera, sovereign of Samos, holder of Imbrasos, receive, Lady,
the birthday-sacrifice, these offerings of calves, which we who
are skilled in the law of the blessed gods know to be far dearest
of all to you.' Thus Maximus prayed while he poured libation;
and she assented firmly, and the threads of the Fates were not
grudging.

IV

Dedication after a storm at sea

When he saw his yard-arm smashed by the north-wind's hurricane, as the gusts disturbed the Carpathian sea by night, Diogenes
vowed, if he escaped death, that in your honour, Boeotian
lord Cabirus, in your holy porch he would hang me, this little
cloak, as votive offering from his stormy voyage. Do you
protect him from poverty too.

IV *A.P.* 6.245 Διοδώρου   Suid. s.vv. ἀήτης (1), βορᾶς (2), λαῖλαψ (2), λώπιον
(4–5 + εὔξατο), ἀλέγοις (6 ἀλ.–πεν.)   caret Pl
2 βορραίηι CSuid.: βορέηι P   3 με Salm.: μῖ P   6 ἀλέκοις Salm.: ἀλέγοις
PSuid. | πενίην CSuid.: -ίηι P

V

ἔρροις, Ἰονίοιο πολυπτοίητε θάλασσα,
   νηλὴς Ἀίδεω πορθμὲ κελαινοτάτου,   2125
ἢ τόccouc κατέδεξο· τίς ἂν τεά, κάμμορε, λέξαι
   αἴσυλα, δυστήνων αἶσαν ὀπιζόμενος;
5 Αἰγέα καὶ Λαβέωνα σὺν ὠκυμόροισιν ἑταίροις
   νηί τε σὺν πάσηι βρύξας ἁλιρροθίηι.

VI

ἡμιτελῆ θάλαμόν τε καὶ ἐγγύθι νυμφικὰ λέκτρα,   2130
   κοῦρε, λιπὼν ὀλοὴν οἶμον ἔβης Ἀίδου,
Θύνιον Ἀστακίην δὲ μάλ' ἤκαχες, ἥ σε μάλιστα
   οἰκτρὰ τὸν ἡβητὴν κώκυεν ἠίθεον,
5 Ἱππάρχου κλαίουσα κακὸν μόρον, εἴκοσι ποίας
   μοῦνον ἐπεὶ βιότου πλήσαο καὶ πίσυρας.   2135

VII

κλίμακος ἐξ ὀλίγης ὀλίγον βρέφος ἐν Διοδώρου
   κάππεσεν, ἐκ δ' ἐάγη καίριον ἀστράγαλον
δινηθεὶς προκάρηνος· ἐπεὶ δ' ἴδεθ' εἷο ἄνακτα
   ἀντόμενον, παιδνὰς αὐτίκ' ἔτεινε χέρας.
5 ἀλλὰ σὺ νηπιάχου δμωός, κόνι, μήποτε βρίθειν   2140
   ὀστέα, τοῦ διετοῦς φειδομένη Κόρακος.

V *A.P.* 7.624 [C] Διοδώρου   [J] εἴς τινας ἐν τῶι Ἰονίωι κόλπωι ναυαγήσαντας
Pl в Διοδώρου
2 νηλὴς PPlᵃᶜ: -λειὴς Plᵖᶜ   3 ἢ τόccouc Pl: ἢ τοὺς coὺς P   5 Αἰγέα post
Brodaeum Huet: ἄλγεα PPl | Λαβέωνα cὺν post Brodaeum Brunck: λα⁕βέων ὅcον
P, λαβέων ὅcον Pl

V

On *Aegeus and Labeo, lost at sea*

A curse upon you, tumultuous sea of Io, pitiless ferry for blackest Hades, so many lives you have taken down. Wretch, who that looks on the fate of the unfortunates could tell the tale of your crimes? You have devoured Aegeus and Labeo together with their early-doomed companions and all their ship sea-beaten.

VI

Death on the eve of marriage

Leaving your bride-chamber half-complete and wedding not far away, young man, you went the fatal way to Hades. And greatly you grieved Bithynian Astacia, who most bitterly bemoaned the young lover in his prime, lamenting Hipparchus' evil doom, since you had completed only four and twenty summers of life.

VII

Death of a slave-child

A little child fell from a little ladder in Diodorus' house, and tumbling head-first broke a fatal vertebra; when he saw his lord coming, he stretched forth his baby hands at once. Earth, never lie heavy on the bones of the infant servitor. Corax was two years old; be gentle to him.

VI *A.P.* 7.627 [C] Διοδώρου   [J] εἴс τινα μέλλοντα γάμωι προсομιλεῖν τελευτή-
саντα   Pl в Διοδώρου
3 Θύνιον P: Θών- Pl   **6** ἐπεὶ Pl: ἐπι P
VII *A.P.* 7.632 [C] Διοδώρου   [J] εἴс παιδίον ἐξολισθῆсαν ἀπὸ κλίμακος   [idem
ad v. 2] εἴс παιδίον πεсὸν ἀπὸ κλίμακος καὶ θανόν   Pl в Διοδώρου
3 δ' Pl: om. P | ἴδεθ' εἶο Opsopoeus: ἴδε θεῖον PPl

VIII

Ἀδρήστειά τε δῖα καὶ ἰχναίη σε φυλάσσοι
παρθένος ἡ πολλοὺς ψευσαμένη Νέμεσις·
δείδια σόν τε φυῆς ἐρατὸν τύπον ἠδὲ σά, κοῦρε,
δήνεα, θεσπεσίης καὶ μένος ἠνορέης,   2145
5 καὶ σοφίην καὶ μῆτιν ἐπίφρονα. τοιάδε τέκνα,
Δροῦσε, πέλειν μακάρων πευθόμεθ' ἀθανάτων.

IX

ἴστω νυκτὸς ἐμῆς ἥ μ' ἔκρυφεν οἰκία ταῦτα
λάινα Κωκυτοῦ τ' ἀμφιγόητον ὕδωρ,
οὔτι μ' ἀνήρ, ἃ λέγουσι, κατέκτανεν ἐς γάμον ἄλλης   2150
παπταίνων †τί μάτην οὔνομα Ῥουφῖνος†,
5 ἀλλά με Κῆρες ἄγουσι μεμορμέναι· οὐ μία δήπου
Παῦλα Ταραντίνη κάτθανεν ὠκύμορος.

X

ἰφθίμωι τόδ' ἐπ' ἀνδρὶ φίλη πόλις ἥινες' Ἀχαιῶι
γράμμα παρ' εὐύδρου νάμασιν Ἀσκανίης·   2155
κλαῦσε δέ μιν Νίκαια, πατὴρ δ' ἐπί οἱ Διομήδης
λάινον ὑψιφαῆ τόνδ' ἀνέτεινε τάφον,
5 δύσμορος, αἰάζων ὀλοὸν κακόν· ἦ γὰρ ἐῴκει
υἱέα οἱ τίνειν ταῦτα κατοιχομένωι.

VIII A.P. 9.405 Διοδώρου [C] εἰς Δροῦσόν τινα εὐχή· †ὁμοία τοῦ προσώπου
αὐτοῦ† Νέμεσις καὶ Ἀδράστεια Pl A Διοδώρου
1 τε Pl: cε P | ἰχναίη CPl: ἠχν- P | φυλάσσοι P^{sscr}Pl: -ει P   3 κοῦρε Pl:
-ρα P

IX A.P. 7.700 [C] Διοδώρου γραμματικοῦ [J] εἰς Ῥουφιανοῦ τινος γυναῖκα
Παῦλαν Ταραντίνην   caret Pl

VIII

The virtues of Drusus

Divine Adrasteia and the tracker-maiden, deceiver of many,
Nemesis,—may they keep you safe. I fear for your body's
lovely form, and your arts, good youth, and the spirit of your
wondrous manhood, and your learning, and your prudent counsel. Such, Drusus, we are told, are the children of the blessed
Immortals.

IX

Paula denies that her husband murdered her

Let them know it, these stone dwellings of my darkness
where I lie hidden, and the waters of Cocytus loud with lamentation: it is false, what they say, that my husband murdered me,
looking to marriage with another ⟨   ⟩. The destined fates
carried me off; surely Paula of Tarentum is not the only one
to die before her time.

X

Epitaph for Achaeus

His beloved city approved this inscription for a man of power,
Achaeus, beside the waters of Ascania's lovely lake. Nicaea
mourned him, and his father Diomedes raised up this tomb of
stone high-shining, unhappy man, lamenting deadly evil; for
surely it was fitting that his son make this payment to himself
when he was dead and gone.

1 ἔκρυφεν Salm.: ἔκρυψεν C, ἔκρυπεν ut vid. P   2 τ᾽ Reiske: om. P
3 κατέκτανεν Salm.: -νε P

X A.P. 7.701 [C] τοῦ αὐτοῦ Διοδώρου [sc. Δ. γραμματικοῦ]   [J] εἰς Ἀχαιὸν
Νικαέα υἱὸν Διομήδους [idem ad v. 4] εἰς Ἀχαιὸν τὸν Νικαέα   Pl B Διοδώρου
1 τόδ᾽ Pl: τῶιδ᾽ P   2 εὐύδρου CPl: εὐέδ- ut vid. P   3 μιν Pl: με P
4 ὑψιφαῆ CPl: ὑψιταφῆ ut vid. P   6 υἱέα οἱ Salm.: υἱέι ὧι PPl

XI

μὴ μέτρει Μάγνητι τὸ πηλίκον οὔνομα τύμβωι   2160
μηδὲ Θεμιστοκλέους ἔργα σε λανθανέτω·
τεκμαίρου Cαλαμῖνι καὶ ὁλκάσι τὸν φιλόπατριν,
γνώσηι δ' ἐκ τούτων μείζονα Κεκροπίης.

XII

θεῖος 'Αριστοφάνευς ὑπ' ἐμοὶ νέκυς· εἰ τίνα πεύθηι,
κωμικός, ἀρχαίης μνῆμα χοροστασίης.   2165

XIII

Αἰσχύλον ἥδε λέγει ταφίη λίθος ἐνθάδε κεῖσθαι   (2166)
τὸν μέγαν οἰκείης τῆλ' ἀπὸ Κεκροπίης
λευκὰ Γέλα Cικελοῖο παρ' ὕδατα. τίς φθόνος, αἰαῖ,
Θηcείδας ἀγαθῶν ἔγκοτος αἰὲν ἔχει;

XIV

τοῦτο Θεμιστοκλεῖ ξένον ἠρίον εἴσατο Μάγνης   2170
λαός, ὅτ' ἐκ Μήδων πατρίδα ῥυσάμενος
ὀθνείην ὑπέδυ χθόνα καὶ λίθον· ἤθελεν οὕτως
ὁ φθόνος, αἱ δ' ἀρεταὶ μεῖον ἔχουσι γέρας.

XI A.P. 7.235 [C] Διοδώρου Ταρcέωc   [J] εἰc Θεμιcτοκλέα τὸν 'Αθηναῖον ἐν
Μαγνηcίαι τελευτήcαντα   Pl A Διοδώρου   εἰc αὐτόν [sc. Θεμιcτοκλέα]
1 τύμβωι CPl: -βου P
XII A.P. 7.38 Διοδώρου [ex Διοδωρι⁸ corr. ut vid.]   εἰc 'Αριcτοφάνην
caret Pl
2 κωμικός Kaibel: -κὸν P | μνῆμα Kaibel: μνᾶ- P

XI

On the tomb of Themistocles at Magnesia

Measure not the name's greatness by his Magnesian tomb, nor forget the deeds of Themistocles. Judge the patriot by Salamis and the ships; from these you shall learn that he is greater than the land of Cecrops.

XII

Epitaph for Aristophanes

Divine Aristophanes lies dead beneath me. Which one, you ask? The comedian, that monument of ancient drama.

XIII

Epitaph for Aeschylus

This tombstone proclaims that Aeschylus the Great lies here, far from his native Cecropia, beside the white waters of Sicilian Gela. What spiteful envy, alas, against the good is this which ever possesses the sons of Theseus?

XIV

On the tomb of Themistocles at Magnesia

The people of Magnesia set up this foreign tomb for Themistocles, when, having saved his fatherland from the Medes, he passed under this alien soil and stone. Envy so willed it; great virtues have less privilege than she.

XIII *A.P.* 7.40 Διοδώρου εἰς τὸν αὐτόν [sc. Αἰσχύλον] Pl B s.a.n. εἰς Αἰσχύλον Suid. s.vv. ἔγκοτον (3 τίς–4), Θησείδας (eadem)
3 Γέλα P (γελᾶ): Γέλας Pl | αἰαῖ Jacobs: αἰὲν PSuid., om. Pl
XIV *A.P.* 7.74 Διοδώρου εἰς τὸν αὐτόν [J] τὸν Θεμιστοκλέα· ἐν Μαγνησίαι τέθαπται τῆι πρὸς Μαιάνδρωι Pl A s.a.n.
1 ξένον Jacobs: κενὸν PPl

XV

Βάκχωι καὶ Μούσηισι μεμηλότα τὸν Διοπείθους
Κεκροπίδην ὑπ᾽ ἐμοί, ξεῖνε, Μένανδρον ἔχω,   2175
†ἐν πυρὶ τὴν ὀλίγην ὃς ἔχει κόνιν†· εἰ δὲ Μένανδρον
δίζηαι, δήεις ἐν Διὸς ἢ μακάρων.

XVI

αἴλινον ὠκυμόρωι με λεχωΐδι τοῦτο κεκόφθαι
τῆς Διοδωρείου γράμμα λέγει σοφίης,
κοῦρον ἐπεὶ τίκτουσα κατέφθιτο· παῖδα δὲ Μήλας   2180
δεξάμενος θαλερὴν κλαῖεν Ἀθηναΐδα
5 Λεσβιάδεσσιν ἄχος καὶ Ἰήσονι πατρὶ λιποῦσαν·
Ἄρτεμι, σοὶ δὲ κυνῶν θηροφόνων ἔμελεν.

XVII

πύργος ὅδ᾽ εἰναλίης ἐπὶ χοιράδος, οὔνομα νήσωι
ταὐτὸν ἔχων, ὅρμου σύμβολόν εἰμι, Φάρος.   2185

XVIII

Ζεύξιδος ἡ χροιή τε καὶ ἡ χάρις, ἐν δέ με μικρῆι   (2186)
κρυστάλλωι τὸ καλὸν δαίδαλον Ἀρσινόηι
γράψας τοῦτ᾽ ἔπορεν Σατυρήιος· εἰμὶ δ᾽ ἀνάσσης
εἰκών, καὶ μεγάλης λείπομαι οὐδ᾽ ὀλίγον.

XV A.P. 7.370 [C] Διοδώρου   [J] εἰς Μένανδρον τὸν ποιητὴν τὸν τῆς νέας κωμωιδίας Pl b Διοδώρου

XVI A.P. 6.348 Διοδώρου Suid. s.v. αἴλινον (1–2)   caret Pl
2 σοφίης PSuid.: -ίας C   3 κατέφθιτο C: κατάφ- P   6 ἔμελεν C: ἔμελλεν P

XV

Epitaph for Menander

Stranger, I hold beneath me the son of Diopeithes, Menander of Cecropia, the favourite of Bacchus and the Muses; ⟨ ⟩; if it be Menander himself you seek, you shall find him in the house of Zeus or of the Blessed.

XVI

Epitaph for a woman dying in child-birth

This inscription, product of Diodorus' art, tells that I was carved in mournful memory of one who died before her time in travail. She perished giving birth to a boy, and Melas took the child, and wept for his blooming Athenais who left lamentations for the women of Lesbos and her father Jason. But you, Artemis, had no care but for your game-slaughtering hounds.

XVII

On the lighthouse at Pharos

A tower here on the sea-girt rock, with the same name as the island, token of anchorage am I, Pharos.

XVIII

On a miniature of Arsinoê

The colour and the charm are worthy of Zeuxis; but it was Satyreius who painted me on a little crystal and gave the pretty work of art to Arsinoê. I am the image of a Queen, and not the least inferior to a larger portrait.

XVII *A.P.* 9.60 [C] Διοδώρου   caret Pl

XVII *A.P.* 9.60 [C] Διοδώρου   caret Pl
2 cύμβολόν Salm.: -λά P

XVIII *A.P.* 9.776 Διοδώρου   εἰc κρύcταλλον γεγλυμμένην   Pl A Διοδώρου   εἰc κρύcταλλον γεγλυμμένην

ΔΙΟΤΙΜΟΥ

I

γραῖα φίλη θρέπτειρα, τί μου προσιόντος ὑλακτεῖς   2190
καὶ χαλεπὰς βάλλεις δὶς τόσον εἰς ὀδύνας;
παρθενικὴν γὰρ ἄγεις περικαλλέα, τῆς ἐπιβαίνων
ἴχνεσι τὴν ἰδίην οἶμον ἴδ᾽ ὡς φέρομαι
5 εἶδος ἐσαυγάζων μοῦνον γλυκύ. τίς φθόνος ὄσσων,
δύσμορε; καὶ μορφὰς ἀθανάτων βλέπομεν.   2195

ΕΠΙΓΟΝΟΥ

I

ἡ πάρος εὐπετάλοισιν ἐν οἰνάνθαις νεάσασα   (2196)
καὶ τετανῶν βοτρύων ῥᾶγα κομισσαμένη
νῦν οὕτω γραιοῦμαι· ἴδ᾽ ὁ χρόνος οἷα δαμάζει·
καὶ σταφυλὴ γήρως αἰσθάνεται ῥυτίδων.

ΕΡΥΚΙΟΥ

I

Γλαύκων καὶ Κορύδων οἱ ἐν οὔρεσι βουκολέοντες,   2200
'Αρκάδες ἀμφότεροι, τὸν κεραὸν δαμάλαν
Πανὶ φιλωρείται Κυλληνίωι αὐερύσαντες
ἔρρεξαν καί οἱ δωδεκάδωρα κέρα
5 ἅλωι μακροτένοντι ποτὶ πλατάνιστον ἔπαξαν
εὐρεῖαν, νομίωι καλὸν ἄγαλμα θεῶι.   2205

I *A.P.* 5.106 Διοτίμου Μιλησίου   [J] εἰς παρθένον ὡραίαν   Pl A ἄδηλον
4 ἰδίην Pl: ἰδίκην P

I *A.P.* 9.261 [C] 'Επιγόνου Θεσσαλονικέως   εἰς ἄμπελον γηράσασαν καὶ μὴ
καρποῦσαν   Pl A 'Επιγόνου Θεσσαλονικέως
2 κομισσαμένη Pl: κομησα- P   3 ὁ P: ὡς Pl

DIOTIMUS

I

A street-scene

Old lady, good nurse, why bark at my approach and cast me
into torments twice as cruel? The girl in your leading is a
beauty. I step in her footprints, but you see I go my own road
too, and I do no more than gaze on her delightful figure.
Wretch, would you grudge a man his eyes? Even Immortals'
forms are ours to look upon.

EPIGONUS

I

An old vine's lament

I that was youthful once among the leafy vines, I whose harvest
was grapes in swelling bunches, am now growing old as you see.
How Time shows his power; even the grape-cluster feels the
wrinkles of old age.

ERUCIUS

I

Sacrifice by oxherds to Pan

Glaucon and Corydon, those ox-herds on the hills, Arcadians
both, in honour of Cyllenian Pan the mountain-lover drew
back the head of a horned calf and sacrificed it, and with a
long-tapering nail they fastened its horns of twelve palms'
length to a broad plane-tree, a fine ornament for the pastoral
god.

I *A.P.* 6.96 [C] Ἐρυκίου   [P] ἀνάθημα τῶι Πανὶ παρὰ Γλαύκωνος καὶ
Κορύδωνος ποιμένων   Suid. s.v. δωδεκαδώρωι (3 Κυλλ.–5)   caret Pl
2 τὸν κεραὸν P: τὴν κεραὴν C | δαμάλαν Stadtmüller: -λην P   5 ἅλωι
Salm.: ἄλλωι ut vid. P, ἄλλωι CSuid. | ποτὶ CSuid.: om. P

II

—βουκόλε, πρὸς τῶ Πανός, ὁ φήγινος, εἰπέ, κολοσσός
οὗτος ὅτωι σπένδεις τὸ γλάγος, ἐστὶ τίνος;
—τῶ λειοντοπάλα Τιρυνθίω· οὐδὲ τὰ τόξα,
νήπιε, καὶ σκυτάλαν ἀγριέλαιον ὁρῆις;
5 —χαίροις, Ἀλκείδα δαμαληφάγε, καὶ τάδε φρούρει
αὔλια κἠξ ὀλίγων μυριόβοια τίθει.

2210

III

ὁ τράγος ὁ Κλήσωνος ὅλαν διὰ πάννυχος ὄρφναν
αἶγας ἀκοιμάτους θῆκε φριμασσόμενος·
ὀδμὰ γάρ μιν ἔτυψε λύκου χιμαροσφακτῆρος
τηλόθε πετραίαν αὖλιν ἀνερχομένου,
5 μέσφα κύνες κοίτας ἀνεγέρμονες ἐπτοίασαν
θῆρα μέγαν, τραγίνους δ' ὕπνος ἔμυσε κόρας.

2215

IV

εὔστοχα θηροβολεῖτε, κυναγέται, οἱ ποτὶ ταύταν
Πανὸς ὀρειώτα νισόμενοι σκοπιάν,
αἴτε λίνοις βαίνοιτε πεποιθότες αἴτε σιδάρωι
αἴτε καὶ ἰξευταὶ λαθροβόλωι δόνακι,
5 κἀμέ τις ὑμείων ἐπιβωσάτω· οἶδα ποδάγραν
κοσμεῖν καὶ λόγχαν καὶ λίνα καὶ καλάμους.

2220

II *A.P.* 9.237 [C] Ἐρυκίου   εἰς ἄγαλμα φήγινον Ἡρακλέους   Pl A Ἐρυκίου
1 τῶ PPl: τοῦ C   3 λειοντοπάλα Pl: λήον τω παλα P   4 σκυτάλαν
Stadtmüller: -λην PPl

III *A.P.* 9.558 Ἐρυκίου   caret Pl
1 πάννυχος P^{ac}: -χον P^{pc}   3 χιμαροσφακτῆρος Brunck: -σφακτος P
4 τηλόθε P^{pc}: -θι P^{ac}   6 τραγίνους Hecker: -νου P

II

On a statue of Heracles

—Ox-herd, in the name of Pan, tell me, this oak-wood statue to which you pour the libation of milk, whose is it?

—It is the Tirynthian lion-wrestler's; cannot you even see his bow, simpleton, and club of wild-olive?

—Hail to you, Alcides, calf-devourer; guard these stables and make them stalls of countless oxen instead of few.

III

Dogs frighten a wolf away from the goats

All night long, throughout the whole time of darkness, Cleson's billy-goat made the she-goats restless with his snorting, for the scent of a goat-slaying wolf had struck him from afar as it came up to the rocky fold; until the dogs, aroused from sleeping, scared the huge beast away, and slumber closed the goat's eyes.

IV

Pan promises success to hunters

Good aim to you in the chase, huntsmen who come to this peak of mountain-dweller Pan, whether you go trusting in nets or in the iron or as fowlers with the reed's secret stroke. And let each one of you call on me by name; I know how to adorn the trap and spear and nets and reeds.

IV *A.P.* 9.824 Ἐρυκίου [Εὐρ- cod.] Pl A Ἐρυκίου εἰς τὸν Πᾶνα Syll.E
2 ὀρειώτα P: ὀρειβάτεω Pl | νισόμενοι P: νισσόμ- Pl   3 αἶτε...αἶτε P: οἶ τε...οἶ τε Pl   4 αἶτε P: οἶ τε Pl   5 ἐπιβωσάτω PᵖᶜPl: -βος- Pᵃᶜ | ποδάγραν Schneider: ποτ' ἄγραν PPl

V

τοῦτο Σάων τὸ δίπαχυ κόλον κέρας 'Ωμβρακιώτας
βουμολγὸς ταύρου κλάσσεν ἀτιμαγέλου,   2225
ὁππότε μιν κνημούς τε κατὰ λασίους τε χαράδρας
ἐξερέων ποταμοῦ φράσσατ' ἐπ' ἀϊόνι
5 ψυχόμενον χηλάς τε καὶ ἰξύας· αὐτὰρ ὁ βούτεω
ἀντίος ἐκ παγέων ἵεθ', ὁ δὲ ῥοπάλωι
γυρὸν ἀπεκράνιξε βοὸς κέρας, ἐκ δέ μιν αἰπᾶς   2230
ἀχράδος εὐμύκωι πᾶξε παρὰ κλισίαι.

VI

'Ατθὶς ἐγώ, κείνη γὰρ ἐμὴ πόλις, ἐκ δέ μ' 'Αθηνῶν
λοιγὸς "Αρης 'Ιταλῶν πρίν ποτ' ἐληίσατο
καὶ θέτο 'Ρωμαίων πολιήτιδα· νῦν δὲ θανούσης
ὀστέα νησαίη Κύζικος ἠμφίασε.   2235
5 χαίροις ἡ θρέψασα καὶ ἡ μετέπειτα λαχοῦσα
χθών με καὶ ἡ κόλποις ὕστατα δεξαμένη.

VII

οὐκέτι συρίγγων νόμιον μέλος ἀγχόθι ταύτας
ἁρμόξηι βλωθρᾶς, Θηρίμαχε, πλατάνου,
οὐδέ σευ ἐκ καλάμων κερααὶ βόες ἁδὺ μέλισμα   2240
δέξονται σκιερᾶι πὰρ δρυὶ κεκλιμένου·
5 ὤλεσε γὰρ πρηστήρ σε κεραύνιος. αἱ δ' ἐπὶ μάνδραν
ὀψὲ βόες νιφετῶι σπερχόμεναι κατέβαν.

V A.P. 6.255 'Ερυκίου   Suid. s.vv. κόλον (1-2, om. Σάων), οὐμβρακιώτης
(1 οὐμβρ.–2 βουμ.), ἀτιμαγέλου (1 κέρας–2, om. οὐμβρ.), βουμολγός (eadem),
κνημοί (3), χαράδρα (3–4), ἰξύν (4 ἐπ'–5), βούτας (5 αὐτὰρ–7 κέρας), ἀπεκράνιξε
(6 ὁ–7 κέρας)   caret Pl
1 'Ωμβρακιώτας Hecker: οὐμ- PSuid.   2 ἀτιμαγέλου CSuid.: ἀτιμεγάλου
P   4 ἐξερέων Hecker: ἐξ ὀρέων PSuid.   6 ἐκ παγέων C: ἐκπλαγέων P, ἐκ
πλαγίων Suid.   7 ἀπεκράνιξε CSuid. (s.v. ἀπεκρ.): -νιζε PSuid. (s.v. βούτ.) |
αἰπᾶς Page: αὐτᾶς P

V

Dedication of a bull's horn

Saon the cow-milker from Ambracia broke off this mutilated horn, two cubits long, from a herd-despising bull. Searching one day along the ridges and bushy ravines he espied it on a river-bank cooling its hooves and flanks. Straight from the stream it rushed to meet the ox-herd; he with his club struck the crooked horn from the bull's head and fastened it from a tall pear-tree beside the loud-lowing byre.

VI

Epitaph for an Athenian woman buried in Cyzicus

'Atthis' am I, for such was my city; but from Athens the Italians' wasting warfare took me captive long ago and made me a dweller in the Romans' city. And now island Cyzicus has covered my bones in death. Farewell, land that nursed me, and land that possessed me thereafter, and land that received me in her bosom at the last.

VII

Epitaph for a neat-herd

No longer near this lofty plane-tree, Therimachus, shall you tune the pipe's pastoral melody, nor shall the horned cattle listen to the sweet song from your reeds as you lie beside the shady oak. A thunderous tempest killed you; and your cattle came down to their fold at nightfall, hurried by the snowstorm.

VI *A.P.* 7.368 [C] Ἐρυκίου [J] εἰς Ἀττικήν τινα γυναῖκα γενομένην Ῥωμαίαν ὑπ' αἰχμαλωσίας καὶ τελευτήσασαν ἐν Κυζίκωι Pl β Ἐρυκίου
2 λοιγὸς P: λυγρὸς Pl, λυγὸς (?) C **4** ἠμφίασε P: ἠμφίεσεν Pl

VII *A.P.* 7.174 [C] Ἐρυκίου [J] εἰς τὸν αὐτόν [sc. Θηρίμαχον κεραυνωθέντα] Pl A Ἐρυκίου εἰς τὸν αὐτόν Suid. s.vv. βλωθρή (1-2), πρηστήρ (5-6)
2 ἀρμόξηι Herwerden: -όζηι PPl **3** καλάμων Scaliger: καμάτων PPl | κερααὶ CPl: -ρειαὶ P **6** νιφετῶι PPlSuid.: νειφ- C

VIII

οὐχ ὅδε δειλαίου Σατύρου τάφος, οὐδ' ὑπὸ ταύτηι,
ὡς λόγος, εὔνηται πυρκαϊῆι Cάτυρος,   2245
ἀλλ' εἴ πού τινα πόντον ἀκούετε, πικρὸν ἐκεῖνον,
τὸν πέλας αἰγινόμου κλυζόμενον Μυκάλης,
5 κείνου δινήεντι καὶ ἀτρυγέτωι ἔτι κεῖμαι
ὕδατι, μαινομένωι μεμφόμενος Βορέηι.

IX

αὖά τοι ἐκτάμνοντι γεράνδρυα, κάμμορε Μίνδων,   2250
φωλὰς ἀραχναίη σκαιὸν ἔτυψε πόδα
νειόθεν ἀντιάσασα, χύδην δ' ἔβρεξε μελαίνηι
σηπεδόνι χλωρὴν σάρκα κατ' ἀστραγάλους·
5 ἐτμήθη δ' ἀπὸ τῆς στιβαρὸν γόνυ, καί σε κομίζει
μουνόποδα βλωθρῆς σκηπάνιον κοτίνου.   2255

X

Γάλλος ὁ χαιτάεις, ὁ νεήτομος, ὡπὸ Τυμώλου
Λύδιος ὀρχηστὰς μάκρ' ὀλολυζόμενος,
ται παρὰ Cαγγαρίωι †τάδε ματέρι τύμπανα ταῦτα†
θήκατο καὶ μάστιν τὰν πολυαστράγαλον
5 ταῦτά τ' ὀρειχάλκου λάλα κύμβαλα καὶ μυρόεντα   2260
βόστρυχον ἐκ λύσσας ἄρτ' ἀναπαυσάμενος.

VIII A.P. 7.397 [C] Ἐρυκίου Θετταλοῦ   [J] εἴς τινα Cάτυρον ναυαγήσαντα ἐν τῆι θαλάσσηι τῆι πλησίον Μυκάλης κατέναντι Cάμου   Pl A Ἐρυκίου
1 δειλαίου PPl^pc: -αιος CPl^ac   2 εὔνηται P: -ναςται Pl   3 ἐκεῖνον CPl: -νων P   4 Μυκάλης CPl: -λας P   5 κείνου Page: -νωι PPl   6 βορέηι PPl^pc: -έην Pl^ac

IX A.P. 9.233 [C] Ἐρυκίου   ἐπί τινι ἀνθρώπωι τέμνοντι δρῦν ὃν ἔτυψε ῥὼξ ἤγουν φαλάγγιον, καὶ ἐξεκόπη τὸν πόδα   Pl B Ἐρυκίου

VIII

Epitaph for Satyrus, lost at sea

Not this the tomb of unhappy Satyrus; nor under this pyre, as the words pretend, is Satyrus laid to rest. But if perchance you have heard of a certain sea,—that cruel one, which surges near goat-pasturing Mycalê,—in its whirling and barren water even now I lie, with a grudge against the mad north-wind.

IX

On a wood-cutter poisoned by a spider

Ill-fated Mindon, as you were uprooting old withered trees, a lurking spider struck your left foot, attacking from below. It drenched the living flesh about the ankle-bones with black decay in overflow. Thereafter the sturdy limb was cut off to the knee, and a staff from a tall wild-olive carries you one-legged.

X

Dedication by a priest of Cybelê

The Gallus, the long-haired, gelded in youth, the Lydian dancer from Tmolus, loud-shrieking, dedicated to the Mother beside the Sangarius these timbrels and this scourge with its many knuckle-bones and these chattering cymbals of copper and a perfumed tress, having now found peace after frenzy.

---

1 Μίνδων P: Μείδ- Pl   3 ἔβρεξε Page: ἔβρυξε PPl   4 σάρκα Pl: σάρκυ
ut vid. P | κατ' P: καὶ Pl   6 σκηπάνιον Pl: σκιπ- P

X *A.P.* 6.234 Ἐρυκίου   Suid. s.vv. Γάλλος (2), ὀρείχαλκος (5-6 βόστρ.+
θήκατο)   caret Pl
1 χαιτάεις P: -τήεις CSuid. | ὠπὸ Τυμώλου P: ὅς ποτε Τμώ- Suid.   3 τᾶι
Reiske: λα P | Σαγγαρίωι Lacroze: Σαιταρίωι P

XI

αἰεί τοι λιπαρῶι ἐπὶ σήματι, δῖε Σοφόκλεις,
    σκηνίτης μαλακοὺς κισσὸς ἄλοιτο πόδας,
αἰεί τοι βούπαισι περιστάζοιτο μελίσσαις
    τύμβος Ὑμηττείωι λειβόμενος μέλιτι,   2265
5 ὡς ἄν τοι ῥείηι μὲν †ἀγανὸς† Ἀτθίδι δέλτωι
    κηρός, ὑπὸ στεφάνοις δ' αἰὲν ἔχηις πλοκάμους.

XII

ἀνίκ' ἀπὸ πτολέμου τρέσσαντά σε δέξατο μάτηρ
    πάντα τὸν ὁπλιστὰν κόσμον ὀλωλεκότα,
αὐτά τοι φονίαν, Δαμάτριε, αὐτίκα λόγχαν   2270
    εἶπε διὰ πλατέων ὠσαμένα λαγόνων
5 'κάτθανε, μηδ' ἐχέτω Σπάρτα ψόγον· οὐ γὰρ ἐκείνα
    ἤμπλακεν εἰ δειλοὺς τοὐμὸν ἔθρεψε γάλα'.

XIII

εἰ καὶ ὑπὸ χθονὶ κεῖται, ὅμως ἔτι καὶ κατὰ πίσσαν
    τοῦ μιαρογλώσσου χεύατε Παρθενίου,   2275
οὕνεκα Πιερίδεσσιν ἐνήμεσε μυρία κεῖνα
    φλέγματα καὶ μυσαρῶν ἀπλυσίην ἐλέγων·
5 ἤλασε καὶ μανίης ἐπὶ δὴ τόσον ὥστ' ἀγορεῦσαι
    πηλὸν Ὀδυσσείην καὶ πάτον Ἰλιάδα.
τοιγὰρ ὑπὸ ζοφίαισιν Ἐρινύσιν ἀμμέσον ἧπται   2280
    Κωκυτοῦ κλοιῶι λαιμὸν ἀπαγχόμενος.

XI *A.P.* 7.36 [C] Ἐρυκίου   ἐπιτύμβιον [P] εἰς Σοφοκλέα [Ἐρυκίου hic add. P,
del. J, qui iterum Ἐρυκίου scr. et del.] [J] τὸν Ἀθηναῖον παῖδα Σοφίλλου   Pl A
Ἐρυκίου   εἰς αὐτόν   Suid. s.vv. ἄλοιτο (1–2), σκηνή (eadem), βούπαις (3–4),
ἀγανόν (5–6) Zonar. s.v. ἄλοιτο
1 Σοφόκλεις CPl: -κλεες P   2 σκηνίτης CPl: -νήτης PSuid.Zonar.
3 περιστάζοιτο CPl: -ζειτο P, –σοιτο Suid.   5 ἀγανὸς PSuid.: ἀένναος Pl
6 ἔχηις Brunck: -εις P, -οις PlSuid.

XII *A.P.* 7.230 [C] Ἐρυκίου Κυζικηνοῦ   εἰς Δημήτριον [pergit idem pag. sequ.
marg. sup.] Ἐρυκίου Κυζικηνοῦ   [J] εἰς Δημήτριον Λακεδαιμόνιον ὑπὸ τῆς

XI

On the tomb of Sophocles

Ever may the stage's ivy, divine Sophocles, dance soft-footed about your shining monument; ever may the bees, the oxen's children, sprinkle your tomb streaming with honey of Hymettus. So may there flow ⟨   ⟩ wax for your Attic writing-tablets, and so may you ever have your hair crowned with garlands.

XII

A Spartan mother kills her cowardly son

When your mother received you a fugitive from battle, all your warrior-adornment lost, Demetrius, herself she drove at once the murderous lance through your broad flanks, saying 'Die, and let Sparta bear no blame; it was no fault of hers, if my milk nourished cowards'.

XIII

An attack on Parthenius

Even though he lies under the earth, yet cease not to pour pitch on foul-mouthed Parthenius for vomiting those myriad angry humours upon the Muses, together with the filth of his loathsome elegies. He went so far in madness as to call the Odyssey a mud-bath and the Iliad a dung-heap; therefore in mid-Cocytus he is caught, in the power of the dark Furies, his throat choked by a dog's collar.

ἰδίας μητρὸς ἀναιρεθέντα   Pl A Ἐρυκίου   Suid. s.vv. τρέσας (1), ὁπλιστής (2)
1 versum marg. sup. denuo scr. J   2 ὁπλιστὰν P: -τὴν Pl   4 διὰ PPl: διαὶ ut vid. C

XIII A.P. 7.377 [C] Ἐρυκίου   εἰς Παρθένιον τὸν Φωκαέα τὸν εἰς τὸν Ὅμηρον παροινήσαντα   caret Pl
2 μιαρογλώσσου P: μυσαρου- C   3 οὕνεκα C: -κε P | ἐνήμεσε C: -μισε P
4 φλέγματα P: φθέγ- J   5 ἐπὶ δὴ P: ἐπεὶ δὴ C, ἐπίη C^γρ   6 πάτον Ap.G.: βάτον J, βοτὸν P   7 ἧπται P: ᾖσται C^γρ   8 ἀπαγχόμενος C: ἀπαχώμ- P

XIV

ὡς βαρὺ τοῦτο, Πρίηπε, καὶ εὖ τετυλωμένον ὅπλον
πᾶν ἀπὸ βουβώνων ἀθρόον ἐκκέχυκας
εἰς γάμον οὐκ ἀνέτοιμον· ἔχει δέ σε δίψα γυναικῶν,
ὦγαθέ, καὶ σπαργαῖς θυμὸν ἅπαντα πόθοις.   2285
5 ἀλλὰ καταπρήυνε τὸν ἐξωιδηκότα φαλλόν
τόνδε καὶ ἀνθηρῆι κρύψον ὑπὸ χλαμύδι·
οὐ γὰρ ἐρημαῖον ναίεις ὄρος, ἀλλὰ παρ' Ἕλλης
ἠιόνα τὴν ἱερὴν Λάμψακον ἀμφιπολεῖς.

ΕΤΡΟΥCΚΟΥ

I

ἡ μία καὶ βιότοιο καὶ Ἄιδος ἤγαγεν εἴσω   2290
ναῦς Ἱεροκλείδην κοινὰ λαχοῦσα τέλη·
ἔτρεφεν ἰχθυβολεῦντα, κατέφλεγε τεθνηῶτα,
σύμπλοος εἰς ἄγρην, σύμπλοος εἰς Ἀίδην.
5 ὄλβιος ὁ γριπεύς· ἰδίηι καὶ πόντον ἐπέπλει
νηὶ καὶ ἐξ ἰδίης ἔδραμεν εἰς Ἀίδην.   2295

ΕΥΗΝΟΥ

I

ἐχθίστη Μούσαις σελιδηφάγε λωβήτειρα
φωλὰς ἀεὶ σοφίης κλέμματα φερβομένη,
τίπτε κελαινόχρως ἱεραῖς ψήφοισι λοχάζηι,
σίλφη, τὴν φθονερὴν εἰκόνα πλαττομένη;
5 φεῦγ' ἀπὸ Μουσάων, ἴθι τηλόσε, μηδ' ὅσον ὄψει   2300
βασκάνωι ἄψηφον δόξαν ἐπεισαγάγηις.

XIV *A.Pl.* (A) 242 Ἐρυκίου   εἰς τὸν αὐτόν   caret P
4 πόθοις Ruhnken: πόροις Pl

I *A.P.* 7.381 [C] Ἐτρούσκου [Ἐτερ- cod.] ἀπὸ Μεσσήνης   [J] εἰς Ἱεροκλείδην
τινὰ ὃν σὺν τῆι ἰδίαι νηὶ κατέκαυσαν   Pl A Ἐτρούσκου Μεσσηνίου
3 τεθνηῶτα CPl: -νειῶτα P

XIV

To Priapus

How heavy, Priapus, and well-calloused a weapon you have
put forth all massy from your groin, ready enough for wedlock.
Thirst for women possesses you, my friend, and all your heart
is bursting with passion. Come, soften this swollen member
down and hide it under your flowered cloak. This is no desert
hill you dwell on; you have the care of holy Lampsacus beside
the shore of Hellê.

ETRUSCUS

I

On a fisherman whose boat served as funeral-pyre

The one ship led Hieroclides into livelihood and into Hades,
assigned a double duty. It fed him fishing, it burned him after
death, ship-mate to the catch, ship-mate to Hades. Happy that
fisherman; in his own ship he sailed the sea, and aided by his
own ship he ran his course to Hades.

EUENUS

I

The book-worm

Detested by the Muses, column-devouring mutilator, hole-
haunter, eternally feeding on pilferings from wisdom's pages,
O black of hue, why lurk in ambush among my sacred accounts,
cockroach, moulding therein your spiteful image? Fly from
the Muses, begone afar, nor with so much as a malicious glance
bring me the repute of one who is of no account.

I *A.P.* 9.251 [C] Εὐήνου γραμματικοῦ   εἰς τοὺς cκώληκαc τοὺς τὰc βίβλους
βιβρώcκονταc ἤγουν cῆταc   caret Pl
6 βαcκάνωι ἄψηφον Page: βάcκανον ἐν ψήφωι P | ἐπειcαγάγηιc Salm.: -αγάγηι P

II

ξεῖνοι, τὴν περίβωτον ἐμὲ πτόλιν, Ἴλιον ἱρήν,
    τὴν πάρος εὐπύργοις τείχεσι κληιзομένην,
αἰῶνος τέφρη κατεδήδοκεν· ἀλλ᾽ ἐν Ὁμήρωι
    κεῖμαι χαλκείων ἕρκος ἔχουσα πυλῶν.   2305
5 οὐκέτι με σκάψει Τρωοφθόρα δούρατ᾽ Ἀχαιῶν,
    πάντων δ᾽ Ἑλλήνων κείσομαι ἐν στόματι.

III

κἤν με φάγηις ἐπὶ ῥίζαν, ὅμως ἔτι καρποφορήσω   (2308)
    ὅccον ἐπιcπεῖcαι coί, τράγε, θυομένωι.

IV

ἅ ποτε παρθενικαῖcιν ἱλαcκομένα παλάμηιcιν   2310
    Κύπριδα cὺν πεύκαιc καὶ γάμον εὐξαμένα
κουριδίουc ἤδη θαλάμωι λύcαcα χιτῶναc
    ἀνδρὸc ἄφαρ μηρῶν ἐξελόχευcα τύπουc·
5 νυμφίοc ἐκ νύμφηc δὲ κικλήcκομαι, ἐκ δ᾽ ⟨Ἀφροδίτηc⟩
    Ἄρεα καὶ βωμοὺc ἔcτεφον Ἡρακλέουc.   2315
Θῆβαι Τειρεcίην ἔλεγόν ποτε, νῦν δ᾽ ἐμὲ Χαλκίc
    τὴν πάρος ἐν μίτραιc ἡcπάcατ᾽ ἐν χλαμύδι.

II A.P. 9.62 [C] Εὐήνου Cικελιώτου   [J] εἰc Ἴλιον τὴν πόλιν ἣν ἐπόρθηcαν
Ἕλληνεc ὅτι διὰ τὸν Ὅμηρον ἀείμνηcτοc μᾶλλον καὶ αἰώνιοc γέγονεν   Pl A Εὐήνου
εἰc Τροίαν   Syll.E
2 τὴν Pl: τὰν P | εὐπύργοιc CPl: ἐν πύρ- P | κληιзομένην Pl: -ναν P   6 cτόματι
P: -ciν Pl

III A.P. 9.75 Εὐήνου [C] Ἀcκαλωνίτου   [J] εἰc ἄμπελον ἣν τράγοc κατέφαγεν
Pl A Εὐήνου   Schol. Ar. Plut. 1129 s.a.n. (unde Suid. s.v. ἀcκὸc Κτηcιφῶντοc)

II

Troy's fame immortal

Me, strangers, the far-famed city, holy Ilium, once renowned for towered walls, the ash of ages has devoured; yet in Homer I rest secure with my fence of brazen gates. No longer shall the Trojan-slaughtering spears of the Achaeans furrow me, but I shall abide on the lips of Hellenes everywhere.

III

The vine's revenge

Though you eat me to the root, yet I shall still bear fruits enough to pour libation, goat, upon you when you are sacrificed.

IV

Change of sex on the wedding-night

I who once with maiden hands supplicated the Cyprian with torches attendant and prayed for marriage, having just unfastened my bridal-robes in the bed-chamber, suddenly brought forth from my thighs the marks of manhood. Now, instead of bride, I have the name of bridegroom; I have given wreaths to Ares and the altars of Heracles instead of Aphrodite. As Thebes of old to Teiresias, so they used to tell, now Chalcis has given greeting to me, formerly in girdles, now in a cloak.

Suet. *Domit.* 14   Kaibel *ep.* 1106 (picto versuum argumento subscriptum epigramma)
2 τράγε omnes excepto P, ubi τάγε in τράγε corr. man. rec.
IV *A.P.* 9.602 Εὐήνου [Εὐΐνου cod.] Ἀθηναίου   caret Pl
3 θαλάμωι Brunck: -μων P   5 post ἐκ δ' vacat P, suppl. Brunck   7 Χαλκίς Lacroze: χαλκός P

V

Ἀτθὶ κόρα μελίθρεπτε, λάλος λάλον ἁρπάξασα
τέττιγ' ἀπτάνοις δαῖτα φέρεις τέκεσιν,
τὸν λάλον ἁ λαλόεσσα, τὸν εὔπτερον ἁ πτερόεσσα,   2320
τὸν ξένον ἁ ξείνα, τὸν θερινὸν θερινά,
5 κοὐχὶ τάχος ῥίψεις; οὐ γὰρ θέμις οὐδὲ δίκαιον
ὄλλυσθ' ὑμνοπόλους ὑμνοπόλοις στόμασιν.

VI

Βάκχου μέτρον ἄριστον ὃ μὴ πολὺ μηδ' ἐλάχιστον·
ἔστι γὰρ ἢ λύπης αἴτιος ἢ μανίης.   2325
χαίρει κιρνάμενος δὲ τρισὶν Νύμφαισι τέταρτος·
τῆμος καὶ θαλάμοις ἐστὶν ἑτοιμότατος.
5 εἰ δὲ πολὺς πνεύσειεν, ἀπέστραπται μὲν Ἔρωτας,
βαπτίζει δ' ὕπνωι γείτονι τοῦ θανάτου.

VII

εἰ μισεῖν πόνος ἐστί, φιλεῖν πόνος, ἐκ δύο λυγρῶν   2330
αἱροῦμαι χρηστῆς ἕλκος ἔχειν ὀδύνης.

VIII

ἢ τὸ δέρας χάλκειον ὅλον βοΐ τᾶιδ' ἐπίκειται   (2332)
ἔκτοθεν ἢ ψυχὰν ἔνδον ὁ χαλκὸς ἔχει.

V A.P. 9.122 [=Pᵃ] [C] ἀδέσποτον   [J] εἰς χελιδόνα τέττιγα καταπιοῦσαν τὸν μουσικὸν μέμψις. μέμφεται τὴν χελιδόνα ὡς καταπιοῦσαν τὸν τέττιγα, δικαίως· ἀμφότεροι γὰρ ὠιδικοί   denuo scr. post 9.339 [=Pᵇ] [C] Εὐήνου εἰς χελιδόνα τέττιγα κατεσθίουσαν Pl ᴮ s.a.n.
2 τέττιγ' ἀπτάνοις Salm. et ut vid. Pᵃ, ubi tantum τέττιγ' ceteris omissis: τέττιγα πτανοῖς PᵇPl   **4** ἁ ξείνα PᵇPl: εὐξείνα Pᵃ | τὸν θερινὸν θερινά Pᵃᵇ: ἀρινὸν ἠερινά Pl   **5** κοὐχὶ Pᵃᵇ: οὐχὶ Pl   **6** ὄλλυσθ' CᵃPl: ὄλλυθ' Pᵃ, ὄλλυσθαι Pᵇ | στόμασιν PᵇPl: -σι Pᵃ

V

The swallow and the cicada

Attic maiden, honey-fed, you chirruper seize the chirruper
cicada, and carry him to feed your wingless babes,—chirruper
preying on chirruper, wingèd on wingèd, summer-guest on
summer-guest,—and will you not drop him at once? It is not
right or just that singers should perish in singers' mouths.

VI

On moderation in drinking

The best measure of Bacchus is that which is neither great nor
very little, for he is the cause of either grief or madness. He likes
to be mixed as a fourth with three Nymphs; and then he is
readiest for the marriage-chamber too. But if he blow strong,
he turns his back on love, and plunges us into sleep the neighbour of death.

VII

The pains of love

If hating is pain, and loving is pain, of two miseries I prefer
the wound of the pain that has benefits.

VIII

On Myron's Cow

Either this is a cow with the skin wholly of bronze clothing
it outside, or the bronze has a soul inside.

VI *A.P.* 11.49 Εὐήνου [Εὐΐνου cod.]   Pl B s.a.n.
3 δὲ τρισὶν Νύμφαισι τέταρτος P: τρισὶ Νύμφαις τέτρατος αὐτός Pl   5 ἀπέ-
στραπτα Pl: ἀπέστραι P   6 βαπτίζει P: -ζεται Pl | τοῦ Pl: τῷ P
VII *A.P.* 12.172 Εὐήνου   Pl A s.a.n.
1 ἐστί Pl: ἐστίν P | λυγρῶν Brunck: λυτρων P, λοιπὸν Pl
VIII *A.P.* 9.717 Εὐήνου [Εὐΐνου cod.]   Pl A Εὐήνου   εἰς τὸ αὐτό
2 ψυχὰν ut vid. Pl (fort. in -ὴν corr.): -χὴν P

IX

αὐτὸς ἐρεῖ τάχα τοῦτο Μύρων· 'οὐκ ἔπλασα ταύταν
τὰν δάμαλιν, ταύτας δ' εἰκόν' ἀνεπλασάμαν.'

2335

X

Παλλὰς καὶ Κρονίδαο συνευνέτις εἶπον ἰδοῦσαι
τὴν Κνιδίην 'ἀδίκως τὸν Φρύγα μεμφόμεθα'.

(2336)

XI

πρόσθε μὲν Ἰδαίοισιν ἐν οὔρεσιν αὐτὸς ὁ βούτας
δέρξατο τὰν κάλλευς πρῶτ' ἀπενεγκαμέναν,
Πραξιτέλης Κνιδίοις δὲ πανωπήεσσαν ἔθηκεν,
μάρτυρα τῆς τέχνης ψῆφον ἔχων Πάριδος.

2340

ΓΕΜΙΝΟΥ

I

ἀντὶ τάφου λιτοῖο θὲς Ἑλλάδα, θὲς δ' ἐπὶ ταύται
δούρατα βαρβαρικᾶς σύμβολα ναυφθορίας,
καὶ τύμβωι κρηπῖδα περίγραφε Περσικὸν Ἄρη
καὶ Ξέρξην· τούτοις θάπτε Θεμιστοκλέα.
5 στάλα δ' ἁ Σαλαμὶς ἐπικείσεται ἔργα λέγουσα
τἀμά. τί με σμικροῖς τὸν μέγαν ἐντίθετε;

2345

IX *A.P.* 9.718 τοῦ αὐτοῦ [sc. Εὐήνου]   Pl A τοῦ αὐτοῦ [sc. Εὐήνου]   εἰς τὸ αὐτό
2 ἀνεπλασάμαν Page: -μην PPl
X *A.Pl.* (A) 165 Εὐήνου   εἰς τὸ αὐτό   caret P
XI *A.Pl.* (A) 166 Εὐήνου   ἕτερον εἰς τὴν ἐν Κνίδωι   caret P

IX

On the same

Perhaps Myron himself will say 'This heifer is not what I moulded, but that whose image I moulded'.

X

On the Cnidian Aphrodite of Praxiteles

Pallas and the consort of the son of Cronos said, when they saw the Cnidian Aphrodite, 'We are wrong to find fault with the Phrygian'.

XI

On the same

In time past on the hills of Ida the cowherd alone beheld her who took the prize for beauty, but Praxiteles has made her all-visible to the Cnidians; he has the vote of Paris to bear witness to his skill.

GEMINUS

I

Epitaph for Themistocles

Put Hellas in place of my humble tomb; then put ships'-timbers on her, tokens of a barbarian fleet destroyed. And paint the Persian army and Xerxes as a base for the tomb all round; with these for company, bury Themistocles. And, for a head-stone, Salamis shall stand thereon proclaiming my deeds. Why lay me, so great, among things so small?

I *A.P.* 7.73 [C] Γεμίνου [ex Γερμινοῦ, quod scr. P, corr.]   [P] εἰς Θεμιστοκλέα Pl A Γερμανικοῦ   εἰς Θεμιστοκλέα

1 ταύται Pl: -ταν P   2 βαρβαρικᾶς Pl: -κὰ P | ναυφθορίας CPl: -ίης P
6 ἐντίθετε CPl: -ται P

II

οὗτος ὁ Κεκροπίδαισι βαρὺς λίθος Ἄρεϊ κεῖμαι,
   ξεῖνε, Φιλιππείης σύμβολον ἠνορέης,
ὑβρίζων Μαραθῶνα καὶ ἀγχιάλου Σαλαμῖνος   2350
   ἔργα Μακηδονίης ἔγχεϊ κεκλιμένα.
5 ὄμνυε νῦν νέκυας, Δημόσθενες· αὐτὰρ ἔγωγε
   καὶ ζωοῖς ἔσομαι καὶ φθιμένοισι βαρύς.

III

ἦ παλίουρος ἐγώ, τρηχὺ ξύλον †ἰὸς† ἐν ἕρκει.
   τίς μ᾽ ἄφορον λέξει, τὴν φορίμων φύλακα;   2355

IV

εἰμὶ μὲν ἐν ποταμοῖς, πελάγει δ᾽ ἴσα μέτρα διώκω,
   Στρυμών, Ἠμαθίης τὸ γλυκερὸν πέλαγος,
βένθος ὁμοῦ καὶ ἄρουρα δι᾽ ὕδατος· ἦ γὰρ ἐγείρω
   ὀμπνιακῶν χαρίτων ἡδύτερον τρίβολον.
5 ἔστι καὶ Ἠμαθίης γόνιμος βυθός· ἄμμι δέ, Νεῖλε,   2360
   κρείσσων ἔσθ᾽ ὁ φέρων τὸν στάχυν, οὐχ ὁ τρέφων.

V

ἡ βάσις ἡ κατέχουσα τὸ βοίδιον ἦι πεπέδηται·
   ἢν δ᾽ ἀφεθῆι ταύτης, φεύξεται εἰς ἀγέλην.
μυκᾶται γὰρ ὁ χαλκός· ἴδ᾽ ὡς ἔμπνουν ὁ τεχνίτας
   θήκατο· κἂν ζεύξηις ἄλλον, ἴσως ἀρόσει.   2365

II *A.P.* 9.288 [C] Γεμίνου   εἰς Φίλιππον τὸν βασιλέα Μακεδονίας ὅτε τοὺς
Ἕλληνας ἐταπείνωσεν   Pl β Γεμίνου
1 Κεκροπίδαισι Pl: -δεσσι P   2 Φιλιππείης Pl^pc: -πίης PPl^ac   4 Μακηδονίης P: -ίοις Pl

II

A monument on the field of Chaeronea

Behold me, stranger, a stone grievous to the sons of Cecrops, dedicated to the War-god, symbol of Philip's valour; I am an insult to Marathon and the deeds of Salamis by the sea, that are humbled by the spears of Macedon. Swear now by your corpses, Demosthenes; yet I shall be grievous to your living and your dead.

III

On a thorn-bush

A thorn-bush am I, rough wood in the ⟨　⟩ fence; who will call me unfruitful, the guardian of the fruitful?

IV

On the river Strymon

I am ranked among rivers, yet the volume which I drive forward is equal to a sea,—I, Strymon, the sweet sea of Emathia. I am both deep-water and ploughland in water; for I give rise to the water-chestnut, sweeter than the blessings of corn. Emathia too has deeps that are fertile; and to us, O Nile, the better stream is that which bears the crop, not that which feeds it.

V

On Myron's Cow

It is the base to which it is bound that holds the heifer back; if it be released from this, it will run away to the herd. For the bronze is lowing: see how alive the artist has made it; if you yoke another to it, it will plough just as well.

III *A.P.* 9.414 Γεμίνου [Γαιμ- P] εἰς παλίουρον [C] θάμνον   caret Pl
1 ἦ Gow: ἡ P   **2** ἄφορον Salm.: -ρῶν P
IV *A.P.* 9.707 Τυλλίου Γεμίνου   Pl A Τυλλίου Γεμίνου   εἰς Cτρυμόνα
V *A.P.* 9.740 Γεμίνου   Pl A Γεμίνου   εἰς τὸ αὐτό
2 δ' P: om. Pl   **3** τεχνίτας P: -της Pl

VI

χείρ με Πολυγνώτου Θασίου κάμεν· εἰμὶ δ' ἐκεῖνος
Σαλμωνεύς, βρονταῖς ὃς Διὸς ἀντεμάνην,
ὅς με καὶ εἰν Ἀίδηι πορθεῖ πάλι καί με κεραυνοῖς
βάλλει μιςῶν μου κοὐ λαλέοντα τύπον.
5 ἴϲχε, Ζεῦ, πρηϲτῆρα, μέθες χόλον, εἰμὶ γὰρ ἄπνους   2370
ὁ ϲκοπός. ἀψύχοις εἰκόϲι μὴ πολέμει.

VII

—Ἥρακλες, ποῦ ϲοι πτόρθος μέγας ἥ τε Νέμειος
χλαῖνα καὶ ἡ τόξων ἔμπλεος ἰοδόκη;
ποῦ ϲοβαρὸν βρίμημα; τί ϲ' ἔπλαϲεν ὧδε κατηφῆ
Λύϲιππος χαλκῶι τ' ἐγκατέμιξ' ὀδύνην;   2375
5 ἄχθηι γυμνωθεὶς ὅπλων ϲέο; τίς δέ ϲ' ἔπερϲεν;
—ὁ πτερόεις, ὄντως εἷς βαρὺς ἄθλος, Ἔρως.

VIII

Φρύνη τὸν πτερόεντα, τὸν εὐτέχνητον Ἔρωτα
μιϲθὸν ὑπὲρ τεχνῶν ἄνθετο Θεϲπιέϲιν.
Κύπριδος ἡ τέχνη, ζηλούμενον, οὐδ' ἐπιμεμφές   2380
δῶρον· ἐς ἀμφοτέρους δ' ἔπρεπε μιϲθὸς Ἔρως.
5 δοιῆς ἐκ τέχνης αἰνέω βροτόν, ὅς γε καὶ ἄλλοις
δοὺς θεὸν ἐν ϲπλάγχνοις εἶχε τελειότερον.

VI *A.Pl.* (A) 30 Γεμίνου   εἰς ἄγαλμα Σαλμωνέως   *A.Pl.* (B) Γεμίνου   caret P
1 Πολυγνώτου Grotius: Πολυκλείτου Pl^AB | Θασίου Pl^B: Θαϲίη Pl^A
VII *A.Pl.* (A) 103 Γεμίνου   εἰς ἄγαλμα τοῦ αὐτοῦ   Loewy *Inschr. gr. Bild.* 534
(1–6)   caret P

VI

Salmoneus in a painting

The hand of Thasian Polygnotus made me. I am that Salmoneus, mad rival of the thunders of Zeus, who destroys me again even in Hades, and strikes me with his bolts, hating even my voiceless figure. Zeus, restrain your fiery blast, put aside your anger, for I, your target, am without breath. Fight not with lifeless images.

VII

On a statue of Heracles

—Where, Heracles, is your great club and your Nemean cloak and quiver full of arrows? Where your proud strength? Why has Lysippus moulded you thus downcast and alloyed the bronze with agony? Are you distressed that you have been stripped of your weapons? Who was it that brought you low?

—It was the wingèd one,—truly one Labour that was too heavy,—the god of Love.

VIII

On a statue of Eros by Praxiteles,
given to Phrynê

It was Phrynê who dedicated to the Thespians this wingèd Eros, this work of fine art in payment for her arts. The art is the Cyprian's, a thing enviable; praiseworthy too was the gift. For both her and him, Eros was a fitting payment. For twofold art I praise the man who gave a god to others, yet kept one still more perfect in his heart.

3 βρίμημα Ruhnken: μίμημα Pl, inscr.   **4** τ’ Brunck: δ’ Pl, inscr.
VIII *A.P.* 6.260 Γεμίνου   Pl A s.a.n.   Suid. s.v. Θεςπιάϲι (1 s.)
2 τεχνῶν Jahn: τέκνων PPlSuid. | Θεςπιέϲιν PSuid. (-έϲι): -άϲι Pl   **3** ζηλού-
μενον Pl: ζητού- P | οὐδ’ Page: οὐκ PPl   **5** αἰνέω βροτόν Pl: αἰνόβροτον P

IX

ἀντί μ' ἔρωτος Ἔρωτα βροτῶι θεὸν ὤπασε Φρύνηι
Πραξιτέλης, μιcθὸν καὶ θεὸν εὑρόμενος·   2385
ἡ δ' οὐκ ἠρνήθη τὸν τέκτονα, δεῖcε γάρ οἱ φρήν
μὴ θεὸc ἀντὶ τέχνης cύμμαχα τόξα λάβηι.
5 ταρβεῖ δ' οὐκέτι που τὸν Κύπριδος ἀλλὰ τὸν ἐκ coῦ,
Πραξίτελες, τέχνην μητέρ' ἐπισταμένη.

ΗΡΑΚΛΕΙΔΟΥ

I

ἄπιςχ' ἄπιςχε χεῖραc ὦ γεωπόνε,   2390
μηδ' ἀμφίταμνε τὰν ἐν ἠρίωι κόνιν·
αὔτα κέκλαυται βῶλοc· ἐκ κεκλαυμέναc
δ' οὗτοι κομάταc ἀναθαλήcεται cτάχυc.

II

λαῖλαψ καὶ πολὺ κῦμα καὶ ἀντολαὶ Ἀρκτούροιο
καὶ cκότοc Αἰγαίου τ' οἶδμα κακὸν πελάγευς,   2395
ταῦθ' ἅμα πάντ' ἐκύκηcεν ἐμὴν νέα, τριχθὰ δὲ κλαcθείς
ἱcτὸc ὁμοῦ φόρτωι κἀμὲ κάλυψε βυθῶι.
5 ναυηγὸν κλαίοιτε παρ' αἰγιαλοῖcι, γονῆες,
Τλησιμένη κωφὴν cτηcάμενοι λίθακα.

IX *A.Pl.* (A) 205 Τυλλίου Γεμίνου   εἰc τὸ αὐτό   caret P
I *A.P.* 7.281 [C] Ἡρακλείδου   [J] ὅμοιον ἐπὶ τῶι αὐτῶι   ἰαμβικόν   Pl B
Ἡρακλείδου
3 κεκλαυμέναc C: -αυcμέναc PPl   4 κομάταc Reiske: κόματος C, κοματος
in κάματος mut. P, κοματὸς Pl | ἀναθαλήcεται Pl: -θαλύc- P | cτάχυc CPl: -υν P

IX

On the same

Praxiteles gave me, a god, to Phrynê, a mortal, the Love-god
in return for love; so he invented guerdon and god in one.
And she refused not the artist; her heart was afraid lest the god
take up his bow as ally in defence of art. The one she fears is no
longer the son of Cypris but the one who came from you,
Praxiteles; his mother, she knows, was Art.

HERACLIDES

I

On a grave in danger from the plough

Hold off, hold off your hands, land-labourer, cleave not about
the dust upon the mound. This soil is soaked in tears; from soil
so tearful no bearded ear shall ever spring again.

II

On a death by ship-wreck

Tempest and mighty wave and rising of Arcturus and darkness
and evil swell of the Aegean sea, all these together confounded
my ship. Split in three, the mast buried me together with my
freight in the deeps. Set up a mute head-stone, O my parents,
and weep on the shore for ship-wrecked Tlesimenes.

II *A.P.* 7.392 [C] Ἡρακλείδου Cινωπέως   [J] εἰc ναυηγὸν Τληcιμένην ἐν τῶι
Αἰγαίωι πελάγει ναυαγήcαντα   Pl A Ἡρακλείδου Cινωπέως
3 πάντ' ἐκύκηcεν P: πάντα κύκ. Pl   5–6 olim tamquam epigramma peculiare
cum lemmate nunc eraso distinxit P   6 κωφὴν P: -φὸν Pl

ONECTOY

I

οὔτε με παρθενικῆς τέρπει γάμος οὔτε γεραιῆς·   2400
τὴν μὲν ἐποικτείρω, τὴν δὲ καταιδέομαι.
εἴη μήτ' ὄμφαξ μήτ' ἀσταφίς· ἡ δὲ πέπειρος
ἐς Κύπριδος θαλάμους †ὥρια καλλοσύνη†.

II

βάκτρον καὶ πήρη καὶ διπλόον εἷμα σοφοῖο
Διογένευς βιότου φόρτος ὁ κουφότατος.   2405
πάντα φέρω πορθμῆϊ, λέλοιπα γὰρ οὐδὲν ὑπὲρ γῆς·
ἀλλά, κύον, σαίνοις, Κέρβερε, τόν με κύνα.

III

'Αρμονίης ἱερὸν φήσεις γάμον, ἀλλ' ἀθέμιστος
Οἰδίποδος· λέξεις 'Αντιγόνην ὁσίην,
ἀλλὰ κασίγνητοι μιαρώτατοι· ἄμβροτος 'Ινώ,   2410
ἀλλ' 'Αθάμας τλήμων· τειχομελὴς κιθάρη,
5 ἀλλ' αὐλὸς δύσμουσος. ἴδ' ὡς ἐκεράσσατο Θήβηι
δαίμων ἐσθλὰ κακοῖς κεἰς ἓν ἔμιξεν ἴσα.

IV

'Ασωπὶς κρήνη καὶ Πηγασὶς ὕδατ' ἀδελφά
ἵππου καὶ ποταμοῦ δῶρα ποδορραγέα·   2415

I *A.P.* 5.20 'Ονέστου   [J] ἐρωτικὴ παραίνεσις   Pl A 'Ονέστου
1 γεραιῆς Pl: γηρ- P   3 ἀσταφίς CPl: ὠταφὶς (?) P
II *A.P.* 7.66 'Ονέστου   εἰς τὸν αὐτόν   Pl A s.a.n. in duo epigrammata divisum,
1–2 εἰς τὸν αὐτόν, 3–4 ὡς ἀπὸ τοῦ Διογένους   Suid. s.v. σαίνεσθαι (4)

HONESTUS

I

On ripeness for marriage

Marriage with either maiden or old woman has no pleasure for me; the one I pity, by the other I am abashed. Let her be neither sour grape nor raisin; the beauty that is ripe is the one in season for the Cyprian's bed-chamber.

II

On Diogenes the Cynic

Stick and wallet and double cloak are the featherweight luggage of philosopher Diogenes' life. I bring the ferryman all I possess; I have left nothing above ground. Come, Cerberus, let dog smile upon Dog.

III

Contrasting themes in Theban legend

You may call the marriage of Harmonia holy; unlawful was that of Oedipus. You may call Antigone saintly; abominable were her brothers. Immortal was Ino; miserable was Athamas. The lyre was for song-built walls; the flute for ill-omened music. See how Fate has compounded good with evil for Thebes, mixing them equally into a single brew.

IV

On the springs Peirenê and Hippocrenê

The fountains of Asopus and Pegasus are sister-streams, gifts of a horse and of a river, broken forth by stamping feet. The one

III *A.P.* 9.216 [C] 'Ονέστου Κορινθίου   εἰς Θήβας τὴν πόλιν ἣν ἔκτισε Κάδμος
Pl A τοῦ αὐτοῦ [sc. 'Ονέστου Κορινθίου]
1 ἀθέμιστος P: -μιτον Pl   5 ἐκεράσσατο Lascaris: -ράσατο PPl   6 κεῖc
Jacobs: δ' εἰc PPl
IV *A.P.* 9.225 [C] 'Ονέστου   εἰς 'Ασωπίδα τὴν κρήνην καὶ Πηγασίδα   caret Pl

χὠ μὲν ἔκοψ᾽ Ἑλικῶνος, ὁ δὲ φλέβας Ἀκροκορίνθου
ἔπληξ᾽. ὢ πτερνῆς εἰς ἴσον εὐστοχίη.

V

ἀμβαίνων Ἑλικῶνα μέγαν κάμες, ἀλλ᾽ ἐκορέσθης
Πηγασίδος κρήνης νεκταρέων λιβάδων·
οὕτως καὶ σοφίης πόνος ὄρθιος· ἢν δ᾽ ἄρ᾽ ἐπ᾽ ἄκρον   2420
τέρμα μόλῃις, ἀρύσῃι Πιερίδων χάριτας.

VI

ἔστην ἐν φόρμιγγι, κατηρείφθην δὲ σὺν αὐλῶι
Θήβη· φεῦ Μούσης ἔμπαλιν ἁρμονίης·
κωφὰ δέ μοι κεῖται λυροθελγέα λείψανα πύργων,
πέτροι μουσοδόμοις τείχεσιν αὐτόμολοι,   2425
5 σῆς χερός, Ἀμφίον, ἄπονος χάρις· ἑπτάπυλον γάρ
πάτρην ἑπταμίτωι τείχισας ἐν κιθάρηι.

VII

παίδων ὃν μὲν ἔκαιεν Ἀρίστιον, ὃν δ᾽ ἐσάκουσε
ναυηγόν, δισσὸν δ᾽ ἄλγος ἔτηξε μίαν.
αἰαῖ, μητέρα Μοῖρα διείλετο, τὴν ἴσα τέκνα   2430
καὶ πυρὶ καὶ πικρῶι νειμαμένην ὕδατι.

V A.P. 9.230 [C] Ὀνέστου   εἰς τὸν Ἑλικῶνα ἢ εἴς τι μουσεῖον   ʒτ   Pl A
Ὀνέστου
3 ἄρ᾽ Pl: ἂν P
VI A.P. 9.250 [C] Ὀνέστου   εἰς Θήβας τὰς ἑπταπύλους ἃς Ἀμφίων καὶ Ζῆθος
μετὰ κιθάρας ὠικοδόμησαν   Pl A Ὀνέστου Κορινθίου
1 κατηρείφθην Pl: κατηριφιην P, κατ᾽ ἠριφίην C   2 Θήβη Pl: -βηι P

cut the veins of Helicon, the other smote those of Acrocorinth. How happy the heel's aim, for both alike!

V

On the labours and rewards of poesy

Climbing great Helicon you wearied, but you had your fill of the nectar-flow of Pegasus' fountain. Thus the labour of Art is uphill, but if you come to the topmost end you shall draw a draught of the Muses' delights.

VI

On Thebes

By the lyre I rose up, the city of Thebes; with the flute I fell in ruins. Alas for the Muse so contrary to harmony! Deaf they lie, the lyre-enchanted relics of my towers, the stones that came unforced for the song-built walls, a gift without labour, Amphion, from your hand; for with the seven-stringed lyre you walled your seven-gated city.

VII

On the death of two sons

Aristion was cremating one of her sons when she heard that the other was ship-wrecked; twofold grief melted her single heart. Alas, Fate divided the mother two ways, her who gave children equally to fire and to the cruel waters.

---

4 πέτροι...αὐτόμολοι Reiske: πέτροις...αὐτομόλοις PPl   5 Ἀμφίων P: -φίον Pl | ἑπτάπυλον Pl: ἑπτάμιτον P

VII *A.P.* 9.292 Ὀνέστου   [C] εἰς Ἀρίστιον γυναῖκα ἧς ἐν μιᾶι ἡμέραι δύο παῖδες τεθνήκαςιν, ὁ μὲν ἐν γῆι ὁ δ' ἐν θαλάσςηι   Pl A Ὀνέστου
1 ἐςάκουςε P: -κουε Pl   3 αἰαῖ Pl: αἴ P

VIII

Μούςης νουθεσίην φιλοπαίγμονος εὕρετο Βάκχος,
ὦ Cικυών, ἐν coὶ κῶμον ἄγων Χαρίτων·
δὴ γὰρ ἔλεγχον ἔχει γλυκερώτατον ἔν τε γέλωτι
κέντρον· χὠ μεθύων ἀcτὸν ἐcωφρόνιcεν.   2435

IX

αὐτοθελὴς ἥδιcτος ἀεὶ πότος· ὃς δέ κ' ἀνάγκηι,
ὑβριcτὴς οἴνωι τ' ἐcτὶ καὶ οἰνοπότηι.
τὸν μὲν γὰρ γαίηι προχέει κρύφα, τὸν δ' ὑπὸ γαίηι
πολλάκι πρὸς Λήθης ἤγαγε πικρὸν ὕδωρ.
5 πουλυμεθεῖc χαίροιτε· τὸ δ' ὁππόcον ἡδὺ ποθῆναι   2440
μέτρον ἐμοὶ πάcης ἄρκιον εὐφροcύνης.

X

A 1   Πολύμν[ια

ἡ Ζηνὸς Διὶ τόνδε Πολύμνια νέκταρος ἀτμόν   (2442)
πέμπω τὴν ὁcίην πατρὶ τίνουcα χάριν.
                'Ονέcτου

XI

A 2   Θάληα

θάλλει ἐπ' εἰρήνης coφίης καλά· τοιγὰρ ἁπάcας
Εἰρήνηι λοιβὰς τάcδε Θάλεια χέω.   2445
                ['Ονέ]cτου

VIII A.P. 11.32 'Ονέcτου   Pl A 'Ονέcτου
4 ἐcωφρόνιcεν Pl: -ιзεν P

VIII

Sicyon the home of satyr-drama

While leading his rout of Graces in your city, Sicyon, Bacchus invented the Comic Muse's moralising. Truly it gives pleasure combined with reproof and a sting amid the laughter; the townsman is chastened by the toper.

IX

On moderation in drinking

The voluntary drink is always pleasantest. That which comes by force does violence to wine and wine-drinker too; the wine it spills unnoticed on the ground, the drinker it often draws to the bitter waters of Lethe underground. A fond farewell to you, deep-drinkers; for me, sufficient measure of all good cheer is just so much as is pleasant to drink.

X–XVIII

On the nine Muses

X

I, Polymnia, daughter of Zeus, send this breath of nectar to Zeus, paying my father the tribute of piety.

XI

The beauties of poesy flourish in peace-time; therefore I, Thalia, pour all these libations to Peace.

IX *A.P.* 11.45 Ὀνέϲτου   Pl A Ὀνέϲτου
5 τὸ Pl: τὰ P
X–XVIII lapides inscriptos ed. Jamot *B.C.H.* 26.130 seqq.

XII

A 3   Τερψιχόρα

κιccὸc Τερψιχόρηι, Βρομίωι δ᾽ ἔπρεψεν ὁ λωτόc,   (2446)
τῆι μὲν ἵν᾽ ἔνθεοc ἧι, τῶι δ᾽ ἵνα τερπνότεροc.
       'Ονέcτου

XIII

A 4   Με[λπο]μέν[α

cύμφθογγόν με λύρηc χορδῆι κεράcαcαν ἀοιδήν   (2448)
λεύccειc ἐν διccοῖc Μελπομένην μέλεcιν.
       'Ονέcτου

XIV

A 5   Καλλιόπα

c]κῆπτρα λόγου, cκήπτρων δὲ δίκη πέλαc οἷc μ[2450
[Κα]λλιόπη πειθοῦc τὸ κράτοc ο[
         [   ]

XV

A 6   ['Ερατώ?]

λιπον ἀλλὰ χορευcε[(2452)
.ανθοβα..[.]ευc ἀπο.[

XVI

A 7   [Κληώ?]

χάριc α[ἷ]c ἐνορῶcα
δέδορκα καλά   2455

XIV 1 μ[ετέδωκα Jamot, μ[εγάλ᾽ αὐχῶ Preuner   2 ὁ[ρθόπολιc Jamot, ο[ὕνεκ᾽ ἔχω Preuner

XII

Ivy is proper for Terpsichore, for Bromios the lotus-flute; to her, that she may be inspired; to him, that he may give the more pleasure.

XIII

Me, Melpomene, you behold blending harmonious song with the lyre-string in twofold music.

XIV

The speaker's staff is a close neighbour of Eloquence, Justice is close neighbour to the speaker's staff ⟨   ⟩ Calliope ⟨   ⟩ the power of persuasion.

XV

XVI

XV ante λιπον et .ανθο- nihil in lapide scriptum
1 χορεύϲε[ι, 2 ἀνθοβαφεῦϲ ἀπὸ γῆϲ suppl. edd.
XVI ante χάριϲ et δέδορκα nihil in lapide scriptum

18-2

XVII

A 8   Ὠρανία

ἀcτέραc ἠρεύνηcα coφῆι φρενί, πατρί τ' ἐοικόc   (2456)
οὔνομ' ἔχω, λέγομαι δ' ἡ Διὸc Οὐρανίη.
    'Ονέcτου

XVIII

A 9   Εὐτέρπα

]†μορc.ινχαρμοcηνδεγειαιν†   (2458)
Εὐτέρπη, κόcμοιc τόνδε cὺ κόcμον ἔχειc.
    'Ονέcτου

XIX

B   ] κιccὸc cτέφο[c   2460
           ]ροιc τερπνοτερ[
    'Ον[έcτου

XX

C 1   τ]ὸν θραcὺν ἐc μολπὴν ἄφθογγον νῦν μ' ἐ[c] ἀοιδήν
      λεῦccε· τί γὰρ Μούcαιc εἰc ἔριν ἠντίαcα;
    π]ηρὸc δ' ὁ Θρήιξ Θάμυριc φόρμιγγι πάρημαι·
    ἀ]λλά, θεαί, μολπῆc ὑμετέρηc ἀίω.   2465
    'Ονέcτου

XXI

C 2 ἡ δοιοὺc cκήπτροιcι θεοὺc αὐχοῦcα Cεβαcτή   (2466)
    Καίcαραc εἰρήνηc διccὰ λέλαμπε φάη·
    ἔπρεψεν δὲ coφαῖc Ἑλικωνιάcιν πινυτόφρων
    cύγχοροc, ἧc γε νόοc κόcμον ἔcωcεν ὅλον.
    'Ονέcτου

XVIII 2 κόcμοιc: κώμοιc coni. Dittenberger | cὺ ed. pr.: ευ lapis

XVII

With subtle mind I searched the stars, and I have a name like my father's; I am called Urania, daughter of Zeus.

XVIII

⟨   ⟩, Euterpe, ⟨   ⟩ this adornment is yours.

XIX

XX

On a statue of Thamyris

Look upon me, the bold one for melody, now mute for song. Why did I come into conflict with the Muses? Maimed beside the lyre I sit, Thamyris of Thrace; yet, goddesses, I hear your melody.

XXI

To Augusta

Augusta, who can boast of two divine sceptred Caesars, set light to twin torches of Peace; fit company for the learnèd Heliconian Muses, a choir-mate of wise counsel, her wisdom was the whole world's saviour.

XX 1 εϲμολπην in lapide legit Keramopoullos, ευμολπην Jamot   **3** πάρημαι Jamot: παριμαι lapis
XXI 3 ἔπρεψεν Wilhelm: επρεπεν lapis

XXII

οὔνομα κηρύccω Τιμοκλέοc, εἰc ἅλα πικρήν   2470
πάντηι cκεπτομένη ποῦ ποτ' ἄρ' ἐcτὶ νέκυc.
αἰαῖ, τὸν δ' ἤδη φάγον ἰχθύεc, ἡ δὲ περιccή
πέτροc ἐγὼ τὸ μάτην γράμμα τορευθὲν ἔχω.

ΜΑΚΚΙΟΥ

I

ἡ χαλεπὴ κατὰ πάντα Φιλίcτιον, ἡ τὸν ἐραcτήν
μηδέποτ' ἀργυρίου χωρὶc ἀναcχομένη,   2475
φαίνετ' ἀνεκτοτέρη νῦν ἢ πάροc. οὐ μέγα θαῦμα
φαίνεcθ'· ἠλλάχθαι τὴν φύcιν οὐ δοκέω.
5 καὶ γὰρ πρηυτέρη ποτὲ γίνεται ἀcπὶc ἀναιδήc,
δάκνει δ' οὐκ ἄλλωc ἢ θανατηφορίην.

II

θερμαίνει μ' ὁ καλὸc Κορνήλιοc· ἀλλὰ φοβοῦμαι   2480
τοῦτο τὸ φῶc ἤδη πῦρ μέγα γινόμενον.

III

ἤλλακτ' ἐξαπίνηc Κορνήλιοc, οὐδ' ἐπὶ λιτῶι
τέρπεται ἡμετέρωι μουcοχαρεῖ βιότωι,

XXII *A.P.* 7.274 [C] Ὀνέcτου Βυζαντίου   [J] εἰc Τιμοκλέα ναυηγόν   Pl B
Ὀνέcτου
2 cκεπτομένη CPl: -νοc P   4 τορευθὲν C: τυρωθ- P, τυπωθ- Pl

I *A.P.* 5.114 Μαικίου   [J] εἰc πόρνην βαρύμιcθον ἐν τῆι νεότητι, γηράcαcαν δὲ
πᾶcιν ὑποκύπτουcαν Pl A τοῦ αὐτοῦ [sc. Φιλοδήμου]
1 Φιλίcτιον P^ac: Φιλήcτιον P^pc, Φιλίcιον Pl   4 ἠλλάχθαι Pl: ἤλλακται P
6 οὐκ ἄλλωc Pl: οὐ καλῶc P

XXII

Epitaph for Timocles, lost at sea

I proclaim the name of Timocles; I scan the cruel sea all around, where can his body be? Alas, the fishes have already devoured him, and I, this useless stone, have this writing carved in vain upon me.

MACCIUS

I

On a courtesan's change of tactics

The hard one in all ways, Philistion, the one who never tolerated a lover without cash, seems now more tolerant than before. It is no great miracle, her seeming so; she has not changed her nature, I fancy. Sometimes the ruthless asp becomes quite tame, but its bite is never other than death-dealing.

II

On his passion for Cornelius

That beauty Cornelius makes me hot; I am frightened of this flame, already growing a great fire.

III

A change in Cornelius

Cornelius is changed all of a sudden, and takes no pleasure in our simple Muse-delighted life. Unsubstantial is the hope from

II *A.P.* 5.117 Μαικίου   [J] ἐρωτομανὲς καὶ γέμον ἀσεβείας [ἀσέβειαν cod.; lemma fort. ad praeced. ep. = Argentarii x referendum]   Pl A τοῦ αὐτοῦ [sc. Μαικίου]
2 γινόμενον P: γιγν- Pl

III *A.P.* 9.411 Μακκίου   παραινετικὸν εἴς τινα φίλον [C] ἤγουν Κορνήλιον τὴν αὑτοῦ φιλίαν ἀνταλλαξάμενον   Pl A s.a.n.
2 μουσοχαρεῖ Pl: -ρῆ P

κούφης δ' αἰωρεῖται ἀπ' ἐλπίδος· οὐκέτι δ' ἡμεῖς
ἧς πάρος, ἀλλ' ἑτέρης Ἐλπίδος ἐκκρέμαται.   2485
5 εἴκωμεν, ψυχή· πεπαλαίσμεθα· μηδὲ βιάζου·
εἰς ἔδαφος τέχνης κείμεθ' ὑπ' ἀργυρέης.

IV

τί στυγνή; τί δὲ ταῦτα κόμης εἰκαῖα, Φιλαινί,
σκύλματα καὶ νοτερῶν σύγχυσις ὀμματίων;
μὴ τὸν ἐραστὴν εἶδες ἔχονθ' ὑποκόλπιον ἄλλην;   2490
εἶπον ἐμοί· λύπης φάρμακ' ἐπιστάμεθα.
5 δακρύεις, οὐ φὴις δέ· μάτην ἀρνεῖσθ' ἐπιβάλληι·
ὀφθαλμοὶ γλώσσης ἀξιοπιστότεροι.

V

ὤμοσ' ἐγὼ δύο νύκτας ἀφ' Ἡδυλίου, Κυθέρεια,
σὸν κράτος, ἡσυχάσειν· ὡς δοκέω δ' ἐγέλας   2495
τοὐμὸν ἐπισταμένη τάλανος κακόν· οὐ γὰρ ὑποίσω
τὴν ἑτέρην, ὅρκους δ' εἰς ἀνέμους τίθεμαι.
5 αἱροῦμαι δ' ἀσεβεῖν κείνης χάριν ἢ τὰ σὰ τηρῶν
ὅρκι' ἀποθνήισκειν, πότνι', ὑπ' εὐσεβίης.

VI

αἰγιαλῖτα Πρίηπε, σαγηνευτῆρες ἔθηκαν   2500
δῶρα παρακταίης σοὶ τάδ' ἐπωφελίης,
θύννων εὐκλώστοιο λίνου βυσσώμασι ῥόμβον
φράξαντες γλαυκαῖς ἐν παρόδοις πελάγευς,

4 ἧς Page: οἱ PPl   5 εἴκωμεν Pl: -κομεν P

IV A.P. 5.130 Μαικίου [in Μακκίου corr. C]   [C] εἰς τὴν ἑταίραν Φιλαινίδα
Pl A τοῦ αὐτοῦ [sc. Μαικίου]
1 εἰκαῖα CPl: ἠκ- P   5 ἐπιβάλληι CPl: -ει vel -εις P

V A.P. 5.133 Μαικίου   [C] εἰς Ἡδύλιον ἑταίραν   Pl A Μαικίου
2 δ' ἐγέλας P: δὲ γελᾶις Pl   3 τάλανος P: spatio vac. relicto om. Pl
4 ἑτέρην Pl: ἑτάρ- P   6 ὅρκι' Pl: ὄργι' P

which he dangles; quite different is the Hope he hangs from, no longer that on which we once depended. Let us yield, my soul; we are out-wrestled; offer no force. We lie thrown to the ground, subdued by the skill of silver.

IV

Philaenis unhappy in love

Why sullen? Why these random pluckings of the hair, Philaenis, and confusion in your flooding eyes? Can it be that you saw your lover holding another in his lap? Tell me; I know the remedy for grief. You weep, and say no; in vain you attempt to deny it; the eyes are trustworthier than the tongue.

V

Hedylion irresistible

I vowed, Cytherea, by your majesty, to sleep two nights apart from Hedylion. And you laughed, I fancy, knowing as you do the malady of my poor heart. For I shall not endure the second night; I cast my vows to the winds. I would rather be impious for her sake than die for piety, Lady, keeping my vows to you.

VI

Dedication by fishermen to Priapus

These gifts, Priapus of the beach, seine-fishers have dedicated to you for your help beside the shore, having fenced round the whirl of tunnies with the linen of well-spun nets in the gray

VI A.P. 6.33 Μαικίου [in Μακκίου corr. C]   [P] ἀνάθημα τῶι Πανὶ παρὰ ἁλιέων Pl A Μαικίου   Suid. s.vv. Πρίαπος (1 s.), σαγήνεια (eadem), βυσσοδομοῦντεc (3–4), ῥόμβον (eadem), φήγινος (5 φηγ. κρατ.), αὐτούργητον (5 καὶ–6 βάθρ.)   Zonar. s.v. ἀκταίη (1s.)
2 παρακταίηc P: παρ' ἀκτ. CPlSuid. Zonar. | ἐπ' ὠφ. C   3 θύννων CPlSuid.: θύνων P | βυccώμαcι CPlSuid.: -ματι P

5 φηγίνεον κρατῆρα καὶ αὐτούργητον ἐρείκης
   βάθρον ἴδ' ὑαλέην οἰνοδόκον κύλικα,   2505
   ὡς ἂν ὑπ' ὀρχησμῶν λελυγισμένον ἔγκοπον ἴχνος
   ἀμπαύσηις ξηρὴν δίψαν ἐλαυνόμενος.

VII

ἀκταίης νησῖδος ἁλιξάντοισι, Πρίηπε,
   χοιράσι καὶ τρηχεῖ τερπόμενε σκοπέλωι,
σοὶ Πάρις ὀστρακόδερμον ὑπ' εὐθήροισι δαμέντα   2510
   ὁ γριπεὺς καλάμοις κάραβον ἐκρέμασεν·
5 σάρκα μὲν ἔμπυρον αὐτὸς ὑφ' ἡμίβρωτον ὀδόντα
   θείς, μάκαρ, αὐτὸ δὲ σοὶ τοῦτο πόρε σκύβαλον.
τῶι σὺ δίδου μὴ πολλά, δι' εὐάγρου δὲ λίνοιο,
   δαῖμον, ὑλακτούσης νηδύος ἡσυχίην.   2515

VIII

γομφιόδουπα χαλινὰ καὶ ἀμφίτρητον ὑπειρκτάν
   κημὸν καὶ γενύων σφίγκτορ' εὐρραφέα
τάνδε τ' ἐπιπλήκτειραν ἀπορρύτοιο διωγμοῦ
   μάστιγα †σκαιοῦ† δῆγμά τ' ἐπιψελίου
5 κέντρα τ' ἐναιμήεντα διωξίπποιο μύωπος   2520
   καὶ πριστὸν ψήκτρης κνῆσμα σιδηρόδετον
διπλοῖς ἀΐόνων ὠρύγμασιν, Ἴσθμιε, τερφθείς
   δῶρα, Πόσειδον, ἔχεις ταῦτα παρὰ Στρατίου.

---

5 ἐρείκης PlSuid.: ἐρίκ- P   7 ὀρχησμῶν Pl^ac: -χισμῶν P, -χηθμῶν Pl^pc
8 ἀμπαύσηις Pl: -σηι P

VII *A.P.* 6.89 Μαικίου Κοΐντου   ἀνάθημα τῶι Πριήπωι παρὰ Πάριδος ἁλιέως
Pl A Μαικίου Κοΐντου   Suid. s.vv. νησίς (1-2 χοιρ., om. Πρίηπε), ἁλιξάντοις
(eadem), ὑλακτούσης (7 s.)
1 ἁλιξάντοισι PSuid.: ἀλεξ- Pl   2 τερπόμενε Brunck: -ναι P, -νος Pl
6 αὐτὸ Pl: -τὸς P   7 μὴ PSuid.: μοι Pl

channels of the sea: an oak-wood mixing-bowl, and a hand-made bench of heath, and a wine-welcoming cup of glass, so that you may rest your weary feet after their twisting in the dance and chase dry thirst away.

VII

Dedication by a fisherman to Priapus

Priapus, rejoicing in the coastal islet's sea-tortured reefs and rugged promontory, to you Paris the fisherman has hung up a shell-skinned crayfish conquered by his good hunting-rod. The flesh, roasted, himself he put under his half-decayed teeth, Blest Spirit, and only this, its refuse, he offered to you. Therefore give him no great gift, divine friend, but appeasement of his growling belly through good catches of his net.

VIII

Dedication of equestrian gear to Poseidon

The teeth-rattling bit, the pierced constraining muzzle, the well-stitched binder of the jaws, this whip the chastiser that goes with rein-free gallop, the bite of the ⟨   ⟩ cavesson, the en-sanguined pricks of the horse-driving goad, and the saw-like iron-bound scrape of the comb, Isthmian Poseidon, rejoicing in the beaches' double roar, these gifts you have from Stratius.

<hr />

VIII *A.P.* 6.233 Μαικίου   [C] ἀνάθημα Cτρατίου τῶι Ποσειδῶνι   Suid. s.vv. γομφίος (1 γομφ. χαλ.), κημός (1 καὶ–2 κημ.), μάστιξ (2 καὶ–ἔυρρ. + μάστιγα), μύωψ (5), ψήκτρα (6)   caret Pl
1 ὑπειρκτάν (vel ὑπερκτάν) Bernhardy: ὑπεικτάν PSuid.   2 γενύων Ap. G.: νεκύων PSuid.   3 τάνδε τ᾿ C: τάνδ᾿ P   6 πριστὸν CSuid.: πρης- P
7 ἀϊόνων Hecker (ἠϊ- Salm.): ἀιώνων P

IX

εὐπέταλον γλαυκὰν ἀναδενδράδα τάνδε παρ' ἄκραις
ἱδρυθεὶς λοφιαῖς Πὰν ὅδ' ἐπισκοπέω.   2525
εἰ δέ σε πορφύροντος ἔχει πόθος, ὦ παροδῖτα,
βότρυος, οὐ φθονέω γαστρὶ χαριζομένωι·
5 ἢν δὲ χερὶ ψαύσηις κλοπίηι μόνον, αὐτίκα δέξηι
ὀζαλέην βάκτρου τήνδε καρηβαρίην.

X

αὐτὸς ἄναξ ἔμβαινε θοῶι πηδήματι ληνοῦ   2530
λακτιστής, ἔργου δ' ἡγέο νυκτερίου·
λεύκωσαι πόδα γαῦρον, ἐπίρρωσαι δὲ χορείης
λάτριν, ὑπὲρ κούφων ζωσάμενος γονάτων,
5 εὔγλωσσον δ' ὀχέτευε κενούς, μάκαρ, ἐς πιθεῶνας
οἶνον ἐπὶ ψαιστοῖς καὶ λασίηι χιμάρωι.   2535

XI

κλαῖε δυσεκφύκτως σφιγχθεὶς χέρας, ἄκριτε δαῖμον,
κλαῖε μάλα στάζων ψυχοτακῆ δάκρυα,
σωφροσύνας ὑβριστά, φρενοκλόπε, ληιστὰ λογισμοῦ,
πτανὸν πῦρ, ψυχᾶς τραῦμ' ἀόρατον, Ἔρως.
5 θνατοῖς μὲν λύσις ἐστὶ γόων ὁ σός, ἄκριτε, δεσμός,   2540
ὧι σφιγχθεὶς κωφοῖς πέμπε λιτὰς ἀνέμοις·
ὃν δὲ βροτοῖς ἀφύλακτος ἐνέφλεγες ἐν φρεσὶ πυρσόν,
ἄθρει νῦν ὑπὸ σῶν σβεννύμενον δακρύων.

IX A.P. 9.249 [C] Μακκίου [ex Μαικίου corr.]   εἰς ἀναδενδράδα ὑπὸ Πανὸς
φυλαττομένην Pl в Μαικίου
2 ἱδρυθεὶς P: -υνθεὶς Pl   5 χερὶ CPl: χερίη P   6 ὀζαλέην P: ἀζ- Pl
X A.P. 9.403 Μακκίου   εἰς ληνόν   caret Pl

IX

On a statue of Pan in a vineyard

Here am I, Pan, seated on the hill-crests, watching over this
leafy gray climbing-vine. If you have a passion for the reddening
cluster, passer-by, I grudge not one who gratifies his hunger;
but if you touch it merely with a thief's fingers, you shall receive
this knobby head-weight of my stick.

X

Dionysus invited to join in the wine-pressing

Yourself, Lord, enter with rapid leap as trampler of the wine-
vat; lead the labour of the night. Make your proud foot show
white, give strength to your dance's servitor, girt up above
your nimble knees. Channel the sweet-voiced wine, Blest
Spirit, into the empty storage-jars in return for cakes and a
shaggy she-goat.

XI

On a statue of Eros in bonds

Weep, undiscerning Spirit, your hands inescapably fettered,
weep your fill, shedding soul-wasting tears, outrager of decency,
sense-deceiver, robber of reason, wingèd fire, the soul's invisible
lesion, Love. To mortals, O undiscerning, your bonds are
their release from groaning; fettered therein, to deaf winds send
your prayers. Look at the torch which you, irresistible to
mortals, have kindled in their hearts, now by your tears being
quenched.

3 χορείης Page: -ην P
XI *A.Pl.* (A) 198 Μαικίου εἰς τὸ αὐτό   caret P
4 πῦρ ψυχᾶς Benndorf: ψυχᾶς πῦρ Pl   5 μὲν Pl^pc: μὲν γὰρ Pl^ac

ΜΑΚΗΔΟΝΙΟΥ

I

ἐχθές μοι cυνέπινε γυνὴ περὶ ἧς λόγος ἔρρει
οὐχ ὑγιής· παῖδες, θραύcατε τὰς κύλικας.   2545

II

κάπρον μὲν χέρcωι Κόδρος ἔκτανε, τὴν δὲ ταχεῖαν   (2546)
εἰν ἁλὶ καὶ χαροποῖc κύμαcιν εἷλ' ἔλαφον·
εἰ δ' ἦν καὶ πτηνὴ θηρῶν φύcιc, οὐδ' ἂν ἐν αἴθρηι
τὴν κείνου κενεὴν Ἄρτεμιc εἶδε χέρα.

III

Cυρρέντου τρηχεῖα μυρίπνοε χαῖρε κονίη   2550
καὶ Πολλεντίνων γαῖα μελιχροτάτη
Ἄcτη θ' ἡ τριπόθητοc, ἀφ' ἧc βρομιώδεα πηλόν
φύρηcαν Βάκχωι τριζυγέεc Χάριτεc·
5 πλούτου καὶ πενίηc κοινὸν κτέαρ, οἷc μὲν ἀνάγκηc
cκεῦοc, τοῖc δὲ τρυφῆc χρῆcι περιccοτέρη.   2555

ΜΥΡΙΝΟΥ

I

ὑψηλῶν ὀρέων ἔφοροι κεραοὶ χοροπαῖκται   (2556)
Πᾶνεc, βουχίλου κράντορεc Ἀρκαδίηc,
εὔαρνον θείητε καὶ εὐχίμαρον Διότιμον
δεξάμενοι λαμπρῆc δῶρα θυηπολίηc.

I *A.P.* 11.39 Μακηδονίου Θεccαλονικέωc   Pl в s.a.n.
II *A.P.* 9.275 [C] Μακηδονίου   εἰc Κόδρον τινὰ κυνηγέτην ἄριcτον   Pl A
Μακεδόνοc
1 ἔκτανε Pl: -νεν P   3 ἐν αἴθρηι schol. Bern.: εναίθρι P, ἀν' αἰθέρα Pl
III *A.P.* 11.27 Μακηδονίου   caret Pl

MACEDONIUS

I

Unhealthy wine-cups

Yesterday my drinking-companion was a woman about whom
there goes an unhealthy tale; slaves, smash the cups.

II

A skilful hunter

Codrus killed a boar on land, the swift deer he took in the sea
and sparkling waves; if the nature of beasts were winged,
Artemis would not have seen him empty-handed in the air
either.

III

A trio of Italian towns celebrated for their clay

Greetings to you, Sorrento's dust, harsh and fragrant, and to
you, Pollenza's honey-sweet earth, and to you, thrice-beloved
Asti, whence the three Graces in unison mixed for Bacchus
his Dionysiac clay; possession alike of wealth and of poverty,
for some the vessel of necessity, for others the superfluous
instrument of luxury.

MYRINUS

I

Dedication by a stock-farmer

Guardians of high mountains, horned dancing merry-makers,
Pans, rulers of Arcadia's fine pasture, make Diotimus rich in
sheep and rich in goats, accepting the gifts of his bright sacrifice.

1 Cυρρέντου Brunck: Cυρέν- P   3 Ἄcτη θ᾽ ἡ τριπόθητος Jacobs: αἷc ται θ᾽
αἱ τριπόθητοι P

1 *A.P.* 6.108 [PC] Μυρίνου   [P] ἀνάθημα τοῖc Παcὶ παρὰ Διοτίμου   Suid. s.vv.
βουχίλου (2), κράντορεc (2 βουχ.–Ἀρκ.)   caret Pl
1 χοροπαῖκται Ap.B.: χαρ- P   2 βουχίλου Suid.: -χείλου P

II

τὴν μαλακὴν Παφίης Cτατύλλιον ἀνδρόγυνον δρῦν   2560
ἕλκειν εἰς 'Αίδην ἡνίκ' ἔμελλε χρόνος,
τὰκ κόκκου βαφθέντα καὶ ὑcγίνοιο θέριστρα
καὶ τοὺς ναρδολιπεῖς ἀλλοτρίους πλοκάμους,
5 φαικάδα τ' εὐτάρcοιcιν ἐπ' ἀcτραγάλοιcι γελῶcαν
καὶ τὴν γρυτοδόκην κοιτίδα παμβακίδων   2565
αὐλούς θ' ἡδὺ πνέοντας ἑταιρείοιc ἐνὶ κώμοιc
δῶρα Πριηπείων θῆκεν ἐπὶ προθύρων.

III

Θύρcιc ὁ κωμήτης, ὁ τὰ νυμφικὰ μῆλα νομεύων,
Θύρcιc ὁ cυρίζων Πανὸc ἴcον δόνακι,
ἔνδιοc οἰνοπότηc cκιερὰν ὑπὸ τὰν πίτυν εὕδει,   2570
φρουρεῖ δ' αὐτὸc ἑλὼν ποίμνια βάκτρον Ἔρωc.
5 ἃ Νύμφαι Νύμφαι, διεγείρατε τὸν λυκοθαρcῆ
βοcκόν, μὴ θηρῶν κύρμα γένηται Ἔρωc.

IV

ὖ τετρηκόcι' ἐcτίν, ἔχειc δὲ cὺ τοὺc ἐνιαυτούc
δὶc τόccουc, τρυφερὴ Λαΐ κορωνεκάβη,   2575
Cιcύφου ὦ μάμμη καὶ Δευκαλίωνοc ἀδελφή·
βάπτε δὲ τὰc λευκὰc καὶ λέγε πᾶcι 'τατᾶ'.

II A.P. 6.254 Μυρίνου   Suid. s.vv. τὰκ κόκκου (3), ὕcτινοc (3), θέριcτρον (3 s.),
τρυτοδόκη (6), βάμβαξ (6), πάμβαξ (6)   caret Pl
3 ὑcγίνοιο C: ὑcτί- PSuid.   4 ναρδολιπεῖc Salm.: ἀνδρολ- PSuid.   6 γρυτο-
δόκην Toup: τρυ- PSuid.   7 αὐλούc Gruter: ἄλλουc P | ἑταιρείοιc Ap.G.:
-ρίοιc P
III A.P. 7.703 [C] Μυρίνου   [J] εἰc Θύρcιν τὸν κωμήτην ὃν ἐπαινεῖ Θεόκριτοc
ὁ Δωρικόc   Pl A Μυρίνου

II

On an effeminate man

When Time was about to drag that rotten trunk, the Paphian's own, Statyllius the effeminate, down to Hades, these gifts he dedicated in the porch of Priapus: his summer-frocks dyed scarlet and purple, his borrowed curls, nard-greasy, the slipper that twinkled about his pretty foot's ankle-bones, his foppery-chest of cottons, his flutes sweet-breathing in harlot-revelries.

III

Thyrsis asleep while Eros guards his flock

Thyrsis the countryman who pastures the sheep of the Nymphs, Thyrsis whose piping is equal to Pan's reed, wine-drinker at noon-tide, sleeps under the shady pine, while Eros himself takes the staff and guards the flocks. Nymphs, O Nymphs, wake up that wolf-defying pasturer, lest Eros become a prey to wild beasts.

IV

On an old harlot

The letter 'u' stands for 'four hundred', but your years are twice as many, my wanton Laïs, crow-Hecuba, O grandmother of Sisyphus and sister of Deucalion; so dye your white hair and cry 'papa' to one and all.

---

3 οἰνοπότης Pl: -τηι P | τὰν PPlᵃᶜ: τὴν Plᵖᶜ   5–6 om. P   6 γένηται Brunck: γένηθ' ὁ Pl

IV *A.P.* 11.67 Μυρίνου   εἰς γραῖαν   Pl A Μυρίνου
1 τετρήκοσι' Pl: τετριήκ- P | ἐστίν P: ἐστι Pl (in ἔτη mut. man. rec.)   2 Λαΐ κορωνεκάβη P: πεντακόρων' Ἑκάβη (πε in rasura) Pl   3 Cιϲύφου P: -φος Pl | μάμμη Pl: μάμη P   4 δὲ Pl: om. P

ΠΑΡΜΕΝΙΩΝΟC

I

ἐс Δανάην ἔρρευсαс, Ὀλύμπιε, χρυсόс, ἵν' ἡ παῖс   (2578)
ὡс δώρωι πειсθῆι, μὴ τρέсηι ὡс Κρονίδην.

II

ὁ Ζεὺс τὴν Δανάην χρυсοῦ, κἀγὼ δὲ сὲ χρυсοῦ·   2580
πλείονα γὰρ δοῦναι τοῦ Διὸс οὐ δύναμαι.

III

⟦παρθενικῆс τάφοс εἴμ' Ἑλέντ₁с, πένθει δ' ἐπ' ἀδελφῶι⟧
Ἅιδηс τὴν Κροκάληс ἔφθαсε παρθενίην·
εἰс δὲ γόουс Ὑμέναιοс ἐπαύсατο, τὰс δὲ γαμούντων
ἐλπίδαс οὐ θάλαμοс κοίμιсεν ἀλλὰ τάφοс.   2585

IV

παρθενικῆс τάφοс εἴμ' Ἑλένηс, πένθει δ' ἐπ' ἀδελφοῦ   (2586)
προφθιμένου διπλᾶ ματρὸс ἔχω δάκρυα.
μνηстῆρсιν δ' ἔλιπον κοίν' ἄλγεα, τὴν γὰρ ἔτ' οὔπω
οὐδενὸс ἡ πάντων ἐλπὶс ἔκλαυсεν ἴсωс.

I *A.P.* 5.33 Παρμενίωνοc   Pl A Παρμενίωνοc
1 ἐс P: εἰс Pl

II *A.P.* 5.34 τοῦ αὐτοῦ [sc. Παρμενίωνοc]   [J] ὅμοιον   Pl A τοῦ αὐτοῦ [sc. Παρμενίωνοc]

III *A.P.* 7.183 [C] Παρμενίωνοc   [J] εἰс Ἑλένην τινὰ παρθένον τελευτήсαcαν caret Pl

PARMENION

I

On Zeus and Danae

You rained as gold on Danae, Olympian, that the girl might
yield as to a gift, not tremble as before the son of Cronos.

II

On the same, applied to a present affair

Zeus took Danae for gold, for gold I take you; I cannot give
more than Zeus.

III

Death of a bride

⟨   ⟩ Hades overtook the maidenhood of
Crocalê. The marriage-song ended in lamentations; not the
bridal-chamber but the tomb laid to rest the hopes of the
wedding-pair.

IV

Epitaph for a young woman

I am the tomb of the maiden Helen. Through mourning over a
brother dead before her, I have her mother's tears twofold. To
her suitors I have left a common grief; the hopes of all alike
lamented her who was not yet anyone's.

1–3 obelis in marg. sin. appositis damnat C   1 ep. sequentis initium perperam huic praefixit P   3 γόους Salm.: γάμους P   4 τάφος C: θάνα-
τος P

IV *A.P.* 7.184 [C] Παρμενίωνος   [J] εἰς τὴν αὐτήν   Pl A Παρμενίωνος
2 διπλᾶ Jacobs: -λόα P

V

φθίσθαι 'Αλέξανδρον ψευδὴς φάτις, εἴπερ ἀληθής   2590
Φοῖβος· ἀνικήτων ἅπτεται οὐδ᾽ 'Αίδης.

VI

ἀρκεῖ μοι χλαίνης λιτὸν σκέπας, οὐδὲ τραπέζαις
δουλεύσω Μουσέων ἄνθεα βοσκόμενος·
μισῶ πλοῦτον ἄνουν, κολάκων τροφόν, οὐδὲ παρ᾽ ὀφρῦν
στήσομαι. οἶδ᾽ ὀλίγης δαιτὸς ἐλευθερίην.   2595

VII

μητρυιῆς δύσμηνις ἀεὶ χόλος, οὐδ᾽ ἐν ἔρωτι   (2596)
ἤπιος· οἶδα πάθη σώφρονcc 'Ιππολύτου.

VIII

οἱ κόρις ἄχρι κόρου κορέσαντό μου, ἀλλ᾽ ἐκορέσθην   (2598)
ἄχρι κόρου καὐτὸς τοὺς κόρις ἐκκορίσας.

IX

παιδὸς ἀφ᾽ ὑψηλῶν κεράμων ὑπὲρ ἄκρα μέτωπα   2600
κύπτοντος, μοῖραν νηπιάχοις ἄφοβον,

V *A.P.* 7.239 Παρμενίωνος   εἰς 'Αλέξανδρον βασιλέα   [J] Παρμενίωνος   εἰς
'Αλέξανδρον τὸν Μακεδόνα   Pl A Παρμενίωνος   εἰς αὐτόν   Suid. s.v. φάτις (1–2)
1 φθίσθαι Pl: φθεῖς- PSuid.
VI *A.P.* 9.43 [C] Παρμενίωνος Μακεδόνος   εἰς τὸν ἐν αὐταρκείαι βιοῦντα
παραίνεσις   Pl A Παρμενίωνος Μακεδόνος
1 τραπέζαις Pl: -3ας P
VII *A.P.* 9.69 [C] Παρμενίωνος Μακεδόνος   Pl A Παρμενίωνος Μακεδόνος
Syll.E
1 δύσμηνις Pl: -νος P

V

On Alexander the Great

False is the report that Alexander perished, if Phoebus be true:
not even Hades takes hold of the unconquerable.

VI

Praise of the simple life

Sufficient for me is my cloak's simple shelter, nor shall I be a
slave to the table, for I feed on the Muses' flowers. I detest
wealth without wit, that nursemaid of flatterers, nor will I
stand to attention beside the supercilious. I know the freedom
of a humble repast.

VII

On step-mothers

A step-mother's temper is ever wrathful, not even gentle in
love; I know what happened to the chaste Hippolytus.

VIII

A tongue-twister

The fleas fed on me till full, but I had my own fill fully flicking
off the fleas.

IX

A mother saves her child

When her child peeped from a high-tiled roof over the edge-
most face (a doom that has no terror for infants), his mother,

VIII *A.P.* 9.113 [C] Παρμενίωνος   [J] εἴc τινα ὑπὸ κόρεων τὴν νύκτα κακῶc
ἀπαλλάξαντα   Pl A Παρμενίωνος Μακεδόνος
1 οἱ CPl: οὐ P | μου Pl: με P
IX *A.P.* 9.114 [C] Παρμενίωνος Μακεδόνος [haec a C bis scripta]   [J] εἰc
παιδίον μέλλον κρημνίζεcθαι ἀφ' ὑψηλῶν κεράμων ὧι ἡ μήτηρ παραcτᾶcα καὶ
τὸν μαζὸν ἐκ τῶν ὄπιcθεν δείξαcα τοῦ θανάτου ἐρρύcατο   Pl A τἀντιπάτρου
Θεccαλονικέωc
2 κύπτοντοc P: κρύ- Pl | μοῖραν Pl: -ρα P

μήτηρ ἐξόπιθεν μαζῶι μετέτρεψε νόημα,
δὶς δὲ τέκνωι ζωὴν ἓν κεχάριστο γάλα.

X

τὸν γαίης καὶ πόντου ἀμειφθείσαισι κελεύθοις
    ναύτην ἠπείρου, πεζοπόρον πελάγους,   2605
ἐν τρισσαῖς δοράτων ἑκατοντάσιν ἔστεγεν ἄρης
    Σπάρτης· αἰσχύνεσθ᾽, οὔρεα καὶ πελάγη.

XI

φημὶ πολυστιχίην ἐπιγράμματος οὐ κατὰ Μούσας
    εἶναι· μὴ ζητεῖτ᾽ ἐν σταδίωι δόλιχον·
πόλλ᾽ ἀνακυκλοῦται δολίχου δρόμος, ἐν σταδίωι δέ   2610
    ὀξὺς ἐλαυνο‚μένοις πνεύματός ἐστι τόνος.

XII

αὑτῶι τις γήμας πιθανὴν τῶι γείτονι ῥέγχει
    καὶ τρέφεται· τοῦτ᾽ ἦν εὔκολος ἐργασία,
μὴ πλεῖν, μὴ σκάπτειν, ἀλλ᾽ εὐστομάχως ἀπορέγχειν
    ἀλλοτρίαι δαπάνηι πλούσια βοσκόμενον.   2615

XIII

λιμοῦ καὶ γραίης χαλεπὴ κρίσις· ἀργαλέον μέν   (2616)
    πεινῆν, καὶ κοίτη δ᾽ ἔστ᾽ ὀδυνηροτέρα.

3 ἐξόπιθεν Pl: -πισθε P | μετέτρεψε Pl: μετέστρ- P   4 ἓν κεχάριστο
L. Dindorf: ἐγκεχ- PPl

X A.P. 9.304 Παρμενίωνος   [C] εἰς Ξέρξην καὶ τοὺς τριακοσίους Σπαρτιάτας
P¦ A Παρμενίωνος
2 πελάγους P: -γευς Pl   3 τρισσαῖς Pl: -οῖς P
XI A.P. 9.342 [C] Παρμενίωνος Μακεδόνος   περὶ τῆς τάξεως τῶν ἐπιγραμμάτων
Pl A Παρμενίωνος

from behind him, turned his thoughts aside by means of her breast; one and the same milk bestowed life twice on the child.

X

On the Spartan dead at Thermopylae

The man who was sailor on land, foot-marcher at sea, on the changed paths of earth and ocean, him the valour of Sparta held off with three hundred spears. Shame upon you, mountains and seas.

XI

Brevity is best in epigrams

I tell you, the epigram of many lines is not in accord with the Muses' will. Seek not the long course in the sprint. The long race has many bends, but sharp is the straining of the breath for those who run in the sprint.

XII

A prudent husband

There is a man who snores and grows fat, after marrying a woman complaisant to his neighbour only. That was a comfortable way to get a living,—not to go sailing or digging but to snore away to your stomach's content, richly fed at another's expense.

XIII

The choice between hunger and the hag

Hard is the choice between hunger and a hag. Hunger is troublesome, but bed is the more painful. Phillis while starving

---

1 φημὶ Pl: φα- P   3 ἀνακυκλοῦται P: -λεῖται Pl | δολίχου Pl: -χὸc P
4 ἐλαυνομένοιc Waltz: -νοc PPl

XII A.P. 11.4 Παρμενίωνος   caret Pl
4 ἀλλοτρίαι Brunck: -ίω P

XIII A.P. 11.65 Παρμενίωνος   caret Pl
2 ἔcτ' ὀδυνηροτέρα Reiske: εἰ τὸ δυν. P

πεινῶν εὔχετο γραῦν, κοιμώμενος εὔχετο λιμόν
Φίλλις. ἴδ' ἀκλήρου παιδὸς ἀνωμαλίην.

XIV

Ὡργεῖος Πολύκλειτος, ὁ καὶ μόνος ὄμμασιν Ἥρην   2620
ἀθρήσας καὶ ὅσην εἶδε τυπωσάμενος,
θνητοῖς κάλλος ἔδειξεν ὅσον θέμις· αἱ δ' ὑπὸ κόλποις
ἄγνωστοι μορφαὶ Ζηνὶ φυλασσόμεθα.

XV

Μήδοις ἐλπισθεῖσα τροπαιοφόρος λίθος εἶναι
ἠλλάχθην μορφὴν καίριον εἰς Νέμεσιν,   2625
ἔνδικος ἱδρυνθεῖσα θεὰ Ῥαμνοῦντος ἐπ' ὄχθαις
νίκης καὶ σοφίης Ἀτθίδι μαρτύριον.

ΦΙΛΙΠΠΟΥ

I

ἄνθεά σοι δρέψας Ἑλικώνια καὶ κλυτοδένδρου
Πιερίης κείρας πρωτοφύτους κάλυκας
καὶ σελίδος νεαρῆς θερίσας στάχυν, ἀντανέπλεξα   2630
τοῖς Μελεαγρείοις ὡς ἴκελον στεφάνοις.
5 ἀλλὰ παλαιοτέρων εἰδὼς κλέος, ἐσθλὲ Κάμιλλε,
γνῶθι καὶ ὁπλοτέρων τὴν ὀλιγοστιχίην.
Ἀντίπατρος πρέψει στεφάνωι στάχυς, ὡς δὲ κόρυμβος
Κριναγόρας, λάμψει δ' ὡς βότρυς Ἀντίφιλος,   2635
Τύλλιος ὡς μελίλωτον, ἀμάρακον ὣς Φιλόδημος,
10 μύρτα δ' ὁ Παρμενίων, ὡς ῥόδον Ἀντιφάνης,

XIV *A.Pl.* (A) 216 Παρμενίωνος   εἰς ἄγαλμα Ἥρας   caret P
XV *A.Pl.* (A) 222 Παρμενίωνος   εἰς τὸ αὐτό   caret Pl
I *A.P.* 4.2 Φιλίππου στέφανος   [J] ἕτερος στέφανος Φιλίππου Θεσσαλονικέως
ὃν ἐποίησεν κατὰ μίμησιν Μελεάγρου, συνῆξεν δὲ καὶ αὐτὸν ἀπὸ τῶν ἐμφερομένων
ποιητῶν· ἐξ Ἀντιπάτρου Ἀντιπάτρου [nomen in altera linea repetitum]

prayed for the hag, abed he prayed for his starvation. Behold the inconsistency of the portionless son.

XIV

On the statue of Hera by Polyclitus

Polyclitus the Argive, he who alone saw Hera with his own eyes and moulded as much as he saw of her, has shown her beauty to mortals so far as is lawful. We, the unknown shapes beneath the folds, are reserved for Zeus.

XV

On the statue of Nemesis at Rhamnus

I, the stone which the Medes hoped would be their trophy-bearer, had my shape timely changed to Nemesis, the righteous goddess seated on the shores of Rhamnus, bearing witness to Attica of victory and of art.

PHILIP

I

On the poets in his 'Garland'

Plucking flowers of Helicon for you, and cutting first-born blooms from Pieria's famous forest, reaping a harvest from recent pages, I in my turn have woven a garland like Meleager's. You know the fame of older poets, noble Camillus; learn also the brief poems of later men. Antipater will adorn the wreath as a head of corn, Crinagoras like ivy-berries; Antiphilus will be bright as a grape-cluster, Tullius like melilot, Philodemus like marjoram, Parmenion myrtle, Antiphanes like

Κριναγόρου ᾿Αντιφίλου Τυλλίου Φιλοδήμου Παρμενίωνος ᾿Αντιφάνους Αὐτομέδοντος Ζωνᾶ Βιάνορος ᾿Αντιγόνου Διοδώρου Εὐήνου καὶ αὐτοῦ Φιλίππου·
ἔγραψεν δ᾿ οὗτος ὁ Φίλιππος τὸν στέφανον πρός τινα Κάμιλλον   caret Pl
3 νεαρῆς Gruter: νεανῆς P   **4** Μελεαγρείοις Gruter: -ρίοις P   **9** Τύλλιος
Gruter: -ίας P

κισσὸς δ' Αὐτομέδων, Ζωνᾶς κρίνα, δρῦς δὲ Βιάνωρ,
  Ἀντίγονος δ' ἐλάη καὶ Διόδωρος ἴον·
Εὐήνωι δάφνην συνεπίπλεκε, τοὺς δὲ περισσούς   2640
  εἴκασον οἷς ἐθέλεις ἄνθεσιν ἀρτιφύτοις.

II

ἔμβολα χαλκογένεια, φιλόπλοα τεύχεα νηῶν,
  Ἀκτιακοῦ πολέμου κείμεθα μαρτύρια·
ἠνίδε, σιμβλεύει κηρότροφα δῶρα μελισσῶν
  ἐσμῶι βομβητῆι κυκλόσε βριθόμενα.   2645
5 Καίσαρος εὐνομίης χρηστὴ χάρις· ὅπλα γὰρ ἐχθρῶν
  καρποὺς εἰρήνης ἀντεδίδαξε τρέφειν.

III

Ζηνὸς καὶ Λητοῦς θηροσκόπε τοξότι κούρη
  Ἄρτεμις, ἢ θαλάμους τοὺς ὀρέων ἔλαχες,
νοῦσον τὴν στυγερὴν αὐθημερὸν ἐκ βασιλῆος   2650
  ἐσθλοτάτου πέμψαις ἄχρις Ὑπερβορέων·
5 σοὶ γὰρ ὑπὲρ βωμῶν ἀτμὸν λιβάνοιο Φίλιππος
  ῥέξει καλλιθυτῶν κάπρον ὀρειονόμον.

IV

οὐκέτι πυργωθεὶς ὁ φαλαγγομάχας ἐπὶ δῆριν
  ἄσχετος ὁρμαίνει μυριόδους ἐλέφας,   2655

12 ἐλάη Gruter: ἐλαίη P
II A.P. 6.236 Φιλίππου   Pl A Φιλίππου   Suid. s.vv. ἔμβολα (1–2), ἠνί (3–4),
σίμβλοι (3–4)
1 τεύχεα Stanley: τείχ- PPlSuid.   3 κηροτρόφα CPlSuid.: -φωι P
5 χρηστὴ Pl: -τῆς P

a rose. Automedon is ivy, Zonas lilies, Bianor the oak-leaf, Antigonus the olive and Diodorus the violet. Weave bay in for Euenus, and liken the rest to what fresh-born flowers you will.

II

Bees' nests among the beaks of ships
dedicated after Actium

Bronze-jaw beaks, ships' voyage-loving armour, we lie here as witnesses to the war at Actium. Behold, the bees' wax-fed gifts are hived in us, weighted all round by a humming swarm. So good is the grace of Caesar's law and order; he has taught the enemy's arms to bear the fruits of peace instead.

III

The Emperor's illness

Archer and spyer of wild life, daughter of Zeus and Leto, Artemis, whose lot is cast in the mountains' dwelling-places, dispatch this very day that hateful sickness away from the best of Emperors, as far as the Hyperboreans. For Philip will offer the smoke of frankincense above your altars, and will make splendid sacrifice of a mountain-roaming boar.

IV

Caesar's chariot drawn by an elephant

He no longer rushes into battle turreted and irresistible, the phalanx-fighting huge-tusked elephant. Through fear he has

III *A.P.* 6.240 Φιλίππου   Pl A Φιλίππου   Suid. s.v. ὑπερβορέων (3–4)
1 κούρη PPl: -ρα C   6 κάπρον P: ταῦρον Pl | ὀρειονόμον P: -μαν Pl
IV *A.P.* 9.285 [C] Φιλίππου Θεσσαλονικέως   εἰς τὸν Καίσαρος ἐλέφαντα τὸν θαυμάσιον [ἐλέφαντα. θαυμάσιον coni. Stadtmüller]   Pl A Φιλίππου
1 φαλαγγομάχας Pl: -χος P

ἀλλὰ φόβωι στείλας βαθὺν αὐχένα πρὸς ζυγοδέσμοις
ἄντυγα διφρουλκεῖ Καίσαρος οὐρανίου.
5 ἔγνω δ' εἰρήνης καὶ θὴρ χάριν· ὄργανα ῥίψας
Ἄρεος εὐνομίης ἀντανάγει πατέρα.

V

Φοῖβον ἀνηναμένη Δάφνη ποτὲ νῦν ἀνέτειλεν   2660
Καίσαρος ἐκ βωμοῦ κλῶνα μελαμπέταλον.
ἐκ δὲ θεοῦ θεὸν εὗρεν ἀμείνονα, Λητοΐδην γὰρ
ἐχθήρασα θέλει Ζῆνα τὸν Αἰνεάδην.
5 ῥίζαν δ' οὐκ ἀπὸ γῆς μητρὸς βάλεν ἀλλ' ἀπὸ πέτρης·
Καίσαρι μὴ τίκτειν οὐδὲ λίθος δύναται.   2665

VI

γαῖαν τὴν φερέκαρπον ὅσην ἔζωκε περίχθων
ὠκεανὸς μεγάλωι Καίσαρι πειθομένην
καὶ γλαυκήν με θάλασσαν ἀπηκριβώσατο Κύπρος
κερκίσιν ἱστοπόνοις πάντ' ἀπομαξαμένη·
5 Καίσαρι δ' εὐξείνωι χάρις ἤλθομεν, ἢν γὰρ ἀνάσσης   2670
δῶρα φέρειν τὰ θεοῖς καὶ πρὶν ὀφειλόμενα.

VII

Λευκάδος αἰπὺν ἔχων ναύταις τηλέσκοπον ὄχθον,
Φοῖβε, τὸν Ἰονίωι λουόμενον πελάγει,
δέξαι πλωτήρων μάζης χεριφυρέα δαῖτα
καὶ σπονδὴν ὀλίγηι κιρναμένην κύλικι   2675

3 φόβωι Pl: φωῖ P | ζυγοδέσμοις P: -μους Pl   5 χάριν CPl: ignotum quid
fuerit in P

V A.P. 9.307 Φιλίππου   [C] εἰς τὸν Καίσαρος βωμὸν διὰ τὸ ἀναβλαστῆσαι ἐν
αὐτῶι δάφνην Pl A Φιλίππου
1 Δάφνη ποτὲ P: ποτὲ Δάφνη Pl | ἀνέτειλεν P: -λε Pl   2 μελαμπέταλον Pl:
-τιλον P   4 θέλει P: φιλεῖ Pl

put his thick neck to the yoke-straps and draws the chariot of divine Caesar. Wild beast though he is, he knows the delights of peace. He has cast off the instruments of war, and raises aloft instead the Father of law and order.

V

A bay-tree grows from an altar

Daphne, who once rejected Phoebus, has now raised up her dark-leafed bough from Caesar's altar. In that god's stead she has found a better god; the son of Leto she loathed, the Zeus descended from Aeneas she desires. She cast her root not from mother-earth but from rock; not even stone can refuse to be fertile for Caesar.

VI

A queen's gifts to Caesar

Modelling all with shuttle labouring on the loom, Kypros made me, a perfect copy of the harvest-bearing earth, all that the land-encircling ocean girdles, obedient to great Caesar, and the gray sea too. We have come as a grateful return for Caesar's hospitality; it was a queen's duty, to bring gifts so long due to the gods.

VII

Prayer for a fair wind to Actium

Phoebus, lord of the steep cliff of Leucas far-seen by sailors, washed by the sea of Io, accept from your voyagers a hand-kneaded feast of barley-cake and libation mixed in a little cup

VI *A.P.* 9.778 Φιλίππου   caret Pl
1 ὅσην Brunck: ὅcη P   3 Κύπρος Cichorius: καρποc P   5 εὐξείνωι
Page: ακεινου P

VII *A.P.* 6.251 Φιλίππου Suid. s.vv. αἰπύ (1), δαῖτας (2 Φοῖβε + 3), χεριφυρέα (eadem), ὀλίγον (4), βραχυφεγγίτης (5 καὶ–cέλαc)   caret Pl
2 ᾿Ιονίωι Salm.: ἠιονίωι P   4 κιρναμένην CSuid.: κρεμαμένην P

5 καὶ βραχυφεγγίτου λύχνου σέλας ἐκ βιοφειδοῦς
  ὄλπης ἡμιμεθεῖ πινόμενον στόματι.
  ἀνθ' ὧν ἱλήκοις, ἐπὶ δ' ἱστία πέμψον ἀήτην
  οὔριον Ἀκτιακοὺς σύνδρομον εἰς λιμένας.

VIII

δούνακας ἀκροδέτους καὶ τὴν ἁλινηχέα κώπην   2680
  γυρῶν τ' ἀγκίστρων λαιμοδακεῖς ἀκίδας
καὶ λίνον ἀκρομόλυβδον ἀπαγγελτῆρά τε κύρτου
  φελλὸν καὶ διςςὰς ςχοινοτενεῖς ςπυρίδας
5 καὶ τὸν ἐγερσιφαῆ πυρὸς ἔγκυον ἔμφλογα πέτρον
  ἄγκυράν τε νεῶν πλαζομένων παγίδα   2685
Πείςων ὁ γριπεὺς Ἑρμῆι πόρεν ἔντρομος ἤδη
  δεξιτερήν, πολλοῖς ἀχθόμενος καμάτοις.

IX

δράγματά σοι χώρου μικραύλακος, ὦ φιλόπυρε
  Δηοῖ, Σωσικλέης θῆκεν ἀρουροπόνος
εὔσταχυν ἀμήσας τὸν νῦν σπόρον. ἀλλὰ καὶ αὖτις   2690
  ἐκ καλαμητομίης ἀμβλὺ φέροι δρέπανον.

X

δίκτυά σοι μολίβωι στεφανούμενα δυσιθάλασσα
  καὶ κώπην, ἅλμης τὴν μεθύουσαν ἔτι,
κητοφόνον τε τρίαιναν, ἐν ὕδασι καρτερὸν ἔγχος,
  καὶ τὸν ἀεὶ φελλοῖς κύρτον ἐλεγχόμενον,   2695

---

6 ὄλπης Salm.: οἰν (ὄίν C) γης P

VIII A.P. 6.5 Φιλίππου εἰς τὸ αὐτό [J] Φιλίππου Θεσσαλονικέως εἰς Πίσωνα
γριπέα Pl A Φιλίππου Syll.E   Suid. s.v. γυρῶν (2)
1 δούνακας PPl: δών- Syll.E   3 ἀκρομόλυβδον Stadtmüller: -λιβδ-
PPlE   5 ἔγκυον PE: ἔγγυον Pl | ἔμφλογα PE: -φογα Pl   7 Πείςων PlE:
Πίς- P   8 ἀχθόμενος Scaliger: αἰθόμ- PPlE

IX A.P. 6.36 Φιλίππου [C] Θεσσαλονικέως   [P] ἀνάθημα Σωσικλέους γεωργοῦ

and meagre-shining lamp's flame that drinks with half-tipsy mouth from a miserly oil-flask. Be gracious in return, and send upon the sails a favourable breeze running with us to the harbours of Actium.

VIII

Dedication by a fisherman

His string-tipped rods and sea-swimming oar, the throat-biting barbs of his curved hooks, the lead-fringed nets, and the cork, spokesman for the weel, and his two rush-plaited creels, and the light-arousing fiery flint, pregnant with flame, and the anchor, that trap for drifting ships,—these Piso the fisherman brought to Hermes, his right hand already tremulous, overburdened with many labours.

IX

Dedication by a farmer

Sheaves from a small-furrowed estate to you, corn-loving Demeter, Sosicles the field-worker has dedicated, having reaped a rich harvest of grain this year. Hereafter also may he bring his sickle blunted from stalk-cutting.

X

Dedication by a fisherman

To you his nets, lead-encircled, sea-plunging, and his oar still soaked in salt water, and his monster-slaying trident, a strong spear in the waters, and his weel ever exposed by floats, and

τῆι Δημήτραι Pl A Φιλίππου Suid. s.vv. ἀμβλύ (3 ἀλλά–4), καλαμητομίης (eadem)
4 φέροι PlSuid. (s.v. ἀμ.): -ρει PSuid. (s.v. καλ.)
X *A.P.* 6.38 Φιλίππου ἀνάθημα τῶι Ποσειδῶνι παρὰ ᾽Αμυντίχου ἁλιέως Pl A Φιλίππου Suid. s.vv. δυσιθάλασσα (δίκτ. δυσιθ.), μεθύουσαν (2)
1 μολίβωι Pl: -λύβδωι P

THE GARLAND OF PHILIP

5 ἄγκυράν τε, νεῶν στιβαρὴν χέρα, καὶ φιλοναύτην
  cπέρμα πυρὸc cώιζειν πέτρον ἐπιcτάμενον,
  ἀρχιθάλαccε Πόcειδον, ᾿Αμύντιχοc ὕcτατα δῶρα
  θῆκατ᾿, ἐπεὶ μογερῆc παύcαθ᾿ ἁλιπλανίηc.

XI

κυκλοτερῆ μόλιβον, cελίδων cημάντορα πλευρῆc,   2700
  καὶ cμίλην, δονάκων ἀκροβελῶν γλυφίδα,
  καὶ †κανονῖδ᾿ ὑπάτην† καὶ τὴν παράθινα κίcηριν,
  αὐχμηρὸν πόντου τρηματόεντα λίθον,
5 Καλλιμένηc Μούcαιc ἀποπαυcάμενοc καμάτοιο
  θῆκεν, ἐπεὶ γήραι κανθὸc ἐπεcκέπετο.   2705

XII

ἄγκυραν ἐμβρύοικον ἐρυcινηίδα
  κώπαc τε διccὰc τοὺc ἀπωcικύματουc
  καὶ δικτύοιc μόλυβδον ἠψιδωμένον
  κύρτουc τε φελλοῖc τοὺc ἐπεcφραγιcμένουc
5 καὶ πῖλον ἀμφίκρηνον ὑδαcιcτεγῆ   2710
  λίθον τε ναύταιc ἑcπέρηc πυρητόκον,
  ἁλὸc τύραννε, cοί, Πόcειδον, ᾿Αρχικλῆc
  ἔθηκε, λήξαc τῆc ἀπ᾿ ἠιόνων ἄληc.

XIII

αὐλὸν καμινευτῆρα τὸν φιλήνεμον
  ῥίνην τε κνηcίχρυcον ὠκυδήκτορα   2715
  καὶ τὸν δίχηλον καρκίνον πυραγρέτην

5 φιλοναύτην Pl: -τιν P   6 cπέρμα Pl: -ματα P
XI A.P. 6.62 Φιλίππου [C] Θεccαλονικέωc   [P] ἀνάθημα ταῖc Μούcαιc παρὰ
Καλλιμένουc καλλιγράφου   Pl A Φιλίππου   Suid. s.vv. cμίλη (2), κανονίc (3
καὶ–ὕπ.), θῖνα (3 καὶ τὴν–4), κίccηριc (4)
2 cμίλην Pl: -λαν PSuid.   3 παράθινα Page: παρὰ θῖνα PPlSuid.   5 καμάτοιο CPl: -τοc (?) P
XII A.P. 6.90 Φιλίππου   ἀνάθημα τῶι Ποcειδῶνι παρὰ Χαρικλέουc [sic]   [C]
ταῦτα τὰ ἰαμβικὰ Φιλίππου Θεccαλονικέωc   Suid. s.vv. βρύχιοc (1), ἄλη (7–8)
caret Pl

his anchor, the ship's firm hand, and that sailor's friend the flint, with its art of preserving the seed of flames,—sea-ruler Poseidon, Amyntichus dedicated these his last gifts, when he had ceased from the toils of sea-roving.

XI

Dedication by a scribe

His disk of lead, marker of the column's margin, and his knife, sharpener of spear-tipped pens, and his ⟨   ⟩ ruler, and his pumice from the beach, dry porous sea-stone,—these to the Muses Callimenes dedicated when his eyes were veiled with age.

XII

Dedication by a fisherman

His anchor that lives in the seaweed and secures the ship, his pair of wave-repelling oars, the lead enmeshed in his nets, and the weels marked above by floats, the rain-proof felt-hat about his head, and the flint that engenders fire for mariners at sunset, —these Archicles dedicated to you, sea-lord Poseidon, having ceased his wanderings from the shore.

XIII

Dedication by a goldsmith

His wind-welcoming furnace-pipe and swift-biting gold-paring file, and the twin crab-claws, his fire-tongs, and these

3 ἠψιδωμένον apogr.: ἠψηδ- P   4 φελλοῖς C: -οὺς P   5 ὑδασιστεγῆ Salm.: -ϲιτεγῆ P, -ϲιτεγγῆ C   7 Πόϲειδον, ’Αρχικλῆϲ CSuid.: ποϲὶ δον αιχι κλῆϲ ut vid. P

XIII A.P. 6.92 Φιλίππου [ut vid., in rasura]   ἀνάθημα τῶι ‘Ερμῆι παρὰ Δημοφῶντοϲ χρυϲοχόου   [C] Φιλίππου Θεϲϲαλονικέωϲ   καὶ ταῦτα ἰαμβικά [haec in rasura; eadem exaraverat P]   Pl A Φιλίππου   Suid. s.vv. αὐλόϲ (1), φιλήνεμοϲ (1), ῥίνη (2)
1 αὐλὸν PSuid.: -λοῦ Pl   3 δίχηλον Pl: -χειλ- P

πτωκὸς πόδας τε τούσδε λειψανηλόγους
ὁ χρυσοτέκτων Δημοφῶν Κυλληνίωι
ἔθηκε, γήραι κανθὸν ἐζοφωμένος.

5

XIV

ἀραξίχειρα ταῦτά σοι τὰ τύμπανα   2720
καὶ κύμβαλ᾽ ὀξύδουπα κοιλοχειλέα
διδύμους τε λωτοὺς κεροβόας, ἐφ᾽ οἷς ποτε
ἐπωλόλυξεν αὐχένα στροβιλίσας,
λυσιφλεβῆ τε σάγαριν ἀμφιθηγέα,
λεοντόδιφρε, σοί, ῾Ρέη, Κλυτοσθένης   2725
ἔθηκε, λυσσητῆρα γηράσας πόδα.

5

XV

κόψας ἐκ φηγοῦ σε τὸν αὐτόφλοιον ἔθηκε
Πᾶνα Φιλοξενίδης, ὁ κλυτὸς αἰγελάτης,
θύσας αἰγιβάτην πολιὸν τράγον ἕν τε γάλακτι
πρωτογόνωι βωμοὺς τοὺς ἱεροὺς μεθύσας·   2730
ἀνθ᾽ ὧν ἐν σηκοῖς διδυμητόκοι αἶγες ἔσονται
γαστέρα, φεύγουσαι τρηχὺν ὀδόντα λύκου.

5

XVI

ξίφη τὰ πολλῶν κνωδάλων λαιμητόμα
πυριτρόφους τε ῥιπίδας συρηνέμους
ἠθμόν τε πουλύτρητον ἠδὲ τετράπουν   2735
πυρὸς γέφυραν, ἐσχάρην κρεηδόκον,

4 λειψανηλόγους Pl: -νολόγους P

XIV *A.P.* 6.94 Φιλίππου [C] Θεσσαλονικέως   [P] ἀνάθημα τῆι ῾Ρέαι παρὰ
Κλυτοσθένους   ὅρα ὅτι καὶ ταῦτα ἐκ τῶν ἰαμβικῶν   Suid. s.vv. τύμπανον (1+6–
῾Ρέη+θῆκε), κύμβαλα (2), σάγαρις (5 λυσ.–σαγ.)   caret Pl
1 ἀραξίχειρα apogr.: ἀραξάχ- PSuid. | σοι P: τοι Suid. et ut vid. Pᵃᶜ
3 λωτοὺς C: λυτ- P   4 στροβιλίσας Reiske: -βηλ- P

XV *A.P.* 6.99 Φιλίππου [C] Θεσσαλονικέως   [P] ἀνάθημα τῶι Πανὶ παρὰ
Φιλοξενίδου ποιμένος   caret Pl

remnant-sweeping hares' feet,—these Demophon the goldsmith dedicated to the Cyllenian, his eyes being dimmed by
age.

XIV

Dedication by a priest of Rhea

These his hand-beaten timbrels and shrill-sounding hollow-
lipped cymbals and pair of flutes with resounding horn, on
which he once made shrieking utterance, twisting his neck
about, and his two-edged vein-dissolving hatchet,—these to you,
lion-charioted Rhea, Clytosthenes dedicated, since his frenzied
feet have grown too old.

XV

Dedication and sacrifice by a goat-herd

Philoxenides the worthy goat-herd struck you unbarked out of
an oak and dedicated you as Pan, having sacrificed an old nanny-
mounting goat and drenched your holy altars in nursing-milk.
In return, his ewes in their pens shall have twin-bearing bellies,
escaping the wolf's jagged fang.

XVI

Dedication by a cook

His swords, throat-cutters of many a beast, his wind-drawing
fire-feeding fans, his riddled strainer, and the fire's four-footed
bridge, his grill to hold the meat, and the ladle that skims

5 ἔϲονται C: om. P

XVI *A.P.* 6.101 Φιλίππου   ἀνάθημα τῶι Ἡφαίϲτωι παρὰ Τιμαϲίωνος μαγείρου
καὶ τοῦτο πάντως τῶν ἰαμβικῶν τυγχάνει   [C] ἰαμβικά   Pl A Φιλίππου   Suid.
s.vv. κνώδαλον (1), ῥιπίζεται (2), ἐϲχάρα (3–4), ζωμήρυϲιϲ (5), κρεάγρα (6)
Zonar. s.v. ζωμήρυϲιϲ
2 ϲυρηνέμουϲ West: πυρην- PPlSuid.   3 ἠθμόν P: ἰθ- Pl   4 ἐϲχάρην P:
-ραν Pl | κρεηδόκον CPl: κρηδ- P

5 ζωμήρυσίν τε τὴν λίπους ἀφρηλόγον
ὁμοῦ κρεάγρηι τῆι σιδηροδακτύλωι,
βραδυσκελὴς Ἥφαιστε, σοὶ Τιμασίων
ἔθηκεν, ἀκμῆς γυῖον ὠρφανωμένος. 2740

XVII

ῥοιὴν ξανθοχίτωνα γεραιόφλοιά τε σῦκα
καὶ ῥοδέας σταφυλῆς ὠμὸν ἀποσπάδιον
μῆλόν θ᾽ ἡδύπνουν λεπτῆι πεποκωμένον ἄχνηι
καὶ κάρυον χλωρῶν ἐκφανὲς ἐκ λεπίδων
5 καὶ σίκυον χλοάοντα, τὸν ἐν φύλλοις πεδοκοίτην, 2745
καὶ πέρκην ἤδη χρυσοχίτων᾽ ἐλάην
σοί, φιλοδαῖτα Πρίηπε, φυτοσκάφος ἄνθετο Δάμων
δένδρεσι καὶ γυίοις εὐξάμενος θαλέθειν.

XVIII

στάθμην ἰθυτενῆ μολιβαχθέα δουριτυπῆ τε
σφῦραν καὶ γυρὰς ἀμφιδέτους ἀρίδας 2750
καὶ στιβαρὸν πέλεκυν στελεχητόμον ἰθύδρομόν τε
πρίονα μιλτείωι στάγματι πειθόμενον
5 τρύπανά θ᾽ ἑλκεσίχειρα τέρετρά τε μιλτοφυρῆ τε
σχοῖνον ὑπ᾽ ἀκρονύχωι ψαλλομένην κανόνι,
σοί, κούρη γλαυκῶπι, Λεόντιχος ὤπασε δῶρον 2755
ἄνθος ἐπεὶ γυίων πᾶν ἀπέδυσε χρόνος.

5 ζωμήρυσίν PlSuid.: -ροῖσιν P   7 σοὶ Pl: σοῦ P   8 ὠρφανωμένος P:
-νισμένος Pl

XVII *A.P.* 6.102 Φιλίππου   ἀνάθημα τῶι Πριήπωι παρὰ Λάμωνος κηπουροῦ
Pl A Φιλίππου   Suid. s.vv. γεραιός (1), ἄχναι (3), σίκυον (5)   Schol. Ar. *Ach.*
519 (5)
4 habent C^marg Pl: versum om. P | κάρυον...ἐκφανὲς C: κάρυα...ἐκφανέ᾽ Pl
5 χλοάοντα Pl: χλοάωντα P, χνοάωντα C, χνοάοντα Suid.Schol.   6 ἐλάην
Pl: -άηι P   7 φιλοδαῖτα Ludwich: -δῖτα Pl, -δῆτα P | Δάμων Brunck: Λάμ-
PPl

the foaming fat, together with his iron-fingered flesh-hook,—
these to you, slow-foot Hephaestus, Timasion dedicated, his
limbs being bereft of their prime.

XVII

Dedication by a fruit-grower

A yellow-coated pomegranate and wrinkly-skin figs and unripe
cutting from a rosy grape-cluster and sweet-scented quince,
fleecy with fine down, and walnut showing forth from green
husk, and fresh cucumber, low-embedded in its leaves, and
gold-coated olive already darkening,—these to you, Priapus,
friend of the feast, Damon the gardener dedicated, praying
that he may flourish in his orchard and in his limbs.

XVIII

Dedication by a carpenter

His taut lead-weighted plumb-line and his plank-smiting ham-
mer and curved bow-drills with cords at each end and stout
stem-hewing axe and straight-running saw, obedient to red
ochre-drops, and hand-twisting augers and gimlets and ochre-
stained line that twangs at the ruler's lightest touch,—this gift
to you, gray-eyed Maiden, Leontichus offered when Time had
stripped all the bloom from his limbs.

XVIII A.P. 6.103 τοῦ αὐτοῦ [C] Φιλίππου   [P] ἀνάθημα τῆι ᾿Αθηνᾶι παρὰ
Λεοντίχου τέκτονος   Pl A Φιλίππου   Suid. s.vv. στάθμη (1–μολ.), σφῦρα
(1 δουρ.–2 σφ.), ἀρίδες (2 καὶ–ἀρ.), πρίων (3 ἰθ.–4), μίλτος (5 μιλτ.–6), ψαλλο-
μένης (eadem)
1 μολιβαχθέα PlSuid.: -λυβ- P   4 πρίονα CPlSuid.: πίονα ut vid. P |
μιλτείωι CPl -τίωι PSuid. | στάγματι PPl: βάμματι Suid.   5 τέρετρά τε Pl:
τέλετρα P (man. rec. in τέρετρά τε corr.) | μιλτοφυρῆ PSuid. (s.v. ψαλλ.): -θυρῆ
Pl, -φυῆ Suid. (s.v. μίλτ.)

XIX

σπερμοφόρον πήρην ὠμαχθέα κώλεσίβωλον
  σφῦραν καὶ γαμψὰς πυρολόγους δρεπάνας
καὶ τριβόλους ὀξεῖς ἀχυρότριβας ἱστοβόην τε
  σὺν γυροῖς ἀρότροις καὶ φιλόγαιον ὕνιν   2760
5 κέντρα τ' ὀπισθονυγῆ καὶ βουστρόφα δεσμὰ τενόντων
  καὶ τρίνακας, ξυλίνας χεῖρας ἀρουροπόνων,
γυῖ' ἀποπηρωθεὶς Λυσίξενος αὔλακι πολλῆι
  ἐκρέμασεν Δηοῖ τῆι σταχυοστεφάνωι.

XX

ὑλισκόπωι με Πανὶ θηρευτὴς Γέλων   2765
ἔθηκε λόγχην, ἧς ἀπέθρισε χρόνος
ἀκμὴν ἐν ἔργωι, καὶ λίνων πολυστρόφων
γεραιὰ τρύχη καὶ πάγας δεραγχέας
5 νευροπλεκεῖς τε κνωδάλων ἐπισφύρους
ὠκεῖς ποδίστρας καὶ τραχηλοδεσπότας   2770
κλοιοὺς κυνούχους· γυῖα γὰρ δαμεὶς χρόνωι
ἀπεῖπεν ἤδη τὴν ὀρεινόμον πλάνην.

XXI

Αἰγύπτου μεδέουσα μελαμβώλου λινόπεπλε
  δαῖμον, ἐπ' εὐιέρους βῆθι θυηπολίας·
σοὶ γὰρ ὑπὲρ σχιδάκων λαγαρὸν ποπάνευμα πρόκειται   2775
  καὶ πολιὸν χηνῶν ζεῦγος ἐνυδροβίων
5 καὶ νάρδος ψαφαρὴ κεγχρίτισιν ἰσχάσιν ἀμφί
  καὶ σταφυλὴ γραίη χὠ μελίπνους λίβανος.

XIX *A.P.* 6.104 τοῦ αὐτοῦ [sc. Φιλίππου]   ἀνάθημα τῆι Δηοῖ παρὰ Λυσιξένου γεωπόνου Pl A Φιλίππου   Suid. s.vv. ὠμαχθής (1–ὠμ.), γαμψόν (2 γαμ.–δρεπ.), ἀχυρμιαί (3 καὶ–ἀχ.), ὕνιν (3 ἱστ.–4), βούπληξ (5), τρίναξ (6)
2 σφῦραν P: -ρην Pl | πυρολόγους PlSuid.: πυριλ- P   4 ὕνιν PlSuid.: -νην P
6 ἀρουροπόνων PSuid.: -νου Pl   7 γυῖ' ἀποπηρωθεὶς Page: γυῖα πεπηρ-PPl

XX *A.P.* 6.107 Φιλίππου   ἀνάθημα τῶι Πανὶ παρὰ Γέλωνος κυνηγοῦ   ἰαμβικὸν καὶ τοῦτο καὶ σκόπει φίλος   Suid. s.v. δεραγχέας πάγας (δ. π.)   caret Pl

XIX

Dedication by a ploughman

His shoulder-burdening seed-bearing wallet and his clod-destroying mallet and crooked corn-gathering sickles and sharp husk-bruising threshers and the pole together with his curved ploughs and the earth-loving share and back-stabbing goads and ox-turning limb-fetters and his winnowing-forks, the field-worker's wooden hands,—maimed of limbs by many a furrow Lysixenus hung these up to corn-wreathed Demeter.

XX

Dedication by a hunter

To forest-watcher Pan the huntsman Gelon dedicated me, his spear, whose point the years have cut off in action, and the agèd rags of his twisted nets, and his neck-throttling nooses, and sinew-plaited swift foot-traps for beasts' ankles, and his neck-mastering hound-constraining collars; for the years have subdued his limbs, and he has now renounced his mountain-pasture wandering.

XXI

Sacrifice and offerings after a safe landing

Queen of Egypt's black earth, linen-robed divinity, come to this holy sacrifice. For you a thin cake is laid upon the sticks and a gray pair of water-dwelling geese and powdery nard beside myriad-seeded figs and an old grape-cluster and the sweet-scented frankincense. If, Queen, you rescue Damis from

---

2 χρόνος C: -νον P   3 λίνων πολυστρόφων Alberti: -νωι -φωι P   6 τραχη-λοδεσπότας Meineke: -δεσμότας P

XXI *A.P.* 6.231 Φιλίππου   Suid. s.vv. μελάμβωλος (1–2 δαῖμ.), λαγαρόν (3), ἐνυδροβίων (4), ψαφαρῆι (5), κεγχρήτιςι (5), ἀσταφίς (6), κεμάς (7–8)   caret Pl
3 πρόκειται CSuid.: -κειμαι P   4 πολιὸν C: -ιῶν PSuid.   5 νάρδος Salm.: -δωι PSuid. | κεγχρίτιςιν Brunck: κεγχρήτ- C (denuoque C^marg) Suid., κεχρήτ- P

εἰ δ᾽ ὡς ἐκ πελάγους ἐρρύσαο Δᾶμιν, ἄνασσα,
κἠκ πενίης, θύσει χρυσόκερων κεμάδα.　　　　2780

XXII

κερκίδας ὀρθρολάλοισι χελιδόσιν εἰκελοφώνους,
Παλλάδος ἱστοπόνου λειομίτους κάμακας,
καὶ κτένα κοσμοκόμην καὶ δακτυλότριπτον ἄτρακτον
σφονδυλοδινήτωι νήματι νηχόμενον
5 καὶ τάλαρον σχοίνοις ὑφασμένον, ὅν ποτ᾽ ὀδόντι　　2785
ἐπλήρου τολύπη πᾶσα καθαιρομένη,
σοί, φιλέριθε κόρη Παλλαντιάς, ἡ βαθύγηρως
Αἰσιόνη πενίης δῶρον ἀνεκρέμασεν.

XXIII

—τίς τὸν ἄχνουν Ἑρμῆν σε παρ᾽ ὑσπλήγεσσιν ἔθηκεν;
—Ἑρμογένης.—τίνος ὤν;—Δαϊμένευς.—ποδαπός;　　2790
—Ἀντιοχεύς.—τιμῶν σε χάριν τίνος;—ὡς συναρωγόν
ἐν σταδίοις.—ποίοις;—Ἰσθμόθι κἠν Νεμέαι.
5 —ἔτρεχε γάρ;—καὶ πρῶτος.—ἑλὼν τίνας;—ἐννέα παῖδας·
ἔπτη δ᾽ ὡς ἂν ἔχων τοὺς πόδας ἡμετέρους.

XXIV

ἄρτι μὲν ἐν θαλάμοις Νικιππίδος ἡδὺς ἐπήχει　　2795
λωτὸς καὶ γαμικοῖς ὕμνος ἔχαιρε κρότοις·

XXII *A.P.* 6.247 Φιλίππου Pl A Φιλίππου Suid. s.vv. ὀρθρογόη (1), λειομίτου (2), κτείς (3 καὶ κτ. κοσμ.), ἄτρακτον (3 καὶ δακτ.–4), τάλαρος (5–6)
1 ὀρθρολάλοισι PlSuid.: ὀρθριλ- P　　2 λειομίτους Pl (c sscr.): -του PSuid. | κάμακας Pl: -κος PSuid.　　3 δακτυλότριπτον CPlSuid.: -ότριβον P
5 σχοίνοις PSuid.: -οισιν Pl | ὀδόντι CSuid.: -τας P, -των Pl

XXIII *A.P.* 6.259 Φιλίππου Pl A Φιλίππου Suid. s.vv. ἄχνους (1), ὕσπληξ (1), στάδιον (4, corruptissime)

poverty as you saved him from the sea, he shall sacrifice a golden-horned kid.

XXII

Dedication by a weaver

Her weaving-shuttles, with voice like early-chattering swallows, loom-labouring Pallas' warp-smoothing shafts, and her tress-arranging comb, and her finger-rubbed spindle swimming with whorl-spun thread, and her reed-plaited basket, which all her tooth-cleansed wool once filled,—these to you, Pallantian maid, lover of wool-workers, Aesionê deep in old age hung up, the offering of her poverty.

XXIII

On a statue of Hermes

—Who set you up, a beardless Hermes, at the starting-gates?—Hermogenes.—Son of whom?—Of Daïmenes.—Of what land? —Of Antioch.—Honouring you for what cause?—As his helper in the sprints.—Which ones?—At the Isthmus and in Nemea.—So he was a runner?—Came in first, too.—Beating whom?—Nine boys; he flew as if he had my feet.

XXIV

Death of a bride

But lately the flute was sounding sweet in the bridal room of Nicippis, and song was merry with the clatter of wedding-

1 ὑσπλήγεσσιν P: -ήγγεσσιν Pl   2 Δαϊμένευς Meineke: δαῖμον ἐὺς P, δαιμο-νέως Cʸᴾ, δαϊμονεῦς Pl   4 'Ισθμόθι κἠν Νεμέαι CPl: ἰσθμότι κἠν εμέαι P
5 ἐλὼν Brunck: ἔχων PPl   6 ἡμετέρους P: ἠερίους Pl
XXIV A.P. 7.186 [C] Φιλίππου   [J] εἰς Νικιππίδα ἐπὶ θαλάμωι τελευτήσασαν
Pl ᴀ Φιλίππου   Suid. s.vv. λωτός (1–2), ἐκώμασεν (3–ἐκώμ.), κώμη (3–4)

θρῆνος δ' εἰς ὑμέναιον ἐκώμασεν, ἡ δὲ τάλαινα
οὔπω πάντα γυνὴ καὶ νέκυς ἐβλέπετο.
5 δακρυόεις Ἀίδη, τί πόσιν νύμφης διέλυσας,
αὐτὸς ἐφ' ἁρπαγίμοις τερπόμενος λέχεσιν;

2800

XXV

ἠπείρωι μ' ἀποδοῦσα νέκυν, τρηχεῖα θάλασσα,
σύρεις καὶ τέφρης λοιπὸν ἔτι σκύβαλον·
κἠν Ἀίδηι ναυηγὸς ἐγὼ μόνος, οὐδ' ἐπὶ χέρσου
εἰρήνην ἔξω φρικαλέης σπιλάδος.
5 ἢ τύμβευε †κενοῦσα† καθ' ὕδατος ἢ παραδοῦσα
γαίηι τὸν κείνης μηκέτι κλέπτε νέκυν.

2805

XXVI

μυλεργάτας ἀνήρ με κἠν ζωᾶς χρόνοις
βαρυβρομήταν εἶχε δινητὰν πέτρον,
πυρηφάτον Δάματρος εὐκάρπου λάτριν,
καὶ κατθανὼν στάλωσε τῶιδ' ἐπ' ἠρίωι
5 σύνθημα τέχνας, ὡς ἔχοι μ' αἰεὶ βαρύν
καὶ ζῶν ἐν ἔργοις καὶ θανὼν ἐπ' ὀστέοις.

2810

XXVII

λατύπος Ἀρχιτέλης Ἀγαθάνορι παιδὶ θανόντι
χερσὶν ὀϊζυραῖς ἡρμολόγησε τάφον·
αἰαῖ πέτρον ἐκεῖνον, ὃν οὐκ ἐκόλαψε σίδηρος,
ἀλλ' ἐτάκη πυκινοῖς δάκρυσι τεγγόμενος.
5 φεῦ στήλη, φθιμένωι κούφη μένε, κεῖνος ἵν' εἴπηι
'ὄντως πατρώιη χεὶρ ἐπέθηκε λίθον'.

2815

XXV A.P. 7.382 [C] Φιλίππου Θεσσαλονικέως [J] εἰς ναυηγόν τινα μὴ
τυχόντα ταφῆς Pl A Φιλίππου
5 versum habent C^marg Pl: om. P | κενοῦσα C: κρατοῦσα Pl
XXVI A.P. 7.394 [C] Φιλίππου Θεσσαλονικέως [J] εἰς μυλεργάτην οὗτινος
ἐπὶ τῶι τάφωι καὶ αὐτὸν τὸν μύλον ἐπέθηκαν caret Pl

dances, when the dirge came riotous upon the marriage-hymn, and the ill-starred girl, not yet a wife in all, was seen a corpse. O tearful Hades, why have you divorced the husband from the bride, you who rejoice in ravished beds?

XXV

A drowned man, buried ashore, reclaimed by the sea

Cruel sea, you gave me up dead to the land, yet carry off even the remnant that is still left of my ashes. I alone suffer shipwreck even in Hades; not even on shore shall I have peace from the frightening storm. Either bury me ⟨   ⟩ in the waters, or give me over to earth and never again steal the corpse that is hers.

XXVI

A miller's grave-stone

The miller owned me in his lifetime too, the deep-roaring revolving stone, wheat-crushing servant of fruitful Demeter, and when he died he made of me a grave-stone on his tomb here, a token of his trade, that he might feel my weight always, in his work when he was alive and on his bones after death.

XXVII

A stone-mason erects a grave-stone for his son

Architeles the mason built with mournful hands a tomb for his dead son Agathanor,—this sorrowful grave-stone not cut by the iron but worn by floods of fast-falling tears. Rest, headstone, lightly on the departed, that he may say 'Truly it was a father's hand that set the stone upon me'.

2 βαρυβρομήταν εἶχε Salm.: βαρυβρομῆς ἀνεῖχε P   3 πυρηφάτον Ap.G.: -του P   5 ἔχοι Page: ἔχει P

XXVII *A.P.* 7.554 [C] Φιλίππου Θεσσαλονικέως   [J] εἰς Ἀγαθάνορα υἱὸν Ἀρχιτέλους   θαυμαστόν   Pl A Φιλίππου

XXVIII

ἡ πυρὶ πάντα τεκοῦσα Φιλαίνιον, ἡ βαρυπενθής
μήτηρ, ἡ τέκνων τρισσὸν ἰδοῦσα τάφον,   2820
ἀλλοτρίαις ὠδῖσιν ἐφόρμισα· ἦ γὰρ ἐώλπειν
πάντως μοι 3ήcειν τοῦτον ὃν οὐκ ἔτεκον·
5 ἡ δ᾽ εὔπαις θετὸν υἱὸν ἀνήγαγον, ἀλλά με δαίμων
ἤθελε μηδ᾽ ἄλλης μητρὸς ἔχειν χάριτα.
κληθεὶς ἡμέτερος γὰρ ἀπέφθιτο· νῦν δὲ τεκούcαιc   2825
ἤδη καὶ λοιπαῖc πένθος ἐγὼ γέγονα.

XXIX

ἠρίθμουν ποτὲ πάντες Ἀριστοδίκην κλυτόπαιδα
ἑξάκις ὠδίνων ἄχθος ἀπωσαμένην.
ἤρισε δ᾽ εἰς αὐτὴν ὕδωρ χθονί· τρεῖς γὰρ ὄλοντο
νούcωι, λειπόμενοι δ᾽ ἤμυcαν ἐν πελάγει.   2830
5 αἰεὶ δ᾽ ἡ βαρύδακρυς ἐπὶ στηλαῖς μὲν ἀηδών,
μεμφομένη δὲ βυθοῖς ἀλκυονὶς βλέπεται.

XXX

Ἰκαρίην ⟨   ⟩ πλώων ἅλα, νηὸς ὀλιcθών
Δᾶμις ὁ Νικαρέτου κάππεσεν εἰς πέλαγος·
πολλὰ πατὴρ δ᾽ ἠρᾶτο πρὸς ἀθανάτους καὶ ἐς ὕδωρ   2835
φθέγγεθ᾽ ὑπὲρ τέκνου κύματα λιccόμενος.
5 ὤλετο δ᾽ οἰκτίcτως βρυχθεὶς ἁλί· κεῖνο δὲ πατρός
ἔκλυεν ἀράων οὐδὲ πάλαι πέλαγος.

XXVIII A.P. 9.254 [C] τοῦ αὐτοῦ Φιλίππου   εἰς Φιλαίνιον γυναῖκα ἧς πάντα
τὰ τέκνα ἐτεθνήκεcαν   Pl A Φιλίππου
1 βαρυπενθήc Scaliger: -θοc PPl   3 ἐφόρμιcα P: ἐφώρ- Pl
XXIX A.P. 9.262 [C] Φιλίππου Θεccαλονικέωc   εἰς Ἀριστοδίκην ἧστινος τὰ
τέκνα τὰ μὲν νόcοc τὰ δὲ πέλαγος ἀπώλεcεν   Pl A τοῦ αὐτοῦ [sc. Φιλίππου]

XXVIII

An unhappy mother

I, Philaenion, who bore all my children for the funeral-fire, deep-mourning mother, witness of my children's threefold burial, found refuge in a stranger's birth-pains. For truly I hoped that this one, whom I did not bear, would live in spite of all. Myself no barren mother, I reared an adopted son; but Fate willed that I should not even enjoy another mother's gift. No sooner was he called mine than he died; so now I am a cause for mourning even to others who have given birth.

XXIX

A mother loses six sons

All men counted Aristodicê a proud mother, six times delivered of her travail's burden. But the waters strove with the earth against her: three died by sickness, the rest perished in the ocean. So for ever that heavy mourner is seen as a nightingale on the gravestones, as a halcyon reproaching the deeps.

XXX

On Damis, lost at sea

Sailing the Icarian sea ⟨   ⟩, falling from his ship, Damis the son of Nicaretus tumbled into the ocean. Many a prayer to the Immortals his father uttered, and called on the waters, imploring the waves for his son's sake. But he perished most pitiably, swallowed by the sea. In time past too that ocean was deaf to a father's prayers.

XXX *A.P.* 9.267 [C] Φιλίππου Θεσσαλονικέως   εἰς Δᾶμίν τινα ἐν τῶι Ἰκαρίωι πελάγει καταποντωθέντα Pl A Φιλίππου
1 Ἰκαρίην πλώων P: Ἰκ. τὸ πάρος πλ. Pl   5 οἰκτίστως Pl: -τωι P | βρυχθεὶς ἁλί P: ἁλὶ βρ. Pl

XXXI

Αἴλιος ὁ θρασύχειρ Ἄρεος πρόμος, ὁ ψελιώσας
αὐχένα χρυσοδέτοις ἐκ πολέμου στεφάνοις,   2840
τηξιμελεῖ νούσωι κεκολουμένος ἔδραμε θυμῶι
ἐς προτέρην ἔργων ἄρσενα μαρτυρίην,
5 ὦσε δ' ὑπὸ σπλάγχνοις πλατὺ φάσγανον, ἓν μόνον εἰπών·
'ἄνδρας ἄρης κτείνει, δειλοτέρους δὲ νόσος'.

XXXII

ἠιόνιον τόδε σῶμα βροτοῦ παντλήμονος ἄθρει   2845
σπαρτόν, ἁλιρραγέων ἐκχύμενον σκοπέλων·
τῆι μὲν ἐρημοκόμης κεῖται καὶ χῆρος ὀδόντων
κόρση, τῆι δὲ χερῶν πενταφυεῖς ὄνυχες
5 πλευρά τε σαρκολιπῆ, ταρσοὶ δ' ἑτέρωθεν ἄμοιροι
νευρῶν καὶ κώλων ἔκλυτος ἁρμονίη.   2850
οὗτος ὁ πουλυμερὴς εἷς ἦν ποτε· φεῦ μακαριστοί
ὅσσοι ἀπ' ὠδίνων οὐκ ἴδον ἠέλιον.

XXXIII

ἥρως Πρωτεσίλαε, σὺ γὰρ πρώτην ἐμύησας
Ἴλιον Ἑλλαδικοῦ θυμὸν ἰδεῖν δόρατος,
καὶ περὶ σοῖς τύμβοις ὅσα δένδρεα μακρὰ τέθηλε   2855
πάντα τὸν εἰς Τροίην ἐγκεκύηκε χόλον·

XXXI A.P. 7.234 [C] Φιλίππου Θεσσαλονικέως   [J] εἰς ἕτερον Αἴλιον Ἀργεῖον στρατίαρχον Pl A Φιλίππου   εἰς αὐτόν   Suid. s.vv. θρασύχειρ (1–πρόμος+ 3–κεκολ.), τηξιμελεῖ (3 s.), κεκολουμένος (eadem)
1 Ἄρεος Brodaeus: Ἄργους PPlSuid. | ὁ ψελιώσας C: ὀψεδιώσας P, ὀψὲ διώσας Pl   3 κεκολουμένος CPl: κεκωλυμένος P   4 προτέρην P: -ρων Pl
XXXII A.P. 7.383 [C] Φιλίππου ὁμοίως   [J] εἰς τινα ναυηγὸν οὗτινος ὅλον τὸ λείψανον διεσπάρη ὑπὸ τῆς θαλάσσης ἐν τῶι αἰγιαλῶι   Pl A τοῦ αὐτοῦ [sc. Φιλίππου]   Pl B Φιλίππου

XXXI

A Roman prefers suicide to death by disease

Aelius, the bold-handed war-leader, the one who braceleted
his neck with the gold bonds of torques won in battle, being
cut down by limb-wasting disease, ran back in his mind to the
past evidence of his manly acts, and drove his broad sword
beneath his vitals, with these words only: 'Men are killed by
the sword, cowards by disease.'

XXXII

On a drowned man washed ashore

See on the beach this body of a man all-unfortunate, with
scattered limbs, washed forth from the sea-beaten rocks. Here
lies the head, hair-stripped and tooth-bereft, there the hand's
five fingers and the flesh-forsaken ribs, apart are the feet deprived of sinews and the limbs' disjointed frame. This man in
many parts was once a whole; happy are those who saw not the
sunlight after the birth-pangs.

XXXIII

On the elms round the tomb of Protesilaus

Hero Protesilaus, as you initiated Ilium first into seeing the
wrath of Hellene spears, so the trees that grow tall around your
tomb are all pregnant with your hatred for Troy. If from their

1 ἠϊόνιον PPl^B: ἠϊόνι Pl^A | cῶμα Huet: cῆμα PPl^{AB}   2 ἐκχύμενον Pl^A:
ἐκχυμένων P, ψυχόμενον Pl^B   4 χερῶν PPl^{AB}: χειρ- C   6 ἔκλυτος PPl^B:
ἔκλιπτος Pl^A   7 πουλυμερὴς CPl^{AB}: πολλυμερῆς P
XXXIII *A.P.* 7.385 [C] Φιλίππου   [J] εἰς Πρωτεσίλαον τὸν ἐν Τροίαι πρῶτον
τελευτήσαντα, ὅτι ἐν τῶι τούτου τάφωι ὅcα φυτὰ βλέπει τὴν Ἴλιον ξηραίνονται
καὶ τῶν φύλλων τὸν κόcμον ἀποβάλλουcι   caret Pl
2 Ἑλλαδικοῦ C: -κῶι P   4 ἐγκεκύηκε Bothe: ἐκκεκ- P

5 Ἴλιον ἢν ἐσίδηι γὰρ ἀπ᾽ ἀκρεμόνων κορυφαίων,
  καρφοῦται πετάλων κόσμον ἀναινόμενα.
  θυμὸν ἐπὶ Τροίηι πόσον ἔζεσας, ἡνίκα τὴν σήν
  σώιζει καὶ στελέχη μῆνιν ἐπ᾽ ἀντιπάλους.   2860

XXXIV

ὦ ξεῖνε, φεῦγε τὸν χαλαζεπῆ τάφον
τὸν φρικτὸν Ἱππώνακτος, οὗ τε χἀ τέφρα
ἰαμβιάζει Βουπάλειον ἐς στύγος,
μή πως ἐγείρηις σφῆκα τὸν κοιμώμενον,
5 ὃς οὐδ᾽ ἐν Ἅιδηι νῦν κεκοίμηκεν χόλον,   2865
  σκάζουσι μέτροις ὀρθὰ τοξεύσας ἔπη.

XXXV

πηρός, ὁ μὲν γυίοις, ὁ δ᾽ ἄρ᾽ ὄμμασιν, ἀμφότεροι δέ
εἰς αὑτοὺς τὸ τύχης ἐνδεὲς ἠράνισαν·
τυφλὸς γὰρ λιπόγυιον ἐπωμάδιον βάρος αἴρων
ταῖς κείνου φωναῖς ἀτραπὸν ὀρθοβάτει.   2870
5 πάντα δὲ ταῦτ᾽ ἐδίδαξε πικρὴ πάντολμος Ἀνάγκη,
  ἀλλήλοις μερίσαι τοὐλλιπὲς εἰς τέλεον.

XXXVI

νηδύι βριθομένην δάμαλιν Λητωίδι κούρηι
στῆσαν νηοκόροι θῦμα χαριζόμενοι,
ἧς Ἀίδην μέλλοντα προέφθασεν εὔστοχος ὠδίς,   2875
πέμφθη δ᾽ εἰς ἀγέλην τεκνογονεῖν ἄφετος.

XXXIV A.P. 7.405 Φιλίππου [C] Μιμνέρμου, οἱ δὲ Φιλίππου [P] εἰς Ἱππώνακτος [J] τάφον τοῦ ἰαμβογράφου [C] ὅστις πρῶτος ἐποίησεν ἴαμβον Pl b
s.a.n. εἰς Ἱππώνακτα
3 ἐς στύγος CPl: ἐστυγὸς P   5 κεκοίμηκεν P: -μικεν Pl
XXXV A.P. 9.11 Φιλίππου, οἱ δὲ Ἰσιδώρου [J] εἰς τυφλὸν καὶ χωλόν, ἀλλήλοις
τὸ ἔλλειπὲς δανεισαμένων Pl A Φιλίππου, οἱ δὲ Ἰσιδώρου

topmost boughs they behold Ilium, they wither and renounce their foliage's beauty. How your anger against Troy must have seethed, when even the tree-trunks preserve your wrath against the foe.

XXXIV

On the tomb of Hipponax

Fly, stranger, from the hailstorm-poet's tomb, the frightful grave of Hipponax, whose very ashes make lampoons for his loathing of Bupalus, lest you arouse the sleeping wasp who has not even now in Hades laid his wrath to rest, the shooter of straight words in limping metre.

XXXV

The lame and the blind help each other

The one was maimed in his legs, the other in his eyes, but each contributed to the other the deficiency of his lot. The blind lifted the lame as a load on his shoulders and walked his path straight by his companion's telling. All this was taught them by Necessity, bitter but all-resourceful, to share what was deficient in each and so to form a whole.

XXXVI

A sacrificial cow spared because pregnant

The temple-keepers placed a heifer with laden belly in honour of Leto's daughter, making gracious sacrifice; but timely-aimed birth-pains came too quick for her impending death, and she was sent to the herd, set free to give birth. For the goddess

4 ὀρθοβάτει P: ὠρ- Pl   6 τέλεον Canter: ἔλεον PPl

XXXVI A.P. 9.22 [C] Φιλίππου Θεσσαλονικέως   [J] εἰς δάμαλιν ἔγκυον μέλλουσαν θύεσθαι τῆι Ἀρτέμιδι καὶ διὰ τὸ παραυτὰ τεκεῖν ἀπολυθεῖσαν Pl A Φιλίππου
1 Λητωΐδι Pl: -δη P   2 θῦμα Pl: θαῦμα P

5 ἡ θεὸς ὠδίνων γὰρ ἐπίσκοπος, οὐδ᾽ ἐδίκαζεν
τικτούσας κτείνειν, ἃς ἐλεεῖν ἔμαθεν.

XXXVII

Ἕβρου Θρηϊκίου κρυμῶι πεπεδημένον ὕδωρ
νήπιος εἰσβαίνων οὐκ ἔφυγεν θάνατον·   2880
ἐς ποταμὸν δ᾽ ἤδη λαγαρούμενον ἴχνος ὀλισθών
κρυμῶι τοὺς ἁπαλοὺς αὐχένας ἀμφεκάρη·
5 καὶ τὸ μὲν ἐξεσύρη λοιπὸν δέμας, ἡ δὲ μένουσα
ὄψις ἀναγκαίην εἶχε τάφου πρόφασιν.
δύσμορος, ἧς ὠδῖνα διείλατο πῦρ τε καὶ ὕδωρ·   2885
ἀμφοτέρων δὲ δοκῶν οὐδενός ἐστιν ὅλως.

XXXVIII

νηὸς ἐπειγομένης ὠκὺν δρόμον ἀμφεχόρευον
δελφῖνες, πελάγευς ἰχθυφάγοι σκύλακες,
καπροφόνος δὲ κύων θηρσὶν κείνους ἰκελώσας
δύσμορος ὡς ἐπὶ γῆν εἰς βυθὸν ἐξέθορεν·   2890
5 ὤλετο δ᾽ ἀλλοτρίης θήρης χάριν, οὐ γὰρ ἐλαφρός
πάντων ἐστὶ κυνῶν ὁ δρόμος ἐν πελάγει.

XXXIX

νῆα μὲν ὤλεσε πόντος, ἐμοὶ δ᾽ ἔπορεν πάλι δαίμων
πλαζομένωι φύσεως νῆα ποθεινοτέρην·
πατρὸς ἰδὼν γὰρ ἐγὼ δέμας εἰς ἐμὲ καίριον ἐλθόν   2895
μουνερέτης ἐπέβην φόρτος ὀφειλόμενος.

5 ἐδίκαζεν P: -ζε Pl

XXXVII A.P. 9.56 [C] Φιλίππου Θεσσαλονικέως   Pl A Φιλίππου
2 εἰσβαίνων Salm.: ἐκβ- PPl   7 διείλατο P: -λετο Pl   8 ὅλως PPl: ὅλος
Pl^{sscr}

XXXVIII A.P. 9.83 [C] Φιλίππου   [idem denuo] Φιλίππου   εἰς κυνηγετικὸν
κύνα [idem tertium] Φιλίππου   [J] εἰς κυνηγετικὸν κύνα, ὅτι κυνὸς ἐν νηὶ

is watcher over birth-pains, and ordains that one should not kill the mother in labour; these are the creatures she is wont to pity.

XXXVII

A boy decapitated by river-ice

A child, entering the frost-bound water of Thracian Hebrus, was overtaken by death. His foot slipped into the river, already thawing, and his soft neck was cut through by the ice. The rest of his body was dragged away, but his head remained, and made necessary cause for burial. Unhappy the woman whose child was divided between fire and water; seeming to belong to both, he belongs to neither wholly.

XXXVIII

A dog leaps into the sea in pursuit of dolphins

Dolphins, the sea's fish-devouring dogs, were dancing around the swift course of a speeding ship, when a boar-slaying hound, likening them to animals, leapt into the deep, poor wretch, as if on to land. So it perished for the sake of a prey not its own; not all dogs have easy running in the sea.

XXXIX

A father's corpse saves his son from drowning

The sea destroyed the ship, but Fate in return gave me as I drifted Nature's still dearer vessel. Seeing my father's body coming opportunely my way, I mounted it, single-scull, its

ἐνυπάρχοντος καὶ τοὺς δελφῖνας θεασαμένου χορεύοντας ἔρριψεν ἑαυτὸν ἐν τῆι θαλάσσηι ὡς ἐπὶ θήραν καὶ ἀπώλετο   Pl A Φιλίππου
2 πελάγευς Pl: -γους P

XXXIX *A.P.* 9.85 [C] Φιλίππου Θεσσαλονικέως   [J] εἴς τινα ναυαγήσαντα μετὰ τοῦ ἰδίου πατρὸς καὶ τοῦ μὲν πρεσβύτου τελευτήσαντος ὁ τούτου υἱὸς ἐπὶ τῶι σώματι τοῦ πατρὸς βασταζόμενος διεσώθη ἐν τῆι χέρσωι   Pl A Φιλίππου
2 φύσεως P: -σιος Pl   3 πατρὸς CPl: -ρὶς P

5 ἤγαγεν εἰς λιμένας δὲ καὶ ἔσπειρεν δὶς ὁ πρέσβυς,
   νήπιον ἐν γαίηι, δεύτερον ἐν πελάγει.

XL

μεμφομένη Βορέην ἐπεπωτώμην ὑπὲρ ἅλμης,
   πνεῖ γὰρ ἐμοὶ Θρήικης ἤπιος οὐδ' ἄνεμος·   2900
ἀλλά με τὴν μελίγηρυν ἀηδόνα δέξατο νώτοις
   δελφὶν καὶ πτηνὴν πόντιος ἡνιόχει.
5 πιστοτάτωι δ' ἐρέτηι πορθμευομένη τὸν ἄκωπον
   ναύτην τῆι στομάτων θέλγον ἐγὼ κιθάρηι.
εἰρεσίην δελφῖνες ἀεὶ Μούσηισιν ἄμισθον   2905
   ἤνυσαν· οὐ ψεύστης μῦθος Ἀριόνιος.

XLI

λιμὸν ὀιζυρὴν ἀπαμυνομένη πολύγηρως
   Νικὼ σὺν κούραις ἠκρολόγει στάχυας,
ὤλετο δ' ἐκ θάλπους· τῆι δ' ἐκ καλάμης συνέριθοι
   νῆσαν πυρκαϊὴν ἄξυλον ἔκ τ' ἀχύρων.   2910
5 μὴ νεμέσα, Δήμητερ, ἀπὸ χθονὸς εἰ βροτὸν οὖσαν
   κοῦραι τοῖς γαίης σπέρμασιν ἠμφίεσαν.

XLII

Ἀδριακοῖο κύτους λαιμὸς τὸ πάλαι μελίγηρυς,
   ἡνίκ' ἐγαστροφόρουν Βακχιακὰς χάριτας,
νῦν κλασθεὶς κεῖμαι νεοθηλέι καρτερὸν ἕρκος   2915
   κλήματι πρὸς τρυφερὴν τεινομένωι καλύβην.

5 ἤγαγεν εἰς λιμένας δὲ P: ἤγαγε δ' εἰς λιμένας με Pl
XL *A.P.* 9.88 [C] Φιλίππου Θεσσαλονικέως   [J] εἰς ἀηδόνα [C: χελιδόνα J]
ὑπ' ἀνέμου ἐμπεσοῦσαν εἰς θάλασσαν καὶ σωθεῖσαν ὑπὸ δελφῖνος   [C] Φιλίππου
[J] ὅτι πεσούσης τῆς ἀηδόνος [C: χελιδόνος J] ἐν θαλάσσηι δελφὶς τοῖς νώτοις
ἐδέξατο, ἡ δὲ κελαδοῦσα τοῦτον ἔτερπεν ἕως εἰς τὴν γῆν ἐξέπεσεν   Pl Α Φιλίππου
3 μελίγηρυν Pl: -γυριν P   8 Ἀριόνιος Pl: Ἀρειόν- P
XLI *A.P.* 9.89 [C] Φιλίππου Θεσσαλονικέως   [J] εἰς γραῦν τινα ταλαίπωρον
καὶ πενιχρὰν ἥτις συνέλεγεν τοὺς ἀπὸ τῶν θεριζόντων πίπτοντας ἀστάχυας ἢ

due and proper freight. The old man carried me to harbour and so gave me life twice,—as an infant on the land, a second time in the sea.

XL

A nightingale rescued by a dolphin

Complaining of Boreas I flew over the salt sea; from Thrace, not even the wind blows kindly for me. But a dolphin took me, the honey-voiced nightingale, on its back; the sea-beast was charioteer for the wingèd one. Ferried by the trustiest of boat-men I charmed the oarless sailor with the lyre of my lips. Dolphins have always done unpaid oar-service to the Muses; the story of Arion is no falsehood.

XLI

The death of Nico

Repelling the misery of hunger, agèd Nico was gathering corn-ears in the company of her girls. She died of the heat, and her fellow-workers heaped her a woodless pyre from stalks and husks. Bear no malice, Demeter, that the girls covered a mortal born of earth with the fruits of earth.

XLII

A wine-jar's neck used to protect a vine

The neck of an Adrian jar, once honey-voiced when I was pregnant with the joys of Bacchus, now broken I lie, a strong protection for a new-blooming vine straining towards a dainty

καὶ ἐτελεύτηϲεν ἐκ τοῦ καύματοϲ καὶ κατεκαύθη μεθ᾽ ὧν ϲυνήγαγεν ἀϲταχύων. ὦ τῆϲ πενίαϲ   Pl A Φιλίππου
4 πυρκαϊὴν Aldus: πῦρ καὶ ἦν PPl | ἔκ τ᾽ ἀχύρων Reiske: ἐκ ϲταχύων PPl
5 οὖϲαν CPl: -ϲαι P

XLII *A.P.* 9.232 [C] Φιλίππου Θεϲϲαλονικέωϲ   ζήτει ἐπὶ τίνι τὸ ἐπίγραμμα Pl B Φιλίππου
1 κύτουϲ CPl: κήτοιϲ P   2 ἡνίκ᾽ P: ἀν- Pl

5 αἰεί τοι Βρομίωι λατρεύομεν· ἢ γεραὸν γάρ
φρουροῦμεν πιστῶς ἢ νέον ἐκτρέφομεν.

XLIII

βαιὸν ἀποπλανίην λιπομήτορα παῖδα κορύπτης
κριὸς ἑλιξόκερως θεῖνε θρασυνόμενος, 2920
κάπρος δ' Ἡράκλειος ἀπορρήξας ἀπὸ δεσμῶν
ἐς νηδὺν κριοῦ πᾶσαν ἔβαψε γένυν,
5 ζωὴν νηπιάχωι δὲ χαρίσσατο. ἆρ' ἀπό γ' Ἥρης
Ἡρακλέης βρεφέων ὤικτισεν ἡλικίην;

XLIV

εὐθαλῆ πλάτανόν με νότου βαρυλαίλαπες αὖραι 2925
ῥίζης ἐξ αὐτῆς ἐστόρεσαν δαπέδοις,
λουσαμένη Βρομίωι δ' ἔστην πάλιν ὄμβρον ἔχουσα
χείματι καὶ θάλπει τοῦ Διὸς ἡδύτερον.
5 ὀλλυμένη δ' ἔζησα· μόνη δὲ πιοῦσα Λυαῖον
ἄλλων κλινομένων ὀρθοτέρη βλέπομαι. 2930

XLV

ἐν Θήβαις Κάδμου κλεινὸς γάμος, ἀλλὰ μυσαχθής
Οἰδίποδος. τελετὰς Εὔιος ἠσπάσατο,
ἃς γελάσας Πενθεὺς ὠδύρατο. τείχεα χορδαῖς
ἔστη, καὶ λωτοῖς ἔστενε λυόμενα.
5 Ἀντιόπης ὁσίη, χαλεπὴ δ' ὠδὶς Ἰοκάστης. 2935
ἦν Ἰνὼ φιλόπαις, ἀλλ' ἀσεβὴς Ἀθάμας.
οἰκτρὸν ἀεὶ πτολίεθρον· ἴδ' ὡς ἐσθλῶν περὶ Θήβας
μύθων καὶ στυγνῶν ἤρκεσεν ἱστορίη.

5 τοι Jacobs: τι P, τι ex το corr. Pl | γάρ Pl: δέ P
XLIII A.P. 9.240 [C] Φιλίππου   ἐπὶ κριῶι μέλλοντι τύψαι παιδίον ἤγουν κορύψαι, ὃν κάπρος τύψας τῶι ὀδόντι ἀπέκτεινεν   Pl A Φιλίππου
1 κορύπτης Pl: Καλύπτρης P   5 ζωὴν Pl: -ὰν P | χαρίσσατο Pl: -ίσατο P | ἀπό γ' Page: ἀπὸ PPl
XLIV A.P. 9.247 [C] Φιλίππου   εἰς πλάτανον ἐκριζωθεῖσαν ὑπὸ ἀνέμων

pergola. We are for ever slaves to Bromios; either we guard him faithfully in old age, or we bring him up young.

XLIII

A boy, attacked by a ram, is saved by a boar

A butting curly-horned ram was fiercely smiting a little far-straying mother-leaving lad, when a Herculean boar broke from its bonds and dipped his whole tusk in the ram's belly. So he gave the child its life; is it because of Hera that Hercules had pity on an infant's tender years?

XLIV

An uprooted tree re-planted and revived with wine

Me, a well-grown plane-tree, tempestuous south-winds laid low on the ground from the very roots. But bathed in wine I stood again upright, enjoying a rainfall sweeter than Heaven's in winter and in summer-heat. In dying I came to life; I alone, by drinking of the wine-god, am seen the straighter, while others sway.

XLV

Contrasting themes in Theban legend

In Thebes, the wedding of Cadmus was noble; of Oedipus, polluted. Bacchus welcomed rites which Pentheus mocked to his sorrow. Walls stood upright to the lyre, but moaned as they crumbled to the pipes. Holy was the travail of Antiope; of Jocasta, grievous. Child-loving was Ino, Athamas impious. A city ever to be pitied; see how amply sufficed the tale of stories good and hateful about Thebes.

[idem ad v. 3] ὑπολαμβάνω ὅτι cκεῦοc οἰνηρὸν αὐτὴν κατεcκεύαcαν Pl A Φιλίππου

1 εὐθαλῆ P: -λέα Pl   2 δαπέδοιc C: -δον (?) P, -δωι Pl

XLV *A.P.* 9.253 [C] Φιλίππου Θεccαλονικέωc εἰc τὰc ἐπταπύλουc Θήβαc ἃc ἐπόλιcε Κάδμοc Pl A Φιλίππου

1 μυcαχθήc P: -θείc Pl   3 ὠδύρατο Pl: ὀδ- P

XLVI

ἠρίθμει πολὺν ὄλβον Ἀριστείδης ὁ πενιχρός
  τὴν ὄιν ὡς ποίμνην, τὴν βόα δ᾽ ὡς ἀγέλην,   2940
⟦ἤμβροτε δ᾽ ἀμφοτέρων· ἀμνὴν λύκος, ἔκτανε δ᾽ ὠδίς
  τὴν δάμαλιν, πενίης δ᾽ ὤλετο βουκόλιον.
5 πηροδέτωι δ᾽ ὅγ᾽ ἱμάντι κατ᾽ αὐχένος ἄμμα πεδήσας
  οἰκτρὸς ἀμυκήτωι κάτθανε πὰρ καλύβηι.⟧

XLVII

καὶ τὸν ἀρουραῖον γυρητόμον αὔλακα τέμνει   2945
  μηροτυπεῖ κέντρωι πειθομένη δάμαλις
καὶ μετ᾽ ἀροτροπόνους ζεύγλας πάλι τῶι νεοθηλεῖ
  πινομένη μόσχωι δεύτερον ἄλγος ἔχει.
5 μὴ θλίψηις αὐτὴν ὁ γεωμόρος· οὗτος ὁ βαιός
  μόσχος, ἐὰν φείσηι, σοὶ τρέφεται δαμάλης.   2950

XLVIII

ὅτ᾽ ἐξ ἀήτου Λίβυος ἀζαοῦς Νότου
συνεζοφώθη πόντος, ἐκ δὲ νειάτων
μυχῶν βυθῖτις ψάμμος ἐξηρεύγετο,
ἱστὸς δὲ πᾶς ὤλισθεν εἰς ἅλα πτύσας,
5 φορτὶς δ᾽ ἔσυρεν ἐς Ἀίδαν πλανώμενον,   2955
ἀρωγοναύτας δαίμονας Λυσίστρατος
ἐλιπάρησεν, οἱ δὲ τῶι νεωκόρωι
μούνωι θάλασσαν ἀγρίαν ἐκοίμισαν.

XLVI A.P. 9.255 [C] τοῦ αὐτοῦ [sc. Φιλίππου]   εἰς Ἀριστείδην τὸν πένητα οὗ πᾶσα κτῆσις βοῦς καὶ πρόβατον ἕν   Pl A Φιλίππου
1–2 post Antipatri Thess. ep. LXVIII A tanquam peculiare epigramma scribit Pl, versibus 3–6 (=LXVIII 3–6) non repetitis
XLVII A.P. 9.274 [C] Φιλίππου   εἰς δάμαλιν ἀροτρεύουσαν ἧς καὶ ὁ μόσχος ἐπηκολούθει μυκώμενος   Pl A Φιλίππου
3 ἀροτροπόνους Scaliger: -νου PPl   **6** μόσχος Pl: μόχθος P | δαμάλης Brodaeus: -λις PPl

XLVI

Suicide of a poor man

Aristides the pauper used to count up his great wealth, reckoning his one sheep as a flock, his cow as a herd. Then he lost both: a wolf killed the sheep, pangs of birth the cow; his poverty's consolation perished. He fastened a knot against his neck with his wallet-binding strap, and died in his misery beside the cabin where no cattle lowed.

XLVII

A cow suckles while ploughing

Obedient to thigh-smiting goad the cow cleaves the curve-cut furrow of the ploughland; and again, after the plough-labour under the yoke, suffers a second pain suckling her new-born calf. Strike her not, you ploughman there; this little calf, if you are merciful, will grow up for you a young ox.

XLVIII

A temple-servant's prayer fulfilled at sea

When the ocean was darkened by the fierce-blowing Libyan south-wind, and the sea-bed sand was belched up from the profoundest deeps, and the whole mast fell into the sea with a splash, and the freighter was dragging him to Hades as he drifted, Lysistratus implored the spirits that rescue sailors, and they lulled the savage sea for their temple-guardian only.

XLVIII *A.P.* 9.290 [C] Φιλίππου Θεσσαλονικέως εἰς Λυσίστρατόν τινα νεωκόρον ἐν ναυαγίαι μόνον σωθέντα   Pl B Φιλίππου
1 ἀzαοῦς Page: αἰzαοῦ P, ἐκ zαοῦς Pl   3 βυθῖτις Pl: -της P | ἐξηρεύγετο Pl: -εύετο P   4 ὤλισθεν Pl: ὄλ- P   5 δ' ἔσυρεν P (δὲ σῦρεν): δ' ἐσύρετ' Pl | ἐς Pl: om. P   6 ἀρωγοναύτας P (ἀρωγὸν αὐτὰς): ἀρωγὸν αὐτᾶι Pl   7 νεωκόρωι Toup: νεηκ- PPl   8 ἐκοίμισαν Pl: -σεν P

XLIX

πουλὺ Λεωνίδεω κατιδὼν δέμας αὐτοδάικτον
Ξέρξης ἐχλαίνου φάρεϊ πορφυρέωι,   2960
κἠκ νεκύων δ' ἤχησεν ὁ τᾶς Cπάρτας πολὺς ἥρως
'οὐ δέχομαι προδόταις μιcθὸν ὀφειλόμενον·
5 ἀcπὶς ἐμοὶ τύμβου κόcμος μέγας· αἶρε τὰ Περcῶν·
ἥξω κεῖς Ἀίδαν ὡς Λακεδαιμόνιος'.

L

ταῦροι πρηυτένοντες ἀροτρευτῆρες ἀρούρης   2965
εἰν ἁλὶ τοὺς γαίης ἀντέχομεν καμάτους·
αὔλακα τὴν ἀcίδηρον ἐν ὕδαcιν ἕλκομεν ἄμφω
μακροτόνων cχοίνων ἄμμα cαγηνόδετον,
5 ἰχθύcι δ' ἐκ cταχύων λατρεύομεν· ἃ ταλαεργοί,
ἤδη κἀν πελάγει καρπὸν ἀροῦcι βόες.   2970

LI

ὠκείαις ἐλάφοιcι κύων ἰcάμιλλα δραμοῦcα
ἔγκυος ἡλκώθη παιδοπόρον γένεcιν,
πᾶcα δὲ cυγκατέμυcε κατουλωθεῖcα χρόνοιcιν·
ἤδη δ' ἡ τοκετῶν ὥριος ἦν βάcανος,
5 πολλὰ δ' ἐπωρύουcαν ἀνὴρ ἐcιδηροτόμηcεν,   2975
καὶ cκύλακες φίλιοι νηδύος ἐξέθορον.
Ἀρτέμιδος λέλυται λοχίων χάρις, ἔμπαλι δ' Ἄρης
ἦρκται μαιοῦcθαι γαστέρας ἡμετέρας.

XLIX A.P. 9.293 Φιλίππου [C] Θεσσαλονικέως   εἰς Λεωνίδην τὸν Cπαρτιάτην
ὅτε Ξέρξης αὐτὸν ὑπεραγαcθεὶς καὶ νεκρὸν ὄντα μετὰ τῆς πορφυρᾶς χλανίδος
ἐcκέπαcεν   Pl b Φιλίππου
2 ἐχλαίνου Lascaris: εὐχλ- PPl   3 κἠκ P: κἀκ Pl | πολὺς P: μέγας Pl
5 ἐμοὶ P: μοι Pl | αἶρε PPl: ἔρρε Pl^γρ   6 ἥξω Pl: κἤξω P | Ἀίδαν Jacobs:
-δην PPl

XLIX

Xerxes and the corpse of Leonidas

Xerxes, having looked down upon the great body of Leonidas self-slain, was cloaking it in a purple robe, when the great hero of Sparta cried even from among the dead 'I reject the reward due to traitors. My shield is my tomb's great adornment. Take away what comes from Persians. I will go even to Hades like a Lacedaemonian.'

L

Oxen draw a fish-net

Gentle-necked oxen, ploughers of the field, we suffer the land's labours in the sea instead. Together we draw in the waters the furrow that is not made by iron; we form the long-stretched ropes' seine-fastening knot, and slave for fish instead of crops. Long-suffering indeed, now oxen must go ploughing for a harvest in the sea too.

LI

A surgical operation

A bitch, running in equal contest with swift deer, being pregnant, was wounded in the womb, her babies' conveyor. Wholly it closed, scarred over by time. And now the hour of birth's ordeal was come, and a man cut her open, loud-howling, and her dear puppies leapt from the womb. The grace of Artemis in child-birth is at an end; Ares instead has begun to be midwife to our bellies.

L A.P. 9.299 Φιλίππου [C] Θεσσαλονικέως   εἰς ταύρους ἕλκοντας ναῦν παρὰ τὸ ῥεῦμα τοῦ ποταμοῦ   Pl A τοῦ αὐτοῦ [sc. Φιλίππου]
3 ἀcίδηρον Pl: -δαρον P   5 ἅ P: οἱ Pl   6 κἄν Pl: κ' ἐν P

LI A.P. 9.311 [C] Φιλίππου Θεσσαλονικέως   εἰς κυνηγετικὴν κύνα ἑλκωθεῖσαν τὸ αἰδοῖον καὶ μέλλουσαν τίκτειν σιδήρωι τμηθεῖσαν ⟨ὥστε⟩ τεκεῖν   Pl A τοῦ αὐτοῦ [sc. Φιλίππου]
2 ἠλκώθη Pl: εἰλκ- P   5 ἐcίδηρο- Pl: ἐcίδαρο- P | -τόμηcεν P: -cε Pl

LII

ἡ ναῦς ἀπ᾽ ἔργων Κύπριδος γομφουμένη
πρὸς τὸν γενάρχην πόντον ἤλυθον θεοῦ·   2980
ἀνὴρ γὰρ ὥρης μ᾽ ἔμπορος τεκτήνατο
καλέςας Ἑταίρην, εἰμὶ γὰρ πᾶςιν φίλη.
5   ἔμβαινε θαρρῶν, μιςθὸν οὐκ αἰτῶ βαρύν·
ἐλθόντα δέχομαι πάντα, βαςτάζω ξένον
⟨   ⟩   2985
ὣς ποτ᾽ ἐπὶ γαίης κἠν βυθῶι μ᾽ ἐρέςςετε.

LIII

βωλοτόμοι μύρμηκες, ὁ γῆς ςτρατός, ἡνίκα τένδον
γειομόρου μελιχρὴν ςμηνοδόκου χάριτα,
μηνίςας ὁ πρέςβυς ἐς ὕδατα κρωςςὸν ἔβαψεν
ἐνθάδε τοὺς ἀπὸ γῆς οὐ δοκέων πελάςειν·   2990
5   οἱ δὲ νέας ⟨   ⟩ ἀχυρίτιδας ἀντιφέροντες
αὐτοκυβερνῆται πρὸς κύτος ἐτρόχαςαν.
ἦ ῥα φίλη γαςτὴρ καὶ βαιοτάτους ἀνέπειςεν
ἐκ χθονὸς εἰς Νύμφας καινοτάτους ἐρέτας.

LIV

Θεςςαλίης εὐίππου ὁ ταυρελάτης χορὸς ἀνδρῶν,   2995
χερςὶν ἀτευχήτοις θηρςὶν ὁπλιζόμενος,
κεντροτυπεῖς πώλους ζεῦξε ςκιρτήματι ταύρων,
ἀμφιβαλεῖν ςπεύδων πλέγμα μετωπίδιον·
5   ἀκρότατον δ᾽ ἐς γῆν κλίνας ἅμα κεύροπον ἅμμα
θηρὸς τὴν τόςςην ἐξεκύλιςε βίην.   3000

LII *A.P.* 9.416 Φιλίππου Θεςςαλονικέως εἰς ναῦν [C] ὁμοίως καὶ αὐτὴν πόρνας
μετάγουςαν τὴν ςφαλερὴν ἐργαςίαν   [J] ἰαμβικὸν τὸ μέτρον Pl в s.a.n.
4 γὰρ Pl: τὰν P   **5** αἰτῶ P^marg Pl: ετῶ P   **6** βαςτάζω Pl: -ων P | ξένον
P^ac Pl: -ων P^pc | post h. v. lacunam statuit Page   **8** μ᾽ Pl: om. P |
ἐρέςςετε P^ac Pl: -ται P^pc denuoque P^marg

LIII *A.P.* 9.438 Φιλίππου εἰς μύρμηκας [C] Φιλίππου Θεςςαλονικέως εἰς
μύρμηκας διαπλεύςαντας ὕδωρ μετὰ ἀχύρων ἕνεκα τοῦ φαγεῖν μέλι Pl A Φιλίππου

LII

On a ship built from the profits of a brothel

I, a ship built from the Cyprian's trade, have come to the sea
that gave that goddess birth. A trafficker in beauty wrought me
and called me 'Courtesan', for I am all men's friend. Board me
cheerfully, I ask no heavy fee. I welcome all comers; I carry
the foreigner ⟨and citizen alike⟩. As once on land, so row me on
the deep.

LIII

A bee-keeper outwitted by ants

When burrowing ants, that army of the soil, were nibbling at
the bee-keeping farmer's sweet delicacy, the old man in anger
plunged the pot in water, thinking that the land-creatures would
not approach there. But they brought a fleet of straw-husks
against it, and ran to the jar self-steered. Their own belly taught
even the tiniest things to take to water from land as new-style
sailors.

LIV

On the Thessalian bull-sports

The bull-chasing band of men from Thessaly, home of fine
horses, armed against wild beasts with hands weaponless,
brought their spur-smitten colts close to the bounding bulls,
eager to fling a forehead-embrace about them. Inclining to the
earth their clinch-hold at the top, bent easily downward, they
overthrew the brute's mighty strength.

1 ὁ γῆς Pl: laesa superficie quid fuerit in P ignotum | ἡνίκα τένδον Jacobs: ἡνίκα
τὴν δε (vel τῆν δε) P, ἡνίκ' ἐc Pl (ubi ἐcύλων suppl. man. rec.)   3 κρωccὸν
Pl: κροcc- P   5 νέαc (lacuna nulla relicta) P: νέαc κούφαc Pl | ἀχυρίτιδαc
Schneider: ἀχυρτίδαc PPl   6 αὐτοκυβερνῆται P: -τὶ Pl | κύτοc P: τάχοc Pl
LIV A.P. 9.543 Φιλίππου   ἀδιανόητον   caret Pl
1 εὐίππου Stadtmüller: -ιππος P   3 κεντροτυπεῖc Schneider: δενδρο- P |
ζεῦξε Reiske: -ξει P   6 τόccην Salm.: τόcην P | ἐξεκύλιcε Brunck: -ληcε P

LV

τίς σε πάγος δυσέρημος ἀνήλιος ἐξέθρεψεν
  Βορραίου Σκυθίης ἄμπελον ἀγριάδα
ἢ Κελτῶν νιφοβλῆτες ἀεὶ κρυμώδεες Ἄλπεις
  τῆς τε σιδηροτόκου βῶλος Ἰβηριάδος,
5 ἢ τοὺς ὀμφακόραγας ἐγείναο, τοὺς ἀπεπάντους   3005
  βότρυας, οἳ στυφελὴν ἐξέχεον σταγόνα;
δίζημαι, Λυκόεργε, τεὰς χέρας, ὡς ἀπὸ ῥίζης
  κλήματος ὠμοτόκου βλαστὸν ὅλον θερίσηις.

LVI

οὐρανὸς ἄστρα τάχιον ἀποσβέσει ἢ τάχα νυκτός
  ἠέλιος φαιδρὴν ὄψιν ἀπεργάσεται   3010
καὶ γλυκὺ νᾶμα θάλασσα βροτοῖς ἀρυτήσιμον ἕξει
  καὶ νέκυς εἰς ζωιῶν χῶρον ἀναδράμεται,
5 ἢ ποτε Μαιονίδαο βαθυκλεὲς οὔνομ᾽ Ὁμήρου
  λήθη γηραλέων ἁρπάσεται σελίδων.

LVII

ἔζευξ᾽ Ἑλλήσποντον ὁ βάρβαρος ἄφρονι τόλμηι,   3015
  τοὺς δὲ τόσους καμάτους πάντας ἔλυσε χρόνος·
ἀλλὰ Δικαιάρχεια διηπείρωσε θάλασσαν
  καὶ βυθὸν εἰς χέρσου σχῆμα μετεπλάσατο.
5 λᾶα, βαθὺ στήριγμα, κατερρίζωσε πέλωρον,
  χερσὶ Γιγαντείαις δ᾽ ἔστασε νέρθεν ὕδωρ.   3020
ἦν δ᾽ ἅλ᾽ ἀεὶ πλώειν· διοδευομένη δ᾽ ὑπὸ ναύταις
  ἄστατος, εἰς πεζοὺς ὡμολόγησε μένειν.

LV *A.P.* 9.561 Φιλίππου [C] εἰς ἄμπελον. σκωπτικόν Pl A Φιλίππου
2 Βορραίου P: ἢ Βορέου Pl   5 ὀμφακόραγας Pl: ὀμφοκόραγας in ὀμφο-
κόρωγας corr. P | ἐγείναο Pl^{pc}: -νατο PPl^{ac} | ἀπεπάντους P^{sscr} (denuoque
P^{marg}) Pl: ἐπὶ πάντους P   8 θερίσηις Pl (et man. rec. in P): -σεις P
LVI *A.P.* 9.575 Φιλίππου εἰς τὸν Ὅμηρον Pl A Φιλίππου εἰς Ὅμηρον

LV

A sour wine

What desert sunless hill of northern Scythia reared you, a wild
vine, or what snow-beaten ever-icy Celtic Alps, or clod of iron-
bearing Iberia, you mother of these sour grapes, these unripened
clusters that have poured forth their acrid juice? I look for your
hands, Lycurgus, to tear up wholly by the roots the crude-
bearing vine-stem's shoot.

LVI

Homer's immortal fame

Heaven shall sooner extinguish the stars, the sun shall sooner
make bright the face of night, the sea shall have sweet water for
mortals to draw, the dead shall hasten back to the land of the
living, before oblivion of his ancient pages shall ever take from
us the wide-renowned name of Homer Maeonides.

LVII

The harbour-mole at Puteoli

The barbarian, with a fool's audacity, yoked the Hellespont,
but Time has undone all those great labours. Now Dicaearchia
has made the sea a mainland and has re-shaped the deeps to the
land's form. She has rooted monstrous stones, a deep foundation,
and with Giants' hands has put the waters in their place below.
One could always sail the sea; inconstant when traversed by
sailors, it has agreed to stay firm for those on foot.

---

1 οὐρανὸς Pl: -νὸν P   3 ἀρυτήσιμον Dorville: ἀροτ- PPl   5 βαθυκλεὲς
Stephanus: βαθὺ κλέος PPl
LVII *A.P.* 9.708 Φιλίππου   Pl A τοῦ αὐτοῦ [sc. Φιλίππου, quod scr. et del. Pl]
Pl B Φιλίππου
1 τόλμηι PPlᴬ: λύσσηι Plᴮ   3 Δικαιάρχεια Plᴮ: -χία PPlᴬ   7 ἦν δ’ ἄλ’
ἀεὶ Salm.: ἦν δ’ ἀλλ’ αἰεὶ P, ἦν δ’ αἰεὶ Plᴬ, μυδαλέη Plᴮ | ὑπὸ Brunck: ἐπὶ PPlᴬᴮ

LVIII

λάθριον ἑρπηστὴν σκολιὸν πόδα, κισσέ, χορεύσας
ἄγχεις τὴν Βρομίου βοτρυόπαιδα χάριν·
δεσμεῖς δ' οὐχ ἡμᾶς, ὀλέκεις δὲ σέ· τίς γὰρ ἕλοιτ' ἂν   3025
κισσὸν ἐπὶ κροτάφοις, μὴ κεράσας Βρόμιον;

LIX

ἡνίκα μὲν καλὸς ἦς, Ἀρχέστρατε, κἀμφὶ παρειαῖς
οἰνωπαῖς ψυχὰς ἔφλεγες ἠϊθέων,
ἡμετέρης φιλίης οὐδεὶς λόγος, ἀλλὰ μετ' ἄλλων
παίζων τὴν ἀκμὴν ὡς ῥόδον ἠφάνισας.   3030
5 ὡς δ' ἐπιπερκάζεις μιαρῇ τριχί, νῦν φίλον ἕλκων
τὴν καλάμην δωρῇ, δοὺς ἑτέροις τὸ θέρος.

LX

γραμματικοί, Μώμου Στυγίου τέκνα, σῆτες ἀκανθῶν,
τελχῖνες βίβλων, Ζηνοδότου σκύλακες,
Καλλιμάχου στρατιῶται, ὃν ὡς ὅπλον ἐκτανύσαντες   3035
οὐδ' αὐτοῦ κείνου γλῶσσαν ἀποστρέφετε,
5 συνδέσμων λυγρῶν θηρήτορες, οἷς τὸ 'μίν' ἢ 'σφίν'
εὔαδε καὶ ζητεῖν εἰ κύνας εἶχε Κύκλωψ,
τρίβοισθ' εἰς αἰῶνα κατατρύζοντες ἀλιτροί
ἄλλων, ἐς δ' ἡμᾶς ἰὸν ἀποσβέσατε.   3040

LVIII A.P. 11.33 Φιλίππου   Pl A Φιλίππου
3 ἕλοιτ' ἂν Jacobs: ὀλεῖται P, ἕλοιτο Pl
LIX A.P. 11.36 Φιλίππου   caret Pl

LVIII

On a vine choked by ivy

Dancing with furtive creeping sidelong foot, ivy, you choke the grape-child delight of Bromios. Yet you do not so much fetter me as destroy yourself; for who would take ivy on his temples without first mixing wine?

LIX

Lost charms of boyhood

When you were handsome, Archestratus, and your wine-red cheeks inflamed the souls of young men, then friendship with me was of no account; you played with others, and threw away your youthful beauty as it were a rose. Now that you are darkening with loathsome hair, you drag me to be your friend; you give me the straw, having given the harvest to others.

LX

On pedants

Grammarians, offspring of Stygian Momus, thorn-worms, demon foes of books, puppies of Zenodotus, armed forces of Callimachus, whom you stretch forth as a shield, yet keep not your tongues even from him; hunters of grim conjunctions, delighting in '*min*' and '*sphin*' and the question whether the Cyclops possessed dogs,—may you wear yourselves out eternally, scoundrels, chattering abuse of others; but against me, put out your venom's fire.

LX *A.P.* 11.321 Φιλίππου Pl A Φιλίππου
1 γραμματικοί Pl: -κοῦ P | ἀκανθῶν Scaliger: ἀπάντων PPl   4 ἀποστρέφετε
P: -ται Pl   6 εἰ κύνας Pl: εἰκόνας P

LXI

χαίροιθ' οἱ περὶ κόσμον ἀεὶ πεπλανηκότες ὄμμα
οἵ τ' ἀπ' Ἀριστάρχου cῆτες ἀκανθολόγοι·
ποῖ γὰρ ἐμοὶ ζητεῖν τίναc ἔδραμεν ἥλιος οἴμους
καὶ τίνος ἦν Πρωτεὺς καὶ τίς ὁ Πυγμαλίων;
5 γινώσκοιμ' ὅσα λευκὸν ἔχει στίχον· ἡ δὲ μέλαινα   3045
ἱστορίη τήκοι τοὺς Περικαλλιμάχους.

LXII

χαῖρε, θεὰ Παφίη· cὴν γὰρ ἀεὶ δύναμιν
κάλλος τ' ἀθάνατον καὶ σέβας ἱμερόεν
πάντες τιμῶσιν θνατοὶ ἐφαμέριοι
ἐν πᾶσιν μύθοις ἔργοισίν τε καλοῖς,   3050
5 πάντηι γὰρ πᾶσιν cὴν δηλοῖς τιμήν.

LXIII

Εὐρώταν ὡς ἄρτι διάβροχον ἔν τε ῥεέθροιc
εἵλκυс' ὁ τεχνίτης ἐν πυρὶ λουcάμενον·
πᾶcι γὰρ ἐν κώλοιc ὑδατούμενος ἀμφινένευκεν
ἐκ κορυφῆc ἐc ἄκρους †ὑγρορἁτων† ὄνυχας.   3055
5 ἃ δὲ τέχνα ποταμῶι cυνεπήρικεν· ἃ τίς ὁ πείcαc
χαλκὸν κωμάζειν ὕδατος ὑγρότερον;

LXIV

ἴδ' ὡς ὁ πῶλος χαλκοδαιδάλωι τέχναι
κορωνιῶν ἔστηκε· δριμὺ γὰρ βλέπων
ὑψαυχενίζει καὶ διηνεμωμέναc   3060

LXI *A.P.* 11.347 Φιλίππου   Pl B s.a.n.
6 Περικαλλιμάχους P: Παρακ- Pl

LXII *A.P.* 13.1 Φιλίππου   πεντάμετρον μόνον   caret Pl
3 τιμῶσιν Boissonade: -cι P   **4** πᾶσιν Brunck: -cι P   **5** πᾶcιν Jacobs:
-cι P

LXI

On the same

A fond farewell to you whose eyes are ever roving round the universe, and you others, thorn-gathering book-worms of Aristarchus' brood. What good is it to me to inquire what paths the sun ran, and who was Proteus' father, and who was Pygmalion? I would know works whose lines are crystal-clear; let the darker learning sap the strength of our super-Callimachuses.

LXII

To Aphrodite

Hail, Paphian goddess. All mortals ephemeral in all noble words and deeds honour your power and deathless beauty and graceful holiness; to all men in all ways you make your majesty manifest.

LXIII

On a bronze figure of the river Eurotas

The artist drew out his Eurotas, bathed in fire, as if just now streaming and in floods; it is fluid in all its limbs, swaying this way and that, and it moves liquidly from head to toe-tips. Art has competed with the river. Who is it that has persuaded bronze to go rioting more fluidly than water?

LXIV

On a statue of a horse by Lysippus

See how the colt stands with head tossing, by the bronze-artist's skill. Fierce-glancing he lifts his neck up and lets freely

LXIII *A.P.* 9.709 τοῦ αὐτοῦ [sc. Φιλίππου] caret Pl
2 τεχνίτης Huschke: -νῆτ- P   4 ἐς Huschke: εἰς P
LXIV *A.P.* 9.777 Φιλίππου εἰς ἵππον χαλκοῦν Pl A τοῦ αὐτοῦ [sc. Φιλίππου] εἰς ἵππον
1 τέχναι P: -νηι Pl

κορυφῆς ἐθείρας οὐρίωκεν ἐς δρόμον.
δοκέω, χαλινοὺς εἴ τις ἡνιοστρόφος
ἐναρμόσηι γένυσσι κἀπικεντρίσηι,
ὁ σὸς πόνος, Λύσιππε, καὶ παρ' ἐλπίδας
τάχ' ἐκδραμεῖται· τᾶι τέχναι γὰρ ἐμπνέει.

3065

5

LXV

τὸν ἐκ Σινώπης εἰ κλύεις Δαμόστρατον
πίτυν λαβόντα τὴν κατ' Ἰσθμὸν ἑξάκις,
τοῦτον δέδορκας, οὗ κατ' εὔγυρον πάλην
ψάμμος πεσόντος νῶτον οὐκ ἐσφράγισεν.
ἴδ' αὖ πρόσωπον θηρόθυμον, ὡς ἔτι
σώιζει παλαιὰν τὴν ὑπὲρ νίκας ἔριν.
λέγει δ' ὁ χαλκός, 'ἃ βάσις με λυσάτω,
χὡς ἔμπνοος νῦν ἕβδομον κονίσομαι'.

3070

5

LXVI

ἴσως με λεύσσων, ξεῖνε, ταυρογάστορα
καὶ στερρόγυιον ὡς Ἄτλαντα δεύτερον
θαμβεῖς ἀπιστῶν εἰ βρότειος ἡ φύσις·
ἀλλ' ἴσθι μ' Ἥραν Λαδικῆα πάμμαχον,
ὃν Cμύρνα καὶ δρῦς Περγάμου κατέστεφεν,
Δελφοί, Κόρινθος, Ἦλις, Ἄργος, Ἄκτιον·
λοιπῶν δ' ἀέθλων ἢν ἐρευνήσηις κράτος,
καὶ τὴν Λίβυσσαν ἐξαριθμήσεις κόνιν.

3075

5

3080

LXVII

ἢ θεὸς ἦλθ' ἐπὶ γῆν ἐξ οὐρανοῦ εἰκόνα δείξων,
Φειδία, ἢ σύ γ' ἔβης τὸν θεὸν ὀψόμενος.

(3082)

---

4 ἐς P: εἰς Pl   5 ἡνιοστρόφος Pl: -φους P   6 ἐναρμόσηι P: -σει
Pl | γένυσσι Pᵖᶜ: -νυσι PᵃᶜPl | κἀπικεντρίσηι P: -ρίσει Pl   8 τᾶι τέχναι
P: τῆι τέχνηι Pl
LXV A.Pl. (A) 25 Φιλίππου Syll.Σπ Φιλίππου caret P
4 ψάμμος Pl et ut vid. Σπᵖᶜ: -μον Σπ   5 αὖ Pl: ἐς Σπ

flow his head's wind-blown mane for the gallop. I fancy, if a
charioteer should fasten the bit on his jaws and goad him, your
work, Lysippus, would soon surprise us by running off. For
art has given it the breath of life.

LXV

On a statue of a wrestler

If you have heard of the man from Sinopê, Damostratus, six
times receiver of the pine-wreath at the Isthmus, that is the man
you see, whose back never had the sand's impress from a fall
in the tortuous wrestling-bout. See too the wild-beast's courage
in his face, how it still keeps its ancient zest for victory. Thus
speaks the bronze: 'Let the pedestal release me, and at once
like a living man I will put the dust on a seventh time.'

LXVI

On a statue of a pancratiast

It may be, stranger, seeing me bull-bellied and solid-limbed
like a second Atlas, you marvel and doubt whether such a nature
was mortal. Know that I am Heras of Laodicea, the pancratiast,
crowned by Smyrna and the oak of Pergamum, Delphi,
Corinth, Elis, Argos, and Actium. If you inquire of my victories in the rest of the games, you will be counting the sands
of Libya.

LXVII

On the statue of Zeus at Olympia by Pheidias

Either the god came to earth from heaven to show you his
likeness, Pheidias, or you went to see the god.

LXVI *A.Pl.* (A) 52 Φιλίππου Syll.Σπ Φιλίππου caret P
1 λεύσσων Pl: λεύσσων Σπ
LXVII *A.Pl.* (A) 81 Φιλίππου εἰς ἄγαλμα caret P

LXVIII

ὤλεσα τὸν Νεμέας θῆρ' ἄπλετον, ὤλεσα δ' ὕδρην
καὶ ταῦρον, κάπρου δ' ἀμφετίναξα γένυν·   3085
ζωστῆρ' ἑλκύσσας πώλους Διομήδεος εἷλον·
χρύσεα μῆλα κλάσας Γηρυόνην ἔλαβον·
5 Αὐγείαν ἐδάην· κεμὰς οὐ φύγεν· ἔκτανον ὄρνις·
Κέρβερον ἠγαγόμην· αὐτὸς Ὄλυμπον ἔχω.

LXIX

Ἥρη τοῦτ' ἄρα λοιπὸν ἔτ' ἤθελε πᾶσιν ἐπ' ἄθλοις,   3090
ὅπλων γυμνὸν ἰδεῖν τὸν θρασὺν Ἡρακλέα.
ποῦ χλαίνωμα λέοντος ὅ τ' εὐροίζητος ἐπ' ὤμοις
ἰὸς καὶ βαρύπους ὄζος ὁ θηρολέτης;
5 πάντα σ' Ἔρως ἀπέδυσε· καὶ οὐ ξένον, εἰ Δία κύκνον
ποιήσας ὅπλων νοσφίσαθ' Ἡρακλέα.   3095

LXX

τίς σου, Κολχὶς ἄθεσμε, συνέγραφεν εἰκόνι θυμόν;
τίς καὶ ἐν εἰδώλωι βάρβαρον εἰργάσατο;
αἰεὶ γὰρ διψᾶις βρεφέων φόνον. ἦ τις Ἰήσων
δεύτερος ἢ Γλαύκη τις πάλι σοι πρόφασις;
5 ἔρρε, καὶ ἐν κηρῶι παιδοκτόνε· σῶν γὰρ ἀμέτρων   3100
ζήλων εἰς ἃ θέλεις καὶ γραφὶς αἰσθάνεται.

LXVIII *A.Pl.* (A) 93 Φιλίππου   εἰς τὸ αὐτό   caret P
3 ἑλκύσσας edd. vett.: -κύσας Pl
LXIX *A.Pl.* (A) 104 Φιλίππου   εἰς τὸ αὐτό   caret P

PHILIP

LXVIII
The labours of Heracles

I destroyed the huge beast of Nemea; I destroyed the Hydra and the bull; I made the boar's teeth chatter. Having snatched the girdle, I captured the horses of Diomedes; having plucked the golden apples, I caught Geryon. I learnt to know Augeas; the hind did not escape me; I slew the birds; I carried Cerberus off; myself, I dwell in Olympus.

LXIX
On a figure of Heracles stripped by Eros

So this was left still for Hera to desire, on top of all his Labours,—to see bold Heracles stripped of his armour. Where are the lion-cloak and loud-whistling arrows on the shoulders and the heavy-footed beast-destroying club? Eros has stripped you of all; nor is it strange that he who made Zeus a swan has parted Heracles from his arms.

LXX
On a picture of Medea

Lawless Colchian, who has portrayed your rage together with your image? Who has made you thus barbarous even in a likeness? You are for ever thirsting for your children's blood; is it some second Jason, or is there again some Glaucê, to be your excuse? Away with you, child-murderess even in the wax; even the paint-brush feels your boundless passions towards what you desire.

1 ἔτ' suppl. Page: om. Pl
LXX A.Pl. (A) 137 Φιλίππου εἰς τὸ αὐτό caret P

LXXI

Κολχίδα, τὴν ἐπὶ παισὶν ἀλάστορα, τραυλὲ χελιδών,
πῶς ἔτλης τεκέων μαῖαν ἔχειν ἰδίων,
ἧς ἔτι κανθὸς ὕφαιμος ἀπαστράπτει φόνιον πῦρ
καὶ πολιὸς γενύων ἀφρὸς ἀποσταλάει,   3105
5 ἀρτιβρεχὴς δὲ σίδηρος ἐφ᾽ αἵματι. φεῦγε πανώλη
μητέρα κἂν κηρῶι τεκνοφονοῦσαν ἔτι.

LXXII

Κύπρι φιλομμειδὴς θαλαμηπόλε, τίς σε μελιχρήν
δαίμονα τοῖς πολέμων ἐστεφάνωσεν ὅπλοις;
σοὶ Παιὰν φίλος ἦν καὶ ὁ χρυσοκόμης Ὑμέναιος   3110
καὶ λιγυρῶν αὐλῶν ἡδυμελεῖς χάριτες.
5 ἐς τί δὲ ταῦτ᾽ ἐνέδυς ἀνδροκτόνα; μὴ θρασὺν Ἄρη
συλήσασ᾽ αὐχεῖς Κύπρις ὅσον δύναται;

LXXIII

—κράμβης ἅψωμαι, Κυλλήνιε;—μή, παροδῖτα.
—τίς φθόνος ἐκ λαχάνων;—οὐ φθόνος, ἀλλὰ νόμος,   3115
ἀλλοτρίων ἀπέχειν κλοπίμους χέρας.—ὢ παραδόξου·
μὴ κλέπτειν Ἑρμῆς καινὸν ἔθηκε νόμον.

LXXI *A.Pl.* (A) 141 Φιλίππου   εἰς τὸ αὐτό   caret P
3 ἀπαστράπτει Schaefer: ἐπ- Pl
LXXII *A.Pl.* (A) 177 Φιλίππου   εἰς τὴν αὐτήν   caret P

LXXI

To a swallow nesting on a picture of Medea

The Colchian, she who took vengeance on her children,—how, twittering swallow, could you bear to have her as nurse to your own babies? Her bloodshot eye still flashes murderous fire, and gray foam dribbles from her jaws, and her sword is fresh-soaked with their blood. Fly from that all-destructive mother, still infant-slaying even in the wax.

LXXII

On a figure of Aphrodite in armour

Cypris, laughter-loving, the bride's waiting-maid, who has crowned you, the goddess of delight, with the weapons of war? To you Paean was dear, and golden-haired Hymen, and the sweet-sounding graces of shrill flutes; why have you put on these man-slaying things? Can it be that you have despoiled bold Ares, to boast how great the power of Cypris is?

LXXIII

Dialogue between a wayfarer and Hermes

—May I lay hands on the cabbage, god of Cyllenê?—Traveller, you may not.—What grudge can come from greens?—No grudge, but the law, that one should keep filching fingers away from others' property.—What a paradox: here is a new law, made by Hermes, 'Thou shalt not steal'.

1 φιλομμειδὴϲ edd. vett.: φιλομει- Pl
LXXIII A.Pl. (A) 193 Φιλίππου εἰϲ ἕτερον τοῦ αὐτοῦ ἐν κήπωι   caret P

LXXIV

συλήσαντες "Ολυμπον ἴδ' ὡς ὅπλοισιν "Ερωτες
κοσμοῦντ' ἀθανάτων σκῦλα φρυασσόμενοι·
Φοίβου τόξα φέρουσι, Διὸς δὲ κεραυνόν, "Αρηος   3120
ὅπλον καὶ κυνέην, 'Ηρακλέους ῥόπαλον,
5 εἰναλίου τε θεοῦ τριβελὲς δόρυ θύρσα τε Βάκχου,
πτηνὰ πέδιλ' 'Ερμοῦ, λαμπάδας 'Αρτέμιδος.
οὐκ ἄχθος θνητοῖς εἴκειν βελέεσσιν 'Ερώτων,
δαίμονες οἷς ὅπλων κόσμον ἔδωκαν ἔχειν.   3125

LXXV

—ὡραίας γ' ἐσορῶ τὰς ἰσχάδας, εἴ γε λαβεῖν μοι
συγχωρεῖς ὀλίγας·—θίγγανε μηδεμιᾶς.
—ὀργίλος ὡς ὁ Πρίηπος.—ἐρῶ σέ τι, κοὐ κενὸς ἥξεις·
ναὶ λίτομαι, δός μοι· καὶ γὰρ ἐγὼ δέομαι·
5 —χρήιζεις γάρ, λέγε μοι, παρ' ἐμοῦ τινος;—ἔστι νόμος που,   3130
δὸς λαβέ.—καὶ θεὸς ὢν ἀργυρίου σὺ γλίχηι;
—ἄλλο τι χρῆμα φιλῶ.—ποῖον τόδε;—τἀμὰ κατέσθων
σῦκα δὸς εὐθύμως ἰσχάδα τὴν ὀπίσω.

LXXVI

ἡ γρηὺς ἡ χερνῆτις, ἡ γυιὴ πόδας
πύστιν κατ' ἐσθλὴν ὕδατος παιωνίου   3135
ἦλθέν ποθ' ἑρπύζουσα σὺν δρυὸς ξύλωι,
τό μιν διεσκήριπτε τὴν τετρωμένην·

LXXIV *A.Pl.* (A) 215 Φιλίππου εἰς τὸ αὐτό   caret P
LXXV *A.Pl.* (A) 240 Φιλίππου εἰς ἕτερον   caret P
3 ἐρῶ σέ τι κοὐ Jacobs: ἐρεῖς ἔτι καὶ Pl
LXXVI *A.P.* 6.203 [C] Λάκωνος, οἱ δὲ Φιλίππου Θεσσαλονικέως   [P] ἀνάθημα

LXXIV

On a portrayal of the Erotes equipped
with the gods' weapons

See how the Loves, having plundered Olympus, array themselves in arms, exulting in their spoils from the Immortals.
They carry the bow of Phoebus, the thunderbolt of Zeus, the
shield and helmet of Ares, the club of Heracles, the three-
pronged spear of the sea-god, the wands of Bacchus, the wingèd
sandals of Hermes, the torches of Artemis. It is no grievance to
mortals that they must yield to the shafts of the Loves, to whose
possession even the gods have given the adornment of their
arms.

LXXV

Dialogue between a wayfarer and Priapus

—I see the figs are ripe, if you will let me take a few...
—Don't touch a single one.—What a temper Priapus has.—Let
me ask you something, and your coming shall not be in vain;
indeed, I implore you, give me, for I too am in need...—Tell
me, is there something you need from me?—There is a law
called 'Give and take'...—You, a god, greedy for cash?—
What I want is something different.—What can that be?—If
you eat my figs, give me with good grace the fig behind you.

LXXVI

An old woman cured of lameness

That old servant-woman, the one lame in the feet, at the good
news of healing waters came crawling one day with her oak

ταῖς Νύμφαις [C] παρὰ [hoc in voc. eras., fort. Λάκωνος, a P scr.] γραὸς
πενιχρᾶς Suid s.vv. γραῦς (1–3), πύςτεις (2 s.), παιώνιον (2 s. ποθ᾽ ἕρπ.),
διεςκήριπτεν (3 s.), οἶκτος (5–7)   caret Pl
1 γυιή Emperius: γυρὴ PSuid.   4 διεςκήριπτε C: -τεν P

5   οἶκτος δὲ Νύμφας εἶλεν, αἵ τ᾽ †ἐρινόμου†
     Αἴτνης παρωρείηισι Συμαίθου πατρός
     ἔχουσι διηέντος ὑγρὸν οἰκίον·   3140
     καὶ τῆς μὲν ἀμφίχωλον ἀρτεμὲς σκέλος
     θερμὴ διεστήριζεν Αἰτναίη λιβάς,
10   Νύμφαις δ᾽ ἔλειπε βάκτρον, αἱ δ᾽ ἐπήινεσαν
     πέμπειν μιν ἀστήρικτον ἡσθεῖσαι δόσει.

LXXVII

ἡ γρηὺς Νικὼ Μελίτης τάφον ἐστεφάνωσε   3145
παρθενικῆς· Ἀίδη, τοῦθ᾽ ὁσίως κέκρικας;

LXXVIII

ἐνθάδε τὴν ἱερὴν κεφαλὴν σορὸς ἥδε κέκευθεν
  Ἀετίου χρηστοῦ ῥήτορος εὐπρεπέος·
ἦλθεν δ᾽ εἰς Ἀίδαο δέμας, ψυχὴ δ᾽ ἐς Ὄλυμπον
⟦τέρπετ᾽ ἅμα Ζηνὶ καὶ ἄλλοισιν μακάρεσσιν,⟧   3150
5 †ἀθάνατον δὲ οὔτε λόγος ποιεῖν οὔτε θεὸς δύναται†.

LXXIX

ἄπαιρέ μου τένοντος, ὦ γεωπόνε,
λέπαδνα καὶ σίδαρον αὐλακεργάταν·
χαλκὸν γὰρ ἁμῶν οὐκ ἐσάρκωσεν Μύρων,
τέχναι δ᾽ ἐζωπόνησεν ὄψιν ἔμπνοον   3155
5 ὡς πολλάκις με κἀπομυκᾶσθαι θέλειν·
εἰς ἔργα δ᾽ οὐκ εἴασε προσδήσας βάσει.

6 παρωρείηισι Συμαίθου Salm.: -σιν εὐμέθου PSuid.
LXXVII *A.P.* 7.187 [=Pᵃ] [C] τοῦ αὐτοῦ [sc. Φιλίππου]   [J] εἰς Μελίτην τινὰ
παρθένον iterum post 7.344 [=Pᵇ] [C] τοῦ αὐτοῦ [sc. Σιμωνίδου]   [J] εἰς
Μελίτην κόρην   Pl A Λεωνίδου
1 ἐστεφάνωσε PᵃPᵇᵖᶜPl: -σεν Pᵇᵃᶜ
LXXVIII *A.P.* 7.362 [J] Φιλίππου Θεσσαλονικέως [P] εἰς Ἀέτιον ῥήτορα
Pl B s.a.n.

stick, which propped her maimed body up. Compassion seized the Nymphs who dwell on the foot-hills of ⟨   ⟩ Etna in the watery home of their whirlpool-sire Symaethus. Etna's hot spring made strong her two lame legs, and she left the Nymphs her stick; so they consented to escort her on her way unsupported, as they rejoiced in her gift.

LXXVII

The young buried by the old

Old Nico wreathed the tomb of maiden Melitê. Hades, was this your judgment righteous?

LXXVIII

Epitaph for a rhetorician

This coffin hides here the holy head of Aëtius, a good and eminent rhetorician. His body went to Hades, his soul to Olympus ⟨   ⟩. But neither eloquence nor god can make a man immortal.

LXXIX

On Myron's Cow

Take the collar from my neck, farmer, and the furrow-working iron. Myron did not turn my bronze to flesh; by his art he created the appearance of life, so that often I would even like to bellow. But he fixed me to my base and so prevented me from going to work.

1 copòc ἥδε κέκευθεν CPl: ἥδε κέκευθε cωρόc P   2 εὐπρεπέοc PPl: ἐκπρ- C
3 ἦλθεν δ' CPl: ἦλθεν P | δέμαc CPl: δόμοιc (potius quam δόμουc) P | ἐc Ὄλυμπον PPl: ἐν Ὀλύμπωι C   4–5 ita P: τέρπετ'…μακάρεccιν om. Pl, qui ex reliquis pentametrum fingit ἀθάνατον ποιεῖ δ' οὐ λόγοc οὔτε θεόc
LXXIX A.P. 9.742 s.a.n.   Pl A Φιλίππου Μακεδόνοc εἰc τὸ αὐτό
2 αὐλακεργάταν Brunck: -τα P, -την Pl   4 τέχναι PᵖᶜPl: -να Pᵃᶜ | δ' ἐξωπόνηcεν P: δέ γ' ἐξεπόνηcεν Pl

LXXX

εἰ τὸ μὲν ἐκδεδάνεικας, ὃ δ᾽ ἄρτι δίδως, ὃ δὲ μέλλεις,   (3158)
οὐδέποτ᾽ εἶ τοῦ σοῦ κύριος ἀργυρίου.

ΦΙΛΟΔΗΜΟΥ

I

τὸν σιγῶντα, Φιλαινί, συνίστορα τῶν ἀλαλήτων   3160
  λύχνον ἐλαιηρῆς ἐκμεθύσασα δρόσου
ἔξιθι, μαρτυρίην γὰρ Ἔρως μόνος οὐκ ἐφίλησεν
  ἔμπνουν· καὶ πτυκτὴν κλεῖε, Φιλαινί, θύρην.
5 καὶ σύ, φίλη Ξανθώ με· σὺ δ᾽, ὦ φιλεράστρια κοίτη,
  ἤδη τῆς Παφίης ἴσθι τὰ λειπόμενα.   3165

II

ἑξήκοντα τελεῖ Χαριτὼ λυκαβαντίδας ὥρας,
  ἀλλ᾽ ἔτι κυανέων σύρμα μένει πλοκάμων,
κἠν στέρνοις ἔτι κεῖνα τὰ λύγδινα κώνια μαστῶν
  ἕστηκεν μίτρης γυμνὰ περιδρομάδος,
5 καὶ χρὼς ἀρρυτίδωτος ἔτ᾽ ἀμβροσίην, ἔτι πειθώ   3170
  πᾶσαν, ἔτι στάζει μυριάδας Χαρίτων.
ἀλλὰ πόθους ὀργῶντας ὅσοι μὴ φεύγετ᾽, ἐρασταί,
  δεῦρ᾽ ἴτε τῆς ἐτέων ληθόμενοι δεκάδος.

LXXX *A.P.* 11.173 Φιλίππου Pl A τοῦ αὐτοῦ [sc. Λουκιλλίου]

I *A.P.* 5.4 Φιλοδήμου   [J] εἰς Φιλαινίδα τὴν νεωτέραν Pl A τοῦ αὐτοῦ [sc. Φιλοδήμου]
4 πτυκτὴν Jacobs: πυκτὴν P, τυκτὴν Pl | θύρην P: -ραν Pl   5–6 om. Pl
5 φίλη P: -λει C | Ξανθώ με C: Ξανθῶι ut vid. P | φιλεράστρια κοίτη J. G. Schneider: -τρι᾽ ἄκοιτις C, -τρια κοίτης P   6 Παφίης C: -φείης P

LXXX

On lending money

If you have lent part, and are just giving part, and are intending to give part, you are at no time master of your own money.

PHILODEMUS

I

The happy lover

The lamp, Philaenis, the silent confidant of our secrets,—make it drink deep of the dew of oil, and then go away. Love alone hates a living witness. And, Philaenis, shut the folding door. As for you and me, beloved Xantho,—O lover-loving bed, now at once learn the rest of the Paphian's arts.

II

'Age cannot wither her...'

Charito is completing her sixty years, but still the long train of her black hair is unchanged, still on her bosom those marble cones of her breasts stand firm, dressed with no circle of corset-band, still her skin without a wrinkle distils ambrosia, still all manner of seduction, still a myriad charms. All lovers who are not afraid of ripe-bursting passion, forget what decade of her years it is, and come this way.

II *A.P.* 5.13 Φιλοδήμου [J] εἰc ἑταίραν τινὰ Χαριτώ. θαυμάcιον Pl A τοῦ αὐτοῦ [sc. Φιλοδήμου] Suid. s.vv. κωνοειδέc (3 s. ἔcτ.), λύγδινα (3 s.)
1 Χαριτώ CPl: -τι P, -τη Csscr | λυκαβαντίδαc P: -βαντοc ἐc Pl   3-4 om. Pl
3 κἢν Suid. edd. vett.: κ' ἐν PSuid.   4 μίτρηc Suid.: μῆτ- P   5 ἀμβρο-
cίην edd. vett.: -ίη PSuid.   6 πᾶcαν P: πᾶcιν C, πάcαc Pl | ἔτι cτάζει PPl: ἀποcτάζει Cγρ   7-8 om. Pl   7 φεύγετ' Salm.: φλέγετ' P

III

ὁccάκι Κυδίλληc ὑποκόλπιος, εἴτε κατ' ἦμαρ
εἴτ' ἀποτολμήcαc ἤλυθον ἑcπέριος,   3175
οἶδ' ὅτι πὰρ κρημνὸν τέμνω πόρον, οἶδ' ὅτι ῥιπτῶ
πάντα κύβον κεφαλῆc αἰὲν ὕπερθεν ἐμῆc.
5 ἀλλὰ τί μοι πλέον ἐcτί; cὺ γὰρ θραcύc, ἠδ' ὅταν ἕλκηιc
πάντοτ', Ἔρωc, ἀρχὴν οὐδ' ὄναρ οἶδα φόβου.

IV

—χαῖρε cύ.—καὶ cύ γε χαῖρε.—τί δεῖ cε καλεῖν;—cὲ δέ;—μήπω 3180
τοῦτο φιλοcπούδει.—μηδὲ cύ.—μή τιν' ἔχειc;
—αἰεὶ τὸν φιλέοντα.—θέλειc ἅμα cήμερον ἡμῖν
δειπνεῖν;—εἰ cὺ θέλειc.—εὖ γε· πόcου παρέcηι;
5 —μηδέν μοι προδίδου.—τοῦτο ξένον.—ἀλλ' ὅcον ἄν cοι
κοιμηθέντι δοκῆι, τοῦτο δόc.—οὐκ ἀδικεῖc.   3185
ποῦ γίνηι; πέμψω.—καταμάνθανε.—πηνίκα δ' ἥξειc;
—ἢν cὺ θέλειc ὥρην.—εὐθὺ θέλω.—πρόαγε.

V

'γινώcκω, χαρίεccα, φιλεῖν πάλι τὸν φιλέοντα
καὶ πάλι γινώcκω τόν με δακόντα δακεῖν·
μή λύπει με λίην cτέργοντά cε μηδ' ἐρεθίζειν
τὰc βαρυοργήτουc cοὶ θέλε Πιερίδαc.'   3190

III *A.P.* 5.25 τοῦ αὐτοῦ [sc. Φιλοδήμου]   [J] εἰc Κυδίλλην τὴν ἑταίραν   Pl A
τοῦ αὐτοῦ [sc. Φιλοδήμου]   Suid. s.v. κύβος (3 οἶδ'–4)
3 πὰρ Pl: παρὰ P   5 cὺ γὰρ Page: γὰρ P, γὰρ οὖν Pl | ἕλκηιc Page: -κηι
PPl   6 οἶδα Boissonade: -δε PPl
IV *A.P.* 5.46 Φιλοδήμου   [J] πρὸc ἑταίραν κατὰ πεῦcιν καὶ ἀπόκριcιν   caret Pl

III

On Cydilla, dangerous but irresistible

Whenever I lie on Cydilla's bosom, whether I come by day or, greatly daring, at dusk, I know I am cutting a path beside a precipice, I know I am tossing all the dice overhead each time. But what good is knowing to me? You are reckless, and whenever you drag me with you, God of Love, I never even know the shadow of fear.

IV

A street-scene

—Good day.—And good day to you.—What is your name?— And what is yours?—Don't be in a hurry about that yet.— Then don't you either.—Are you engaged?—To anyone who fancies me.—Will you dine with me today?—If it is your wish.—Good. And what will your company cost me?—Give me nothing in advance...—That's most unusual.—...Only give me what you think right after you have slept with me.— You're very honest. Where will you be? I will send for you.— You can find out.—When will you arrive?—Whatever time you like.—The present moment is what I like.—Then lead the way.

V

A lovers' quarrel

'My charmer, I know how to love the lover in return, I know how to bite the biter back. Do not vex me too much; I am in love with you. Do not of your own will provoke the Muses;

---

2 φιλοcπούδει Kaibel: -δοc P | μηδὲ Dübner: μήτε P   3 αἰεὶ C: ἀεὶ P
4 δειπνεῖν: -πλεῖν ut vid. P

V *A.P.* 5.107 Φιλοδήμου [J] εἰc ἑταίραν ὑπερήφανον   Pl A ἄδηλον
1 γινώcκω P: γιγν- Pl | πάλι Scaliger: πάνυ PPl   2 γινώcκω P: γιγν-
Pl   3 ἐρεθίζειν P: -ζε Pl   4 coὶ P: μὴ Pl

5 τοῦτ' ἐβόων αἰεὶ καὶ προύλεγον, ἀλλ' ἴσα πόντωι
  Ἰονίωι μύθων ἔκλυες ἡμετέρων.
  τοιγὰρ νῦν cὺ μὲν ὧδε μέγα κλαίουσα βαΰζοις,
  ἡμεῖς δ' ἐν κόλποις ἥμεθα Ναϊάδος.   3195

VI

ἠράσθην Δημοῦς Παφίης γένος· οὐ μέγα θαῦμα·
καὶ Cαμίης Δημοῦς δεύτερον· οὐχὶ μέγα·
καὶ πάλι Νυσιακῆς Δημοῦς τρίτον· οὐκέτι ταῦτα
παίγνια· καὶ Δημοῦς τέτρατον Ἀργολίδος.
5 αὐταί που Μοῖραί με κατωνόμασαν Φιλόδημον,   3200
  ὡς αἰεὶ Δημοῦς θερμὸς ἔχοι με πόθος.

VII

καὶ νυκτὸς μεσάτης τὸν ἐμὸν κλέψασα cύνευνον
ἦλθον καὶ πυκινῆι τεγγομένη ψακάδι·
τοὔνεκ' ἐν ἀπρήκτοισι καθήμεθα, κοὐχὶ λαλεῦντες
εὕδομεν ὡς εὕδειν τοῖc φιλέουσι θέμις;   3205

VIII

μικκὴ καὶ μελανεῦcα Φιλαίνιον, ἀλλὰ cελίνων
οὐλοτέρη καὶ μνοῦ χρῶτα τερεινοτέρη
καὶ κεστοῦ φωνεῦcα μαγώτερα καὶ παρέχουσα
πάντα καὶ αἰτῆcαι πολλάκι φειδομένη.
5 τοιαύτην cτέργοιμι Φιλαίνιον ἄχρις ἂν εὕρω   3210
  ἄλλην, ὦ χρυcέη Κύπρι, τελειοτέρην.

5 τοῦτ' P: ταῦτ' Pl   7 βαΰζοις P: -ζεις Pl   8 ἥμεθα Pl: ἡμέραι P, ἡμέρα
C | Ναϊάδος C: Νηϊάδος Pl, ἀϊάδος P

VI A.P. 5.115 Φιλοδήμου [J] γραμματικοῦ πολλὰς Δημοῦς φιλήσαντος, διὰ
τοῦτο καὶ Φιλοδήμου Pl A τοῦ αὐτοῦ [sc. Φιλοδήμου]
1 Δημοῦς CPl: Δημούςης ut vid. P   3 πάλι Νυσιακῆς C: πάλι Ν**ιακῆς P,
πάλιν Ἀσιακῆς Pl   6 ἔχοι P: -ει Pl

they are angry with you.' Thus would I cry aloud all day and give you warning, but the sea of Io paid as much heed to my words as you did. So now you may howl and cry your heart out as you do, while I rest on the bosom of Naias.

VI

Philodemus, 'lover of Demo'

I fell in love with Demo, born in Paphos; no great wonder. Secondly with Demo of Samos; still, no great wonder. Then again with Demo of Nysa third; there it ceased to be a joke. And fourthly with Demo of Argolis: I suppose the Fates themselves named me 'Philodemus', that I might always be hotly in love with a Demo.

VII

An inactive lover

I cheated my husband and came, in the middle of the night, soaked in the heavy rain too. So must we only sit, and nothing done, not talking and sleeping as lovers ought to sleep?

VIII

The charms of Philaenion

Small and swarthy is Philaenion, but curlier-haired than celery, her skin tenderer than down, her voice more enchanting than Aphrodite's girdle. She grants every favour and often spares to ask a fee. May such a Philaenion be my beloved, golden Aphrodite,—until I find another more perfect.

VII *A.P.* 5.120 Φιλοδήμου [J] εἰς τὴν ἑαυτοῦ μοιχαλίδα νυκτὸς πρὸς αὐτὸν ἐλθοῦσαν caret Pl

VIII *A.P.* 5.121 τοῦ αὐτοῦ [sc. Φιλοδήμου] [J] εἰς Φιλέννιον ἑταίραν ἔπαινος. θαυμάσιος Pl A τοῦ αὐτοῦ [sc. Φιλοδήμου] Suid s.vv. μαγώτερα (1 ἀλλὰ–3 μαγ.), μνοῦς (2 καὶ–τερ.), κεστός (3–μαγ.)
1 Φιλαίνιον Pl: -λέννιον P 2 μνοῦ PSuid.: ἀμνοῦ Pl

IX

νυκτερινὴ δίκερως φιλοπάννυχε φαῖνε, Cελήνη,
φαῖνε δι᾽ εὐτρήτων βαλλομένη θυρίδων·
αὔγαζε χρυσέην Καλλίστιον. ἐς τὰ φιλεύντων
ἔργα κατοπτεύειν οὐ φθόνος ἀθανάτηι.
5 ὀλβίζεις καὶ τήνδε καὶ ἡμέας, οἶδα, Cελήνη·
καὶ γὰρ σὴν ψυχὴν ἔφλεγεν Ἐνδυμίων.

3215

X

οὔπω σοι καλύκων γυμνὸν θέρος οὐδὲ μελαίνει
βότρυς ὁ παρθενίους πρωτοβολῶν χάριτας,
ἀλλ᾽ ἤδη θοὰ τόξα νέοι θήγουσιν Ἔρωτες,
Λυσιδίκη, καὶ πῦρ τύφεται ἐγκρύφιον.
5 φεύγωμεν, δυσέρωτες, ἕως βέλος οὐκ ἐπὶ νευρῆι·
μάντις ἐγὼ μεγάλης αὐτίκα πυρκαϊῆς.

3220

XI

ψαλμὸς καὶ λαλιὴ καὶ κωτίλον ὄμμα καὶ ᾠδή
Ξανθίππης καὶ πῦρ ἄρτι καταρχόμενον,
ὦ ψυχή, φλέξει σε· τὸ δ᾽ ἐκ τίνος ἢ πότε καὶ πῶς
οὐκ οἶδα· γνώσηι, δύσμορε, τυφομένη.

3225

XII

ὦ ποδός, ὦ κνήμης, ὦ τῶν ἀπόλωλα δικαίως
μηρῶν, ὦ γλουτῶν, ὦ κτενός, ὦ λαγόνων,

IX *A.P.* 5.123 Φιλοδήμου   [C] εἰς Καλλίστιον τὴν ἑταίραν   caret Pl
4 φθόνος C: φόβος P
X *A.P.* 5.124 τοῦ αὐτοῦ [sc. Φιλοδήμου]   [C] εἰς Λυσιδίκην παρθένον   Pl A
τοῦ αὐτοῦ [sc. Φιλοδήμου]
3 θήγουσιν CPl: -σαι ut vid. P   6 μεγάλης P: πολλῆς Pl

IX

Lovers in the moonlight

Shine, Lady of the night, two-horned, lover of night-long
revelry, shine, Moon, through latticed windows falling; shed
your light on golden Callistion. We bear no malice, that a
goddess should spy upon the deeds of lovers. You count us
happy, both her and me, I know it, Moon; your own soul was
set on fire by Endymion.

X

To Lysidicê, whose charms are not yet mature

Your summer-fruit is not yet bare of the bud, nor dark yet is
the grape that puts forth its early maiden-charms; but already
the youthful Loves are whetting their swift arrows, Lysidicê,
and a fire is smouldering hidden. Ill-starred lovers, let us fly
before the shaft is on the string. I prophesy a mighty blaze in a
moment.

XI

The talents of Xanthippê

Xanthippê's harping, and her talking, and her eyes that say so
much, and her singing, and her flame lately starting will burn
you up, my soul. But why, and when, and how, I know not;
you will learn, unhappy soul, when you are afire.

XII

The charms of an Italian girl outweigh her defects

O foot, O leg, O thighs, my just undoing, O buttocks, O scallop,
O flanks, O shoulders, O breasts, O slender neck, O hands, O

XI *A.P.* 5.131 Φιλοδήμου [C] εἰc Ξανθίππην ὁμοίωc Pl A τοῦ αὐτοῦ [sc.
Φιλοδήμου]
1 λαλιὴ Pl: -ιῆι P

XII *A.P.* 5.132 τοῦ αὐτοῦ [sc. Φιλοδήμου] [C] εἰc τὴν αὐτὴν Ξανθίππην
μανίαc μεστὸν καὶ θαυμαστικόν Pl A τοῦ αὐτοῦ [sc. Φιλοδήμου] Suid. s.v.
ῥαδινή (1 ὢ ποδ.–κνήμ. + 3 ὢ τοῦ–τραχ.)

ὦ ὤμοιν, ὦ μαστῶν, ὦ τοῦ ῥαδινοῖο τραχήλου,   3230
  ὦ χειρῶν, ὦ τῶν μαίνομαι ὀμματίων,
5 ὦ κατατεχνοτάτου κινήματος, ὦ περιάλλων
  γλωττισμῶν, ὦ τῶν θῦέ με φωναρίων·
εἰ δ' 'Οπικὴ καὶ Φλῶρα καὶ οὐκ ἄιδουσα τὰ Cαπφοῦς,
  καὶ Περσεὺς 'Ινδῆς ἠράcατ' 'Ανδρομέδης.   3235

XIII

δακρύεις, ἐλεεινὰ λαλεῖς, περίεργα θεωρεῖς,   (3236)
  ζηλοτυπεῖς, ἅπτηι πολλάκι, πυκνὰ φιλεῖς·
ταῦτα μέν ἐcτιν ἐρῶντος. ὅταν δ' εἴπω 'παράκειμαι'
  †καὶ cὺ μένειc† ἁπλῶς οὐδὲν ἐρῶντος ἔχεις.

XIV

Ξανθὼ κηρόπλαcτε μυρόχροε μουcοπρόcωπε,   3240
  εὔλαλε, διπτερύγων καλὸν ἄγαλμα Πόθων,
ψῆλόν μοι χερcὶν δροcιναῖς μύρον· ἐν μονοκλίνωι
  δεῖ με λιθοδμήτωι, δεῖ ποτε πετριδίωι
5 εὔδειν ἀθανάτως πουλὺν χρόνον. ἆιδε πάλιν μοι,
  Ξανθάριον, ναὶ ναὶ τὸ γλυκὺ τοῦτο μέλος.   3245

XV

Κύπρι γαληναίη φιλονύμφιε, Κύπρι δικαίων
  cύμμαχε, Κύπρι Πόθων μῆτερ ἀελλοπόδων,

---

3 ὦ ὤμοιν Jacobs: ὤμοιν P, ὦ ὠμῶν Pl   5 κατατεχνοτάτου P: κακοτ-
Pl   6 γλωττιcμῶν CPl: γλωτιc- P | θῦ' ἐμὲ P (θύεμε): κλῶμαι Pl   7 οὐκ
ἄιδουcα CPl: οὐ καὶ ἰδοῦcα (?) P

XIII A.P. 5.306 Φιλοδήμου   Pl A Φιλοδήμου
4 μένειc P: μένηις Pl | οὐδὲν ἐρῶντος ἔχεις C (iterumque Cγρ in marg.) Pl:
ἐρῶντος οὐδὲν ἔχεις P

darling eyes that have driven me mad, O skilfullest vibrations, O incomparable kisses, O whispered words that were the death of me,—what though she be an Oscan, and with a name like 'Flora', unable to sing the verse of Sappho? Did not Perseus love Andromeda, though she was an Indian?

XIII

An inactive lover

You weep, you talk in piteous tones, you cannot keep your eyes off me, you are jealous, you touch me often, you keep on kissing me. All that is like a lover. But when I say 'Here I lie beside you; ⟨what are you waiting for?'⟩ then you simply have nothing of the lover in you.

XIV

To Xantho

Xantho, little waxwork doll, skin-scented, with a Muse's face, sweet of voice, the wingèd Passions' pretty pride and joy, pluck me a fragrance from the lyre with those dewy fingers; in lonely-bedded rock-built cavelet I am doomed, yes doomed some day to sleep a time unending-long. Sing me again, my little Xantho, —yes, yes, that is the song, the one all sweetness.

XV

A prayer to Aphrodite

Cypris, lady of calm seas, lover of bridegrooms, Cypris, comrade-in-arms of the righteous, Cypris, mother of stormy

XIV *A.P.* 9.570 Φιλοδήμου   caret Pl
1 Ζανθὼ κηρόπλαστε Huschke: ξανθοκηρόπλαστε P   **3** ψῆλόν Pᵖᶜ (scilicet litt. η in marg. adscripta): ψιλον Pᵃᶜ | χερσὶν Schneider: -σὶ P   **4** δεῖ ποτε Kaibel: δὲ ποτι P   post v. 4 versus duo suppositicios add. P
XV *A.P.* 10.21 Φιλοδήμου   Pl A Φιλοδήμου
1 δικαίων P: -αίοις Pl

Κύπρι, τὸν ἡμίσπαστον ἀπὸ κροκέων ἐμὲ παστῶν,
   τὸν χιόσι ψυχὴν Κελτίσι νιφόμενον,
5 Κύπρι, τὸν ἡσύχιόν με, τὸν οὐδενὶ κοῦφα λαλεῦντα,   3250
   τὸν σέο πορφυρίωι κλυζόμενον πελάγει,
Κύπρι φιλορμίστειρα φιλόργιε, σῶιζέ με, Κύπρι,
   Ναϊακοὺς ἤδη, δεσπότι, πρὸς λιμένας.

XVI

Δημώ με κτείνει καὶ Θέρμιον, ἡ μὲν ἑταίρη
   †Δημὼ ἡ† δ' οὔπω Κύπριν ἐπισταμένη·   3255
καὶ τῆς μὲν ψαύω, τῆς δ' οὐ θέμις. οὐ μὰ σέ, Κύπρι,
   οὐκ οἶδ' ἣν εἰπεῖν δεῖ με ποθεινοτέρην.
5 Δημάριον λέξω τὴν παρθένον· οὐ γὰρ ἕτοιμα
   βούλομαι, ἀλλὰ ποθῶ πᾶν τὸ φυλασσόμενον.

XVII

ἑπτὰ τριηκόντεσσιν ἐπέρχονται λυκάβαντες,   3260
   ἤδη μοι βιότου σχιζόμεναι σελίδες·
ἤδη καὶ λευκαί με κατασπείρουσιν ἔθειραι,
   Ξανθίππη, συνετῆς ἄγγελοι ἡλικίης,
5 ἀλλ' ἔτι μοι ψαλμός τε λάλος κῶμοί τε μέλονται
   καὶ πῦρ ἀπλήστωι τύφεται ἐν κραδίηι·   3265
αὐτὴν ἀλλὰ τάχιστα κορωνίδα γράψατε, Μοῦσαι,
   ταύτην ἡμετέρης, δεσποτίδες, μανίης.

XVIII

ἠράσθην, τίς δ' οὐχί; κεκώμακα, τίς δ' ἀμύητος
   κώμων; ἀλλ' ἐμάνην· ἐκ τίνος; οὐχὶ θεοῦ;

---

3 κροκέων Pl: -καίων P   4 νιφόμενον Brunck: νειφ- PPl   5 οὐδενὶ P:
οὐδὲν Pl | κοῦφα Brunck: κωφὰ PPl   8 Ναϊακοὺς Jacobs: Ναϊκακοὺς P,
'Ρωμαϊκοὺς Pl | δεσπότι Pl: -τη P

XVI A.P. 12.173 Φιλοδήμου   App. B.-V. 11 (om. 5-6)   caret Pl
XVII A.P. 11.41 Φιλοδήμου   Pl в s.a.n.
2 βιότου Pl: βρότου P   3 spat. vac. relicto om. Pl   4 Ξανθίππη

racing passions, me, Cypris, half-torn from saffron bridal-
chamber, my soul blizzarded by Celtic snows, me, Cypris, the
peaceable, whose word all men might trust, me now awash on
your dark-blue sea, Cypris, lover of harbour's rest, lover of
secret rites, bring me safe, Cypris, now, mistress, to the haven
of Naias.

XVI

The maiden preferred to the courtesan

Demo and Thermion are the death of me, the one a courtesan
⟨   ⟩ the other still ignorant of love. The one I fondle, the
other I may not; by your majesty I vow, Cyprian, I know not
which to call the more desirable. I will say it is little Demo, the
maiden; for I do not want the ready-made, but yearn for all
that is barred and bolted.

XVII

The age of discretion

Seven years come to join thirty, so many pages already torn
from my life. Already too, Xanthippê, white hairs besprinkle
me, announcers of discretion's years. Yet still the lyre-song's
voice and revelry are dear to me, and the fire smoulders in my
insatiable heart. Come, Muses, my sovereigns, quickly write
this same 'Finis' to my insanity.

XVIII

'Lusisti satis...'

I loved, as who has not? I revelled, and who is not initiate in
revelry? But I went mad,—by whose will, if not a god's? Let

Salm.: -ίπη P, -ίππης Pl   6 τύφεται ἐν Jacobs: τύφετ' ἐν P, τύφετ' ἐνὶ Pl
7-8 om. Pl

XVIII *A.P.* 5.112 Φιλοδήμου   [J] ὅτι ἐν νεότητι ἐρωτόληπτος ὢν ἐν τῶι γήραι
μόλις ἐσωφρόνησε   Pl A τοῦ αὐτοῦ [sc. Φιλοδήμου]
1 κεκώμακα P: -κε Pl   2 θεοῦ Pl: θῦ P

ἐρρίφθω, πολιὴ γὰρ ἐπείγεται ἀντὶ μελαίνης   3270
    θρὶξ ἤδη, cυνετῆc ἄγγελοc ἡλικίηc.
5 καὶ παίζειν ὅτε καιρόc, ἐπαίξαμεν· ἡνίκα καὶ νῦν
    οὐκέτι, λωϊτέρηc φροντίδοc ἁψόμεθα.

XIX

Ἰνοῦc ὦ Μελικέρτα cύ τε γλαυκὴ μεδέουcα
    Λευκοθέη πόντου δαῖμον ἀλεξίκακε   3275
Νηρήιδων τε χοροὶ καὶ κύματα καὶ cύ, Πόcειδον,
    καὶ Θρήϊξ ἀνέμων πρηύτατε Ζέφυρε,
5 ἵλαοί με φέροιτε διὰ πλατὺ κῦμα φυγόντα
    cῶιον ἐπὶ γλυκερὴν ἠιόνα Πειραέωc.

XX

ἤδη καὶ ῥόδον ἐcτὶ καὶ ἀκμάζων ἐρέβινθοc   3280
    καὶ καυλοὶ κράμβηc, Cωcύλε, πρωτότομοι
καὶ μαίνη †ζαλαγεῦcα† καὶ ἀρτιπαγὴc ἁλίτυροc
    καὶ θριδάκων οὔλων ἀβροφυῆ πέταλα·
5 ἡμεῖc δ᾽ οὔτ᾽ ἀκτῆc ἐπιβαίνομεν οὔτ᾽ ἐν ἀπόψει
    γινόμεθ᾽ ὡc αἰεί, Cωcύλε, τὸ πρότερον·   3285
καὶ μὴν Ἀντιγένηc καὶ Βάκχιοc ἐχθὲc ἔπαιζον,
    νῦν δ᾽ αὐτοὺc θάψαι cήμερον ἐκφέρομεν.

XXI

λευκοΐνουc πάλι δὴ καὶ ψάλματα καὶ πάλι Χίουc
    οἴνουc καὶ πάλι δὴ cμύρναν ἔχειν Cυρίην
καὶ πάλι κωμάζειν καὶ ἔχειν πάλι διψάδα πόρνην   3290
    οὐκ ἐθέλω· μιcῶ ταῦτα τὰ πρὸc μανίην.

3 πολιὴ C: πολιῆι P, πολλὴ Pl   6 λωϊτέρηc P: λωοτ- Pl
XIX *A.P.* 6.349 Φιλοδήμου   caret Pl
6 γλυκερὴν post Dorvillium (-ρὰν) Kaibel: γλυκὺν P | ἠιόνα Πειραέωc C: ϊον ἀπειραεοc P
XX *A.P.* 9.412 Φιλοδήμου   [C] εἰc Cωcύλον τινὰ φίλον   Pl A Φιλοδήμου

it all go; already gray hair comes hurrying in place of black, announcer of discretion's years. When it was time for play, we played; now that it is no longer so, we will apply ourselves to higher thoughts.

XIX
Prayer for a safe sea-passage

Melicertes, son of Ino, and you, sea-green Leucothea, queen of the ocean, spirit evil-averting, and choirs of Nereids, and waves, and you, Poseidon, and Thracian Zephyr, gentlest of winds, be favourable and bear me over the broad waters, escaping safe to the Piraeus' welcome shore.

XX
Death interrupts a holiday

Already roses and chick-peas are at their best, Sosylus, and first-cut cabbage-stalks, and ⟨   ⟩ sprats, and fresh-set salty cheese, and delicate leaves of curly lettuces; but you and I go not upon the beach, nor are we to be found at the belvedere, as always, Sosylus, in times past. It is but yesterday that Antigenes and Bacchius were enjoying life, and now today we are carrying them out for burial.

XXI
Virtuous pleasures preferred to the extravagant

I want no more white-violet garlands or lyre-song, no more Chian wines and no more Syrian frankincense, no more revelry and no more tipsy courtesans. I hate those things; they lead to

2 καυλοί Pl: -λοῖο P | πρωτότομοι Page: -μου PPl   3 ἀλίτυρος PᵃᶜPl: ἀλὶ τυρός Pᵖᶜ   4 ἀβροφυῆ Scaliger: ἀφρο- PPl   6 γινόμεθ' P: γιγν- Pl
XXI *A.P.* 11.34 Φιλοδήμου   caret Pl
1 δὴ Apogr. Voss.: δει P   2 δὴ Apogr. Voss.: δεῖ P   3 ἔχειν Brunck: -ει P

5 ἀλλά με ναρκίσσοις ἀναδήσατε καὶ πλαγιαύλων
  γεύσατε καὶ κροκίνοις χρίσατε γυῖα μύροις
  καὶ Μιτυληναίωι τὸν πνεύμονα τέγξατε Βάκχωι
  καὶ συζεύξατέ μοι φωλάδα παρθενικήν.   3295

XXII

κράμβην Ἀρτεμίδωρος, Ἀρίσταρχος δὲ τάριχον,
  βολβίσκους δ' ἡμῖν δῶκεν Ἀθηναγόρας,
ἡπάτιον Φιλόδημος, Ἀπολλοφάνης δὲ δύο μνᾶς
  χοιρείου, καὶ τρεῖς ἦσαν ἀπ' ἐχθὲς ἔτι·
5 †ὠιὸν† καὶ στεφάνους καὶ σάμβαλα καὶ μύρον ἡμῖν   3300
  λάμβανε, παῖ· δεκάτης εὐθὺ θέλω παράγειν.

XXIII

αὔριον εἰς λιτήν σε καλιάδα, φίλτατε Πείσων,
  ἐξ ἐνάτης ἕλκει μουσοφιλὴς ἔταρος
εἰκάδα δειπνίζων ἐνιαύσιον· εἰ δ' ἀπολείψεις
  οὔθατα καὶ Βρομίου Χιογενῆ πρόποσιν,   3305
5 ἀλλ' ἑτάρους ὄψει παναληθέας, ἀλλ' ἐπακούσηι
  Φαιήκων γαίης πουλὺ μελιχρότερα.
ἢν δέ ποτε στρέψηις καὶ ἐς ἡμέας ὄμματα, Πείσων,
  ἄξομεν ἐκ λιτῆς εἰκάδα πιοτέρην.

XXIV

τὴν πρότερον †θυμέλην† μήτ' ἔμβλεπε μήτε παρέλθηις·   3310
  νῦν ἄπαγε, δραχμῆς †εἰς κολοκορδόκολα†.
καὶ σῦκον δραχμῆς ἓν γίνεται· ἢν δ' ἀναμείνηις,
  χίλια. τοῖς πτωχοῖς ὁ χρόνος ἐστὶ θεός.

XXII *A.P.* 11.35 τοῦ αὐτοῦ [sc. Φιλοδήμου]   caret Pl
5 στεφάνους Brunck: -νος P   6 παῖ Meineke: καὶ P
XXIII *A.P.* 11.44 Φιλοδήμου   caret Pl

madness. But wreathe me with narcissus, give me a sample of the cross-flute, anoint my limbs with saffron unguents, moisten my lungs with wine of Mytilenê, and unite me with a stay-at-home maiden.

XXII

Preparations for a dinner-party

Artemidorus has given us cabbage, Aristarchus salt fish, Athenagoras baby onions, Philodemus a small liver, Apollophanes two pounds of pork (and there were three left over from yesterday). Get us 〈 〉, my lad, and garlands and slippers and unguent; I want to bring dinner in at four o'clock sharp.

XXIII

An invitation to dine

Tomorrow from three o'clock, my dear Piso, your poetic friend drags you to his humble cottage, giving a dinner for the anniversary of the Twentieth. If you find no udders or Chiosborn draughts of wine, yet you shall see true friends, yet you shall hear things far sweeter than Phaeacia did. And if ever you turn your eyes even toward me, Piso, we shall celebrate a richer instead of a humbler Twentieth.

XXIV

Prices are lowered by plenty

Neither look at nor enter the former 〈 〉; for the present 〈 〉. A single fig may cost a drachma; you may get a thousand if you bide your time. Time is the beggar's god.

2 ἕταρος Salm.: -ρις P   3 ἀπολείψεις Brunck: -ψηις P
XXIV A.P. 10.103 Φιλοδήμου   Pl A s.a.n.
3 ἐν γίνεται Scaliger: ἐγγίνεται P, ἐγγίγν- Pl

XXV

πέντε δίδωσιν ἑνὸς τῆι δεῖναι ὁ δεῖνα τάλαντα
καὶ βινεῖ φρίccων καὶ μὰ τὸν οὐδὲ καλήν·   3315
πέντε δ' ἐγὼ δραχμὰς τῶν δώδεκα Λυσιανάσσηι,
καὶ βινῶ πρὸς τῶι κρείccονα καὶ φανερῶc.
5 πάντως ἤτοι ἐγὼ φρένας οὐκ ἔχω ἢ τό γε λοιπόν
τοὺς κείνου πελέκει δεῖ διδύμους ἀφελεῖν.

XXVI

ἐνθάδε τῆς τρυφερῆς μαλακὸν ῥέθος, ἐνθάδε κεῖται   3320
Τρυγόνιον cαβακῶν ἄνθεμα cαλμακίδων,
ἧι καλύβη καὶ δοῦμος ἐνέπρεπεν, ἧι φιλοπαίγμων
cτωμυλίη, μήτηρ ἣν ἐφίληcε θεῶν,
5 ἣ μούνη cτέρξαcα τὰ Κύπριδος ἡμιγυναίκων
ὄργια καὶ φίλτρων Λαΐδος ἁψαμένη.   3325
φῦε κατὰ cτήληc, ἱερὴ κόνι, τῆι φιλοβάκχωι
μὴ βάτον ἀλλ' ἁπαλὰς λευκοΐων κάλυκαc.

XXVII

ὁ πρὶν ἐγὼ καὶ πέντε καὶ ἐννέα, νῦν, Ἀφροδίτη,
ἓν μόλις ἐκ πρώτης νυκτὸς ἐς ἥλιον.
οἴμοι καὶ τοῦτ' αὐτὸ κατὰ βραχύ, πολλάκι δ' ἤδη   3330
ἡμιθαλές, θνήιcκει· τοῦτο τὸ Τερμέριον.
5 ὦ γῆρας γῆρας, τί ποθ' ὕcτερον ἢν ἀφίκηαι
ποιήcεις, ὅτε νῦν ὧδε μαραινόμεθα;

XXV *A.P.* 5.126 Φιλοδήμου   [C] τωθαcτικὸν ἐπί τινι ἐρῶντι cαπρῶι καὶ
πολλὰ παρεχομένωι ταῖc ἑταίραιc   caret Pl
3 δραχμὰς Reiske: δραγμᾶc P | Λυcιανάccηι Reiske: τῆι Λυc. P
XXVI *A.P.* 7.222 [C] Φιλοδήμου   [J] εἰc Τρυγόνιον ἑταίραν τοῦ Cαβακῶν [C:
Cακῶν J] ἔθνουc ὁρμωμένην   Pl A Φιλοδήμου   Suid. s.vv. ῥέθοc (1–2 Τρυγ.),
cαβακῶν (2)

XXV

The worse and the better bargain in love

What's his name gives what's her name five talents for a single favour, and has her in fear and trembling, an ugly girl too, goodness knows. Now I give Lysianassa five drachmas for twelve favours, and what is more I have a better wench and do it openly. The fact must be, either I am out of my senses, or he ought in future to have his manhood chopped off with an axe.

XXVI

Epitaph for an effeminate priest of Cybelê

Here lie that lady-like creature's tender limbs, here lies Trygonion, idol of nerveless emasculates, well suited to the cabin and the council and their playful gossip; whom the Mother of the gods loved, who alone among the effeminates adored the Cyprian's rites and took to the seductions of a Laïs. Holy earth, put forth against this orgy-lover's headstone not brambles but the delicate buds of white-violets.

XXVII

An impotent lover

I who in time past was good for five or nine times, now, Aphrodite, hardly manage once from early night to sunrise. The thing itself,—already often only at half-strength,—is gradually dying. That's the last straw. Old age, old age, what will you do later when you come to me, if even now I am as languid as this?

2 cαβακῶν CPl: **cακῶν P   5 ἡμιγυναίκων Paton: ἀμφὶ γυναικῶν PPl
6 ἀψαμένη CPl: -να P   8 λευκοΐων CPl: -όϊον P
XXVII *A.P.* 11.30 Φιλοδήμου   caret Pl
3 τοῦτ' αὐτὸ Jacobs: τοῦτο P   4 ἡμιθαλές Page: -θανές P | Τερμέριον Pauw:
-μόριον P

XXVIII

Ἀντικράτης ἤιδει τὰ σφαιρικὰ μᾶλλον Ἀράτου
πολλῶι, τὴν ἰδίην δ' οὐκ ἐνόει γένεσιν·   3335
δϲτάζειν γὰρ ἔφη πότερ' ἐν Κριῶι γεγένηται
ἢ Διδύμοις ἢ τοῖς Ἰχθύσιν ἀμφοτέροις.
5 εὕρηται δὲ σαφῶς ἐν τοῖς τρισί· καὶ γὰρ ὀχευτής
καὶ μῶρος μαλακός τ' ἐστὶ καὶ ὀψοφάγος.

XXIX

τρισσοὺς ἀθανάτους χωρεῖ λίθος· ἁ κεφαλὰ γάρ   3340
μανύει τρανῶς Πᾶνα τὸν αἰγόκερων,
στέρνα δὲ καὶ νηδὺς Ἡρακλέα, λοιπὰ δὲ μηρῶν
καὶ κνήμας Ἑρμῆς ὁ πτερόπους ἔλαχεν.
5 θύειν ἀρνήσηι, ξένε, μηκέτι· τοῦ γὰρ ἑνός coι
θύματος οἱ τρισσοὶ δαίμονες ἁπτόμεθα.   3345

XXX

Hor. *Serm.* 1.2.119 seqq.

            parabilem amo uenerem facilemque.
illam 'post paulo', 'sed pluris', 'si exierit uir',
Gallis, hanc Philodemus ait sibi, quae neque magno
stet pretio neque cunctetur cum est iussa uenire.

XXVIII *A.P.* 11.318 Φιλοδήμου   Pl B s.a.n.
2 ἰδίην δ' P: δ' ἰδίην Pl   6 μαλακός τ' Pl: μαλακῶς P

XXVIII

The nativity of Anticrates

Anticrates knew the doctrine of the spheres far better than
Aratus did, but was ignorant of his own nativity. He was uncertain, he said, whether he was born under the Ram or the
Twins or the pair of Fishes. Clearly we can detect him in all
three; for he is a lecher and a fool, an effeminate and a glutton.

XXIX

On a statue combining Pan, Heracles, and Hermes

The stone has room for three immortals; the head shows
clearly Pan the goat-horned, the breast and belly show Heracles,
while the rest of him, thighs and legs, belong to wing-footed
Hermes. Stranger, refuse no longer to make sacrifice; we are
three gods to lay hands on your single offering.

XXX

The complaisant woman preferred to the coy

' *The Venus I love is procurable and complaisant. The one who says
"A little later" or "Only it will cost you more" or "If my husband
goes out",—let the Galli have her, said Philodemus, claiming for
himself the woman who is neither high-priced nor slow to come when
bidden.*'

XXIX *A.Pl.* (A) 234 Φιλοδήμου   εἰς ἕτερον ἄγαλμα Πανός   caret P
4 κνήμας Page: -μης Pl

ΠΟΛΕΜΩΝΟC

I

ἑπτὰ βοῶν cφραγῖδα βραχὺc λίθοc εἶχεν ἴαcπιc   (3346)
   ὡc μίαν, ὡc πάcαc ἔμπνοα δερκομέναc·
καὶ τάχα κἂν †ἀπέρεψε† τὰ βοίδια, νῦν δὲ κέκλειται
   τῆι χρυcῆι μάνδρηι τὸ βραχὺ βουκόλιον.

II

ἡ πτωχῶν χαρίεccα πανοπλίη ἀρτολάγυνοc   3350
   αὕτη καὶ δροcερῶν ἐκ πετάλων cτέφανοc
καὶ τοῦτο φθιμένοιο προάcτιον ἱερὸν ὀcτεῦν
   ἐγκεφάλου, ψυχῆc φρούριον ἀκρότατον.
5 'πῖνε', λέγει τὸ γλύμμα, 'καὶ ἔcθιε καὶ περίκειcο
   ἄνθεα· τοιοῦτοι γινόμεθ' ἐξαπίνηc'.   3355

III

ἢ τὸ φιλεῖν περίγραψον, Ἔρωc, ὅλον ἢ τὸ φιλεῖcθαι   (3356)
   πρόcθεc, ἵν' ἢ λύcηιc τὸν πόθον ἢ κεράcηιc.

ΚΟΙΝΤΟΥ

I

᾽Ακρεῖται Φοίβωι, Βιθυνίδοc ὃc τόδε χώρηc
   κράcπεδον αἰγιαλοῖc γειτονέον cυνέχει,
Δᾶμιc ὁ κυρτευτήc, ψάμμωι κέραc αἰὲν ἐρείδων,   3360
   φρουρητὸν κήρυκ' αὐτοφυεῖ cκόλοπι

I *A.P.* 9.746 Πολέμωνοc βαcιλέωc εἰc δακτύλιον Pl A Πολέμωνοc βαcιλέωc εἰc ἕτερον
1 cφραγῖδα P: cφρηγ- Pl   3 κέκλειται P: -ειcται Pl
II *A.P.* 11.38 Πολέμωνοc βαcιλέωc   Pl B s.a.n. *C.I.G.* II 7298 (5 s.)

POLEMON

I

On a stone engraved with cows

The little stone of jasper had a seal of seven cows as one, all as if with the breath and light of life. Perhaps they would have wandered off, those cattle; as it is, the little herd is confined in the golden byre.

II

'Memento mori'

Here is the beggar's joy, his bread-flask panoply, and a wreath of dewy leaves, and here is a sacred bone, the dead brain's outpost, lofty citadel of the soul. 'Drink' says the carving 'and eat and put flowers about you, for like to this we suddenly become.'

III

Love must be mutual

Either delete Loving altogether, God of Love, or insert Being Loved, so that you may either dissolve my desire or blend it.

QUINTUS

I

Dedication by a fisherman

To Phoebus of the Cape, who guards this fringe of Bithynian land neighbouring the shores, Damis the weel-fisher, ever thrusting the horn into the sand, has dedicated a Triton-shell

---

III *A.P.* 5.68 [C] Λουκιλλίου, οἱ δὲ Πολέμωνος τοῦ Ποντικοῦ   Pl A Λουκιλλίου Syll.E εἰς Ἔρωτα

I *A.P.* 6.230 Κοίντου   caret Pl
1 Ἀκρεῖται Valesius: ἀρίτα P   **2** γειτονέον cυνέχει Salm.: γειτονέουcιν ἔχεις C, γειτονέοιcιν ἔχοιc P

5 θῆκε γέρας λιτὸν μέν, ἐπ' εὐσεβίηι δ' ὁ γεραιός
εὐχόμενος νούςων ἐκτὸς ἰδεῖν ᾿Αίδην.

CABINOY

I

ʒμίνθος ὁ παντοίης δαιτὸς λίχνος, οὐδὲ μυάγρης
δειλός, ὁ κἀκ θανάτου κέρδεα ληιʒόμενος,   3365
νευρολάλον Φοίβου χορδὴν θρίσεν· ἡ δ' ἐπὶ πῆχυν
ἑλκομένη θηρὸς λαιμὸν ἀπεβρόχιςεν.
5 τόξων εὐςτοχίην θαυμάʒομεν· ὃς δὲ κατ' ἐχθρῶν
ἤδη καὶ κιθάρην εὔςτοχον ὅπλον ἔχει.

II

Πανὶ Βίτων χίμαρον, Νύμφαις ῥόδα, θύρςα Λυαίωι,   3370
τριςςὸν ὑπ' εὐπετάλοις δῶρον ἔθηκε φόβαις.
δαίμονες ἀλλὰ δέχοιςθε κεχαρμένοι, αὔξετε δ' αἰεί
Πὰν ἀγέλην, Νύμφαι πίδακα, Βάκχε γάνος.

CKEYOΛA

I

αἱ χίμαροι, τί ποτ' ἄρα τὰ μὲν θύμα καὶ τιθύμαλλα
λείπετε καὶ χλοερὴν αἰγίνομον βοτάνην,   3375
γυρὰ δ' ἐπ' ἀλλήλαις ςκιρτήματα γαῦρα τίθεςθε
ἀμφὶ τὸν ὑλιβάτην ἀλλόμεναι Νόμιον;
5 οὐκ ἀπὸ πυγμαχίης ἀποπαύςετε, μή ποτ' ἀπεχθής
ἀντήςηι κορύνη χειρὸς ἀπ' αἰπολικῆς;

I A.P. 9.410 [C] Τυλλίου Cαβηνοῦ [in rasura; incertum quid scripserit P]
εἰς μῦν φαγόντα κιθάρας χορδὴν καὶ περιπλακέντα ἐν αὐτῆι καὶ ἀποπνιγέντα
Pl A Τυλλίου Γεμίνου
I ʒμίνθος Wiegand: cμ- PPl   6 εὔςτοχον Pl: ἄςτ- P

II A.P. 6.158 Cαβίνου [C] γραμματικοῦ   Pl A Cαβίνου   Suid. s.vv. θύρςος(1 s.),
φοίβη (2), γάνος (4)

protected by natural spikes; a slight gift indeed, but with piety, as in old age he prayed to see death without disease.

SABINUS

I

On a mouse, strangled by a lyre-string

A mouse, that glutton for every kind of feast, not even shy of the trap, that pirate of profit even from death, snapped one of Phoebus' string-vocal chords; recoiling to the bridge, it strangled the creature's throat. We marvel at the bow's good aiming; the god now has the cithara also as a weapon of good aim against his enemies.

II

A triple dedication to Pan

To Pan a kid, to the Nymphs roses, wands to Bacchus,—triple the gift that Biton has dedicated under the leafy foliage. Divinities, do you but accept with gladness and ever give increase, Pan to his flock, Nymphs to his well, Bacchus to his wine.

SCAEVOLA

I

Goats frolic round a statue of Pan

My goats, why leave the thyme and spurge and green goat-pasture grass, and start high-spirited leaps upon each other in a ring, jumping around the forest-wanderer, the Pastor? Give over your boxing-matches, or the hated club shall come to meet you from the goat-herd's hand.

2 φόβαις Pl: φοίβαις CSuid., φοίβωι P   4 πίδακα PlSuid.: πήδ- P

I *A.P.* 9.217 [C] Μουκίου Cκευόλα   εἰc αἰγῶν ποίμνιον διὰ τὸ cκιρτᾶν ἐν ταῖc νομαῖc   caret Pl
3 ἀλλήλαιc Salm.: -λαιcι P   6 αἰπολικῆc Salm.: αἰπολικᾶc P

ΣΕΚΟΥΝΔΟΥ

I

ὁλκὰς ἀμέτρητον πελάγους ἀνύσασα κέλευθον   3380
καὶ τοσάκις χαροποῖς κύμασι νηξαμένη,
ἣν ὁ μέλας οὔτ᾽ Εὖρος ἐπόντισεν οὔτ᾽ ἐπὶ χέρσον
ἤλασε χειμερίων ἄγριον οἶδμα Νότων,
5 ἐν πυρὶ νῦν ναυηγὸς ἐγὼ χθονὶ μέμφομ᾽ ἀπίστωι,
νῦν ἁλὸς ἡμετέρης ὕδατα διζομένη.   3385

II

ἡ τὸ πάλαι Λαῒς πάντων βέλος οὐκέτι Λαΐς,   (3386)
ἀλλ᾽ ἐτέων φανερὴ πᾶσιν ἐγὼ Νέμεσις·
οὐ μὰ Κύπριν· τί δὲ Κύπρις ἔμοιγ᾽ ἔτι πλὴν ὅσον ὅρκος;
γνώριμον οὐδ᾽ αὐτῆι Λαΐδι Λαῒς ἔτι.

III

τίπτε τὸν ὀγκηστὴν βραδύπουν ὄνον ἄμμιγ᾽ ἐν ἵπποις   3390
γυρὸν ἀλωειναῖς ἐξελάατε δρόμον;
οὐχ ἅλις ὅττι μύλοιο περίδρομον ἄχθος ἀνάγκηι
σπειρηδὸν σκοτόεις κυκλοδίωκτος ἔχω,
5 ἀλλ᾽ ἔτι καὶ πώλοισιν ἐρίζομεν; ἦ ῥ᾽ ἔτι λοιπόν
νῦν μοι τὴν σκολιὴν αὐχένι γαῖαν ἀροῦν.   3395

I *A.P.* 9.36 [C] Σεκούνδου   [J] εἰς ἑτέραν ὑπὸ πυρὸς καταφθαρεῖσαν ἧς οὐκ
ἐκυρίευσε θάλασσα   Pl A Σεκούνδου
1 ἀμέτρητον Page: -του PPl | πελάγους P: πολέμου Pl   2 τοσάκις Pl:
τοσσά- P   6 ὕδατα Pl: -τος P

II *A.P.* 9.260 [C] Σεκούνδου Ταραντίνου   εἰς Λαΐδα τὴν ἑταίραν διὰ τὸ γηρά-
σκειν   Pl B Ἐπιγόνου
3 ἔμοιγ᾽ Jacobs: ἐμοῦ P   versus corruptus in Pl, οὐ μὰ Κύπριν οὐδὲ Κύπρις ἔτι

SECUNDUS

I

On a ship destroyed by fire ashore

A ship that completed measureless ocean-paths and swam so many times in the sparkling waves; whom neither the black east-wind submerged nor savage swell of the stormy south-winds drove ashore; now wrecked in flames, now looking for the waters of my sea I reproach the treacherous land.

II

Laïs has lost her beauty

The Laïs of times past, an arrow in every heart, no longer Laïs am I, but plain to every eye the Nemesis of the years. By the Cyprian—and what is the Cyprian still to me, except a name to swear by?—not even to Laïs herself is Laïs still a thing to recognise.

III

On a donkey, taken from the mill
to help in threshing

Why drive me forth on the round track together with threshing-mares, your braying slow-footed donkey? Is it not enough that, blindfolded and circle-driven, round upon round, I bear perforce the millstone's revolving weight, but yet I must compete with horses? No doubt it remains for me to plough with my neck the recurving earth.

ἐμοὶ ὅσον ὅρκος   Schol. ἐν ἄλλωι οὕτως· οὐ με Κύπριν· τί δὲ Κύπρις ἐμοὶ πλέον ἢ ὅσον ὅρκος;
III *A.P.* 9.301 Cεκούνδου   [C] εἰς ὄνον ἐν ἅλωνι ἀναγκαζόμενον μετὰ ἵππων cυμπατεῖν τοὺς ἀcτάχυαc   Pl A Cεκούνδου
1 ὀγκηcτὴν Pl: -κιcτ- P PPl   **2** δρόμον Pl: -μωι P   **3** ἀνάγκηι Reiske: -κηc PPl   **6** νῦν P: ἦν Pl

IV

σκυλοχαρεῖς ἴδ᾽ Ἔρωτας, ἴδ᾽ ὡς βριαροῖσιν ἐπ᾽ ὤμοις
ὅπλα φέρουσι θεῶν νήπι᾽ ἀγαλλόμενοι,
τύμπανα καὶ θύρσον Βρομίου, Ζηνὸς δὲ κεραυνόν,
ἀσπίδ᾽ Ἐνυαλίου καὶ κόρυν ἠύκομον,
5 Φοίβου δ᾽ εὔτοξον φαρέτρην, Ἁλίου δὲ τρίαιναν,   3400
καὶ cθεναρὸν χειρῶν Ἡρακλέους ῥόπαλον.
τί πλέον ἀνθρώποισιν, Ἔρως ὅτε καὶ πόλον εἶλε,
τεύχεα δ᾽ ἀθανάτων Κύπρις ἐληίcατο;

CΕΡΑΠΙѠΝΟC

I

—τοῦ τούcτεῦν;—φωτὸς πολυεργέος.—ἦ ῥά τις ἦcθα
ἔμπορος ἢ τυφλοῦ κύματος ἰχθυβόλος.   3405
—ἄγγειλον θνητοῖcιν ὅτι cπεύδοντες ἐς ἄλλας
ἐλπίδας, εἰς τοίην ἐλπίδα λυόμεθα.

ΘΑΛΛΟΥ

I

ἀσπίδα μὲν Πρόμαχος, τὰ δὲ δούρατα θῆκεν Ἀκοντεύς,
τὸ ξίφος Εὐμήδης, τόξα δὲ ταῦτα Κύδων,
Ἱππομέδων τὰ χαλινά, κόρυν δ᾽ ἀνέθηκε Μελάντας,   3410
κνημῖδας Νίκων, κοντὸν Ἀριστόμαχος,
5 τὸν θώρηκα Φιλῖνος· ἀεὶ δ᾽, Ἄρες βροτολοιγέ,
cκῦλα φέρειν δώιης πᾶσιν ἀπ᾽ ἀντιπάλων.

IV *A.Pl.* (A) 214 Cεκούνδου εἰς ἀγάλματα Ἐρώτων   caret P
2 ἀγαλλόμενοι Brunck: -να Pl

I *A.P.* 7.400 [C] Cεραπίωνος Ἀλεξανδρέως   [J] ἐπιτύμβιον ἀνώνυμον εἰς ὀcτᾶ
ἀνθρώπεια κείμενα ἀτημέλητα Pl A Cεραπίωνος

IV

On the Erotes, equipped with the weapons
of the gods

Look at the Loves, delighting in their spoils; see how in childish pride they carry on sturdy shoulders the weapons of the gods,— timbrels and wand of Bromios, thunderbolt of Zeus, shield and plumed helmet of Enyalios, quiver of Phoebus full of arrows, the sea-god's trident, the strong club of Heracles' hands. How shall mortals prevail, when Love has captured Heaven, and the Cyprian has despoiled the immortals of their arms?

SERAPION

I

Epitaph for a labourer

—Whose skull is this?
—Of a hard-labouring man.
—Some trader, no doubt, or fisherman of the blind waves.
—Give this message to mortals, that while we go chasing other hopes, such is the hope to which we are reduced.

THALLUS

I

Dedication by warriors to Ares

Promachus dedicated the shield, Aconteus the spears, Eumedes the sword, Cydon these bows, Hippomedon the bridle-bits, Melantas dedicated the helmet, Nicon the greaves, Aristomachus the pike, Philinus the corslet. Ever grant to all, man-destroyer Ares, that they carry off spoils from their adversaries.

1 τοῦ τούϲτεῦν Page: τοῦτ' ὀϲτεῦν PPl

1 *A.P.* 6.91 Θαλοῦ [C] Μιληϲίου [P] ἀνάθημα τῶι ῎Αρει παρά τινων Suid. s.v. βροτολοιγόϲ (5 ῎Αρεϲ–6) caret Pl

II

ἑσπερίοις μέγα χάρμα καὶ ἠώιοις περάτεσσι
Καῖσαρ, ἀνικάτων ἔκγονε Ῥωμυλιδῶν,
αἰθερίην γένεσιν σέο μέλπομεν, ἀμφὶ δὲ βωμοῖς
γηθοσύνους λοιβὰς σπένδομεν ἀθανάτοις.
5 ἀλλὰ σὺ παππώιοις ἐπὶ βήμασιν ἴχνος ἐρείδων
εὐχομένοις ἡμῖν πουλὺ μέλοις ἐπ᾽ ἔτος.

3415

III

δύσδαιμον Κλεάνασσα, σὺ μὲν †γάμωι ἔπλεο κούρωι
ὥριον† ἀκμαίης οἷά τ᾽ ἐφ᾽ ἡλικίης·
ἀλλὰ τεοῖς θαλάμοισι γαμοστόλος οὐχ Ὑμέναιος
οὐδ᾽ Ἥρης ζυγίης λαμπάδες ἠντίασαν,
5 πένθιμος ἀλλ᾽ Ἀίδης ἐπεκώμασεν, ἀμφὶ δ᾽ Ἐρινύς
φοίνιος ἐκ στομάτων μόρσιμον ἧκεν ὄπα·
ἤματι δ᾽ ὧι νυμφεῖος ἀνήπτετο λαμπάδι παστάς,
τούτωι πυρκαϊῆς, οὐ θαλάμων, ἔτυχες.

3420

3425

IV

δισσὰ φάη, Μίλητε, τεῆς βλαστήματα γαίης
Ἰταλὶς ὠκυμόρους ἀμφεκάλυψε κόνις·
πένθεα δὲ στεφάνων ἠλλάξαο, λείψανα δ᾽ αἰαῖ
ἔδρακες ἐν βαιῆι κάλπιδι κευθόμενα.
5 φεῦ πάτρα τριτάλαινα, πόθεν πάλιν ἢ πότε τοίους
ἀστέρας αὐχήσεις Ἑλλάδι λαμπομένους;

3430

II *A.P.* 6.235 Θάλλου   caret Pl
1 περάτεσσι C: -ιν (?) P   5 παππώιοις C: -ῶος P   6 μέλοις P: μένοις C et
denuo C^γρ | ἐπ᾽ ἔτος C: ἔπετ᾽ ἔτος (?) P
III *A.P.* 7.188 [C] Ἀντωνίου Θάλλου   [J] εἰς Κλεάνασσαν ἐν τῶι θαλάμωι

II

On Caesar's birthday

Great joy to the farthest West and East, Caesar, descendant of Romulus' unconquerable sons, your heavenly birth we sing, and around the altars we pour glad libations to the Immortals. Do you tread firm in your grandfather's steps, and be the subject of our prayers for many a year.

III

Death of a bride

Ill-starred Cleanassa, ⟨a maiden ripe for marriage were you⟩, as in the prime of youth; but there came to your bed-chamber no marriage-making Hymen nor torches of connubial Hera. Death and mourning broke riotous in, and a murderous Fury sped from her lips an utterance of doom. On the day when the bridal-chamber was lit by the torch, thereon you got no marriage-bed but a funeral-pyre.

IV

Death of two famous Milesians

Twin lights, Miletus, offspring of your soil, Italian dust has covered, swiftly doomed. Garlands you have changed for grief, their relics you have seen, alas, in a little urn concealed. O thrice unhappy fatherland, whence and when in future shall you boast of such stars shining upon Hellas?

πυρποληθεῖσαν, μᾶλλον δὲ ἀναρπασθεῖσαν   Suid. s.vv. Ἐρινύς (5 ἀμφὶ–6), μόρσιμον (eadem), φοίνιος (eadem), νυμφεῖος οἶκος (7 s.)   caret Pl
IV *A.P.* 7.373 [C] Θαλλοῦ Μιλησίου   [J] εἰς δύο τινὰς Μιλησίους ἐν Ἰταλίαι τελευτήσαντας· οἶμαι δ' ὅτι σοφούς   Pl A Θαλλοῦ
3 ἠλλάξαο Pl: -ξω P

V

ἁ χλοερὰ πλατάνιστος ἴδ' ὡς ἔκρυψε φιλεύντων
ὄργια τὰν ἱερὰν φυλλάδα τεινομένα,   3435
ἀμφὶ δ' ἄρ' ἀκρεμόνεccιν ἑοῖc κεχαριcμένος Ὥραιc
ἡμερίδος λαρῆc βότρυc ἀποκρέμαται.
5 οὕτως, ὦ πλατάνιcτε, φύοιc, χλοερὰ δ' ἀπὸ cεῖο
φυλλὰc ἀεὶ κεύθοι τοὺc Παφίηc ἑτάρους.

ZΩNA

I

ἀρτιχανῆ ῥοιάν τε καὶ ἀρτίχνουν τόδε μῆλον   3440
καὶ ῥυτιδόφλοιον cῦκον ἐπομφάλιον
πορφύρεόν τε βότρυν μεθυπίδακα πυκνόρρωγα
καὶ κάρυον χλωρῆc ἀρτίδορον λεπίδοc
5 ἀγροιώτηι τῶιδε μονοcτόρθυγγι Πριήπωι
θῆκεν ὁ καρποφύλαξ δενδριακὴν θυcίην.   3445

II

Δηοῖ λικμαίηι καὶ ἐναυλακοφοίτιcιν Ὥραιc
Ἡρῶναξ πενιχρῆc ἐξ ὀλιγηροcίηc
μοῖραν ἀλωίτα cτάχυος πάνcπερμά τε ταῦτα
ὄcπρι' ἐπὶ πλακίνου τοῦδ' ἔθετο τρίποδοc,
5 ἐκ μικρῶν ὀλίγιcτα· πέπατο γὰρ οὐ μέγα τοῦτο   3450
κληρίον ἐν λυπρῆι τῆιδε γεωλοφίηι.

V A.P. 9.220 [C] Θαλοῦ Μιληcίου   εἴc τιναc ἐπὶ [fort. ὑπὸ voluit] πλατάνωι
φιλοῦνταc   caret Pl
3 ἄρ' Salm.: ἂν P

I A.P. 6.22 s.a.n.   ἀνάθημα ἑτέρου κηπουροῦ τῶι Πριήπωι   Pl A Ζωνᾶ Suid.
s.vv. ἀρτιχανῆ (1), ῥυτίc (2), πιδακίων (3), ἀντίδορον (4), ἀγροιώτηc (5),
Πρίαπος (5 s.)   An. Par. Cramer 4.87.29
3 πορφύρεόν Pl: -ρίαν PSuid. | μεθυπίδακα PlSuid.: -πήδ- P | πυκνόρρωγα P:
-ρρωγον Pl, -ρράγα Suid.   4 χλωρῆc PSuid.: λεπτῆc Pl, etiam χλωρὸν

V

Love under a plane-tree

The green plane-tree, see how it has concealed the lovers'
mysteries, spreading its sacred foliage; about its branches hangs
the sweet vine's cluster, the delight of the Hours. So may you
grow, plane-tree, and may your green foliage ever give cover
to the Paphian's comrades.

ZONAS

I

Dedication of fruits

A new-split pomegranate and this new-downy quince and
wrinkly-skinned navel-fig and purple grape-cluster wine-
fountaining, thick-berried, and walnut new-skinned from its
green husk,—these the fruit-guardian dedicated to this rustic
single-shaft Priapus as sacrificial offering from the trees.

II

Dedication by a farmer

For winnower Demeter and the furrow-frequenting Hours,
from his pauper's scanty ploughland Heronax placed on this
flat-topped tripod a portion of threshed corn and these veget-
ables of all seeds, out of small store slightest offerings; for it is
no large allotment he owns here on this bitter hill-crest.

Suid. | ἀρτίδορον Toup: ἀντί- PPlSuid.   5 ἀγροιώτηι Pl: -ώτα P, -ῶτα C,
-ῶται et -ῶτα Suid.

II *A.P.* 6.98 Ζωνᾶ ἀνάθημα τῆι Δηοῖ παρά Ἡρώνακτος   Suid. s.vv. λικμᾶν
(1–3 τε), ὀλιγηροσίη (2 πεν.–3 στάχ.), λυπρή (5 πέπ.–6), γεώλοφον (eadem),
πέπατο (eadem)   caret Pl
1 ἐναυλακοφοίτιcιν CSuid.: -φοιτίαν (?) P | Ὥραιc CSuid.: -ρηc (?) P
3 ἀλωίτα Ap.B.: ἀλωεῖται P, ἀλοεῖται Suid.   4 ὅcπρι' Reiske: ὃc πρὶν P
5 πέπατο PSuid.: πέπαυτο C, γρ. πέπαcτο idem in marg.

III

τοῦτό τοι, ὑλειῶτα, κατ᾽ ἀγριάδος πλατάνοιο
δέρμα λυκορραίστας ἐκρέμασεν Τελέσων
καὶ τὰν ἐκ κοτίνοιο καλαύροπα, τάν ποκα τῆνος
πολλάκι ῥομβητὰν ἐκ χερὸς ἠκροβόλει.   3455
5 ἀλλὰ τύ, Πὰν βουνῖτα, τὰ μὴ πολύολβά τε δέξαι
δῶρα καὶ εὐαγρεῖ τῶιδε πέτασσον ὄρος.

IV

᾽Αίδηι ὃς ταύτης καλαμώδεος ὕδατι λίμνης
κωπεύεις νεκύων βᾶριν †ἑλὼν ὀδύνην†,
τῶι Κινύρου τὴν χεῖρα βατηρίδος ἐμβαίνοντι   3460
κλίμακος ἐκτείνας δέξο, κελαινὲ Χάρον·
5 πλάζει γὰρ τὸν παῖδα τὰ σάνδαλα, γυμνὰ δὲ θεῖναι
ἴχνια δειμαίνει ψάμμον ἐπ᾽ ἠιονίην.

V

ψυχράν σευ κεφαλᾶς ἐπαμήσομαι αἰγιαλῖτιν
θῖνα κατὰ κρυεροῦ χευάμενος νέκυος·   3465
οὐ γάρ σευ μήτηρ ἐπιτύμβια κωκύουσα
εἶδεν ἁλίξαντον σὸν μόρον εἰνάλιον·
5 ἀλλά σ᾽ ἐρημαῖοί τε καὶ ἄξεινοι πλαταμῶνες
δέξαντ᾽, Αἰγαίης γείτονες ἠιόνος·
ὥστ᾽ ἔχε μὲν ψαμάθου μόριον βραχύ, πουλὺ δὲ δάκρυ,   3470
ξεῖν᾽, ἐπεὶ εἰς ὀλοὴν ἔδραμες ἐμπορίην.

III *A.P.* 6.106 [= Pᵃ] Ζωνᾶ   ἀνάθημα τῶι Πανὶ παρὰ Τελέσωνος κυνηγοῦ denuo
post 6.255 [= Pᵇ] Ζωνᾶ Pl A Ζωνᾶ Suid. s.vv. ὑλειώτης (1 s.), λυκορραίστης (2),
κότινος (3 s.)
1 τοι Pᵇ: coι PᵃPlSuid. | ἀγριάδος PᵇPlSuid.: ἀγρειάδ- Pᵃ   2 λυκορραί-
ϲταϲ Page: -της PPlSuid.   4 χερὸς PᵇPl: χειρ- PᵃSuid.   5 βουνῖτα
Pl: -νεῖτα Pᵃᵇ   6 εὐαγρεῖ Pᵃ: -γρηι Pᵇ, -γρεῖν Pl | τῶιδε πέτασσον ὄρος
Pᵃᵇ: τῶιδ᾽ ἐπίνευσον ὄρει Pl
IV *A.P.* 7.365 ⟦εἰc, del. C⟧ Ζωνᾶ Cαρδιανοῦ τοῦ καὶ Διοδώρου ⟦εἰϲ ἀκρίδα,

III

Dedication by a hunter

This skin, Woodlander, the wolf-slayer Teleson hung for you on a plane-tree in the fields, and his staff of wild-olive, which he used often to shoot whirling from his hand. Do you, hill-god Pan, accept his gifts, though not of great riches, and open to him the mountain for good hunting.

IV

Description of a scene on a sepulchral monument

Black Charon, who in the waters of this reedy lake are rowing for Hades the boat of corpses ⟨   ⟩, to the son of Cinyras as he comes aboard stretch forth your hand from the mounting-ladder and take him in. His sandals make the child stumble, and he is afraid to set his naked footprints on the sand of the shore.

V

On a shipwrecked sailor

Cold shingle from the shore will I heap upon your head, pouring it over your frozen corpse; for no mother wailing over your tomb beheld your sea-tortured corpse amid the waters, only the solitary inhospitable flats that neighbour the Aegean shore received you. So, stranger, take your brief portion of sand, with many a tear, for fatal was the trading to which you ran.

---

del. J‖ [J] εἰc Κινύρου παῖδα [idem ad v. 3] εἰc Κινύραν νεώτερον caret Pl
1 'Αίδηι Jacobs: -δη P **2** κωπεύεις C: -εύηι P | ὀδύνην P: -νης C **3** ἐμβαί-
νοντι P: ἐκβ- C **4** Χάρον C: -ριν P **5** δὲ θεῖναι Ap.B.: δὲ θῆναι C, δεθῆναι P
V *A.P.* 7.404 [C] Ζωνᾶ Cαρδιανοῦ [J] εἴc τινα ἔμπορον ναυαγήcαντα καὶ ἐπὶ
ψάμμου ταφῆc εὐμοιρήcαντα Pl в Ζανοῦ
3 ceυ Pl: cου P **4** ἀλίξαντον Jacobs: ἀλιξάντων P, 'Αλεξάντη Pl
6 δέξαντ' Αἰγαίηc Scaliger et Reiske: δέξονται γαίηc PPl | ἠϊόνος J: -νεc PPl
7 ἔχε μὲν Reiske: ἐχέμεν PPl | ψαμάθου CPl: -ουc P

VI

αἱ δ᾽ ἄγετε ξουθαὶ cιμβληίδεc ἄκρα μέλιccαι
φέρβεcθ᾽ ἢ θυμέων ῥικνὰ περικνίδια
ἢ πετάλαc μάκωνοc ἢ ἀcταφιδίτιδα ῥῶγα
ἢ ἴον ἢ μάλων χνοῦν ἐπικαρπίδιον·   3475
5 πάντα περικνίξαcθε καὶ ἄγγεα κηρώcαcθε,
ὄφρα μελιccοcόοc Πὰν ἐπικυψέλιοc
γεύcηται τὸ μὲν αὐτόc, ὁ δὲ βλιcτηρίδι χειρί
καπνώcαc βαιὰν κῦμμι λίπηι μερίδα.

VII

ὦνερ, τᾶν βαλάνων τὰν ματέρα φείδεο κόπτειν,   3480
φείδεο, γηραλέαν δ᾽ ἐκκεράιζε πίτυν
ἢ πεύκαν ἢ τάνδε πολυcτέλεχον παλίουρον
ἢ πρῖνον καὶ τὰν αὐαλέαν κόμαρον·
5 τηλόθι δ᾽ ἴcχε δρυὸc πέλεκυν, κοκύαι γὰρ ἔλεξαν
ἁμῖν ὡc πρότεραι ματέρεc ἐντὶ δρύεc.   3485

VIII

Νύμφαι ἐποχθίδιαι Νηρηίδεc, εἴδετε Δάφνιν
χθιζόν, ἐπαχνιδίαν ὡc ἀπέλουcε κόμαν,
ὑμετέραιc λιβάδεccιν ὅτ᾽ ἔνθορε cειριόκαυτοc
ἠρέμα φοινιχθεὶc μᾶλα παρηίδια;
5 εἴπατέ μοι, καλὸc ἦν; ἢ ἐγὼ τράγοc οὐκ ἄρα κνάμαν   3490
μοῦνον ἐγυιώθην, ἀλλ᾽ ἔτι καὶ κραδίαν;

VI *A.P.* 9.226 [C] Ζωνᾶ Cαρδιανοῦ   εἰc cίμβλα μελιccῶν ὡc ἀπὸ τοῦ μελιccοκόμου
Pl A Ζωνᾶ
1 αἱ Brunck: αἰ P, εἰ Pl   2 θυμέων P: -μων Pl   3 μάκωνοc P: -νac Pl |
ἀcταφιδίτιδα Pl: ἀcταφειτιδικὰ P, ἀcταφειτιδι C | ῥῶγα P: ῥᾶγα Pl   6 μελιc-
cοcόοc PᵃᶜPl: -cύαc Pᵖᶜ   8 βαιὰν Page: βαιὴν PPl | λίπηι Pl: -πει P
VII *A.P.* 9.312 [C] Ζωνᾶ Cαρδιανοῦ   εἰc δρῦν ἥμερον παραίνεcιc μὴ κόπτειν διὰ

VI

To honey-bees

Come, tawny hive-bees, feed on the heads, whether wrinkly morsels of thyme or petals of poppy or berry of dried grape or violet or down on the fruit of quinces. Nibble round them all and make vessels of wax; so may Pan, the bee-saviour and hive-keeper, taste a part himself and, smoking you out with honey-gathering hand, leave a small share for you also.

VII

Why the oak should not be felled

Forbear, man, to cut the mother of the acorns; forbear, and lay low the agèd stone-pine or sea-pine or this many-stemmed paliurus or holm-oak or the dry arbutus. Keep your axe far from the oak, for our ancestors have declared that oaks were once upon a time our mothers.

VIII

Pan asks the Nymphs about Daphnis

Nymphs of the shore, Nereids, did you see Daphnis yesterday when he washed his dusty hair; when, burnt by the Dog-star, he leapt into your waters, the apples of his cheeks lightly reddened? Tell me, was he beautiful? Or am I a goat deformed not only in leg but in heart too?

τὸν μῦθον τὸν φάσκοντα ἀπὸ δρυὸς καὶ πέτρας τὰς τῶν ἀνθρώπων γενέσεις Pl A Ζωνᾶ
1 τᾶν P: τῶν Pl   **4** καὶ Jacobs: ἢ PPl   **6** ἐντὶ Pl: ἦν τι P
VIII *A.P.* 9.556 Ζωνᾶ caret Pl
1 Νηρηΐδες P text.: δινηΐδες P marg.   **2** κόμαν Page: κόμην P text., κόνιν P marg.   **4** παρηΐδια Ppc: -ηΐδα Pac   **6** κραδίαν Brunck: -ίην P

IX

δός μοι τοὔκ γαίης πεπονημένον ἁδὺ κύπελλον,　(3492)
ἇς γενόμην καὶ ὑφ' ἇι κείσομ' ἀποφθίμενος.

ΑΔΕΣΠΟΤΑ

I

ἐσχατιαὶ Λιβύων Νασαμωνίδες, οὐκέτι θηρῶν
ἔθνεσιν ἠπείρου νῶτα βαρυνόμεναι　　　　　3495
ἦχος ἐρημαίαισιν ἐπὶ πτύρεσθε λεόντων
ὠρυγαῖς ψαμάθους ἄχρις ὑπὲρ Νομάδων·
5 φῦλον ἐπεὶ νήριθμον ἐν ἰχνοπέδαισιν ἀγρευθέν
ἐς μίαν αἰχμηταῖς Καῖσαρ ἔθηκεν ὁ παῖς.
αἱ δὲ πρὶν ἀγραύλων ἐγκοιτάδες ἀκρώρειαι　　3500
θηρῶν νῦν ἀνδρῶν εἰσι βοηλασίαι.

II

Ἰκάρου ὦ νεόφοιτον ἐς ἠέρα πωτηθέντος
Ἰκαρίη πικρῆς τύμβε κακοδρομίης,
ἀβάλε μήτε σε κεῖνος ἰδεῖν μήτ' αὐτὸς ἀνεῖναι
Τρίτων Αἰγαίου νῶτον ὑπὲρ πελάγευς·　　　3505
5 οὐ γάρ σοι σκεπανή τις ὑφόρμισις οὔτε βόρειον
ἐς κλίτος οὔτ' ἀγὴν κύματος ἐς νοτίην.
ἔρροις, ὦ δύσπλωτε κακόξενε, σεῖο δὲ τηλοῦ
πλώοιμι στυγεροῦ τόσσον ἀπ' Ἀίδεω.

IX A.P. 11.43 Ζωνᾶ Pl в s.a.n.
2 ἇι Pl: ὧι P

I A.P. 7.626 [C] ἀδέσποτον　[J] ὅτι Καῖσαρ ἐξεκάθηρε τὴν Λιβύην τῶν ἐνοι-
κούντων θηρίων καὶ ἐποίησεν οἰκεῖσθαι　[idem ad v. 5] ὅτι τὰς ἐσχατιὰς τῆς
Λιβύης τὰς πλησίον Νασαμώνων ὁ Καῖσαρ ἡμέρωσεν　caret Pl
3 ἦχος C: ἦχοι P | ἐπιπτύρεσθε C: ἐπιπτύσσεσθε P　　5 νήριθμον Salm.: ἀνί-
ρηθμον P

IX

The philosophic drinker

Give me the sweet cup wrought of the clay wherefrom I came
and whereunder I shall lie in death.

ANONYMOUS EPIGRAMS

I

On lions in the Roman arena

Nasamonian extremities of Libya, no longer do you shudder,
your mainland-surface burdened with tribes of beasts, at the
sound of lions when they roar in the deserts even beyond the
sands of the Nomads; for their countless race, trapped in foot-
fetters, the boy-Caesar has put face to face with spearmen. The
mountain-ridges, once lairs for wild-dwelling beasts, are now
cattle-droves for men.

II

A curse on the Icarian sea

Icaria, tomb of the bitter ill-voyaging of Icarus flown to the
new-frequented sky, would that he had not set eyes on you,
and that Triton himself had not raised your back above the
Aegean sea. For you have no sheltered anchorage, neither towards the northern clime nor to the southern breaking of the
waves. A curse upon you, dangerous, inhospitable, and may
I sail as far from your hated self as from Hades.

II *A.P.* 7.699 [C] ἀδέσποτον [J] εἴς τινα ἐν τῶι Ἰκαρίωι πελάγει κινδυνεύσαντα,
οὐ μὴν καὶ τελευτήσαντα, πλὴν ὅτι τὴν Ἰκαρίην θάλασσαν ἰσχυρῶς ἐπιμέμφεται
caret Pl
I νεόφοιτον P: -φυτον (?) C   5 οὔτε Reiske: οὐδὲ P | βόρειον Salm.: -ος P
6 ἀγὴν P: ἄγειν C   8 τόccον Page: ὄccον P

III

ὁ Ζεὺς πρὸς τὸν Ἔρωτα, 'βέλη τὰ σὰ πάντ' ἀφελοῦμαι',   3510
χὼ πτανός, 'βρόντα, καὶ πάλι κύκνος ἔσηι'.

IV

Λευκάδος ἀντί με Καῖσαρ ἲδ' Ἀμβρακίης ἐριβώλου
Θυρρείου τε πέλειν ἀντί τ' Ἀνακτορίου
Ἄργεος Ἀμφιλόχου τε καὶ ὁππόσα ῥαίσατο κύκλωι
ἄστε' ἐπιθρώσκων δουρομανὴς πόλεμος   3515
5 εἵσατο Νικόπολιν θείην πόλιν, ἀντὶ δὲ νίκης
Φοῖβος ἄναξ ταύτην δέχνυται Ἀκτιάδος.

III *A.P.* 9.108 [C] ἀδέσποτον [J] εἰς τὸν Δία τωθαστικὸν ὡς ἀπὸ τοῦ Ἔρωτος
Pl A ἀδέσποτον

388

III

Eros superior to Zeus

Zeus to Eros: 'I will take all your arrows away.' The wingèd one: 'Thunder, and you shall be a swan again.'

IV

The founding of Nicopolis

To replace Leucas and fertile Ambracia and Thyrrheum and Anactorium and Amphilochian Argos and as many cities as spear-mad war leapt upon and shattered round about, Caesar founded me, Nicopolis, city divine; and lord Phoebus receives this in return for the victory at Actium.

IV *A.P.* 9.553 s.a.n. ὡραῖον caret Pl

II

DOUBTFUL CLAIMANTS

ΑΛΦΕΙΟΥ

I

νηῶν ὠκυπόρων ὃς ἔχεις κράτος, ἵππιε δαῖμον,
καὶ μέγαν Εὐβοίης ἀμφιβρέμηι σκόπελον,
οὔριον εὐχομένοισι δίδου πλόον Ἄρεος ἄχρις   3520
ἐς πόλιν ἐκ Cυρίης πείσματα λυσαμένοις.

II

Λητοῦς ὠδίνων ἱερὴ τροφέ, τὴν ἀσάλευτον
Αἰγαίωι Κρονίδης ὥρμισατ' ἐν πελάγει,
οὔ νύ σε δειλαίην, μὰ τεούς, δέσποινα, βοήσω
δαίμονας, οὐδὲ λόγοις ἕψομαι Ἀντιπάτρου,   3525
5 ὀλβίζω δ' ὅτι Φοῖβον ἐδέξαο καὶ μετ' Ὄλυμπον
Ἄρτεμις οὐκ ἄλλην ἢ σὲ λέγει πατρίδα.

III

κλεῖε, θεός, μεγάλοιο πύλας ἀκμῆτας Ὀλύμπου·
φρούρει, Ζεῦ, ζαθέαν αἰθέρος ἀκρόπολιν·
ἤδη γὰρ καὶ πόντος ὑπέζευκται δορὶ Ῥώμης   3530
καὶ χθών, οὐρανίη δ' οἶμος ἔτ' ἐστ' ἄβατος.

I *A.P.* 9.90 [C] Ἀλφειοῦ Μιτυληναίου   [J] εὐχὴ πρὸς τὸν Ποσειδῶ παρά τινων πλεόντων ἀπὸ Cυρίας   caret Pl
2 Εὐβοίης Ap.G.: -βοίβης P | ἀμφιβρέμηι Stadtmüller: -κρεμὴ P   4 λυσαμένοις Reiske: -νους P

II *A.P.* 9.100 [C] Ἀλφειοῦ Μιτυληναίου   [J] εἰς Δῆλον τὴν νῆσον ἔπαινος ὅτι ἐν αὐτῆι ἐγεννήθη ὅ τε Ἀπόλλων καὶ ἡ Ἄρτεμις   [ad v. 3] εἰς Δῆλον τὴν νῆσον τὴν τροφὸν Ἀρτέμιδος καὶ Ἀπόλλωνος   Pl A Ἀλφειοῦ Μιτυληναίου

ALPHEUS

I

Prayer for a safe voyage to Rome

Lord of horses, who hold power over swift ships and roar around the great crag of Euboea, grant a calm sailing as far as Ares' city for your suppliants, who have loosed their stern-cables from Syria.

II

Praise of Delos

Holy nurse of Leto's travail, whom the son of Cronos anchored unshakable in the Aegean sea, by your gods I vow, sovereign Lady, I shall not cry you miserable, or follow the words of Antipater. I count you happy that you took Phoebus in, and that Artemis, after Olympus, calls no other but you her fatherland.

III

Rome is supreme by land and sea

Bolt great Olympus' unwearied gates, O god; guard the sky's holy acropolis, O Zeus. Already sea and land are subdued to the spear of Rome; the path to heaven remains untrodden.

3 μὰ τεούς Pl: μα τέου C, μαστέου ut vid. P   4 δαίμονας Pl: -νος P
6 Ἄρτεμις Pl: -μιν C, -μι P | λέγει PᵖᶜPl: -γειν PᵃᶜC

III A.P. 9.526 Ἀλφειοῦ Μιτυληναίου   εἰς τὴν τύχην Ῥωμαίων   Pl A Ἀλφειοῦ Μιτυληναίου
4 οἶμος Pl et in fine versus P: ὅμως in textu P

IV

οὐ στέργω βαθυληίους ἀρούρας,
οὐκ ὄλβον πολύχρυσον οἶα Γύγης·
αὐτάρκους ἔραμαι βίου, Μακρῖνε,
τὸ μηθὲν γὰρ ἄγαν ἄγαν με τέρπει.   3535

V

Πανὶ κασιγνήτων ἱερὴ τριάς, ἄλλος ἀπ᾽ ἄλλης,
ἄνθετ᾽ ἀπ᾽ οἰκείης σύμβολον ἐργασίης·
Πίγρης ὀρνίθων, ἁλίων ἀπομοίρια Κλείτωρ,
ἔμπαλιν ἰθυτόνων Δᾶμις ἀπὸ σταλίκων.
5 ἀνθ᾽ ὧν εὐαγρίην τῶι μὲν χθονός, ὧι δὲ διδοίης   3540
ἐξ ἁλός, ὧι δὲ νέμοις ἠέρος ὠφελίην.

VI

οὔρεά μευ καὶ πόντον ὑπὲρ τύμβοιο χάρασσε
καὶ μέσον ἀμφοτέρων μάρτυρα Λητοΐδην
ἀενάων τε βαθὺν ποταμῶν ῥόον, οἵ ποτε ῥείθροις
Ξέρξου μυριόναυν οὐχ ὑπέμειναν ἄρη.   3545
5 ἔγγραφε καὶ Σαλαμῖνα, Θεμιστοκλέους ἵνα σῆμα
κηρύσσηι Μάγνης δῆμος ἀποφθιμένου.

VII

χειμερίοις νιφάδεσσι παλυνομένη τιθὰς ὄρνις
τέκνοις εὐναίας ἀμφέχεε πτέρυγας,

IV A.P. 9.110 [C] Ἀλφειοῦ Μιτυληναίου   [J] παραίνεσις εἰς τὸ βιοῦν ἐν
αὐταρκίαι   3τ τὸ μέτρον τοῦ ἐπιγράμματος   Pl A Ἀλφειοῦ Μιτυληναίου
Drac. metr. 33.17 (1 s.) Ἀλφειοῦ
V A.P. 6.187 Ἀλφ(ε)ιοῦ Μιτυληναίου εἰς τὸ αὐτό [C] Ἀλκαίου Pl A Ἀλφειοῦ
Μιτυληναίου εἰς τὸ αὐτό Suid. s.vv. στάλικας (4), ὠφελείας (6 ὧι–ὠφ.)
1 ἄλλος Pl: ἄλλης P   4 ἰθυτόνων CSuid.: -τονῶν P, -τενῶν Pl   5 τῶι
μὲν P: ὧι μὲν Pl

IV

On self-sufficiency and moderation

I have no love for deep harvest-fields or wealth of gold like
Gyges; self-sufficient is the life I long for, Macrinus. The rule
'Nothing in excess' gives me excessive joy.

V

Dedications by three brothers

To Pan a pious trinity of brothers dedicated a token from his
proper trade, each from his own,—Pigres of birds, Cleitor a
portion of fish, Damis again from his upright hunting-stakes.
Give in return good hunting, to the one from the land, to the
other from the sea, to the other grant help from the sky.

VI

On the tomb of Themistocles at Magnesia

Engrave above my tomb mountains and sea, and, between them,
Apollo my witness, and deep streams of ever-flowing rivers,
whose waters once succumbed to Xerxes' myriad vessels of war.
Inscribe also Salamis, so that the people of Magnesia may proclaim that this is the tomb of dead Themistocles.

VII

Maternal love in the poultry-yard

A domestic hen, sprinkled with winter snowflakes, spread her
wings as a nest about her brood till the cold from the sky killed

VI *A.P.* 7.237 [C] Ἀλφ⟨ε⟩ιοῦ Μιτυληναίου   Pl a Ἀλφειοῦ Μιτυληναίου   εἰς τὸν
αὐτὸν Θεμιστοκλέα
1 μευ P^{pc}Pl: μέν μευ P^{ac} 4 ἄρη CPl: ἄρην P   6 κηρύccηι Pl: -ει P
VII *A.P.* 9.95 [C] Ἀλφειοῦ Μιτυληναίου   [J] εἰς ὄρνιν τρέφουcαν νεοττοὺς καὶ
ἐν χειμῶνι τούτους ταῖς πτέρυξι cκεπάcαcαν ὑπὸ χιόνος καλυφθεῖcαν †ἀπέθανεν·
μέμφεται οὖν Πρόκνην καὶ Μήδειαν ὡς τὰ ἴδια τέκνα ἀπεκτονυίας   Pl a Ἀλφειοῦ
1 χειμερίοις P: -ίαις Pl | παλυνομένη P: -να Pl

μέσφα μιν οὐράνιον κρύος ὤλεσεν· ἦ γὰρ ἔμεινεν   3550
αἴθριος, οὐρανίων ἀντίπαλος νεφέων.
5 Πρόκνη καὶ Μήδεια, κατ' "Αιδος αἰδέσθητε
μητέρες ὀρνίθων ἔργα διδασκόμεναι.

VIII

'Ανδρομάχης ἔτι θρῆνον ἀκούομεν, εἰσέτι Τροίην
δερκόμεθ' ἐκ βάθρων πᾶσαν ἐρειπομένην   3555
καὶ μόθον Αἰάντειον ὑπὸ στεφάνηι τε πόληος
ἔκδετον ἐξ ἵππων "Εκτορα συρόμενον
5 Μαιονίδεω διὰ μοῦσαν, ὃν οὐ μία πατρὶς ἀοιδόν
κοσμεῖται, γαίης δ' ἀμφοτέρης κλίματα.

IX

ἡρώων ὀλίγαι μὲν ἐν ὄμμασιν, αἱ δ' ἔτι λοιπαί   3560
πατρίδες οὐ πολλῶι γ' αἰπύτεραι πεδίων·
οἵην καὶ σέ, τάλαινα, παρερχόμενός γε Μυκήνην
ἔγνων †αἰπολίου† παντὸς ἐρημοτέρην,
5 αἰπολικὸν μήνυμα· γέρων δέ τις 'ἡ πολύχρυσος'
εἶπεν 'Κυκλώπων τῆιδ' ἐπέκειτο πόλις'.   3565

X

"Αργος, 'Ομηρικὲ μῦθε, καὶ 'Ελλάδος ἱερὸν οὖδας
καὶ χρυσέη τὸ πάλαι Περσέος ἀκρόπολι,
ἐσβέσθ' ἡρώων κείνων κλέος, οἵ ποτε Τροίης
ἤρειψαν κατὰ γῆς θειόδομον στέφανον.

3 οὐράνιον CPl: -ιος P   4 αἴθριος Jacobs: αἰθέρος PPl

VIII A.P. 9.97 [C] 'Αλφειοῦ Μιτυληναίου   [J] εἰς "Ομηρον τὸν ποιητὴν ὅτι διὰ
τὴν εὐμουσίαν αὐτοῦ πᾶσα πόλις ἀντέχεται αὐτοῦ ὡς ἰδίου πολίτου   Pl A
'Αλφειοῦ Μιτυληναίου   εἰς αὐτόν
2 βάθρων Pl: βαράθρων P   4 ἔκδετον Reiske: ἠδὲ τὸν PPl   6 δ' CPl:
om. P

IX A.P. 9.101 [C] 'Αλφειοῦ Μιτυληναίου   [J] εἰς Μυκήνην τὴν 'Αγαμέμνονος

her; for she stayed in the open air, defiant of the clouds in the sky. Procnê and Medea, blush for shame in Hades; let a hen's action teach you mothers a lesson.

VIII

On Homer's Iliad

Still we hear Andromache's lament, still we see Troy all shattered from its foundations, and the battle-tumult of Ajax, and Hector bound to horses and dragged beneath the city's coronal, through the poetry of Maeonides, whom not one country honours as its singer but regions of both continents.

IX

A visit to Mycenae

Few are the father-cities of heroes before our eyes, and those yet remaining are not much higher than their plains. Such were you also, unhappy Mycenê, when I passed by and recognised you, more deserted than any ⟨   ⟩, a herdsman's show-piece. 'Rich in gold', thus spoke some agèd man, 'here stood the Cyclopean city.'

X

Troy has outlived the Argive palaces

Argos, Homeric legend, and holy soil of Hellas, and once-golden acropolis of Perseus, you have extinguished the fame of those heroes who of old brought low to the ground Troy's

καὶ Μενελάου πόλιν τὴν ποτε πολύχρυσον νυνὶ δὲ ἔρημον οὖσαν καὶ μηδὲ ἴχνος πόλεως cῴζουcαν Pl A ᾽Αντιπάτρου Θεccαλονικέωc εἰc τὸ αὐτό
1 ἐν ὄμμαcιν Pl: ὀνόματι P | δ᾽ ἔτι Reiske: δέ τε PPl   2 πολλῶι γ᾽ Jacobs: πολλῶν PPl   3 γε Stephanus: τε PPl

X *A.P.* 9.104 [C] ᾽Αλφειοῦ Μιτυληναίου   [J] εἰc τὴν αὐτὴν πόλιν καὶ εἰc τὸ ῎Αργος καὶ τὴν ὅλην ῾Ελλάδα, καὶ ὅτι ἐcβέcθη τὰ τῶν ἡρώων οἵτινεc τὴν Τροίαν ἐξεπόρθηcαν Pl A ᾽Αλφειοῦ Μιτυληναίου
4 ἤρειψαν Pl: -ριψ- P

5 ἀλλ' ἡ μὲν κρείςςων ἐςτὶν πόλις, αἱ δὲ πεςοῦςαι   3570
δείκνυςθ' εὐμύκων αὔλια βουκολίων.

XI

τλήμονες οἷς ἀνέραστος ἔφυ βίος, οὔτε γὰρ ἔρξαι
εὐμαρὲς οὔτ' εἰπεῖν ἔςτι τι νόςφι Πόθων.
καὶ γὰρ ἐγὼ νῦν εἰμι λίην βραδύς, εἰ δ' ἐπίδοιμι
Ξεινόφιλον, στεροπῆς πτήςομαι ὀξύτερος.   3575
5 τοὔνεκεν οὐ φεύγειν γλυκὺν Ἵμερον ἀλλὰ διώκειν
πᾶςι λέγω· ψυχῆς ἐςτιν Ἔρως ἀκόνη.

XII

ἁρπάςομαι πυρόεςςαν, Ἔρως, ⟨χερὸς⟩ ἐκ ςέο πεύκην,
ςυλήςω δ' ὤμων ἀμφικρεμῆ φαρέτρην,
εἴ γ' ἐτύμως εὕδεις, πυρὸς ἔγγονε, καὶ ςέο φῶτες   3580
πρὸς βαιὸν τόξων εὐνομίην ἄγομεν.
5 ἀλλὰ καὶ ὣς ςε δέδοικα, δολοπλόκε, μή τινα κεύθηις
εἰς ἐμέ, κἢν ὕπνωι πικρὸν ὄνειρον ἴδηις.

ΑΝΤⲰΝΙΟΥ

I

ἡ πρὶν ἐγὼ Περςῆος ἀκρόπτολις αἰθερίοιο,
ἡ πικρὸν Ἰλιάδαις ἀςτέρα θρεψαμένη,   3585
αἰπολίοιςιν ἔναυλον ἐρημαίοιςιν ἀνεῖμαι
τίςαςα Πριάμου δαίμοςιν ὀψὲ δίκας.

5 ἐςτὶν πόλις P: ἐςτὶ πτόλις Pl   6 εὐμύκων Lascaris: -μήκ- PPl
XI A.P. 12.18 Ἀλφειοῦ Μιτυληναίου   Syll.S s.a.n   caret Pl
XII A.Pl. (A) 212 Ἀλφειοῦ   εἰς τὸ αὐτό   caret P
1 χερὸς suppl. edd. vett.: lacuna relicta om. Pl

god-built coronal. The stronger city is Troy: you who have fallen are pointed at as stalls of lowing cattle.

XI

Life without love is dullness

Wretched are they whose life is loveless; without the soft passions, neither deed nor word comes easily. All too sluggish am I this moment, but if I set eyes on Xeinophilus, sharper than lightning I shall fly. So I command all men, do not run from sweet Desire but chase him; Love is the whetstone of the soul.

XII

On a statue of Eros asleep

I shall snatch the fiery pine-torch, Eros, from your hand and steal from your shoulders the quiver that hangs around them, if truly you are asleep, Fire's progeny, and we mortals have a moment's peace from your bow and arrows. Yet even so I dread you, guile-weaver, lest you have one hidden, destined for me, and even in sleep see a cruel dream.

ANTONIUS

I

The ruins of Mycenae

I, once the acropolis of aery Perseus, nurse of a star so hateful to the sons of Ilos, forsaken am I, a fold for lonely goat-flocks, at long last paying atonement to the avenging spirits of Priam.

I *A.P.* 9.102 [C] Ἀντωνίου Ἀργείου [J] εἰς τὴν αὐτὴν πόλιν Μυκήνας καὶ ὅτι πρὸ τῶν Ἀτρειδῶν Περσέως ἐχρημάτιζε Pl B Ἀντωνίου Ἀργείου
I ἀκρόπτολις Pl: ἀκρέπτ- P   3 ἀνεῖμαι Pl: ἀνεῖσα P

ΑΡΧΙΑ

I

νήπι᾽ Ἔρως, πόρθει με τὸ κρήγυον, εἷς με κένωσον
πᾶν σὺ βέλος, λοιπὴν μηκέτ᾽ ἀφεὶς γλυφίδα,
ὡς ἂν μοῦνον ἕλοις ἰοῖς ἐμέ, καί τινα χρήιζων   3590
ἄλλον ὀιστεῦσαι μηκέτ᾽ ἔχοις ἀκίδα.

II

φεύγειν δεῖ τὸν Ἔρωτα· κενὸς πόνος, οὐ γὰρ ἀλύξω   (3592)
πεζὸς ὑπὸ πτηνοῦ πυκνὰ διωκόμενος.

III

ὁπλίζευ, Κύπρι, τόξα καὶ εἰς σκοπὸν ἥσυχος ἐλθέ
ἄλλον, ἐγὼ γὰρ ἔχω τραύματος οὐδὲ τόπον.   3595

IV

σοὶ τάδε, Πὰν σκοπιῆτα, παναίολα δῶρα σύναιμοι
τρίζυγες ἐκ τρισσῆς θέντο λινοστασίης,
δίκτυα μὲν Δᾶμις θηρῶν, Πίγρης δὲ πετηνῶν
λαιμοπέδας, Κλείτωρ δ᾽ εἰναλίφοιτα λίνα.
5 ὧν τὸν μὲν καὶ ἐσαῦθις ἐν ἠέρι, τὸν δ᾽ ἔτι θείης   3600
εὔστοχον ἐν πόντωι, τὸν δὲ κατὰ δρυόχους.

I *A.P.* 5.58 Ἀρχίου [J] εἰς Ἔρωτα caret Pl
1 πόρθει Page: -θεῖς P | κρήγυον Reiske: κρίγυον C, κρίσιον (?) P, γρ. κήρινον sscr. C   4 ἔχοις Jacobs: -εις P
II *A.P.* 5.59 τοῦ αὐτοῦ [sc. Ἀρχίου] [J] ὁμοίως Pl A s.a.n.
1 δεῖ P: δὴ Pl

400

ARCHIAS

I

Love's victim

Infant Love, destroy me in good earnest, empty every dart upon me, no longer leave a shaft. So shall you conquer none but me with your arrows, and when you need to shoot another man you shall no longer have a barb.

II

Love is inescapable

I must fly from Love,—but it is labour lost; I shall not escape, a runner close pursued by a flyer.

III

Aphrodite's victim

Arm yourself, Cypris, with your bow and go to some other target in peace of mind; in me is not even space for a wound.

IV

Dedications by three brothers

To you, Pan the highlander, three brothers from three kinds of snaring have dedicated these splendid gifts,—Damis his meshes for beasts, Pigres his neck-fetters for birds, Cleitor his sea-roaming nets. Make the one hereafter also of good aim in the air, the other again in the sea, the other in the thickets.

III *A.P.* 5.98 ἄδηλον, οἱ δὲ ᾽Αρχίου   Pl A tamquam finis epigrammatis 5.67 (τοῦ αὐτοῦ, sc. Νικάρχου, Pl; Καπίτωνος P)
2 οὐδὲ P: ὧδε Pl

IV *A.P.* 6.16 ᾽Αρχίου εἰς τὸ αὐτό   [C] τῶι Πανὶ παρὰ τριῶν ἀδελφῶν ἁλιέων Pl A ᾽Αρχίου εἰς τὸ αὐτό   Suid. s.vv. σκοπιήτης (1 s.), δρύοχοι (5 τὸν δ᾽–6)
2 τρισσῆς PlSuid.: -ᾶς P   **3** πετηνῶν P: πετειν- Pl

V

ἀγραύλωι τάδε Πανὶ βιαρκέος ἄλλος ἀπ' ἄλλης
αὔθαιμοι τρισσοὶ δῶρα λινοστασίης,
Πίγρης μὲν δειραχθὲς ἐΰβροχον ἄμμα πετηνῶν,
Δᾶμις δ' ὑλονόμων δίκτυα τετραπόδων,
5 ἄρκυν δ' εἰναλίων Κλείτωρ πόρεν· οἷς σὺ δι' αἴθρας
καὶ πελάγευς καὶ γᾶς εὔστοχα πέμπε λίνα.

3605

VI

ταῦτά σοι ἔκ τ' ὀρέων ἔκ τ' αἰθέρος ἔκ τε θαλάσσας
τρεῖς γνωτοὶ τέχνας σύμβολα, Πάν, ἔθεσαν·
ταῦτα μὲν εἰναλίων Κλείτωρ λίνα, κεῖνα δὲ Πίγρης
οἰωνῶν, Δᾶμις τὰ τρίτα τετραπόδων.
5 οἷς ἅμα χερσαίηισιν, ἅμ' ἠερίηισιν ἐν ἄγραις,
Ἀγρεῦ, ἅμ' ἐν πλωταῖς ὡς πρὶν ἀρωγὸς ἴθι.

3610

VII

τρίζυγες, οὐρεσίοικε, κασίγνητοι τάδε τέχνας
ἄλλος ἀπ' ἀλλοίας σοὶ †τάδε†, Πάν, ἔθεσαν·
καὶ τὰ μὲν ὀρνίθων Πίγρης, τὰ δὲ δίκτυα θηρῶν
Δᾶμις, ὁ δὲ Κλείτωρ εἰναλίων ἔπορεν.
5 τῶν ὁ μὲν ἐν ξυλόχοισιν, ὁ δ' ἠερίηισιν ἐν ἄγραις
αἰέν, ὁ δ' ἐν πελάγεσσ' εὔστοχον ἄρκυν ἔχοι.

3615

V *A.P.* 6.179 Ἀρχίου ἀνάθημα τῶι Πανὶ παρὰ τριῶν ἀδελφῶν θηρευτῶν Pl A
τοῦ αὐτοῦ [sc. Ἀρχίου] εἰς τὸ αὐτό Suid. s.vv. βιαρκέος (1 βιαρκ.–2),
δειραχθές (3 δειρ.–πετ.)
3 Πίγρης CPl: -ις P | πετηνῶν PlᵃᶜSuid.: πετανῶν P, πετεινῶν Plᵖᶜ 4 ὑλο-
νόμων Pl: ὑλαν- P 5 πόρεν Pl: -ρε P | αἴθρας P: -ης Pl 6 πελάγευς καὶ
γᾶς P: γ. καὶ π. Pl

VI *A.P.* 6.180 τοῦ αὐτοῦ [sc. Ἀρχίου] εἰς τὸ αὐτό Pl A τοῦ αὐτοῦ [sc.
Ἀρχίου] εἰς τὸ αὐτό

V

On the same

To rustic Pan three brothers offer these gifts, each from different life-sustaining snares,—Pigres has brought his throat-oppressing slip-knot noose for birds, Damis his nets for forest-roaming quadrupeds, Cleitor his toils for sea-denizens. Do you send them successful netting by air and sea and land.

VI

On the same

From hills, from sky, from sea these tokens of their craft three brothers have dedicated, Pan, to you,—Cleitor these nets for sea-denizens, Pigres those for birds, Damis the third for quadrupeds. Go their helper as before, Hunter, at once in the chase by land, by air, by water.

VII

On the same

Mountain-dweller, three brothers have dedicated, Pan, these offerings to you, each from a different craft,—Pigres has brought the nets for birds, Damis those for beasts, Cleitor those for sea-denizens. Ever may the one have a snare of good aim in the thickets, the second in chase aloft, the third in the seas.

1 θαλάccαc CPl: -ηc P   2 τέχναc P: -ηc Pl   3 Πίγρηc CPl: -ιc P
5 χερcαίηιcιν Pl: -αίαιcιν P   6 πλωταῖc P: -οῖc Pl
VII *A.P.* 6.181 τοῦ αὐτοῦ [sc. ᾿Αρχίου]   εἰc τὸ αὐτό   Pl A τοῦ αὐτοῦ [sc.
᾿Αρχίου]   εἰc τὸ αὐτό
1 οὐρεcίοικε Pl: οὐρέcιοι· καὶ P   3 Πίγρηc CPl: -ιc P   5 ὁ μὲν CPl: μὲν
P | ἠερίηιcιν Pl^{pc}: -ίοιcιν PPl^{ac}   6 αἰέν Pl: εἶεν P | πελάγεcc᾿ Page: -γει PPl |
εὔcτοχον ἄρκυν CPl^{pc}: ἄρκυν εὔcτοχον P, εὔcτοχον ἄγραν Pl^{ac}

VIII

αἱ τρισσαὶ Σατύρη τε καὶ Ἡράκλεια καὶ Εὐφρώ   3620
θυγατέρες Ξούθου καὶ Μελίτης Σάμιαι,
ἁ μὲν ἀραχναίοιο μίτου πολυδινέα λάτριν
ἄτρακτον δολιχᾶς οὐκ ἄτερ ἀλακάτας,
5 ἁ δὲ πολυσπαθέων μελεδήμονα κερκίδα πέπλων
εὔθροον, ἁ τριτάτα δ᾽ εἰροχαρῆ τάλαρον,   3625
οἷς ἔσχον χερνῆτα βίον δηναιόν, Ἀθάνα
πότνια, ταῦθ᾽ αἱ σαὶ σοὶ θέσαν ἐργάτιδες.

IX

σάνδαλα ταῦτα Βίτιννα, πολυπλέκτου δὲ Φιλαινίς
πορφύρεον χαίτας ῥύτορα κεκρύφαλον,
ξανθὰ δ᾽ Ἀντίκλεια νόθον κεύθουσαν ἄημα   3630
ῥιπίδα τὰν μαλερὸν θάλπος ἀμυνομέναν,
5 λεπτὸν δ᾽ Ἡράκλεια τόδε προκάλυμμα προσώπου
τευχθὲν ἀραχναίηις εἴκελον ἀρπεδόσιν,
ἁ δὲ καλὸν σπείρημα περισφυρίοιο δράκοντος
οὔνομ᾽ Ἀριστοτέλεω πατρὸς ἐνεγκαμένα·   3635
ἅλικες ἀγλαὰ δῶρα, γαμοστόλε, σοὶ τάδε, Κύπρι,
10 ὤπασαν αἱ γυάλων Ναυκράτιδος ναέται.

X

ταῦτα σαγηναίοιο λίνου δηναιὰ Πριήπωι
λείψανα καὶ κύρτους Φιντύλος ἐκρέμασεν

VIII *A.P.* 6.39 Ἀρχίου ἀνάθημα τῆι Ἀθηνᾶι παρὰ τριῶν ἀδελφῶν γυναικῶν
Pl A Ἀρχίου Suid. s.vv. ἄτρακτον (3 ἀραχν.–4), μίτος (eadem), ἀράχνειον
(3 ἀραχν.–4 ἄτρ.), πολυσπαθής (5), μελεδήματα (5), τάλαρος (6 ἁ–τάλ.),
χερνῆτις (7 s.)
1 Ἡράκλεια C^(γρ)Pl: Εὔκλεια P   2 Ξούθου PPl: Ξάνθ- C   4 ἀλακάτας
CPlSuid.: -της P   6 τριτάτα CPlSuid.: -τη P   8 σοὶ CPlSuid.: om. P

IX *A.P.* 6.207 [PC] Ἀρχίου   [P] εἰς τὸ αὐτό   Suid. s.vv. κεκρύφαλον (2),
ῥύτορα (2), μαλερόν (4), ἀρπεδόσι (5 τόδε–6)   caret Pl
1 πολυπλέκτου Toup: -πλεγκτόν P | δὲ Jacobs: τε P   3–5 ita C marg.:

404

VIII

Dedication of spinning and weaving instruments

The trio Satyrê and Heracleia and Euphro, daughters of Xouthos and Melitê, Samians, the one her spindle, whirling servant of the spidery thread, not without the long distaff, the other her tuneful comb, care-taker of close-woven robes, the third her basket rejoicing in wool,—wherewith they long maintained a life of labour, Lady Athena, these things your hire-women have dedicated to you.

IX

Dedications by five women of Naucratis

Bitinna, these sandals; Philaenis, a purple net, protector of much-braided hair; blonde Anticleia, the fan that hides a counterfeit breeze, defence against the violence of heat; Heracleia, this delicate veil for the face, fashioned like spider's threads; and she who bears the name of her father Aristoteles, the lovely serpent-coils about her ankles,—all of one age, these dwellers in the low-land of Naucratis have given these splendid offerings, Aphrodite, to you, the marriage-president.

X

Dedication by a fisherman

Phintylus has hung up for Priapus these long-lived remnants of his seine-net, and his weels, and crookèd barb fastened to horse-

in unum contraxit P (ξανθὰ δ' 'Αντίκλεια τόδε προκάλυμμα προσώπου)
3 κεύθουσαν ἄημα Toup: -σα νόημα C   4 μαλερὸν...ἀμυνομέναν Suid.:
-ρὰν... -νην C   6 ἀρπεδόσιν CSuid.: ἀρπηδ- P   10 Ναυκράτιδος
Ap.B.: -τίδες P

X A.P. 6.192 [C] 'Αρχίου [P] ἀνάθημα τῶι Πριήπωι παρὰ Φιντύλου Suid.
s.vv. γαμψόν (3 s.), τριτάνυστον (5 καὶ-τριτ.), φελλός (5 ἀβάπτ.–6), ἰαυθμοί
(7 s. οὐδ'–τειρ.)   caret Pl
1 δηναιὰ Salm.: δίν- P | Πριήπωι P: Πριάπ- C   2 Φιντύλος C: incertum quid
lateat in P

καὶ γαμψὸν χαίτηισιν ἐφ᾽ ἱππείηισι πεδηθέν   3640
ἄγκιστρον, κρυφίην εἰναλίοισι πέδην,
5 καὶ δόνακα τριτάνυστον ἀβάπτιστόν τε καθ᾽ ὕδωρ
φελλὸν ἀεὶ κρυφίων σῆμα λαχόντα βόλων·
οὐ γὰρ ἔτι στείβει ποσὶ χοιράδας οὐδ᾽ ἐπιαύει
ἠϊόσιν μογερῶι γήραϊ τειρόμενος.   3645

XI

Τρωιάδι Πελλαναῖος ἀνηέρτησεν Ἀθάναι   (3646)
αὐλὸν ἐριβρεμέταν Μίκκος Ἐνυαλίου,
ὧι ποτε καὶ θυμέληισι καὶ ἐν πολέμοισιν ἔμελψεν
πρόσθε, τὸ μὲν στοναχᾶς σῆμα, τὸ δ᾽ εὐνομίας.

XII

οὐδὲ νέκυς ναυηγὸς ἐπὶ χθόνα Θῆρις ἐλασθείς   3650
κύμασιν ἀγρύπνων λήσομαι ἠϊόνων·
ἦ γὰρ ἁλιρρήκτοις ὑπὸ δειράσιν ἀγχόθι πόντου
δυςμενέος ξείνων χερσὶν ἔκυρσα τάφου·
5 αἰεὶ δὲ βρομέοντα καὶ ἐν νεκύεσσι θαλάσσης
ὁ τλήμων ἄϊω δοῦπον ἀπεχθόμενον.   3655
μόχθων οὐδ᾽ Ἀίδης με κατεύνασεν, ἡνίκα μοῦνος
οὐδὲ θανὼν λείηι κέκλιμαι ἡσυχίηι.

XIII

—εἰπέ, γύναι, τίς ἔφυς.—Πρηξώ.—τίνος ἔπλεο πατρός;
—Καλλιτέλευς.—πάτρας δ᾽ ἐκ τίνος ἐσσί;—Σάμου.

---

6 βόλων Suid.: -λῶν P   8 τειρόμενος CSuid.: πειρ- P
XI *A.P.* 6.195 [P] Ἀρχίου [C] Ἀρχίου γραμματικοῦ [P] ἀνάθημα τῆι
Ἀθηνᾶι παρὰ Παλληναίου   caret Pl
1 Πελλαναῖος Holsten: Παλλ- P   2 ἐριβρεμέταν C: ἀρι- P | Μίκκος Ap.G.:
ϲμικρὸν P   3 ὧι Reiske: ἅι P   4 εὐνομίας Jacobs: -ίης P

hair, hidden trap for sea-denizens, and his triply stretched cane-rod, and his cork, unsinkable in the water, ever serving as indicator of the unseen catch. Oppressed by the pains of age, he treads the crags no longer underfoot nor slumbers on the beaches.

XI

Dedication by a trumpeter

To Athena of Troy Miccus of Pellenê hung up the loud-thundering flute of the war-god, which in time past he sounded at altars and in battle, the one as a token of lamentation, the other of law and order.

XII

Epitaph for a drowned man buried on the beach

Not even in death shall I, Theris, driven shipwrecked to land by the waves, forget the unsleeping shores; for close to my enemy the ocean, under spray-beaten crags, at strangers' hands I got my tomb. So evermore, poor wretch, even among the dead I hear the hated sea-thunder roaring. Not even Hades has given me rest from troubles, since I alone am not laid in calm repose, not even in death.

XIII

Epitaph for a woman dying in child-birth

—Tell, lady, who you are.—Prexo.—Who was your father?—Calliteles.—From what country do you come?—Samos.—Who

XII *A.P.* 7.278 [C] Ἀρχίου Βυζαντίου   [J] εἰς ναυηγὸν ἀνώνυμον   ἄλλο θαυμαστόν   Pl β Ἀρχίου
1 Θῆρις Pl: θηρςὶν P   3 ὑπὸ δειράσιν P: ποτὶ χοιράσιν Pl   4 ξείνων Pl: -νου P   6 ἀπεχθόμενον P: ἐπερχόμενον Pl   7 οὐδ' P: δ' οὐδ' Pl | κατεύνασεν Pl: κατέναυσεν P   8 λείηι PPl: τελείηι C
XIII *A.P.* 7.165 [C] Ἀντιπάτρου Cιδωνίου, οἱ δὲ Ἀρχίου   [J] εἰς τὴν αὐτήν caret Pl

—μνᾶμα δέ cου τίc ἔτευξε;—Θεόκριτοc, ὅc με cύνευνον   3660
ἤγετο.—πῶc δ᾽ ἐδάμηc;—ἄλγεcιν ἐν λοχίοιc.
5 —εἰν ἔτεcιν τίcιν εὖcα;—δὶc ἔνδεκα.—παῖδα δὲ λείπειc;
—νηπίαχον, τριccῶν Καλλιτέλην ἐτέων.
—ζωῆc τέρμαθ᾽ ἵκοιτο μετ᾽ ἀνδράcι.—καὶ cέο δοίη
παντὶ Τύχη βιότωι τερπνόν, ὁδῖτα, τέλοc.   3665

XIV

Ἄιδοc ὦ νεκυηγὲ κεχαρμένε δάκρυcι πάντων,
ὃc βαθὺ πορθμεύειc τοῦτ᾽ Ἀχέροντοc ὕδωρ,
εἰ καί cοι βέβριθεν ὑπ᾽ εἰδώλοιcι καμόντων
ὁλκάc, μὴ προλίπηιc Διογένη με κύνα.
5 ὀλπὴν καὶ cκίπωνα φέρω καὶ διπλόον εἶμα   3670
καὶ πήρην καί cοι ναυτιλίηc ὀβολόν·
καὶ ζωὸc τάδε μοῦνον, ἃ καὶ νέκυc ὧδε κομίζω,
εἶχον, ὑπ᾽ ἠελίου δ᾽ οὔτι λέλοιπα φάει.

XV

—καὶ γενέταν τοῦ νέρθε καὶ οὔνομα καὶ χθόνα φώνει,
cτάλα, καὶ ποίαι κηρὶ δαμεὶc ἔθανε.   3675
—†πατήρ† μὲν Πρίαμοc, γᾶ δ᾽ Ἴλιον, οὔνομα δ᾽ Ἕκτωρ,
ὦνερ, ὑπὲρ πάτραc δ᾽ ὤλετο μαρνάμενοc.

XVI

μοῦνοc ἐναιρομένοιcιν ὑπέρμαχον ἀcπίδα τείναc
νηυcὶ βαρὺν Τρώων, Αἶαν, ἔμειναc ἄρη,

XIV A.P. 7.68 Ἀρχίου   εἰc τὸν αὐτόν [J] Διογένην   Pl A ὡc ἀπὸ τοῦ αὐτοῦ [sc. Διογένουc]   Suid. s.v. καμόντων (3 s. ὁλκάc)
1 κεχαρμένε CPl: -νοc P   7 μοῦνον CPl: -να P
XV A.P. 7.140 Ἀρχίου [J] Μακεδόνοc   [P] εἰc τὸν αὐτόν [sc. Ἀλέξανδρον τὸν Μακεδόνα]   Pl A Ἀρχίου   εἰc αὐτόν
2 ἔθανε P: -νεν Pl   3 πατὴρ μὲν P: γεννήτωρ Pl   4 ὦνερ P: ὦ ξέν᾽ Pl

made your tomb?—Theocritus, who took me for wife.—How did you die?—In pains of child-birth.—At what age?—Twenty-two.—Do you leave a child?—An infant of three years, Calliteles.—May he reach the end of life among grown men.—And may Fortune give to all your life, wayfarer, a happy ending.

XIV

Diogenes the Cynic on his way to Hades

Corpse-carrier of Hades, rejoicing in all men's tears, ferryman of this deep water of Acheron, though your boat be heavy-laden with the ghosts of the departed, yet leave not me behind, Diogenes the Cynic. I carry a flask and staff and double cloak and wallet and your obol for the voyage. And that which my corpse thus brings is all I had in life; I have left nothing beneath the sun's light.

XV

Epitaph for Hector

—Grave-stone, declare the father and name and land of him below, and by what doom he died overthrown.
—His father was Priam, his country Ilium; his name, sir, was Hector, and he died fighting for his fatherland.

XVI

Praise of Ajax

Alone you held your champion shield before the dying, Ajax, and withstood the Trojans' fighting, so heavy upon the ships;

XVI A.P. 7.147 [C] 'Αρχίου [P] εἰς τὸν αὐτόν [J] Αἴαντα [P] 'Αρχίου [J] τὸν Τελαμῶνος [hic 'Αρχίου τὸν Τελα erasit C, idem τὸν Τελα supra μῶνος scripsit] τὸν ἔξοχον Ἑλλήνων ἀρχόν, ἀλλὰ διὰ κενὴν δόξαν μαινόμενος ἑαυτὸν ἀπέσφαξεν Pl A 'Αρχίου εἰς αὐτόν   Suid. s.vv. ἐναίρειν (1 s.), χερμαδίωι (3), πάταγος (4)
1 ὑπέρμαχον PlSuid.: -χος P   2 Αἴαν Brunck: αἰὲν PPlSuid. | ἔμεινας CPl: -ναν P | ἄρη PPl: -ην C, idem in -η correxit

οὐδέ σε χερμαδίων ὦσεν κτύπος, οὐ νέφος ἰῶν,   3680
    οὐ πῦρ, οὐ δοράτων, οὐ ξιφέων πάταγος,
5 ἀλλ᾽ αὔτως προβλής τε καὶ ἔμπεδος ὡς τις ἐρίπνα
    ἱδρυθεὶς ἔτλης λαίλαπα δυσμενέων.
εἰ δέ σε μὴ τεύχεσσιν ᾿Αχιλλέος ὥπλισεν ῾Ελλάς
    ἄξιον ἀντ᾽ ἀρετᾶς ὅπλα ποροῦσα γέρας,   3685
Μοιράων βουλῆισι τάδ᾽ ἄμπλακεν, ὡς ἂν ὑπ᾽ ἐχθρῶν
10   μή τινος, ἀλλὰ σὺ σῆι πότμον ἕληις παλάμηι.

XVII

αἰωρῆι θήρειον ἱμασσόμενος δέμας αὔραις,
    τλᾶμον, ἀορτηθεὶς ἐκ λασίας πίτυος·
αἰωρῆι, Φοίβωι γὰρ ἀνάρσιον εἰς ἔριν ἔστης,   3690
    πρῶνα Κελαινίτην ναιετάων Σάτυρε·
5 σεῦ δὲ βοὰν αὐλοῖο μελίβρομον οὐκέτι Νύμφαι
    ὡς πάρος ἐν Φρυγίοις οὔρεσι πευσόμεθα.

XVIII

Θρήικας αἰνείτω τις ὅτι στοναχεῦσι μὲν υἷας
    μητέρος ἐκ κόλπων πρὸς φάος ἐρχομένους,   3695
ἔμπαλι δ᾽ ὀλβίζουσιν ὅσους αἰῶνα λιπόντας
    ἀπροϊδὴς Κηρῶν λάτρις ἔμαρψε μόρος·
5 οἱ μὲν γὰρ ζώοντες ἀεὶ παντοῖα περῶσιν
    ἐς κακά, τοὶ δὲ κακῶν εὗρον ἄκος φθίμενοι.

3 ὦσεν P: -σε PlSuid.　　5 ἐρίπνα P: -νη Pl　　6 ἱδρυθεὶς P: ἱδρυνθ- Pl
8 ἀρετᾶς P: -ῆς Pl　　9 ἄμπλακεν P: ἤμ- Pl　　10 σὺ σῆι P: τεῆι Pl

XVII *A.P.* 7.696 [C] ᾿Αρχίου Μιτυληναίου　　[J] εἰς Σάτυρον κρεμασθέντα διὰ
τὸ ἐρίσαι ᾿Απόλλωνι　ὅμοιον τῶι Μαρσύαι　Pl в ᾿Αρχίου

nor rattle of stones drove you back, nor cloud of arrows, nor fire, nor din of spears and swords. But even so, firm-fixed as a cliff, standing forward and steadfast, you endured the hurricane of your foes. If Hellas armed you not in the harness of Achilles, giving you the weapons that were the honour worthy of your valour, she erred thus by the will of the Fates; that you might take your doom from no enemy, but at your own hand.

XVII

On Marsyas

There you hang, your beast-like body scourged by the winds, poor wretch, suspended from a shaggy pine. There you hang, Satyr that dwelt on Celaenae's headland, because you stood up to unseemly strife with Phoebus; and we Nymphs shall no longer hear, as in time past, the loud sweet call of your flute on the Phrygian hills.

XVIII

A Thracian custom

Let all men praise the Thracians, since they bewail their sons as they come forth from their mothers' wombs to the daylight, and on the contrary call happy all who leave life by arrest of the Fates' servitor, Death unforeseen. For the living ever pass to all manner of misery, but the others have found in death their misery's cure.

1 θήρειον Pl: -ρίον P   4 Κελαινίτην Brunck: -νήτην P, -νῖτιν Pl   6 ὡς Pl: τὼς P | Φρυγίοις CPl: -ίαις P | πευσόμεθα Pl et man. rec. in P: -σόμενον P

XVIII *A.P.* 9.111 [C] Ἀρχίου Μιτυληναίου [J] ἔπαινος Θραικῶν ὅτι γεννωμένων μὲν ἀνθρώπων ὀδύρονται, τελευτώντων δὲ χαρμόσυνα καὶ τελετὰς ἄγουσιν Pl A Ἀρχίου

XIX

ὁ πρὶν ἀελλοπόδων λάμψας πλέον Ἀετὸς ἵππων,   3700
ὁ πρὶν ὑπαὶ μίτραις κῶλα καθαψάμενος,
ὃν Φοίβου χρησμωιδὸς ἀέθλιον ἔστεφε Πυθώ
ὀρνύμενον πτανοῖς ὠκυπέταις ἴκελον,
5 καὶ Νεμέη βλοσυροῖο τιθηνήτειρα λέοντος
Πῖσά τε καὶ δοιὰς ἠιόνας Ἰσθμὸς ἔχων,   3705
νῦν κλοιῶι δειρὴν πεπεδημένος οἷα χαλινῶι
καρπὸν ἀλεῖ Δηοῦς ὀκριόεντι λίθωι,
ἴσαν μοῖραν ἔχων Ἡρακλέι· καὶ γὰρ ἐκεῖνος
10 τόσσ᾽ ἀνύσας δούλαν ζεῦγλαν ἐφηρμόσατο.

XX

ἁ πάρος ἀντίφθογγον ἀποκλάγξασα νομεῦσι   3710
πολλάκι καὶ δρυτόμοις κίσσα καὶ ἰχθυβόλοις,
πολλάκι δὲ κρέξασα πολύθροον, οἷά τις ἀχώ,
κέρτομον ἀντωιδοῖς χείλεσιν ἁρμονίαν,
5 νῦν εἰς γᾶν ἄγλωσσος ἀναύδητός τε πεσοῦσα
κεῖμαι μιμητὰν ζᾶλον ἀνηναμένα.   3715

XXI

πρὶν μὲν ἐπὶ χλωροῖς ἐριθηλέος ἔρνεσι πεύκας
ἥμενος ἢ σκιερᾶς ἀκροκόμου πίτυος
ἔκρεκες εὐτάρσοιο δι᾽ ἰξύος ἀχέτα μολπάν
τέττιξ, οἰονόμοις τερπνότερον χέλυος.

XIX *A.P.* 9.19 [C] Ἀρχίου Μιτυληναίου   [J] εἰς ἵππον ἀθλοφόρον γηράσαντα
καὶ ἀντὶ στεφάνων καὶ νίκης μύλην ἀνταλλαξάμενον   Pl A Ἀρχίου
1 bis scriptum in P   2 μίτραις CPl: μήτ- P   5 Νεμέη Pl: -ηι P | τιθηνήτειρα
CPl: -τῆρα P   7 κλοιῶι P: κλοιὸν Pl | δειρὴν edd. vett.: -ρῆ PPl | χαλινῶι
Pl: -νὸν P   8 ἀλεῖ Casaubon: ἐλαῖ P, ἐλᾶι Pl   9 ἴσαν P: -ην Pl   10
δούλαν P: -ην Pl
XX *A.P.* 7.191 [C] Ἀρχίου   [J] εἰς κίσσαν τὸ ὄρνεον διὰ τὸ εἶναι αὐτὸ ὠιδικόν

XIX

On a champion race-horse

'Eagle', who was once most brilliant of storm-swift horses, who once had limbs bound below with chaplets, by Phoebus' oracular Pytho crowned champion, racing like a swift-winged bird, by Nemea too, nurse of the fierce lion, and by Pisa and the Isthmus with its twin beaches,—now, his neck fettered with a collar as if by the bridle, he grinds Demeter's corn with the rugged stone, suffering a fate like Heracles'; for he too, after so many accomplishments, put on the yoke of slavery.

XX

Epitaph for a jay

I, the jay, who often in time past screamed back in answer to herdsmen and woodcutters and fishermen, and often struck up a manifold strain of mockery with lips that gave note for note, as good as any echo, now tongueless and voiceless I lie fallen to the ground, renouncing my zeal for mimicry.

XXI

Epitaph for a cicada

In bygone days perched on green branches of luxuriant fir, or of shade-pine with crown of foliage, you would strike up a melody, tuneful cicada, along your fine-winged waist, to shep-

PlΑ'Αρχίου εἰc κίccαν   Suid. s.vv. ἀντίφθογγον (1 s.), κερτόμιος (3 s.), ἀντωιδή (3–6), ἀγλωccία (5 s.)
1 ἀποκλάγξαcα PSuid.: -κλάξ- Pl   2 κίccα PlSuid.: κίccαι P   3 δὲ P: δὴ Pl, utrumque Suid.
XXI A.P. 7.213 [C] 'Αρχίου [J] εἰc τέττιγα ὑπὸ μυρμήκων ἀναιρεθέντα Pl a
'Αρχίου εἰc τὸ αὐτό   Suid. s.vv. ἐριθηλέος (1), ἰξύν (3 s.), ἀπροϊδής (6), Μαιονίδαc (7 s.)
1 χλωροῖc P: χλοερ- PlSuid. | πεύκαc CPlSuid.: -ηc PSuid.

5 νῦν δέ σε μυρμάκεσσιν ὑπ' εἰνοδίοισι δαμέντα   3720
  Ἄιδος ἀπροϊδὴς ἀμφεκάλυψε μυχός.
εἰ δ' ἑάλως, συγγνωστόν, ἐπεὶ καὶ κοίρανος ὕμνων
  Μαιονίδας γρίφοις ἰχθυβόλων ἔθανεν.

XXII

οὐκέτι παφλάζοντα διαΐσσων βυθὸν ἅλμης,
  δελφίς, πτοιήσεις εἰναλίων ἀγέλας,   3725
οὐδὲ πολυτρήτοιο μέλος καλάμοιο χορεύων
  ὑγρὸν ἀναρρίψεις ἅλμα παρὰ σκαφίcιν,
5 οὐδὲ σύ γ', ἀφρηστά, Νηρηΐδας ὡς πρὶν ἀείρων
  νώτοις πορθμεύσεις Τηθύος εἰς πέρατα·
ἦ γὰρ ἴσον πρηῶνι Μαλείης ὡς ἐκυκήθη   3730
  κῦμα, †πολυψάμμους ὦσεν ἐπὶ ψαμάθους†.

XXIII

ἕν ποτε παμφαίνοντι μέλαν πτερὸν αἰθέρι νωμῶν
  σκορπίον ἐκ γαίης εἶδε θορόντα κόραξ,
ὃν μάρψων ὤρουσεν, ὁ δ' ἀΐξαντος ἐπ' οὔδας
  οὐ βραδὺς εὐκέντρωι πέζαν ἔτυψε βέλει,   3735
5 καὶ ζωῆς μιν ἄμερσεν. ἴδ' ὡς ὃν ἔτευχεν ἐπ' ἄλλωι
  ἐκ κείνου τλήμων αὐτὸς ἔδεκτο μόρον.

XXIV

αὐτὸς σὺν κίχλαισιν ὑπὲρ φραγμοῖο διωχθείς
  κόσσυφος ἠερίης κόλπον ἔδυ νεφέλης,

XXII A.P. 7.214 [C] τοῦ αὐτοῦ [sc. Ἀρχίου] [J] εἰς δελφῖνα ἐκβρασθέντα ὑπὸ
τῆς θαλάσσης ἐν τῆι χέρσωι   Suid. s.vv. Τηθύς (5 s.), πρῆνες (7 s.)   caret Pl
1 ἅλμης P: -μας C   **4** ἀναρρίψεις Ap.B.: -ψαις P   **5-6** hoc loco Schaefer:
post 7-8 P   **5** Νηρηΐδας Suid.: Νιρ- P   **7** ἦ Suid. (ἢ): εἰ P | πρηῶνι
C: πρίωνι P

XXIII A.P. 9.339 [C] Ἀρχίου Μιτυληναίου   εἰς κόρακα καὶ σκορπίον ὃν ὁ κόραξ
μέλλων ἐσθίειν ὑπ' αὐτοῦ πληγεὶς ἀνηιρέθη   Pl A Ἀρχίου

herds more joy-giving than the lyre. But now, vanquished by wayside ants, unforeseen the pit of Hades has enveloped you. Yet your downfall is pardonable; for even the lord of song, Maeonides, was killed by mere fishermen's riddles.

XXII

Epitaph for a dolphin

Dolphin, no longer darting through the bubbling deeps of the brine shall you startle the flocks of sea-denizens, nor dancing to the pierced reed's music shall you fling up a leap in the water beside the boats, nor lifting the Nereids on your back as in time past, foam-cleaver, shall you ferry them to the ends of Ocean. For a wave, stirred as high as the headland of Malea, thrust you ⟨upon the sandy shore⟩.

XXIII

The raven and the scorpion

Once upon a time, plying his black wings in the shining sky, a raven saw a scorpion dart up from underground. He swooped to catch it, but as he rushed down to earth it was quick to strike his foot with pointed dart; and so it robbed him of life. See how the doom he was making for another, from that other the poor creature himself received.

XXIV

The song-bird is sacrosanct

A blackbird sank into the bosom of a net in the air, himself together with thrushes chased over a fence. These the cord

---

1 μέλαν πτερὸν Brunck: μελάντερον P, μελάντερος Pl   4 εὐκέντρωι Pl: ἐν κέν- P | πέζαν Pl: πέξαν P   5 ζωῆς μιν Pl: ζωᾶς μὲν P | ὡς ὂν Scaliger: ὅccον PPl

XXIV A.P. 9.343 [C] Ἀρχίου εἰς κόττυφον δίκτυον ὑπαλύξαντα Pl A Ἀρχίου
1 αὐτὸς Page: -ταῖς PPl | κίχλαιcιν P: -ληιcιν Pl

καὶ τὰς μὲν cυνοχηδὸν ἀνέκδρομος ὤχμαcε θῶμιγξ,   3740
  τὸν δὲ μόνον πλεκτῶν αὖθι μεθῆκε λίνων.
5 ἱρὸν ἀοιδοπόλων ἔτυμον γένος· ἦ ἄρα πολλήν
  καὶ κωφαὶ πτανῶν φροντίδ᾿ ἔχουcι πάγαι.

XXV

εὔφημος γλώccηι παραμείβεο τὰν λάλον Ἠχώ
  κοὐ λάλον, ἤν τι κλύω, τοῦτ᾿ ἀπαμειβομέναν·   3745
εἰς cὲ γὰρ ὃν cὺ λέγεις cτρέψω λόγον, ἢν δὲ cιωπᾶις
  cιγήcω· τίς ἐμεῦ γλῶccα δικαιοτέρη;

XXVI

Ἑρμῆ Κωρυκίων ναίων πόλιν, ὦ ἄνα χαίροις   (3748)
  Ἑρμῆ καὶ λιτῆι προσγελάcαις ὁcίηι.

XXVII

τοῦδέ με κυμοπλῆγος ἐπὶ σκοπέλοιο Πρίηπον   3750
  ναῦται Θρηϊκίου θέντο πόρου φύλακα,
πολλάκις οἷς ἦιξα ταχὺς καλέουσιν ἀρωγός,
  ξεῖνε, κατὰ πρύμνης ἡδὺν ἄγων Ζέφυρον.
5 τοὔνεκεν οὔτ᾿ ἄκνισον, ὅπερ θέμις, οὔτ᾿ ἐπιδευῆ
  εἴαρος ἀθρήσεις βωμὸν ἐμὸν στεφάνων,   3755
ἀλλ᾿ αἰεὶ θυόεντα καὶ ἔμπυρον· οὐδ᾿ ἑκατόμβη
  τόccον ὅcον τιμὴ δαίμοcιν ἀνδάνεται.

5 ἱρὸν Lascaris: ἱερὸν PPl | πολλήν Pl: -ὴ P   6 πτανῶν P: πτην- Pl
XXV A.P. 9.27 [C] Ἀρχίου, οἱ δὲ Παρμενίωνος   [J] εἰς τὴν Ἠχὼ διὰ τὸ
ὑcτερόφωνον καὶ ὅτι τὸ ἀκροτέλευτον ἀποκρίνεται Pl A Ἀρχίου εἰς Ἠχώ

gripped fast-held without escape; him alone it rele
from the woven threads. Sacrosanct truly is the race
even insensate traps have great regard for birds.

XXV
Echo

Pass by me with words of good omen on your lips; I am
the talkative un-talkative, answering back only what I
The word you speak I shall return to you; if you are sil
shall be still. What tongue is juster than mine?

XXVI
Sacrifice to Hermes in Corycus

Hermes, dweller in the Corycians' city, lord Hermes, rejoic
and smile upon our simple sacrifice.

XXVII
Priapus, patron of seafarers

Me, Priapus, on this sea-beaten rock the sailors placed as guardian
of the Thracian strait; and often I hastened, stranger, as swift
helper to their call, bringing the delightful west-wind down
astern. Therefore, as is right, you will not see my altar without
savour of sacrifice or wanting in garlands in the spring, but
ever fragrant and alight; not even a hecatomb is so pleasing to
the gods as honour due.

XXVI *A.P.* 9.91 [C] ᾿Αρχίου νεωτέρου   [J] εἰς ῾Ερμῆν τὸν ἐν Κωρυκίωι εὐχή
caret Pl
1 Κωρυκίων Brunck: -ύκιον P
XXVII *A.P.* 10.7 ᾿Αρχίου   Pl A ᾿Αρχίου
1 κυμοπλῆγος P: κυματοπ- Pl   5 ἄκνισον P: -ισσον Pl   7 οὐδ᾿ P: ἐν δ᾿ Pl

XXVIII

βαιὸс ἰδεῖν ὁ Πρίηποс ἐπαιγιαλίτιδα ναίω
χηλὴν †αἰθυίαс οὔποτε ἀντιβίαс†
φοξόс, ἄπουс, οἷόν κεν ἐρημαίηιсιν ἐπ’ ἀκταῖс   3760
ξέссειαν μογερῶν υἱέεс ἰχθυβόλων·
5 ἀλλ’ ἤν τιс γριπεύс με βοηθόον ἢ καλαμευτήс
φωνήсηι, πνοιῆс ἵεμαι ὀξύτεροс.
λεύссω καὶ τὰ θέοντα καθ’ ὕδατοс. ἦ γὰρ ἀπ’ ἔργων
δαίμονεс, οὐ μορφᾶс, γνωcτὸν ἔχουсι τύπον.   3765

XXIX

Πᾶνά με τὸν δειρῆс ἐπὶ λιссάδοс αἰγιαλίτην,
Πᾶνα τὸν εὐόρμων τῆιδ’ ἔφορον λιμένων
οἱ γριπῆεс ἔθεντο· μέλω δ’ ἐγὼ ἄλλοτε κύρτοιс,
ἄλλοτε δ’ αἰγιαλοῦ τοῦδε сαγηνοβόλοιс.
5 ἀλλὰ παράπλει, ξεῖνε, сέθεν δ’ ἐγὼ οὔνεκα ταύτηс   3770
εὐπλοΐηс πέμψω πρηὺν ὄπιсθε νότον.

XXX

τὰс βοῦс καὶ τὸν ἴαсπιν ἰδὼν περὶ χειρὶ δοκήсειс   (3772)
τὰс μὲν ἀναπνείειν, τὸν δὲ χλοηκομέειν.

XXXI

χάλκεοс. ἀλλ’ ἄθρηсον ὅсον θράсοс ἄνυсε κάπρου
ὁ πλάсταс ἔμπνουν θῆρα τυπωсάμενοс,   3775

XXVIII A.P. 10.8 τοῦ αὐτοῦ [sc. ’Αρχίου]   Pl A ’Αρχίου
2 αἰθυίαс P: -θυαс Pl | ἀντιβίαс P: -ίηс Pl   3 κεν Pl: εκεν P   4 ξέссειαν
Pl: -εια, om. compendio quo litt. ν indicare solet, P
XXIX A.P. 10.10 ’Αρχίου νεωτέρου   caret Pl
1 τὸν δειρῆс Jacobs: τόνδ’ ἱερῆс P | λιссάδοс Huschke: διсс- P | αἰγιαλίτην
Huschke: -τηс P

XXVIII

On the same

Small to look at, I, Priapus, dwell on the breakwater by the beach ⟨   ⟩, head pointed, feet wanting, such as the sons of toiling fishermen might carve on deserted shores. Yet if any fisher with net or line calls me to help him, swifter than the wind I rush. What runs over the water also I see. Truly it is from their deeds, not from their shapes, that the character which spirits have is recognised.

XXIX

Pan, patron of seafarers

Me, Pan, the shore-dweller on my smooth ridge, Pan the over-seer of harbours of good anchorage, the fishermen placed here. Sometimes I care for their weels, sometimes for the seine-fishers of this shore. Stranger, sail by; in aid of this fair passage I will send a gentle south-wind behind you.

XXX

On a gem engraved with cows

Seeing the cows and jasper on your finger, you will fancy the former breathe, the latter to be green with grass.

XXXI

On a bronze statue of the Calydonian boar

Only a bronze; but see what boldness the sculptor fashioned for the boar, moulding an animal alive, its neck-hairs bristling,

---

XXX *A.P.* 9.750 Ἀρχίου   εἰc βόαc ἐν δακτυλίωι   Pl A Ἀρχίου   ὅμοιον εἰc δακτύλιον
1 τὸν Pl: τὴν P

XXXI *A.P.* 15.51 Ἀρχίου   εἰc τὸν Καλυδώνιον cῦν   Pl A s.a.n.   εἰc τὸν Καλυδώνιον κάπρον
1 ἄνυcε P: ἤν- Pl

χαίτας αὐχενίους πεφρικότα, θηκτὸν ὀδόντα
βρύχοντα, γλήναις φρικτὸν ἱέντα σέλας,
5 ἀφρῶι χείλεα πάντα δεδευμένον. οὐκέτι θάμβος
εἰ λογάδα στρατιὴν ὤλεσεν ἡμιθέων.

XXXII

μηκέτι ταυροβόροιο βαρὺ βρύχημα λέοντος   3780
πτήσσετε, ληϊνόμοι γειαρόται Νεμέης·
ἢ γὰρ ὑφ' Ἡρακλῆος ἀριστάθλοιο δέδουπεν
αὐχένα θηροφόνοις ἀγχόμενος παλάμαις.
5 ποίμνας ἐξελάσασθε, πάλιν μυκηθμὸν ἀκούοι
Ἠχὼ ἐρημαίης ἐνναέτειρα νάπης.   3785
καὶ σύ, λεοντόχλαινε, πάλιν θωρήσσεο ῥινῶι,
Ἥρης πρηΰνων μισονόθοιο χόλον.

XXXIII

Ἠχὼ πετρήεσσαν ὁρᾶις, φίλε, Πανὸς ἑταίρην
ἀντίτυπον φθογγὴν ἔμπαλιν αἰδομένην,
παντοίων στομάτων λάλον εἰκόνα, ποιμέσιν ἡδύ   3790
παίγνιον· ὅσσα λέγεις, ταῦτα κλύων ἄπιθι.

XXXIV

αὐτὰν ἐκ πόντοιο τιθηνητῆρος Ἀπελλῆς
τὰν Κύπριν γυμνὰν εἶδε λοχευομέναν,
καὶ τοίαν ἐτύπωσε διάβροχον ὕδατος ἀφρῶι,
θλίβουσαν θαλεραῖς χερσὶν ἔτι πλόκαμον.   3795

XXXII *A.Pl.* (A) 94 Ἀρχίου   εἰς τὸν αὐτὸν φονεύοντα τὸν ἐν Νεμέαι λέοντα
caret P
7 θωρήσσεο edd. vett.: -ήσσε Pl

grinding its sharp teeth, with eyeballs darting fearful flames, lips all wet with foam. No longer a marvel, if it destroyed a chosen host of demigods.

XXXII

On a portrayal of Heracles and the Nemean lion

Cringe no longer at the deep roar of the bull-devouring lion, herdsmen and ploughmen of Nemea; it has fallen beneath Heracles, the victor in Labours, its neck strangled by his beast-slaughtering hands. Drive out your flocks; let Echo, dwelling in the lonely glen, hear again the lowing of cattle. And do you, the lion-cloaked, arm yourself again with a hide, appeasing the anger of bastard-hating Hera.

XXXIII

On a portrayal of Echo

It is Echo of the rocks you see, my friend, the comrade of Pan, singing back in a voice the counterpart of yours, talking image of every kind of tongue, the shepherds' pleasant play-mate. Whatever you speak, you may hear it spoken, and so go your way.

XXXIV

On the 'Aphrodite Anadyomene' of Apelles

Apelles saw Cypris herself being born naked from the ocean that reared her, and such he modelled her, still pressing with fresh hands her tresses drenched in the water's foam.

XXXIII *A.Pl.* (A) 154 Λουκιανοῦ, οἱ δὲ 'Αρχίου εἰς τὸ αὐτό   caret P
XXXIV *A.Pl.* (A) 179 'Αρχίου   εἰς τὸ αὐτό   caret P

ΦΛΑΚΚΟΥ

I

ἀργύρεον νυχίων με cυνίcτορα πιcτὸν ἐρώτων
οὐ πιcτῆι λύχνον Φλάκκοc ἔδωκε Νάπηι,
ἧc παρὰ νῦν λεχέεccι μαραίνομαι, εἰc ἐπιόρκου
παντοπαθῆ κούρηc αἴcχεα δερκόμενοc.
5 Φλάκκε, cὲ δ' ἄγρυπνον χαλεπαὶ τείρουcι μέριμναι,   3800
ἄμφω δ' ἀλλήλων ἄνδιχα καιόμεθα.

II

ῥοικοcκελῆ δίχαλον †ἀμμοδυόταν†
ὀπιcθοβάμον' ἀτράχηλον ὀκτάπουν
νήκταν ἐρυμνόνωτον ὀcτρακόχροα
τῶι Πανὶ τὸν πάγουρον ὁρμιηβόλοc   3805
5 ἄγραc ἀπαρχὰν ἀντίθηcι Κώπαcοc.

III

λαίλαπα καὶ μανίην ὀλοῆc προφυγόντα θαλάccηc
ναυηγὸν Λιβυκαῖc κείμενον ἐν ψαμάθοιc
οὐχ ἑκὰc ἠϊόνων πυμάτωι βεβαρημένον ὕπνωι
γυμνὸν ἀπὸ cτυγερῆc ὡc κάμε ναυφθορίηc   3810
5 ἔκτανε λυγρὸc ἔχιc. τί μάτην πρὸc κύματ' ἐμόχθει
τὴν ἐπὶ γῆc φεύγων μοῖραν ὀφειλομένην;

I *A.P.* 5.5 Cτατυλλίου Φλάκκου   [J] εἰc ἑταίραν τινά   caret Pl
2 Φλάκκοc C: Φλάκιοc (?) P | ἔδωκε Νάπηι Salm.: ἔδωκεν ἄπνη P   3–6 bis
scripti: post lacunam relictam P, in lacuna J   3 εἰc Bothe: τῆc PJ   5
τείρουcι P: τήρ- J (quod in τείρ- mutat C)
II *A.P.* 6.196 Cτατυλλίου Φλά⟨κκου⟩   [C] Φλάκκου ἰαμβικόν   [P] ἀνάθημα

FLACCUS

I

A faithless girl

A silver lamp, faithful accomplice of the night's amours, to faithless Napê Flaccus gave me. Now beside her bed I waste away, looking on the all-suffering shamelessness of that perjured girl. And you, Flaccus, unsleeping, are oppressed by cruel cares; far from each other, we are both aflame.

II

Dedication of a crab

Crook-legged, double-clawed, sand-burrower, backward-walker, neckless, eight-footed, swimmer strong-backed, shell-skinned,—this crab as first-fruit of his catch the line-caster Copasus dedicates to Pan.

III

A man saved from shipwreck is killed by a snake

Fled from the tempest and fury of the destructive sea, the shipwrecked man, lying on the Libyan sands, not far from the beaches, weighed down by his last sleep, naked, exhausted as he was from his vessel's hateful wreck, was killed by a deadly viper. Why would he vainly labour against the waves, escaping a doom that was appointed him on land?

τῶι Πανὶ παρὰ Κωπάσου   Pl A Cτατυλλίου Φλάκκου   Suid. s.v. ὀπιcθοβάμων (2 ὀπ.–3 νήκτ.)
1 ῥοικοcκελῆ Sternbach: ῥοιβο- P, ῥαιβο- CPl | δίχαλον P: -χηλ- Pl   3 νήκταν Brunck: νήκταν τ᾽ PPl | ὀcτρακόχροα CPl: -χροον P
III *A.P.* 7.290 [C] Cτατυλλίου Φλάκκου   [J] ἕτερον εἰc ναυηγὸν ὑπὸ ἔχεωc δηχθέντα   Pl A ⟨C⟩τατυλ⟨λ⟩ίου Φλάκκου

IV

"Εβρου χειμερίοις ἀταλὸς κρυμοῖσι δεθέντος
κοῦρος ὀλισθηροῖς ποσσὶν ἔθραυσε πάγον·
τοῦ παρασυρομένοιο περιρραγὲς αὐχέν᾽ ἔκοψεν   3815
θηγαλέον ποταμοῦ Βιστονίοιο τρύφος.
5 καὶ τὸ μὲν ἡρπάσθη δίναις μέρος, ἡ δὲ τεκοῦσα
λειφθὲν ὕπερθε τάφωι μοῦνον ἔθηκε κάρα,
μυρομένη δὲ τάλαινα ᾽τέκος, τέκος᾽ εἶπε ᾽τὸ μέν σου
πυρκαϊή, τὸ δέ σου πικρὸν ἔθαψεν ὕδωρ᾽.   3820

V

Οἰδίποδες διссοί σε καὶ Ἠλέκτρα βαρύμηνις
καὶ δείπνοις ἐλαθεὶς Ἀτρέος Ἥλιος
ἄλλα τε πουλυπαθέσσι, Σοφόκλεες, ἀμφὶ τυράννοις
ἄξια τῆς Βρομίου βύβλα χοροιτυπίης
5 ταγὸν ἐπὶ τραγικοῖο κατήινησαν θιάσοιο   3825
αὐτοῖς ἡρώων φθεγξάμενον στόμασι.

VI

πένθιμον ἡνίκα πατρὶ Πολυξείνης ὑμέναιον
ἤνυσεν ὀγκωτοῦ Πύρρος ὕπερθε τάφου,
ὧδε πολυκλαύτοιο κόμας λακίσασα καρήνου
Κισσηὶς τεκέων κλαῦσε φόνους Ἑκάβη·   3830
5 ᾽πρόσθε μὲν ἀξονίοις φθιτὸν εἴρυσας Ἕκτορα δεσμοῖς,
νῦν δὲ Πολυξείνης αἷμα δέχηι φθίμενος·

IV *A.P.* 7.542 [C] Φλάκκου [J] εἰς παιδίον διερχόμενον τὸν ποταμὸν Ἕβρον κρυσταλλωθέντα καὶ τοῦ πάγου περιρραγέντος ἐξολισθῆσαν διεκόπη τὴν κεφαλὴν ὑπὸ τοῦ παγέτου καὶ τέθνηκεν Pl A Φλάκκου

1 δεθέντος P: πεδηθείς Pl   **2** κοῦρος CPl: -ρας (?) P   **3** ἔκοψεν P: -ψε
Pl   **6** τάφωι Reiske: -φου PPl   **7** μυρομένη Pl: -να P

V *A.P.* 9.98 [C] Cτατυλλίου Φλάκκου [J] εἰς Σοφοκλέα τὸν τῶν τραγωιδιῶν
ποιητὴν ἔπαινος δι᾽ ὅλου τοῦ ἐπιγράμματος   caret Pl

IV

On a boy decapitated by river-ice

A stripling boy, his feet slipping, broke through the ice of
Hebrus bound by winter's frosts. As he was swept away, a
sharp and jagged fragment from the Bistonian river struck
through his neck. One part of him was seized by the flood;
his head—alone left above the surface—his mother laid in the
grave. Poor woman, she wept and said 'My child, my child,
one part of you the funeral-pyre, the other the cruel waters
have entombed'.

V

Praise of Sophocles

Two plays on Oedipus, Electra's grievous wrath, the sun put
to flight by the feast of Atreus, and other books worthy of
Dionysus' choral dance on kings of manifold sufferings,—these
have approved you, Sophocles, as leader of the Tragic company;
you, who have spoken with your heroes' very lips.

VI

Hecuba's lament

When Pyrrhus fulfilled in his father's honour that mournful
marriage to Polyxena above the high-piled tomb, thus Hecuba
the daughter of Cisseus lamented her children's slaughter,
rending the hair from her head of many sorrows: 'First you
dragged Hector dead in axle-bonds, now in your grave
you receive the blood of Polyxena. Son of Aeacus, why were you

1 ϲε Salm.: τε P   4 χοροιτυπίηϲ Heringa: χαρ- P   5 ἐπὶ Heringa:
ἐπεὶ P | κατήινηϲαν Page: -ήνεϲαν C, -ήρεϲαν (?) P

VI A.P. 9.117 [C] Ϲτατυλλίου Φλάκκου   [J] ἐπὶ τῶι τάφωι 'Αχιλλέωϲ ὅτε
Πύρροϲ τὴν Πολυξένην ἐϲφαγίαϲεν ἡνίκα ἡ ταλαίπωροϲ 'Εκάβη ἐπὶ τοῦ ἰδίου
κόλπου τὸ αἷμα τῆϲ θυγατρὸϲ ὑπεδέξατο   Pl A Ϲτατυλλίου Φλάκκου
3 πολυκλαύτοιο Ppc: -κλαύϲτ- PacPl   5 ἀξονίοιϲ Pl: εὐξενίοιϲ P   6 φθί-
μενοϲ Pl: -νηϲ P

Αἰακίδη, τί τοσοῦτον ἐμὴν ὠδύσσαο νηδύν;
παισὶν ἔφυς γὰρ ἐμοῖς ἤπιος οὐδὲ νέκυς'.

VII

—σιγήσας ἄρυσαι.—τίνος οὔνεκα;—μηκέτ' ἀρύου.   3835
—τεῦ χάριν;—Ἡσυχίης ἡδὺ λέλογχα ποτόν.
—δύσκολος ἡ κρήνη.—γεῦσαι, καὶ μᾶλλον ἐρεῖς με
δύσκολον.—ὢ πικροῦ νάματος.—ὢ λαλιῆς.

VIII

χρυσὸν ἀνὴρ εὑρὼν ἔλιπεν βρόχον, αὐτὰρ ὁ χρυσόν
ὃν λίπεν οὐχ εὑρὼν ἧψεν ὃν εὗρε βρόχον.   3840

IX

χρυσὸν ἀνὴρ ὁ μὲν εὗρεν, ὁ δ' ὤλεσεν· ὧν ὁ μὲν εὑρών   (3841)
ῥῖψεν, ὁ δ' οὐχ εὑρὼν λυγρὸν ἔδησε βρόχον.

X

ἄρτι γενειάζων ὁ καλὸς καὶ στερρὸς ἐρασταῖς   (3843)
παιδὸς ἐρᾶι Λάδων· σύντομος ἡ Νέμεσις.

7 ὠδύσσαο Pl: ὠδύσαο P
VII A.P. 9.37 [C] ⟨Στα⟩τυλλίου Φλάκκου   [J] εἰς πηγὴν ἐπώνυμον Ἡσυχίας
Pl A Στατυλλίου Φλάκκου
2 Ἡσυχίης P: -χίοις Pl
VIII A.P. 9.44 Στατυλλίου Φλάκκου   [J] ὅτι ὁ τὸν χρυσὸν κρύψας μὴ εὑρών
ἀνῆψεν ὃν ἀντὶ τοῦ χρυσοῦ εὗρε βρόχον   [C] Πλάτωνος τοῦ μεγάλου   Pl A

426

so enraged against my motherhood? Not even your corpse has mercy on my children.'

VII

A fountain named 'Quietude'

—Be silent when you draw from me.—Why?—Stop drawing. —Why so?—I am owner of the sweet draught of Quietude. —What a disagreeable fountain.—Taste, and you will call me still more disagreeable.—What a bitter flow.—What a chatter-box.

VIII

The gold and the noose

A man finding gold left a noose; but he who did not find the gold which he had left fastened the noose which he found.

IX

On the same

One man found gold, the other lost it; the loser fastened the deadly noose which the finder had thrown aside.

X

Time's revenge

Just as his beard begins to grow, Ladon, that beauty so harsh to lovers, is in love with a boy. Nemesis makes short work.

Ϲτατυλλίου Φλάκκου Syll.E Πλάτωνοϲ Diog.L. 3.33 ἄλλο [sc. Πλάτωνόϲ] I versum a P scriptum denuo scr. C [=C²] εὑρὼν CC²: om. P | ἔλιπεν P: -πε C²Pl
IX *A.P.* 9.45 [C] Ϲτατυλλίου Φλάκκου   [J] τοῦτο εἰϲ ἄνθρωπον διὰ πενίαν μέλλοντα ἀπάγξαϲθαι ὃϲ ἐν τῶι δένδρωι ἐν ὧι τὸν βρόχον ἀνάψειν ἔμελλεν χρυϲὸν εὑρὼν κεκρυμμένον ἀπῆλθε καταλείπων τὸν βρόχον Pl A Πλάτωνοϲ, οἱ δὲ Ἀντιπάτρου
X *A.P.* 12.12 Φλάκκου caret Pl

XI

cῶόν μοι Πολέμωνα μολεῖν, ὅτ᾽ ἔπεμπον, Ἄπολλον,   3845
ἠιτούμην θυσίην ὄρνιν ὑποσχόμενος·
ἦλθε δέ μοι Πολέμων λάσιος γένυν· οὐ μὰ σέ, Φοῖβε,
ἦλθεν ἐμοί, πικρῷ δ᾽ ἐξέφυγέν με τάχει.
5 οὐκέτι coι θύω τὸν ἀλέκτορα. μή με σοφίζου,
κωφήν μοι cταχύων ἀντιδιδοὺc καλάμην.   3850

XII

εἴ μοι cωιζόμενοc Πολέμων ὃν ἔπεμπον ἀνέλθοι
⟨   ⟩
νῦν δ᾽ αὐτῶι Πολέμων ἀνασώιζεται· †οὐκέτ᾽ ἀφῆcαι†,
Φοῖβε, δαcὺc δ᾽ ἧκων οὐκέτι cῶοc ἐμοί.
5 αὐτὸc ἴcωc cκιάcαι γένυν εὔξατο· θυέτω αὐτόc,   3855
ἀντία ταῖcιν ἐμαῖc ἐλπίcιν εὐξάμενοc.

XIII

cαῖc ἴκελον προύπεμπον ἐγὼ Πολέμωνα παρειαῖc,
ἢν ἔλθηι, θύcειν ὄρνιν ὑποcχόμενοc,
ὃν δέχομαι φθονεροῖc, Παιάν, φρίccοντα γενείοιc,
οὐ τούτου τλήμων εἴνεκεν εὐξάμενοc.   3860
5 οὐδὲ μάτην τίλλεcθαι ἀναίτιον ὄρνιν ἔοικεν·
ἢ cυντιλλέcθω, Δήλιε, καὶ Πολέμων.

XI A.P. 12.25 Cτατυλλίου Φλάκκου   caret Pl
I Ἄπολλον Brunck: Ἀπόλλω P   4 ἦλθεν ἐμοί Brunck: ἦλθε δέ μοι P
XII A.P. 12.26 τοῦ αὐτοῦ [sc. Cτατυλλίου Φλάκκου]   caret Pl

XI

On Polemon's beard

That Polemon return to me safe, I prayed when I saw him off,
Apollo, promising a bird as sacrifice. Polemon has come back to
me, but shaggy-chinned; in your name I swear, Phoebus, he has
not come back to me, he has put himself beyond my reach with
cruel quickness. That cock I sacrifice to you no longer. Think
not to deceive me, giving me dull straw instead of corn.

XII

On the same

If Polemon should return to me safe, as I saw him off ⟨
            ⟩. Now Polemon is saved, but only for himself;
no longer ⟨   ⟩, Phoebus; returning all shaggy, he is no
longer saved for me. Perhaps he himself prayed for his chin's
shadowing; so let him make sacrifice himself, as he prayed the
contrary of my hopes.

XIII

On the same

I saw Polemon off, his cheeks like yours, Apollo, and I promised
to sacrifice a bird when he returned. I receive him back bristling
with spiteful beard: it was not for that I prayed, poor fool, nor
is it right that some blameless bird should be plucked to no
purpose,—or let Polemon too be plucked, Lord of Delos.

2 om. P (est v. 1 paginae ultimus, v. 3 pag. sequentis primus)   5 cκιάcαι
Brunck: κιάcαι P

XIII *A.P.* 12.27 τοῦ αὐτοῦ [sc. Cτατυλλίου Φλάκκου]   caret Pl
3 δέχομαι Salm.: δεμοχαι P   4 τούτου Salm.: τοιούτου P

XIV

εὕδεις, ἀγρύπνους ἐπάγων θνητοῖσι μερίμνας,
εὕδεις, ἀτηρῆς ἃ τέκος Ἀφρογενοῦς,
οὐ πεύκην πυρόεσσαν ἐπηρμένος οὐδ᾽ ἀφύλακτον   3865
ἐκ κέραος ψάλλων ἀντιτόνοιο βέλος.
5 ἄλλοι θαρσείτωσαν· ἐγὼ δ᾽, ἀγέρωχε, δέδοικα
μή μοι καὶ κνώσσων πικρὸν ὄνειρον ἴδηις.

ΓΛΑΥΚΟΥ

I

ἁ Βάκχα Παρία μέν, ἐνεψύχωσε δ᾽ ὁ γλύπτας
τὸν λίθον· ἀνθρώισκει δ᾽ ὡς βρομιαζομένα.   3870
ὦ Σκόπα, ἁ θεοποιὸς †ἐμήσατο μήσατο† τέχνα
θαῦμα, χιμαιροφόνον Θυιάδα μαινομέναν.

II

ἡ Βάκχη Κρονίδην Σάτυρον †ἔθετο†, εἰς δὲ χορείαν   (3873)
θρώισκει μαινομένην ὡς βρομιαζόμενος.

III

καὶ τὸν ἀπὸ Τρηχῖνος ἰδὼν πολυώδυνον ἥρω   3875
τόνδε Φιλοκτήτην ἔγραφε Παρράσιος·
ἔν τε γὰρ ὀφθαλμοῖς ἐσκληκόσι κωφὸν ὑποικεῖ
δάκρυ, καὶ ὁ τρύχων ἐντὸς ἔνεστι πόνος.
5 ζωογράφων ὦ λῶιστε, σὺ μὲν σοφός, ἀλλ᾽ ἀναπαῦσαι
ἄνδρα πόνων ἤδη τὸν πολύμοχθον ἔδει.   3880

XIV A.Pl. (A) 211 Στατυλλίου Φλάκκου   εἰς Ἔρωτα κοιμώμενον   caret P
I A.P. 9.774 Γλαύκου Ἀθηναίου   εἰς Βάκχην   Pl A Γλαύκου Ἀθηναίου
1 Παρία Pl: -ρίνα P   4 Θυιάδα Pᵖᶜ: Θυάδα PᵃᶜPl

XIV

On a statue of Eros asleep

You slumber, bringing sleepless cares to mortals; you slumber, child of ruinous Aphrodite, neither with fiery torch uplifted nor twanging from straining bow the shaft that none can guard against. Let others take heart; for myself, proud boy, I am afraid, lest even in sleep you see a cruel dream.

GLAUCUS

I

On a statue of a Bacchant by Scopas

The Bacchant is of Parian marble, but the sculptor has given the stone a soul; she leaps up as if possessed by Bromios. What a miracle, Scopas, your god-creating art has contrived,—a goat-slaying Thyiad in a frenzy.

II

On a portrayal of Zeus dancing with Bacchants

The Bacchant has made the son of Cronos a Satyr; he leaps into the frenzied dance as if possessed by Bromios.

III

On a painting of Philoctetes by Parrhasius

Having seen him too, the tormented hero from Trachis, Parrhasius painted this Philoctetes. In his dry eyes a tear dwells mutely, and the wasting pain is within him. O best of painters, skilful indeed are you, but it was time to give the long-suffering man a rest from pain.

II *A.P.* 9.775 τοῦ αὐτοῦ [sc. Γλαύκου] εἰς τὸ αὐτό Pl в Γλαύκου ᾿Αθηναίου
I ἔθετο P: θέτο Pl   2 μαινομένην Jacobs: -νος PPl

III *A.Pl.* (Α) 111 Γλαύκου εἰς εἰκόνα Φιλοκτήτου   caret P

ΙCΙΔΩΡΟΥ

I

ἰξῶι καὶ καλάμοισιν ἀπ' ἠέρος αὐτὸν ἔφερβεν
Εὔμηλος λιτῶς ἀλλ' ἐν ἐλευθερίηι·
οὔποτε δ' ὀθνείην ἔκυσεν χέρα γαστρὸς ἔκητι·
τοῦτο τρυφὴν κείνωι, τοῦτ' ἔφερ' εὐφροσύνην.
5 τρὶς δὲ τριηκοστὸν ζήσας ἔτος ἐνθάδ' ἰαύει   3885
παισὶ λιπὼν ἰξὸν καὶ πτερὰ καὶ καλάμους.

II

τὸ χῶμα τύμβος ἐστίν· ἀλλὰ τὼ βόε
ἐπίσχες οὗτος τὰν ὕνιν τ' ἀνάσπασον.
κινεῖς σποδὸν γάρ· ἐς δὲ τοιαύταν κόνιν
μὴ σπέρμα πυρῶν ἀλλὰ χεῦε δάκρυα.   3890

III

οὐ χεῖμα Νικόφημον, οὐκ ἄστρων δύσις,
ἁλὸς Λιβύσσης κύματ' οὐ κατέκλυσεν.
ἀλλ' ἐν γαλήνης φεῦ τάλας ἀνηνέμωι
πλόωι πεδηθεὶς ἐφρύγη δίψευς ὕπο.
5 καὶ τοῦτ' ἀήτεων ἔργον· ἃ πόσον κακόν   3895
ναύταισιν ἢ πνέοντες ἢ μεμυκότες.

I *A.P.* 7.156 [C] 'Ισιδώρου Αἰγεάτου   [J] εἰς Εὔμηλον ἰξευτήν   Pl A 'Ισιδώρου
Αἰγεάτου   Pl B 'Ισιδώρου
3 οὔποτε δ' CPl: οὔποτ' P

II *A.P.* 7.280 [C] 'Ισιδώρου Αἰγεάτου   ἀπὸ ναυηγοῦ πρὸς γεωπόνον   [J] εἰς
τάφον ἐπὶ χώρας κείμενον ἀροτρευομένης   ἰαμβικόν   Pl A 'Ισιδώρου Αἰγεάτου
ἀπὸ ναυηγοῦ πρὸς γεωπόνον

ISIDORUS

I

Epitaph for a fowler

With lime and reeds Eumelus kept himself fed from the sky, simply, but in freedom. He never kissed a stranger's hand for hunger's sake. This brought him his luxuries, this his delights. Having lived thrice a thirtieth year he reposes here, leaving for his children lime, feathers, and reeds.

II

On a tomb in danger from the plough

This mound is a tomb; hold your pair of oxen, fellow, lift up the ploughshare. What you are disturbing is ashes; upon such dust pour tears, not seed of corn.

III

Death by thirst at sea

Nor storms nor setting of stars nor waves of the Libyan sea drowned Nicophemus, but in calm weather's windless sailing enchained, poor wretch, he was burnt up by thirst. This too is the winds' work; how great an evil to sailors, whether blowing or with lips closed fast.

1 ἐcτίν CPl: -τί P | τὼ Pl: τῶι P   2 οὗτοc CPl: -τωc P | τὰν P: τὴν Pl | τ᾽ CPl: om. P   3 κινεῖc CPl: incertum quid fuerit in P

III *A.P.* 7.293 [C] ᾽Icιδώρου Αἰγεάτου   [J] εἰc Νικόφημον ναυαγήcαντα ὑπὸ δίψουc ἐν τῆι θαλάccηι   Pl A ᾽Icιδώρου

1 δύcιc CPl: -cειc P   2 Λιβύccηc CPl: -βήccηc P | κύματ᾽ οὐ Salm.: κύματοc PPl   3 γαλήνηc Page: -νηι PPl   4 δίψευc P: -ψηc Pl   5 ἅ πόcον CPl: ἀπὸ cῶν P

IV

ἔκ με γεωμορίης Ἐτεοκλέα πόντιος ἐλπίς
εἵλκυσεν ὀθνείης ἔμπορον ἐργασίης.
νῶτα δὲ Τυρσηνῆς ἐπάτευν ἁλός, ἀλλ' ἅμα νηί
πρηνιχθεὶς κείνης ὕδασιν ἐγκατέδυν
5 ἀθρόον ἐμβρίσαντος ἀήματος. οὐκ ἄρ' ἀλωάς
αὐτὸς ἐπιπνείει κεἰς ὀθόνας ἄνεμος.

3900

V

πούλυπον ἀγρεύσας ποτὲ Τύννιχος ἐξ ἁλὸς εἰς γῆν
ἔρριψεν δείσας θηρὸς ἱμαντοπέδην·
ἀλλ' ὅ γ' ἐφ' ὑπνώοντα πεσὼν συνέδησε λαγωόν
φεῦ τάχα θηρευτὰς ἄρτι φυγόντα κύνας.
5 ἀγρευθεὶς ἤγρευσεν· ὁ δ' εἰς ἅλα Τύννιχος ἰχθύν
ἧκε πάλιν ζωόν, λύτρα λαγωὸν ἔχων.

3905

ΛΑΥΡΕΑ

I

Αἰολικὸν παρὰ τύμβον ἰών, ξένε, μή με θανοῦσαν
τὰν Μιτυληναίαν ἔννεπ' ἀοιδοπόλον·
τόνδε γὰρ ἀνθρώπων ἔκαμον χέρες, ἔργα δὲ φωτῶν
ἐς ταχινὴν ἔρρει τοιάδε ληθεδόνα·
5 ἢν δέ με Μουσάων ἐτάσῃς χάριν, ὧν ἀφ' ἑκάστης
δαίμονος ἄνθος ἐμῇ θῆκα παρ' ἐννεάδι,
γνώσεαι ὡς Ἀίδεω σκότον ἔκφυγον, οὐδέ τις ἔσται
τῆς λυρικῆς Σαπφοῦς νώνυμος ἠέλιος.

3910

3915

IV *A.P.* 7.532 [C] Ἰσιδώρου Αἰγεάτου   [J] εἰς Ἐτεοκλέα ναυηγὸν ἐν τῶι
Τυρρηνικῶι πελάγει ναυαγήσαντα Pl b Ἰσιδώρου
3 ἀλλ' ἅμα νηί Pl: ἀλλά με νηί P   5 ἐμβρίσαντος Scaliger: ἐκβ- PPl
6 αὐτὸς: αὐτὸς P, ωὗτὸς Pl

V *A.P.* 9.94 [C] Ἰσιδώρου Αἰγεάτου   [J] εἰς πολύπουν καὶ λαγωόν. προεγράφη
ἐν τοῖς ἔμπροσθεν· ⟨κεῖται add. man. rec.⟩ δισσῶς Pl a Ἰσιδώρου Αἰγεάτου

mine. O Ilium, how Nemesis has cared for you; since now, when Mycenê is no longer to be seen, you live, and live as a city.

PINYTUS

I

Epitaph for Sappho

The tomb holds the bones and the dumb name of Sappho; but immortal are the utterances of her art.

POLYAENUS OF SARDIS

I

On a fawn killed by snake-poison in the dam's milk

A cruel viper struck the nursing udder of a lately-calving doe, 〈   〉 full; her fawn plucked at the teat, poison-tainted, and swallowed the incurable bitter milk from the deadly wound. Death passed from one to the other; straightway by pitiless doom the breast took away the gift which the womb had brought.

JULIUS POLYAENUS

I

Prayer for release from exile

Though many-voiced there ever fill your hearing either fears in prayer present or thanks for prayer past, Zeus, governor of Scheria's holy ground, yet listen to me also and assent with truthful promise: that here and now be the end of my banishment, and that I live in my fatherland at rest from my long labours.

---

2 εἰδοῦϲα P: οἰδοῦϲα Pl | πικρὸϲ Pl: -ὸν P   4 ἔβροξε P: -ρωξε Pl   5 νηλέι Pl: -λαίηι P

I *A.P.* 9.7 Ἰουλίου Πολυαίνου   [J] εἴϲ τινα ἐπὶ ξένηϲ εὐξάμενον ἐν τῆι ἰδίαι πατρίδι τελευτῆϲαι καὶ ζῆϲαι τὸν ὑπόλοιπον χρόνον   Pl A Ἰουλίου Πολυαίνου   3 Cχερίηϲ Lascaris: χερίηϲ PPl

II

ἐλπὶς ἀεὶ βιότου κλέπτει χρόνον, ἡ πυμάτη δέ   (3953)
ἠὼς τὰς πολλὰς ἔφθασεν ἀσχολίας.

III

(a) πολλάκις εὐξαμένωι μοι ἀεὶ θυμῆρες ἔδωκας   3955
τέκμαρ ἀκυμάντου, Ζεῦ πάτερ, εὐπλοΐης·
δοίης μοι καὶ τοῦτον ἐπὶ πλόον, ἠδὲ σαώσαις
ἤδη καὶ καμάτων ὅρμισον εἰς λιμένα.

(b) οἶκος καὶ πάτρη βιότου χάρις, αἱ δὲ περισσαί
φροντίδες ἀνθρώποις οὐ βίος ἀλλὰ πόνος.   3960

ΠΟΜΠΗΙΟΥ

I

ἡ τὸ καλὸν καὶ πᾶσιν ἐράσμιον ἀνθήσασα,
ἡ μούνη Χαρίτων λείρια δρεψαμένη,
οὐκέτι χρυσοχάλινον ὁρᾶι δρόμον ἠελίοιο
Λαΐς, ἐκοιμήθη δ' ὕπνον ὀφειλόμενον,
5 κώμους καὶ τὰ νέων ζηλώματα καὶ τὰ ποθεύντων   3965
κνίσματα καὶ μύστην λύχνον ἀπειπαμένη.

II A.P. 9.8 s.a.n.   Pl A 'Ιουλίου Πολυαίνου
1 βιότου P: -τοιο Pl

III (a) A.P. 9.9 τοῦ αὐτοῦ [sc. 'Ιουλίου Πολυαίνου]   [J] ὁμοίως ἐπί τινι εὐξαμένωι
εὐπλοίην καὶ εἰς τὴν ἑαυτοῦ πατρίδα ὑποστροφήν   Pl B 'Ιουλιανοῦ
3 δοίης P: δώιης Pl | ἐπὶ Page: ἔτι PPl | σαώσαις Lascaris: -σοις P, -σας Pl
4 καὶ PPl^ac: κἀκ Pl^pc | λιμένα Schmidt: -νας PPl

II

On Hope

Hope ever steals life's time away, and the last dawn outraces our many businesses.

III

(*a*) *Prayer for a safe voyage*

Often I have prayed, and ever have you granted a welcome pledge, Father Zeus, of fair sailing on waveless seas. Grant it me for this passage also, and protect me now and bring me to anchor in a haven from troubles.

(*b*) *No place like home*

Home and fatherland are life's delight. Cares beyond them are not man's life but his labour.

POMPEIUS

I

The death of Laïs

She whose flowering was so beautiful and to all men desirable, she who alone gathered the lilies of the Graces, Laïs no longer looks on the sun's gold-bridled course, but is laid to rest in her appointed sleep, having said farewell to revels and young men's jealousies and lovers' chafings and the bedroom-lamp her confidant.

(*b*) *A.P.* ibidem, tamquam eiusdem epigrammatis distichon ultimum   bis scriptum in Pl tamquam peculiare epigramma, Pl A Παλλαδᾶ, Pl B ᾽Ιουλιανοῦ
1 βιότου PPl^A: -τοιο Pl^B

I *A.P.* 7.219 [C] Πομπηίου νεωτέρου   [J] εἰς τὴν αὐτὴν Λαΐδα τὴν Κορινθίαν
Pl A Πομπηίου νεωτέρου   Suid. s.vv. λείρια (2), χρυσοχάλινον (3), ζηλώματα (5 s.), κνίσματα (5 καὶ τὰ ποθ.–6)
3 δρόμον PPl: φάος Suid.

II

εἰ καὶ ἐρημαίη κέχυμαι κόνις ἔνθα Μυκήνη,
    εἰ καὶ ἀμαυροτέρη παντὸς ἰδεῖν σκοπέλου,
Ἴλου τις καθορῶν κλεινὴν πόλιν, ἧς ἐπάτησα
    τείχεα καὶ Πριάμου πάντ᾽ ἐκένωσα δόμον,   3970
5 γνώσεται ἔνθεν ὅσον πάρος ἔσθενον· εἰ δέ με γῆρας
    ὕβρισεν, ἀρκοῦμαι μάρτυρι Μαιονίδηι.

II *A.P.* 9.28 [C] Πομπηίου, οἱ δὲ Μάρκου νεωτέρου   [J] εἰς Μυκήνας τὴν

442

II

On the ruins and fame of Mycenae

Though I, Mycenê, lie heaped here as desert dust, though I be dismaller than any crag to view, yet one who surveys the famous city of Ilos,—whose walls I trampled, and made empty all the house of Priam,—shall learn therefrom how mighty I was in time past. If old age has done me insult, I am content with Homer for my witness.

’Αγαμέμνονος πόλιν ἔπαινος   Pl A Πομπηίου, οἱ δὲ Μάρκου νεωτέρου εἰς
τὴν Μυκήνην

443

INDEXES

I. INDEX OF SOURCES

ANTHOLOGIA PALATINA

BOOK 4
2	Philip I	line 2628

BOOK 5
3	Antipater VII	109
4	Philodemus I	3160
5	Flaccus I	3796
13	Philodemus II	3166
16	Argentarius I	1301
20	Honestus I	2400
25	Philodemus III	3174
30	Antipater VI	103
31	Antipater CXII	705
32	Argentarius II	1307
33	Parmenion I	2578
34	Parmenion II	2580
46	Philodemus IV	3180
58	Archias I	3588
59	Archias II	3592
63	Argentarius III	1311
68	Polemon III	3356
89	Argentarius IV	1313
98	Archias III	3594
102	Argentarius V	1319
104	Argentarius VI	1323
105	Argentarius VII	1329
106	Diotimus I	2190
107	Philodemus V	3188
108	Crinagoras XIV	1841
109	Antipater LIII	359
110	Argentarius VIII	1333
111	Antiphilus XII	855
112	Philodemus XVIII	3268
113	Argentarius IX	1339
114	Maccius I	2474
115	Philodemus VI	3196
116	Argentarius X	1345
117	Maccius II	2480
118	Argentarius XI	1351
119	Crinagoras I	1773
120	Philodemus VII	3202
121	Philodemus VIII	3206
122	Diodorus II	2106
123	Philodemus IX	3212
124	Philodemus X	3218
125	Bassus I	1587
126	Philodemus XXV	3314
127	Argentarius XII	1355

128	Argentarius XIII	line 1361
129	Automedon I	1509
130	Maccius IV	2488
131	Philodemus XI	3224
132	Philodemus XII	3228
133	Maccius V	2494
306	Philodemus XIII	3236
307	Antiphilus XIII	861
308	Antiphilus XIV	865

BOOK 6
5	Philip VIII	2680
10	Antipater XXXIX	283
16	Archias IV	3596
22	Zonas I	3440
33	Maccius VI	2500
36	Philip IX	2688
38	Philip X	2692
39	Archias VIII	3620
62	Philip XI	2700
88	Antiphanes I	725
89	Maccius VII	2508
90	Philip XII	2706
91	Thallus I	3408
92	Philip XIII	2714
93	Antipater XXXII	247
94	Philip XIV	2720
95	Antiphilus XV	871
96	Erucius I	2200
97	Antiphilus XXI	909
98	Zonas II	3446
99	Philip XV	2727
100	Crinagoras VIII	1809
101	Philip XVI	2733
102	Philip XVII	2741
103	Philip XVIII	2749
104	Philip XIX	2757
105	Apollonides I	1125
106	Zonas III	3452
107	Philip XX	2765
108	Myrinus I	2556
109	Antipater LIV	363
158	Sabinus II	3370
161	Crinagoras X	1819
179	Archias V	3602
180	Archias VI	3608
181	Archias VII	3614
186	Diocles II	2084
187	Alpheus V	3536
192	Archias X	3638

445

195	Archias XI	line 3646
196	Flaccus II	3802
198	Antipater C	633
199	Antiphilus XVI	877
201	Argentarius XVII	1379
203	Philip LXXVI	3134
207	Archias IX	3628
208	Antipater IX	119
209	Antipater X	125
227	Crinagoras III	1781
228	Adaeus I	1
229	Crinagoras IV	1787
230	Quintus I	3358
231	Philip XXI	2773
232	Crinagoras XLII	2014
233	Maccius VIII	2516
234	Erucius X	2256
235	Thallus II	3414
236	Philip II	2642
237	Antistius I	1101
238	Apollonides II	1131
239	Apollonides III	1137
240	Philip III	2648
241	Antipater XLIII	303
242	Crinagoras IX	1813
243	Diodorus III	2112
244	Crinagoras XII	1829
245	Diodorus IV	2118
246	Argentarius XVIII	1385
247	Philip XXII	2781
248	Argentarius XXIII	1419
249	Antipater XLV	313
250	Antiphilus I	783
251	Philip VII	2672
252	Antiphilus II	791
253	Crinagoras XLIII	2022
254	Myrinus II	2560
255	Erucius V	2224
256	Antipater CX	693
257	Antiphilus XXII	915
258	Adaeus II	5
259	Philip XXIII	2789
260	Geminus VIII	2378
261	Crinagoras V	1793
291	Antipater CI	639
333	Argentarius XIV	1365
335	Antipater XLI	293
345	Crinagoras VI	1797
348	Diodorus XVI	2178
349	Philodemus XIX	3274
350	Crinagoras XIII	1835

BOOK 7

15	Antipater LXXIII	481
16	Pinytus I	3939
17	Laurea I	3909
18	Antipater XII	135
36	Erucius XI	2262

38	Diodorus XII	line 2164
39	Antipater XIII	141
40	Diodorus XIII	2166
49	Bianor I	1645
51	Adaeus III	11
65	Antipater LXXVII	497
66	Honestus II	2404
68	Archias XIV	3666
73	Geminus I	2342
74	Diodorus XIV	2170
75	Antipater LXXIV	483
136	Antipater LV	373
140	Archias XV	3674
141	Antiphilus XXIII	921
147	Archias XVI	3678
156	Isidorus I	3881
165	Archias XIII	3658
168	Antipater CII	647
174	Erucius VII	2238
175	Antiphilus XXIV	929
176	Antiphilus XXV	935
180	Apollonides IV	1143
183	Parmenion III	2582
184	Parmenion IV	2586
185	Antipater XVI	157
186	Philip XXIV	2795
187	Philip LXXVII	3145
188	Thallus III	3420
191	Archias XX	3710
213	Archias XXI	3716
214	Archias XXII	3724
216	Antipater XVII	163
219	Pompeius I	3961
222	Philodemus XXVI	3320
230	Erucius XII	2268
233	Apollonides XX	1237
234	Philip XXXI	2839
235	Diodorus XI	2160
236	Antipater CXV	723
237	Alpheus VI	3542
238	Adaeus IV	17
239	Parmenion V	2590
240	Adaeus V	21
243	Bassus II	1591
252	Antipater LVI	375
274	Honestus XXII	2470
278	Archias XII	3650
280	Isidorus II	3887
281	Heraclides I	2390
286	Antipater XIV	145
287	Antipater LVIII	383
288	Antipater LX	397
289	Antipater XXVI	221
290	Flaccus III	3807
293	Isidorus III	3891
294	Laurea II	3917
305	Adaeus XI	47
362	Philip LXXVIII	3147

		line				line
364	Argentarius XXI	1407	632	Diodorus VII	2136
365	Zonas IV	3458	633	Crinagoras XVIII	1867
366	Antistius II	1109	634	Antiphilus XIX	895
367	Antipater LXIII	413	635	Antiphilus XXVIII	953
368	Erucius VI	2232	636	Crinagoras XLIV	2030
369	Antipater XLIX	337	637	Antipater LXI	401
370	Diodorus XV	2174	638	Crinagoras XLV	2036
371	Crinagoras XV	1847	639	Antipater LIX	391
372	Bassus III	1597	640	Antipater LVII	377
373	Thallus IV	3428	641	Antiphilus XVII	883
374	Argentarius XIX	1393	642	Apollonides VIII	1163
375	Antiphilus XXVI	941	643	Crinagoras XIX	1873
376	Crinagoras XVI	1853	644	Bianor IV	1661
377	Erucius XIII	2274	645	Crinagoras XX	1877
378	Apollonides V	1149	666	Antipater XI	129
379	Antiphilus III	797	671	Bianor V	1667
380	Crinagoras XL	1999	692	Antipater CVII	675
381	Etruscus I	2290	693	Apollonides IX	1167
382	Philip XXV	2801	694	Adaeus VI	23
383	Philip XXXII	2845	696	Archias XVII	3688
384	Argentarius XXXI	1469	699	Adespota II	3502
385	Philip XXXIII	2853	700	Diodorus IX	2148
386	Bassus IV	1603	701	Diodorus X	2154
387	Bianor II	1649	702	Apollonides XII	1185
388	Bianor III	1655	703	Myrinus III	2568
389	Apollonides VI	1153	705	Antipater L	343
390	Antipater LXII	407	741	Crinagoras XXI	1883
391	Bassus V	1607	742	Apollonides XIII	1191
392	Heraclides II	2394	743	Antipater LXVII	433
393	Diocles I	2078			
394	Philip XXVI	2807	BOOK 9		
395	Argentarius XX	1401	1	Polyaenus Sard. I	3941
396	Bianor VI	1669	3	Antipater CVI	669
397	Erucius VIII	2244	7	Polyaenus Jul. I	3947
398	Antipater LXV	423	8	Polyaenus Jul. II	3953
399	Antiphilus XXVII	947	9	Polyaenus Jul. III	3955
400	Serapion I	3404	10	Antipater XVIII	169
401	Crinagoras XLI	2006	11	Philip XXXV	2867
402	Antipater LXVI	429	13B	Antiphilus XXIX	959
403	Argentarius XXXII	1477	14	Antiphilus XXX	965
404	Zonas V	3464	19	Archias XIX	3700
405	Philip XXXIV	2861	22	Philip XXXVI	2873
530	Antipater XXII	197	23	Antipater LXXI	465
531	Antipater XXIII	201	26	Antipater XIX	175
532	Isidorus IV	3897	27	Archias XXV	3744
534	Automedon XII	1581	28	Pompeius II	3967
542	Flaccus IV	3813	29	Antiphilus XXXI	973
554	Philip XXVII	2813	30	Bassus XI	1643
622	Antiphilus XVIII	889	34	Antiphilus XXXII	979
623	Aemilianus I	53	35	Antiphilus L	1093
624	Diodorus V	2124	36	Secundus I	3380
625	Antipater XXXIII	251	37	Flaccus VII	3835
626	Adespota I	3494	43	Parmenion VI	2592
627	Diodorus VI	2130	44	Flaccus VIII	3839
628	Crinagoras XVII	1859	45	Flaccus IX	3841
629	Antipater LXXVI	493	46	Antipater CIV	659
630	Antiphilus IV	803	56	Philip XXXVII	2879
631	Apollonides VII	1159	58	Antipater XCI	583

59	Antipater XLVI	*line* 317		222	Antiphilus XXXVII	*line* 1011
60	Diodorus XVII	2184		223	Bianor VII	1675
62	Euenus II	2302		224	Crinagoras XXIII	1897
69	Parmenion VII	2596		225	Honestus IV	2414
71	Antiphilus XXXIII	985		226	Zonas VI	3472
72	Antipater XCV	609		227	Bianor VIII	1683
73	Antiphilus V	809		228	Apollonides XIV	1195
75	Euenus III	2308		229	Argentarius XXIV	1427
76	Antipater LXXX	515		230	Honestus V	2418
77	Antipater CXI	699		231	Antipater XXXV	261
81	Crinagoras XXII	1891		232	Philip XLII	2913
82	Antipater XV	151		233	Erucius IX	2250
83	Philip XXXVIII	2887		234	Crinagoras XLVIII	2054
84	Antiphanes II	729		235	Crinagoras XXV	1911
85	Philip XXXIX	2893		236	Bassus VI	1611
86	Antiphilus XXXIV	991		237	Erucius II	2206
87	Argentarius XXII	1411		238	Antipater LXXXIII	535
88	Philip XL	2899		239	Crinagoras VII	1803
89	Philip XLI	2907		240	Philip XLIII	2919
90	Alpheus I	3518		241	Antipater LII	353
91	Archias XXVI	3748		242	Antiphilus XX	901
92	Antipater II	81		243	Apollonides XV	1203
93	Antipater XXXI	243		244	Apollonides XVI	1209
94	Isidorus V	3903		245	Antiphanes III	735
95	Alpheus VII	3548		246	Argentarius XXV	1433
96	Antipater XXI	191		247	Philip XLIV	2925
97	Alpheus VIII	3554		248	Boethus I	1767
98	Flaccus V	3821		249	Maccius IX	2524
100	Alpheus II	3522		250	Honestus VI	2422
101	Alpheus IX	3560		251	Euenus I	2296
102	Antonius I	3584		252	Bianor IX	1691
103	Mundus I	3931		253	Philip XLV	2931
104	Alpheus X	3566		254	Philip XXVIII	2819
107	Antipater CXIV	717		255	Philip XLVI	2939
108	Adespota III	3510		256	Antiphanes IV	741
109	Diocles III	2090		257	Apollonides XVII	1217
110	Alpheus IV	3532		258	Antiphanes V	747
111	Archias XVIII	3694		259	Bianor X	1697
112	Antipater V	99		260	Secundus II	3386
113	Parmenion VIII	2598		261	Epigonus I	2196
114	Parmenion IX	2600		262	Philip XXIX	2827
117	Flaccus VI	3827		263	Antiphilus XLVII	1073
122	Euenus V	2318		264	Apollonides XVIII	1223
143	Antipater XCIII	597		265	Apollonides XIX	1231
149	Antipater LXVIII	441		266	Antipater CVIII	681
150	Antipater LXVIII^A	447		267	Philip XXX	2833
156	Antiphilus XXXV	997		268	Antipater XXIV	209
161	Argentarius XV	1369		269	Antipater CIX	687
178	Antiphilus VI	815		270	Argentarius XXVI	1441
186	Antipater CIII	653		271	Apollonides X	1173
192	Antiphilus XXXVI	1003		272	Bianor XI	1701
215	Antipater XXV	215		273	Bianor XII	1707
216	Honestus III	2408		274	Philip XLVII	2945
217	Scaevola I	3374		275	Macedonius II	2546
218	Aemilianus II	57		276	Crinagoras XLVI	2042
219	Diodorus I	2100		277	Antiphilus VII	821
220	Thallus V	3434		278	Bianor XIII	1713
221	Argentarius XXXV	1495		279	Bassus VII	1617

448

280	Apollonides xxi	*line* 1243
281	Apollonides xxii	1251
282	Antipater xxvii	225
283	Crinagoras xxvi	1917
284	Crinagoras xxxvii	1981
285	Philip iv	2654
286	Argentarius xvi	1373
287	Apollonides xxiii	1255
288	Geminus ii	2348
289	Bassus viii	1623
290	Philip xlviii	2951
291	Crinagoras xxvii	1923
292	Honestus vii	2428
293	Philip xlix	2959
294	Antiphilus xxxviii	1017
295	Bianor xiv	1719
296	Apollonides xxiv	1261
297	Antipater xlvii	325
298	Antiphilus xxxix	1023
299	Philip l	2965
300	Adaeus vii	27
301	Secundus iii	3390
302	Antipater lxix	453
303	Adaeus viii	33
304	Parmenion x	2604
305	Antipater xxxvi	267
306	Antiphilus xl	1029
307	Philip v	2660
308	Bianor xv	1725
309	Antipater lxiv	419
310	Antiphilus xli	1037
311	Philip li	2971
312	Zonas vii	3480
339	Archias xxiii	3732
342	Parmenion xi	2608
343	Archias xxiv	3738
403	Maccius x	2530
404	Antiphilus xlii	1043
405	Diodorus viii	2142
406	Antigonus i	67
407	Antipater xxxiv	257
408	Antipater cxiii	711
409	Antiphanes vi	753
410	Sabinus i	3364
411	Maccius iii	2482
412	Philodemus xx	3280
413	Antiphilus viii	827
414	Geminus iii	2354
415	Antiphilus xliii	1051
416	Philip lii	2979
417	Antipater lxx	459
418	Antipater lxxxii	527
419	Crinagoras xxix	1935
420	Antipater li	349
421	Antipater xxviii	231
422	Apollonides xi	1179
423	Bianor xvi	1731
428	Antipater i	75

429	Crinagoras ii	*line* 1777
430	Crinagoras xxxviii	1987
438	Philip liii	2987
439	Crinagoras xlvii	2048
513	Crinagoras xlix	2060
516	Crinagoras xxx	1941
517	Antipater iv	93
526	Alpheus iii	3528
541	Antipater xliv	307
542	Crinagoras xxxix	1995
543	Philip liv	2995
544	Adaeus ix	37
545	Crinagoras xi	1823
546	Antiphilus ix	833
548	Bianor xvii	1739
549	Antiphilus xliv	1059
550	Antipater xciv	603
551	Antiphilus x	841
552	Antipater xlii	299
553	Adespota iv	3512
554	Argentarius xxxiii	1485
555	Crinagoras xxxi	1947
556	Zonas viii	3486
557	Antipater lxxix	509
558	Erucius iii	2212
559	Crinagoras xxxii	1955
560	Crinagoras xxxiii	1961
561	Philip lv	3001
562	Crinagoras xxiv	1903
570	Philodemus xiv	3240
575	Philip lvi	3009
602	Euenus iv	2310
706	Antipater lxxxi	521
707	Geminus iv	2356
708	Philip lvii	3015
709	Philip lxiii	3052
717	Euenus viii	2332
718	Euenus ix	2334
728	Antipater lxxxiv	541
732	Argentarius xxxvi	1501
740	Geminus v	2362
742	Philip lxxix	3152
746	Polemon i	3346
750	Archias xxx	3772
756	Aemilianus iii	63
774	Glaucus i	3869
775	Glaucus ii	3873
776	Diodorus xviii	2186
777	Philip lxiv	3058
778	Philip vi	2666
790	Antipater xcii	591
791	Apollonides xxv	1267
792	Antipater lxxxv	543
824	Erucius iv	2218

BOOK 10

4	Argentarius xxviii	1451
7	Archias xxvii	3750

8	Archias XXVIII	line 3758
10	Archias XXIX	3766
17	Antiphilus XI	849
18	Argentarius XXIX	1459
19	Apollonides XXVI	1273
20	Adaeus X	43
21	Philodemus XV	3246
22	Bianor XVIII	1745
23	Automedon III	1523
24	Crinagoras XXXIV	1965
25	Antipater XL	287
100	Antiphanes VII	759
101	Bianor XIX	1749
102	Bassus IX	1631
103	Philodemus XXIV	3310

BOOK II

4	Parmenion XII	2612
20	Antipater XX	185
23	Antipater XXXVIII	277
24	Antipater III	87
25	Apollonides XXVII	1279
26	Argentarius XXVII	1447
27	Macedonius III	2550
28	Argentarius XXX	1463
29	Automedon II	1517
30	Philodemus XXVII	3328
31	Antipater XXXVII	273
32	Honestus VIII	2432
33	Philip LVIII	3023
34	Philodemus XXI	3288
35	Philodemus XXII	3296
36	Philip LIX	3027
37	Antipater XCVI	615
38	Polemon II	3350
39	Macedonius I	2544
40	Antistius III	1113
41	Philodemus XVII	3260
42	Crinagoras XXXV	1969
43	Zonas IX	3492
44	Philodemus XXIII	3302
45	Honestus IX	2436
46	Antimedon I	73
49	Euenus VI	2324
50	Automedon IV	1529
65	Parmenion XIII	2616
66	Antiphilus LI	1095
67	Myrinus IV	2574
72	Bassus X	1637
158	Antipater XCVII	621
168	Antiphanes VIII	765
173	Philip LXXX	3158
219	Antipater XCVIII	629
224	Antipater XCIX	631
248	Bianor XX	1755
318	Philodemus XXVIII	3334
319	Automedon V	1535
320	Argentarius XXXIV	1491

321	Philip LX	line 3033
322	Antiphanes IX	771
324	Automedon VI	1541
325	Automedon VII	1549
326	Automedon X	1569
327	Antipater VIII	115
346	Automedon VIII	1553
347	Philip LXI	3041
348	Antiphanes X	777
361	Automedon IX	1561
364	Bianor XXI	1761
415	Antipater CV	665

BOOK 12

12	Flaccus X	3843
18	Alpheus XI	3572
24	Laurea III	3923
25	Flaccus XI	3845
26	Flaccus XII	3851
27	Flaccus XIII	3857
34	Automedon XI	1575
35	Diocles IV	2096
172	Euenus VII	2330
173	Philodemus XVI	3254

BOOK 13

1	Philip LXII	3047

BOOK 15

51	Archias XXXI	3774

ANTHOLOGIA PLANUDEA

25	Philip LXV	3066
30	Geminus VI	2366
40	Crinagoras XXXVI	1975
49	Apollonides XXVIII	1285
50	Apollonides XXIX	1289
52	Philip LXVI	3074
61	Crinagoras XXVIII	1929
75	Antipater XLVIII	331
81	Philip LXVII	3082
93	Philip LXVIII	3084
94	Archias XXXII	3780
103	Geminus VII	2372
104	Philip LXIX	3090
111	Glaucus III	3875
131	Antipater LXXXVI	547
133	Antipater LXXXVII	557
136	Antiphilus XLVIII	1079
137	Philip LXX	3096
141	Philip LXXI	3102
143	Antipater XXIX	237
147	Antiphilus XLIX	1087
154	Archias XXXIII	3788
165	Euenus X	2336
166	Euenus XI	2338

176	Antipater LXXXVIII	*line* 567		222	Parmenion XV	*line* 2624
177	Philip LXXII	3108		234	Philodemus XXIX	3340
179	Archias XXXIV	3792		235	[Apollonides] XXXI	1295
184	Antipater XXX	239		239	Apollonides XXX	1291
193	Philip LXXIII	3114		240	Philip LXXV	3126
197	Antipater LXXXIX	573		241	Argentarius XXXVII	1503
198	Maccius XI	2536		242	Erucius XIV	2282
199	Crinagoras L	2062		243	Antistius IV	1119
205	Geminus IX	2384		273	Crinagoras LI	2070
211	Flaccus XIV	3863		276	Bianor XXII	1763
212	Alpheus XII	3578		290	Antipater LXXVIII	503
214	Secundus IV	3396		296	Antipater LXXII	473
215	Philip LXXIV	3118		305	Antipater LXXV	487
216	Parmenion XIV	2620		333	Antiphilus XLV	1063
220	Antipater XC	577		334	Antiphilus XLVI	1069

INSCRIPTIONS

BCH 26 (1902) 130 seqq.   Honestus X–XXI   2442–2469

II. INDEX OF EPIGRAMMATISTS

Adaeus	*lines* 1–52	Glaucus	*lines* 3869–3880
Aemilianus	53–66	Heraclides	2390–2399
Alpheus	3518–3583	Honestus	2400–2473
Antigonus	67–72	Isidorus	3881–3908
Antimedon	73–74	Laurea	3909–3930
Antipater	75–724	Maccius	2474–2543
Antiphanes	725–782	Macedonius	2544–2555
Antiphilus	783–1100	Mundus	3931–3938
Antistius	1101–1124	Myrinus	2556–2577
Antonius	3584–3587	Parmenion	2578–2627
Apollonides	1125–1300	Philip	2628–3159
Archias	3588–3795	Philodemus	3160–3345
Argentarius	1301–1508	Pinytus	3939–3940
Automedon	1509–1586	Polemon	3346–3357
Bassus	1587–1644	Polyaenus Sard.	3941–3946
Bianor	1645–1766	Polyaenus, Jul.	3947–3960
Boethus	1767–1772	Pompeius	3961–3972
Crinagoras	1773–2077	Quintus	3358–3363
Diocles	2078–2099	Sabinus	3364–3373
Diodorus	2100–2189	Scaevola	3374–3379
Diotimus	2190–2195	Secundus	3380–3403
Epigonus	2196–2199	Serapion	3404–3407
Erucius	2200–2289	Thallus	3408–3439
Etruscus	2290–2295	Zonas	3440–3493
Euenus	2296–2341	Adespota	3494–3517
Flaccus	3796–3868		
Geminus	2342–2389		